D1717667

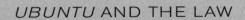

UBUNTU AND THE LAW

just ideas

transformative ideals of justice in ethical and political thought

series editors

Drucilla Cornell

Roger Berkowitz

Kenneth Michael Panfilio

UBUNTU AND THE LAW

AFRICAN IDEALS AND
POSTAPARTHEID JURISPRUDENCE

Edited by Drucilla Cornell and Nyoko Muvangua

FORDHAM UNIVERSITY PRESS

NEW YORK   2012

Copyright © 2012 Fordham University Press

All rights reserved. No part of this publication may be reproduced, stored in a retrieval system, or transmitted in any form or by any means—electronic, mechanical, photocopy, recording, or any other—except for brief quotations in printed reviews, without the prior permission of the publisher.

Fordham University Press has no responsibility for the persistence or accuracy of URLs for external or third-party Internet websites referred to in this publication and does not guarantee that any content on such websites is, or will remain, accurate or appropriate.

Fordham University Press also publishes its books in a variety of electronic formats. Some content that appears in print may not be available in electronic books.

Library of Congress Cataloging-in-Publication Data

   Ubuntu and the law : African ideals and postapartheid jurisprudence / edited by Drucilla Cornell and Nyoko Muvangua.
      p. cm. — (Just Ideas)
      Includes bibliographical references and index.
      ISBN 978-0-8232-3382-3 (cloth : alk. paper)
      1. Law—South Africa—Philosophy.   2. Post-apartheid era—South Africa.
   3. Customary law—South Africa.   4. Ubuntu (Philosophy)   I. Muvangua, Nyoko.
II. Cornell, Drucilla.

KTL440.U28   2012
349.68—dc23

                                    2011037015

Printed in the United States of America

14 13 12 5 4 3 2 1

First edition

This book is dedicated to Justice Yvonne Mokgoro, whose life and work on the Constitutional Court embody the spirit of *ubuntu*. Her legacy will always be the spirit of *ubuntu*.

Contents

PART II   Articles on *uBuntu*

Preface

The dignity jurisprudence of South Africa may well be the most sophisticated in the world.

How and why we respect dignity has been given both secular philosophical justifications as well as religious justifications in the development of both International Human Rights law and the law of Canada and Germany. But in South Africa there is a South African ethical notion, *ubuntu*, which also gives shape and defines the meaning of dignity as both ethically and legally important. Both dignity and *ubuntu* are integrally tied to an ethical ideal of what it means to be a human being, and therefore one would expect that there is a resonance between the two. And yet to reduce *ubuntu* to any of the secular or religious European conceptions of dignity would be to miss its own contribution to giving shape and meaning to dignity. Respect for dignity lies at the very heart of the ethical relationship demanded by *ubuntu*; *ubuntu,* however, is irreducible to that respect.

In certain crucial areas of law, such as socioeconomic rights, *ubuntu* has shown its ability to help define obligations and even democratic practices, and must be part of working through the conflict-ridden situations often found in the demand for socioeconomic rights. Thus, *ubuntu* clearly demands respect and recognition of the dignity of all others. Furthermore, the relationship between *ubuntu* and dignity must be recognized, as they both have come to play an important role in the jurisprudence of the new South Africa, which is both rich and generative.

uBuntu, indeed, can help us think about the significance of dignity in the new South Africa, both as a legal concept and an ethical ideal. It is also particularly important to recognize *ubuntu* as a South African ideal since this Constitution is, indeed, an African one. This respect for African ideals, notions of law and conceptions of jurisprudence is long overdue, but that alone is not the reason *ubuntu* deserves to be recognized. As we have suggested, *ubuntu* has been necessary in the development of crucial areas of the Constitution, such as socioeconomic rights. The debate and discussion over the relationship between dignity and *ubuntu* must continue, and we hope that this casebook, as well as the forthcoming *Dignity Jurisprudence of the Constitutional Court of South Africa: Cases and Materials*, will promote that dialogue. For these reasons both of these books are indispensable and inseparable companions for the further development of the rich and complex jurisprudence demanded of the new South Africa.

Where footnotes in this publication are double cited, the first number is electronically generated, consecutively, in accordance with the pages of the book. The second number is the footnote in the original case.

Acknowledgments

We want to thank the Constitutional Court of South Africa for its generous support of both this casebook and the *Dignity Jurisprudence of the Constitutional Court of South Africa* casebook. Sam Fuller and Drucilla Cornell particularly want to thank Justice Albie Sachs for his astute and insightful criticisms of our introduction.

We also want to thank Justice Yvonne Mokgoro for her inspirational support for the *uBuntu* Project.

Without the support of the National Research Foundation, under the auspices of Drucilla Cornell's chair in Customary Law, Indigenous Values and the Dignity Jurisprudence; we would not have had the support to complete this challenging project.

We want to thank all those who have participated in the research of this book: Sam Fuller, Sheldon Laing, Katherine Kopkowski, Chuma Himonga, Tom Bennett, and Kathryn Serafino-Dooley. A project of this magnitude always demands collaborative effort, and we have been honored by the support and the spirit with which it has been given.

A very special thank you goes to Justice Laurie Ackermann of the South African Constitutional Court and now retired, for his assistance with the Latin translations. Thank you also to Zandi Zondi and Lebo Ramma for helping with the African language phrase translations in the Glossary.

Without Dorothy Pietersen's care and attention, we would not have had the energy to complete this project.

Finally, we are greatly indebted to Diana Dunbar, who dedicated hours of her time to carefully proofreading the entire manuscript.

UBUNTU AND THE LAW

Introduction

uBuntu has seen a revival in constitutional jurisprudence in the last several years. As will be confirmed, *ubuntu* never lapsed as an important value and ideal in the Magistrate Courts and even the Supreme Courts of South Africa. Nonetheless, the history of *ubuntu* and its relationship to the Constitution of the new South Africa has been haunted by controversy in both the legal academy and, indeed, in the courts themselves. However, before turning to the jurisprudential history of *ubuntu* in South Africa we need to discuss *ubuntu* as a philosophical and ethical concept, particularly as this relates to questions of the meaning of law, legal obligation, and the understanding of the social bond.

John Murungi has beautifully described the heart of African jurisprudence:

Each path of jurisprudence represents an attempt by human beings to tell a story about being human. Unless one discounts the humanity of others, one must admit that one has something in common with all other human beings. To discount what one has in common with other human beings is to discount oneself as a human being. *What is essential to law is what secures human beings in their being.* The pursuit and the preservation of what is human and what is implicated by being human are what, in a particular understanding, is signified by African jurisprudence. Being African is a sign of being African, and being African is a sign of being human. African jurisprudence is a signature. In this signature lies not only what is essential about African jurisprudence, but also what is essential about the Africanness of African jurisprudence. To learn how to decipher it, which, in a sense, implies learning how to decipher oneself, paves the way to a genuine understanding.[1]

Our purpose in this short introduction is to introduce readers to how Murungi understands the way in which African jurisprudence informs the actualization of *ubuntu* in the most significant constitutional cases that have recently revived *ubuntu* as an active and central constitutional principle. But before we turn to the cases we need to examine two concepts fundamental to any understanding of law: the notion of the person and the idea of legal legitimacy, and the conception of the social bond that makes it possible. In Western jurisprudence, the social bond is understood as an experiment in the imagination in which we seek to conceive why individuals would concede any of their natural liberty and agree to the limiting of their liberty (whereby liberty is defined as a lack of restraint) by joining together with others to form a legal system. Hobbes, for example, argues that the state of nature and natural liberty are philosophical fictions that help us delineate the conditions of a positive legal system that would make it worthwhile for human beings to accept the coercion and restraint that any actual legal system has to impose.[2] For Hobbes, we agree to leave the state of nature because we exist in a world of horrific violence and brutality. Thus, as vulnerable human beings, we concede to the "Leviathan," the authority to undergird the legal system so long as it protects our basic rights and provides us with basic security and a world of stability so that we can know what to expect. Hobbes's idea of the social contract runs like a golden thread through much of the great writers and defenders of legal positivism, such as H. L. A. Hart in his minimalist notion of natural law.[3]

Immanuel Kant, in his essay "On the Common Saying: This May Be True in Theory but Does Not Apply in Practice,"[4] argues that the Hobbesian conception of the social contract will always falter. Hobbes's social contract imagines vulnerable human beings forsaking their natural liberty and yielding to the coercive power of the sovereign and of the positive law only because of the drive for security and the protection of expectation. Thus, simply put, if the only basis for abiding by a legal system is fear and security, and there is no moral reason to do so, then there will always be a rational reason for opting out of the social contract.

Famously, Kant defended the proposition that human beings could postulate themselves as free in the realm of practical reason, and they could do so by laying down a law unto themselves, and regulating their behavior by this law. Kant explains that this law is the categorical imperative and the ultimate moral law, which integrally connects freedom and morality, for it is our ability to regulate ourselves through reason alone, in the practical sense, that we represent ourselves as free from all the pulls of our day-to-day desires that drive us and indeed knock us about like bits of flotsam and jetsam. The relationship between the realm of internal freedom (of morality), and the realm of external freedom (of right or *Recht*), has long been debated in Kantian scholarship. But clearly, and despite Kant's own waffling on the matter, there must be a connection between the two. If there were no connection, then there would be no moral ground for the realm of external freedom in which we coordinate our ends with one another. Kant's hypothetical experiment in the imagination, in which we configure the conditions in which human beings could aspire to the great ideal of the Kingdom of Ends, turns on the possibility that as creatures of practical reason we can harmonize our interests. The dignity of human beings, for Kant, is precisely to be found in the possibility offered to us by our practical reason that we can, at least, aspire to live together guided by the great regulative ideal of the Kingdom of Ends.

But even the great Kantian hypothetical experiment of the imagination, in which we configure the conditions of a social contract, rooted in the respect for all other human beings, still begins with imagined individuals, even if moral individuals. It is still individuals who agree to accept some form of coercion, even if rooted in Kant's basic understanding of right, which is that individuals are allowed the greatest possible space for their freedom, as long as it can be harmonized with the freedom of all others in the social contract. *uBuntu*, alternatively, does not conceive of a social bond as one that precedes through an imagined social contract. *uBuntu* is both the African principle of transcendence for the individual, and the law of the social bond.

In *ubuntu* human beings are intertwined in a world of ethical relations and obligations from the time they are born. The social bond, then, is not imagined as one of separate individuals (as in both of the versions of the social contract just described). This inscription by the other is fundamental in that we are born into a language, a kinship group, a tribe, a nation. But this inscription is not simply reduced to a social fact. We come into the world obligated to others, and in turn these others are obligated to us, to the individual. Thus, it is a profound misunderstanding of *ubuntu* to confuse it with simple-minded communitarianism. It is only through the engagement and support of others that we are able to realize a true individuality and rise above our biological distinctiveness into a fully developed person whose uniqueness is inseparable from the journey to moral and ethical development. Ifeanyi Menkiti captures this in the following passage:

> In the stated journey of the individual toward personhood, let it therefore be noted that the community plays a vital role both as a catalyst and as prescriber of norms. The idea is that in order to transform what was initially biologically given into full personhood, the community, of necessity, has to step in, since the individual, himself or herself, cannot carry through the transformation unassisted. But then what are the implications of this idea of a biologically given organism having first to go through a process of social and ritual transformation, so as to attain the full complement of excellences seen as definitive of the person?
>
> One conclusion appears inevitable, and it is to the effect that personhood is the sort of thing which has to be achieved, the sort of thing at which the individuals could fail. I suppose that another way of putting the matter is to say that the approach to persons in traditional thought is generally speaking a maximal, or more exacting, approach, insofar as it reaches for something beyond

such minimalist requirements as the presence of consciousness, memory, will, soul, rationality or mental function. The project of being or becoming persons, it is believed, is a truly serious project that stretches beyond the raw capacities of the isolated individual, and it is a project which is laden with the possibility of triumph, but also of failure.[5]

If the community is committed to individuation and the achievement of a unique destiny for each person, the person in turn is obligated to enhance the community that supports him or her, not simply as an abstract duty that is correlated with a right, but as a form of participation that allows the community to strive for fidelity to what D. A. Masalo has called *participatory difference*. For Masalo this participatory difference recognizes that each one of ourselves is different, but also that each one is called on to make a difference by contributing to the creation and sustenance of a humane and ethical community. The great African philosopher, Kwasi Wiredu, has extended this argument by developing it to include a principle, which he has called *sympathetic impartiality*, as we seek to imagine ourselves, if not in the shoes of others, as beings like ourselves.[6] For Wiredu, the principle of sympathetic impartiality is one that we develop in association with others and is part of our cognitive and moral training in personhood. The problem, then, of how we can develop such a connection to otherness is explained precisely because we are ethically intertwined with others and therefore they are in a profound sense part of ourselves. This point is elucidated by Justice Langa in *MEC for Education: KwaZulu-Natal and Others v. Pillay and Others*:

> The notion that "we are not islands unto ourselves" is central to the understanding of the individual in African thought. It is often expressed in the phrase *umuntu ngumuntu ngabantu* which emphasises "communality and the interdependence of the members of a community" and that every individual is an extension of others. According to Gyekye, "an individual human person cannot develop and achieve the fullness of his/her potential without the concrete act of relating to other individual persons." This thinking emphasises the importance of community to individual identity and hence to human dignity. Dignity and identity are inseparably linked as one's sense of self-worth is defined by one's identity. Cultural identity is one of the most important parts of a person's identity precisely because it flows from belonging to a community and not from personal choice or achievement. And belonging involves more than simple association; it includes participation and expression of the community's practices and traditions.[7]

This point is further encapsulated by Masalo when he states that "human nature is community based. Their cognitive and moral capacities are developed by and in the context of their sociality."[8]

We can understand, then, that our ethical relationship to others is inseparable from how we are both embedded and supported by a community that is not outside each one of us, but is inscribed in us. The inscription of the other also calls the individual out of himself or herself back towards the ancestors, forwards towards the community, and further towards relations of mutual support for the potential of each one of us. The famous phrase *umuntu ngumuntu ngabantu* means "a person is a person by or through other people." We have seen, however, that this does not imply any simple notion of communitarianism, or of social cohesion. Each one of us is called to become our own person and make a difference so as to realize the ethical quality of humanness and support such a quality of humanness in others. Although I am supported by others, and an ethical action is by definition ethical because it is an action in a relation to another being, it is still up to me to realize my own personal destiny and to become a person, in the ethical and moral sense of the word. Thus, it is humanity, and not just my community, that is at stake in my ethical action. If I relate to another person in a manner that lives up to *ubuntu* then there is at least an ethical relationship between the two of us. And, of course, if we relate to others around us, through both participatory difference and sympathetic impartiality, then we will have helped to create an ethical, and thus *human*, community. The concept of a person in African jurisprudence is an ethical concept. A self-regarding or self-interested human being is one that has not only fallen away from his own sociality with others but also has lost touch with who he is as an ethical human being. One crucial aspect of doing justice to such a person is that we, who are participating in an ethical community, help that individual to get back in touch with himself or herself. Thus, cohesion and harmony are not the ultimate good, because they must always be submitted to the doing of justice. Again, to quote Murungi:

> Certainly, in Africa, but not only in Africa, personhood is social. African jurisprudence is a part of African social anthropology. Social cohesion is an essential element of African jurisprudence. Areas of jurisprudence such as criminology and penology, law of inheritance, and land law, for example, focus on the preservation of and promotion of social cohesion. This cohesion is a cohesion that is tempered by justice. Justice defines a human being as a human being. Thus, injustice in Africa is not simply a matter of an individual breaking a law that is imposed on him or her by other individuals, or by a collection of individuals who act in the name of the state. It is a violation of the individual's duty to him or herself, a violation of the duty of the individual to be him or herself—the duty to be a social being.[9]

Critics of *ubuntu*, some of whom are included in this book, have argued that *ubuntu* is a form of social cohesion that denies what we have just called participatory difference and, worse yet, is inherently hierarchical, and indeed patriarchal. We want to note that there are examples in the case law that work against such a generalization.

In the High Court decision of *Bhe and Others v. The Magistrate, Khayelitsha and Others*, Justice Ngwenya argued against the constitutionality of primogeniture, as it was rigidly codified in the official written customary law. He also noted that "it lacks basic humanity, which is the hallmark of *ubuntu*" (Justice Ngwenya's judgment is included in this casebook).[10]

These critics make the mistake of reducing *ubuntu* to an ethical ontology of a purportedly shared world. What is missed in this criticism is precisely the activism inherent in participatory difference. This activism is inherent in the ethical demand to bring about a humane world. *uBuntu* clearly has an aspirational and ideal edge—there is no end to a struggle to bring about a humane world, and to become a person in that humane world, and who makes a difference in it. Yet, it must not be misunderstood as a regulative ideal in the Kantian sense. In Kant the great ideas of reason, including the Kingdom of Ends, can only be represented as aesthetic ideas. A famous example of our time is John Rawls's aesthetic idea, the "Veil of Ignorance," which can be interpreted as a configuration of the noumenal self, and indeed, the noumenal self as a legislator in the Kingdom of Ends.[11] But the great ideas, though they can be represented as aesthetic ideas, always remain other to what is, precisely because in Kant there are limits to the accomplishments of theoretical reason. It is through practical reason that we try to configure the demands of a moral world that is always other to what is (and must remain so because the split in ourselves, between the noumenal and phenomenal aspects of being finite creatures) and yet, we can guide ourselves by those aspirations drawn out in the best aesthetic representations of a moral world. In African jurisprudence, as we have tried to offer in our brief summary of it, there is no split between the phenomenal and the noumenal, as there is in Kant. And therefore, *ubuntu* is not, in the strict Kantian sense, a regulative ideal. *uBuntu* is materialized in ethical actions and, more specifically, in the enactment of justice between individuals in conflict. This enactment materializes a more humane world.

Mabogo More brings together the different aspects of *ubuntu* in his own profound and yet succinct definition:

> In one sense *ubuntu* is a philosophical concept forming the basis of relationships, especially ethical behaviour. In another sense, it is a traditional politico-ideological concept referring to socio-political action. As a moral or ethical concept, it is a point of view according to which moral practices are founded exclusively on consideration and enhancement of human well-being; a preoccupation with "human." It enjoins that what is morally good is what brings dignity, respect, contentment, and prosperity to others, self and the community at large. *uBuntu* is a demand for respect for persons no matter what their circumstances may be.
>
> In its politico-ideological sense it is a principle for all forms of social or political relationships. It enjoins and makes for peace and social harmony by encouraging the practice of sharing in all forms of communal existence.[12]

As a result, doing justice under *ubuntu* does not make a rigid distinction between civil and social-economic rights. Again, to remind the reader of John Murungi's powerful statement: "what is essential to law is what secures human beings in their being."[13]

We have quoted extensively from a number of renowned African philosophers and specialists in African jurisprudence in part as a response to Justice Mokgoro's profound call to legal academics in South Africa to acknowledge the importance of African philosophy and jurisprudence.[14]

UBUNTU AND THE INTERIM CONSTITUTION

Even if we have effectively shown the richness of *ubuntu*, both philosophically and ethically, the question remains whether *ubuntu*, as one understanding of the law, can be operationalized as both a grounding ethic of the South African Constitution and a justiciable principle.

In *Azanian Peoples Organisation (AZAPO) and Others v. President of the Republic South Africa and Others* 1996 (8) BCLR 1015 (CC) the court recognized the constitutional status of *ubuntu* and the epilogue in which it was included. The word *ubuntu* was omitted entirely from the final Constitution, perhaps only to the exception of paragraph 22 of Schedule 6 which preserves the epilogue of the Interim Constitution, and therefore a shadow of *ubuntu*, for the purposes of the Promotion of National Unity and Reconciliation Act (Act 34 of 1995).[15] It is important to note that *ubuntu* was only introduced into the Interim Constitution in the epilogue. The purpose of the epilogue was to provide a basis for amnesty and the formulation of a Truth and Reconciliation Commission.

We will begin our discussion of *ubuntu* under the Interim Constitution with the decision in *S v. Makwanyane*, the case in which the Constitutional Court struck down the legality of the death penalty under the Interim Constitution. We initiate this discussion with Justice Mokgoro's judgment because in her judgment she not only philosophically defines *ubuntu*, but she also seeks to show how *ubuntu* underscores a particular reading of the right to life and the right to dignity. First, however, let us introduce Justice Mokgoro's own definition of *ubuntu*:

> Generally, *ubuntu* translates as humaneness. In its most fundamental sense, it translates as *personhood* and *morality*. Metaphorically, it expresses itself in *umuntu ngumuntu ngabantu*, describing the significance of group solidarity on survival issues so central to the survival of communities. While it envelops the key values of group solidarity, compassion, respect, human dignity, conformity to basic norms and collective unity, in its fundamental sense it denotes humanity and morality. Its spirit emphasises respect for human dignity, marking a shift from confrontation to conciliation.[16]

We can see how Justice Mokgoro's definition resonates with that given by Mabogo More. First, *ubuntu* is clearly an ethical concept in her definition. As we discussed earlier, the African notion of the person is inherently normative. Thus, note how in Justice Mokgoro's definition *humaneness*, in the second sentence, is translated as both personhood and morality. As we have seen, because *ubuntu* defines human beings as intertwined with others from the beginning of life, and personhood as an ethical journey undertaken only with the support of others, it makes sense to draw attention to this connection between personhood and morality as Justice Mokgoro does in her definition.

Secondly, Justice Mokgoro's definition also reflects *ubuntu* as a political-ideological concept in the meaning given to that phrase by Mabogo More. Thus, note that Justice Mokgoro explicitly draws the connection between *ubuntu* and the building of democracy. The term democracy carries many meanings. In some cases it is reduced to the right to vote, and with it some form of representation and majority rule. In an essay by George Carew, the author makes a strong argument that there can be found in African traditions a strong commitment to what he defines as deliberative democracy and direct face-to-face participation. Deliberative democracy is essential in new African states that are premised on the need for political, economic and social transformation. Carew states:

> Deliberative politics, as I have argued, emphasises dialogue and mutual consideration and respect as the base on which citizens can come to an understanding about the public good. Thus the practice of this form of politics would presuppose that transformation in a way has occurred in such attitudes as are envisaged by, say, liberal egoists, who hold that politics is only about self-interest and the market. But how exactly might such a transformation occur? What crucial move or moves could lead to the moralisation of social relations?[17]

As we have discussed earlier, *ubuntu* does indeed moralize social relations. It is through dialogic participation that human beings both develop their own personhood as well as create shared representations of reality that allow a common world, and in modern language, the development of the notion of "the public good." Thus, for Justice Mokgoro, part of the building of democracy, certainly in the deliberative sense, in the rainbow heritage of South Africa, demands that no voice is silenced or group excluded in the effort to create a new South Africa—a new shared public world.

Thirdly, Justice Mokgoro refers us back to Murungi's reminder that what is essential to law in African jurisprudence "is what secures human beings in their being."[18] Thus, Justice Mokgoro emphasizes that the expression *umuntu ngumuntu ngabantu* speaks directly to survival issues, and that such survival is dependent on mutual support. But nothing about this notion of interdependency, or more strongly put, inscription by the other, means that dignity and the equal worth of human beings is not recognized. Indeed, if one reads More's definition carefully *ubuntu* is integrally connected to respect for persons, with the important reminder that because one is put in an extremely vulnerable position this respect is not one that is deserved or one that can be lost. As might be expected, given what we have discussed about *ubuntu*, Justice Mokgoro explicitly appeals to *ubuntu* as the law of law that must govern and ground the legal order of South Africa. As Mokgoro eloquently points out:

> Not only is the notion of *ubuntu* expressly provided for in the epilogue of the Constitution, the underlying idea and its values are also expressed in its preamble. These values underlie, first and foremost, the whole idea of adopting a Bill of Rights and Freedoms in a new legal order. They are central to the coherence of all the rights entrenched in Chapter 3—where the right to life and the right to respect for protection of human dignity are embodied in sections 9 and 10 respectively.[19]

In a series of interviews Justice Mokgoro has emphasized that even if the word *ubuntu* was omitted from the final Constitution its spirit could not be, because it is an ethical ground upon which a future of reconstruction and reconciliation can be built that goes way beyond the actual institutionalization of a Truth and Reconciliation Commission.[20] Neglecting to give *ubuntu* a prominent place in the final constitution, beyond its remnant as a shadow of the epilogue, did have negative implications for the development of a rich and complex *ubuntu* jurisprudence, that is, until somewhat recently. We are seeing a revival of *ubuntu*, both as a grounding ideal of the entire Constitution and, indeed, as a justiciable constitutional principle that has had major implications in the private law. But let us return to Justice Mokgoro's judgment.

Justice Mokgoro connects the right to dignity and the right to life through *ubuntu*. Mere biological life, into which we are all born, is not a human life under *ubuntu*. Simply existing is not what gives a human being inherent worth. Each of us, famously, has our own placenta, and therefore a unique biological life. But what develops this biological singularity is the respect and support that is given to all human beings so that they can achieve a unique personal life. Of course, if you kill someone that is the end of the journey. But it is the recognition of dignity that is crucial for a human life and this is why even a reprehensible criminal remains a human being and must not be thrown out of the reach of humanity.

There is yet another aspect of Justice Mokgoro's notion of *ubuntu* that reflects it as a politico-ideological concept in that the state is seen as a representative of *all* of its people. The state, however, is not simply a political representative, which, in a sense, is obvious, but it is also a moral representative. To quote Justice Mokgoro:

> The state is a moral representative of its people and in many ways sets the standard for moral values within society. If it sanctions by law punishment for killing by killing, it sanctions vengeance by law. If it does so with a view to

deterring others, it dehumanises the person and objectifies him or her as a tool for crime control. This objectification through the calculated killing of a human being, to serve state objectives, strips the offender of his or her human dignity and dehumanises such a person constituting a violation of section 10 of the Constitution.[21]

One accusation against *ubuntu* is that it is not specific enough as an ethical or moral ideal to be used as the ground of the modern Constitution that gives form to the meaning of the respect for dignity. But, *ubuntu* as an ethical, as well as a politico-ideological concept, is always integral to a social bond. *uBuntu*, in a profound sense, encapsulates the moral relations demanded by human beings who must live together. As we have seen it implies both a fundamental moralization of social relations, and this moralization of social relations is never changing. But the actual demands of *ubuntu* must change, since *ubuntu* is inseparable from a relationship between human beings that is always present, yet it is also connected to how we are always changing in those relationships, and our needs changing with them. The aspirational aspect of *ubuntu* is that we must strive together to achieve a public good and a shared world so that we can harmonize our individual interests. It is *ubuntu*'s embeddedness in our social reality that makes it a transformative concept at its core. But this transformation can never be taken away from the moralization of social relationships. It would have been absurd 500 years ago to put forward the argument that *ubuntu* demands access to electricity, since there was no access to electricity at all. Now, however, it is not at all absurd to make such an argument. Indeed, electricity is integral in securing a human life in modern society. Again, to turn to Murungi's definition that "law secures human beings in their being," law in the sense of doing justice does not separate between civil and social economic rights. Both are necessary for the securing and protection of our humanity in the moral sense that is echoed in Justice Mokgoro's judgment and in the writings of all the other African philosophers that are mentioned in this book.

Justice Mokgoro begins her judgment with an explicit call that the Constitution recognize and respect the indigenous values and ideals as these values can be explicitly developed to interpret the Bill of Rights. Again, we can see how this call to both incorporate indigenous values, and to be explicit about how these values are incorporated, both reflects the necessary respect for the formerly silenced majority of South Africans and promotes dialogue and communication. This promotion of dialogue is itself crucial to the moralization of social relations that is integral to the realization of *ubuntu*.

We began our discussion with Justice Mokgoro's judgment. For Justice Langa the moralization of social relations is crucial to the substantive revolution demanded by the new Constitution, both in its values and in its law. In this sense, for Langa, *ubuntu* lies at the very heart of the ethos of the new culture that is constituted in the very phrase "the new South Africa." Indeed, Justice Langa argues the following:

Implicit in the provisions and tone of the Constitution are the values of a more mature society, which relies on moral persuasion rather than force; on example rather than coercion. In this new context, then, the role of the State becomes clear. For good or for worse, the State is a role model for our society. Our culture of respect for human life and dignity, based on the values reflected in the Constitution, has to be engendered, and the State must take the lead. In acting out this role, the State not only preaches respect for the law and that killing must stop, but it demonstrates in the best way possible, by example, society's own regard for human life and dignity by refusing to destroy that of the criminal. Those who are inclined to kill need to be told why it is wrong. The reason surely must be the principle that the value of human life is inestimable, and it is a value, which the State must uphold by example as well. As pointed out by Mr Justice Schaefer of the Supreme Court of Illinois: "The methods we employ in the enforcement of our criminal law have aptly been called the measures by which the quality of our civilisation may be judged."[22]

Although Justice Mokgoro does so more explicitly, Justice Langa also echoes that *ubuntu* is the law of law in the new South Africa as it points away from a society in which relations between human beings were fundamentally immoral. Indeed, Justice Langa emphasizes the aspirational edge of *ubuntu*, not only in violent crimes, which he argues are the antithesis of *ubuntu*, but also against the historical horror show of apartheid, in which, as he writes "life became cheap, almost worthless."[23] Indeed, he argues, the dehumanization of all South Africans under apartheid lead to a call to return to *ubuntu*, and that this call for a return to *ubuntu* was integral to the overcoming of apartheid.[24] For Justice Langa the new society must express its condemnation of crime so as to aspire to the new moralization of social relations that underlies our Constitution. Whilst Justice Langa concludes that the death penalty is inconsistent with the right to life, the right to human dignity, and the right to not be subjected to cruel, inhumane and degrading punishment, *ubuntu* was not just an add-on to his finding that the death penalty is unconstitutional, because if the state is a role model then it must not behave in a way that is the antithesis of *ubuntu*. So, for the state to come down to the level of the murderer, it effectively undermines the ethos of the entire Constitution.

In Justice Madala's judgment we once again hear that *ubuntu*, even if it only appears in the postamble, is the law of law of the new South Africa. But, Justice Madala also makes an important addition to the discussion of *ubuntu*. Most of the judgments discuss three theories that justify punishment: deterrence, prevention, and retribution. For Justice Madala we do not punish individuals so as to keep them off the streets, or, at least, that cannot be the only goal. Justice Madala argues that the death penalty is against another idea of punishment: rehabilitation. As noted in Mabogo More's definition, all persons must be respected, no matter what their circumstances. No one can simply be thrown out of humanity as no good. Thus, for Justice Madala *ubuntu* demands that we take seriously rehabilitation as the ultimate purpose of punishment in the name of restorative justice, a concept for Justice Madala, that is integral to *ubuntu* and that gives meaning to the word *new* in the *new* South Africa. In this regard Justice Madala states the following:

> As observed before, the death penalty rejects the possibility of rehabilitation of the convicted persons, condemning them as "no good," once and for all, and drafting them to the death row and the gallows. One must then ask whether such a rejection of rehabilitation as a possibility accords with the concept of *ubuntu*.[25]

In Justice Madala's judgment *ubuntu* is explicitly used to justify the finding that the death penalty is unconstitutional:

> In my view, the death penalty does not belong to the society envisaged in the Constitution, is clearly in conflict with the Constitution generally and runs counter to the concept of *ubuntu;* additionally and just as importantly, it violates the provisions of section 11(2) of the Constitution and, for those reasons, should be declared unconstitutional and of no force and effect.[26]

Justice Mahomed develops what we are going to term here a *jurisprudence of memory*. The past of apartheid is remembered through the rights it violated. These violated rights are part of what lead to a society that is eaten up by violence and terrible suffering. It is against this jurisprudential memory, when combined with the ethos of the new South Africa, that the fate of the death penalty must be determined. As we have seen, over and over again now, *ubuntu* insists that no person is ever completely beyond the pale of humanity. Like Justice Mokgoro, Justice Mahomed also emphasizes that it is not only the person that is killed that is denied dignity; it is the community that kills him and that effectively undermines the ethos of the new state that is underscored by *ubuntu*.

The then President of the Constitutional Court, Arthur Chaskalson, writing for the majority, also referred to *ubuntu* in his judgment. He does so in his argument as to why the death penalty cannot be saved by the limitations clause, section 33(1) of the Interim Constitution. More specifically, he gives less weight to retribution than he does to deterrence and prevention in the balancing process called for by the limitations clause. Even if Justice Chaskalson indicates that *ubuntu* has primary application in the effort at political conciliation he recognizes that, "it is not without relevance to the enquiry we are called upon to undertake in the present case."[27]

Some critics of the *ubuntu* decision, such as Johan van der Walt, have asked: if *ubuntu* has been such an important overriding ethical and politico-ideological conception, why was the death penalty allowed in certain African tribes? Justice Sachs, in his concurrence with the death penalty decision, argues through a complex historical analysis that the death penalty was not the most pervasive penalty, even for heinous crimes, in South African tribal life.[28] Van der Walt criticizes Justice Sachs for not taking into account certain sayings or parables that seem to run against his account of African jurisprudence:

> Northern Sotho sayings such as *setopo ka setopa*, a corpse for a corpse, *letgotlo le lefa ka setopo*, a mouse pays with its carcass (meaning a murderer pays with his life) and the Tswana saying *botshelô bo tswêlwê ke botshelô, thlôgô ke thlôgô*, a life yields to a life, a head to a head, clearly reflect this endorsement in African languages. Should Justice Sachs not at least have discussed and qualified incisively these sayings so as convincingly to dismiss their relevance before embarking on his rather rosy portrayal of African jurisprudence?[29]

We are not attempting to answer van der Walt's question with additional historical evidence in a bid to support Justice Sachs. The deeper point, as we noted earlier, is that *ubuntu* is about the moralization of social relations, and what this means precisely changes with the social bond it seeks to create or maintain. The task before the new South Africa is to move away from a society in which ethical relations between human beings have been completely shattered. The task then is explicitly restorative, but in a unique sense. The sense in which it is restorative demands respect for the indigenous values and ideals that were ridiculed during apartheid. Thus, in that sense, we must restore these values and ideals, but that does not mean that such restoration must be done uncritically. Nor, more importantly, can we simply take one context and overlay it against another. *uBuntu* as the law of law of the new South Africa seeks nothing less than to restore ethical relationships between human beings. It is against that ethical mission that *ubuntu* must be read. *An eye for an eye* was once thought to be a legitimate way of thinking about punishment in many European countries. One only needs to think of Michel Foucault's book, *Discipline and Punish: The Birth of the Prison*, for an explication of how the death penalty was imposed in Europe in its most horrifying forms for what we would now see as small crimes. And whilst the saying *an eye for an eye* is still common to the English language, the death penalty has been abolished in the United Kingdom and the European Union.

So then, what does *ubuntu* mean for the death penalty in the new South Africa? After reading these judgments it should be clear that *ubuntu* shapes the reasons why the death penalty is a violation of life, dignity and the right to be free from inhumane and degrading conduct.

THE RE-COGNITION OF *UBUNTU* UNDER THE FINAL CONSTITUTIONAL ORDER

So far we have been discussing *ubuntu* when it had constitutional status in the epilogue of the Interim Constitution. As we have also noted, *ubuntu* only remains as a shadow in the final Constitution even in spite of the fact that it remains the fundamental value of the majority of South Africans. Thus, it is not surprising that *ubuntu* continued to be used at all levels of the judiciary, as the reader can see in the cases compiled in this book. But there has, inevitably, been confusion as to what the precise role of *ubuntu* is now that it has lost its literal status on the face of the document that is the final Constitution. For the sake of clarity *ubuntu* does need to be re-cognized both as a grounding ideal and as a justiciable principle. As is clearly evident from the cases that shall be reviewed this re-cognition is clearly under way and has clearly had an impact on statutory law, private law, and indeed, on the interpretation of the rights enshrined in the Bill of Rights.

RESTORATIVE JUSTICE AND SENTENCING UNDER THE CRIMINAL LAW

As we have already noted, Justice Madala in his concurring judgment in *S v. Makwanyane* argued that *ubuntu* favors the theory of punishment that is rooted in restorative justice, which seeks to rehabilitate the wrongdoer. Historically, African customary law did not make a firm distinction between criminal and civil law, in that the goal of both was always to seek to reconcile the wronged person with the wrongdoer, so that often compensation or some form of community service would be the appropriate remedy in what, in the Western criminal justice model, would be considered a criminal matter.[30]

Restorative justice, as opposed to retributive justice and other forms of punishment, seeks rehabilitation, not only of the wrongdoer, but also of the rift that has taken place in the community because of the wrongdoer's act, thereby restoring and undergirding the ethical commitments of the community. Thus, under restorative justice, the punishment does not only have to fit the crime, but also the criminal.[31]

uBuntu determines that you can never separate the criminal from the society in which he lives and that society's ethical commitments. Thus, *ubuntu* demands a system of justice that seeks to heal the rift in the society caused by the wrongdoing—a system of restorative justice.

Justice Madala's theory has come to fruition in the judicial innovation of recent criminal cases in our high courts. For example, in *S v. Shilubane*, the court raised the possibility of using section 300 of the Criminal Procedure Act[32] as a tool to aid a model of restorative justice, which would see an accused in a case of petty theft being able to pay compensation to the victim for the theft, in combination with a suspended sentence. However, for Justice Bosielo, this *ubuntu*-informed remedy of compensation was not an option, *in casu*, because the requirement in section 300 that the complainant consent to the compensation could not be met. But, for our purposes, the importance of Justice Bosielo's decision is not section 300 *per se*, but rather its demonstration of a movement in the courts to interpret existing remedies as gateways to restorative justice. This innovative judicial movement towards restorative justice is reflected in the following excerpt from Justice Bosielo's judgment:

> Inasmuch as it is critical for the maintenance of law and order that criminals be punished for their crimes, it is important that presiding officers impose sentences that are humane and balanced. There is abundant empirical evidence that retributive justice has failed to stem the ever-increasing wave of crime. It is furthermore counter-productive if not self-defeating, in my view, to expose an accused like the one, *in casu*, to the corrosive and brutalising effect of prison life for such a trifling offence. The price which civil society stands to pay in the end by having him emerge out of prison a hardened criminal, far outweighs the advantages to be gained by not sending him to jail.
>
> I am of the view that courts must seriously consider alternative sentences like community service as a viable alternative to direct imprisonment, particularly where the accused is not such a serious threat to society that he requires to be taken away from society for its protection. I am particularly fortified in my view by the strong sentiments (with which I respectfully agree) expressed by the former Deputy Minister of Correctional Services, Ms Cheryl Gillwald in the edition of the now defunct *This Day* newspaper of 17 August 2004 under the heading 'Crime and Punishment,' where she in an illuminating manner stated:
>
> "Incarceration only becomes a deterrent when society perceives the justice system to be efficient, consistent and effective. Rather than focusing on internment, sentencing should focus on what the most effective rehabilitation route would be for the offender, taking into account the gravity of the offence, assessment of the individual and his/her history, social and employment circumstances."
>
> Speaking for myself such an approach to sentencing will benefit our society immensely by excluding the possibility of warped sentences being imposed routinely on people who do not deserve them.[33]

Another *ubuntu*-informed innovation towards restorative justice can be found in the matter of *S v. Joyce Maluleke*. Here Justice Bertelsmann went so far as to use the remedy of an apology, at the request of the deceased's mother, in combination with a suspended sentence, in a homicide trial.

Although neither one of these cases directly referred to *ubuntu*, we would like to make the point that Justice Sachs has explicitly connected this kind of thinking about restorative justice to *ubuntu*. Therefore we feel that it is important that this move in criminal law towards innovative remedies be understood within the broader context of *ubuntu* thinking. Furthermore, as Justice Sachs emphasizes, criminal justice is not the only area in which *ubuntu* can or should play an important legal role in the new South Africa.

SOCIOECONOMIC RIGHTS

Thino Bekker, in a thoughtful article included in this volume, makes the argument that the *Port Elizabeth*[34] case clearly brought *ubuntu* to bear on not only issues of the private law of property and the rights protected in sections 25 and 26 of the Constitution, but also on the interpretation of the piece of legislation that is commonly known as PIE.[35] This, for Bekker, is what he calls the revitalization of *ubuntu*. Bekker also worries that Justice Sachs seemed to make no new contribution to the understanding of *ubuntu* "or the potential role that it may play in future adjudication."[36]

We, however, read the case differently in that we see the entirety of Justice Sachs's reasoning to be based on *ubuntu*. First of all, Justice Sachs argues that sections 25 and 26 of the Constitution (dealing with property and housing rights, respectively) must be read together. More importantly, he interprets section 26(3) in such a manner that the relationship between the right to own property and the right to have a home puts a specific obligation on the courts to grapple with what are inevitably competing rights situations involving conflict so as to bring about as much reconciliation as possible between the opposing sides. The approach then clearly moves beyond the idea that law announces a winner in a contested advocacy setting. Indeed Justice Sachs argues the following:

> In sum, the Constitution imposes new obligations on the courts concerning rights relating to property not previously recognised by the common law. It counterposes to the normal ownership rights of possession, use and occupation, a new and equally relevant right not arbitrarily to be deprived of a home. The expectations that ordinarily go with title could clash head-on with the genuine despair of people in dire need of accommodation. The judicial function in these circumstances is not to establish a hierarchical arrangement between the different interests involved, privileging in an abstract and mechanical way the rights of ownership over the right not to be dispossessed of a home, or vice versa. Rather it is to balance out and reconcile the opposed claims in as just a manner as possible taking account of all the interests involved and the specific factors relevant in each particular case.[37]

In this paragraph Justice Sachs is appealing to both the ethical and the politico-ideological aspects of *ubuntu* emphasized in More's definition of *ubuntu*. But Justice Sachs does so in a specific and important way. His argument here is that *ubuntu* imposes an obligation on the courts to seek reconciliation, which is based on the enhancement of the well being of all the people of South Africa. *uBuntu* is actually brought to bear on the definition of judicial responsibility.

Justice Sachs then proceeds to give a precise reading of PIE, which includes, first, the need to give extensive contextual analysis of the circumstances of the occupation of the land. Secondly, he gives an analysis of the meaning of another aspect of the statute, which makes it relevant to consider how long the occupiers have been on the land. This analysis demands that we look at how settled the families that occupy the land are in both their homes and in their communities. Thirdly, he carefully examines how one should interpret the "availability of suitable alternative accommodation or land," as it appears in section 6(3) of PIE. Here Justice Sachs makes it clear that it is not enough to have a solution that works in theory. To quote Justice Sachs, and here again we see his reliance on *ubuntu* both as an ethical and politico-ideological concept:

> The Constitution requires that everyone must be treated with care and
> concern; if the measures, though statistically successful, fail to respond to the
> needs of the most desperate, they may not pass the test.[38]

He then further interprets the sections of PIE, which require the consideration of all relevant circumstances, and what the court must have regard to when developing those circumstances. Here again the spirit of *ubuntu* demands that the court have an obligation to actually inform itself of the situation of the occupiers and the suffering that would be imposed upon them if they were to be evicted. Again, what Sachs is emphasizing is the obligation of the court to move beyond the limited positivist notion of what is expected of the judiciary in terms of more conventional notions of rules of evidence and procedure. To quote Justice Sachs:

> The obligation on the court is to "have regard to" the circumstances, that is,
> to give them due weight in making its judgement as to what is just and equi-
> table. The court cannot fulfil its responsibilities in this respect if it does not
> have the requisite information at its disposal. It needs to be fully apprised of
> the circumstances before it can have regard to them. It follows that although
> it is incumbent on the interested parties to make all relevant information
> available, technical questions relating to onus of proof should not play an un-
> duly significant role in its enquiry. The court is not resolving a civil dispute as
> to who has rights under land law; the existence of unlawfulness is the founda-
> tion for the enquiry, not its subject matter.[39]

Next, of course, Justice Sachs turns to the obligation of the court to find an equitable solution. The definition of "just and equitable" should not turn on some technical internal examination of what those terms have meant in the ordinary provisions of land law. Instead, Justice Sachs argues, that the necessary reconciliation that must be achieved between the rule of law and the achievement of equality cannot be done if the court does not go beyond its normal function and must instead, as he has repeated several times, pursue the situation of the occupiers. As he earlier argued, the goal here is not some technical hierarchy between sections 25 and 26, but the achievement of a just and equitable outcome that hopefully reconciles the parties and, to the degree that it is possible, protects the well being of the most vulnerable. Thus, *ubuntu* as we have earlier referred to it as the law of law, demands for Justice Sachs an interpretation of both PIE and its specific clauses and the constitutional rights of sections 25 and 26. At this point he writes:

> Thus, PIE expressly requires the court to infuse elements of grace and compassion into the formal structures of law. It is called upon to balance competing interests in a principled way and to promote the constitutional vision of a caring society based on good neighbourliness and shared concern. The Constitution and PIE confirm that we are not islands unto ourselves. The spirit of *ubuntu*, part of the deep cultural heritage of the majority of the population, suffuses the whole constitutional order. It combines individual rights with a communitarian philosophy. It is a unifying motif of the Bill of Rights, which is nothing if not a structured, institutionalised and operational declaration in our evolving society of the need for human interdependence, respect and concern.[40]

Note that Justice Sachs argues that first, *ubuntu* is a unifying motif of the Bill of Rights—that is, the law of law. Second, he notes that it is a structured, institutionalized declaration. What does he mean by that? As we have interpreted his judgment, *ubuntu* profoundly structures the entire analysis that he offers, not only of the Constitution and of PIE, but also of judicial obligation. *uBuntu* is institutionalized as both an ethical and social politico-ideological concept in More's sense. Indeed, the role of mediation is not read as simply a way to save money in Justice Sachs's judgment. It is, for him, an important factor that must be taken into account as to whether or not it was tried before the eviction took place. And how do Justice Sachs's analyses of mediation rely on *ubuntu*? Mediation, for Justice Sachs, becomes an important part of how one analyzes what is a just and equitable solution when land is unlawfully occupied precisely because it promotes sustainable reconciliations and the possibility of finding a mutually acceptable solution.

It is important to emphasize that this sustainable reconciliation is only possible through direct participatory democracy in which everyone in the community must have a voice and must be heard. Thus participatory democracy is organic to the communities in conflict and it is the actual voices of the human beings involved in the conflict that must be heard in order to enable a genuine reconciliation of the parties.

uBuntu is operational in all of the aspects of this judgment that we have just mentioned: it underscores the interpretation of the Constitution and what this interpretation means, and an analysis of the specific terms of PIE. *uBuntu* operationalizes certain obligations that must be imposed upon the judiciary. Further, through the status that Justice Sachs gives to mediation, obligations are also imposed upon the parties in the name of *ubuntu*.

Indeed, in the *City of Johannesburg v. Rand Properties*[41] judgment, High Court Justice Jajbhay closely follows the structure of Justice Sachs's argument in the *Port Elizabeth* case. He underscores the centrality of *ubuntu* as it defines a broad view of the ideal of humanity. To begin with, Justice Jajbhay returns us to some of the common themes we have heard echoed both in our philosophical elaboration of *ubuntu*, and in the cases we have discussed; themes such as interconnectedness, and the ethical notion of humanity, and the responsibility that results from our inevitable interpolation by others. Whilst the decision of the High Court in *City of Johannesburg v. Rand Properties* was overturned we feel that Justice Jajbhay, in the quote that follows, accurately emphasized how *ubuntu* resists some of the worst aspects of the values, or lack thereof, of neoliberal capitalism, and indeed further develops Justice Sachs's reliance on *ubuntu* in the *Port Elizabeth* case. What this quote emphasizes, and, of course, what neoliberalism denies, in particular, is our interconnectedness and the obligations that flow from understanding our intertwinement with one another:

> *uBuntu* speaks to our interconnectedness, our common humanity and the responsibility to each that flows from our connection. This in turn must be interpreted to mean that in the establishment of our constitutional values we must not allow urbanisation and the accumulation of wealth and material possessions to rob us of our warmth, hospitality and genuine interests in each other as human beings. *uBuntu* is a culture which places some emphasis on the commonality and on the interdependence of the members of the community. It recognises a person's status as a human being, entitled to unconditional respect, dignity, value and acceptance from the members of the community that such a person may be a part of. In South Africa, *ubuntu* must become a notion with particular resonance in the building of our constitutional democracy.
>
> The absence of adequate housing for the Respondents and any subsequent eviction will drive them in a vicious circle, to the depravation of their employment, their livelihood, and therefore their right to dignity, perhaps even their right to life. The right to work is one of the most precious liberties that an individual possesses. An individual has as much right to work as the individual has to live, to be free and to own property. To work means to eat and consequently, to live. This constitutes an encompassing view of humanity. The applicant's suggestion that the Respondents be relocated to an informal settlement flies in the face of the concept that a "person is a person through persons" (*ubuntu*).[42]

Justice Jajbhay clearly relies on and develops Justice Sachs's conception of *ubuntu* and its role in socioeconomic cases. However, the High Court focused on section 26 arguments and held that the city had failed to meet its obligation to create and implement a program that would give the Respondents adequate housing in the inner city. The Constitutional Court overturned the High Court insofar as it refused to deal with the resident's broader claim, which was accepted by the High Court, that the city lacked a comprehensive housing program, as required by the decision in *Grootboom*. Thus, the quote from the High Court decision still accurately reflects the centrality given to *ubuntu* in the *Port Elizabeth* case. And, moreover Justice Yacoob, in the Constitutional Court's decision for *City of Johannesburg v. Rand Properties*, although not using the word *ubuntu*, takes Justice Sachs's constitutionalization of mediation a step further, as required by *ubuntu*, demanding a meaningful engagement between the parties, which can require direct interaction. This is emphasized by Justice Yacoob in the following extract from the judgment:

> Engagement has the potential to contribute towards the resolution of disputes and to increase understanding and sympathetic care if both sides are willing to participate in the process. People about to be evicted may be so vulnerable that they may not be able to understand the importance of engagement and may refuse to take part in the process. If this happens, a municipality cannot walk away without more. It must make reasonable efforts to engage and it is only if these reasonable efforts fail that a municipality may proceed without appropriate engagement. It is precisely to ensure that a city is able to engage meaningfully with poor, vulnerable or illiterate people that the engagement process should preferably be managed by careful and sensitive people on its side.[43]

As we noted earlier, Thino Bekker worried that Justice Sachs only used the word *ubuntu* once in his judgment, and we understand his concern that when *ubuntu* is used it must be made as explicit as possible as to exactly how it is functioning in the judgment at hand. Certainly, Justice Jajbhay acknowledges aspects of *ubuntu* that were left implicit in Justice Sachs's judgment. And yet, as we have tried to show, Justice Sachs's entire judgment can and should be read through *ubuntu* as a "structured, institutionalised and operational declaration."[44] But our deeper point is that even when *ubuntu* is not referred to, such as in the *Khosa* case, which is included in this book, it is still used as the spirit of judicial reflection, subsuming the manner in which the judiciary meets its mandates under the new constitutional dispensation. That said, it is important at this crucial stage in the development of the South African constitutional democracy that *ubuntu* is recognized as one possible understanding of the law of law in the new South Africa. This understanding of *ubuntu* need not be in competition with dignity. However, it does give a different form to dignity, even as the *Grundnorm* of the Constitution, than the one defended in more Kantian interpretations of the Constitution, such as that offered by Justice Ackermann. It is, of course, also important, as we have seen in our reading and interpretation of Justice Sachs's judgment, that the judiciary develops *ubuntu* as a justiciable principle for the Bill of Rights, statutes, and indeed the private law.

THE IMPACT OF *UBUNTU* ON PRIVATE LAW

In Justice Mokgoro's majority judgment in the *Dikoko* case she finds that the quantum of damages could potentially affect the relationship between dignity and freedom of expression, and therefore excessive monetary awards could have a chilling effect on freedom of expression. Therefore, the quantum of damages is a constitutional issue. Indeed, Justice Mokgoro finds the quantum of damages in this case to be inappropriate and would have issued an order that the damages award of the High Court must indeed be lowered. For us, the true significance of the *Dikoko* case is not simply that the quantum of damages is a constitutional issue for Justice Mokgoro. Justice Mokgoro defends an alternative to that of damages for a person whose personality rights have been impaired by another. She returns to a remedy, *amende honorable*, considered in this case by the High Court. Justice Mokgoro uses the following quote from Melius de Villiers that was used in the High Court judgment:

> In the systems of jurisprudence founded on Roman law a legal remedy has
> been introduced which was not entirely unknown to the Romans, known as
> the *amende honorable*. . . . *this remedy took two forms. In the first place, there is
> the palinode, recantation or retraction,* that is, a declaration by the person who
> uttered or published the defamatory words or expressions concerning another,
> to the effect that he withdraws such words or expressions as being untrue; and
> it is applied when such words or expressions are in fact untrue. In the second
> place there is the *deprecation* apology, which is an acknowledgement by the
> person who uttered or published concerning another anything which if
> untrue would be defamatory, or who committed a real injury, that he has
> done wrong and a prayer that he may be forgiven.[45]

For Justice Mokgoro the harm of defamation is often one that cannot be adequately satisfied by damages, and indeed it is not really money that is sought. Further, in a case such as this one, damages can actually cause serious financial harm to the defamer and, as we noted earlier, also inhibit freedom of expression. Yes, Justice Mokgoro writes that a public apology is often less costly than an award for damages, but note again that her defense of this remedy is not simply done as a cost saving device, but goes straight to the heart of the wrong in a defamation case. If what is sought is restoration of reputation then that can be better done by a public apology. Of course she also shows concern for the financial harm imposed on defamers who may well not be wealthy themselves. Thus, for Justice Mokgoro, the restoration of reputation and, indeed, the need to protect against inappropriate claims of defamation would underscore the need to make a contextual determination of precisely how the defamation has harmed the individual and indeed what role damages would play in the restoration of reputation. Once again we see Justice Mokgoro appealing to external factors so as to make adequate judgments about the appropriate remedy. And this again highlights, as was done in the *Port Elizabeth* case, a notion of judicial responsibility. Thus, for Justice Mokgoro, this responsibility of the judge is not only to take careful consideration of the context into account, but more importantly to do so through *ubuntu*:

> In our constitutional democracy the basic constitutional value of human dig-
> nity relates closely to *ubuntu* or *botho*, an idea based on deep respect for the
> humanity of another. Traditional law and culture have long considered one
> of the principal objectives of the law to be the restoration of harmonious hu-
> man and social relationships where they have been ruptured by an infraction
> of community norms. It should be a goal of our law to emphasise, in cases of
> compensation for defamation, the re-establishment of harmony in the
> relationship between the parties, rather than to enlarge the hole in the defen-
> dant's pocket, something more likely to increase acrimony, push the parties
> apart and even cause the defendant financial ruin. The primary purpose of a
> compensatory measure, after all, is to restore the dignity of a plaintiff who
> has suffered the damage and not to punish a defendant. A remedy based on
> the idea of *ubuntu* or *botho* could go much further in restoring human
> dignity than an imposed monetary award in which the size of the victory is
> measured by the quantum ordered and the parties are further estranged
> rather than brought together by the legal process. It could indeed give better
> appreciation and sensitise a defendant as to the hurtful impact of his or her
> unlawful actions, similar to the emerging idea of restorative justice in our
> sentencing laws.[46]

As we have already seen, for Justice Mokgoro a public apology emphasizes restorative as opposed to retributive justice. To refer to More's definition once more, *ubuntu* enjoins us to seek to repair shattered relationships, as well as, in the case of defamation, to restore one's reputation. We need to emphasize here that the court seeks remedies that promote, rather than further undermine, restorative justice. For Justice Mokgoro judicial obligation demands innovative remedies for the wrong of defamation in the name of the restorative justice demanded by *ubuntu*:

> The goal should be to knit together shattered relationships in the community
> and encourage across-the-board respect for the basic norms of human and so-
> cial inter-dependence. It is an area where courts should be pro-active, encour-
> aging apology and mutual understanding wherever possible.[47]

Justice Sachs, in his concurring opinion, further develops the connection between judicial obligation to develop innovative remedies and the importance of this being done through the restorative justice commanded by *ubuntu*. As Justice Sachs argues:

> Although *ubuntu-botho* and the *amende honorable* are expressed in different languages intrinsic to separate legal cultures, they share the same underlying philosophy and goal. Both are directed towards promoting face-to-face encounter between the parties, so as to facilitate resolution in public of their differences and the restoration of harmony in the community. In both legal cultures the center-piece of the process is to create conditions to facilitate the achievement, if at all possible, of an apology honestly offered, and generously accepted.
>
> Thus, although I believe the actual award made by the High Court in this matter was way over the top, and accordingly associate myself with Mokgoro J's minority finding in this regard, my concern is not restricted to the excessiveness of the amount. It lies primarily with the fact that the law, as presently understood and applied, does far too little to encourage repair and reconciliation between the parties. In this respect the High Court can-not be faulted. The concerns expressed above were not raised in the papers or addressed in argument before it. The Court was simply working with a well-tried remedy in the ordinary way. Unfortunately, the hydraulic pressure on all concerned to go with the traditional legal flow inevitably produces a set of rules that are self-referential and self-perpetuating. The whole forensic mindset, as well as the way evidence is led and arguments are presented, is functionally and exclusively geared towards enlarging or restricting the amount of damages to be awarded, rather than towards securing an apology. In my view, this fixed concentration on quantum requires amendment. Greater scope has to be given for reparatory remedies.[48]

Referring to the present case at hand Justice Sachs points out a trap that inheres in the "hydraulic pressure" to only focus on money in defamation cases. As Justice Sachs points out, if Mr. Dikoko had actually apologized to Mr. Mokhatla he would have, in doing so, left himself open to being liable for even greater damages. Thus, as is further noted, the relationship between the two was worsened and the rupture between the two was entrenched rather than healed. Neither Justice Mokgoro nor Justice Sachs ar-gues against damages. Indeed both understand the role that damages can play, and must play, in *some* defamation cases. Even so, as Justice Sachs concludes:

> What is needed, then, is more flexibility and innovation concerning the rela-tion between apology and money awards. A good beginning for achieving greater remedial suppleness might well be to seek out the points of overlap

between *ubuntu–botho* and the *amende honorable*, the first providing a new spirit, the second a time-honoured legal format. Whatever renovatory modalities are employed, and however significant to the outcome the facts will have to be in each particular case, the fuller the range of remedial options available the more likely will justice be done between the parties. And the greater the prospect of realising the more humane society envisaged by the Constitution.[49]

Both Justice Sachs and Justice Mokgoro focus on restorative justice and the need to take into account what would actually repair the relationship between the parties. Thus, the focus is on the actual relationship between the persons involved and therefore what would be appropriate to order as a remedy would have to take into account the need to do justice between individuals. The need to do justice between individuals has now been brought into contract law in the *Barkhuizen*[50] case. Justice Ngcobo, for the majority, stressed the importance of freedom of contract, as this freedom is integral to the respect of the dignity of persons. In a profound sense, then, freedom of contract is grounded in the respect for dignity of all persons. But if it is *ubuntu* that gives meaning to dignity, even in the exercise of the freedom of the will actualized in the contractual relationship, the court must also take into account whether or not a specific contract actually was rooted in respect for dignity. To make the next step in the analysis, Justice Ngcobo turns to *ubuntu* in that *ubuntu* demands that values like justice and reasonableness must be taken into account when assessing any specific contract, and the actual relations of power between the parties. As Justice Ngcobo underscores, *ubuntu* must redefine the notions of justice, fairness and equity in contract law in terms of their legal significance. Indeed, as Justice Ngcobo notes:

> In general, the enforcement of an unreasonable or unfair time limitation clause will be contrary to public policy. Broadly speaking, the test announced in *Mohlomi* is whether a provision affords a claimant an adequate and fair opportunity to seek judicial redress. Notions of fairness, justice and equity, and reasonableness cannot be separated from public policy. Public policy takes into account the necessity to do simple justice between individuals. Public policy is informed by the concept of *ubuntu*. It would be contrary to public policy to enforce a time limitation clause that does not afford the person bound by it an adequate and fair opportunity to seek judicial redress.[51]

The important thing to note here is that it is through *ubuntu* that good faith comes to be more than a value that is applied indirectly in contract law, and instead is now used to develop good faith so as to allow it to be a principle that can be invoked directly to attack a contractual provision, formerly agreed to by the contracting parties. Thus Justice Ngcobo explicitly disagrees with the Supreme Court of Appeal to the extent that the Supreme Court's dicta on the matter can be interpreted as denying that a clause will be found unconstitutional by the mere fact that it is unreasonable and unfair. Indeed, Justice Ngcobo makes the following statement:

> Thus if a court finds that a time limitation clause does not afford a contracting party a reasonable and fair opportunity to approach a court, it will declare it to be contrary to public policy, and therefore invalid.[52]

Therefore, it is crucial for the Constitutional Court to engage in a principle balancing process between the importance of dignity in contractual relations, and at the same time, the need to do justice between the parties so that there will be an actual examination of the power of relations between the individuals as well as the assessment of certain kinds of clauses in standard form contract, for example, as to whether these are consistent with the doing of *ubuntu*. Thus, it is *ubuntu* that gives legal significance to the idea of a countervailing notion of justice that must be taken into account in any individual contract. Justice Ngcobo recognizes this in the following passage:

> Public policy imports the notions of fairness, justice and reasonableness. Public policy would preclude the enforcement of a contractual term if its enforcement would be unjust or unfair. Public policy, it should be recalled "is the general sense of justice of the community, the boni mores, manifested in public opinion." Thus where a claimant seeks to avoid the enforcement of a time limitation clause on the basis that non-compliance with it was caused by factors beyond his or her control, it is inconceivable that a court would hold the claimant to such a clause. The enforcement of the time limitation clause in such circumstances would result in an injustice and would no doubt be contrary to public policy. As has been observed, while public policy endorses the freedom of contract, it nevertheless recognises the need to do simple justice between the contracting parties. To hold that a court would be powerless in these circumstances would be to suggest that the hands of justice could be tied; in my view, the hands of justice can never be tied under our constitutional order.[53]

Again it is important to note that *ubuntu* is not an aside, but indeed gives shape to the demands of justice and reasonableness so that a harsh contract would inevitably be against public policy in that it breaks down the respect for persons implied in freedom of contract and further undermines the necessary examination of individual circumstances so as to know whether there was actually an expression of free will in the contractual relationship. It is important to note then that *ubuntu* is actually giving a moral meaning to public policy. In this particular case, since *ubuntu* demands justice between individuals, Justice Ngcobo looked closely at the circumstances of the individuals and thus concluded that the enforcement of this particular clause against this particular Applicant was not unjust.

Justice Sachs, in his dissent, like Justice Ngcobo, directly connects the right to contract with free expression of the will and volition. But, as he powerfully argues, the evolution of contract law has been in the direction of recognizing that the technical approach of the Supreme Court of Appeal can actually undermine, rather than reinforce, the volition of more powerless people to enter into contracts on their own terms. For example, Justice Sachs argues strongly that standard form contracts, with their small print, cannot truly be traced to volition on the part of the contracting party because they often come in the form of a take-it-or-leave-it basis. To quote Justice Sachs on standard form contracts:

> Standard form contracts are contracts that are drafted in advance by the supplier of goods or services and presented to the consumer on a "take-it-or-leave-it" basis, thus eliminating opportunity for arm's length negotiations. They contain a common stock of contract terms that tend to be weighted heavily in favour of the supplier and to operate to limit or exclude the consumer's normal contractual rights and the supplier's normal contractual obligations and liabilities. Not only is the consumer frequently unable to resist the terms in a standard form contract, but he or she is often unaware of their existence or unable to appreciate their import. Onerous terms are often couched in obscure legalese and incorporated as part of the "fine print" of the contract.[54]

It is important to underscore that Justice Sachs does not disagree with the reasoning of Justice Ngcobo as it entails that justice deploys *ubuntu* and gives shape to the legal significance of the constitutional ideal of dignity. For both Justice Sachs and Justice Mokgoro dignity is one of the central reasons for respecting the right to a contract in the first place. He disagrees with the specific conclusion in this case because he argues that time limitation clauses, such as the one in this case, should always be found to be unconstitutional as fundamentally unfair and therefore against public policy. Although Justice Sachs does not explicitly use the word *ubuntu* his elaboration does not negate Justice Ngcobo's reasoning about *ubuntu*'s place in contract law as it gives legal significance to good faith, unreasonableness, and indeed the idea of public policy. Indeed, he uses Justice Ngcobo's reasoning to reach a different conclusion.[55]

Justice Sachs emphasizes that the problem with standard form contracts is not only that they can make use of fine print to trap the vulnerable, but also that they can infringe upon the constitutional right of access to the court. This is part and parcel of why when such contracts do limit the right of access to the courts they should be found unfair.

The re-cognition of *ubuntu*, as seen from the above cases, is certainly taking place in the Constitutional Court of South Africa. We have little doubt that this re-cognition will influence the development of *ubuntu* in the lower courts of South Africa. But, as we have seen, *ubuntu*, even if it gives form and new meaning to legal principles such as unfairness and public policy, can never be reduced to any one of its formulations in any area of law. For, as Justice Ngcobo reminds us, as the law of law, it demands nothing less than that we do justice to individuals, and this effort to do justice to individuals' demands reformulation of constitutional principles and, indeed, principles of the private law.

Over and over again we have referred to John Murungi's insight that "law is what secures human beings in their being." But, ultimately it is also about opening and protecting a space for a kind of dialogue about what it means to be a human being:

> What African jurisprudence calls for is an ongoing dialogue among Africans on being human, a dialogue that of necessity leads to a dialogue with other human beings. This dialogue is not an end in itself. It is a dialogue with an existential implication. It aims at living in accordance with what one is, which implies living in accordance with what one ought to be. Although one is what one is, one is what one is dialogically. To be dialogical, which necessarily is to engage others, leaves open what one is, and calls for dwelling in this openness.[56]

In any society there is always conflict, and people are inevitably wounding each other in their engagements. So there can never be any end to the dialogue about what justice means in a given context. In South Africa there has been a traumatic rip in the relations between people. The particular devastation of colonialism leaves a gaping wound in the social bond, and yet it is the all-too-evident exposure of each one of us to that wound that brings us into the healing process. At stake in our own engagement with each other in the new South Africa is our own humanity, understood ethically, for the wound is not out there, it is within each one of us. As we have emphasized throughout this introduction, we become human only in our relationships with others. And thus there is a call to participate in the dialogue of what restorative justice might mean. In the cases we have discussed the call to restorative justice has demanded reformulations of constitutional and private law. But of course, it is not simply judges who are called to do justice; we are all called.

... any man's death diminishes me, because I am involved in mankind, and therefore never send to know for whom the bell tolls; it tolls for thee.

John Donne

I

Legal Cases

This part provides summaries of legal cases as well as excerpts from the original court judgments, which are presented unedited in their original form—preserving the judges' personal styles, typographical errors, and spelling patterns of International English.

uBuntu, Restorative Justice,
and the Constitutional Court

THE MANDELA CASE

S v. Mandela [2001] JOL 7754 (C)

Case Summary

FACTS

The facts of this case weave a complex matrix of events that led to the murder of two deceased by gang members in KTC, Cape Town.

The accused, in this case, Mr. Mandela, was a member of a gang who was charged with two counts of the crime of murder, two contraventions of Act 75 of 1969, insofar as he was charged with unlawful possession of a firearm and ammunition and one charge of arson. The accused entered a plea of not guilty on all five counts and advanced the defense of compulsion in respect of all the charges, save for the charge of arson.

LEGAL HISTORY

The case appeared before the High Court.

LEGAL ISSUES

The issue to be determined by the court was whether, in relation to charges two to four, the accused could successfully rely on the defense of compulsion for a full acquittal?

DECISION

In consideration of the accused's defense of compulsion Justice Davis considered the decision of Judge of Appeal Rumpff (as he then was) in *S v. Goliath* 1972 (3) SA 1 (A), distinguishing the facts of *Goliath* from the actions of the accused *in casu*. Justice Davis held that the constitutional right to life of the person who is safeguarding his own life at the expense of another results in an "exquisite balance between the conflict between the two rights bearers of this most precious of rights." Justice Davis went on to hold that, given the delicacy of this balance, the court would only be able to find that the accused lacked *culpa* due to compulsion or necessity in instances where "the danger of the death cannot be averted, save by acts of heroism which extend beyond the capacity that should, and can, be demanded of the reasonable person."

In this regard the court found that, on the evidence, there was "no immediacy of life threatening compulsion as there was in the case of *Goliath*" and therefore, that there was nothing to warrant a finding that the accused could not have taken some action so as to warn victims in either murder or in some way prevent the murders. Justice Davis went on to reason that if the court were to accept the defense of compulsion or necessity when it was clear that the accused could have taken measures short of heroism to prevent the harm, then it would be setting a very low bench mark in a constitutional democracy that demands more from its members. Justice Davis held further that because we now live in a "constitutional community, based on fundamental principles including those of freedom, dignity, *ubuntu*, and respect for life; the acceptance of so base a threshold would be tantamount to a lowering of regard for life and an undermining of the very fabric of the attempt to build a constitutional community, where each and every person is deserving of equal concern and respect and in which community grows, sourced in the principle of *ubuntu*."

The learned judge went on to say that even if, as counsel for the defense suggested, the judgment of Jansen JA could be read as the incorporation in South African law of a normative test to replace the physiological (subjective) test that is currently employed by the courts to determine culpability, it was nevertheless not objectively reasonable, applying the standards of the reasonable gang member of Khayelitsha, not to have taken steps that may have been available to avert the murders.

In an *obiter* statement, in keeping with the community theme developed in this judgment, Justice Davis went on to question the accountability of the investigatory agencies for the absence of the other members of the gang who acted with Mr. Mandela, but who failed to appear as his co-accused in this trial.

Justice Davis

. . .

The accused pleaded not guilty to all the charges.

. . .

When the defence opened its case, Mr Mandela changed his plea in respect of counts 1 to 4, to that of guilty. However, as he persisted with the same defence of compulsion, nothing changed and he had, in effect, continued to plead that he was not guilty.

The essence of his testimony before the court confirmed the version that he had given Magistrate van Reenen. He had met Mr Ntamo, to whom he referred as "the boss," in 1996. Mr Ntamo had offered him a place to stay in KTC. In June 1997, at the time of the establishment of the NCF, he was advised by Mr Ntamo to make a choice as to which of the ANC or NCF he should support. He confirmed that Ms Gexu wanted to acquire a house and that he had informed her that he was the owner of an additional house in Samora Machel and that she could acquire that house from him. He then appeared to consult with Mr Ntamo about houses in Delft and arranged for Ms Gexu to meet Mr Ntamo, whereupon she gave him R1500 as a deposit on this house.

He was then called to Mr Ntamo's house where he met Messrs Hewu, James as well as Mr Ntamo. They instructed him to arrange for Ms Gexu to be present at Nyanga bus terminus on the following day. He was also instructed at the time that this would be part of a plan that would eventually lead him to shooting Nomhle Gexu. He testified that he had never killed anyone before, but he was informed that if he did not do so they would employ force upon him to fatal effect. He claimed that the motivation for this attack was to cast greater suspicion upon members of the NCF and hence ensure that the DP would perceive the NCF to be the enemy.

Mr Hewu fetched Mr Mandela on the appointed day. They arrived at the house of "the boss" who was not there. After a wait of some two hours Mr Ntamo arrived. There was some anxiety about the delay. Mr Tira then took out a firearm from a trunk full of arms and gave it to Mandela. Tira had his own firearm. They then fetched Nomhle Gexu at the bus terminus and drove to Delft. Gexu, Tira and Mandela sat in the front of the car, which Tira drove. The car stopped because Tira informed them that there was a shortcut by the use of a footpath. At the appointed moment, Tira bent to tie his shoelace and Mr Mandela, recognising the necessary sign, fired two shots, with fatal effect. They then ran away. People who had heard the shots being fired, apprehended them, and Tira explained that the shots came from a gun employed by a farmer who had threatened them, claiming that they had been trespassers.

Mr Mandela then testified that upon the following morning he went to Tira's house. Ms Gexu's family were looking for her. They knew that Mandela had arranged to have an appointment with Ms Gexu regarding the acquisition of a house. Tira and Mandela went to see Ntamo and it was there that the plan was hatched to use Crime Stop as a means of deflecting the anxiety of the Gexu family. Mr Mandela confirmed that he had phoned Crime Stop and left his telephone number with Crime Stop. When an official from Crime Stop phoned, Mandela claimed that Nomhle Gexu had been kidnapped.

After initially being arrested for the kidnapping of Ms Gexu, Mandela was then released. Shortly thereafter another meeting took place, this time at the house of Tira. At this particular meeting where Mr Ntamo, Mr James, Mr Landingwe were present Mandela was informed that Mr Mbewana must be killed. Mandela testified that he was not prepared to kill Mr Mbewana, he had just been released, he had been suspected of murdering Nomhle Gexu, and he was anxious about an involvement. Mr Ntamo informed him that they had another person to do the dastardly deed but that he must assist him. A further meeting was held to plan the event and he was informed at that meeting that he must call at Mr Mbewana's house and accompany him to Mr Mjodo's house. When he came back to Mr Mbewana's house he did the necessary and it was at this point that Mr Mbewana gave him a jacket.

Mr Mandela had gone to his part of the dwelling when he emerged. Mr Mbewana had left the house. He followed upon the heels of Mbewana. They walked through a passage that would take them to the house. There they found a white Toyota Cressida. Siwa emerged from the car and instructed Mr Mbewana to get into the rear. Siwa, Tira and Cira were all in the car. Tira informed Mr Mandela that he also was required to get into the motor car. The car slowly moved in the direction of NY5 cemetery. When they reached the cemetery, Siwa said to Mr Mbewana, "Get out of the car you dog." Mr Mbewana at this point enquired about what it was that they required. He was pushed out of the car, a shot went off and he was killed. Mr Mandela claims that he was sitting in the car and that it was Tira who had fired the fatal shot. When they left the cemetery Mr Mandela was instructed that he must go to the police station and report that there had been dagga and arms in the house of Tyobeka, and he dutifully proceeded to the Nyanga Police Station. As Captain Coetzee, to whom he had already informed, was not present, he returned to Mr Mbewana's house. En route he saw Tira who called him into his house. Tira told him that he should have waited at the police station. He testified that on the morning following the death of Mbewana he had been driven by Tira, accompanied by Cira, to the flat at Malunga Park. When they arrived Ntamo was waiting. He gave Mandela a written statement in terms of which he would depose to the story relating to the kidnapping of Mr Mbewana in a motor car vehicle belonging to Mr Jezile (a car that earlier evidence had confirmed was unable to be driven). After giving this statement to the police Mandela was taken to a meeting, apparently of the community police forum where he followed earlier instructions and mentioned a number of people from the NCF who had been involved in the murder of Mbewana. He was later congratulated by Ntamo who assured him that he would be afforded the benefits of a witness protection programme.

Much of the balance of his testimony related to his being placed in the witness protection programme. The essence of the evidence, which he gave before the court, did not differ markedly from that of the statement, to which I have already made reference.

EVALUATION

Mr *Naudé* who appeared on behalf of the State, concentrated most of his argument on an attack upon the defence of compulsion. He emphasised the anomaly in Mr

Mandela's evidence regarding the fact that as a police informer he had been unable to explain why he had shown so little confidence in the police, including Captain Coetzee, or Inspector Broad for whom he supplied information, as to why he had not informed them of the plans which he claimed had been hatched by Mr Ntamo and his colleagues. Mandela's explanation was that Mr Ntamo had told him that if he failed to co-operate with Ntamo and his colleagues, he would be killed and that Cape Town was too small a place for him to hide. This, Mr *Naudé* submitted, provided no evidential basis to justify a defence of compulsion. Of particular significance was Mandela's admission, reluctantly given under cross-examination, that he was aware in the case of both deceased, that a plan had been made to murder them and he was aware when he instructed Nomhle Gexu to meet him at the bus terminus, as well as when he lured Mr Mbewana in the direction of Tira's car, that a plan was being implemented to kill both people. In short he conceded that he was part of the murderous plan.

Mr *Naudé* also referred to the certain aspects of the evidence of Miki Bonjulu the girlfriend of Mr Mandela, whom he had promised to marry. Although Mr Mandela had expressed anxiety about both he and Miki's plight in the light of the threats pursuant to his involvement in the two murders, he had never provided her with a clear, coherent version as to the nature of the threats made by Ntamo. Nowhere in Ms Bonjulu's evidence was there any indication that she was aware of the nature or cause of the danger in which Mr Mandela claimed he had been when he testified in court. It is highly unlikely that he would not have told the woman whom he was to marry and who had met Ntamo (contrary to the latter's denial) as to the reason why he was in trouble, that is Ntamo. For these reasons Mr *Naudé* contended that there was an absence of compulsion necessary to ground a defence. Indeed Mr *Naudé* went so far to submit that Mandela was a member of a "moord bende," the other members allegedly being Hewu, James, Sira and Ntamo. For this reason alone there was no evidence to justify that Mr Mandela's life was threatened. He was a willing member of this "moord bende." As a willing participant he had not been threatened. In any event there is an insufficient basis of evidence to sustain an argument that he would have been killed by Mr Ntamo if he had failed to co-operate with what Mr *Naudé* referred to as the "moord bende."

In short, Mr *Naudé* urged that there was no evidence to suggest that he had done any more than participate consciously in the murder of Mr Mbewana, knowing full well that he had lured Mr Mbewana into Tira's car for the express purpose of ensuring his death. Similarly, he had acted intentionally to cause the death of Nomhle Gexu without any measure of compulsion. Mr *Naudé* went further to suggest that the torn jacket with which Mr Mandela had returned to the Mbewana household was indicative that he had participated in the struggle, which ensued before Mr Mbewana had been shot. In his evidence Mandela had been particularly vague about the reaction of Mr Mbewana when he had been ordered into the Cressida. Indeed he went so far as to suggest that the man who was being driven to his own execution did not enquire about the purpose of the trip until threatened at the cemetery.

In support of the submission regarding the implications of Mandela's membership of a gang, Mr *Naudé* referred to the decision in *S v Bradbury* 1967 (1) SA 387 (A) at 404H where Holmes JA said:

> "As a general proposition a man who voluntarily and deliberately becomes a member of a criminal gang with knowledge of its disciplinary code of vengeance, cannot rely on compulsion as a defence, or fear as an extenuation."

In *S v Lungele and Another* 1999 (2) SACR 597 (SCA), Olivier JA, in considering the criminal liability of a person who was one of a gang involved in a robbery where another member of the gang killed an employee of the business which had been the subject of the robbery, said:

> "In my view the inference is inescapable that the first Appellant did foresee the possibility of the death of an employee of Scotts: he knew that at least two of his co-conspirators were armed with firearms; he knew that Scotts is in the main street of Port Elizabeth, and that it is immediately opposite a police station; and he knew that the robbery would take place in broad daylight. He nevertheless participated in the robbery, helping to subdue some of the victims. The State has consequently proved the necessary *mens rea* in the form of *dolus eventualis* beyond reasonable doubt" (at 603C–D).

In my view, this finding is of application to the present case. In his own version, Mr Mandela associated with the other members of a gang and played a key role in the implementation of the plan that he well knew was designed to murder Mr Mbewana and Ms Gexu. Absent a defence of compulsion. The same approach adopted in both *Bradbury* and *Lungele* is of application and he should be convicted on all the first four counts. Although Mr *Vismer*, who appeared on behalf of Mr Mandela, correctly referred to the relative coherence of Mandela's version as opposed to that of Ntamo, Tira *et al*, on Mr Mandela's own version he must be found guilty unless a defence of compulsion can be properly raised.

. . .

If Mr Mandela's own version is accepted as the foundation of the case, the court is still required to investigate whether there is a satisfactory basis for a finding of compulsion necessary to justify an acquittal. . . . On that evidence Mr Mandela participated in the crimes; whether he has a defence depends upon an analysis of the evidence viewed in the context of the law relating to compulsion.

COMPULSION

As Prof Burchell in *The South African Criminal Law and Procedure* Vol 1 3 Ed writes at 84:

> "The defence of necessity arises when, confronted with the choice between suffering some evil and breaking the letter of the law in order to avoid it, the accused chooses the latter alternative. The term 'necessity' is used here to cover this dilemma situation when it is brought about by the forces surrounding circumstances or by human agency (compulsion, duress and coercion) since the law is the same in both instances."

Van der Westhuizen *Noodstand as Reg Verdedigingsgrond in die Strafreg* LLD thesis (1979) submits that in principle there can be no distinction at all between necessity and compulsion, a view which is supported by De Wet and Swanepoel *Strafreg* at 81–92.

The most difficult aspect of this defence concerns the taking of life. In *S v Goliath* 1972 (3) SA 1 (A) the Appellate Division held that compulsion could, depending on the circumstances of the particular case, constitute a complete defence to a charge of murder.

. . .

As Burchell observes, however:

> "Clearly *Goliath*'s case does not mean that our Courts will likely accept compulsion as a complete defence in the future. As Rumpff, JA said 'whether an acquittal is justified will depend on the particular circumstances of each case and the whole factual matrix will have to be carefully examined and adjudicated upon with the greatest care'" (at page 97).

In regard to the factual situation of *Goliath*, Goliath (who was 18 years old) was walking with "X" when they came across the deceased. "X" demanded a cigarette and money from the deceased. When the deceased desisted "X" stabbed him and ordered Goliath to bind him. After being threatened with his own life Goliath acceded to the demand whereupon "X" stabbed him until he died. An inference appeared to have been drawn that Goliath could not have avoided the threats to his life by fleeing. Moreover, Goliath's role in the crime was limited to assisting the principal offender by binding the deceased's hands behind his back and stripping him of his clothes.

The relatively low standard adopted by the Appellate Division in *Goliath*'s case regarding the conduct to be expected of an accused who pleads the defence of necessity has not found universal favour. Thus, in *R v Gotz* (1992) 1 All ER 832 (HL) the House of Lords, following an earlier decision in *R v Howe* 1986 (1) QB 626

(HL) at 641 refused to allow duress as a defence for attempted murder and went on to question the appropriateness of such a defence in a climate of violence and terror. Lord Jauncey expressed the view that duress would be more appropriately dealt with at the stage of mitigation.

. . .

In the context of South Africa, the current climate of violence and blatant disregard for human life would tend to provide a reason to curb the defence when life is involved. But this factor must be counter-balanced against the right to life enshrined in section 1 of the Republic of South Africa Constitution Act 108 of 1996. A person who is faced with the most agonising of choice of safeguarding his own right to life at the expense of another's right to life may be regarded as not having the requisite *mens rea* (although he may have *culpa* when he fails an objective test). However, given the exquisite balance between the conflict between the two right bearers of this most precious of rights, a court can only find necessity to be a defence, such that the accused then lacks the requisite culpability, in circumstances where the danger of death cannot be averted, save by acts of heroism which extend beyond the capacity that should, and can, be demanded of the reasonable person.

In this particular case, Mr *Naudé* submitted that other options short of heroism were available to Mr Mandela. He could have contacted the police, at the very least Inspector Broad, for whom he had informed and provided evidence in the past and in whom he must have had some confidence. There is regrettably some evidence, to which Mr *Vismer* correctly referred, which would justify Mr Mandela's lack of confidence in other police officials in the area. For example, Inspector Adonis testified about what he regarded as "a fishy business" in respect of the prosecution of this case. He testified that he had been placed in charge of the investigation. Initially he had arrested Messrs Diko, Tyobeka and Mngika in connection with the death of Mr Mbewana. Inspector Adonis explained that he had been pressurised by members of the community police forum, of which Mr Hewu in particular, was a prominent member, to make these arrests. He testified that he had experienced considerable difficulty obtaining co-operation from his fellow police officers in ensuring access to Mr Mandela, who was clearly a key witness. Although this difficulty was explained adequately by Sergeant Ngcobo, who was also called as a witness by the defence, certain problems remain unexplained.

. . .

There was no clear evidence, however, that Mr Mandela could not have warned either victim; that he could not at least have ensured that the victims would have had an opportunity to flee. In his case, thus, the standard of heroism was hardly required for him to save a life. As Mr *Naudé* correctly submitted he had a choice of either informing the deceased or Inspector Broad, or taking some step in the time available to ensure that the deaths did not occur. There was no immediacy of life threatening compulsion as there was in the case of *Goliath*. Were a court to accept so low a standard in finding the existence of such a defence it would be guilty of demanding very little from members of our society, which is now a constitutional community, based on fundamental principles including those of freedom, dignity, *ubuntu* and respect for life. Were the defence of necessity to be extended as far as Mr *Vismer* urges, it would represent a lowering of regard for life and an undermining of the very fabric of the attempt to build a constitutional community, where each and every person is deserving of equal concern and respect and in which community grows sourced in the principle of *ubuntu*.

. . .

I took him to mean in this regard a view, which looks somewhat more objectively at the question of culpability than would the psychological test with which courts generally work.

. . .

Thus, Jansen JA enquired as to how a court should determine the blameworthiness of an accused that had killed another person under coercion, had nevertheless acted intentionally and with an awareness of unlawfulness (at 797H). The answer, which the learned Judge gave, was to adopt an objective test employing the conduct of an average person as the standard of what should be expected of an accused. He explicitly referred to this approach as the "normative" one. He said that if it could not have been expected of the accused to do otherwise than to have killed the deceased, he could not be blamed and had to be found not guilty. If, however, it could have been expected of him to have acted differently, he could be so blamed (at 798E–F).

. . .

Even if this theory is adopted, the problem remains; did Mr Mandela's conduct comply with the standard that society can expect from an average person, in this case an average person living in the turbulent context of Khayelitsha?

Given the evidence, which has been placed before the court, no other conclusion can reasonably be drawn but that Mr Mandela should be found guilty of both charges of murder. On his own version no explanation was given as to why he had not taken alternative steps. His own version must be tested against that of his own girlfriend, who never heard the detailed anxieties of which Mr Mandela suddenly expressed in this Court. On his own evidence he never explained why he could not have gone to Inspector Broad or why he could not have escaped out of Cape Town and away from the alleged threat of Mr Ntamo. Simply to refer to Ntamo's claim that Cape Town was not big enough for the two of them cannot be used as a serious defence in a court of law.

On the basis of his own version of how he employed a gun loaded with ammunition to kill Nomhle Gexu, it follows from this evidence that he also must be found guilty of charges 2 and 3.

THE *MALULEKE* CASE

Case can be accessed online at http://www.restorativejustice.org.

Case Summary

Facts

The accused, a widowed mother of four minor children, had been convicted of the murder of the deceased, a member of the accused's extended family and a member of the "small, close-knit community" within which the accused lived. The accused had assisted her husband (who, as a co-accused, died before trial) in the "sustained assault" of the deceased after the deceased had been caught in the accused's home, apparently trying to commit theft.

Legal History

This is a judgment on sentencing that follows on the conviction of the accused in the Northern Circuit of the Transvaal Division of the High Court at Lephalele.

Legal Issue

The court had to consider several factors in mitigation of sentence, including the question of whether and to what extent a restorative justice-informed remedy of an apology to the deceased's mother, which is a remedy already provided for in African customary law, may become an alternative to a retributive justice model.

Decision

Justice Bertelsmann determined that there were many factors *in casu* that would work in mitigation of the severe sentence that usually follows the crime of murder. Among the factors to be weighed against the severity of the offence of murder, were, *inter alia*:

1. The accused's four minor children were fully dependent upon the accused, an unemployed mother, herself fully dependent on the benefits of a child grant, and the responsibility on the accused had further been exacerbated by the death of her husband, formerly her co-accused, who had lost the benefit of his pension due to incarceration at the time of his death;
2. The accused was a first-time offender who had never before shown a tendency towards violence of the sort carried out on the deceased and she had not been identified as a further threat to society;
3. The accused showed remorse for her actions, and the facts showed that, prior to the judgment on sentencing, the accused and the deceased's mother had begun communicating, perhaps thereby facilitating the apology referred to in the judgment.

Justice Bertelsmann held that there existed, albeit few in number, precedents indicating that imprisonment need not be the only option; "[c]ommunity service coupled with suitable conditions has been imposed upon accused who were convicted of the intentional taking of another's life before, eg *S v Potgieter* 1994(1) SACR 61 (A)."

In the process of finding evidence in mitigation of sentence, counsel for the defence asked the accused whether she had taken steps in compliance with African customary law, of sending an elder member of her family to the family of the deceased in order to offer an apology on behalf of the accused. The accused indicated that she had not done so. In cross-examination, however, it was shown that the deceased's mother would not be averse to accepting such an apology, adding only that the apology be qualified by an explanation by the accused as to why she had killed her child. Justice Bertelsmann said that "this answer [of the deceased's mother] enabled the court to involve the community in the sentencing and rehabilitation process."

The accused was sentenced to a suspended period of imprisonment of eight years. Importantly, the court held that the decision to suspend the sentence for three years was based on the condition that "the accused apologised according to custom to the mother of the deceased and her family within a month after the sentence having been imposed." Justice Bertelsmann further held that even absent the condition of the apology, the court would probably not have sent the accused to prison due to the other factors (listed *supra*) that existed in mitigation of sentence. However, the emphasis of Justice Bertelsmann's remarks placed great value on the possibility of the apology as "an opportunity to begin to heal the wounds that the commission of the crime caused to the family of the deceased and the community at large."

Justice Bertelsmann thus considered the benefits of "reparation, healing and rehabilitation" that restorative justice, as a criminal justice model, has to offer in the sentencing of an accused. Justice Bertelsmann noted that the model of restorative justice placed emphasis on both the victim and the accused and his or her place in his or her own community. It was further emphasized that restorative justice seeks, primarily, to reestablish the integrity of the community. Thus, focus is placed on the offender taking responsibility for the crime as a member of the community. Justice Bertelsmann argued that "a supple restorative justice approach creates promising possibilities of introducing customary law principles into the formal criminal justice system." Here emphasis is placed on recognition of the relevance of 'our African heritage.'[1]

The court concluded that "[r]estorative justice in South Africa is still in its infancy," explaining that there were relatively few precedents, at the time of judgement, that would have aided Justice Bertelsmann in his sentencing. Relying, therefore, on the recommendations by Justice Bosielo (Justice Shongwe concurring) in *S v. Shilubane* [2005] JOL 15671 (T), Justice Bertelsmann held that:

[R]estorative justice, seen in the context of an innovative approach to sentencing, may become an important tool in reconciling the victim and the offender and the community and the offender. It may provide a whole range of supple alternatives to imprisonment. This would ease the burden on our overcrowded correctional institutions.[2]

Justice Bertelsmann

[1] The accused, who was accused number 1 during the trial, was convicted of murder in the High Court of the Northern Circuit of the Transvaal Provincial Division, at Lephalele. She had been charged together with several other accused. The victim was a young person who broke into her house in a small village in the Limpopo Province.

[2] The other accused were acquitted.

[3] The accused had caused the death of the deceased by participating actively, together with her husband, in a sustained assault upon the deceased after he had been apprehended in her home into which he had broken with the apparent intent to commit theft.

[4] Her husband, who was originally charged with her, died before the start of the trial.

[5] The accused lives in a small, close-knit community. The deceased was in fact part of her extended family and well known to her.

[6] The sentencing of the accused presented particular problems. On the one hand, she is guilty of a very serious offence, the result of a sustained and brutal attack upon a youthful transgressor who was trussed up before the assault started and could neither defend nor protect himself.

[7] On the other hand, the accused has four minor children who are dependent on her. She is unemployed, and her only income is a child grant.

[8] She is a widow and does not receive a pension because her husband was under suspension from the police at the time of his demise.

[9] The accused is a first offender. There is no suggestion that there exists any danger of the crime being repeated, nor is there any indication that the accused is a person normally given to violent conduct.

[10] There was evidence that she regretted and still regrets the death of the victim.

[11] She therefore is clearly not a person against whom society needs to be protected.

[12] In spite of these considerations, the crime of murder calls for a severe sentence. This does not mean that incarceration is the only option. Community service coupled with suitable conditions has been imposed upon accused who were convicted of the intentional taking of another's life before, eg *S v Potgieter* 1994(1) SACR 61 (A).

[13] During evidence in mitigation, the defence investigated the question whether the accused had, prior to the trial, complied with the traditional custom of her com-

munity of apologising for the taking of the deceased's life by sending an elder member or members of her family to the family of the deceased.

. . .

[17] When the accused was asked whether she had complied with this custom, she answered in the negative.

[18] As far as this Court is aware, the failure to comply with this custom would normally be regarded as adding insult to injury by the family of the victim. The state and the defence approached the issue on the same basis during the trial.

[19] The state called the victim's mother to inform the court of the hurt and loss that the deceased's family had suffered. In cross-examination, counsel for the defence enquired from her whether she would be prepared to receive a senior representative from the accused's family in order to attempt to restore the broken relationship between the families.

[20] The deceased's mother answered in the affirmative, adding, "But she must tell me why she killed my child."

[21] This answer enabled the Court to involve the community in the sentencing and rehabilitation process.

[22] The Court sentenced the accused to 8 (eight) years imprisonment, all of which was suspended for a period of 3 (three) years on condition that, *inter alia*, the accused apologized according to custom to the mother of the deceased and her family within a month after the sentence having been imposed.

[23] The Court would not have sent the accused to jail in the light of the strong mitigating factors that were present in this instance, even without the possibility of introducing an observance of custom into the sentencing and rehabilitation process.

[24] But once this opportunity presented itself, a suitable sentence could be imposed that also created an opportunity to begin to heal the wounds that the commission of the crime caused to the family of the deceased and to the community at large. As it happened, the accused and the deceased's mother started talking to each other before the Court had formally adjourned.

[25] The particular circumstances of this case created the opportunity to introduce the principles of restorative justice into the sentencing process.

[26] Restorative justice has been developed by criminal jurists and social scientists as a new approach to dealing with crimes, victims and offenders. It emphasises the need for reparation, healing and rehabilitation rather than harsher sentences, longer terms of imprisonment, adding to overcrowding in jails and creating greater risks of recidivism.

"While improving the efficiency of the criminal justice system is necessary, applying harsher punishment to offenders has been shown internationally to have little success in preventing crime. Moreover, both these approaches are flawed in that they overlook important requirements for the delivery of justice, namely:

considering the needs of victims;
helping offenders to take responsibility on an individual level; and
nurturing a culture that values personal morality and encourages people to
take responsibility for their behaviour.

Considering that crime rates in South Africa remain high and that government's focus appears to be on punishment rather than justice, a different approach is needed." (Per Mike Batley and Traggy Maepa in: *Beyond Retribution—Prospects for Restorative Justice in South Africa,* page 16.)

. . .

[28] Various definitions are quoted in this article of what restorative justice is aimed at, and the author says on page 7:

"the most comprehensive definition comes from Canada and goes thus:
(by Robert Cormier) 'Restorative justice is an approach to justice that focuses
on repairing the harm caused by crime while holding the offender responsible for his or he actions, by providing an opportunity for the parties directly
affected by the crime—victim(s), offender and community—to identify
and address their needs in the aftermath of the crime, and seek a resolution
that affords healing, reparation and reintegration, and prevents further
harm.'"

[29] The author underlines that restorative justice shifts the focus of the criminal process from retribution to healing and re-establishing societal bonds. It concentrates on the development of the offender.

[30] Batley and Maepa underline that a supple restorative justice approach creates promising possibilities of introducing customary law principles into the formal criminal justice system:

"Although restorative justice may be considered a fairly new approach to
criminal justice, a number of countries such as Canada and New Zealand
have discovered that the ethnic heritage of their indigenous people has much
to offer the modern criminal justice system. This heritage typically addresses
major shortcomings in the modern system, such as the need to ensure that
an offender really does acknowledge personal responsibility, that he or she is
reintegrated back into the society, and that the needs of those who have been
affected by crime are addressed.

Although it is generally not well integrated into the South African criminal justice system, our African heritage is relevant. While there are a number of differences between ethnic groups in this country, some of the central features of African legal systems that become evident are:

> A concern to shame the offender and then to reincorporate him or her back into the community once the initial expression of community repugnance has been demonstrated;
> Avoiding as far as possible the segregation of the offender or his or her marginalisation into a sub-community of similar social rejects;
> A recognition that the supernatural plays a part in justice;
> A focus on community affairs aimed at reconciling the parties and restoring harmonious relations within the community, and
> Ensuring that the families of the involved parties are always fully involved."
> (*loc. cit.*)

[31] Restorative justice in South Africa is still in its infancy. Anecdotal evidence exists of successful pilot projects that have been launched to help offenders to take responsibility for their actions and to begin a reconciliation process with the victims, such as the project at the Rooigrond prison in the North-West Province, where rape offenders sentenced to long terms of imprisonment were reconciled with their victims and a healing process was thereby started. The victims and the offenders met within the confines of the prison after advance counselling. The offenders apologized to the victims in an effort to enable the latter to find closure of the relevant incident and its consequences. Acceptance of the apology should encourage the offenders in their rehabilitation.

[32] I have been able to find only one South African judgment in which there has been a conscious recognition of the advantages of restorative justice: *S v Shilubane* 2005 JOL 15671 (T), by Bosielo J, Shongwe J (as he was then), concurring. It is obvious that restorative justice cannot provide a single and definitive answer to all of the ills of crime and its consequences. Restorative justice cannot ensure that society is protected against offenders who have no wish to reform, and who continue to endanger our communities.

[33] But on the other hand restorative justice, properly considered and applied, may make a significant contribution in combating recidivism by encouraging offenders to take responsibility for their actions and assist the process of their ultimate reintegration into society thereby.

[34] In addition, restorative justice, seen in the context of an innovative approach to sentencing, may become an important tool in reconciling the victim and the offender and the community and the offender. It may provide a whole range of supple

alternatives to imprisonment. This would ease the burden on our overcrowded correctional institutions.

[35] Restorative justice has received more attention in *inter alia* Zimbabwe than in South Africa to date. In *S v Shariwa* [2003] JOL 11015 (ZH), Ndou J, said the following:

> "the convicted person should not be visited with punishment to the point of being broken. . . . Whatever the gravity of the crime and the interests of society, the most important factors in determining the sentence are the person, and the character and circumstances of the crime. . . . Imprisonment, originally a mere matter of detention until a debt is paid or a trial determined, has now become the most usual punishment for most crimes, except for minor offences for which non—custodial sentences are imposed. This is so because despite the various associations of benevolent men and women and experts in penology, no practical alternative has worked in most jurisdictions.
>
> In our jurisdiction there has been a paradigm shift. First, over the years our superior courts have emphasised that a sentence of imprisonment is a severe and rigorous form of punishment, which should be imposed only as a last resort and where no other form of punishment will do. Second, there have been concerted efforts to shift from the more traditional methods dealing with crime and the offender towards a more restorative form of justice that takes into account the interests of both society and the victim, ie community service . . ."

[36] The learned judge deals with sentencing guidelines in Zimbabwe, which determine that community service should be considered in all cases warranting an effective prison sentence of 24 months or less.

[37] These sentiments are echoed by Bosielo J in *S v Shilubane* 2005 [JOL 15671(T)]. The learned Judge says:

> "The accused herein stole 7 fowl from the complainant which according to his admissions, he cooked. Self-evidently the loss of the complainant amounts to R216.00 (two hundred and sixteen rand) which is the value of the seven fowls reflected on the charge sheet. I have little doubt in my mind that, in line with new philosophy of restorative justice, that the complainant would have been more pleased to receive compensation for his loss. An order of compensation coupled with a suspended sentence would, in my view, have satisfied the basic triad and the primary purposes of punishment . . .
>
> Unless presiding officers become innovative and pro-active in opting for other alternative sentences to direct imprisonment, we will not be able to solve the problem of overcrowding in our prisons. Inasmuch as it is critical for the maintenance of law and order that criminals be punished for their crimes,

it is important that the presiding officer impose sentences which are humane and balanced. There is abundant empirical evidence that retributive justice has failed to stem the ever-increasing wave of crime. It is furthermore counterproductive if not self-defeating, in my view, to expose an accused like the one, *in casu*, to the corrosive and brutalising effect of prison life for such a trifling offence. The price which civil society stands to pay in the end by having him emerge out of prison a hardened criminal, far outweighs the advantages to be gained by sending him to jail . . . I am of the view that courts must seriously consider alternative sentences like community service as a viable alternative to direct imprisonment, particularly where the accused is not such a serious threat to the society that he requires to be taken away from society for its protection."

See further *Zulu v S* 2003 JOL 116 at 7 (ZH).

[38] The incorporation of the principles of traditional justice into the South African criminal justice system must be approached with circumspection. While it is generally appreciated that African legal systems did not know prisons, it would be dangerous indeed for a Judge, not versed in traditional customs, to make assumptions that could prove to be grievously wrong and the incorrect application of which would do more harm than good.

[39] There appears to be little reason why similar results could not be achieved in South Africa.

[40] Eventually, legislative intervention may be required to recognise aspects of customary law—but this should not deter courts from investigating the possibility of introducing exciting and vibrant potential alternative sentences into our criminal justice system.

THE *MASETLHA* CASE

Masetlha v. The President of the Republic of South Africa and Another 2008 (1) BCLR 1 (CC)

Case Summary

FACTS

On 14 December 2004, upon appointment by the then President of South Africa, Thabo Mbeki, Mr. Masetlha became the director general (DG) of the National Intelligence Agency. The appointment was for a period of three years and, as per the letter of appointment, was made in terms of the Intelligence Services Act as read with the Public Services Act.

In August 2005, the media reported on what became known as the "Macozoma affair," thus called because Mr. Macozoma, a businessman, had been placed under surveillance by the NIA in what Deputy Chief Justice Moseneke termed "a clumsy blunder by field operatives." Mr. Macozoma complained to the Minister of the

National Intelligence Agency, who then requested that the DG furnish him with a formal account concerning the surveillance in order to answer to the complaint. In his formal account, the Applicant claimed that he neither had knowledge of nor had he given authorization for the surveillance, and claimed that he had only become aware thereof after the complaint had reached the minister in September 2005. He further laid the blame of the error at the door of his subordinate, the deputy director general (DDG) and several field operatives under the DDG's command. The minister, being dissatisfied with the account ordered a further investigation into the affair. The investigation culminated in a report by the Inspector-General of Intelligence stating the unlawfulness of the surveillance. Also included in the report were recommendations and suggestions that the DG was deliberatively noncooperative with the investigation and that disciplinary proceedings should be instituted against the DG for insubordinate and incompetent conduct in relation to the operation. Thereafter, the Minister, the DG and the Inspector-General met to discuss the outcomes of the report whereafter a letter containing some of the report's recommendations was written by the minister to the President. On October 20, 2005, the DG met with the President and minister during which meeting a letter was read to the DG by the minister, detailing that the DG had been suspended as the DG of the NIA.

Importantly, there was no mention, at the time that the decision to suspend the DG came from the President. Confirmation that the decision emanated from the President himself came on November 15, following the formal procedure of the Presidential Minute, which is necessary to give the decision "legal significance . . . as a decision of the President."

Meanwhile, on November 12, following the meeting with the President and the minister, the Applicant sought an urgent application to review the terms of the suspension, claiming that the suspension was unlawful.

Before the Applicant could refute the procedure of the Presidential Minute, the President moved unilaterally to amend the terms of office of the DG which would terminate within two days of having been given notice, and would amount to termination of his employment twenty-one months and nine days before the three year original period. The Applicant was, however, offered full compensation with benefits for the time outstanding in terms of his original terms of office. Importantly here, in terms of the separate majority judgment of Justice Sachs, the President asserted that the decision to unilaterally amend the Applicant's term of office, was made because the "relationship between him, as head of state and of the national executive, and Mr. Masetlha as head of the Agency, had disintegrated irreparably."

Therefore, the present case is the application by the Applicant for a declarator that the President had no power to make the amendments unilaterally and that the Applicant still remained the incumbent head of the NIA, or that, in the alternative, he be reinstated as such.

LEGAL HISTORY

This case came by way of application for direct leave to appeal to the Constitutional Court against the judgment of Judge Du Plessis, in the court *a quo*, denying the Applicant's two review applications.

LEGAL ISSUES

Of the five issues canvassed by the court in this decision, the two that are relevant to Justice Sachs's reasoning concerning *ubuntu* are: "whether the presidential decision to amend the Applicant's term of office or to dismiss him is constitutionally permissible" and the related issue of the validity of the earlier (and at this point, perhaps moot) suspension. Crucially the court had to decide on issues surrounding the doctrine of *functus officio*, or, as Deputy Chief Justice Moseneke stated, "whether the power to appoint implies the power to dismiss or to amend the terms of office so as to end it."

DECISION

The majority decided, per the Deputy Chief Justice Moseneke, that the constitutional power to make an appointment such as that of the Applicant had not been deliberately omitted from the Constitution and that it was a necessary correlative of the power to appoint. This the Deputy Chief Justice held on the reasoning that "[w]ithout the competence to dismiss, the President would not be able to remove the head of the Agency without his or her consent before the end of the term of office, whatever the circumstances might be. That would indeed lead to an absurdity and severely undermine the constitutional pursuit of the security of this country and its people."

The Deputy Chief Justice further argued that there would be no irregularities of procedural fairness due to the special legal relationship between the parties and that the power exercised here by the President was merely an executive power, finding its source in the Constitution and in the relevant legislation. Therefore, any challenge on section 33 rights and PAJA would fail, which, the court reiterated, would not leave a complete absence of challenge since all exercise of public power is still subject to constitutional review for legality.

In his separate but concurring judgment, Justice Sachs concurs with the reasoning of the Deputy Chief Justice except with the extent to which Justice Moseneke relies upon the law of contract to govern the relationship between the President and the head of the NIA.

Justice Sachs states that, since the relationship between the President and the appellant is *sui generis* and "at all times suffused with a constitutional dimension," it is the Constitution's governance of all exercises of public power that is determinative here. To this end, Justice Sachs goes on to hold that while the President was "lawfully entitled to amend the terms of the appointment to bring it to an immediate end" it would not mean that Mr. Masetlha would be denied any remedy at all. He would still have recourse to the right to fair labour practice by relying directly on the constitutional provisions of the section 23.

Justice Sachs holds further that as fairness is a matter for determination on a case-by-case basis, the facts *in casu* render the termination fair since it had been legitimately based on a loss of trust that had previously been present in the *sui generis* relationship between the two parties.

However, on the issue of fairness, Justice Sachs held that one of the elements of fairness "required that Mr Masetlha be consulted on the manner in which the termination was to be publicly communicated . . . [which would] presuppose the display of appropriate concern for reputational consequences." Here Justice Sachs linked the Applicant's interest in "fair dealing" with the concept of civility, stating that the two could not be separated. Further expanding upon the concept of civility, Justice Sachs had the following to say:

> Civility in a constitutional sense involves more than just courtesy or good manners. It is one of the binding elements of a constitutional democracy. It presupposes tolerance for those with whom one disagrees and respect for the dignity of those with whom one is in dispute. Civility, closely linked to *ubuntu*-botho, is deeply rooted in traditional culture, and has been widely supported as a precondition for the good functioning of contemporary democratic societies. . . . The Constitution the emerged therefore presupposes that public power will be exercised in a manner that is not arbitrary and not unduly disrespectful of the dignity of those adversely affected by the exercise.

Deputy Chief Justice Moseneke

INTRODUCTION

[1] This case raises intricate questions on the constitutional validity of two decisions of the President of the Republic. He first suspended and later terminated Mr Masetlha's employment as head and Director-General of the National Intelligence Agency (the Agency). The President did so by unilaterally amending his term of office so that it expired within two days of the notice and just over 21 months earlier than the original term. The termination of employment was accompanied by an offer to pay Mr Masetlha his full monthly salary, allowances and benefits for the unexpired period and other moneys that may be due to an incumbent at the expiry of a term of office.

[2] Mr Masetlha has impugned the decisions as constitutionally impermissible. He has declined the financial pay-out and presses on with the claim to be re-instated to his post.

[3] These issues reach us by way of an application for leave to appeal directly to this Court against the decision of Du Plessis J sitting in the Pretoria High Court. That Court dismissed two review applications brought by Mr Masetlha against the

President on the grounds that his dismissal from employment constituted lawful executive action and that the dispute over the suspension had been rendered moot by the dismissal.

[4] In this Court, Mr Masetlha seeks a declarator that the President has no power to suspend him from his post or to alter unilaterally his terms of employment. In the alternative, he asks for an order setting aside the two decisions as irregular. It must be said that Mr Masetlha does not concede that the decision of the President to change the terms of his appointment in effect amounts to his dismissal as head of the Agency. Nonetheless, at its core, his claim is for specific performance. It is a claim to be re-instated as Director-General and head of the Agency.

[5] Mr Masetlha asks, in the alternative, that, should this Court not find in his favour on the disputes that are not capable of resolution on motion papers, the factual averments underpinning the disputes should be referred to oral evidence.

. . .

[9] On 31 August 2005 the so-called "Macozoma affair" broke into the public domain. Mr Macozoma is a businessman. At issue were the circumstances under which he came to be placed under surveillance by agents of the Agency. It is common cause that the surveillance was a clumsy blunder by field operatives of the Agency. The applicant insists that, as head of the Agency, he had not authorised and was not aware of the surveillance until the field operatives were exposed and Mr Macozoma had lodged a complaint with the Minister. The complaint reached the Minister on the 5 September 2005. The Minister had not been informed before then that Mr Macozoma was under surveillance.

[10] The Minister requested Mr Masetlha to account formally on the surveillance operation. Mr Masetlha reported in writing that the surveillance did occur but that it was done without his knowledge and in error, attributable to Mr Njenje, the deputy Director-General of the Agency, and certain field operatives under Mr Njenje's command. The Minister proclaimed himself dissatisfied with explanations given to him by Mr Masetlha and instructed the Inspector-General of Intelligence (Inspector-General)[3] [4] to investigate the circumstances that gave rise to the surveillance.

[11] On 17 October 2005, the Inspector-General prepared a written report in which he informed the Minister that the surveillance of Mr Macozoma was unauthorised and unlawful and that it had not been undertaken for the reasons given by the Agency operatives but for another purpose. The report notes that Mr Masetlha had deliberately sought to mislead the Inspector-General's investigation team and the Minister in this regard. In addition, the Inspector-General recommended that disciplinary steps be taken against the applicant for failing to exercise the required degree of management and oversight on the surveillance operation. On the same day, the Minister convened a meeting attended by the Inspector-General and the applicant. At the meeting, the Minister read out the outcome of the investigation by and recommendations of the Inspector-General and he advised that he had made certain recommendations to the President for his consideration.

[12] For the sake of completeness, I record that after receiving the report of the Inspector-General, the Minister suspended and thereafter dismissed Mr Njenje and another senior member of the Agency, Mr Mhlanga, for their reported role in the "Macozoma affair." Following his suspension, Mr Njenje threatened to institute legal proceedings.

[13] Within two days of the disclosure of the Inspector-General's report and meeting with the Minister, on 19 October 2005, the applicant was summoned to a meeting with the President and the Director-General within the Presidency, Reverend Chikane. At that meeting, the President urged the applicant to persuade Mr Njenje to stall his intended court case until the President had met with him. Mr Masetlha, in turn, raised his concerns regarding the suspension of two of his subordinates. A further meeting, which would include the Minister and the Inspector-General, was arranged for the following day at the official residence of the President. Mr Masetlha explains that he left the meeting of 19 October 2005 with the distinct impression that the President wanted to reach an amicable arrangement with Mr Njenje and Mr Mhlanga. According to him, the President appeared to understand the concerns raised that the investigation by the Inspector-General had been flawed.

[14] The following day, on 20 October 2005, Mr Masetlha attended the planned follow-up meeting at the official residence of the President. . . . The President said that it was no longer necessary to proceed with matters raised the previous day. . . . The Minister read out a letter dated 20 October 2005 and addressed to the applicant. It bore the signature of the Minister and informed Mr Masetlha that he was suspended from his position as the Director-General of the Agency. At no stage during the meeting did the Minister or the President suggest that the decision to suspend Mr Masetlha had been taken by the President.

[15] Three weeks later, on 12 November 2005, the applicant launched an urgent application in the High Court against the Minister and the President, seeking to review and set aside the suspension as unlawful.[4] [5] However, three days later, on 15 November 2005, the President recorded, as his own decision, the suspension of the applicant with effect from 20 October 2005. This he did by way of a Presidential Minute. The Constitution requires that a decision by the President, if it is to have legal consequences, must be in writing.[5] [6] The Presidential Minute was therefore an indispensable step to give legal significance to the suspension as a decision of the President.

[16] The applicant, however, does not accept that it is the President who made the suspension decision. . . .

[17] On 10 March 2006, the Applicant initiated a fresh application directed at setting aside the suspension at the President's instance. The founding papers carried attacks on the integrity of the President. He also accused the President of lying. On 20 March 2006 and before filing an answering affidavit to the second suspension application, the President amended the applicant's term of office so that it expired

on 22 March 2006. This meant that the term of office was to expire within two days of the notice and 21 months and nine days earlier than the original term.

[18] In making the decision, the President asserted that the relationship of trust between him, as head of state and of the national executive, and Mr Masetlha, as head of the Agency, had disintegrated irreparably . . . The letter also made the point that the applicant would be remunerated in terms of section 37(2)(d) of the PSA[6] [7] for the remainder of his term of office before its amendment . . .

[19] In a letter dated 22 March 2006, Minister Fraser-Moleketi informed the applicant that he would be paid his full monthly remuneration for the remaining 21 months and nine days as well as specified benefits due at the expiry of the term of office . . .

[20] Consistent with his stance that the President had not lawfully terminated or amended his term of office, Mr Masetlha declined the cumulative salary, allowances, benefits and conditions tendered by Minister Fraser-Moleketi . . . he repaid to the government the amount that Minister Fraser-Moleketi had caused to be deposited into his banking account.

[21] On 27 March 2005, the applicant initiated another application in which he sought a declaratory order that the President had no power to amend his term of office unilaterally and that he remains the head of the Agency. In the alternative, the applicant asked for an order re-instating him as Director-General of the Agency. The suspension and the amendment applications were consolidated and heard together.

In the High Court

[22] The High Court dismissed both review applications. It found that section 3(3)(a) of ISA, the legislative provision which provides for the appointment of the head of intelligence services, simply echoes section 209(2) of the Constitution, which is the original source of the power to appoint the head of the Agency and that, although the power to appoint is provided for in legislation, it remained located in the Constitution itself. It is perhaps convenient to recite now the provision of section 209(2) of the Constitution:

> "The President as head of the national executive must appoint a woman or a man as head of each intelligence service established in terms of subsection (1), and must either assume political responsibility for the control and direction of any of those services, or designate a member of Cabinet to assume that responsibility."

[23] The High Court considered the crucial inquiry to be whether the dismissal of the applicant is an exercise of executive power, particularly because the Constitution and applicable legislative provisions are silent on the dismissal of a head of an intelligence service. The Court found that the power to appoint includes the power

to dismiss. The power to dismiss is implicit in section 209(2) of the Constitution and is an executive power in terms of section 85(2)(e) of the Constitution. The Court reasoned that the authority to dismiss is therefore not susceptible to judicial review under the provisions of the Promotion of Administrative Justice Act (PAJA).[7]
[8] However, it observed, this did not mean that the President's decision is beyond the reach of judicial review on any basis. The decision of the President to dismiss must conform to the principle of legality. Therefore, the power to dismiss may not be exercised in bad faith, arbitrarily or irrationally.

[24] On the facts, the Court found that, in order for the President to fulfil his role as head of the national executive, he must subjectively trust the head of a national intelligence service. Therefore the irreparable breakdown of the relationship of trust between the President and the head of the Agency constituted a lawful and rational basis for the dismissal. Having concluded that the dismissal was constitutionally justifiable, the Court found that the disputes on the suspension decision had become academic and, on that basis, dismissed the application challenging the validity of the suspension.

THE ISSUES
[25] There are five main issues . . .

First, whether leave to appeal should be granted.

The second issue is whether the presidential decision to amend the Applicant's term of office or to dismiss him is constitutionally permissible.

The third issue raises the validity of the decision to suspend the Applicant from his post.

The fourth issue relates to the appropriate remedy, if any.

Lastly, there is the question whether any aspects of this case should, at the request of the Applicant, be referred to oral evidence.

. . .

[28] We are here confronted with an enquiry into the constitutional and legislative source and reach of the power of the President to appoint or dismiss a state functionary, in this case being the head of the Agency. The enquiry will compel us to probe whether the power to amend a term of employment or to dismiss is located within section 209(2) of the Constitution, read with section 3(3)(a) of ISA and section 12(2) of the PSA or within all of these provisions read together, and whether the provisions are capable of being construed harmoniously. Clearly, the task at hand calls for a construction of the constitutional provisions and legislation that give effect to them.[8] Whatever the origin or contours of the public power in issue, we are also called upon to decide whether the authority is executive power or administrative action reviewable under PAJA. It seems to me beyond contestation that important constitutional issues fall to be resolved in this application.

. . .

CONSTITUTIONAL AND LEGISLATIVE SETTING

. . .

[32] A collective pursuit of national security is integral to the primary constitutional object of establishing a constitutional state based on democratic values, social justice and fundamental human rights . . .

"National security must reflect the resolve of South Africans, as individuals and as a nation, to live as equals, to live in peace and harmony, to be free from fear and want and to seek a better life."9 [11]

[33] The security services of the Republic consist of a single defence force; a single police service and any intelligence services established in terms of the Constitution and must be structured and regulated by national legislation.10 [12] Predictably, one of the important principles prescribed is that national security must be pursued in compliance with the law.11 [13] . . . Besides the rule of law imperative, this constitutional injunction is also inspired by and deeply rooted in a repudiation of our past in which security forces were, for the most part, law unto themselves; they terrorised opponents of the government of the day with impunity and often in flagrant disregard of the law.

[34] Whilst located within Chapter 11 of the Constitution, the provisions of section 209(1) are narrowly tailored to establish and regulate intelligence services other than an intelligence division of the defence force or the police service . . . Section 209(2) provides for the President's power to appoint a head of each intelligence service . . . section 209 is silent on the power of the President to suspend or dismiss a head of an intelligence service.

[35] The national legislation envisaged in section 209(1) of the Constitution is ISA. It came into operation during February 2003 but has transitional provisions that preserve the link and continuity with past intelligence services.12 [17] . . . Section 3(3)(b) of ISA makes it clear that the Director-General is the head and accounting officer of the intelligence service. However, ISA makes no express provision for the suspension or alteration of the terms of employment or dismissal of the head of an intelligence service, including the Agency.

[36] This position may be contrasted with the powers conferred on the Minister by the same legislation. Section 4 of ISA requires the Minister to create, in consultation with the President, the posts of Deputy Director-General within the Agency. The Minister also bears the responsibility to create posts of assistant Director-General, all directorates, divisions and other lower post structures . . . It is however clear from the provisions of ISA13 that the Minister may regulate the suspension and dismissal of the Deputy Director-General and members of the Agency of a lower rank but has no similar power in relation to the Director-General and head of the Agency.

[37] The head of the Agency is part of the public service for the Republic. The basic values and principles governing public administration are, in turn, prescribed by Chapter 10 of the Constitution . . .

[38] The terms of employment of the head of an intelligence service, including the Agency, are regulated by both the PSA and ISA. Regrettably, the interplay between the provisions of these two statutes in this particular context is complex and less than clear. The starting point for understanding this interplay should be section 2(3) of the PSA, which provides:

> "Where persons employed in the . . . Agency . . . are not excluded from the
> provisions of this Act, those provisions shall apply only in so far as they are
> not contrary to the laws governing their service, and those provisions shall not
> be construed as derogating from the powers or duties conferred or imposed
> upon the . . . Agency . . ."

[39] It follows that the provisions of the PSA apply to the conditions of service of a head and members of the Agency when they are not at odds with the provisions of ISA . . . section 3B(1)(a) and sections 12(2), (3) and (4). Section 3B provides generally for the appointment and "other career incidents" of heads of national departments . . .

. . .

[41] It appears plain that, in the case of the head of the Agency, the President is the relevant executing authority.[14] [24] In other words, the manner in which the term of office of the head of the Agency may be amended or indeed terminated before its expiry may form part of the service agreement between the executing authority and the head of the Agency.

[42] It is, however, significant that outside this possible contractual process of termination, the PSA does not make provision for dismissal of the Director-General of the Agency . . . Another point of difference is that a discharge of an officer or employee under the PSA is subject to the applicable provisions of the Labour Relations Act.[15] [25] On the other hand, section 2(b) of the Labour Relations Act[16] [26] and section 3(1)(a) of the Basic Conditions of Employment Act[17] [27] expressly excludes members of the Agency from the scope of their application.

THE DECISION TO AMEND CONDITIONS OF SERVICE OR TO DISMISS

[43] In this Court, the applicant put up a rather spirited criticism of the decision of the High Court on two main grounds, each with several strands. The first is that the decision to dismiss or to alter was not taken under section 209(2) of the Constitution. The applicant contends that the President purported to take the decision in terms of section 12(2) of the PSA, which does not confer express authority on the President or on anyone else to do so. The kernel of the argument is that the dismissal was done without lawful authority. However, if section 12(2) of the PSA confers implied authority to amend or dismiss, then its exercise is the implementation of legislation and thus falls to be reviewed and set aside under PAJA as procedurally unfair.

[44] The second main contention is that section 209(2) of the Constitution, even if read together with section 3(3)(a) of ISA, does not vest in the President the power to reduce or end the period of office of the head of the Agency. To this main argument, there are several strands.

[45] Firstly is that the invocation of section 209(2) of the Constitution, as a provision, which confers the requisite power on the President, is an afterthought and a belated and impermissible attempt to re-characterise his decision after the event. Second, these provisions do not confer on the President the implied power to dismiss. Third, even if the power to dismiss is to be implied, it must be sourced, not from the Constitution but from section 3(3)(a) of ISA, which vests in the President the power to appoint the head of the Agency. Since the exercise of such power would be the implementation of legislation, it would amount to administrative action for the purposes of PAJA. Fourth, if any implied power to dismiss is conferred by section 209(2) of the Constitution, it is, in any event, subject to the procedural fairness requirement. And, lastly, the manner in which the power to dismiss under section 209 was exercised is inconsistent with the principle of legality. I now turn to look at these arguments closely.

. . .

[48] Another important consideration is that the import of the text of the President's letter dated 20 March 2006, addressed to the Applicant, is not open to doubt. In it the President states:

> ". . . I have decided to amend your current term of office as head of the said Agency to expire on 22 March 2006. You will be remunerated, in terms of section 37(2)(d) of the Public Service Act, 1994, for the remainder of your term of office before its amendment."

[49] Second, the President's letter seeks to amend the term of appointment and does so in deliberate terms in order to achieve a compassionate financial outcome for the applicant. This it achieves by making the term of office expire prematurely. The truth of the matter is that, in substance, the amendment brings to an end the appointment and is accompanied by an offer to place the applicant in the same financial position he would have been in had his contract of service run its full course. To that extent, the applicant is right that this was the outcome that the President sought to reach through the mechanics of an alteration of the period of office under sections 12(2) and (4) of the PSA.

. . .

[52] It is however beyond doubt that, although the decision is couched in the language of an alteration of conditions of service, it is in effect a decision to bring to an end the applicant's term of office or to dismiss him. The blatant effect of the amendment of the term of office is to extinguish it . . . This does not however change the fact that the President sought to use the provisions of the PSA and, in

particular, sections 12(2) and (4) read with section 37(2)(d), as a manner of terminating the term of office. The sharp question is whether these provisions of the PSA alone or together with other constitutional and legislative provisions authorise the dismissal of the head of the Agency. It is to that question that I now turn.

. . .

[56] It is so that the President and Mr Masetlha did not agree on "any grounds upon, and the procedures according to which the services of the head of department may be terminated before the expiry of his or her term of office . . ."[18] [30] . . . Additional terms may be concluded on particular tasks and performance criteria of the head of department. Similarly, the termination procedure, before the expiry of the term of service, may be agreed upon as an additional provision to the prescribed contract under section 12(2).

. . .

[58] In my view, this contention of the applicant is unsound on several grounds. It omits to make a necessary distinction between the substantive power to appoint and dismiss a head of an intelligence service, on the one hand, and the resultant contract of employment, which is regulated by the provisions of section 12 of the PSA. The operative constitutional and legislative framework does make that distinction. The power, if any, to appoint and dismiss a head of an intelligence service is located in section 209(2) of the Constitution, read with section 3(3) of ISA and section 3B(1)(a) of the PSA. However, these provisions in themselves do not regulate how the appointment to and termination of office should happen. The manner and form of appointment that the legislature has chosen is a contract of service which, in the case of the head of the Agency, is regulated by sections 12(2) and (4) of the PSA.

. . .

[61] But even more importantly, nothing in the wording of section 12 of the PSA compels the parties to agree on any terms of the service agreement beyond the essential elements thereof, as it is the case between the President and Mr Masetlha. It seems to me therefore that the section provides for a contractual framework for the manner of appointment of the head of department under section 12(2) and also implicitly for the termination of his or her term of office, even in the absence of a specific and agreed procedure contemplated in section 12(4)(c) of the PSA.

[62] In other words, if the alteration or termination of the service contract were not regulated by an express contractual provision, it would be regulated by implied contractual terms.[19] [31] This means that neither contracting party may change the agreement unilaterally . . . The contract of employment is for a fixed period of three years. Therefore, it may not be terminated as a matter of contract before the expiry of the period unless there is material breach of the contract by the employee.

[63] As I have said earlier, the power to appoint and the power to dismiss, if any, is not located in section 12(2) of the PSA . . . The power and indeed obligation of the President to appoint the head of an intelligence service is not sourced from a

private law relationship. It is a public law power. In other words, this dispute between the parties is not merely about a breach or wrongful termination of an employment contract. It is rather about whether public authority has been exercised in a constitutionally valid manner . . .

[64] The public power at stake derives from Chapter 11 of the Constitution and the operative legislation, which are intended to advance national security through the control and establishment of intelligence services. In particular, the provisions of section 209 . . .

[65] Thus, the procedural and permissive requirements of sections 12(2) and (4) of the PSA must not be read alone, but in conjunction with the constitutional and operative legislative scheme that I have described at length.[20] [33] . . . The source of that power is not section 12(2) of the PSA. It is section 209(2) of the Constitution, which is mirrored in the specific provision dealing with the appointment of the head of an intelligence service in section 3(3) of ISA. Of course, section 3B of the PSA also gives the general power of appointment of a head of department to the President.

Does the power to appoint under section 209(2) of the Constitution and section 3(3)(a) of ISA imply a power to dismiss?

[66] The next question is whether the power to appoint implies the power to dismiss or to amend the terms of office so as to end it . . .

[67] . . . I cannot accept that the power to dismiss has been deliberately omitted from the Constitution or that it is unnecessary.

[68] . . . Without the competence to dismiss, the President would not be able to remove the head of the Agency without his or her consent before the end of the term of office, whatever the circumstances might be. That would indeed lead to an absurdity and severely undermine the constitutional pursuit of the security of this country and its people. That is why the power to dismiss is an essential corollary of the power to appoint and the power to dismiss must be read into section 209(2) of the Constitution. There is no doubt that the power to appoint under section 209(2) of the Constitution and the power under ISA implies a power to dismiss.

[69] Of course, section 3(3)(a) of ISA is the legislation contemplated in section 209(1) of the Constitution. It is couched in terms similar to section 209(2) and it too is silent on the power to dismiss. However, that power must be present because it is implied in and flows from the empowering constitutional provision. But that does not alter or destroy, as the applicant will have us accept, the constitutional character of the power to dismiss a head of the Agency . . .

[70] It follows that the power that the Respondent utilised to dismiss the applicant is located in section 209(2) of the Constitution read with section 3(3)(a) of ISA . . .

. . .

[72] I have no doubt that, in all the circumstances, the President had the requisite power under section 209(2) of the Constitution read with section 3(3)(a)

of ISA and was entitled to take a decision to bring to an end the appointment of Mr Masetlha as Director-General of the Agency. However, as will become apparent later, the power to employ and to dismiss the Director-General of the Agency should not be conflated with the contractual implications of terminating his fixed term employment contract prematurely.

. . .

[74] The question then is whether the power to appoint and the correlative power to dismiss a head of the Agency as conferred by section 209(2) of the Constitution is subject to a requirement of procedural fairness. The unfairness that the Applicant complains of lies in that the President did not afford him an opportunity to be heard before the impending dismissal . . .

[75] It is so that the *audi principle* or the right to be heard, which is derived from tenets of natural justice, is part of the common law. It is inspired by the notion that people should be afforded a chance to participate in the decision that will affect them and more importantly an opportunity to influence the result of the decision . . . In my view however, the special legal relationship that obtains between the President as head of the national executive, on the one hand, and the Director-General of an intelligence agency, on the other, is clearly distinguishable from the considerations relied upon in *Zenzile*. One important distinguishing feature is that the power to dismiss is an executive function that derives from the Constitution and national legislation.

[76] . . . Furthermore, it is important to understand that section 1 of PAJA expressly excludes, from the purview of "administrative action," executive powers or functions of the President referred to in section 85(2)(e) . . .

[77] . . . The power to dismiss—being a corollary of the power to appoint—is similarly executive action that does not constitute administrative action; particularly in this special category of appointments . . . These powers to appoint and to dismiss are conferred specially upon the President for the effective business of government and, in this particular case, for the effective pursuit of national security . . .

[78] This does not, however, mean that there are no constitutional constraints on the exercise of executive authority. The authority conferred must be exercised lawfully, rationally and in a manner consistent with the Constitution.[21] Procedural fairness is not a requirement . . .

[81] It is therefore clear that the exercise of the power to dismiss by the President is constrained by the principle of legality . . . Firstly, the President must act within the law and in a manner consistent with the Constitution. He or she therefore must not misconstrue the power conferred. Secondly, the decision must be rationally related to the purpose for which the power was conferred . . .

[82] I agree with the High Court that ordinarily a dismissal of a head of an intelligence service on the basis of irretrievable loss of trust on the part of his principal, in this case the President, would not be arbitrary or irrational . . . In this case, nothing suggests that the President acted arbitrarily or without sufficient reason.

. . .

[86] . . . It follows that in order to fulfil his duty in relation to national security, the President must subjectively trust the head of the intelligence services. Once the President had apprised himself of the facts from the Minister . . . the President concluded that he had lost trust in the Applicant and that it was in the national interest to terminate his appointment as head of the Agency. In my view, that breakdown of the relationship of trust constitutes a rational basis for dismissing the Applicant from his post as Director General of the Agency.

The Underlying Contract of Employment

[87] As we have seen earlier, the President had the requisite power to make the decision to dismiss the applicant or to amend his term of office so as to end it. I can find no cause to hold that the exercise of that power is not in accordance with the law. This does not however mean that a contract of employment between Mr Masetlha and the government comes to naught. The question is what the legal consequences are of the premature termination of the underlying contract of employment.

[88] Although it is clear that there has been a break-down in trust, that alone is not a sufficient ground to justify a unilateral termination of a contract of employment. It must however be said that the irretrievable breach of trust will be relevant for purposes of remedy. The ordinary remedies for breach of contract are either re-instatement or full payment of benefits for the remaining period of the contract.[22] In my view, even if the contract of employment were terminated unlawfully, Mr Masetlha would not be entitled to re-instatement as a matter of contract. Re-instatement is a discretionary remedy in employment law, which should not be awarded here because of the special relationship of trust that should exist between the head of the Agency and the President.[23] [47]

. . .

[91] . . . To the extent that the mainstay of his claim is to be re-instated as Director-General of the Agency, his claim must fail. From that must follow that Mr Masetlha's residual or alternative remedy is full payment of salary, allowances and benefits of his post for the remaining period of his contract.

[92] . . . I would accordingly dismiss the appeal and uphold the decision of the High Court that the suspension dispute has been rendered moot by the decision on the dismissal of the applicant.

. . .

Remedy

[97] In its bare bones, the relief asked for by Mr Masetlha is to be re-instated as Director-General of the Agency. I have come to the conclusion that the President was entitled to dismiss him but, given the underlying contract of employment between Mr Masetlha and the government, it was open to him to claim specific performance in the form of re-instatement or full payment of salary, allowance and benefits that

attach to his post for the unexpired term of the contract. For reasons that I have advanced, I hold that this is not an appropriate case to order re-instatement . . .

[98] This is so because it would not be proper to foist upon the President a Director-General of an important intelligence agency he does not trust . . .

. . .

[100] This does not arise. Absent an order for the re-instatement of Mr Masetlha, the state remains duty-bound to place Mr Masetlha in exactly the same position as he would have been had he served his full term as Director-General of the Agency. It is quite clear that Mr Masetlha declined the tender in order not to prejudice his claim for re-instatement as Director-General. Now that that claim has failed, there is no reason in law why he should not be paid the amount and benefits which the state had detailed in the letter from Minister Fraser-Moleketi to him dated 22 March 2006 and marked "AR3" in the application papers.

[101] . . . I plan to make an order, which will allow the parties to approach this Court or any other court of competent jurisdiction, on supplemented papers, for a speedy resolution regarding the extent of the applicant's remuneration and benefits owing.

Justice Sachs

[226] I support the order proposed by Moseneke DCJ and much of his reasoning. I agree that the power both to appoint and to dismiss the head of the National Intelligence Agency (NIA) is derived from the Constitution. I differ, however, in relation to the extent to which his judgment applies ordinary incidents of contract law to the consequences of the breakdown of the relationship between the President and Mr Masetlha. To my mind, the relationship between the President and the head of the NIA is at all times suffused with a constitutional dimension. I do not believe that the scant contractual details in this matter govern the issues raised, but rather that the case must be decided in the context of a constitutionally controlled public power having been exercised.

[227] The relationship at issue is different from that which the President would have with, say, his private secretary, or his gardener, where the ordinary incidents of contract law within a public administration legal regime could play a major role. It is a relationship created in a constitutional setting; its fundamental content is dictated by performance of identified constitutional responsibilities; its possible modes of termination are governed by constitutional criteria; and, I believe, the consequences of termination should be regulated by constitutional requirements. In this respect, I agree with the broad approach to legality adopted by Ngcobo J, though I do not accept his finding that the contract with Mr Masetlha was unlawfully terminated because of a lack of prior consultation.

[228] The starting point of my enquiry is the *sui generis* (of its own special kind) nature of the relationship between the President and the head of the NIA. The Constitution expressly empowers the President, as the head of the national executive, di-

rectly to appoint three functionaries, each with a leading role to play in security: the National Director of Public Prosecutions,[24] [1] the National Commissioner of Police[25] [2] and the head of the NIA.[26] [3] . . .

. . .

[230] Yet it cannot be that in a constitutional state, the secret service is so secret that its functioning takes place outside the realm of law. Our Constitution eschews autocracy, and it is unthinkable that a senior public figure straddling the divide between the public administration and government, and expressly commanded to work within the law,[27] [13] should oblige him- or herself to function in a legal void without any rights at all.

[231] Moseneke DCJ would fill the vacuum by invoking the ordinary principles of contract law. In my view, however, the equivalent of terms and conditions should be inferred in each case from the special nature of the specific relationship between the President and the appointees established by the Constitution, in this case the head of the NIA. At the very heart of the special relationship is the need for confidence on the part of the President in the dependability of the intelligence passed on to him. Once the basis of that reliance evaporates, the whole foundation of the relationship disappears . . . A great deal of subjective discretion is therefore necessarily built in to the appreciation by the President of the work of the head of the NIA. Absent the trust, the core of the relationship is negated.[28] [14]

[232] The issue presented by this case, then, is not based on something on which the President did not rely, namely, an allegation of breach of contract by Mr Masetlha. The basic question is whether the substratum of the relationship had vanished, entitling the President to terminate the appointment because its primary purpose and *raison d'être* (reason for coming into existence) had been obliterated. In my view, the facts show that it had, entitling the President to revoke the appointment.

[233] In the circumstances, then, I would hold that the President was lawfully entitled to amend the terms of the appointment to bring it to an immediate end. This does not mean that Mr Masetlha had been without any protection at all. He never lost his right to a fair labour practice. Though the mechanisms established by the LRA were not available to him, he was still entitled under section 23 of the Constitution to be treated fairly.[29] [15] Fairness in the circumstances was largely dictated by the nature of the work to be performed and the wide discretion given to the President to determine whether the requisite degree of trust had been destroyed . . . But short of such irrational motivation, the fairness of the termination itself must be seen as having flown from the fact that the basic confidence that the President needed for the relationship to continue had been irretrievably lost. Revocation of the appointment in these circumstances was accordingly not unfair, and the President could then lawfully terminate the relationship.

. . .

[235] Fairness of the termination, however, is not the end of the enquiry. Fairness required that in the absence of fault being alleged and established, Mr Masetlha

should not be deprived of the material benefits he would have received had the relationship proceeded to full term. This was in fact attended to on what were referred to as compassionate grounds. In my view, more than compassion was involved—the President was legally bound to pay out Mr Masetlha for the remainder of his term.

[236] . . . People live not by bread alone; indeed, in the case of career functionaries, reputation and bread are often inseparable.

[237] The general public too had an interest. Constitutionally created institutions need constantly to be nurtured if they are to function well. This requires that those who exercise public power should avoid wherever possible acting in a manner which may unduly disturb public confidence in the integrity of the incumbents of these institutions.

[238] In this regard, it is my view that fair dealing and civility cannot be separated. Civility in a constitutional sense involves more than just courtesy or good manners. It is one of the binding elements of a constitutional democracy. It presupposes tolerance for those with whom one disagrees and respect for the dignity of those with whom one is in dispute. Civility, closely linked to *ubuntu-botho*, is deeply rooted in traditional culture, and has been widely supported as a precondition for the good functioning of contemporary democratic societies.[30] Indeed, it was civilised dialogue in extremely difficult conditions that was the foundation of our peaceful constitutional revolution. The Constitution that emerged therefore presupposes that public power will be exercised in a manner that is not arbitrary and not unduly disrespectful of the dignity of those adversely affected by the exercise.

[240] I would conclude, then, as follows: given the loss of trust bearing on the central task of the head of the NIA, as is evident from the papers, the termination by the President of the appointment of Mr Masetlha as head of the NIA was not unlawful; the offer to pay him out for the balance of the period of his appointment should not be characterised as an act of grace or compassion, but as compliance with a legal obligation; and to the extent that any reputational damage to Mr Masetlha might have been caused by the manner in which the proceedings unfolded, the judgments in this matter establish that the basis for the termination of Mr Masetlha's incumbency was simply an irretrievable breakdown of trust, and not dismissal for misconduct.

uBuntu Under the Interim Constitution:
Life, Death, and *uBuntu*

THE *MAKWANYANE* CASE

S v. Makwanyane 1995 (6) BCLR 665 (CC)

Case Summary

FACTS

Two accused had been convicted on four counts of murder, for which they were sentenced to death on each count, as well as one count of attempted murder and one count of robbery with aggravating circumstances, for which they were sentenced to long term imprisonment.

The matter was appealed to the Appellate Division of the Supreme Court. The court dismissed the appeal for convictions and sentences. The Appellate Division was of the opinion that the accused deserved the most severe punishment that could be afforded in law. The most severe punishment at that time was the death penalty. Therefore, further hearing of the appeals against the death sentences were postponed until the Constitutional Court had determined the constitutionality of the death sentence.

It was contended on behalf of the two accused that the imposition of the death penalty for murder was a cruel, inhuman or degrading punishment, and that it was also inconsistent with the right to life provision—section 9 of the Interim Constitution. The argument was that the death sentence was incapable of correction in the case of error, its application was arbitrary, and it negated the essential content of the right to life.

The Attorney General contended on behalf of the State that the death penalty is a necessary and acceptable form of punishment which is not cruel, inhuman or degrading within the meaning of section 11(2) of the Interim Constitution, which prohibited cruel, inhuman, or degrading treatment or punishment. He argued further that if the drafters of the Interim Constitution had wished to make the death penalty unconstitutional, they would have done so expressly. According to the Attorney General, the issue was thus for Parliament to decide.

The Attorney General argued further that the death penalty served as a deterrent to violent crime, much more than life imprisonment, and it met society's need for retribution in the case of heinous crimes. The Attorney General argued that what is cruel, inhuman, or degrading depends on contemporary attitudes of society, and that South African society regarded the death penalty as an acceptable form of punishment; thus rendering it not cruel, inhuman, or degrading within the meaning of section 11(2). To the extent that it infringed fundamental rights, the limitation of such rights was justified in terms of section 33 of the Interim Constitution.

Legal History

This case originated in the Witwatersrand High Court, in which the accused were convicted and sentenced. It then went to the Appellate Division of the Supreme Court for an appeal against the sentences.

Legal Issues

The question before the Constitutional Court was whether the death penalty as a form of punishment for murder was justifiable under the new constitutional order.

Dispensation

Justice Chaskalson (who was president of the Constitutional Court at the time), writing for the majority, struck down the death penalty, maintaining that it was cruel, inhuman, and degrading (section 11(2)), and that it violated the right to life (section 9) and the right to human dignity (section 10).

The Attorney General submitted that the death penalty was an issue for Parliament to decide. Justice Chaskalson reviewed that history of the negotiated settlement of the new constitutional order, which ultimately left the decision about the death penalty as one to be decided by the Constitutional Court.

Justice Chaskalson relied on the *S v. Zuma* case to argue that a purposive and generous approach should be adopted when interpreting the Constitution. Further, Justice Chaskalson argued that section 11(2) should not be construed in isolation, but in the light of other related provisions of Chapter 3 of the Interim Constitution and that the history and background to the adoption of the Constitution itself should be taken into account. Punishment had to be in accordance with section 9 (the right to life), section 10 (the right to respect for and protection of one's dignity) and section 8 (the right to equality before the law).

Justice Chaskalson then sought to apply the ordinary meaning of the words of section 11(2) to find that the death penalty was cruel, inhuman, and degrading.

The arbitrariness inherent in the application of the death sentence was a factor that had to be taken into account. Although section 227(1)(a) of the Criminal Procedure Act 51 of 1977 may not *prima facie* be discriminatory, its application may reveal it to be discriminatory in effect. It was necessary to accept that uncertainty as a feature in all legal proceedings, and the possibility of error could not be totally excluded. Where error resulted in unjust imprisonment, the error could be rectified if discovered; but the killing of an innocent person was irremediable. Attempts to temper this horror of extermination by allowing wide rights of appeal and review lead to the "death row phenomenon" and a delay in carrying out or setting aside the sentence. To design a system that avoids arbitrariness and delay in carrying out a sentence was exceedingly difficult, if not impossible. That such delay was cruel and inhuman was emphasized by Justice Chaskalson in the majority judgment.

The further legal issue was whether the death sentence was a justifiable limitation of the above rights in terms of section 33(1) of the Interim Constitution. The South African Constitution deals with the limitation of fundamental rights through an explicit limitations clause, section 33(1). This limitation clause in turn demands a two-staged approach. First, the court must find whether there was a violation of a fundamental right, and second, the court must find whether this violation of a fundamental right is justifiable according to the criteria set out in section 33(1); these criteria are whether the infliction of death as a form of punishment for murder could be shown to be reasonable, necessary, and consistent with the other requirements of section 33 of the Interim Constitution.

Justice Chaskalson considers three desirable goals of punishment: deterrence, retribution, and prevention, and concludes that none of these three could override the fundamental rights established in section 11(2), as well as sections 8, 9, and 10 of the Interim Constitution. For Justice Chaskalson, the evidence on deterrence is inconclusive as to whether or not death has any greater deterrent effect than life imprisonment. Life imprisonment also guarantees prevention, particularly when there is no parole, since it removes the criminal from the streets. Lastly, Justice Chaskalson strongly argues that retribution should not be given undue weight in the balancing process provided by the criteria of the limitations clause. Quoting the postamble of the Interim Constitution, Justice Chaskalson argues that *ubuntu* would weigh against retribution as an acceptable goal for punishment.

He thus concludes the case as follows:

[144] The rights to life and dignity are the most important of all human rights, and the source of all other personal rights in Chapter 3. By committing ourselves to a society founded on the recognition of human rights we are required to value these two rights above all others. And this must be demonstrated by the State in everything that it does, including the way it punishes criminals. This is not achieved by objectifying murderers and putting them

to death to serve as an example to others in the expectation that they might possibly be deterred thereby.

[145] In the balancing process the principal factors that have to be weighed are on the one hand the destruction of life and dignity that is a consequence of the implementation of the death sentence, the elements of arbitrariness and the possibility of error in the enforcement of capital punishment, and the existence of a severe alternative punishment (life imprisonment) and, on the other, the claim that the death sentence is a greater deterrent to murder, and will more effectively prevent its commission, than would a sentence of life imprisonment, and that there is a public demand for retributive justice to be imposed on murderers, which only the death sentence can meet.

JUSTICE ACKERMANN

Justice Ackermann argued that greater emphasis must be placed on the inevitably arbitrary nature of a decision to impose the death penalty in supporting the conclusion that it conflicted with section 11(2).

The Interim Constitution marked a move from a past characterized by much that was arbitrary and unequal in the operation of the law to a dispensation where state action had to be susceptible to rational justification. The obligation to ensure that the criminal does not strike again is integrally tied to the elimination of the death penalty. However, the consequences of the death sentence as a form of punishment differ radically from any other type of sentence. Whatever the scope of the right to life entrenched in section 9 of the Interim Constitution, it must encompass the right not to be deliberately put to death by the State in a way that was arbitrary and unequal. The death penalty is a violation of section 9 and section 11(2) of the Interim Constitution, because it cannot be cleansed of arbitrariness and thus unequal application.

If the death penalty is abolished, which it must be, then there is an obligation on the part of the State to protect society from being harmed by crime.

JUSTICE DIDCOTT

Justice Didcott concluded that capital punishment violated the right to life entrenched in section 9 and the prohibition against cruel, inhuman, and degrading punishment entrenched in section 11(2). Without deciding on a comprehensive and exact definition of what was encompassed by the right to life, such right must include at the very least the right not to be put to death by the State deliberately. As to section 11(2), the ordeal suffered by criminals awaiting and experiencing execution was intrinsically cruel, inhuman, and degrading. Following the two-step procedure established by section 33(1), Justice Didcott established that the death penalty could be justified by that clause. If it could be established for certain that it was a unique deterrent against future crimes, then the death sentence would pass constitutional muster. The question was not, however, whether the death penalty had a deterrent effect, but whether that effect was significantly greater than any alternative sentence available. Without enough empirical proof it was not possible to determine the extent to which capital punishment worked as a deterrent. The inherent arbitrariness of its application was intolerable because of the irreversibility of the punishment stemming from the inability to remedy a mistake that is discovered after the person has been put to death. This defect disallowed capital punishment to be salvaged through the limitations clause.

JUSTICE KENTRIDGE

Justice Kentridge agreed with Justice Chaskalson that a decision could be reached without giving an authoritative interpretation of section 33(1)(b) of the Interim Constitution, which provides that no statutory limitation on another Constitutional right shall "negate the essential content of the right in question."

Like Justice Chaskalson, Justice Kentridge argues that the essential content of the right to life has to be decided carefully and its implications can only be drawn out in future cases before the court. Justice Kentridge then offers two possible interpretations to section 33(1)(b) of the Interim Constitution. The first is that section 33(1)(b) "subjectively" applies to the right to life in the case of the death penalty because by ending a life, you automatically negate the essence of the right to life. The second approach is to examine the law, which is sought to be justified under the limitations clause—section 33 of the Interim Constitution. For Justice Kentridge, the decisive issue was whether the death penalty was a cruel, inhuman, or degrading punishment. However revolting the act of cruelty committed against a victim, it did not follow that the State should respond to the murderer's cruelty with a deliberate and matching cruelty of its own. In general civilized democratic societies had found the death penalty to be unacceptably cruel, inhuman, and degrading. The State ought to be "institutionalised civilisation." The new South Africa in particular should represent this idea. The deliberate execution of a human, however depraved his conduct, mitigates against the emerging ideal of the new South Africa. The elimination of the death penalty does not imply a lenient attitude towards crime. But such elimination does entail the realization that even the worst and most vicious criminals were not excluded from the protection of the Constitution.

JUSTICE KRIEGLER

Justice Kriegler argued that the issue was not the moral question of whether the death penalty ought to be abolished or retained. The only question before the Constitutional Court was a legal question: Was there an infringement of fundamental rights? Section 9 of the Interim Constitution plainly indicated that the State could not deliberately deprive a person of his life. Accordingly section 277(1) of the Criminal Procedure Act 51 of 1977 was liable to be struck down unless saved by the limitations clause, section

33 of the Interim Constitution. Justice Kriegler was satisfied that it was not saved by section 33 of the Interim Constitution, as it did not meet the requirements of the limitations clause. No empirical study had demonstrated that capital punishment had greater deterrent force than a lengthy sentence of imprisonment. Without certainty of the deterrent value of capital punishment, it could not be reasonable to allow state imposition of the death penalty. Thus for Justice Kriegler, it was unnecessary to decide whether the death penalty conflicted with other fundamental rights.

JUSTICE O'REGAN

Justice O'Regan[1] forcefully argued that the death penalty did not only constitute cruel and inhuman punishment, but that it also violated the right to life and the right to human dignity; sections 9 and 10 of the Interim Constitution, respectively.

She also argued that in interpreting the right to life clause, the court should take into account the purpose for which the right was protected in the Constitution. While existence is a precondition for any right in the Constitution, the right to life was included in the Constitution not only as a mere anchor for all other rights. It connotes a human life. For Justice O'Regan, the right to life is meaningless without dignity, because the right to life embodies human dignity.

Within the context of the South African past, the right to human dignity is of vital importance, because the brutal reality of apartheid denied the common humanity we all share. For Justice O'Regan, the extension of Chapter 3 rights to all human beings, including criminals was the hallmark of the new Constitutional dispensation. Not only was the execution of the criminal a violation of his or her dignity, the manner in which the execution takes place and the death row phenomenon is in itself a violation of dignity. Like the other justices, Justice O'Regan was unconvinced that deterrence could be used to weigh against the founding rights of dignity, and the right to a life in which one's dignity is respected. Thus, once again, the death penalty could not be saved by the societal goal of punishment for criminals, as it had to be evaluated by the criteria of the limitations clause.

JUSTICE SACHS

Justice Sachs sought to expand on two aspects of the majority judgment. Firstly, Justice Sachs was critical of the majority judgment, as it places greater reliance on the protection against cruel, inhuman, or degrading punishment than it did on the right to life and the right to dignity. Justice Sachs argued forcefully that the starting point of an analysis of the death penalty should be section 9; the right to life. The words of section 9 were clear, unqualified, and binding on the state. He then noted that while section 33 of the Interim Constitution permitted a limitation of the right to life, the death penalty did not limit the right to life, it annihilated human life.

Secondly, Justice Sachs was concerned about the source of the values that the court, in its interpretation of the Constitution, is supposed to promote. In his judgment Justice Sachs noted again that the Constitution mandates the court, in interpreting the Bill of Rights, to do so in a manner that promotes values of an open and democratic society. Justice Sachs observed that one such value is that all societies and communities must be taken into account and their interests equally considered in matters of such burning importance as the death penalty. He further argued that due to the evil of history that was founded on the contempt of blackness, recognition of the values of the black Africans was long overdue. It was distressing for Justice Sachs that the South African law reports and legal publications contained extremely limited citations to African jurisprudence. In a constitutional dispensation, it is ethically crucial that the court take into account African jurisprudence and indigenous values. Deep respect for African values is indeed demanded by the spirit of the epilogue of the Interim Constitution.

We begin with Justice Mokgoro's judgment because her judgment expresses the most developed elaboration of *ubuntu* as it gives shape to the constitutional right of dignity and life. See also the paragraph of Justice Chaskalson in which he uses *ubuntu* further. See Justice Sachs as he defends the need to deploy African values in constitutional law.

Justice Mokgoro

. . .

[300] I am in agreement with the judgment of Chaskalson P, its reasoning, and its conclusions, and I concur in the order that gives effect to those conclusions. I give this brief concurring opinion to highlight what I regard as important: namely that, when our Courts promote the underlying values of an open and democratic society in terms of section 35 when considering the constitutionality of laws, they should recognise that indigenous South African values are not always irrelevant nor unrelated to this task. In my view, these values are embodied in the Constitution and they impact directly on the death penalty as a form of punishment.

[301] Now that constitutionalism has become central to the new emerging South African jurisprudence, legislative interpretation will be radically different from what it used to be in the past legal order. In that legal order, due to the sovereignty of Parliament, the supremacy of legislation and the absence of judicial review of Parliamentary statutes, Courts engaged in simple statutory interpretation, giving effect to the clear and unambiguous language of the legislative text—no matter how unjust the legislative provision. The view of the Court in *Bongopi v Council of State, Ciskei* 1992 (3) SA 250 (Ck) at 265H–I, as per Pickard CJ is instructive in this regard:

> "This Court has always stated openly that it is not the maker of laws. It will enforce the law as it finds it. To attempt to promote policies that are not to be found in the law itself or to prescribe what it believes to be the current public attitudes or standards in regard to these policies is not its function."

[302] With the entrenchment of a Bill of Fundamental Rights and Freedoms in a supreme Constitution, however, the interpretative task frequently involves making constitutional choices by balancing competing fundamental rights and freedoms. This can often only be done by reference to a system of values extraneous to the constitutional text itself, where these principles constitute the historical context in which the text was adopted and which help to explain the meaning of the text. The Constitution makes it particularly imperative for Courts to develop the entrenched fundamental rights in terms of a cohesive set of values, ideal to an open and democratic society. To this end, common values of human rights protection the world over and foreign precedent may be instructive.

[303] While it is important to appreciate that in the matter before us the Court had been called upon to decide an issue of constitutionality and not to engage in debate on the desirability of abolition or retention, it is equally important to appreciate that the nature of the Court's role in constitutional interpretation, and the duty placed on courts by section 35, will of necessity draw them into the realm of making necessary value choices.

[304] The application of the limitation clause embodied in section 33(1) to any law of general application which competes with a Chapter 3 right is essentially also an exercise in balancing opposing rights. To achieve the required balance will of necessity involve value judgments. This is the nature of constitutional interpretation. Indeed section 11(2), which is the counterpart of section 15(1) of the Constitution of Zimbabwe,[2] [47] and provides protection against cruel, inhuman or degrading punishment, embodies broad idealistic notions of dignity and humanity. If applied to determine whether the death penalty was a form of torture, treatment or punishment which is cruel, inhuman or degrading it also involves making value choices, as was held per Gubbay CJ in *Catholic Commission for Justice and Peace, Zimbabwe v Attorney General, Zimbabwe* 1993 94) SA 239 (ZS) at 241. In order to guard against what Didcott J, in his concurring judgment terms the trap of undue subjectivity, the interpretation clause prescribes that courts seek guidance in international norms and foreign judicial precedent, reflective of the values, which underlie an open and democratic society based on freedom and equality. By articulating rather than suppressing values, which underlie our decisions, we are not being subjective. On the contrary, we set out in a transparent and objective way the foundations of our interpretative choice and make them available for criticism. Section 35 seems to acknowledge the paucity of home-grown judicial precedent upholding human rights, which is not surprising considering the repressive nature of the past legal order. It requires courts to proceed to public international law and foreign case law for guidance in constitutional interpretation, thereby promoting the ideal and internationally accepted values in the cultivation of Human Rights jurisprudence for South Africa. However, I am of the view that our own (ideal) indigenous value systems are a premise from which we need to proceed and are not wholly unrelated to our goal of a society based on freedom and equality. This, in my view too, is the relevance of the

submissions of Adv *Davids*, appearing as *amicus curiae* on behalf of the Black Advocates' Forum, albeit that these submissions were inappropriately presented.

[305] In *Dudgeon v United Kingdom* (1982) 4 EHRR 149, the European Court of Human Rights, per Walsh J, expressed the view that:

> ". . . in a democracy the law cannot afford to ignore the moral consensus of he community. If the law is out of touch with the moral consensus of the community, whether by being either too far below it or too far above it, the law is brought into contempt" (at 184).

Although this view was expressed in relation to the legislative process, in as far as courts have to comply with the requirements of section 35 of the Constitution the approach it embodies, is not wholly inapplicable in constitutional adjudication. Enduring values, however, are not the same as fluctuating public opinion. In his argument before the Court, the Attorney General submitted that:

> ". . . the overwhelming public opinion in favour of the retention of the death sentence is sufficiently well-known to be accepted as the true voice of the South African society. This opinion of the South African public is evidenced by newspaper articles, letters to newspapers, debates in the media and representations to the authorities . . ."

The described sources of public opinion can hardly be regarded as scientific. Yet even if they were, constitutional adjudication is quite different from the legislative process, because "the Court is not a politically responsible institution"[3] [48] to be seized every five years by majoritarian opinion. The values intended to be promoted by section 35 are not founded on what may well be uninformed or indeed prejudiced public opinion. One of the functions of the Court is precisely to ensure that vulnerable minorities are not deprived of their constitutional rights.

[306] In support of her main contention, Adv *Davids* quite appropriately expressed concern for the need to consider the value systems of the formerly marginalised sectors of society in creating a South African jurisprudence. However, for reasons outlined in the concurring opinion of Sachs J, the issue was regrettably not argued. Indeed even if her submissions might not have influenced the final decision of the Court, the opportunity to present and argue properly adduced evidence of those undistorted values historically disregarded in South African judicial law-making would have created an opportunity of important historical value, injecting such values into the mainstream of South African jurisprudence. The experience would, in my view, also have served to emphasise that the need to develop an all-inclusive South African jurisprudence is not only incumbent upon the judiciary, let alone the Constitutional Court. The broad legal profession, academia and those sectors of organised civil society particularly concerned with public interest law,

have an equally important responsibility and role to play by combining efforts and resources to place the required evidence in argument before the Courts. It is not as if these resources are lacking; what has been absent has been the will, and the acknowledgement of the importance of the material concerned.

[307] In interpreting the Bill of Fundamental Rights and Freedoms, as already mentioned, an all-inclusive value system, or common values in South Africa, can form a basis upon which to develop South African Human Rights jurisprudence. Although South Africans have a history of deep divisions characterised by strife and conflict, one shared value and ideal that runs like a golden thread across cultural lines, is the value of *ubuntu*—a notion now coming to be generally articulated in this country. It is well accepted that the transitional Constitution is a culmination of a negotiated political settlement. It is a bridge between a history of gross violations of human rights and humanitarian principles, and a future of reconstruction and reconciliation. The post-amble of the Constitution expressly provides:

". . . there is a need for understanding but not for vengeance, a need for reparation but not for retaliation, a need for *ubuntu* but not for victimisation . . ."

Not only is the notion of *ubuntu* expressly provided for in the epilogue of the Constitution, the underlying idea and its accompanying values are also expressed in the preamble. These values underlie, first and foremost, the whole idea of adopting a Bill of Fundamental Rights and Freedoms in a new legal order. They are central to the coherence of all the rights entrenched in Chapter 3—where the right to life and the right to respect for and protection of human dignity are embodied in sections 9 and 10 respectively.

[308] Generally, *ubuntu* translates as *humaneness*. In its most fundamental sense, it translates as *personhood* and *morality*. Metaphorically, it expresses itself in *umuntu ngumuntu ngabantu*, describing the significance of group solidarity on survival issues so central to the survival of communities. While it envelops the key values of group solidarity, compassion, respect, human dignity, conformity to basic norms and collective unity, in its fundamental sense it denotes humanity and morality. Its spirit emphasises respect for human dignity, marking a shift from confrontation to conciliation.[4] [49] In South Africa *ubuntu* has become a notion with particular resonance in the building of a democracy. It is part of our "rainbow" heritage, though it might have operated and still operates differently in diverse community settings. In the Western cultural heritage, respect and the value for life, manifested in the all-embracing concepts of *humanity* and *menswaardigheid* are also highly priced. It is values like these that section 35 requires to be promoted. They give meaning and texture to the principles of a society based on freedom and equality.

[309] In American jurisprudence, Courts have recognised that the dignity of the individual in American society is the supreme value. Even the most evil offender, it has been held, "remains a human being possessed of a common human dignity"

(*Furman v Georgia* 408 US 238 at 273 (1972)), thereby making the calculated process of the death penalty inconsistent with this basic, fundamental value. In Hungarian jurisprudence, the right to life and the right to human dignity are protected as twin rights in section 54(1) of that Constitution.[5] [50] They are viewed as an inseparable unity of rights. Not only are they regarded as a unity of indivisible rights, but they also have been held to be the genesis of all rights. In international law, on the other hand, human dignity is generally considered the fountain of all rights. The International Covenant on Civil and Political Rights (1966) GA Res 2200 (XXI), 21 UN GAOR SUPP (no 16) at 62, UN DOC A/6316 (1966), in its preamble, makes references to "the inherent dignity of all members of the human family" and concludes that "human rights derive from the inherent dignity of the human person." This, in my view, is not different from what the spirit of *ubuntu* embraces.

[310] It is common cause, however, that the legal system in South Africa, and the socio-political system within which it operated, has for decades traumatised the human spirit. In many ways, it trampled on the basic humanity of citizens. We cannot in all conscience declare, as did a United States Supreme Court Justice in *Furman v Georgia* 408 US 238 (1972) at 296 with reference to the American context, that respect for and protection of human dignity has been a central value in South African jurisprudence. We cannot view the death penalty as fundamentally inconsistent with our harsh legal heritage. Indeed, it was an integral part of a system of law enforcement that imposed severe penalties on those who aspired to achieve the values enshrined in our Constitution today.

[311] South Africa now has a new Constitution however, which creates a constitutional state. This state is in turn founded on the recognition and protection of basic human rights, and although this constitutes a revolutionary change in legal terms, the idea is consistent with the inherited traditional value systems of South Africans in general—traditional values which hardly found the chance to bring South Africa on par with the rest of the world. As this Constitution evolves to overcome the culture of gross human rights violations of the past, jurisprudence in South Africa will simultaneously develop a culture of respect for and protection of basic human rights. Central to this commitment is the need to revive the value of human dignity in South Africa, and in turn re-define and recognise the right to and protection of human dignity as a right, concomitant to life itself and inherent in all human beings, so that South Africans may also appreciate that "even the vilest criminal remains a human being" (*Furman v Georgia* (*supra*)). In my view, life and dignity are like two sides of the same coin. The concept of *ubuntu* embodies them both.

[312] In the past legal order, basic human rights in South Africa, including the right to life and human dignity, were not protected in a bill of fundamental rights and freedoms, in a supreme constitution, as is the case today. Parliament then was sovereign, and could pass any law it deemed fit. Legislation was supreme, and due to the absence of judicial review, no court of law could set aside any statute or its

provision on grounds of violating fundamental rights. Hence, section 277 of the Criminal Procedure Act 51 of 1977 could survive untested to this day.

[313] Our new Constitution, unlike its dictatorial predecessor, is value-based. Among other things, it guarantees the protection of basic human rights, including the right to life and human dignity, two basic values supported by the spirit of *ubuntu* and protected in sections 9 and 10 respectively. In terms of section 35, this Constitution now commits the State to base the worth of human beings on the ideal values espoused by open democratic societies the world over and not on race, colour, political, economic and social class. Although it has been argued that the currently high level of crime in the country is indicative of the breakdown of the moral fabric of society, it has not been conclusively shown that the death penalty, which is an affront to these basic values, is the best available practical form of punishment to reconstruct that moral fabric. In the second place, even if the end were desirable, that would not justify the means. The death penalty violates the essential content of the right to life embodied in section 9, in that it extinguishes life itself. It instrumentalises the offender for the objectives of State policy. That is dehumanising. It is degrading and it violates the rights to respect for and protection of human dignity embodied in section 10 of the Constitution.

[314] Once the life of a human being is taken in the deliberate and calculated fashion that characterises the described methods of execution the world over, it constitutes the ultimate cruelty with which any living creature could ever be treated. This extreme level of cruel treatment of a human being, however despicably such person might have treated another human being, is still inherently cruel. It is inhuman and degrading to the humanity of the individual, as well as to the humanity of those who carry it out.

[315] Taking the life of a human being will always be reprehensible. Those citizens who kill deserve the most severe punishment, if it deters and rehabilitates and therefore effectively addresses deviance of this nature. Punishment by death cannot achieve these objectives. The high rate of crime in this country is indeed disturbing and the State has a duty to protect the lives of all citizens—including those who kill. However, it should find more humane and effective integrated approaches to manage its penal system, and to rehabilitate offenders.

[316] The State is representative of its people and in many ways sets the standard for moral values within society. If it sanctions by law punishment for killing by killing, it sanctions vengeance by law. If it does so with a view to deterring others, it dehumanises the person and objectifies him or her as a tool for crime control. This objectification through the calculated killing of a human being, to serve State objectives, strips the offender of his or her human dignity and dehumanises such a person, constituting a violation of section 10 of the Constitution.

[317] Although the Attorney General placed great reliance on the deterrent nature of the death penalty in his argument, it was conceded that this has not been conclusively proven. It has also not been shown that this form of punishment was

the best available option for the rehabilitation of the offender. Retaining the death penalty for this purpose is therefore unnecessary. Section 277(1) which authorises the death penalty under these unnecessarily inhuman and degrading circumstances is inconsistent with the right to life and human dignity embodied in sections 9 and 10 of the Constitution, respectively, and is in direct conflict with the values that section 35 aims to promote in the interpretation of these sections. Taking the life of a person under such deliberate and calculated circumstances, with the methods already described in the judgment of Chaskalson P, is cruel, inhuman or degrading treatment or punishment. It is inconsistent with section 11(2) of the Constitution. In my view, therefore, the death penalty is unconstitutional. Not only does it violate the right not to be subjected to cruel, inhuman or degrading treatment or punishment, it also violates the right to life and human dignity

. . .

Justice Chaskalson

[130] Retribution ought not to be given undue weight in the balancing process. The Constitution is premised on the assumption that ours will be a constitutional state founded on the recognition of human rights.[6] [159] The concluding provision on national unity and reconciliation contains the following commitment:

> "The adoption of this Constitution lays the secure foundation for the people of South Africa to transcend the divisions and strife of the past, which generated gross violations of human rights, the transgression of humanitarian principles in violent conflicts and a legacy of hatred, fear, guilt and *revenge.*
>
> These can now be addressed on the basis that there is a need for understanding but *not for vengeance*, a need for reparation but *not for retaliation*, a need for *ubuntu* but *not for victimisation.*" (Emphasis mine.)

[131] Although this commitment has its primary application in the field of political reconciliation, it is not without relevance to the enquiry we are called upon to undertake in the present case. To be consistent with the value of *ubuntu* ours should be a society that "wishes to prevent crime . . . (not) to kill criminals simply to get even with them."

. . .

Justice Langa

. . .

[217] For the reasons set out in Didcott J's judgement, I place more emphasis on the right to life. Section 9 of the Constitution proclaims it in unqualified terms. It is the most fundamental of all rights,[7] [36] the supreme human right.[8] [37] I do not consider it necessary or desirable to define the exact scope of the right, save to make two points, namely:

(a) It does mean that every person has the right not to be deliberately put to death by the State as punishment, as envisaged in section 277 of the Criminal Procedure Act.

(b) I do not exclude the application of the limitations clause to the right to life. Any law that seeks to limit the right will have to comply with the requirements of section 33(1) of the Constitution. For the reasons set out in Chaskalson P's judgment, the requirements have not been met; the State has been unable to justify the limitation, which is imposed on the right to life by section 277 of the Criminal Procedure Act. I cannot accept that it is "reasonable," as required by section 33(1) of the Constitution, to override what is the most fundamental of all rights, without clear proof that the deterrence value of the penalty is substantially higher than that which the imposition of a suitably long period of imprisonment has. This has not been proved. Because of the view I take, I find it unnecessary to deal with the other requirements of section 33(1) of the Constitution.

[218] The emphasis I place on the right to life is, in part, influenced by the recent experiences of our people in this country. The history of the past decades has been such that the value of life and human dignity has been demeaned. Political, social and other factors created a climate of violence resulting in a culture of retaliation and vengeance. In the process, respect for life and for the inherent dignity of every person became the main casualties. The State has been part of this degeneration, not only because of its role in the conflicts of the past, but also by retaining punishments which did not testify to a high regard for the dignity of the person and the value of every human life.

[219] The primacy of the right to life and its relationship to punishment needs to be emphasised also in view of our constitutional history. The doctrine of parliamentary sovereignty meant, virtually, that the State could do anything, enact any law, subject only to procedural correctness.[9] [38]

[220] When the Constitution was enacted, it signalled a dramatic change in the system of governance from one based on rule by Parliament to a constitutional state in which the rights of individuals are guaranteed by the Constitution. It also signalled a new dispensation, as it were, where rule by force would be replaced by democratic principles and a governmental system based on the precepts of equality and freedom.

[221] It may well be that for millions in this country; the effect of the change has yet to be felt in a material sense. For all of us though, a framework has been created in which a new culture must take root and develop.

[222] Implicit in the provisions and tone of the Constitution are values of a more mature society, which relies on moral persuasion rather than force; on example rather than coercion. In this new context, then, the role of the State becomes clear. For good or for worse, the State is a role model for our society.[10] [39] A culture of

respect for human life and dignity, based on the values reflected in the Constitution, has to be engendered, and the State must take the lead. In acting out this role, the State not only preaches respect for the law and that the killing must stop, but it demonstrates in the best way possible, by example, society's own regard for human life and dignity by refusing to destroy that of the criminal. Those who are inclined to kill need to be told why it is wrong. The reason surely must be the principle that the value of human life is inestimable, and it is a value, which the State must uphold by example as well. As pointed out by Mr Justice Schaefer of the Supreme Court of Illinois:[11] [40]

> "The methods we employ in the enforcement of our criminal law have aptly been called the measures by which the quality of our civilisation may be judged."

[223] The ethos of the new culture is expressed in the much-quoted provision on national unity and reconciliation that forms part of the Constitution. Chaskalson P quotes the various components of it in paragraphs 7 and 130 of his judgment. It describes the Constitution as a "bridge" between the past and the future; from "the past of a deeply divided society characterised by strife, conflict, untold suffering and injustice, and a future founded on the recognition of human rights . . . for all South Africans . . ."; and finally, it suggests a change in mental attitude from vengeance to an appreciation of the need for understanding, from retaliation to reparation and from victimisation to *ubuntu*. The Constitution does not define this last-mentioned concept.

[224] The concept is of some relevance to the values we need to uphold. It is a culture, which places some emphasis on communality and on the interdependence of the members of a community. It recognises a person's status as a human being, entitled to unconditional respect, dignity, value and acceptance from the members of the community such person happens to be part of. It also entails the converse, however. The person has a corresponding duty to give the same respect, dignity, value and acceptance to each member of that community. More importantly, it regulates the exercise of rights by the emphasis it lays on sharing and co-responsibility and the mutual enjoyment of rights by all. It is perhaps best illustrated in the following remarks in the judgment of the Court of Appeal of the Republic of Tanzania in *DPP v Pete*,[12] [41]

> "The second important principle or characteristic to be borne in mind when interpreting our Constitution is a corollary of the reality of co-existence of the individual and society, and also the reality of co-existence of rights and duties of the individual on the one hand, and the collective of communitarian rights and duties of society on the other. In effect this co-existence means that the rights and duties of the individual are limited by the rights and duties of society, and *vice versa*."

[225] An outstanding feature of *ubuntu* in a community sense is the value it puts on life and human dignity. The dominant theme of the culture is that the life of another person is at least as valuable as one's own. Respect for the dignity of every person is integral to this concept. During violent conflicts and times when violent crime is rife, distraught members of society decry the loss of *ubuntu*. Thus heinous crimes are the antithesis of *ubuntu*. Treatment that is cruel, inhuman or degrading is bereft of *ubuntu*.

[226] We have all been affected, in some way or other, by the "strife, conflict, untold suffering and injustice" of the recent past. Some communities have been ravaged much more than others. In some, there is hardly anyone who has not been a victim in some way or who has not lost a close relative in senseless violence. Some of the violence has been perpetrated through the machinery of the State, in order to ensure the perpetuation of a *status quo* that was fast running out of time. But all this was violence on human beings. Life became cheap, almost worthless.

[227] It was against a background of the loss of respect for human life and the inherent dignity, which attaches to every person that a spontaneous call has arisen among sections of the community for a return to *ubuntu*. A number of references to *ubuntu* have already been made in various texts but largely without explanation of the concept.[13] It has however always been mentioned in the context of it being something to be desired, a commendable attribute which the nation should strive for.

[228] At first blush, it may sound odd that the issue of the right to life is being decided on the basis of persons condemned to death for killing other human beings. In this regard, it is relevant to note that there are some 400 people presently under sentence of death for acts of violence. That in itself means that there are probably an equivalent number of victims whose lives have been prematurely, violently, terminated. They died without having had any recourse to law. For them there was no "due process."

. . .

[231] The violent acts of those who destroy life cannot be condoned, neither should anyone think that the abolition of the sentence of death means that the crime is regarded as anything but one of extreme seriousness. The sentence itself was an indication of society's abhorrence for the cruel and inhuman treatment of others. That moral outrage has been expressed in the strongest terms that society could muster.

. . .

[233] The Constitution constrains society to express its condemnation and its justifiable anger in a manner that preserves society's own morality. The State should not make itself guilty of conduct, which violates that which it is in the community's interests to nurture. The Constitution, in deference to our humanity and sense of dignity, does not allow us to kill in cold blood in order to deter others from killing. Nor does it allow us to "kill criminals simply to get even with them."[14] We are not to stoop to the level of the criminal.

[234] It follows from the remarks that as a "punishment" the death penalty is a violation of the right to life. It is cruel, inhuman *and* degrading. It is also a severe affront to human dignity. The "death row phenomenon" merely aggravates the position. Section 277 of the Criminal Procedure Act cannot be saved by the provisions of section 33(1) of the Constitution in respect of any of the rights affected. The punishment is not reasonable on any basis. In view of the available alternative sentence of a long term of imprisonment, it is also unnecessary.

. . .

Justice Madala

[237] The Constitution in its post-amble declares:

> ". . . there is a need for understanding but not vengeance, and for reparation but not for retaliation, a need for *ubuntu* but not victimisation."

The concept *ubuntu* appears for the first time in the post-amble, but it is a concept that permeates the Constitution generally and more particularly Chapter 3, which embodies the entrenched fundamental human rights. The concept carries in it the ideas of humaneness, social justice and fairness.

[238] It was argued by Mr *Bizos*, on behalf of the Government, that the post-amble enjoins the people of South Africa to open a new chapter which envisages the country playing a leading role in the upholding of human rights. He submitted further, that the Government favoured the abolition of the death penalty because it believed that such punishment could not be reconciled with the fundamental rights contained in the Constitution, and that its application diminished the dignity of our society as a whole.

[239] In my rejection of the death penalty as a form of punishment, I do not intend, nor do my colleagues, to condone murder, rape, armed robbery with aggravating circumstances and those other crimes which are punishable by a sentence of death in terms of section 277 of the Criminal Procedure Act 51 of 1977. These criminal acts are, and remain, as heinous, vicious and as reprehensible as they ever were, and do not belong in civilised society. The death penalty is a punishment, which involves so much pain and suffering that civilised society ought not to tolerate it even in spite of the present high rate of crime. And society ought to tolerate the death penalty even less when considering that it has not been proved that it has any greater deterrent effect on would-be murderers than life imprisonment.

[240] The aspect of irrevocability of the death penalty has been canvassed adequately in the judgment of Chaskalson P and I propose to say no more on that score (see paragraphs 26 and 54).

[241] As observed before, the death penalty rejects the possibility of rehabilitation of the convicted persons, condemning them as "no good," once and for all, and

drafting them to the death row and the gallows. One must then ask whether such rejection of rehabilitation as a possibility accords with the concept of *ubuntu*.

[242] One of the relative theories of punishment (the so-called purposive theories) is the reformative theory, which considers punishment to be a means to an end, and not an end in itself—that end being the reformation of the criminal as a person, so that the person may, at a certain stage, become a normal law-abiding and useful member of the community once again. The person and the personality of the offender are the point of focus rather than the crime, although the crime is, however, not forgotten. And in terms of this theory of punishment and as a necessary consequence of its application, the offender has to be imprisoned for a long period for the purpose of rehabilitation. By treatment and training the offender is rehabilitated, or, at the very least, ceases to be a danger to society.

[243] This, in my view, accords fully with the concept of *ubuntu*, which is so well enunciated in the Constitution.

[244] Our Courts have found room for the exercise of *ubuntu*, as appears from the many cases where they have found that despite the heinousness of the offence and the brutality with which it was perpetrated, there were factors in the offenders' favour, indicating that they were, in spite of the criminal conduct of which they were convicted, responsible members of society, and were worthy and capable of rehabilitation. (See *S v Mbotshwa* 1993 (2) SACR 468 (A) at 468J–469F; *S v Ramba* 1990 (2) SACR 334 (A) at 335H–336E; *S v Ngcobo* 1992 (2) SACR 515 (A) at 515H-516A; Contra: *S v Bosman* 1992 (1) SACR 115 (A) at 116G–117F).

[245] Against *ubuntu* must be seen the other side, the inhuman side of mankind, in terms of which the death penalty violates section 11(2) of the Constitution in that it is "cruel, inhuman or degrading treatment or punishment."

[246] In *Catholic Commission for Justice and Peace in Zimbabwe v Attorney General, Zimbabwe* 1993 (4) SA 239 (ZSC) at 268E–H, Gubbay CJ observed:

> "The moment he enters the condemned cell, the prisoner is enmeshed in a dehumanising environment of near hopelessness. He is in a place where the sole object is to preserve his life so that he may be executed. The condemned prisoner is 'the living dead' . . . He is kept only with other death sentence prisoners—with those whose appeals have been dismissed and who await death or reprieve; or those whose appeals are still to be heard or are pending judgment. While the right to an appeal may raise the prospect of being allowed to live, the intensity of the trauma is much increased by knowledge of its dismissal. The hope of a reprieve is all that is left. Throughout all this time the condemned prisoner constantly broods over his fate. The horrifying spectre of being hanged by the neck and the apprehension of being made to suffer a painful and lingering death is, if at all, never far from mind. Grim accounts exist of hangings not properly performed."

[247] Convicted persons in death row invariably find themselves there for a long time as they make every effort to exhaust all possible review avenues open to them. All this time they are subjected to a fate of ever increasing fear and distress. They know not what their future is and whether their efforts will come to nought; they live under the sword of Damocles—they will be advised any day about their appointment with the hangman. It is true that they might have shown no mercy at all to their victims, but we do not and should not take our standards and values from the murderer. We must, on the other hand, impose our standards and values on the murderer.

[248] In the afore-mentioned Zimbabwe case, the Court concluded that the incarceration of the condemned person under these conditions was in conflict with the provisions of section 15(1) of the Zimbabwe Constitution, which like our Constitution, has entrenched guarantees against torture or inhuman and degrading punishment.

[249] The so-called "death row phenomenon" also came under attack in the case of *Soering v United Kingdom* (1989) 11 EHRR 439.

From the statistics supplied by the Attorney General and from what one gleans daily from the newspapers and other media, we live at a time when the high crime rate is unprecedented, when the streets of our cities and towns rouse fear and despair in the heart, rather than pride and hope, and this in turn, robs us of objectivity and personal concern for our brethren. But, as Marshall J put it in *Furman v Georgia (supra)* at 371:

"The measure of a country's greatness is its ability to retain compassion in time of crisis."

[250] This, in my view, also accords with *ubuntu*—and calls for a balancing of the interest of society against those of the individual, for the maintenance of law and order, but not for dehumanising and degrading the individual.

[251] We must stand tallest in these troubled times and realise that every accused person who is sent to jail is not beyond being rehabilitated—properly counselled—or, at the very least, beyond losing the will and capacity to do evil.

. . .

[260] In my view, the death penalty does not belong to the society envisaged in the Constitution, is clearly in conflict with the Constitution generally and runs counter to the concept of *ubuntu*; additionally and just as importantly, it violates the provisions of section 11(2) of the Constitution and, for those reasons, should be declared unconstitutional and of no force and effect.

Justice Mahomed

[261] I have had the privilege of reading the full and erudite judgment of Chaskalson P in this matter. I agree with the order proposed by him and in general with the

reasons given by him for that order. Regard being had, however, to the crucial circumstances of the debate on capital punishment, and the multiplicity of potential constitutional factors and nuances which impact on its resolution, I think it is desirable for me to set out briefly some of my responses to this debate in order to explain why I have come to the conclusion that capital punishment is prohibited by the Constitution.

[262] All constitutions seek to articulate, with differing degrees of intensity and detail, the shared aspirations of a nation; the values which bind its people, and which discipline its government and its national institutions; the basic premises upon which judicial, legislative and executive power is to be wielded; the constitutional limits and the conditions upon which that power is to be exercised; the national ethos which defines and regulates that exercise; and the moral and ethical direction which that nation has identified for its future. In some countries, the Constitution only formalises, in a legal instrument, a historical consensus of values and aspirations evolved incrementally from a stable and unbroken past to accommodate the needs of the future. The South African Constitution is different: it retains from the past only what is defensible and represents a decisive break from, and a ringing rejection of, that part of the past which is disgracefully racist, authoritarian, insular, and repressive and a vigorous identification of and commitment to a democratic, universalistic, caring and aspirationally egalitarian ethos, expressly articulated in the Constitution. The contrast between the past, which it repudiates, and the future, to which it seeks to commit the nation, is stark and dramatic. The past institutionalised and legitimised racism. The Constitution expresses in its preamble the need for a "new order . . . in which there is equality between . . . people of all races." Chapter 3 of the Constitution extends the contrast, in every relevant area of endeavour (subject only to the obvious limitations of section 33). The past was redolent with statutes, which assaulted the human dignity of persons on the grounds of race and colour alone; section 10 constitutionally protects that dignity. The past accepted, permitted, perpetuated and institutionalised pervasive and manifestly unfair discrimination against women and persons of colour; the preamble, section 8 and the postamble seek to articulate an ethos which not only rejects its rationale but unmistakenly recognises the clear justification for the reversal of the accumulated legacy of such discrimination. The past permitted detention without trial; section 11(1) prohibits it. The past permitted degrading treatment of persons; section 11(2) renders it unconstitutional. The past arbitrarily repressed the freedoms of expression, assembly, association and movement; sections 15, 16, 17, and 18 accord to these freedoms the status of "fundamental rights." The past limited the right to vote to a minority; section 21 extends it to every citizen. The past arbitrarily denied to citizens on the grounds of race and colour, the right to hold and acquire property; section 26 expressly secures it. Such a jurisprudential past created what the postamble to the Constitution recognises as a society "characterised by strife, conflict, untold suffering and injustice." What the Constitution expressly aspires to

do is to provide a transition from these grossly unacceptable features of the past to a conspicuously contrasting:

"future founded on the recognition of human rights, democracy and peaceful
co-existence and development opportunities for all South Africans,
irrespective of colour, race, class, belief, or sex."

[263] The postamble to the Constitution gives expression to the new ethos of the nation by a commitment to "open a new chapter in the history of our country," by lamenting the transgressions of "human rights" and "humanitarian principles" in the past, and articulating a:

"need for understanding, but not for vengeance, a need for reparation but not retaliation, a need for *ubuntu* but not for victimisation."

"The need for *ubuntu*" expresses the ethos of an instinctive capacity for and enjoyment of love towards our fellow men and women; the joy and the fulfil-ment involved in recognising their innate humanity; the reciprocity this gen-erates in interaction within the collective community; the richness of the creative emotions which it engenders and the moral energies which it releases both in the givers and the society which they serve and are served by.

[264] It is against this historical background and ethos that the constitutionality of capital punishment must be determined.

[265] The death penalty sanctions the deliberate annihilation of life. As I have previously said it:

"is the ultimate and the most incomparably extreme form of punishment . . . It is the last, the most devastating and the most irreversible recourse of the crimi-nal law, involving as it necessarily does, the planned and calculated termination of life itself; the destruction of the greatest and most precious gift which is be-stowed on all humankind" (*S v Mhlongo* 1994 (1) SACR 584 (A) at 587e–g).

This "planned and calculated termination of life itself" was permitted in the past, which preceded the Constitution. Is it *now* permissible? Those responsible for the enactment of the Constitution, could, if they had so wished, have treated the issue as a substantially political and moral issue justifying a political choice, clearly expressed in the Constitution, either retaining or prohibiting the death sentence. They elected not to do so, leaving it to this Court to resolve the issue, as a constitu-tional issue.

[266] The differences between a political election made by a legislative organ and decisions reached by a judicial organ, like the Constitutional Court, is crucial.

The legislative organ exercises a political discretion, taking into account the *political preferences* of the electorate that votes political decision-makers into office. Public opinion therefore legitimately plays a significant, sometimes even decisive, role in the resolution of a public issue such as the death penalty. The judicial process is entirely different. What the Constitutional Court is required to do in order to resolve an issue, is to examine the relevant provisions of the Constitution, their text and their context; the interplay between the different provisions; legal precedent relevant to the resolution of the problem both in South Africa and abroad; the domestic common law and public international law impacting on its possible solution; factual and historical considerations bearing on the problem; the significance and meaning of the language used in the relevant provisions; the content and the sweep of the ethos expressed in the structure of the Constitution; the balance to be struck between different and sometimes potentially conflicting considerations reflected in its text; and by a judicious interpretation and assessment of all these factors to determine what the *Constitution* permits and what it prohibits.

[267] Adopting that approach, I am satisfied that the death penalty as a form of punishment violates crucial sections of the Constitution and that it is not saved by the limitations permitted in terms of section 33. I wish briefly to set out my reasons for that conclusion.

[268] In the first place, it offends section 9 of the Constitution, which prescribes in peremptory terms that "every person shall have the right to life." What does that mean? What is a "person"? When does "personhood" and "life" begin? Can there be a conflict between the "right to life" in section 9 and the right of a mother to "personal privacy" in terms of section 13 and her possible right to the freedom and control of her body? Does the "right to life," within the meaning of section 9, preclude the practitioner of scientific medicine from withdrawing the modern mechanisms which mechanically and artificially enable physical breathing in a terminal patient to continue, long beyond the point, when the "brain is dead" and beyond the point when a human being ceases to be "human" although some unfocussed claim to qualify as a "being" is still retained? If not, can such a practitioner go beyond the point of passive withdrawal into the area of active intervention? When? Under what circumstances?

[269] It is, for the purposes of the present case, unnecessary to give to the word "life" in section 9 a comprehensive legal definition, which will accommodate the answer to these and other complex issues, should they arise in the future, it is possible to approach the constitutionality of the death sentence by a question with a sharper and narrower focus, thus:

> "Does the right to life guaranteed by section 9, include the right of every
> person, not to be deliberately killed by the State, through a systematically
> planned act of execution sanctioned by the State as a mode of punishment and
> performed by an executioner remunerated for this purpose from public funds?"

The answer to that question is in my view: "Yes, every person has that right." It immediately distinguishes that right from some other obvious rights referred to in argument, such as for example the right of a person in life-threatening circumstances to take the life of the aggressor in self-defence or even the acts of the State, in confronting an insurrection or in the course of war.

[270] The deliberate annihilation of the life of a person, systematically planned by the State, as a mode of punishment, is wholly and qualitatively different. It is not like the act of killing in self-defence, an act justifiable in the defence of the clear right of the victim to the preservation of his life. It is not performed in a state of sudden emergency, or under the extraordinary pressures, which operate when, insurrections are confronted or when the State defends itself during war. It is systematically planned long after—sometimes years after—the offender has committed the offence for which he is to be punished, and whilst he waits impotently in custody, for his date with the hangman. In its obvious and awesome finality, it makes every other right, so vigorously and eloquently guaranteed by Chapter 3 of the Constitution, permanently impossible to enjoy. Its inherently irreversible consequence makes any reparation or correction impossible, if subsequent events establish, as they have sometimes done, the innocence of the executed or circumstances which demonstrate manifestly that he did not deserve the sentence of death.

[271] The death sentence must, in some measure, manifest a philosophy of indefensible despair in its execution, accepting as it must do, that the offender it seeks to punish is so beyond the pale of humanity as to permit of no rehabilitation, no reform, no repentance, no inherent spectre of hope or spirituality; nor the slightest possibility that he might one day, successfully and deservedly be able to pursue and to enjoy the great rights of dignity and security and the fundamental freedoms protected in Chapter 3 of the Constitution, the exercise of which is possible only if the "right to life" is not destroyed. The finality of the death penalty allows for none of these redeeming possibilities. It annihilates the potential for their emergence. Moreover, it cannot accomplish its objective without invading in a very deep and distressing way, the guarantee of human dignity afforded by section 10 of the Constitution, as the person sought to be executed spends long periods in custody, anguished by the prospect of being "hanged by the neck until he is dead" in the language of section 279(4) of Act 51 of 1977. The invasion of his dignity is inherent. He is effectively told: "You are beyond the pale of humanity. You are not fit to live among humankind. You are not entitled to life. You are not entitled to dignity. You are not human. We will therefore annihilate your life." (See the observations of Brennan J in *Trop v Dulles* 356 US 84 at 100.)

[272] It is not necessarily only the dignity of the person to be executed that is invaded. Very arguably the dignity of all of us, in a caring civilisation, must be compromised, by the act of repeating, systematically and deliberately, albeit for a wholly different objective, what we find to be so repugnant in the conduct of the offender in the first place (see *Furman v Georgia* 408 US 238 at 273 (1972) [Brennan J concurring]).

. . .

[277] In my view, the death sentence does indeed constitute cruel, inhuman or degrading punishment within the meaning of those expressions in section 11(2).

[278] Undoubtedly, this conclusion does involve in some measure a value judgment, but it is a value judgment which requires objectively to be formulated, having regard to the ordinary meaning of the words used in section 11(2); its consistency with the other rights protected by the Constitution and the constitutional philosophy and humanism expressed both in the preamble and the postamble to the Constitution; its harmony with the national ethos which the Constitution identifies; the historical background to the structures and objectives of the Constitution; the discipline of proportionality to which it must legitimately be subject; the effect of the death sentence on the right to life protected by the Constitution; its inherent arbitrariness in application; its impact on human dignity; and its consistency with constitutional perceptions evolving both within South Africa and the world outside with which our country shares emerging values central to the permissible limits and objectives of punishment in the civilised community.

[279] I have dealt with some of these issues, in analysing the proper approach to the interpretation of the Constitution, and in focusing on the rights protected by sections 8, 9, and 10 of the Constitution. Some of the other issues relevant to the exercise have been dealt with in the comprehensive judgment of the President and the persuasive comments of some of my colleagues.

[280] Applying the relevant considerations which emerge from the proper approach in assessing whether capital punishment is "cruel, inhuman or degrading punishment," I share the conclusions arrived at by the United Nations Committee on Human Rights, and the Hungarian Constitutional Court, (Decision 23/1990 (X31) AB) that the death sentence is cruel and degrading punishment and the conclusion of the Californian Supreme Court that it is "impermissibly cruel" (*People v Anderson* 493 P 2d 880 (1972)).

[281] In my view, it also constitutes *inhuman* punishment. It invades irreversibly the humanity of the offender by annihilating the minimum content of the right to life protected by section 9; by degrading impermissibly the humanity inherent in his right to dignity; by the inevitable arbitrariness with which its objective is implemented, by the continuing and corrosive denigration of his humanity in the long periods preceding his formal execution; by the inescapable denial of his humanity inherently involved in a sentence which directs his elimination from society.

[282] I am accordingly of the view that the death penalty does *prima facie* invade the right to life; the right to equality; the right to dignity; and the right not to be subject to cruel inhuman or degrading punishment, respectively protected by sections 8, 9, 10, and 11(2) of the Constitution.

. . .

[296] Is there any other basis on which the death penalty can be justified? The only serious alternative basis suggested in argument was that it is justifiable as an act

of retribution. Retribution has indeed constituted one of the permissible objects of criminal punishment because there is an inherent legitimacy about the claim that the individual victims and society generally should, and are entitled to, enforce punishment as an expression of their moral outrage and sense of grievance. I have, however, some serious difficulties with the justification of the *death sentence* as a form of retribution. The proper approach is not to contrast the legitimacy of the death sentence as a form of retribution against no retribution at all. That is plainly untenable and manifestly indefensible. The relevant contrast is between the death sentence and the alternative of a very lengthy period of imprisonment, in appropriate cases. It is difficult to appreciate why a sentence which compels the offender to spend years and years in prison, away from his family, in conditions of deliberate austerity and rigid discipline, substantially and continuously impeding his enjoyment of the elementary riches and gifts of civilised living, is not an effective and adequate expression of moral outrage. The unarticulated fallacy in the argument that it is not is the proposition that it must indeed be equivalent in form to the offence committed. That is an impermissible argument. The burning of the house of the offender is not a permissible punishment for arson. The rape of the offender is not a permissible punishment of a rapist. Why should murder be a permissible punishment for murder? Indeed, there are good reasons why it should not, because its execution might desensitise respect for life *per se*. More crucially, within the context of the South African Constitution, it appears to be at variance with its basic premise and ethos, which I analysed earlier in this judgment. On these considerations, I find it difficult to hold that the death sentence has been demonstrated by the State to be "justifiable in an open and democratic society based on freedom and equality."

. . .

Justice Sachs

[358] The second issue that caused me special concern was the source of the values that we are to apply in assessing whether or not capital punishment is a cruel, inhuman or degrading punishment as constitutionally understood. The matter was raised in an *amicus curiae* brief and argued orally before us by Ms *Davids* on behalf of the Black Advocates Forum.

[359] Her main contention was that we should not pronounce on the subject of capital punishment until we had been apprised by sociological analysis of the relevant expectations, sensitivities and interests of society as a whole. In the past, she stated, the all-white minority had imposed Eurocentric values on the majority, and an all-white judiciary had taken cognisance merely of the interests of white society. Now, for the first time, she added, we had the opportunity to nurture an open and democratic society and to have due regard to an emerging national consensus on values to be upheld in relation to punishment.

[360] Many of the points she made had a political rather than a legal character, and as such should have been directed to the Constitutional Assembly rather than

to the Constitutional Court. Nevertheless, much of her argument has a bearing on the way this Court sees its functions, and deserves the courtesy of a reply.

[361] To begin with, I wish firmly to express my agreement with the need to take account of the traditions, beliefs and values of all sectors of South African society when developing our jurisprudence.

[362] In broad terms, the function given to this Court by the Constitution is to articulate the fundamental sense of justice and right shared by the whole nation as expressed in the text of the Constitution. The Constitution was the first public document of legal force in South African history to emerge from an inclusive process in which the overwhelming majority were represented. Reference in the Constitution to the role of public international law (sections 35(1) and 231) underlines our common adherence to internationally accepted principles. Whatever the status of earlier legislation and jurisprudence may be, the Constitution speaks for the whole of society and not just one section.

[363] The preamble, postamble and the principles of freedom and equality espoused in sections 8, 33 and 35 of the Constitution, require such amplitude of vision. The principle of inclusivity shines through the language provisions in section 3, and underlies the provisions, which led to the adoption of the new flag and anthem, and the selection of public holidays.

[364] The secure and progressive development of our legal system demands that it draw the best from all the streams of justice in our country. This would include benefiting from the learning of those Judges who in the previous era managed to articulate a sense of justice that transcended the limits of race, as well as acknowledging the challenging writings of academics such as the late Dr Barend van Niekerk, who bravely broke the taboos on criticism of the legal system.[15] [59]

[365] Above all, however, it means giving long overdue recognition to African law and legal thinking as a source of legal ideas, values and practice. We cannot, unfortunately, extend the equality principle backwards in time to remove the humiliations and indignities suffered by past generations, but we can restore dignity to ideas and values that have long been suppressed or marginalised.

[366] Redressing the balance in a conceptually sound, methodologically secure and functionally efficient way, will be far from easy. Extensive research and public debate will be required. Legislation will play a key role; indeed, the Constitution expressly acknowledges situations where legal pluralism based on religion can be recognised (section 14(3)), and where indigenous law can be applied (section 181). Constitutional Principle XIII declares that ". . . Indigenous law, like common law, shall be recognised and applied by the Courts, subject to the fundamental rights contained in the Constitution and to legislation dealing specifically therewith."

[367] Yet the issue raised by Ms *Davids* goes beyond the question of achieving recantation of different systems of personal law.

[368] In interpreting Chapter 3 of the Constitution, which deals with fundamental rights, all Courts must promote the values of an open and democratic society based

on freedom and equality (section 35(1)). One of the values of an open and democratic society is precisely that the values of all sections of society must be taken into account and given due weight when matters of public import are being decided. Ms *Davids'* concern is that when it comes to interpreting Chapter 3, and in particular, the concept of punishment, the values of only one section of the community are taken into account.

[369] Paul Sieghart points out: "*the hallmarks of a democratic society are pluralism, tolerance and broadmindedness. Although individual interests must on occasion be subordinated to those of a group, democracy does not mean that the views of a majority must always prevail: a balance must be achieved which ensures the fair and proper treatment of minorities and avoids any abuse of a dominant position.*"[16] [60]

The principle that cognisance must be taken of minority opinions should apply with at least equal force to majority opinions; if one of the functions of the Constitution is to protect unpopular minorities from abuse, another must surely be to rescue the majority from marginalisation.

[370] In a democratic society such as we are trying to establish, this is primarily the task of Parliament, where the will of the majority can be directly expressed within the framework of a system of fundamental rights. Our function as members of this Court—as I see it—is, when interpreting the Constitution, to pay due regard to the values of all sections of society, and not to confine ourselves to the values of one portion only, however, exalted or subordinate it might have been in the past.

[371] It is a distressing fact that our law reports and legal textbooks contain few references to African sources as part of the general law of the country. That is no reason for this Court to continue to ignore the legal institutions and values of a very large part of the population, moreover, of that section that suffered the most violations of fundamental rights under previous legal regimes, and that perhaps has the most to hope for from the new constitutional order.

[372] Appropriate source material is limited and any conclusions that individual members of this Court might wish to offer would inevitably have to be tentative rather than definitive. We would certainly require much fuller research and argument than we had in the present case. The paucity of materials, however, is a reason for putting the issue on the agenda, not a justification for postponing it.

[373] The evolution of core values in all sections of the community is particularly relevant to the characterisation of what at any moment are regarded as cruel, inhuman and degrading punishments (section 11(2)). In my view, section 35(1) requires this Court not only to have regard to public international law and foreign case law, but also to all the dimensions of the evolution of South African law which may help us in our task of promoting freedom and equality. This would require reference not only to what in legal discourse is referred to as "our common law" but also to traditional African jurisprudence.

[374] I must stress that what follows relates to matters not properly canvassed in argument. The statements I make should not be regarded as an attempt on my part

to "lay down the law" on subjects that might well be controversial. Rather, the materials are presented for their possible relevance to the search for core and enduring values consistent with the text and spirit of the Constitution. It is unfortunate they were not placed before us to enable their reliability and their merits to be debated; they are intended to indicate that, speaking for myself, these are the kinds of scholarly sources which I would have regarded as helpful in determining questions such as the present one, if Ms *Davids* had presented them to us rather than complain about their absence. I might add that there is nothing to indicate that had these sources been properly presented and subjected to the rigorous analysis, which our judicial procedure calls for, the decision of this Court would have been different. There does not appear to be any foundation for her plea that we postpone the matter. On the contrary, the materials that I will refer to point to a source of values entirely consistent with the overall thrust of the President's judgment, and, in particular, with his reference to the constitutionally acknowledged principle of *ubuntu*.[17] [61]

[375] Our libraries contain a large number of studies by African and other scholars of repute, which delineate in considerable detail how disputes were resolved and punishments meted out in traditional African society. There are a number of references to capital punishment and I can only repeat that it is unfortunate that their import was never canvassed in the present matter.

[376] In the first place, the sources indicate that it is necessary to acknowledge that systems of law enforcement based on rational procedures were well entrenched in traditional society. In his classic study of the Tsonga-speaking people, Henri Junod observes that ". . . The Bantus possess a strong sense of justice. They believe in social order and in the observance of the laws, and, although these laws were not written, they are universal and perfectly well known."[18] [62] The *Cape Law Journal*, in a long and admiring report on what it refers to as a Kaffir Law Suit, declares that in a typical trial "the Socratic method of debate appears in all its perfection."[19] [63] John Henderson Soga points out those offences were considered to be against the community or tribe rather than the individual, and punishment of a constructive or corrective nature was administered for disturbing the balance of tribal life.[20] [64]

[377] More directly for our purposes, the materials suggest that amongst the Cape Nguni, the death penalty was practically confined to cases of suspected witchcraft, and was normally spontaneously carried out after accusation by the diviners.[21] [65] Soga says that the death penalty was never imposed, the reasoning being as follows: "Why sacrifice a second life for one already lost?"[22] [66] Professor ZK Mathews is in broad agreement.[23] [67] The *Cape Law Journal* notes that summary executions were usually inflicted for assault on the wives of chiefs or aggravated cases of witchcraft, but otherwise the death sentence "seldom followed even murder, when committed without the aid of supernatural powers; and as banishment, imprisonment and corporal punishment are all unknown in (African) jurisprudence,

the property of the people constitutes the great fund out of which debts of justice are paid."[24] [68]

[378] Similar approaches were apparently followed in other African communities. The Sotho King Moshoeshoe was said to be well known for his opposition to capital punishment, even for supposed witchcraft,[25] [69] as was Montshiwa during his long reign as King of the Barolong.[26] [70] The absence of capital punishment among the Zulu people apparently angered Shepstone, Lieutenant Governor of Natal. Donald Morris writes as follows:

[379] "Hearken to Shepstone on November 25, 1850, substituting capital punishment for the native system of cattle fines in the case of murder:

[380] *'. . . Know ye all . . . a man's life has no price: no cattle can pay for it. He who intentionally kills another, whether for Witchcraft or otherwise, shall die himself.'*"[27] [71]

[381] Thus, if these sources were reliable, it would appear that the relatively well-developed judicial processes of indigenous societies did not in general encompass capital punishment for murder. Such executions as took place were the frenzied, extra-judicial killings of supposed witches, a spontaneous and irrational form of crowd behaviour that has unfortunately continued to this day in the form of necklacing and witch burning. In addition, punishments by military leaders in terms of military discipline were frequently of the harshest kind and accounted for the lives of many persons. Yet, the sources referred to above indicate that, where judicial procedures were followed, capital punishment was in general not applied as a punishment for murder.

[382] In seeking the kind of values that should inform our broad approach to interpreting the Constitution, I have little doubt as to which of these three contrasted aspects of tradition we should follow and which we should reject. The rational and humane adjudicatory approach is entirely consistent with and re-enforcing of the fundamental rights enshrined in our Constitution; the exorcist and militarist concepts are not.

[383] We do not automatically invoke each and every aspect of traditional law as a source of values, just as we do not rely on all features of the common law. Thus, we reject the once powerful common law traditions associated with patriarchy and the subordination of servants to masters, which are inconsistent with freedom and equality, and we uphold and develop those many aspects of the common law, which feed into and enrich the fundamental rights enshrined in the Constitution. I am sure that there are many aspects and values of traditional African law, which will also have to be discarded or developed in order to ensure compatibility with the principles of the new constitutional order.

. . .

[389] Historically, constitutionalism was a product of the age of enlightenment. It was associated with the overthrow of arbitrary power and the attempt to ensure that Government functioned according to established principles and processes and in the light of enduring values. It came together with the abolition of torture and

the opening up of dungeons. It based itself on the twin propositions that all persons had certain inherent rights that came with their humanity, and that no one had a God-given right to rule over others.

[390] The second great wave of constitutionalism after World War II, was also a reaction to gross abuse of power, institutionalised inhumanity and organised disrespect for life. Human rights were not merely declared to exist: against the background of genocide and crimes against humanity committed in the name of a racial ideology linked to State sovereignty, firm constitutional limits were placed on State power. In particular, the more that life had been cheapened and the human personality disregarded, the greater the entrenchment of the rights to life and dignity.

[391] Constitutionalism in our country also arrives simultaneously with the achievement of equality and freedom, and of openness, accommodation and tolerance. When reviewing the past, the framers of our Constitution rejected not only the laws and practices that imposed domination and kept people apart, but those that prevented free discourse and rational debate, and those that brutalised us as people and diminished our respect for life.

[392] Accordingly, the idealism that we uphold with this judgment is to be found not in the minds of the Judges, but in both the explicit text of the Constitution itself, and the values it enshrines. I have no doubt that even if, as the President's judgment suggests, the framers subjectively intended to keep the issue open for determination by this Court, they effectively closed the door by the language they used and the values they required us to uphold. It is difficult to see how they could have done otherwise. In a founding document dealing with fundamental rights, you either authorise the death sentence or you do not. In my view, the values expressed by section 9 are conclusive of the matter. Everyone, including the most abominable of human beings, has the right to life, and capital punishment is therefore unconstitutional.

For the judgments of Justices Ackermann, Didcott, Kentridge, Kriegler and O'Regan as well as Justice Sachs's interpretation on the Right to Life see The Dignity Jurisprudence of the South African Constitutional Court.

Horizontality, Reconciliation, and *uBuntu*

THE *BALORO* CASE

Baloro and Others v. University of Bophuthatswana and Others 1995 (8) BCLR 1018 (B)

Case Summary

FACTS

The Applicants in this matter were four academics, who were non-South Africans, and who had academic positions at the University of Bophuthatswana. The Respondents in this matter were the University of Bophuthatswana (the University), the acting Vice Chancellor of the University (the second Respondent), and the third Respondent was the University of Bophuthatswana Staff Association, a body that had representation on the staffing committee of the University, which was responsible for assessing candidates for promotion.

The Applicants immigrated to South Africa in order to perform the duties for which they were hired. They relied in good faith on the policy of the University that promised to be nondiscriminatory on the basis of race, sex, nationality, or creed.

The University usually applied for the renewal of the Applicants' work permits on their behalf, but in 1994 when their permits were up for renewal, the Applicants were instructed by the University to apply for the renewal of their work permits on their own. Their applications were, however, supported by letters of recommendation from the acting Vice Chancellor of the University. But while the applications for their work permits were pending before the Department of Home Affairs, the staffing committee demanded that the University withdraw their recommendation letters. As a result, the recommendation letters were withdrawn. The committee argued that hiring foreign workers in postapartheid South Africa deprived South Africans of employment opportunities, and served as an obstacle to the Reconstruction and Development Program.

The Applicants had also applied for promotion, but the staffing committee did not consider their applications. Instead, the committee informed them that the University had agreed on a suspension of the hiring and or promotion of non-South Africans. The Applicants argued that the University's suspension of hiring and promoting foreign nationals was discriminatory and unlawful. Their argument was based on section 8(2) of the Interim Constitution, which prohibited discrimination on grounds of social origin. More specifically, their argument was that section 8(2) prohibited the University from unfairly discriminating against the Applicants. The Applicants argued that section 35 of the Interim Constitution (which governs the interpretation of the Interim Constitution) favored a generous interpretation. A broad interpretation would necessitate a finding that the Bill of Rights applied both vertically (against the state), and horizontally (against individuals).

Legal History
The case was heard in what was then the Bophuthatswana High Court.

Legal Issue
The legal issue was whether the South African Bill of Rights applied both vertically and horizontally, and therefore, whether or not the claim for discrimination could be validly upheld.

Dispensation
The court found that the fundamental rights applied horizontally as well as vertically, but that their horizontal application was subject to limitations. There were, in other words, criteria that were to be used in order to determine whether fundamental rights were horizontally applicable.

The court came to this conclusion by first elucidating the intention of the drafters of the Interim Constitution. In drafting the Constitution, the drafters intended to create a new South Africa in which the discriminations and inequalities of the apartheid would be corrected.

The court also reviewed the language of section 7 of the Interim Constitution (dealing with the application of the Bill of Rights) and noted that the absence of a reference to "State" in section 7(4)(a) pointed to an interpretation that favored a horizontal application of the Bill of Rights. Further, the court reviewed the language of section 35(3) of the Interim Constitution. This section states that: "In the interpretation of any law and the application and development of the common law and customary law, a Court shall have due regard to the spirit, purport and objects of this Chapter."

The court then noted that the reference to *any law* indicated that the Bill of Rights should apply horizontally.

As previously stated, the court argued that the horizontal application of the Bill of Rights was not without limits. Freedom of choice and principles of privacy had to be respected. The court noted, however, that there was no preexisting formula or criteria to determine whether the Bill of Rights was horizontally applicable. The creation of this formula therefore, necessitated the court to lay new foundations. The criteria developed by the court comprised three inquiries:

Is the activity a "public function" that is operating in the public domain?

Is the activity so linked or "intertwined" with public action that the private actor becomes equated with the public domain?

Has the conduct of the private actor (persons) complained of, been approved, authorised or encouraged by the State or public institutions in an adequate manner so as to be responsible for it?

In applying these criteria to the case before it, the court found that the University, to the degree that it was an institution of learning, was in the public domain, and that its activities were intertwined with public action. The Bill of Rights was therefore horizontally applicable to the situation.

The court also emphasized its mandate in terms of section 35(1) of the Interim Constitution, which was to interpret the Bill of Rights in a manner that promoted the foundational values of an open democracy.

Judge President Friedman

. . .

THE VERTICALITY OF CHAPTER 3

It was a matter of contention among parties participating in the multi-party negotiating process whether the provisions of Chapter 3 should be enforceable against the State and its organs only or whether they should bind both the State and private social institutions and persons. In the end it was agreed that the chapter should operate vertically only but that provision be made for seepage to horizontal relationships. As a result a subsection was included in the interpretation clause requiring a Court of law applying and developing the existing law to have due regard to the spirit, purport and objects of Chapter 3 (section 35(3)). To allay fears that the predominantly vertical operation of Chapter 3 may be construed as authorising "privatised apartheid," a provision was also included in the limitation clause (section 33) permitting measures designed to prohibit unfair discrimination by (private) bodies and persons not explicitly bound by the chapter (section 33(4)). I shall elaborate on these provisions in the next presentation.

THE SCOPE OF CHAPTER 3

Section 7(2) provides that Chapter 3 shall apply to all law in force and all administrative acts performed during the period of its operation. "All law in force" does not only refer to legislation but also to the common law and customary law. "Administrative acts performed" includes, apart from legislative administrative acts, administrative decisions as well as acts performed to implement and execute decisions. From this follows that administrative decisions taken before the commencement of the Constitution cannot be challenged in terms of Chapter 3 while administrative acts performed to implement or execute such decisions can.

JURISTIC PERSONS

Section 7(3) provides that all juristic persons are entitled to the rights entrenched in Chapter 3 where, and to the extent that the nature of the rights, permit. The fear existed among some of the negotiators at Kempton Park that corporations might abuse this provision to try and constitutionalise (and thereby over-complicate) issues, which should rather be adjudicated on another basis. Does a juristic person, for instance, have a "dignity" or a "privacy" of its own? And should it be possible for companies, whose activities are restricted by (say) environmental legislation, to claim that they are being discriminated against? In view of these concerns it was thought that a wording, which requires an analysis of the nature of the right in question, is more restrictive than one requiring an analysis of the nature of the juristic person itself. An entity can, in other words, more readily be "humanised" or "personalised" than a right.

Without a provision such as section 7(3), Chapter 3 would at any rate have been out of step with other bills of rights of recent origin.

The basic concern of the Constitution, namely to transform the South African legal system into one concerned with openness, accountability, democratic principles, human rights and reconciliation and reconstruction (*Qozeleni's* case (*supra*) at 634B–F; *Phato's* case (*supra*) at 16–25), would in particular instances call for explicit application of the provisions of Chapter 3 of the Constitution between individuals themselves. After all, the "past of a deeply divided society characterised by strife, conflict, untold suffering and injustice" (words used in the "unity and reconciliation" section of the Constitution) is not merely a history of repressive State action against individuals, but it is also a history of structural inequality and injustice on racial and other grounds, gradually filtering through to virtually all spheres of society since the arrival of European colonists some three and a half centuries ago, and it will probably take generations to correct the imbalance. But the development of the law by the Courts is by its very nature dependent on litigation and therefore likely to be incremental and perhaps slow, hence the provision for State intervention also, by virtue of section 33(4), to prohibit unfair discrimination by private persons and bodies" (at 31B–G).

In *Motala and Another v University of Natal* 1995 (3) BCLR 374 (D) Hurt J rejected the view expressed by Van Dijkhorst J in *De Klerk's* case (*supra*), that were the entrenched rights to be applied *inter personas*, it would have a chaotic effect on the common law. Hurt J concluded on this aspect at 382F–H in the following terms:

> "It must, in my respectful view, be the task of the Courts, armed with the powers conferred on them by sections 7, 33 and 35 (and not the task of Parliament) to define the limits of the entrenched rights where they appear to encroach upon each other and at the same time to blend them into the common law, modifying the latter wherever necessary so as to achieve a harmonious amalgam.
>
> It goes without saying that many of the entrenched rights are, by their very nature, exclusively 'vertical' in their operation. But many of them are, in my view, not. For the purpose of furnishing these reasons I need only say that I consider that the rights entrenched in sections 8(1), 8(2) and 32, which are the only entrenched rights in issue before me, are enforceable not only against the State or its organs as defined, but also against individuals, natural or juristic, who may be disposed to threaten them or interfere with the exercise of them."

I respectfully agree with the conclusions arrived at by Van Schalkwyk, Froneman and Hurt J, namely that there exists a horizontal application in regard to the fundamental rights contained in the Constitution.

The Constitution contains a most vivid and elaborate illustration of a vision of fundamental rights, expanded almost to the limits for the manifold application of human rights to life in this country by the government and the Courts, in order that principles of justice operate in the formation of an egalitarian society. As the great philosopher Kant said: "If justice is subverted, man's existence on earth is of no value."

The provisions of national unity and reconciliation are, and I quote:

> "National Unity and Reconciliation
>
> This Constitution provides a historic bridge between the past of a deeply divided society characterised by strife, conflict, untold suffering and injustice, and a future founded on the recognition of human rights, democracy and peaceful co-existence and development opportunities for all South Africans, irrespective of colour, race, class, belief or sex.
>
> The pursuit of national unity, the well being of all South African citizens and peace require reconciliation between the people of South Africa and the reconstruction of society.
>
> The adoption of this Constitution lays the secure foundation for the people of South Africa to transcend the divisions and strife of the past, which

generated gross violations of human rights, the transgression of humanitarian principles in violent conflicts and a legacy of hatred, fear, guilt and revenge.

These can now be addressed on the basis that there is a need for understanding but not for vengeance, a need for reparation but not for retaliation, a need for *ubuntu* but not for victimisation."

There is a desire by the legislature to establish a new society in this country on the foundation of new and noble aspirations. There is a quest for new development through the application of just laws, and a new mode of life in this country. There is an expression of faith, and of affirming moral values emphatically in a new and just society, and the invariable and necessary characteristics for this purpose, are protected in the legislation to safeguard the values contained in the Constitution.

It is clear that the administration of justice and the law in action touch human life and society in many aspects and situations.

If the application of the said rights is founded on verticality only, then clearly large corporations, multinational conglomerates often with more wealth, power and influence that "organs of State," who may practice discrimination, would be immune from the application of Chapter 3. What about large private hospitals, schools and private universities who might practice elements of discrimination, are they also immune? Clearly not. It could never have been the intention to combat discrimination on the level of the State only, and allow it to continue and proliferate on other levels.

   . . .

(3) If the fundamental rights are restricted to a purely vertical application, negative results must flow between the government and the individual or between the individual and corporations or private institutions, such as referred to herein, which will cause further social ills or problems.

(4) The provisions of section 33(4) encroach distinctly on the domain of private law, certainly in regard to unfair discrimination, which is the horizontal dimension. See *SA Law Commission Final Report on Group and Human Rights (supra)* at 124, and the examples there quoted; for example, a restaurant owner would be entitled to refuse admission to a person improperly dressed. But a school, whether public or private, would not be entitled to refuse a pupil admission on the grounds of the pupil's race or colour. This would amount to unfair discrimination.

(5) As has been illustrated, in the United States in order to combat race discrimination, the horizontal dimension of fundamental rights are applied.

In his article *Racial Discrimination: The Role of the Civil Law* in *Current Legal Problems* Volume 41 at 244, Sir Nicholas Browne-Wilkinson says the following:

"The first question is whether the enforcement of civil rights can provide an effective remedy to racial discrimination. I think the answer is affirmatively 'yes', as the experience in the United States has demonstrated. In the course of the years, decisions given in class actions under Title 7 have been at the very forefront of the civil rights movement. Only as a result of such civil actions has desegregation occurred, equal education opportunities been obtained and a substantial shift towards equality of economic opportunity been achieved. This success has been due to vigorous, well-informed and serious black civil rights lawyers working in conjunction with equally vigorous, well-informed serious white lawyers, who have the additional advantage of wealth and status. Generously funded public organizations also aided such litigation. Cases came before federal Courts presided over by judges of great moral (and sometimes physical) courage who construed the legislation in a purposive manner with a view to achieving the object of the Civil Rights Act. Those Courts had the ability to handle the large class actions, giving rise to awards of damages sufficiently large to make even the biggest corporation pause to reflect whether it might not be cheaper, in the long run, to abandon racially discriminatory practices."

To these damages, the American Courts could, and did, add mandatory orders, regulating the future ethnic balance. To the American ethnic minorities the Courts have given redress for unlawful discrimination on the same basis as redress for any other legal wrong. The Courts are perceived by the ethnic minorities to be their protectors.

Contrast this with what Martin Luther King Jr said before leading protest marches through Birmingham, Alabama:

"We are now confronted with recalcitrant forces in the Deep South that will use the Courts to perpetuate the unjust and illegal system of racial separation. . . . This is raw tyranny under the guise of maintaining law and order. We cannot in all good conscience obey such an injunction. . . . We do this not out of any disrespect for the law but out of the highest respect for *the law*. This is not an attempt to evade or defy the law or engage in chaotic anarchy. Just as in all good conscience we cannot obey unjust laws; neither can we respect the unjust use of the Courts." (Emphasis mine.)

Section 35 makes provision for a horizontal application of the fundamental rights, in order to:

". . . promote the values which underlie an open and democratic society based on freedom and equality."

This cannot be achieved if the application of section 7 is to be of a vertical dimension only.

Therefore in applying the principles enunciated in (ii) and (iii) hereof and section 8(2) (*supra*) an overwhelming case has been made out that the Applicants have been discriminated against because they are not South African nationals.

Amnesty, Reconciliation, and *uBuntu*

THE AZAPO CASE

Azanian Peoples Organisation and Others v. President of the Republic of South Africa and Others 1996 (8) BCLR 1015 (CC)

Case Summary

FACTS

In this case, the Azanian Peoples Organisation (AZAPO), including Stephen Biko's widow challenged section 27 of the Promotion of National Unity and Reconciliation Act 34 of 1995. This Act established the famous Truth and Reconciliation Commission. Section 27 provided a conditional grant of amnesty if the applicant engaged in full disclosure of any role played during apartheid, such as torture. This role had to be for a political purpose. The Applicants argued that section 27 denied them the fundamental right to a trial, which was guaranteed in the Interim Constitution by section 22. For our purposes here, *AZAPO* is a particularly important case because it constitutionalized the epilogue of the Interim Constitution, giving it equal status to all other constitutional provisions. Famously, *ubuntu* was included in the epilogue, even if mainly to justify the need for the Truth and Reconciliation Commission.

Not only was criminal amnesty granted, but civil amnesty was also granted.

LEGAL HISTORY

The case received wide attention not only because Biko's widow was one of the Applicants, but also because many of the other Applicants were, like Biko's widow, survivors of brutal violence done to them.

LEGAL ISSUE
The issue was whether or not section 27 could meet constitutional muster under the Interim Constitution.

DISPENSATION
The court powerfully argued that there was a constitutional mandate to set up a Truth and Reconciliation Commission and that such a mandate would be undermined in its effort to seek the truth about what had actually happened to the victims of apartheid, many of who had simply gone missing. Although the court recognized the intense feelings on the part of those who wanted to seek retribution against the perpetrators who had so horribly wronged their families, the court ultimately held that the legislature in adopting section 20 had not exceeded its powers.

Deputy President Mahomed

[1] For decades South African history has been dominated by a deep conflict between a minority, which reserved for itself all control over the political instruments of the State and a majority who sought to resist that domination. Fundamental human rights became a major casualty of this conflict as the resistance of those punished by their denial was met by laws designed to counter the effectiveness of such resistance. The conflict deepened with the increased sophistication of the economy, the rapid acceleration of knowledge and education and the ever increasing hostility of an international community steadily outraged by the inconsistency which had become manifest between its own articulated ideals after the Second World War and the official practices which had become institutionalised in South Africa through laws enacted to give them sanction and teeth by a parliament elected only by a privileged minority. The result was a debilitating war of internal political dissension and confrontation, massive expressions of labour militancy, perennial student unrest, punishing international economic isolation, widespread dislocation in crucial areas of national endeavour, accelerated levels of armed conflict and a dangerous combination of anxiety, frustration and anger among expanding proportions of the populace. The legitimacy of law itself was deeply wounded as the country haemorrhaged dangerously in the face of this tragic conflict that had begun to traumatise the entire nation.

[2] During the eighties it became manifest to all that our country with all its natural wealth, physical beauty and human resources was on a disaster course unless that conflict was reversed. It was this realisation which mercifully rescued us in the early nineties as those who controlled the levers of State power began to negotiate a different future with those who had been imprisoned, silenced, or driven into exile in consequence of their resistance to that control and its consequences. Those negotiations resulted in an interim Constitution[1] committed to a transition towards a more just, defensible and democratic political order based on the protection of fundamental human rights. It was wisely appreciated by those involved in the preceding

negotiations that the task of building such a new democratic order was a very difficult task because of the previous history and the deep emotions and indefensible inequities it had generated; and that this could not be achieved without a firm and generous commitment to reconciliation and national unity. It was realised that much of the unjust consequences of the past could not ever be fully reversed. It might be necessary in crucial areas to close the book on that past.

[3] This fundamental philosophy is eloquently expressed in the epilogue to the Constitution, which reads as follows:

"National Unity and Reconciliation

This Constitution provides a historic bridge between the past of a deeply divided society characterised by strife, conflict, untold suffering and injustice, and a future founded on the recognition of human rights, democracy and peaceful co-existence and development opportunities for all South Africans, irrespective of colour, race, class, belief or sex.

The pursuit of national unity, the well being of all South African citizens and peace require reconciliation between the people of South Africa and the reconstruction of society.

The adoption of this Constitution lays the secure foundation for the people of South Africa to transcend the divisions and strife of the past, which generated gross violations of human rights, the transgression of humanitarian principles in violent conflicts and a legacy of hatred, fear, guilt and revenge.

These can now be addressed on the basis that there is a need for understanding but not for vengeance, a need for reparation but not for retaliation, a need for *ubuntu* but not for victimisation.

In order to advance such reconciliation and reconstruction, amnesty shall be granted in respect of acts, omissions and offences associated with political objectives and committed in the course of the conflicts of the past. To this end, Parliament under this Constitution shall adopt a law determining a firm cut-off date, which shall be a date after 8 October 1990 and before 6 December 1993, and providing for the mechanisms, criteria and procedures, including tribunals, if any, through which such amnesty shall be dealt with at any time after the law has been passed.

With this Constitution and these commitments we, the people of South Africa, open a new chapter in the history of our country."

Pursuant to the provisions of the epilogue, Parliament enacted during 1995 what is colloquially referred to as the Truth and Reconciliation Act. Its proper name is the Promotion of National Unity and Reconciliation Act 34 of 1995 ("the Act").

[4] The Act establishes a Truth and Reconciliation Commission. The objectives of that Commission are set out in section 3. Its main objective is to "promote national unity and reconciliation in a spirit of understanding which transcends the

conflicts and divisions of the past." It is enjoined to pursue that objective by "establishing as complete a picture as possible of the causes, nature and extent of the gross violations of human rights" committed during the period commencing 1 March 1960 to the "cut-off date."[2] For this purpose the Commission is obliged to have regard to "the perspectives of the victims and the motives and perspectives of the persons responsible for the commission of the violations."[3] It also is required to facilitate:

> ". . . the granting of amnesty to persons who make full disclosure of all the relevant facts relating to acts associated with a political objective . . ."[4]

The Commission is further entrusted with the duty to establish and to make known "the fate or whereabouts of victims" and of "restoring the human and civil dignity of such victims" by affording them an opportunity to relate their own accounts of the violations and by recommending "reparation measures" in respect of such violations[5] and finally to compile a comprehensive report in respect of its functions, including the recommendation of measures to prevent the violation of human rights.[6]

[5] Three committees are established for the purpose of achieving the objectives of the Commission.[7] The first committee is the Committee on Human Rights Violations, which conducts enquiries pertaining to gross violations of human rights during the prescribed period, with extensive powers to gather and receive evidence and information.[8] The second committee is the Committee on Reparation and Rehabilitation, which is given similar powers to gather information and receive evidence for the purposes of ultimately recommending to the President suitable reparations for victims of gross violations of human rights.[9] The third and the most directly relevant committee for the purposes of the present dispute is the Committee on Amnesty.[10] This is a committee, which must consist of five persons of which the chairperson must be a judge.[11] The Committee on Amnesty is given elaborate powers to consider applications for amnesty.[12] The Committee has the power to grant amnesty in respect of any act, omission or offence to which the particular application for amnesty relates, provided that the applicant concerned has made a full disclosure of all relevant facts and provided further that the relevant act, omission or offence is associated with a political objective committed in the course of the conflicts of the past, in accordance with the provisions of sections 20(2) and 20(3) of the Act.[13] These subsections contain very detailed provisions pertaining to what may properly be considered to be acts "associated with a political objective." Subsection (3) of section 20 provides as follows:

> "Whether a particular act, omission or offence contemplated in subsection (2) is an act associated with a political objective, shall be decided with reference to the following criteria:

(a) The motive of the person who committed the act, omission or offence;

(b) the context in which the act, omission or offence took place, and in particular whether the act, omission or offence was committed in the course of or as part of a political uprising, disturbance or event, or in reaction thereto;

(c) the legal and factual nature of the act, omission or offence, including the gravity of the act, omission or offence;

(d) the object or objective of the act, omission or offence, and in particular whether the act, omission or offence was primarily directed at a political opponent or State property or personnel or against private property or individuals;

(e) whether the act, omission or offence was committed in the execution of an order of, or on behalf of, or with the approval of, the organisation, institution, liberation movement or body of which the person who committed the act was a member, an agent or a supporter; and

(f) the relationship between the act, omission or offence and the political objective pursued, and in particular the directness and proximity of the relationship and the proportionality of the act, omission or offence to the objective pursued, but does not include any act, omission or offence committed by any person referred to in subsection (2) who acted—

  (i) for personal gain: Provided that an act, omission or offence by any person who acted and received money or anything of value as an informer of the State or a former state, political organisation or liberation movement, shall not be excluded only on the grounds of that person having received money or anything of value for his or her information; or

  (ii) out of personal malice, ill-will or spite, directed against the victim of the acts committed."

[6] After making provision for certain ancillary matters, section 20(7) (the constitutionality of which is impugned in these proceedings) provides as follows:

"(7) (a) No person who has been granted amnesty in respect of an act, omission or offence shall be criminally or civilly liable in respect of such act, omission or offence and no body or organisation or the State shall be liable, and no person shall be vicariously liable, for any such act, omission or offence.

(b) Where amnesty is granted to any person in respect of any act, omission or offence, such amnesty shall have no influence upon the criminal liability of any other person contingent upon the liability of the first-mentioned person.

(c) No person, organisation or state shall be civilly or vicariously liable for an act, omission or offence committed between 1 March 1960 and the cut-off date by a person who is deceased, unless amnesty could not have been granted in terms of this Act in respect of such an act, omission or offence."

Section 20(7) is followed by sections 20(8), 20(9) and 20(10) which deal expressly with both the formal and procedural consequences of an amnesty in the following terms:

"(8) If any person—

   (a) has been charged with and is standing trial in respect of an offence constituted by the act or omission in respect of which amnesty is granted in terms of this section; or

   (b) has been convicted of, and is awaiting the passing of sentence in respect of, or is in custody for the purpose of serving a sentence imposed in respect of, an offence constituted by the act or omission in respect of which amnesty is so granted, the criminal proceedings shall forthwith upon publication of the proclamation referred to in subsection (6) become void or the sentence so imposed shall upon such publication lapse and the person so in custody shall forthwith be released.

(9) If any person has been granted amnesty in respect of any act or omission which formed the ground of a civil judgment which was delivered at any time before the granting of the amnesty, the publication of the proclamation in terms of subsection (6) shall not affect the operation of the judgment in so far as it applies to that person.

(10) Where any person has been convicted of any offence constituted by an act or omission associated with a political objective in respect of which amnesty has been granted in terms of this Act, any entry or record of the conviction shall be deemed to be expunged from all official documents or records and the conviction shall for all purposes, including the application of any Act of Parliament or any other law, be deemed not to have taken place: Provided that the Committee may recommend to the authority concerned the taking of such measures as it may deem necessary for the protection of the safety of the public."[14]

[7] What is clear from section 20(7), read with sections 20(8), (9) and (10), is that once a person has been granted amnesty in respect of an act, omission or offence:

   (a) the offender can no longer be held "criminally liable" for such offence and no prosecution in respect thereof can be maintained against him or her;

(b) such an offender can also no longer be held civilly liable personally for any damages sustained by the victim and no such civil proceedings can successfully be pursued against him or her;

(c) if the wrongdoer is an employee of the State, the State is equally discharged from any civil liability in respect of any act or omission of such an employee, even if the relevant act or omission was effected during the course and within the scope of his or her employment; and

(d) other bodies, organisations or persons are also exempt from any liability for any of the acts or omissions of a wrongdoer which would ordinarily have arisen in consequence of their vicarious liability for such acts or omissions.

[8] The Applicants sought in this Court to attack the constitutionality of section 20(7) on the grounds that its consequences are not authorised by the Constitution. They aver that various agents of the State, acting within the scope and in the course of their employment, have unlawfully murdered and maimed leading activists during the conflict against the racial policies of the previous administration and that the Applicants have a clear right to insist that such wrongdoers should properly be prosecuted and punished, that they should be ordered by the ordinary Courts of the land to pay adequate civil compensation to the victims or dependants of the victims and further to require the State to make good to such victims or dependants the serious losses which they have suffered in consequence of the criminal and delictual acts of the employees of the State. In support of that attack Mr *Soggot SC*, who appeared for the Applicants together with Mr *Khoza*, contended that section 20(7) was inconsistent with section 22 of the Constitution, which provides that

"[e]very person shall have the right to have justiciable disputes settled by a Court of law or, where appropriate, another independent or impartial forum."

He submitted that the Amnesty Committee was neither "a Court of law" nor an "independent or impartial forum" and that in any event the Committee was not authorised to settle "justiciable disputes." All it was simply required to decide was whether *amnesty* should be granted in respect of a particular act, omission or offence.

[9] The effect of an amnesty undoubtedly impacts upon very fundamental rights. All persons are entitled to the protection of the law against unlawful invasions of their right to life, their right to respect for and protection of dignity and their right not to be subject to torture of any kind. When those rights are invaded those aggrieved by such invasion have the right to obtain redress in the ordinary Courts of law and those guilty of perpetrating such violations are answerable before such Courts, both civilly and criminally. An amnesty to the wrongdoer effectively obliterates such rights.

[10] There would therefore be very considerable force in the submission that section 20(7) of the Act constitutes a violation of section 22 of the Constitution, if there was nothing in the Constitution itself which permitted or authorised such violation. The crucial issue, therefore, which needs to be determined, is whether the Constitution, indeed, permits such a course. Section 33(2) of the Constitution provides that

> "[s]ave as provided for in subsection (1) or any other provision of this Constitution, no law, whether a rule of common law, customary law or legislation, shall limit any right entrenched in this Chapter."

Two questions arise from the provisions of this subsection. The first question is whether there is "any other provision in this Constitution" which permits a limitation of the right in section 22 and secondly if there is not, whether any violation of section 22 is a limitation which can be justified in terms of section 33(1) of the Constitution which reads as follows:

> "The rights entrenched in this Chapter may be limited by law of general application, provided that such limitation—
>
> (a) shall be permissible only to the extent that it is—
>   (i)   reasonable; and
>   (ii) justifiable in an open and democratic society based on freedom and equality; and
> (b) shall not negate the essential content of the right in question, and provided further that any limitation to—
>   (aa) a right entrenched in section 10, 11, 12, 14(1), 21, 25 or 30(1)(d) or (e) or (2); or
>   (bb) a right entrenched in section 15, 16, 17, 18, 23 or 24, in so far as such right relates to free and fair political activity, shall, in addition to being reasonable as required in paragraph (a)(i), also be necessary."

[11] Mr *Marcus*, who together with Mr *D Leibowitz* appeared for the Respondents, contended that the epilogue, which I have previously quoted, is indeed a "provision of this Constitution" within the meaning of section 33(2). He argued that any law conferring amnesty on a wrongdoer in respect of acts, omissions and offences associated with political objectives and committed during the prescribed period, is therefore a law properly authorised by the Constitution.

[12] It is therefore necessary to deal, in the first place, with the constitutional status of the epilogue. In the founding affidavit in support of the application for direct access to this Court made by the Deputy President of the first applicant, reliance

was placed on the Constitutional Principles contained in schedule 4 to the Constitution and it was submitted that

> "[the] Constitutional Principles in Schedule 4 enjoy a higher status to that of other sections of the Constitution, in that, in terms of section 74(1) of the Constitution, it is not permissible to amend the Constitutional Principles and they shall be included in the final Constitution.
>
> To the extent that, therefore, the post-end clause is in conflict with Constitutional Principle VI, the latter should prevail."

Constitutional Principle VI provides that

> "[t]here shall be a separation of powers between the legislature, executive and the judiciary, with appropriate checks and balances to ensure accountability, responsiveness and openness."

[13] During oral argument before us this submission was wisely not pressed by counsel for the Applicants. Even assuming in favour of the Applicants that there is some potential tension between the language of section 20(7) of the Act and Constitutional Principle VI, it can be of no assistance to the Applicants in their attack on the status of the epilogue. The purpose of schedule 4 to the Constitution is to define the principles with which a new constitutional text adopted by the Constitutional Assembly must comply.[15] The new constitutional text has no force and effect unless the Constitutional Court has certified that the provisions of the text comply with these Constitutional Principles.[16]

[14] The Constitutional Principles have no effect on the *status* of the epilogue. That status is determined by section 232(4) of the Constitution, which provides as follows:

> "In interpreting this Constitution a provision in any Schedule, including the provision under the heading *'National Unity and Reconciliation,'* to this Constitution shall not by reason only of the fact that it is contained in a Schedule, have a lesser status than any other provision of this Constitution which is not contained in a Schedule, and such provision shall for all purposes be deemed to form part of the substance of this Constitution."

The epilogue, therefore, has no lesser status than any other part of the Constitution. As far as section 22 is concerned it therefore would have the same effect as a provision within section 22 itself, which enacted that:

> "Nothing contained in this subsection shall preclude Parliament from adopting a law providing for amnesty to be granted in respect of acts, omissions

and offences associated with political objectives committed during a defined period and providing for the mechanisms, criteria and procedures, including tribunals, if any, through which such amnesty shall be dealt with at any time after the law has been passed."

What is clear is that Parliament not only has the authority in terms of the epilogue to make a law providing for amnesty to be granted in respect of the acts, omissions and offences falling within the category defined therein but that it is in fact obliged to do so. This follows from the wording in the material part of the epilogue which is that "Parliament under this Constitution *shall* adopt a law" providing, *inter alia*, for the "mechanisms, criteria and procedures . . . through which . . . amnesty shall be dealt with."

[15] It was contended that even if this is the proper interpretation of the status of the epilogue and even if the principle of "amnesty" is authorised by the Constitution, it does not authorise, in particular, the far-reaching amnesty which section 20(7) allows. In his heads of argument on behalf of the Applicants, Mr *Soggot* conceded that the wording of the epilogue provides

". . . a clear indication that the Constitution contemplates the grant of amnesty in respect of offences associated with political objectives and committed in the course of the conflicts of the past, including offences involving gross violations of human rights."

At the commencement of oral argument Mr *Soggot* informed us, however, that he had been instructed by his clients to withdraw this concession and he therefore did not abandon the submission that section 20(7) was unconstitutional in all respects and that Parliament had no constitutional power to authorise the Amnesty Committee to indemnify any wrongdoer either against criminal or civil liability arising from the perpetration of acts falling within the categories described in the legislation.

AMNESTY IN RESPECT OF CRIMINAL LIABILITY

[16] I understand perfectly why the Applicants would want to insist that those wrongdoers who abused their authority and wrongfully murdered, maimed or tortured very much loved members of their families who had, in their view, been engaged in a noble struggle to confront the inhumanity of apartheid, should vigorously be prosecuted and effectively be punished for their callous and inhuman conduct in violation of the criminal law. I can therefore also understand why they are emotionally unable to identify themselves with the consequences of the legal concession made by Mr *Soggot* and if that concession was wrong in law I would have no hesitation whatsoever in rejecting it.

[17] Every decent human being must feel grave discomfort in living with a con-

sequence which might allow the perpetrators of evil acts to walk the streets of this land with impunity, protected in their freedom by an amnesty immune from constitutional attack, but the circumstances in support of this course require carefully to be appreciated. Most of the acts of brutality and torture which have taken place have occurred during an era in which neither the laws which permitted the incarceration of persons or the investigation of crimes, nor the methods and the culture, which informed such investigations, were easily open to public investigation, verification and correction. Much of what transpired in this shameful period is shrouded in secrecy and not easily capable of objective demonstration and proof. Loved ones have disappeared, sometimes mysteriously and most of them no longer survive to tell their tales. Others have had their freedom invaded, their dignity assaulted or their reputations tarnished by grossly unfair imputations hurled in the fire and the crossfire of a deep and wounding conflict. The wicked and the innocent have often both been victims. Secrecy and authoritarianism have concealed the truth in little crevices of obscurity in our history. Records are not easily accessible; witnesses are often unknown, dead, unavailable or unwilling. All that often effectively remains is the truth of wounded memories of loved ones sharing instinctive suspicions, deep and traumatising to the survivors but otherwise incapable of translating themselves into objective and corroborative evidence which could survive the rigours of the law. The Act seeks to address this massive problem by encouraging these survivors and the dependants of the tortured and the wounded, the maimed and the dead to unburden their grief publicly, to receive the collective recognition of a new nation that they were wronged, and crucially, to help them to discover what did in truth happen to their loved ones, where and under what circumstances it did happen, and who was responsible. That truth, which the victims of repression seek so desperately to know, is, in the circumstances, much more likely to be forthcoming if those responsible for such monstrous misdeeds are encouraged to disclose the whole truth with the incentive that they will not receive the punishment which they undoubtedly deserve if they do. Without that incentive there is nothing to encourage such persons to make the disclosures and to reveal the truth that persons in the positions of the Applicants so desperately desire. With that incentive, what might unfold are objectives fundamental to the ethos of a new constitutional order. The families of those unlawfully tortured, maimed or traumatised become more empowered to discover the truth, the perpetrators become exposed to opportunities to obtain relief from the burden of a guilt or an anxiety they might be living with for many long years, the country begins the long and necessary process of healing the wounds of the past, transforming anger and grief into a mature understanding and creating the emotional and structural climate essential for the "reconciliation and reconstruction" which informs the very difficult and sometimes painful objectives of the amnesty articulated in the epilogue.

[18] The alternative to the grant of immunity from criminal prosecution of offenders is to keep intact the abstract right to such a prosecution for particular

persons without the evidence to sustain the prosecution successfully, to continue to keep the dependants of such victims in many cases substantially ignorant about what precisely happened to their loved ones, to leave their yearning for the truth effectively unassuaged, to perpetuate their legitimate sense of resentment and grief and correspondingly to allow the culprits of such deeds to remain perhaps physically free but inhibited in their capacity to become active, full and creative members of the new order by a menacing combination of confused fear, guilt, uncertainty and sometimes even trepidation. Both the victims and the culprits who walk on the "historic bridge" described by the epilogue will hobble more than walk to the future with heavy and dragged steps delaying and impeding a rapid and enthusiastic transition to the new society at the end of the bridge, which is the vision that informs the epilogue.

[19] Even more crucially, but for a mechanism providing for amnesty, the "historic bridge" itself might never have been erected. For a successfully negotiated transition, the terms of the transition required not only the agreement of those victimized by abuse but also those threatened by the transition to a "democratic society based on freedom and equality."[17] If the Constitution kept alive the prospect of continuous retaliation and revenge, the agreement of those threatened by its implementation might never have been forthcoming, and if it had, the bridge itself would have remained wobbly and insecure, threatened by fear from some and anger from others. It was for this reason that those who negotiated the Constitution made a deliberate choice, preferring understanding to vengeance, reparation over retaliation, *ubuntu*[18] over victimisation.[19]

. . .

[21] The result, at all levels, is a difficult, sensitive, perhaps even agonising, balancing act between the need for justice to victims of past abuse and the need for reconciliation and rapid transition to a new future; between encouragement to wrongdoers to help in the discovery of the truth and the need for reparations for the victims of that truth; between a correction in the old and the creation of the new. It is an exercise of immense difficulty interacting in a vast network of political, emotional, ethical and logistical considerations. It is an act calling for a judgment falling substantially within the domain of those entrusted with lawmaking in the era preceding and during the transition period. The results may well often be imperfect and the pursuit of the act might inherently support the message of Kant that "out of the crooked timber of humanity no straight thing was ever made"[20] [21] There can be legitimate debate about the methods and the mechanisms chosen by the lawmaker to give effect to the difficult duty entrusted upon it in terms of the epilogue. We are not concerned with that debate or the wisdom of its choice of mechanisms but only with its constitutionality. That, for us, is the only relevant standard. Applying that standard, I am not satisfied that in providing for amnesty for those guilty of serious offences associated with political objectives and in defining the mechanisms through which and the manner in which such amnesty may be secured by such of-

fenders, the lawmaker, in section 20(7), has offended any of the express or implied limitations on its powers in terms of the Constitution.

[22] South Africa is not alone in being confronted with a historical situation which required amnesty for criminal acts to be accorded for the purposes of facilitating the transition to, and consolidation of, an overtaking democratic order. Chile, Argentina and El Salvador are among the countries which have in modern times been confronted with a similar need. Although the mechanisms adopted to facilitate that process have differed from country to country and from time to time, the principle that amnesty should, in appropriate circumstances, be accorded to violators of human rights in order to facilitate the consolidation of new democracies was accepted in all these countries and truth commissions were also established in such countries.

. . .

AMNESTY IN RESPECT OF THE CIVIL LIABILITY
OF INDIVIDUAL WRONGDOERS

[33] Mr *Soggot* submitted that Chapter 3 of the Constitution, and more particularly section 22, conferred on every person the right to pursue, in the ordinary Courts of the land or before independent tribunals, any claim which such person might have in civil law for the recovery of damages sustained by such a person in consequence of the unlawful delicts perpetrated by a wrongdoer. He contended that the Constitution did not authorise Parliament to make any law, which would have the result of indemnifying (or otherwise rendering immune from liability) the perpetrator of any such delict against any claims made for damages suffered by the victim of such a delict. In support of that argument he suggested that the concept of "amnesty," referred to in the epilogue to the Constitution, was, at worst for the Applicants, inherently limited to immunity from criminal prosecutions. He contended that even if a wrongdoer who has received amnesty could plead such amnesty as a defence to a criminal prosecution, such amnesty could not be used as a shield to protect him or her from claims for delictual damages suffered by any person in consequence of the act or omission of the wrongdoer.

[34] There can be no doubt that in some contexts the word "amnesty" does bear the limited meaning contended for by counsel. Thus one of the meanings of amnesty referred to in *The Oxford English Dictionary* is ". . . a general overlooking or pardon of past offences, by the ruling authority"[21] [34] and in similar vein, *Webster's Dictionary* gives as the second meaning of amnesty "a deliberate overlooking, as of an offense."[22] [35] *Wharton's Law Lexicon* also refers to amnesty in the context "by which crimes against the government up to a certain date are so obliterated that they can never be brought into charge.[23] [36]

[35] I cannot, however, agree that the concept of amnesty is inherently to be limited to the absolution from criminal liability alone, regardless of the context and regardless of the circumstances. The word has no inherently fixed technical meaning.

Its origin is to be found from the Greek concept of "amnestia" and it indicates what is described by Webster's Dictionary[24] [37] as "an act of oblivion." The degree of oblivion or obliteration must depend on the circumstances. It can, in certain circumstances, be confined to immunity from criminal prosecutions and in other circumstances be extended also to civil liability. Describing the effects of amnesty in treaties concluded between belligerent parties, a distinguished writer states:

> "An amnesty is a complete forgetfulness of the past; and as the treaty of peace is meant to put an end to every subject of discord, the amnesty should constitute its first article. Accordingly, such is the common practice at the present day. But though the treaty should make no mention of it, the amnesty is necessarily included in it, from the very nature of the agreement.
>
> Since each of the belligerents claims to have justice on his side, and since there is no one to decide between them (Book III, § 188), the condition in which affairs stand at the time of the treaty must be regarded as their lawful status, and if the parties wish to make any change in it the treaty must contain an express stipulation to that effect. Consequently all matters not mentioned in the treaty are to continue, as they happen to be at the time the treaty is concluded. This is also a result of the promised amnesty. *All the injuries caused by the war are likewise forgotten; and no action can lie on account of those for which the treaty does not stipulate that satisfaction shall be made; they are considered as never having happened.*
>
> But the effect of the settlement or amnesty can not be extended to things which bear no relation to war terminated by the treaty. Thus, claims based upon a debt contracted, or an injury received, prior to the war, but which formed no part of the motives for undertaking the war, remain as they were, and are not annulled by the treaty, unless the treaty has been made to embrace the relinquishment of all claims whatsoever. The same rule holds for debts contracted during the war, but with respect to objects which have no relation to it, and for injuries received during the war, but not as a result of it." (*My emphasis.*)[25] [38]

[36] What are the material circumstances of the present case? As I have previously said, what the epilogue to the Constitution seeks to achieve by providing for amnesty is the facilitation of "reconciliation and reconstruction" by the creation of mechanisms and procedures which make it possible for the truth of our past to be uncovered. Central to the justification of amnesty in respect of the criminal prosecution for offences committed during the prescribed period with political objectives, is the appreciation that the truth will not effectively be revealed by the wrongdoers if they are to be prosecuted for such acts. That justification must necessarily and unavoidably apply to the need to indemnify such wrongdoers against civil claims for payment of damages. Without that incentive the wrongdoer cannot be encouraged

to reveal the whole truth which might inherently be against his or her material or proprietary interests. There is nothing in the language of the epilogue which persuades me that what the makers of the Constitution intended to do was to encourage wrongdoers to reveal the truth by providing for amnesty against criminal prosecution in respect of their acts but simultaneously to discourage them from revealing that truth by keeping intact the threat that such revelations might be visited with what might in many cases be very substantial claims for civil damages. It appears to me to be more reasonable to infer that the legislation contemplated in the epilogue would, in the circumstances defined, be wide enough to allow for an amnesty which would protect a wrongdoer who told the truth, from both the criminal and the civil consequences of his or her admissions.

[37] This conclusion appears to be fortified by the fact that what the epilogue directs is that "amnesty shall be granted in respect of acts, omissions and offences . . ."

If the purpose was simply to provide mechanisms in terms of which wrongdoers could be protected from criminal prosecution in respect of offences committed by them, why would there be any need to refer also to "acts and omissions" in addition to offences? The word "offences" would have covered both acts and omissions in any event.

[38] In the result I am satisfied that section 20(7) is not open to constitutional challenge on the ground that it invades the right of a victim or his or her dependant to recover damages from a wrongdoer for unlawful acts perpetrated during the conflicts of the past. If there is any such invasion it is authorised and contemplated by the relevant parts of the epilogue.

The Effect of Amnesty on Any Potential Civil Liability of the State

[39] Mr *Soggot* contended forcefully that whatever be the legitimate consequences of the kind of amnesty contemplated by the epilogue for the criminal and civil liability of the wrongdoer, the Constitution could not justifiably authorise any law which has the effect of indemnifying the State itself against civil claims made by those wronged by criminal and delictual acts perpetrated by such wrongdoers in the course and within the scope of their employment as servants of the State. Section 20(7) of the Act, he argued, had indeed that effect and was therefore unconstitutional to that extent.

[40] This submission has one great force. It is this. If the wrongdoer in the employment of the State is not personally indemnified in the circumstances regulated by the Act, the truth might never unfold. It would remain shrouded in the impenetrable mysteries of the past, leaving the dependants of many victims with a grief unrelieved by any knowledge of the truth. But how, it was argued, would it deter such wrongdoers from revealing the truth if such a revelation held no criminal or civil consequences for them? How could such wrongdoers be discouraged from disclosing the truth if their own liberty and property was not to be threatened by such

revelations, but the State itself nevertheless remained liable to compensate the families of victims for such wrongdoings perpetrated by the servants of the State?

[41] This is a serious objection, which requires to be considered carefully. I think it must be conceded that in many cases, the wrongdoer would not be discouraged from revealing the whole truth merely because the consequences of such disclosure might be to saddle the State with a potential civil liability for damages arising from the delictual acts or omissions of a wrongdoer (although there may also be many cases in which such a wrongdoer, still in the service of the State, might in some degree be inhibited or even coerced from making disclosures implicating his or her superiors).

[42] The real answer, however, to the problems posed by the questions which I have identified, seems to lie in the more fundamental objectives of the transition sought to be attained by the Constitution and articulated in the epilogue itself. What the Constitution seeks to do is to facilitate the transition to a new democratic order, committed to "reconciliation between the people of South Africa and the reconstruction of society." The question is how this can be done effectively with the limitations of our resources and the legacy of the past.

[43] The families of those whose fundamental human rights were invaded by torture and abuse are not the only victims who have endured "untold suffering and injustice" in consequence of the crass inhumanity of apartheid which so many have had to endure for so long. Generations of children born and yet to be born will suffer the consequences of poverty, of malnutrition, of homelessness, of illiteracy and disempowerment generated and sustained by the institutions of apartheid and its manifest effects on life and living for so many. The country has neither the resources nor the skills to reverse fully these massive wrongs. It will take many years of strong commitment, sensitivity and labour to "reconstruct our society" so as to fulfill the legitimate dreams of new generations exposed to real opportunities for advancement denied to preceding generations initially by the execution of apartheid itself and for a long time after its formal demise, by its relentless consequences. The resources of the State have to be deployed imaginatively, wisely, efficiently and equitably, to facilitate the reconstruction process in a manner which best brings relief and hope to the widest sections of the community, developing for the benefit of the entire nation the latent human potential and resources of every person who has directly or indirectly been burdened with the heritage of the shame and the pain of our racist past.

[44] Those negotiators of the Constitution and leaders of the nation who were required to address themselves to these agonising problems must have been compelled to make hard choices. They could have chosen to direct that the limited resources of the State be spent by giving preference to the formidable delictual claims of those who had suffered from acts of murder, torture or assault perpetrated by servants of the State, diverting to that extent, desperately needed funds in the crucial areas of education, housing and primary health care. They were entitled to permit a

different choice to be made between competing demands inherent in the problem. They could have chosen to direct that the potential liability of the State be limited in respect of any civil claims by differentiating between those against whom prescription could have been pleaded as a defence and those whose claims were of such recent origin that a defence of prescription would have failed. They were entitled to reject such a choice on the grounds that it was irrational. They could have chosen to saddle the State with liability for claims made by insurance companies which had compensated institutions for delictual acts performed by the servants of the State and to that extent again divert funds otherwise desperately needed to provide food for the hungry, roofs for the homeless and black boards and desks for those struggling to obtain admission to desperately overcrowded schools. They were entitled to permit the claims of such school children and the poor and the homeless to be preferred.

[45] The election made by the makers of the Constitution was to permit Parliament to favour "the reconstruction of society" involving in the process a wider concept of "reparation," which would allow the State to take into account the competing claims on its resources but, at the same time, to have regard to the "untold suffering" of individuals and families whose fundamental human rights had been invaded during the conflict of the past. In some cases such a family may best be assisted by a reparation which allows the young in this family to maximise their potential through bursaries and scholarships; in other cases the most effective reparation might take the form of occupational training and rehabilitation; in still other cases complex surgical interventions and medical help may be facilitated; still others might need subsidies to prevent eviction from homes they can no longer maintain and in suitable cases the deep grief of the traumatised may most effectively be assuaged by facilitating the erection of a tombstone on the grave of a departed one with a public acknowledgement of his or her valour and nobility. There might have to be differentiation between the form and quality of the reparations made to two persons who have suffered exactly the same damage in consequence of the same unlawful act but where one person now enjoys lucrative employment from the State and the other lives in penury.

[46] All these examples illustrate, in my view, that it is much too simplistic to say that the objectives of the Constitution could only properly be achieved by saddling the State with the formal liability to pay, in full, the provable delictual claims of those who have suffered patrimonial loss in consequence of the delicts perpetrated with political objectives by servants of the State during the conflicts of the past. There was a permissible alternative, perhaps even a more imaginative and more fundamental route to the "reconstruction of society," which could legitimately have been followed. This is the route, which appears to have been chosen by Parliament through the mechanism of amnesty and nuanced and individualised reparations in the Act. I am quite unpersuaded that this is not a route authorised by the epilogue to the Constitution.

[47] The epilogue required that a law be adopted by Parliament which would provide for "amnesty" and it appreciated the "need for reparation," but it left it to Parliament to decide upon the ambit of the amnesty, the permissible form and extent of such reparations and the procedures to be followed in the determination thereof, by taking into account all the relevant circumstances to which I have made reference. Parliament was therefore entitled to decide that, having regard to the resources of the State, proper reparations for those victimised by the unjust laws and practices of the past justified formulae which did not compel any irrational differentiation between the claims of those who were able to pursue enforceable delictual claims against the State and the claims of those who were not in that position but nevertheless deserved reparations.

[48] It was submitted by Mr *Soggot* that the reference to the "need for reparation" in the epilogue is contained only in the fourth paragraph of the epilogue and does not appear in the directive to Parliament to adopt a law "providing for the mechanisms, criteria and procedures, including tribunals, if any, through which . . . amnesty shall be dealt with. . . ." He argued from this that what the makers of the Constitution must have contemplated was that the ordinary liability of the State, in respect of damages sustained by others in consequence of the acts of the servants of the State, remained intact, and was protected by section 22 of the Constitution. In my view, this is a fragmentary and impermissible approach to the structure of the epilogue. It must be read holistically. It expresses an integrated philosophical and jurisprudential approach. The very first paragraph defines the commitment to the "historic bridge" and the second paragraph expands on the theme of this bridge by elevating "the pursuit of national unity, . . . reconciliation between the people of South Africa and the reconstruction of society." It then goes on in the third paragraph, in very moving and generous language, to "secure" the "foundation" of the nation by transcending "the divisions and strife of the past, which generated gross violations of human rights" and elects, in eloquent terms in the next paragraph, to make the historic choice in favour of understanding above vengeance, *ubuntu* over victimisation and "a need for reparation but not for retaliation." This philosophy then informs the fifth paragraph which directs Parliament to adopt a law providing for amnesty and is introduced by the words "[i]n order to advance such reconciliation and reconstruction, amnesty shall be granted. . . ." The reference to "*such* reconciliation and reconstruction" embraces the continuing radiating influence of the preceding paragraphs including the reference to "the need for reparation." Approached in this way, the reparations authorised in the Act are not alien to the legislation contemplated by the epilogue. Indeed, they are perfectly consistent with, and give expression to, the extraordinarily generous and imaginative commitment of the Constitution to a philosophy, which has brought unprecedented international acclaim for the people of our country. It ends with the deep spirituality and dignity of the last line:

"Nkosi sikelel' iAfrika—God seën Suid-Afrika" (God bless South Africa)

THE INDEMNITY OF ORGANISATIONS AND PERSONS IN RESPECT OF CLAIMS BASED ON VICARIOUS LIABILITY

[49] It was not contended by Mr *Soggot* that even if the State was properly rendered immune against claims for damages in consequence of delicts perpetrated by its servants, acting within the scope and in the course of their employment, individuals and organisations should not enjoy any similar protection in respect of any vicarious liability arising from any unlawful acts committed by their servants or members. He was correct in that attitude. Apart from the fact that the wrongdoers concerned might be discouraged from revealing the truth which implicated their employers or organisations on whose support they might still directly or indirectly depend, the Constitution itself could not successfully have been transacted if those responsible for the negotiations which preceded it and the political organisations to which they belonged, were going to remain vulnerable to potentially massive claims for damages arising from their vicarious liability in respect of such wrongful acts perpetrated by their agents or members. The erection of the "historic bridge" would never have begun.

CONCLUSION

[50] In the result, I am satisfied that the epilogue to the Constitution authorised and contemplated an "amnesty" in its most comprehensive and generous meaning so as to enhance and optimise the prospects of facilitating the constitutional journey from the shame of the past to the promise of the future. Parliament was, therefore, entitled to enact the Act in the terms which it did. This involved more choices apart from the choices I have previously identified.[26] [39] They could have chosen to insist that a comprehensive amnesty manifestly involved an inequality of sacrifice between the victims and the perpetrators of invasions into the fundamental rights of such victims and their families, and that, for this reason, the terms of the amnesty should leave intact the claims which some of these victims might have been able to pursue against those responsible for authorising, permitting or colluding in such acts, or they could have decided that this course would impede the pace, effectiveness and objectives of the transition with consequences substantially prejudicial for the people of a country facing, for the first time, the real prospect of enjoying, in the future, some of the human rights so unfairly denied to the generations which preceded them. They were entitled to choose the second course. They could conceivably have chosen to differentiate between the wrongful acts committed in defence of the old order and those committed in the resistance of it, or they could have chosen a comprehensive form of amnesty, which did not make this distinction. Again they were entitled to make the latter choice. The choice of alternatives legitimately fell within the judgment of the lawmakers. The exercise of that choice does not, in my view, impact on its constitutionality. It follows from these reasons that section 20(7) of the Act is authorised by the Constitution itself and it is unnecessary to consider the relevance and effect of section 33(1) of the Constitution.

ORDER

[51] In the result, the attack on the constitutionality of section 20(7) of the Promotion of National Unity and Reconciliation Act 34 of 1995 must fail. That was the only attack, which was pursued on behalf of the Applicants in this Court. It accordingly follows that the application must be, and is, refused.

Justices Chaskalson P, Ackermann, Kriegler, Langa, Madala, Mokgoro, O'Regan, and Sachs concurred in the judgment of Mahomed DP.

uBuntu, Socioeconomic Rights, and Personhood

THE *PORT ELIZABETH MUNICIPALITY* CASE

Port Elizabeth Municipality v. Various Occupiers 2004 (12) BCLR 1268 (CC)

Case Summary

FACTS

This case concerned an application for eviction sought by the Port Elizabeth Municipality against various persons who had unlawfully occupied privately owned land. These persons had come to occupy this land due to a previous eviction from another piece of land.

The occupants had made it clear that they would be willing to move if suitable alternative living arrangements were provided by the Municipality. To this end, the Municipality suggested that the occupiers move to Walmer Township. The occupiers objected to this suggestion on the basis that the township was overcrowded, crime-ridden and therefore unsuitable, especially for their children.

The Municipality argued that it was not obliged to provide alternative housing to the Respondents. It argued further that it had put in place a comprehensive housing program, and granting the occupiers housing under this program would amount to permitting them to "jump the queue"—it would allow them to get housing before those that had already applied for housing.

LEGAL HISTORY

The Eastern Cape Local Division High Court was the court of first instance in this matter, and it granted the eviction order on grounds that such an order was in the public interest. It ordered that the Sheriff demolish the informal settlements with police assistance (if need be); and further, that the occupiers pay the costs of the legal proceedings.

On appeal, the Supreme Court of Appeal set aside the order for eviction, and agreed with the Respondents that the Applicant was under an obligation to provide alternative suitable living arrangements.

The Municipality applied to the Constitutional Court for leave to appeal and to have the eviction order restored.

Furthermore, the Municipality sought a ruling that it was not constitutionally obliged to find alternative accommodation or land when seeking an order of eviction of unlawful occupiers.

Legal Issues

The legal issues were threefold: whether leave to appeal to the Constitutional Court should be granted; whether the eviction order should be upheld; and whether the Municipality was constitutionally obliged to provide alternative suitable living arrangements.

Dispensation

Writing for a unanimous court, Justice Sachs dismissed the application for leave to appeal. Through an appeal to *ubuntu*, Justice Sachs argued that when interpreting the Constitution, section 25 (which protects the right to private property) and section 26 (which protects the right to housing) must be read together in order to find a fair, equitable, and compassionate outcome in a situation such as this one where there is a conflict between the right to private property and the right to housing. The Prevention of Illegal Eviction from and Unlawful Occupation of Land Act 19 of 1998 (PIE) must be interpreted against this constitutional background, and more specifically with reference to the compassionate solution demanded by *ubuntu*.

Section 26(3) of the Constitution states that "no one may be evicted from their home, or have their home demolished, without an order of court made after considering all relevant circumstances." PIE is an amplification of both sections 25 and 26 of the Constitution and must be read against the background of both these provisions, which are informed by the overarching principle of *ubuntu*.

Justice Sachs listed a number of factors that must be taken into consideration before an application for an eviction order can succeed. He emphasized that one crucial factor is whether or not consultation or mediation had been tried so as to give the poor their voice in the proceedings.

Justice Sachs argued that there was a qualified constitutional duty to provide alternative land when seeking an eviction order. The court made it clear that great reluctance will be shown to grant an eviction order unless it was shown that reasonable efforts were made to provide suitable housing for the occupants.

The leave to appeal was dismissed and the eviction overturned. The Municipality had to pay the costs of the legal proceedings.

Justice Sachs

. . .

[11] The Prevention of Illegal Eviction from and Unlawful Occupation of Land Act 19 of 1998 (PIE) was adopted with the manifest objective of overcoming the above abuses and ensuring that evictions in future took place in a manner consistent with the values of the new constitutional dispensation. Its provisions have to be interpreted against this background.

[12] PIE not only repealed PISA but in a sense inverted it: squatting was decriminalised and the eviction process was made subject to a number of requirements, some necessary to comply with certain demands of the Bill of Rights. The overlay between public and private law continued, but in reverse fashion, with the name, character, tone and context of the statute being turned around. Thus the first part of the title of the new law emphasised a shift in thrust from prevention of illegal squatting to prevention of illegal eviction. The former objective of reinforcing common-law remedies while reducing common-law protections, was reversed so as to temper common-law remedies with strong procedural and substantive protections; and the overall objective of facilitating the displacement and relocation of poor and landless black people for ideological purposes was replaced by acknowledgment of the necessitous quest for homes of victims of past racist policies. While awaiting access to new housing development programmes, such homeless people had to be treated with dignity and respect.

[13] Thus, the former depersonalised processes that took no account of the life circumstances of those being expelled were replaced by humanised procedures that focused on fairness to all. People once regarded as anonymous squatters now became entitled to dignified and individualised treatment with special consideration for the most vulnerable. At the same time the second part of the title established that unlawful occupation was also to be prevented. The Courts now had a new role to play, namely, to hold the balance between illegal eviction and unlawful occupation. Rescuing the Courts from their invidious role as instruments directed by statute to effect callous removals, the new law guided them as to how they should fulfil their new complex and constitutionally ordained function: when evictions were being sought, the Courts were to ensure that justice and equity prevailed in relation to all concerned.

The Broad Constitutional Matrix for the Interpretation of PIE

[14] In this context PIE cannot simply be looked at as a legislative mechanism designed to restore common-law property rights by freeing them of racist and authoritarian provisions, though that is one of its aspects. Nor is it just a means of

promoting judicial philanthropy in favour of the poor, though compassion is built into its very structure. PIE has to be understood, and its governing concepts of justice and equity have to be applied, within a defined and carefully calibrated constitutional matrix.

[15] As with all determination about the reach of constitutionally protected rights, the starting and ending point of the analysis must be to affirm the values of human dignity, equality and freedom.[1] [11] One of the provisions of the Bill of Rights that has to be interpreted with these values in mind is section 25, which reads:

"Property
(1) No one may be deprived of property except in terms of law of general application and no law may permit arbitrary deprivation of property."[2] [12]

The blatant disregard manifested by racist statutes for property rights in the past makes it all the more important that property rights be fully respected in the new dispensation, both by the state and by private persons. Yet such rights have to be understood in the context of the need for the orderly opening-up or restoration of secure property rights for those denied access to or deprived of them in the past.

[16] As Ackermann J pointed out in *First National Bank*,[3] [13] subsections (4) to (9) of section 25 underlined the need for and aimed at redressing one of the most enduring legacies of racial discrimination in the past, namely the grossly unequal distribution of land in South Africa. The details of these provisions had to be borne in mind whenever section 25 was being construed, because they emphasised that under the Constitution the protection of property as an individual right was not absolute but subject to societal considerations. His judgment went on to state:

"The preamble to the Constitution indicates that one of the purposes of its adoption was to establish a society based, not only on 'democratic values' and 'fundamental human rights' but also on 'social justice.' Moreover the Bill of Rights places positive obligations on the State in regard to various social and economic rights. Van der Walt (1997) aptly explains the tensions that exist within section 25:

'[T]he meaning of section 25 has to be determined, in each specific case, within an interpretative framework that takes due cognisance of the inevitable tensions which characterise the operation of the property clause. This tension between individual rights and social responsibilities has to be the guiding principle in terms of which the section is analysed, interpreted and applied in every individual case.'

The purpose of section 25 has to be seen both as protecting existing private property rights as well as serving the public interest, mainly in the sphere of land reform but not limited thereto, and also as striking a proportionate balance between these two functions . . . When considering the purpose and content of the property clause it is necessary, as Van der Walt (1997) puts it '. . . to move away from a static, typically private-law conceptualist view of the constitution as a guarantee of the status quo to a dynamic, typically public-law view of the constitution as an instrument for social change and transformation under the auspices [and I would add 'and control'] of entrenched constitutional values.'

That property should also serve the public good is an idea by no means foreign to pre-constitutional property concepts."[4] [14]

[17] The transformatory public-law view of the Constitution referred to by Van der Walt is further underlined by section 26, which reads:

"Housing

(1) Everyone has the right to have access to adequate housing.

(2) The State must take reasonable legislative and other measures, within its available resources, to achieve the progressive realisation of this right.

(3) No one may be evicted from their home, or have their home demolished, without an order of Court made after considering all the relevant circumstances. No legislation may permit arbitrary evictions."

Section 26(3) evinces special constitutional regard for a person's place of abode. It acknowledges that a home is more than just a shelter from the elements. It is a zone of personal intimacy and family security. Often it will be the only relatively secure space of privacy and tranquillity in what (for poor people in particular) is a turbulent and hostile world. Forced removal is a shock for any family, the more so for one that has established itself on a site that has become its familiar habitat. As the United Nations Housing Rights Programme report points out:

"To live in a place, and to have established one's own personal habitat with peace, security and dignity, should be considered neither a luxury, a privilege nor purely the good fortune of those who can afford a decent home. Rather, the requisite imperative of housing for personal security, privacy, health, safety, protection from the elements and many other attributes of a shared humanity, has led the international community to recognise adequate housing as a basic and fundamental human right."[5] [15]

[18] It is not only the dignity of the poor that is assailed when homeless people are driven from pillar to post in a desperate quest for a place where they and their families can rest their heads. Our society as a whole is demeaned when State action intensifies rather than mitigates their marginalisation. The integrity of the rights-based vision of the Constitution is punctured when governmental action augments rather than reduces denial of the claims of the desperately poor to the basic elements

of a decent existence. Hence the need for special judicial control of a process that is both socially stressful and potentially conflictual.

[19] Much of this case accordingly turns on establishing an appropriate constitutional relationship between section 25, dealing with property rights, and section 26, concerned with housing rights. The Constitution recognises that land rights and the right of access to housing and of not being arbitrarily evicted, are closely intertwined. The stronger the right to land, the greater the prospect of a secure home. Thus, the need to strengthen the precarious position of people living in informal settlements is recognised by section 25 in a number of ways. Land reform is facilitated,[6] [16] and the State is required to foster conditions enabling citizens to gain access to land on an equitable basis;[7] [17] persons or communities with legally insecure tenure because of discriminatory laws are entitled to secure tenure or other redress;[8] [18] and persons dispossessed of property by racially discriminatory laws are entitled to restitution or other redress.[9] [19] Furthermore, sections 25 and 26 create a broad overlap between land rights and socio-economic rights, emphasising the duty on the State to seek to satisfy both, as this Court said in *Grootboom*.[10] [20]

[20] There are three salient features of the way the Constitution approaches the interrelationship between land hunger, homelessness and respect for property rights. In the first place, the rights of the dispossessed in relation to land are not generally delineated in unqualified terms as rights intended to be immediately self-enforcing. For the main part they presuppose the adoption of legislative and other measures to strengthen existing rights of tenure, open up access to land and progressively provide adequate housing. Thus, the Constitution is strongly supportive of orderly land reform, but does not purport to effect transfer of title by constitutional fiat.[11] [21] Nor does it sanction arbitrary seizure of land, whether by the State or by landless people.[12] [22] The rights involved in section 26(3) are defensive rather than affirmative. The landowner cannot simply say: this is my land; I can do with it what I want, and then send in the bulldozers or sledgehammers.

[21] A second major feature of this cluster of constitutional provisions is that through section 26(3) they expressly acknowledge that eviction of people living in informal settlements may take place, even if it results in loss of a home.

[22] A third aspect of section 26(3) is the emphasis it places on the need to seek concrete and case-specific solutions to the difficult problems that arise. Absent the historical background outlined above, the statement in the Constitution that the Courts must do what Courts are normally expected to do, namely, take all relevant factors into account, would appear otiose (superfluous), even odd. Its use in section 26(3), however, serves a clear constitutional purpose. It is there precisely to underline how non-prescriptive the provision is intended to be. The way in which the Courts are to manage the process has accordingly been left as wide open as constitutional language could achieve, by design and not by accident, by deliberate purpose and not by omission.

[23] In sum, the Constitution imposes new obligations on the Courts concerning rights relating to property not previously recognised by the common law. It counterposes to the normal ownership rights of possession, use and occupation, a new and equally relevant right not arbitrarily to be deprived of a home. The expectations that ordinarily go with title could clash head-on with the genuine despair of people in dire need of accommodation.[13] [23] The judicial function in these circumstances is not to establish a hierarchical arrangement between the different interests involved, privileging in an abstract and mechanical way the rights of ownership over the right not to be dispossessed of a home, or vice versa. Rather it is to balance out and reconcile the opposed claims in as just a manner as possible taking account of all the interests involved and the specific factors relevant in each particular case.

THE STRUCTURE OF PIE

[24] PIE provides some legislative texture to guide the Courts in determining the approach to eviction now required by section 26(3) of the Constitution. Its preamble makes clear that it was enacted to do so.[14] [24] Its central operative provisions are section 4, which deals with evictions sought by owners or persons in charge of property,[15] [25] and section 6, which is concerned with eviction proceedings brought by organs of state. There is considerable difference in detail between the two provisions. They emphasise that a distinction has to be made on the basis of whether the application for eviction is brought by the owner of property or by the Municipality. This case deals with proceedings brought under section 6 by the Municipality and does not require us to consider whether it would have taken a different form if it had been brought directly by owners themselves under section 4. Despite their differences both sections emphasise the central role Courts have to ensure equity after considering all relevant circumstances.

[25] Section 6, the governing provision in the present matter, reads:

"6. Eviction at instance of organ of State.—

(1) An organ of State may institute proceedings for the eviction of an unlawful occupier from land which falls within its area of jurisdiction, except where the unlawful occupier is a mortgagor and the land in question is sold in a sale of execution pursuant to a mortgage, and the Court may grant such an order if it is just and equitable to do so, after considering all the relevant circumstances, and if—

   (a) the consent of that organ of State is required for the erection of a building or structure on that land or for the occupation of the land, and the unlawful occupier is occupying a building or structure on that land without such consent having been obtained; or

   (b) it is in the public interest to grant such an order.

   (2) For the purposes of this section, "public interest" includes the interest
       of the health and safety of those occupying the land and the public in
       general.
   (3) In deciding whether it is just and equitable to grant an order for evic-
       tion, the Court must have regard to—
       (a) the circumstances under which the unlawful occupier occupied
           the land and erected the building or structure;
       (b) the period the unlawful occupier and his or her family have
           resided on the land in question; and
       (c) the availability to the unlawful occupier of suitable alternative ac-
           commodation or land."

Simply put, the ordinary prerequisites for the Municipality to be in a position to
apply for an eviction order are that the occupation is unlawful and the structures are
either unauthorised, or unhealthy or unsafe.[16] [26] Contrary to the pre-constitutional
position, however, the mere establishment of these facts does not require the Court
to make an eviction order. In terms of section 6, they merely trigger the Court's discretion. If they are proved, the Court then may (not must) grant an eviction order
if it is just and equitable to do so. In making its decision it must take account of all
relevant circumstances, including the manner in which occupation was effected, its
duration and the availability of suitable alternative accommodation or land.

"The Circumstances of the Occupation of the Land"
[26] A distinction could be drawn between occupation with the consent of the
landowner but involving structures that do not meet with by-law requirements, a
health hazard, and occupation in the face of landowner opposition. Different considerations could arise depending on whether the land occupied is public or privately
owned. In the case of public land, the State generally has further land to meet its obligations in terms of section 26 of the Constitution, while in the case of privately
owned land there is normally no alternative land available unless the State takes
steps to acquire some. On the other hand, private land may be derelict, with the
owners having little practical interest in its utilisation, while public land may have
been set-aside for important public purposes, including the provision of housing.
The motivation for settling on the land could be of importance. The degree of
emergency or desperation of people, who have sought a spot on which to erect their
shelters, would always have to be considered. Furthermore, persons occupying land
with at least a plausible belief that they have permission to be there can be looked
at with far greater sympathy than those who deliberately invade land with a view to
disrupting the organised housing programme and placing themselves at the front of
the queue. The public interest requires that the legislative framework and general
principles which govern the process of housing development should not be undermined and frustrated by the unlawful and arbitrary actions of a relatively small
group of people.[17] [27] Thus the well-structured housing policies of a municipality

could not be allowed to be endangered by the unlawful intrusion of people at the expense of those inhabitants who may have had equal claims to be housed on the land earmarked for development by the Applicant. Municipalities represent all the people in their area and should not seek to curry favour with or bend to the demands of individuals or communities, whether rich or poor. They have to organise and administer their affairs in accordance with the broader interests of all the inhabitants.

"The Period the Unlawful Occupier and His or Her Family have been on the Land"
[27] Section 6 does not make the explicit distinction that section 4 does between occupation for less than six months and occupation for longer. Clearly, however, eviction proceedings speedily undertaken would be more readily sustained than those instituted after a long period of occupation without objection. PIE does not envisage any set formula connecting time to stability, such as that which would be necessary for prescription or a statute of limitations. Its concern is with time as an element of fairness. Justice and equity require showing special concern when settled communities or individuals are faced with being uprooted. The longer the unlawful occupiers have been on the land, the more established they are on their sites and in the neighbourhood, the more well settled their homes and the more integrated they are in terms of employment, schooling and enjoyment of social amenities, the greater their claim to the protection of the Courts. A Court will accordingly be far more cautious in evicting well-settled families with strong local ties, than persons who have recently moved on to land and erected their shelters there. And should it decide that eviction is called for in the former case, it will be especially astute to ensure that equitable arrangements are made to diminish its negative impact.

[28] Section 6(3) states that the availability of a suitable alternative place to "The Availability of Suitable Alternative Accommodation or Land" is something to which regard must be had, and is not an inflexible requirement. *There is therefore no unqualified constitutional duty on local authorities to ensure that in no circumstances should a home be destroyed unless alternative accommodation or land is made available. In general terms, however, a Court should be reluctant to grant an eviction against relatively settled occupiers unless it is satisfied that a reasonable alternative is available, even if only as an interim measure pending ultimate access to housing in the formal housing programme.*[18] [28]

[29] The availability of suitable alternative accommodation will vary from municipality to municipality and be affected by the number of people facing eviction in each case. The problem will always be to find something suitable for the unlawful occupiers without prejudicing the claims of lawful occupiers and those in line for formal housing. In this respect it is important that the actual situation of the persons concerned be taken into account. It is not enough to have a programme that works in theory. The Constitution requires that everyone must be treated with care and concern; if the measures though statistically successful, fail to respond to the needs of those most desperate, they may not pass the test.[19] [29] In a society

founded on human dignity, equality and freedom it cannot be presupposed that the greatest good for the many can be achieved at the cost of intolerable hardship for the few, particularly if by a reasonable application of judicial and administrative statecraft such human distress could be avoided. Thus it would not be enough for the municipality merely to show that it has in place a programme that is designed to house the maximum number of homeless people over the shortest period of time in the most cost effective way. The existence of such a programme would go a long way towards establishing a context that would ensure that a proposed eviction would be just and equitable. It falls short, however, from being determinative of whether and under what conditions an actual eviction order should be made in a particular case.

"Considering all the Relevant Circumstances"
[30] There is nothing in section 6 to suggest that the three specifically identified circumstances are intended to be the only ones to which the Court may refer in deciding what is just and equitable. They are peremptory but not exhaustive. It is clear both from the open-ended way in which they are framed and from the width of decision-making involved in the concept of what is just and equitable, that the Court has a very wide mandate and must give due consideration to all circumstances that might be relevant. Thus the particular vulnerability of occupiers referred to in section 4 (the elderly, children, disabled persons and households headed by women) could constitute a relevant circumstance under section 6. Similarly, justice and equity would take account of the extent to which serious negotiations had taken place with equality of voice for all concerned. What is just and equitable could be affected by the reasonableness of offers made in connection with suitable alternative accommodation or land, the time scales proposed relative to the degree of disruption involved, and the willingness of the occupiers to respond to reasonable alternatives put before them.

[31] The combination of circumstances may be extremely intricate, requiring a nuanced appreciation of the specific situation in each case. Thus, though there might be a sad uniformity in the conditions of homelessness and desperation, which lead to unlawful occupations, on the one hand, and the frustration of landowners at being blocked by intruders from enjoyment of their property, on the other, the actual details of the relationships involved are capable of infinite variation.[20] [30] It is not easy to classify the multitude of places and relationships involved. This is precisely why, even though unlawfulness is established, the eviction process is not automatic and why the Courts are called upon to exercise a broad judicial discretion on a case-by-case basis. Each case accordingly has to be decided not on generalities but in the light of its own particular circumstances. Every situation has its own history, its own dynamics, its own intractable elements that have to be lived with (at least for the time being), and its own creative possibilities that have to be explored as far as reasonably possible. The proper application of PIE will therefore depend on the facts of each

case, and each case may present different facts that call for the adoption of different approaches.

"Must have Regard to the Circumstances"

[32] The obligation on the Court is to "have regard to" the circumstances, that is, to give them due weight in making its judgment as to what is just and equitable. The Court cannot fulfil its responsibilities in this respect if it does not have the requisite information at its disposal. It needs to be fully apprised of the circumstances before it can have regard to them. It follows that although it is incumbent on the interested parties to make all relevant information available, technical questions relating to onus of proof should not play an unduly significant role in its enquiry. The Court is not resolving a civil dispute as to who has rights under land law; the existence of unlawfulness is the foundation for the enquiry, not its subject matter. What the Court is called upon to do is to decide whether, bearing in mind the values of the Constitution, in upholding and enforcing land rights it is appropriate to issue an order which has the effect of depriving people of their homes.[21] [31] Of equal concern, it is determining the conditions under which, if it is just and equitable to grant such an order, the eviction should take place.[22] [32] Both the language of the section and the purpose of the statute require the Court to ensure that it is fully informed before undertaking the onerous and delicate task entrusted to it. In securing the necessary information, the Court would therefore be entitled to go beyond the facts established in the papers before it. Indeed when the evidence submitted by the parties leaves important questions of fact obscure, contested or uncertain, the Court might be obliged to procure ways of establishing the true state of affairs, so as to enable it properly to "have regard" to relevant circumstances.

"Just and Equitable"

[33] In *Port Elizabeth Municipality v Peoples Dialogue on Land and Shelter and Others*,[23] [33] a case with some similarities to the present, section 6 was helpfully analyzed by Horn AJ. He pointed out that in matters brought under PIE one is dealing with two diametrically opposed fundamental interests. On the one hand there is the traditional real right inherent in ownership reserving exclusive use and protection of property by the landowner. On the other hand there is the genuine despair of people in dire need of adequate accommodation. It was with this regard that the legislature had by virtue of its provisions of PIE set about implementing a procedure, which envisaged the orderly and controlled removal of informal settlements. It is the duty of the Court in applying the requirements of the Act to balance these opposing interests and bring out a decision that is just and equitable. He went on to say that the use of the term "just and equitable" relates to both interests, that is what is just and equitable not only to the persons who occupied the land illegally but to the landowner as well. He held that the term also implies that a Court, when deciding on a matter of this nature, would be obliged to break away from a purely

legalistic approach and have regard to extraneous factors such as morality, fairness, social values and implications and circumstances which would necessitate bringing out an equitably principled judgment.

[34] Finally Horn AJ went on to emphasise that each case would have to be decided on its own facts. Hopefully once the housing shortage had been overcome incidents of unlawful invasion of property by desperate communities in search of accommodation would disappear. In the interim the Courts would do the best they could and apply criteria that were just and equitable and acceptable to all concerned. What remained essential, he concluded, was that removals be done in a fair and orderly manner and preferably with a specific plan of resettlement in mind.

[35] The approach by Horn AJ has been described both judicially and academically as sensitive and balanced.[24] [34] I agree with that description. The phrase "just and equitable" makes it plain that the criteria to be applied are not purely of the technical kind that flow ordinarily from the provisions of land law. The emphasis on justice and equity underlines the central philosophical and strategic objective of PIE. Rather than envisage the foundational values of the rule of law and the achievement of equality as being distinct from and in tension with each other, PIE treats these values as interactive, complementary and mutually reinforcing. The necessary reconciliation can only be attempted by a close analysis of the actual specifics of each case.

[36] The Court is thus called upon to go beyond its normal functions, and to engage in active judicial management according to equitable principles of an ongoing, stressful and law-governed social process. This has major implications for the manner in which it must deal with the issues before it, how it should approach questions of evidence, the procedures it may adopt, the way in which it exercises its powers and the orders it might make.[25] [35] The Constitution and PIE require that in addition to considering the lawfulness of the occupation the Court must have regard to the interests and circumstances of the occupier and pay due regard to broader considerations of fairness and other constitutional values, so as to produce a just and equitable result.

[37] Thus, PIE expressly requires the Court to infuse elements of grace and compassion into the formal structures of the law. It is called upon to balance competing interests in a principled way and promote the constitutional vision of a caring society based on good neighbourliness and shared concern. The Constitution and PIE confirm that we are not islands unto ourselves. The spirit of *ubuntu*, part of the deep cultural heritage of the majority of the population, suffuses the whole constitutional order.[26] [36] It combines individual rights with a communitarian philosophy.

It is a unifying motif of the Bill of Rights, which is nothing if not a structured, institutionalised and operational declaration in our evolving new society of the need for human interdependence, respect and concern.

[38] The inherited injustices at the macro level will inevitably make it difficult for the Courts to ensure immediate present-day equity at the micro level. The judiciary cannot of itself correct all the systemic unfairness to be found in our society.

Yet it can at least soften and minimise the degree of injustice and inequity, which the eviction of the weaker parties in conditions of inequality of necessity entails. As the authors of the minority judgment in the second abortion case in the German Federal Constitutional Court pointed out, there are some problems based on contradictory values that are so intrinsic to the way our society functions that neither legislation nor the Courts can "solve" them with "correct" answers.[27] [37] When dealing with the dilemmas posed by PIE, the Courts must accordingly do as well as they can with the evidential and procedural resources at their disposal.

MEDIATION

[39] In seeking to resolve the above contradictions, the procedural and substantive aspects of justice and equity cannot always be separated. The managerial role of the Courts may need to find expression in innovative ways. Thus one potentially dignified and effective mode of achieving sustainable reconciliations of the different interests involved is to encourage and require the parties to engage with each other in a proactive and honest endeavour to find mutually acceptable solutions. Wherever possible, respectful face-to-face engagement or mediation through a third party should replace arms-length combat by intransigent opponents.

[40] Compulsory mediation[28] [38] is an increasingly common feature of modern systems. It should be noted, however, that the compulsion lies in participating in the process, not in reaching a settlement. In South Africa, mediation or conciliation are compulsory in many cases before labour disputes are brought before a Court.[29] [39] Mediation in family matters, too, though not compulsory, is increasingly common in many jurisdictions.[30] [40]

[41] Thus, those seeking eviction should be encouraged not to rely on concepts of faceless and anonymous squatters automatically to be expelled as obnoxious social nuisances. Such a stereotypical approach has no place in the society envisaged by the Constitution; justice and equity require that everyone is to be treated as an individual bearer of rights entitled to respect for his or her dignity. At the same time those who find themselves compelled by poverty and landlessness to live in shacks on the land of others, should be discouraged from regarding themselves as helpless victims, lacking the possibilities of personal moral agency. The tenacity and ingenuity they show in making homes out of discarded material, in finding work and sending their children to school, are a tribute to their capacity for survival and adaptation. Justice and equity oblige them to rely on this same resourcefulness in seeking a solution to their plight and to explore all reasonable possibilities of securing suitable alternative accommodation or land.

[42] Not only can mediation reduce the expenses of litigation, it can help avoid the exacerbation of tensions that forensic combat produces. By bringing the parties together, narrowing the areas of dispute between them and facilitating mutual give-and-take, mediators can find ways around sticking-points in a manner that the adversarial judicial process might not be able to do. Money that otherwise might be

spent on unpleasant and polarising litigation can better be used to facilitate an out-come that ends a stand-off, promotes respect for human dignity and underlines the fact that we all live in a shared society.

[43] In South African conditions, where communities have long been divided and placed in hostile camps, mediation has a particularly significant role to play. The process enables parties to relate to each other in pragmatic and sensible ways, building up prospects of respectful good neighbourliness for the future. Nowhere is this more required than in relation to the intensely emotional and historically charged problems with which PIE deals. Given the special nature of the competing interests involved in eviction proceedings launched under section 6 of PIE, absent special circumstances it would not ordinarily be just and equitable to order eviction if proper discussions, and where appropriate, mediation, have not been attempted.

[44] In the light of the above considerations, parties to this appeal were given an opportunity to address argument on the legality and propriety of this Court itself or-dering mediation. The Chief Justice issued further directions on this topic.[31] [41] Neither party, however, indicated unqualified support for mediation. The Munici-pality's response was that while section 7 of PIE[32] [42] placed no obligation on a mu-nicipality to appoint a mediator, there was sufficient indication in PIE and the Constitution for a Court to make such an order as a precursor to granting an eviction order. It accordingly favoured an eviction order, to be suspended while mediation was being tried. The occupiers' answer, on the other hand, was that none of the express powers given to the Court by PIE conferred authority on the Court to order parties to subject themselves to mediation as a precursor to the granting of an eviction order. They contended that if the Municipality had truly wished to go to mediation, it could have done so prior to launching its application; having failed in the SCA, it should not be entitled to a second bite of the cherry, and should stand or fall by its evidence in the application for eviction. Should the application for leave to appeal be refused, however, the occupiers undertook then to participate in any process of mediation suggested by the Municipality, provided that a mediator be ap-pointed by a Member of the Executive of the Eastern Cape provincial government.

[45] In my view, section 7 of PIE is intended to be facilitative rather than ex-haustive. It does not purport, either expressly or by necessary implication, to limit the very wide power entrusted to the Court to ensure that the outcome of eviction proceedings will be just and equitable. As has been pointed out, section 26(3) of the Constitution and PIE, between them, give the Courts the widest possible discretion in eviction proceedings, taking account of all relevant circumstances. One of the relevant circumstances in deciding whether an eviction order would be just and eq-uitable would be whether mediation has been tried.[33] [43] In appropriate circum-stances the Courts should themselves order that mediation be tried.

[46] It appears that from the beginning the parties have been at loggerheads with each other. The Municipality's position has been that it would consider negotiating with the occupiers only once an eviction order has been granted. The occupiers for

their part have acknowledged that they will have to move, but have not accepted the proposal that they move to Walmer, where they claim that conditions are bad and they might be subjected to further eviction. There are only nine households and three single persons to be dealt with. Each family situation has its own particularities, and the possibilities of individualised responses rather than a blanket solution could not be ruled out. The endless war of attrition between the parties has been to no-one's advantage. The Municipality could have explored the potential of the landowners to make a contribution towards a solution.

[47] The question arises whether it is permissible or appropriate for this Court to order mediation when its use or non-use has not been considered either by the Court of first instance or by the SCA. By the time an appeal is heard some of the advantages of mediation are lost. There is no saving on forensic expense, no avoidance of the law's delay, and no minimisation of litigious rancour. Further, the chances of successful mediation are usually at their highest when the outcome of litigation is at its most uncertain. In the present matter neither party supports it unconditionally at this stage. Not without hesitation, I have come to the conclusion that too much water has flowed under the bridge to make it appropriate that mediation be attempted now. The fact that mediation has not been tried will, however, be an important factor in determining whether it is just and equitable for an eviction order to be made. With this consideration in mind, I turn to consider the Municipality's appeal against the decision of the SCA.

Should the Decision of the SCA Be Overturned?

[48] It is necessary now to consider whether the application for leave to appeal should be granted. In considering this question it is important to identify the relevant facts of this case to which the legal principles identified above must be applied. The Municipality launched motion proceedings to seek the eviction of the occupiers. Many of the facts it alleged in its founding affidavits were disputed by the occupiers in response. Accordingly we must accept those facts asserted by the Applicant that remain undenied by the respondent, together with the facts as alleged by the Respondents.[34] [44]

[49] The occupiers have built shacks on privately owned land in the suburb of Lorraine, in Port Elizabeth. It is clear that the shacks were erected without the necessary approval from the Municipality. Accordingly, the requirement of section 6(1)(a) of the Act is met.[35] [45] The occupiers assert that eight of the respondent families have resided on the land for eight years[36] [46] (as at August 2000 when the answering affidavits were signed), three of them for four years[37] [47] and only one family for two years.[38] [48] They aver that most of them moved to the land in Lorraine after having been evicted from land in Glenroy, Port Elizabeth. They also state that they are willing to move again but want to do so only if they are provided with a piece of land upon which to live "without fear of further eviction" until they are provided with housing in terms of the Municipality's housing scheme. In this

short tale, the hard realities of urbanisation and homelessness in South Africa are captured.

[50] The occupiers claim that when they moved onto the land they were given permission to do so by a woman whom they assumed to be the owner. The Municipality, in reply, filed affidavits on behalf of all the owners of the erven concerned indicating that the current occupiers do not have permission to reside on the land. These specific and emphatic denials must be accepted to establish that the occupiers, even if they were once given permission to occupy the land by an owner, no longer have permission to do so. However, the owners do not assert that they require the land for their own personal use at this stage.

[51] It is clear from the Municipality's affidavits that the land is vacant land, upon which some trees and bushes are growing, but that the owners are not using it at present for any productive purpose. The Municipality wishes the occupiers to move because firstly, it has received a petition signed by 1600 members of the public requesting the Municipality to move the occupiers, and secondly because it asserts that the conditions in which the occupiers are occupying the land constitute a health risk because of the absence of toilet facilities. The Municipality indicates that it has no obligation to house these particular families. It states that it has established a "four peg housing programme" to provide site and service facilities to the homeless in its area and that the Applicants can apply to be part of that programme, though it admits it will take some time for them to be provided with appropriate site and service facilities.

[52] The occupiers deny that their occupation of the land creates a health risk. They state that they use pit latrines which are hygienic. They also state that they obtain water on a daily basis from a gentleman at the nearby Riding Club, though the Municipality, in turn denies this allegation. The occupiers also admit that they are willing to register for the "four peg housing scheme" but are concerned about where they should live in the meanwhile.

[53] In determining whether the Municipality is entitled to obtain the eviction of the occupiers, the three criteria mentioned in section 6 of the Act must be considered: the circumstances under which the unlawful occupier occupied the land and erected the structures; the period the occupier has resided on the land, and the availability of suitable alternative land. It is clear from what has been said above that the occupiers moved onto the land with what they considered to be the permission of the owner and that they have been there for a long period of time. Eight children are attending local schools in the area and several of the adults have work nearby.

[54] The Municipality, in its founding affidavit, pointed to two possible sites as suitable alternative land: the first was Walmer, which the occupiers reject as being overcrowded and unsafe; the second is Greenbushes, which the occupiers reject as being too far away for them to go to their work and for their children to school in the Lorraine area. It is quite clear that the Municipality has not entered into any discussions with the Respondents, who are a relatively small group of people (only 68),

to identify their particular circumstances or needs. The occupiers do mention two areas, Seaview and Fairview, as potentially suitable alternative land, but the Municipality does not address these suggestions in their reply. Indeed in their reply the Municipality states bluntly:

"... [the] Applicant is under no duty to make suitable alternative land available for this particular group of people over and above its existing Housing Programme as set out in Applicant's Founding Affidavit and I repeat Applicant's invitation to Respondents to register under the Applicant's Housing Programme in order to be eligible for benefits under the scheme."

The Municipality also states:

"It is respectfully submitted on behalf of the Applicant that what the Respondents have sought to do is unilaterally occupy private land and then, when requested to vacate, the Respondents have alleged that they have nowhere else to go and the Applicant must solve their problem by providing alternative land."

[55] These paragraphs capture the nub of the Municipality's case. It asserts that having established a four peg housing programme, it need do no more to accommodate individually homeless families such as the occupiers than offer them registration in that housing programme which, it admits, may not provide housing for the occupiers for some years. It is not accurate, however, on the facts before us to define the occupiers as "queue jumpers." They are a community who are homeless, who have been evicted once, and who found land to occupy with what they considered to be the permission of the owner where they have been residing for eight years. This is a considerable period of time. The Municipality now seeks to evict them without any discussion with them, or consideration of their request that they be provided with security of tenure on a suitable piece of land pending their accommodation in the housing programme.

[56] In considering whether it is "just and equitable" to make an eviction order in terms of section 6 of the Act, the responsibilities that municipalities, unlike owners, bear in terms of section 26 of the Constitution are relevant. As *Grootboom* (*supra*) indicates,[39] [49] municipalities have a major function to perform with regard to the fulfilment of the rights of all to have access to adequate housing. Municipalities, therefore, have a duty systematically to improve access to housing for all within their area. They must do so on the understanding that there are complex socio-economic problems that lie at the heart of the unlawful occupation of land in the urban areas of our country. They must attend to their duties with insight and a sense of humanity. Their duties extend beyond the development of housing schemes, to treating those within their jurisdiction with respect. Where the need to evict

people arises, some attempts to resolve the problem before seeking a Court order will ordinarily be required.

[57] From the papers it appears that the Municipality in this matter took no action against the occupiers for years and then acted precipitately to secure an eviction. The Municipality took only cursory steps to ascertain the circumstances of the occupiers, and to establish whether they had made any effort to apply for housing. It took no steps to seek to address the problems of the occupiers at all before launching eviction proceedings, despite the fact that the land was not needed by the owners or the Municipality, and despite the fact that the occupiers are a small group of people who have resided on the land for a considerable time.

[58] Much of the argument in this Court turned on whether or not the Municipality had established on the papers that Walmer was an area under its control, so that the suggestion it made that the occupiers could relocate to Walmer established the availability of suitable alternative land within the definition of section 6(3)(c) of the Act. It is not appropriate to determine the question of eviction on the precise legal status of Walmer. The real question in this case is whether the Municipality has considered seriously or at all the request of these occupiers that they be provided with suitable alternative land upon which they can live "without fear of eviction" until provided with housing by the Municipality. The thrust of the SCA judgment makes this clear. The lack of information concerning the status of Walmer highlighted the failure of the Municipality to show that it had responded reasonably to the dire situation of the occupiers. The availability of suitable alternative accommodation is a consideration in determining whether it is just and equitable to evict the occupiers, it is not determinative of that question.

[59] To sum up: in the light of the lengthy period during which the occupiers have lived on the land in question, the fact that there is no evidence that either the Municipality or the owners of the land need to evict the occupiers in order to put the land to some other productive use, the absence of any significant attempts by the Municipality to listen to and consider the problems of this particular group of occupiers, and the fact that this is a relatively small group of people who appear to be genuinely homeless and in need, I am not persuaded that it is just and equitable to order the eviction of the occupiers.

[60] In the circumstances, the application for leave to appeal fails and the Municipality is ordered to pay the costs of the Respondents, including the costs of two counsels.

[61] It remains only to be said that this decision in no way precludes further efforts to find a solution to a situation that is manifestly unsatisfactory to all concerned. In cases like the present it is particularly important that the Municipality not appear to be aligned with one side or the other. It must show that it is equally accountable to the occupiers and to the landowners. Its function is to hold the ring and to use what resources it has in an even-handed way to find the best possible solutions. If it cannot itself directly secure a settlement it should promote a solution through the appointment

of a skilled negotiator acceptable to all sides, with the understanding that the mediation proceedings would be privileged from disclosure. On the basis of this judgment a Court involved in future litigation involving occupiers should be reluctant to accept that it would be just and equitable to order their eviction if it is not satisfied that all reasonable steps had been taken to get an agreed, mediated solution.

THE ORDER

The application for leave to appeal is dismissed with costs, including the costs of two counsels.

CITY OF JOHANNESBURG V. RAND PROPERTIES

City of Johannesburg v. Rand Properties (Pty) Ltd and Others 2006 (2) All SA 240 (W)

The High Court judgment was overturned by the Constitutional Court to the degree that the High Court held that the Municipality had failed to meet its constitutional obligations under section 26 to create and implement a comprehensive housing plan. We include the case because Justice Jajbhay both relies on and develops Justice Sachs's jurisprudential use of *ubuntu* in *Port Elizabeth*. As we will see, Justice Yacoob introduces the concept of meaningful engagement, which can be interpreted as a form of operational *ubuntu*, stronger even than the call for mediaton in Justice Sachs's judgment in *Port Elizabeth*. Thus even though Justice Yacoob does not explicitly use the word *ubuntu*, we include his judgment because it is rooted in Justice Sachs's previous deployment of *ubuntu*.

Case Summary

FACTS

Several applications brought by the City of Johannesburg, for the eviction of a large number of people from the inner city were heard together. The applications were based on the National Building Regulations and Building Standards Act 103 of 1977, as well as on the National Health Act 61 of 2003, and the City's fire by-laws.

The Respondents objected to the applications on various grounds, and among them was that evicting the occupants from the building would render them homeless.

The rights implicated in such an eviction were: the right to housing (section 26 of the Constitution), and the right to human dignity (section 10 of the Constitution).

LEGAL HISTORY

The Witwatersrand Local High Court was the court of first instance for this matter.

LEGAL ISSUES

At issue was whether the Applicant was under an obligation to provide alternative housing to the occupants, or take reasonable steps to ensure that they would have shelter once evicted from the buildings.

DISPENSATION

The court held that rendering the occupants of these buildings homeless adversely affected their right to life, freedom, and security. Moreover, rendering them homeless goes to the heart of their human dignity, as housing forms an indispensable part of ensuring human dignity. The court elucidated that the right to housing as enshrined in the Constitution does not mean that the State is placed under a duty to provide housing on demand. But, the right does place a duty on the State to protect and improve houses and neighborhoods. It was also noted that the present-day South African society is riddled with inequalities that detract from people's ability to live with a semblance of human dignity and fulfill their full potential as human beings. On this reasoning, the court strongly urged the State to favor the poor people in our society, as they are the most vulnerable and need the most assistance in attaining their full potential. Such an approach would be consistent with the Constitution's directive that elements of our common humanity be weaved into the formal structures of the law through an appeal to *ubuntu*.

It was therefore incumbent on the City of Johannesburg to ensure that the more than three hundred people that it sought to evict had housing that was not a threat to their health and livelihoods. In the words of the court, the sole criteria for living in the inner city should not depend on affordability or the size of one's pocket. The values that our Constitution demands is that the positions and voices of the poor are heard as part of the criteria in judging whether eviction is constitutionally acceptable.

Justice Jajbhay

. . .

[25] In the present matter I intend dealing with the fundamental rights of access to adequate housing enshrined in section 26 of the Constitution, enjoyed by the Respondents in matters such as the present. Accordingly, and for the reasons that I have arrived at my conclusion, I do not deem it necessary to deal with any of the other prayers sought in either the Applicant's application or the Respondents' counter-application.

THE APPLICANT'S CONSTITUTIONAL AND STATUTORY OBLIGATIONS

[26] The historical, social and political background highlighted in *Modder East Squatters v Modderklip Boerdery (Pty) Ltd*; *President of the Republic of South Africa v Modderklip Boerdery (Pty) Ltd* as well as in *Port Elizabeth Municipality v Various Occupiers*, coupled with the relevant constitutional and legal provisions indicate that eviction is fundamentally a constitutional matter. The historical, contextual approach to eviction under our new constitutional order has now been accepted unequivocally by the Constitutional Court. In matters such as the present the municipalities' constitutional duty; to promote a safe and healthy environment towards the general public has to be reconciled with the State's constitutional duty towards the poor and

the destitute such as the present Respondents. The Constitution emphasises the need for concrete and case-specific solutions.

[27] In the decision of *Government of the Republic of South Africa v Grootboom*, the Constitutional Court demonstrated a new commitment to finding ways of enforcing the social and economic rights guaranteed in the Constitution. In so doing, we have now moved away from an insistence on the mere rationality of state actions to a standard that requires the State and other relevant stake holders to act reasonably to fulfil their constitutional duties regarding social and economic rights.

[28] In the *Port Elizabeth Municipality* case (*supra*) Sachs J emphasised that:

> "(I)n sum, the Constitution imposes new obligations on the Courts concerning rights relating to property not previously recognised by the common law. It counterposes to the normal ownership rights of possession, use and occupation, a new and equally relevant right not arbitrarily to be deprived of their home. The expectations that ordinarily go with title could clash head-on with the genuine despair of people in dire need of accommodation. The judicial function in these circumstances is not to establish a hierarchical arrangement between the different interests involved, privileging in an abstract and mechanical way the rights of ownership over the right not to be dispossessed of their home, or vice versa. Rather, it is to balance out and reconcile the opposed claims in as just a manner as possible, taking account of all the interests involved and the specific factors relevant in each particular case."

The same may be said about the competing rights and obligations *vis à vis* a municipality and occupiers such as the Respondents in the present matter.

[29] In matters such as the present, the mere establishment by a municipality that occupation is unhealthy or unsafe does not automatically require a Court to make an eviction order. This merely triggers the Court's discretion. The degree of emergency and desperation of the people who have been living for many years in these squalid conditions will always have to be considered. Where occupiers have been occupying the buildings for some time, (such as in the present instance) has to be looked at with far greater sympathy than those who deliberately invade the buildings with a view to disrupting a housing regeneration programme contemplated by a municipality.

[30] Mokgoro J emphasised that section 26 of the Constitution must be seen as making a decisive break from the past. The Constitution emphasises the importance of adequate housing and in particular security of tenure in our new constitutional democracy. The indignity suffered as a result of evictions from homes, forced removals and the relocation to land often wholly inadequate for housing needs has to be replaced with a system in which "the State must strive to provide access to adequate housing for all and, where that exists, refrain from permitting people from being removed unless it can be justified." The learned Justice emphasised in that

case, that the underlying problem, is not about greed, wickedness or carelessness but poverty. The same can be said here:

"What is really a welfare problem gets converted into a property one. People at the lower end of the market are quadruply vulnerable: they lack income and savings to pay for the necessities of life; they have poor prospects of raising loans, since their only asset is a State-subsidised house; the consequences of inability to pay, under the law as its stands, can be drastic because they live on the threshold of being cast back into the ranks of the homeless in informal settlements, with little chance of escape; and they can easily find themselves at the mercy of conscienceless persons ready to abuse the law for purely selfish gain."

[31] Under the previous insensitive and oppressive order, the scope of evictions based on the stronger right to possession was exercised in an inhumane and arbitrary fashion. The state was garbed with the power to remove people from land and property when State security, public health or the public interest demanded and justified such callous action. Powers of this nature existed in different forms.

[32] So for example, *Vena v George Municipality* illustrates a situation where the local authority made use of the provision in the Act that considered occupiers as (unlawful squatters) if the structures they occupied, which were invariably self-built shacks did not comply with building regulations. Informal housing of this nature never complied with the regulations, and thus the local authorities were allowed to evict and remove the occupiers at will.

[33] The Prevention of Illegal Squatting Act obliged landowners to evict "unlawful squatters" from their land. This promoted a political agenda of the apartheid regime by introducing a vague and wide-ranging definition of "unlawful squatting." It also granted draconian powers of eviction and forced removal to state owners, land owners and the police, and ousted the Court's jurisdiction to review these actions.

[34] Thus, the regulation and movement of human beings in the inner city *inter alia* was differentiated on the basis of race. Those affected almost in all instances by the oppressive legislation were African people. This constituted a source of grave assault on the dignity of Black people. "It resulted in the creation of large, well-established and affluent white urban areas co-existing side by side, with crammed pockets of impoverished and insecure black ones."

[35] Sachs J in the *Port Elizabeth Municipality* case explains that:

"PISA, accordingly, gave the universal social phenomenon of urbanisation and intensely racialised South African character. Everywhere the landless poor flocked to urban areas in search of a better life. This population shift was both a consequence of and a threat to the policy of racial segregation. PISA was to prevent and control what was referred to as squatting on public or private land by criminalising it and providing for a simplified eviction process. The powers to enforce politically motivated, legislatively sanctioned and state sponsored eviction and forced removals became a cornerstone of apartheid land law. This marked a major shift, both quantitatively and qualitatively (politically). Evictions could be sought by local government and achieved by use of criminal rather than civil law. It was against this background and to deal with these injustices, that section 26(3) of the Constitution was adopted and new statutory arrangements made."

[36] Whilst it is not necessary for me to deal with the constitutionality of section 12(4)(b) of the NBRA, for the reasons that I have already explained, I must pause to state that this section must be read as if "subject to section 26(3) of the Constitution." In other words the Applicant cannot be allowed to arbitrarily "evacuate" occupiers such as the Respondents without engaging in the due process. This was correctly conceded by Mr Du Plessis SC on behalf of the Applicant. The procedure suggested by Mr Du Plessis SC in respect of notices afforded in terms of the NBRA will have to be tested in the ordinary motion Court. I do not believe that it is necessary for me to pronounce on the validity of the suggested procedure at this point. However I am encouraged by the pursuance of a consultative process.

[37] Section 26(3) of the Constitution prohibits eviction from and demolishing of homes without a Court order. This constitutional principle has been introduced in a range of reform laws that specify the qualifications for allowing evictions and the requirements for carrying them out lawfully.

[38] Sachs J in the *Port Elizabeth Municipality* case emphasised:

"that a third aspect of section 26(3) is the emphasis it places on the need to seek concrete and case specific solutions to the difficult problems that arise. Absent the historical background outlined above, the statement in the Constitution that the Courts must do what Courts are normally expected to do namely, take all relevant factors into account would appear otiose (superfluous) even odd. Its use in section 26(3) however, serves a clear constitutional purpose. It is there precisely to underline how non-prescriptive the provision is intended to be. The way in which the Courts are to manage the process has, accordingly, been left as wide open as constitutional language could achieve, by design and not by accident, by deliberate purpose and not by omission."

Our Constitution imposes an obligation on these Courts in matters such as the present to balance out and reconcile the opposing claims in a just manner, taking account of all the interests involved and the specific factors relevant in each particular case.

. . .

[62] Our Constitution requires a Court in matters such as the present to weave the elements of humanity and compassion within the fabric of the formal structures

of the law. It calls upon us to balance competing interests in a principled way and to promote the constitutional vision of a caring society based on good neighbourliness and shared concern. Our Constitution retains from the past only what is defensible and represents a decisive break from, and a ringing rejection of that part of the past which is disgracefully racist, authoritarian, insular and repressive, and vigorous identification of and commitment to a democratic, universalistic, caring and aspirationally egalitarian ethos. This statement articulates a spirit of *ubuntu,* which is part of the deep cultural heritage of the majority of the population.

[63] In South Africa the culture of *ubuntu* is the capacity to express compassion, justice, reciprocity, dignity, harmony and humanity in the interests of building, maintaining and strengthening the community. *uBuntu* speaks to our inter-connectedness, our common humanity and the responsibility to each that flows from our connection. This in turn must be interpreted to mean that in the establishment of our constitutional values we must not allow urbanisation and the accumulation of wealth and material possessions to rob us of our warmth, hospitality and genuine interests in each other as human beings. *uBuntu* is a culture, which places some emphasis on the commonality and on the interdependence of the members of the community. It recognises a person's status as a human being, entitled to unconditional respect, dignity, value and acceptance from the members of the community of which such a person may be a part. In South Africa, *ubuntu* must become a notion with particular resonance in the building of our constitutional democracy.

[64] The absence of adequate housing for the Respondents and any subsequent eviction will drive them in a vicious circle, to the deprivation of their employment, their livelihood, and therefore their right to dignity, perhaps even their right to life. The right to work is one of the most precious liberties that an individual possesses. An individual has as much right to work as the individual has to live, to be free and to own property. To work means to eat and consequently to live. This constitutes an encompassing view of humanity. The Applicant's suggestion that the Respondents be relocated to an informal settlement flies in the face of the concept that a "person is a person through persons" (*ubuntu*). Recent experience has shown that this alternative is fundamentally skewed. Occupiers of shacks in these informal settlements have not only lost their possessions through floods and fire but also their lives.

WORMALD NO AND OTHERS V. KAMBULE

Wormald NO and Others v. Kambule 2005 (4) All SA 629 (SCA)

Case Summary

FACTS

The Respondent had been in occupation of a certain residential property since 2001, and did not pay rent or hold a lease on the property. She claimed that she had a right to occupy the said property, and that this right derived from a customary marriage that she had concluded with one Baduza (the deceased).

> "The second Appellant, a Close Corporation which had the deceased as its sole member, is the registered owner of the property. The first Appellant represents his co-Appellants in these proceedings, in his capacity as the executor, *nomine officio*, in the massed estate of the deceased and his surviving civil law spouse, the third Appellant, and consequently, the sole member of the second Appellant in terms of section 29 of the Close Corporation Act 69 of 1984."

The Appellants argued that Respondent was in unlawful occupation of the property as it belonged to the Close Corporation, an entity separate from her deceased husband.

The Appellants further argued that the Respondent's right to live on the property derived from her being the deceased's "housekeeper" and that the resulting claim to occupancy terminated on his death. On this basis, the Applicants sought an eviction order against the Respondent.

The Respondent denied that she was a mere housekeeper, and asserted her marriage to the deceased, and that she was now a widow.

Legal History

This case initiated in the Eastern Cape High Court, where the court dismissed an application launched by the Appellants. In this application, the Appellants sought an eviction order against the Respondent from the occupied property. In seeking an eviction order, the Applicants relied on provisions of the Prevention of Illegal Eviction and Unlawful Occupation of Land Act (PIE). The High Court dismissed the application for eviction.

The High Court also refused to grant a requested order declaring invalid a customary marriage that the Respondent had allegedly entered into with the deceased. The Appellants appealed the High Court decision to the Supreme Court of Appeal.

Legal Issues

The Supreme Court of Appeal had thus to determine: whether the Respondent was an unlawful occupier as defined by PIE and should be evicted; and whether the alleged customary union between the deceased and the Respondent was *de jure* a valid marriage.

Dispensation

With respect to the Respondent's claim that she had acquired a right to reside on the property, the court held that the customary law duty of a husband to provide a dwelling for his wife does not amount to a bestowal of *dominium* over the contested land. The Respondent in this case was thus not entitled to the land.

But the court went on to consider whether it would be just and equitable to grant the eviction order. In so doing, the court relied on Justice Sachs's judgment in the *Port Elizabeth Municipality* case. In the latter case, Justice Sachs held that PIE required that elements of grace and compassion be weaved into the formal structures of the law. He asserted further that it is incumbent upon any court to balance competing interests in a principled way and promote the constitutional vision of a caring society based on good neighborliness and shared concern.

The court argued that it had met the constitutional mandate recognized by Port Elizabeth that the values of grace and compassion be weaved into the formal structures of the law. The court examined the Respondent's position in society and found that because she was affluent, it was in accordance with justice and fairness that the eviction order be confirmed.

However, the court did not rule definitively on whether or not her customary marriage was fulfilled. Thus nothing barred her from a further claim that her customary marriage was indeed valid, permitting her to claim from the deceased's estate as a widow.

Justice Combrick concurred with the decision of Justice Maya on the issue of eviction, but argued that a customary marriage is only valid if it is registered.

Acting Justice Maya

. . .

[7] After considering these facts and the relevant law, Chetty J held that the deceased and the Respondent had concluded a customary marriage and complied with all the requirements for the recognition of such a marriage; that the deceased purchased the property acting in his capacity as the second Appellant's sole member and as its ". . . embodiment [and thus bound to it] to provide the Respondent with a home during the subsistence of their customary marriage"; that the customary marriage vested the Respondent, as the deceased's widow, with a personal servitude of *usus* or *habitatio* in respect of the residential property with which her deceased spouse had provided her and that the customary marriage was not rendered invalid by the fact of its non-registration in accordance with the Transkei Marriage Act 21 of 1978. He concluded that the Respondent was not an unlawful occupier as envisaged in section 1 of PIE. It is these findings that the Appellants contest.

[8] It is common cause between the parties that the provisions of PIE are applicable. Section 4 thereof governs eviction proceedings brought by "the owner or person in charge" of the land in issue and contains both procedural and substantive provisions. Subsections (2), (3), (4) and (5) set out the procedural requirements which, it is common cause, the Appellants duly complied with.

[9] Subsections (6), (7) and (8) contain the substantive provisions and read as follows:

"(6) If an unlawful occupier has occupied the land in question for less than six months at the time when the proceedings are initiated, a Court may grant an order for eviction if it is of the opinion that it is just and equitable to do so, after considering all the relevant circumstances, including the rights and needs of the elderly, children, disabled persons and households headed by women.

(7) If an unlawful occupier has occupied the land for more than six months at the time when the proceedings are initiated, a Court may grant an order for eviction if it is of the opinion that it is just and equitable to do so, after considering all the relevant circumstances, including, except where the land is sold in a sale of execution pursuant to a mortgage, whether land has been made available or can reasonably be made available by a municipality or other organ of state or another land owner for the relocation of the unlawful occupier, and including the rights and needs of the elderly, children, disabled persons and households headed by women.

(8) If the Court is satisfied that all the requirements of this section have been complied with and that no valid defence has been raised by the unlawful occupier, it must grant an order for the eviction of the unlawful occupier, and determine—

(a) a just and equitable date on which the unlawful occupier must vacate the land under the circumstances; and

(b) the date on which an eviction order may be carried out if the unlawful occupier has not vacated the land on the date contemplated in paragraph (a)."

[10] An "unlawful occupier" is defined in section 1 of PIE as follows:

"a person who occupies land without the express or tacit consent of the owner or person in charge, or without any other right in law to occupy such land, excluding a person who is an occupier in terms of the Extension of Security of Tenure Act, 1997, and excluding a person whose informal right to land, but for the provisions of this Act, would be protected by the provisions of the Interim Protection of Informal Land Rights Act, 1996 (Act 31 of 1996)."

[11] An owner is in law entitled to possession of his or her property and to an ejectment order against a person who unlawfully occupies the property except if that right is limited by the Constitution, another statute, a contract or on some or other legal basis. *Brisley v Drotsky* 2002 (4) SA 1 (SCA). In terms of section 26(3) of the Constitution, from which PIE partly derives, (*Cape Killarney Property Investments (Pty) Ltd v Mahamba and Others* 2001 (4) SA 1222 (SCA) at 1229E), "no one may be evicted from their home without an order of Court made after consideration of all the relevant circumstances." PIE therefore requires a party seeking to evict another from land to prove not only that he or she owns such land and that the

other party occupies it unlawfully, but also that he or she has complied with the procedural provisions and that on a consideration of all the relevant circumstances [and, according to the *Brisley* case (*supra*) to qualify as relevant the circumstances must be legally relevant], an eviction order is "just and equitable."

[12] As previously indicated, the essential basis for the Respondent's opposition to the eviction proceedings is the alleged customary marriage and the deceased's alleged intention to bind the second Appellant to provide her with lifelong use of the property and that, furthermore, it would not be just and equitable to evict her.

[13] Assuming but without deciding whether in fact that there was such a marriage in the instant case, it must be considered that whilst it is so that in customary law a husband and, upon his death, his heir, has a duty to maintain his wife or widow, as the case may be, and provide her with residential and agricultural land, she does not, at any stage, acquire real rights in such land. The *dominium* vests in the husband's or his heir's estate. TW Bennett *Customary Law in South Africa* (2004) at 347; *Xulu v Xulu* 1938 NAC 46 (N&T). The wife does not, therefore, have a right to demand to occupy any land of her choice, even to the detriment of the estate, as the Respondent seeks to do in the present matter.

[14] Furthermore, customary law, significantly a legal system to which the concept of a mortgage bond is alien, makes no provision for a situation such as the present, where a "widow" is laying claim to property belonging to a third party which is also bonded. It would clearly be untenable in law to extend the right of a customary law wife or widow to maintenance to confer real rights in respect of such property, particularly against the wishes of the bondholder. It is also significant that there is not the slightest indication in the papers that the second Appellant was established for the purpose of providing support to the Respondent. All that its founding statement reflects is that it was formed with the objective of "purchasing and investing in immovable property." Apart from the Respondent's bare assertion that the deceased bought the property for her (which is difficult to reconcile with the deceased's omission to either register the property in her name or to grant her membership in the second Appellant or even to provide for her in his will), there are no allegations of an intention to donate the property to her or grant her lifelong use thereof or transfer any rights whatsoever in relation to the property to her. In the absence of such evidence the Court *a quo* erred, in my view, in finding that the deceased "bound [the second Appellant] to provide the Respondent with a home during the subsistence of their customary marriage" and that the second Appellant consequently granted her a right of *usus* or *habitatio* to endure for her lifetime.

[15] It must be borne in mind that the effect of PIE is not to expropriate the landowner and that it cannot be used to expropriate someone indirectly. The landowner retains the protection against arbitrary deprivation of property under section 25 of the Bill of Rights. PIE serves merely to delay or suspend the exercise of the landowner's full proprietary rights until a determination has been made whether it is just and equitable to evict the unlawful occupier and under what con-

ditions. *Ndlovu v Ngcobo; Bekker and Another v Jika* 2003 (1) SA 113 (SCA) paragraph 17. In the light of the aforegoing remarks, the Court *a quo* erred in finding that a right to occupy the property accrued as a result of the alleged customary marriage. The Respondent's occupation of the property has no legal basis and is, thus, unlawful.

[16] As regards the declaratory order that was sought by the Appellants concerning the validity of the customary marriage, it is well established that a Court has discretion to grant or to withhold declaratory relief and that it will not deal with abstract, hypothetical or academic questions in proceedings for declaratory relief. The declaratory order that was sought is superfluous to the Appellant's claim for eviction and no proper reason has been advanced for us to consider granting it.

[17] It now remains to consider whether it would be just and equitable to grant an eviction order. Sachs J, dealing with the concept "just and equitable" in the context of PIE in *Port Elizabeth Municipality v Various Occupiers* 2005 (1) SA 217 (CC), referred with approval to the comments of Horn AJ in *Port Elizabeth Municipality v Peoples Dialogue on Land and Shelter and Others* 2000 (2) SA 1074 (SE) stating in paragraph 33:

". . . [I]n matters brought under PIE; one is dealing with two diametrically opposed fundamental interests. On the one hand, there is the traditional real right inherent in ownership, reserving exclusive use and protection of property by the landowner. On the other hand, there is the genuine despair of people in dire need of adequate accommodation. . . . It is the duty of the Court, in applying the requirements of the Act, to balance these opposing interests and bring out a decision that is just and equitable. . . . The use of the term "just and equitable" relates to both interests, that is, what is just and equitable not only to persons who occupied the land illegally but to the landowner as well."

The learned Judge continued at paragraphs 36 and 37:

"[36] The Court is thus called upon to go beyond its normal functions and to engage in active judicial management according to equitable principles of an ongoing, stressful and law-governed social process. This has major implications for the manner in which it must deal with the issues before it, how it should approach questions of evidence, the procedures it may adopt, the way in which it exercises its powers and the orders it might make. The Constitution and PIE require that, in addition to considering the lawfulness of the occupation, the Court must have regard to the interests and circumstances of the occupier and pay due regard to broader considerations of fairness and other constitutional values, so as to produce a just and equitable result.

[37] Thus, PIE expressly requires the Court to infuse elements of grace and compassion into the formal structures of the law. It is called upon to balance

competing interests in a principled way and to promote the constitutional vision of a caring society based on good neighbourliness and shared concern. The Constitution and PIE confirm that we are not islands unto ourselves. The spirit of *ubuntu,* part of a deep cultural heritage of the majority of the population, suffuses the whole constitutional order. It combines individual rights with a communitarian philosophy. It is a unifying motif of the Bill of Rights, which is nothing if not a structured, institutionalised and operational declaration in our evolving new society of the need for human interdependence, respect and concern."

See also *Land en Landbouontwikkelingsbank van Suid-Afrika v Conradie* 2005 (4) SA 506 (SCA) at 513C.

[18] The nature of the discretion, which a Court employs in this exercise, is described in the *Bekker* case *(supra)* where Harms JA held at paragraph 18:

"The Court, in determining whether or not to grant an order or in determining the date on which the property has to be vacated (s 4(8)), has to exercise a discretion based upon what is just and equitable. The discretion is one in the wide and not narrow sense (cf *Media Workers Association of South Africa and Others v Press Corporation of South Africa Ltd ("Perskor")* 1992 (4) SA 791 (A) at 800, *Knox D'Arcy Ltd and Others v Jamieson and others* 1996 (4) SA 348 (A) at 360G–362G). [*Port Elizabeth Municipality v Various Occupiers (supra)* at paragraph 31]. A Court of first instance, consequently, does not have a free hand to do whatever it wishes to do and a Court of appeal is not hamstrung by the traditional grounds of whether the Court exercised its discretion capriciously or upon a wrong principle, or that it did not bring its unbiased judgment to bear on the question, or that it acted without substantial reasons."

[19] Apart from relying on the alleged customary marriage, the only averment made by the Respondent to counter the eviction is that she is a 59 year-old single woman. The Appellants' allegation that she has no dependants was not placed in dispute. No suggestion was made that she is indigent. The contrary may, in fact, be inferred from her demand for "suitable and reasonable alternative accommodation having regard to her station in life." As indicated above, the Appellants tendered, even before the eviction proceedings were launched, to provide her with a two bedroomed flat, in a local hotel owned by the estate. This offer was rejected on the basis that the flat was in a dilapidated condition. A similar offer of a "renovated" flat was repeated during the hearing in this Court. It was also rejected, out of hand. Whilst the value and financial status of the estate (and the second Appellant) and whether it can continue with the bond repayments is unknown, the Respondent, except for a vague, unsubstantiated contention that the deceased was a wealthy man, bearing

in mind that the entire purchase price of the property was financed by a bank, did not deny the Appellants' allegations that the debt exceeds the current market value of the property and that such repayments are prejudicing the estate. Her concession that she cannot occupy the property indefinitely seems to support these allegations.

[20] It is clear that she is not in dire need of accommodation and does not belong to the poor and vulnerable class of persons whose protection was obviously foremost in the Legislature's mind when it enacted PIE. To my mind, her situation is essentially no different from that of the "affluent tenant" occupying luxurious premises, who is holding over, discussed in the *Bekker* case (*supra*) (paragraph 17), in respect of whom the Court held that the "relevant circumstances" prescribed in section 4(7) of PIE do not arise "save that the applicant is the owner, that the lease has come to an end and that the tenant is holding over."

[21] For all the above reasons, it seems to me that it would be just and equitable to grant the eviction order. Having said that, it must be emphasised that if the Respondent were able to establish that she was indeed married to the deceased by customary law, that fact would be a valid basis for a maintenance claim against the estate. In that case, even if the estate, through the executor, has evinced a negative attitude towards her intended maintenance claim, nothing precludes her from pursuing this option in an appropriate forum. It seems proper, in all the circumstances, to allow her to remain on the property for a reasonable period whilst she pursues such a claim, should she so wish. It appears to me, due regard being had to the estate's tender to provide her with refurbished accommodation (for life if it was found that she was married to the deceased, or for six months to a year if it was found there was no marriage) and the expense that it would incur towards that end, that the estate would not be unduly prejudiced by such an order.

[22] As counsel correctly submitted, it seems fair in all the circumstances of the case that the estate should bear the costs of the proceedings. I am further satisfied, and counsel did not contend otherwise, that the employment of two counsel was warranted.

THE *KHOSA* AND *MAHLAULE* CASES

Khosa and Others v. Minister of Social Development and Others; Mahlaule and Another v. Minister of Social Development and Others 2004 (6) BCLR 569 (CC)

Case Summary
We include the *Khosa* case in this text because even though Justice Mokgoro does not explicitly use the word *ubuntu,* her reasoning in the judgment reflects the value of *ubuntu* in her insistence that permanent residents are members of our community—to deny them their humanity would undermine the *ubuntu* of the entire community.

FACTS

The Constitutional Court consolidated two separate cases relating to constitutional challenges involving the Social Assistance Act 59 of 1992. The provisions of the Social Assistance Act reserved social grants for South African citizens only. Both Applicants in this case were South African permanent residents who were destitute and would have qualified for the social grant, but for the fact that they were not South African citizens.

LEGAL HISTORY

This case originated in the Witwatersrand High Court. In the *Khosa* matter, the High Court declared section 4(b)(ii) of the Social Assistance Act to be invalid, and in the *Mahlaule* matter, the High Court declared subsection 3(c) of the Social Assistance Act to be invalid, to the degree that both provisions were inconsistent with the Constitution. The effect of these orders was to oblige the State to provide social assistance under the Act to all "residents" who qualified for such assistance, irrespective of their citizenship. The High Court argued that without a narrow construction of permanent residence, the State was under an obligation to provide assistance to both citizens and permanent residents.

The case was then sent to the Constitutional Court for confirmation of constitutional invalidity of the said provisions.

LEGAL ISSUES

The legal issue was whether the High Court was justified in declaring the provisions of the Social Assistance Act as unconstitutional, to the degree that these provisos did not include permanent residents?

DISPENSATION

Writing for the majority of the court, Justice Mokgoro noted that an exemption of noncitizens receiving social grants was inconsistent with section 27 of the Constitution, which accords everyone the right of access to health care, water, shelter, and social security. She noted further that the exclusion of noncitizens receiving social grants violated sections 9 and 10 of the Constitution.

Justice Mokgoro strongly emphasized that the wording of section 27 of the Constitution grants socioeconomic rights to *everyone*. To the degree that the State excluded permanent residents from benefiting under the Act whilst the Constitution bestowed the right on everyone, the conduct of the State (under the Act) was inconsistent with the Constitution. Such inconsistency could not be saved by section 36 of the Constitution—the limitations clause. Justice Mokgoro distinguished between permanent residents who were required to meet the obligations based on their long-standing participation in the community and thus were distinguished from more temporary residents who had no such obligations.

Ultimately, the court ordered that the words *permanent resident* be read into the relevant sections of the Act after the word *citizen.*

Justice Mokgoro

. . .

MAIN CONTENTIONS OF THE PARTIES

[38] The Applicants contended that the exclusion of all non-citizens from the scheme is inconsistent with the State's obligations under section 27(1)(c) of the Constitution to provide access to social security to "everyone." The relevant parts of section 27 of the Constitution provide:

"Health care, food, water and social security—

  (1) Everyone has the right to have access to—

  . . .

    (c) social security, including, if they are unable to support themselves and their dependants, appropriate social assistance.

  (2) The State must take reasonable legislative and other measures, within its available resources, to achieve the progressive realisation of each of these rights."

[39] They also argued that the exclusion limited their right to equality and was unfair under section 9 of the Constitution and that the limitation was unjustifiable under section 36 of the Constitution. They further contended that their right to life under section 11 of the Constitution and their right to dignity under section 10 were infringed without justification. In so far as the grants in favour of children were concerned, they contended that the exclusion also infringed the rights that children have under section 28 of the Constitution. The Respondents essentially advanced reasons that motivated and, so it was submitted, justified the decision to exclude all non-citizens, including permanent residents. These arguments will be dealt with in detail later in this judgment.

THE APPROACH TO CLAIMS FOR SOCIO-ECONOMIC RIGHTS

[40] The socio-economic rights in our Constitution are closely related to the founding values of human dignity, equality and freedom.[40] [45] Yacoob J observed in *Government of the Republic of South Africa and Others v Grootboom and Others* that the proposition that rights are interrelated and are all equally important, has immense human and practical significance in a society founded on these values.[41] [46]

[41] In this case we are concerned with these intersecting rights, which reinforce one another at the point of intersection. The rights to life and dignity, which are

intertwined in our Constitution,[42] [47] are implicated in the claims made by the Applicants. This Court in *Dawood* said:

> "Human dignity . . . informs constitutional adjudication and interpretation at a range of levels. It is a value that informs the interpretation of many, possibly all, other rights . . . Section 10, however, makes it plain that dignity is not only a *value* fundamental to our Constitution it is a justiciable and enforceable *right* that must be respected and protected. In many cases, however, where the value of human dignity is offended, the primary constitutional breach occasioned may be of a more specific right such as the right to bodily integrity, the right to equality or the right not to be subjected to slavery, servitude or forced labour."[43] [48]

[42] Equality is also a foundational value of the Constitution and informs constitutional adjudication in the same way as life and dignity do. Equality in respect of access to socio-economic rights is implicit in the reference to "everyone" being entitled to have access to such rights in section 27. Those who are unable to survive without social assistance are equally desperate and equally in need of such assistance.

[43] This Court has dealt with socio-economic rights on four previous occasions.[44] [49] What is clear from these cases is that section 27(1) and section 27(2) cannot be viewed as separate or discrete rights creating entitlements and obligations independently of one another. Section 27(2) exists as an internal limitation on the content of section 27(1) and the ambit of the section 27(1) right can therefore not be determined without reference to the reasonableness of the measures adopted to fulfil the obligation towards those entitled to the right in section 27(1).[45] [50]

[44] When the rights to life, dignity and equality are implicated in cases dealing with socio-economic rights, they have to be taken into account along with the availability of human and financial resources in determining whether the State has complied with the constitutional standard of reasonableness. This is, however, not a closed list and all relevant factors have to be taken into account in this exercise. What is relevant may vary from case to case depending on the particular facts and circumstances.

What makes this case different to other cases that have previously been considered by this Court is that, in addition to the rights to life and dignity, the social-security scheme put in place by the State to meet its obligations under section 27 of the Constitution raises the question of the prohibition of unfair discrimination.

[45] It is also important to realise that even where the State may be able to justify not paying benefits to everyone who is entitled to those benefits under section 27 on the grounds that to do so would be unaffordable, the criteria upon which they choose to limit the payment of those benefits (in this case citizenship) must be consistent with the Bill of Rights as a whole. Thus if the means chosen by the Legislature to give effect to the State's positive obligation under section 27 unreasonably limits other constitutional rights, that too must be taken into account.

The Ambit of the Right of Access to Social Security in Terms of section 27(1)(c)

[46] The socio-economic rights in sections 26[46] [51] and 27 of the Constitution are conferred on "everyone" by subsection (1) in each of those sections. In contrast, the Sate's obligations in respect of access to land apply only to citizens.[47] [52] Whether the right in section 27 is confined to citizens only or extends to a broader class of persons therefore depends on the interpretation of the word "everyone" in that section. The Applicants relied on section 25 of the Constitution, as well as various other rights in the Bill of Rights,[48] [53] to argue that "everyone" in section 27 included non-citizens and therefore also (for the purposes of this case) permanent residents.

[47] This Court has adopted a purposive approach to the interpretation of rights.[49] [54] Given that the Constitution expressly provides that the Bill of Rights enshrines the rights of "all people in our country,"[50] [55] and in the absence of any indication that the section 27(1) right is to be re-stricted to citizens as in other provisions in the Bill of Rights, the word "everyone" in this section cannot be construed as referring only to "citizens."[51] [56]

The Reasonableness of the Legislative Scheme

[48] A Court considering the reasonableness of legislative or other measures taken by the Sate will not enquire into whether other more desirable or favourable measures could have been adopted, or whether public resources could have been better spent.[52] [57] A wide range of possible measures could be adopted by the Sate to meet its obligations and many of these may meet the requirement of reasonableness. Once it is shown that the measures do so, this requirement would be met.

[49] In dealing with the issue of reasonableness, context is all important. We are concerned here with the right to social security and the exclusion from the scheme of permanent residents who, but for their lack of citizenship, would qualify for the benefits provided under the scheme. In considering whether that exclusion is reasonable, it is relevant to have regard to the purpose served by social security, the impact of the exclusion on permanent residents and the relevance of the citizenship requirement to that purpose. It is also necessary to have regard to the impact that this has on other intersecting rights. In the present case, where the right to social assistance is conferred by the Constitution on "everyone" and permanent residents are denied access to this right, the equality rights entrenched in section 9 are directly implicated.

The Purpose of Providing Access to Social Security to Those in Need

[50] The Sate did not suggest that the exclusion of permanent residents was a temporary measure, nor did it argue that the exclusion was an incident of attempts by it progressively to realise everyone's right of access to social security. The Sate's case is rather that non-citizens have no legitimate claim of access to social security and it

therefore excluded them from the scheme that it put in place. It is that proposition that has to be tested against the constitutional standard of reasonableness demanded by section 27(2).

[51] Those who seek assistance must meet stringent means tests prescribed by regulations made under the Act. Grants are made to those in need, including vulnerable persons. According to Mr Madonsela, the Director-General of the Department of Social Development, the legislation is part of the government's strategy to combat poverty. He says also that the legislation is directed at realising the relevant objectives of the Constitution and the Reconstruction and Development Programme, and giving effect to South Africa's international obligations.

[52] The right of access to social security, including social assistance, for those unable to support themselves and their dependants is entrenched because as a society we value human beings and want to ensure that people are afforded their basic needs. A society must seek to ensure that the basic necessities of life are accessible to all if it is to be a society in which human dignity, freedom and equality are foundational.[53] [58]

THE REASONABLENESS OF CITIZENSHIP AS A CRITERION OF DIFFERENTIATION

[53] It is necessary to differentiate between people and groups of people in society by classification in order for the State to allocate rights, duties, immunities, privileges, benefits or even disadvantages and to provide efficient and effective delivery of social services. However, those classifications must satisfy the constitutional requirement of "reasonableness" in section 27(2). In this case, the State has chosen to differentiate between citizens and non-citizens. That differentiation, if it is to pass constitutional muster, must not be arbitrary or irrational nor must it manifest a naked preference. There must be a rational connection between that differentiating law and the legitimate government purpose it is designed to achieve. A differentiating law or action, which does not meet these standards, will be in violation of section 9(1) and section 27(2) of the Constitution.

[54] The Respondents averred that citizenship is a requirement for social benefits in "almost all developed countries."[54] [59] That may be so in respect of certain benefits. But unlike ours, those countries do not have constitutions that entitle "everyone" to have access to social security, nor are their immigration and welfare laws necessarily the same as ours.

[55] The Respondents contended that immigrants, before entering the country, are required to show self-sufficiency in order to qualify for permanent residence status. They are only restricted from accessing the right in question for a temporary period of five years, after which they can apply for citizenship by reason of naturalisation. On receipt of citizenship, they would have a right to social security. In their submission, any infringement of the right was therefore only of a temporary nature. They did not,

however, offer any justification for denying the right to permanent residents during this five-year period.

[56] In essence, the Constitution properly interpreted provides that a permanent resident need not be a citizen in order to qualify for access to social security. Justifying the restriction of that right of access by the fact that the South African Citizenship Act 88 of 1995 allows them to apply under exceptional circumstances for naturalisation,[55] [60] and thereby obtain access to the grants in question is not reasonable. Besides, it is doubtful whether the need for a social grant will be viewed as an "exceptional circumstance" sufficient to waive the normal requirements for naturalisation considering that the Immigration Act 13 of 2002 requires, in terms of sections 25 to 28, that a person applying for permanent residence in South Africa either be self-sufficient or have a supporting sponsor. The decision to grant naturalisation under the South African Citizenship Act may well be subject to administrative discretion and would therefore be beyond the control of the Applicants.[56] [61]

[57] The Respondents argued that the State has an obligation toward its own citizens first, and that preserving welfare grants for citizens only creates an incentive for permanent residents to naturalise. This argument, commonly found in American jurisprudence, is based on the social contract assumption that non-citizens are not entitled to the full benefits available to citizens.[57] [62] The argument, however, does not accord with the stated legislative intention in the Immigration Act, which provides that:

> "The holder of a permanent residence permit has all the rights, privileges, duties and obligations of a citizen save for those rights, privileges, duties and obligations which a law or the Constitution explicitly ascribes to citizenship."[58] [63]

FINANCIAL CONSIDERATIONS

[58] I accept that the concern that non-citizens may become a financial burden on the country is a legitimate one and I accept that there are compelling reasons why social benefits should not be made available to all who are in South Africa irrespective of their immigration status. The exclusion of all non-citizens who are destitute, however, irrespective of their immigration status, fails to distinguish between those who have become part of our society and have made their homes in South Africa, and those who have not. It also fails to distinguish between those who are being supported by sponsors who arranged their immigration and those who acquired permanent residence status without having sponsors to whom they could turn in case of need.

[59] It may be reasonable to exclude from the legislative scheme workers who are citizens of other countries, visitors and illegal residents, who have only a tenuous link with this country. The position of permanent residents is, however, quite different to

that of temporary or illegal residents. They reside legally in the country and may have done so for a considerable length of time. Like citizens, they have made South Africa their home. While citizens may leave the country indefinitely without forfeiting their citizenship, permanent residents are compelled to return to the country (except in certain circumstances) at least once every three years.[59] [64] While they do not have the rights tied to citizenship, such as political rights and the right to a South African passport, they are, for all other purposes mentioned above, in much the same position as citizens. Once admitted as permanent residents they can enter and leave the country.[60] [65] Their homes and no doubt in most cases their families too, are in South Africa. Some will have children born in South Africa. They have the right to work in South Africa,[61] [66] and even owe a duty of allegiance to the State.[62] [67] For these reasons, I exclude temporary residents and it would have been appropriate for the High Court to do so.

[60] The Respondents also sought to deny the benefit to permanent residents on the grounds that this would impose an impermissibly high financial burden on the State. The Respondents relied for this point on an affidavit deposed to by Mr Kruger, the Chief Director of Social Services in the National Treasury. According to him, the development of a system of social grants has been a key pillar of the government's strategy to fight poverty and promote human development. This has led to a substantial and rapid increase in expenditure on social grants. In the last three years alone the expenditure, excluding costs of administration, has increased from R16.1 billion to R26.2 billion. It is contemplated that over the next three years grants will increase from R26.2 billion to R44.6 billion. In addition, provision has to be made for expenditure on other socio-economic programmes. Mr Kruger says that if provision has to be made for the expenditure necessary to give effect to the High Court order, the costs will be large and will result in shortfalls in provincial budgets particularly in the poorer provinces.

[61] Mr Kruger indicates that there is a paucity of information concerning the number of persons who might qualify for grants if they are extended to permanent residents. He refers to various classes of persons who have been exempted from the normal immigration requirements and have been accorded permanent residence status. They include Mozambican refugees and various persons from members of the Southern African Development Community and other African countries. He estimates that there are at least 260 000 such persons currently in South Africa. Most of these permanent residents have been living in South Africa for a considerable period of time. In the case of the Applicants, they have all been in South Africa since 1993 or longer. The Respondents were unable, however, to furnish this Court with information relating to the numbers who hold permanent resident status, or who would qualify for social assistance if the citizenship barrier were to be removed.

[62] There is thus no clear evidence to show what the additional cost of providing social grants to aged and disabled permanent residents would be. Taking into account certain assumptions relating to the composition of the groups and numbers

of dependants, Mr Kruger concludes that the additional annual cost of including permanent residents in grants in terms of sections 3, 4 and 4B could range between R243 million and R672 million. The possible range demonstrates the speculative nature of the calculations, but even if they are taken as providing the best guide of what the cost may be, they do not support the contention that there will be a huge cost in making provision for permanent residents. Approximately one fifth of the projected expenditure is in respect of child grants and the unconstitutionality of the citizenship requirement in that section of the Act has already been conceded by the Respondents. The remainder reflects an increase of less than 2% on the present cost of social grants (currently R26.2 billion) even on the higher estimate. Bearing in mind that it is anticipated that the expenditure on grants will, in any event, increase by a further R18.4 billion over the next three years without making provision for permanent residents, the cost of including permanent residents in the system will be only a small proportion of the total cost.

Self-sufficiency

[63] Another reason given for excluding permanent residents from the scheme was the promotion of the immigration policy of the State, which seeks to exclude persons who may become a burden on the State and thereby to encourage self-sufficiency among foreign nationals.

[64] Limiting the cost of social welfare is a legitimate government concern. If it is considered necessary to control applications for permanent residence by excluding those who may become a burden on the State, that too is permissible, but it must be done in accordance with the Constitution and its values. The State can protect itself against persons becoming financial burdens by thorough, careful consideration in the admission of immigrants, or by taking adequate security from those admitted, or by demanding such security or guarantees from their sponsors at the time the immigrants are allowed into the country or are permitted to stay as permanent residents. It would not necessarily be unreasonable in such circumstances to require a permanent resident to look in the first instance to his or her sponsor for support, and to permit a claim on the security system only if, notwithstanding the security or guarantee, that fails.

[65] At the time the immigrant applies for admission to take up permanent residence the State has a choice. If it chooses to allow immigrants to make their homes here it is because it sees some advantage to the State in doing so. Through careful immigration policies it can ensure that those admitted for the purpose of becoming permanent residents are persons who will profit, and not be a burden to, the State. If a mistake is made in this regard, and the permanent resident becomes a burden, that may be a cost we have to pay for the constitutional commitment to developing a caring society, and granting access to socio-economic rights to all who make their homes here. Immigration can be controlled in ways other than allowing immigrants to make their permanent homes here, and then abandoning them to destitution if

they fall upon hard times. The category of permanent residents who are before us are children and the aged, all of whom are destitute and in need of social assistance. They are unlikely to earn a living for themselves. While the self-sufficiency argument may hold in the case of immigrants who are viable in the job market and who are still in the process of applying for permanent resident status, the argument is seemingly not valid in the case of children and the aged who are already settled permanent residents and part of South African society.

[66] Respondents relied in their argument on the decision of a United States appellate Court in *City of Chicago v Shalala*.[63] [68] In that case it was held that the relevant legislative provisions, which disqualified non-citizens, who were legal permanent residents from participation in the scheme, were not inconsistent with the equal protection clause of the US Constitution.[64] [69] In reaching its decision the Court applied a rational basis standard of review, holding that there was a rational connection between the federal government's immigration policy and its welfare policy of encouraging the self-sufficiency of immigrants.

[67] The test for rationality is a relatively low one. As long as the government purpose is legitimate and the connection between the law and the government purpose is rational and not arbitrary, the test will have been met.[65] [70] Despite the failure of many of the Respondents' arguments with respect to the purpose of the exclusion of permanent residents from the social-assistance scheme, I am prepared to assume that there is a rational connection between the citizenship provisions of the Act and the immigration policy it is said to support. But that is not the test for determining constitutionality under our Constitution. Section 27(2) of the Constitution sets the standard of reasonableness, which is a higher standard than rationality.[66] [71]

Is There Unfair Discrimination?

[68] The fact that the differentiation between citizens and non-citizens may have a rational basis does not mean that it is not an unfairly discriminatory criterion to use in the allocation of benefits. If the differentiation is based on a ground listed in section 9(3)[67] [72] of the Constitution a rebuttable presumption that the discrimination is unfair is created by section 9(5).[68] [73] However, where, as in this case, the ground for the differentiation is not itself listed but is analogous to such listed grounds, there is no presumption in favour of unfairness and the unfairness first has to be established.

[69] In *President of the Republic of South Africa and Another v Hugo*,[69] [74] Goldstone J stated that:

> "At the heart of the prohibition of unfair discrimination lies a recognition
> that the purpose of our new constitutional and democratic order is the estab-
> lishment of a society in which all human beings will be accorded equal dig-
> nity and respect regardless of their membership of particular groups. The
> achievement of such a society in the context of our deeply inegalitarian past

will not be easy, but that that is the goal of the Constitution should not be forgotten or overlooked.

. . .

To determine whether that impact was unfair it is necessary to look not only at the group who has been disadvantaged but at the nature of the power in terms of which the discrimination was effected and, also at the nature of the interests which have been affected by the discrimination."

[70] Citizenship is not a ground of differentiation that is specified in section 9(3) of the Constitution. In *Hoffmann v South African Airways* this Court held that "at the heart of the prohibition of unfair discrimination is the recognition that under our Constitution all human beings, regardless of their position in society, must be accorded equal dignity."[70] [75] To be considered an analogous ground of differentiation to those listed in section 9(3) the classification must, therefore, have an adverse effect on the dignity of the individual, or some other comparable effect.[71] [76]

[71] In *Larbi-Odam*[72] [77] the Court found that discrimination on the basis of citizenship in the context of permanent employment amounted to unfair discrimination. With respect to permanent residents the Court had the following to say:

"[Permanent residents] have been selected for residence in this country by the Immigrants Selection Board, some of them on the basis of recruitment to specific posts. Permanent residents are generally entitled to citizenship within a few years of gaining permanent residency, and can be said to have made a conscious commitment to South Africa.[73] [78]

Moreover, permanent residents are entitled to compete with South Africans in the employment market. As emphasised by the Appellants, it makes little sense to permit people to stay permanently in a country, but then to exclude them from a job they are qualified to perform."

With regard to the vulnerability of permanent residents, the Court in *Larbi-Odam* found that first, foreign citizens are a minority in all countries, and have little political muscle. Secondly, the Court felt that citizenship is a personal attribute, which is difficult to change. The Respondents argued in this Court that citizenship is not a matter within the discretion of the Minister of Home Affairs, and that the State would be compelled to grant citizenship to persons who have resided in South Africa for five years and who satisfy the other criteria required for citizenship by naturalisation. Even if that were true (and it is not necessary to decide the point) it remains so that citizenship is typically not within the control of the individual and is, at least temporarily, a characteristic of personhood not alterable by conscious action and in some cases not alterable except on the basis of unacceptable costs. It is also true, as was noted in *Larbi-Odam* (*supra*) that in the South African context individuals were deprived of rights or benefits ostensibly on the basis of citizenship, but in reality in circumstances where citizenship was governed by race. Differentiation on the grounds of citizenship is clearly on a ground analogous to those listed in section 9(3) and therefore amounts to discrimination.[74] [79]

[72] With this said, one must now determine whether that discrimination is unfair. The determining factor regarding the unfairness of the discrimination is its impact on the person discriminated against.[75] [80] Relevant considerations in this regard include:

> "(a) the position of the complainants in society and whether they have suffered in the past from patterns of disadvantage, whether the discrimination in the case under consideration is on a specified ground or not;
>
> (b) the nature of the provision or power and the purpose sought to be achieved by it. If its purpose is manifestly not directed, in the first instance, at impairing the complainants in the manner indicated above, but is aimed at achieving a worthy and important societal goal, such as, for example, the furthering of equality for all, this purpose may, depending on the facts of the particular case, have a significant bearing on the question whether complainants have in fact suffered the impairment in question . . .
>
> (c) with due regard to (a) and (b) above, and any other relevant factors, the extent to which the discrimination has affected the rights or interests of complainants and whether it has led to an impairment of their fundamental human dignity or constitutes an impairment of a comparably serious nature."[76] [81]

These factors do not constitute a closed list and it is their cumulative effect that must be examined and in respect of which a determination must be made as to whether the discrimination is unfair.[77] [82]

[73] In *Brink v Kitshoff NO*, O'Regan J, with the concurrence of all the members of the Court, stated:

> "Section 8 was adopted then in the recognition that discrimination against people who are members of disfavoured groups can lead to patterns of group disadvantage and harm. Such discrimination is unfair: it builds and entrenches inequality amongst different groups in our society. The drafters realised that it was necessary both to proscribe such forms of discrimination and to permit positive steps to redress the effects of such discrimination. The need to prohibit such patterns of discrimination and to remedy their results are the primary purposes of section 8 and, in particular, subsections (2), (3) and (4)."[78] [83]

[74] There can be no doubt that the Applicants are part of a vulnerable group in society and, in the circumstances of the present case, are worthy of constitutional protection. We are dealing, here, with intentional, statutorily sanctioned unequal

treatment of part of the South African community. This has a strong stigmatising effect. Because both permanent residents and citizens contribute to the welfare system through the payment of taxes, the lack of congruence between benefits and burdens created by a law that denies benefits to permanent residents almost inevitably creates the impression that permanent residents are in some way inferior to citizens and less worthy of social assistance.[79] [84] Sharing responsibility for the problems and consequences of poverty equally as a community represents the extent to which wealthier members of the community view the minimal well-being of the poor as connected with their personal well-being and the well-being of the community as a whole.[80] [85] In other words, decisions about the allocation of public benefits represent the extent to which poor people are treated as equal members of society.[81] [86]

[75] Social grants in terms of section 3 of the Act can be claimed by "an aged person, a disabled person or a war veteran." Child-support grants in terms of section 4 can be claimed by the primary care-giver of the child, and care-dependency grants can be claimed by the parent or foster parent of a care-dependent child. In terms of section 1 of the Act, a care-dependent child is one who requires and receives permanent home care owing to his or her severe mental or physical disability.

The Impact of the Exclusion

[76] The exclusion of permanent residents in need of social-security programmes forces them into relationships of dependency upon families, friends and the community in which they live, none of whom may have agreed to sponsor the immigration of such persons to South Africa. These families or dependants, who may be in need of social assistance themselves, are asked to shoulder burdens not asked of other citizens. The denial of the welfare benefits therefore impacts not only on permanent residents without other means of support, but also on the families, friends and communities with whom they have contact. Apart from the undue burden that this places on those who take on this responsibility, it is likely to have a serious impact on the dignity of the permanent residents concerned who are cast in the role of supplicants.

[77] As far as the Applicants are concerned, the denial of the right is total and the consequences of the denial are grave. They are relegated to the margins of society and are deprived of what may be essential to enable them to enjoy other rights vested in them under the Constitution. Denying them their right under section 27(1) therefore affects them in a most fundamental way. In my view this denial is unfair.

[78] Section 4(b)(ii) of the Act, which deals with child-support grants, requires both the adult and the child to be South African citizens. In the case of care-dependency grants, section 4B(b)(ii) requires that both the parent and the child be South African citizens. However, there is no citizenship requirement in respect of foster parents of a care-dependent child. Foster-child grants in terms of section 4A are also not subject to a citizenship requirement. The children referred to in section 4(b)(ii) and 4B(b)(ii) may have been born in South Africa and may be citizens, but if the

primary care-giver or parent, excluding foster parents, is not a South African citizen, the grant is not payable. The Respondents did not seek to support these provisions, which discriminate against children on the grounds of their parents' nationality. It was therefore conceded that citizenship is an irrelevant consideration in assessing the needs of the children concerned. Moreover the denial of support in such circumstances to children in need trenches upon their rights under section 28(1)(c) of the Constitution.[82] [87]

Evaluation

[79] It is now necessary to weigh up the competing considerations taking into account the intersecting rights that are involved in the present case. Of crucial importance to this analysis is the fact that the Constitution provides that "everyone" has the right to have access to social security if they are unable to support themselves and their dependants. We are concerned here with a scheme that has been put in place by the State to provide access to social security to persons unable to support themselves and their dependants. The only challenge to the scheme is that it denies access to non-citizens. There is no suggestion that the scheme is otherwise inappropriate or inconsistent with the Constitution.

[80] I have already indicated that the exclusion of permanent residents from the scheme is discriminatory and unfair and I am satisfied that this unfairness would not be justifiable under section 36 of the Constitution. The relevant considerations have been traversed above and need not be repeated. What is of particular importance in my view, however, and can be stressed again, is that the exclusion of permanent residents from the scheme is likely to have a severe impact on the dignity of the persons concerned, who, unable to sustain themselves, have to turn to others to enable them to meet the necessities of life and are thus cast in the role of supplicants.

[81] The denial of access to social assistance is total, and for as long as it endures, permanent residents unable to sustain themselves or to secure meaningful support from other sources will be relegated to the margins of society and deprived of what may be essential to enable them to enjoy other rights vested in them under the Constitution. Denying permanent residents access to social security therefore affects them in a most fundamental way.

[82] In my view the importance of providing access to social assistance to all who live permanently in South Africa and the impact upon life and dignity that a denial of such access has, far outweighs the financial and immigration considerations on which the State relies. For the same reasons, I am satisfied that the denial of access to social grants to permanent residents who, but for their citizenship, would qualify for such assistance does not constitute a reasonable legislative measure as contemplated by section 27(2) of the Constitution.

[83] There is a difficulty in applying section 36 of the Constitution to the socio-economic rights entrenched in sections 26 and 27 of the Constitution. Sections 26 and 27 contain internal limitations, which qualify the rights. The State's obligation

in respect of these rights goes no further than to take "reasonable legislative and other measures within its available resources to achieve the progressive realisation" of the rights. If a legislative measure taken by the State to meet this obligation fails to pass the requirement of reasonableness for the purposes of sections 26 and 27, section 36 can only have relevance if what is "reasonable" for the purposes of that section, is different to what is "reasonable" for the purposes of sections 26 and 27.

[84] This raises an issue which has been the subject of academic debate but which has not as yet been considered by this Court.[83] [88] We heard no argument on the matter and do not have the benefit of a judgment of the High Court. In the circumstances, it is undesirable to express any opinion on the issue unless it is necessary to do so for the purposes of the decision in this case. In my view it is not necessary to decide the issue. Even if it is assumed that a different threshold of reasonableness is called for in sections 26 and 27 than is the case in section 36, I am satisfied for the reasons already given that the exclusion of permanent residents from the scheme for social assistance is neither reasonable nor justifiable within the meaning of section 36.

[85] The Constitution vests the right to social security in "everyone." By excluding permanent residents from the scheme for social security, the legislation limits their rights in a manner that affects their dignity and equality in material respects. Dignity and equality are founding values of the Constitution and lie at the heart of the Bill of Rights. Sufficient reason for such invasive treatment of the rights of permanent residents has not been established. The exclusion of permanent residents is therefore inconsistent with section 27 of the Constitution.

REMEDY

[86] For the reasons given above, we do not confirm the order of the High Court and we find section 3(c), prior to amendment by the Welfare Laws Amendment Act, to be unconstitutional. It was the submission of the Respondents that we find sections 4(b)(ii) and 4B(b)(ii) of the Act, as amended by the Welfare Laws Amendment Act, unconstitutional and that we strike them both down, coupled with an order suspending invalidity. Section 4B(b)(ii) as it appears in section 3 of the Welfare Laws Amendment Act is not yet in force. Although this new section will become part of the Act when it is promulgated, it has been passed as part of the Welfare Laws Amendment Act. Thus, the High Court's determination of the impugned section as a provision of the Social Assistance Act was technically not in order. Since the impugned section was before the High Court it is necessary for it to be considered in these confirmation proceedings. However, in view of the fact that the new provision is currently contained in the Welfare Laws Amendment Act, making, in the strict sense, that Act the subject of constitutional challenge, the order regarding this issue should be directed at the Welfare Laws Amendment Act and not the Social Assistance Act. For the same reasons as in the case of section 3(c), we do not confirm the order of the High Court and also find section 4(b)(ii)

to be unconstitutional. The constitutionality of section 4B(b)(ii), as it appears in section 3 of the Welfare Laws Amendment Act is discussed below.

[87] Once the Court has found constitutional inconsistency,[84] [89] it must declare invalidity to the extent of the inconsistency. The Court may then make an order, which is "just and equitable."[85] [90] In this case, the impugned provisions are inconsistent with the Constitution in that they exclude permanent residents from access to social security on the basis that they are non-citizens. The declaration of invalidity therefore does not affect the full extent of the impugned provisions. In such circumstances, the approach of this Court has been to declare only the relevant part of the impugned legislation inconsistent with the Constitution.[86] [91]

[88] When Courts consider a remedy following a declaration of invalidity of a statute, the question of remedial precision, which relates directly to respect for the role of the Legislature, is an important consideration.[87] [92] As permanent residents are not included in the allocation of social grants in section 4(b)(ii) of the Act, remedying the defect with the necessary precision would require the reading-in of the curing words, rather than striking down the impugned provisions and suspending the declaration of invalidity, as submitted by the Respondents. Suspending the declaration of in-validity would, in my view, not constitute a "just and equitable order" as contemplated by section 172(1)(b) of the Constitution. There is every reason not to delay payment of social grants any further to the Applicants and those similarly situated. Even if this Court were to grant interim relief to the Applicants during the period of suspension, other permanent residents would be barred from applying until the end of the period of suspension. Striking down without an order of suspension is not appropriate either, as it would make the grants instantly available to all residents including visitors within South Africa who satisfy the other criteria.

[89] Reading in the words "or permanent resident" after "South African citizen" in section 3(c) and "or permanent residents" after "South African citizens" in section 4(b)(ii) offers the most appropriate remedy as it retains the right of access to social security for South African citizens while making it instantly available to permanent residents.

HOFFMANN V. SOUTH AFRICAN AIRWAYS

Hoffmann v. South African Airways 2000 (11) BCLR 1211 (CC)

Case Summary

FACTS

The Appellant sought employment with the Respondent, South African Airways (SAA) to employ him as a cabin attendant. The Appellant's application for employment was rejected when it was discovered that he was HIV positive. Although the Respondent had a policy of nondiscrimination against people who were HIV positive, it still did not accept people who were HIV positive as cabin attendants. The

argument was that HIV positive persons were unable to meet some of the health requirements for that job, and this would place the airline at a disadvantage.

The Appellant launched a case in the High Court, where he sought an order
compelling the Respondent to employ him as a cabin attendant. The Appellant argued that he was unfairly discriminated against by the Respondent.

LEGAL HISTORY

This case was launched in the Witwatersrand High Court, where the Applicant's
challenge against the Respondent failed. He was, however, granted leave to appeal
the court's decision to the Constitutional Court.

LEGAL ISSUES

Two questions were put before the court in this regard: whether SAA's practice violated any provision in the Bill of Rights; and if so, what would be the appropriate
relief in this case.

DISPENSATION

The court found that SAA's practice was in violation of the equality clause in the
Constitution—section 9. The court unanimously upheld the appeal and set aside
the order of the High Court. Further, it set aside the decision of the Respondent not
to employ the Appellant, and ordered the Respondent to offer the Appellant employment as a cabin attendant. If the Appellant failed to accept such an offer within
thirty days, the offer would lapse.

Justice Ngcobo noted that the discrimination against HIV-positive persons who
seek jobs as flight attends violates section 9 of the Constitution. He also argued that
discrimination is an assault on the person's dignity, and further insisted that *ubuntu*
demands that vulnerable people be treated with compassion and understanding.

Justice Ngcobo

. . .

[27] At the heart of the prohibition of unfair discrimination is the recognition
that under our Constitution all human beings, regardless of their position in
society, must be accorded equal dignity.[88] [20] That dignity is impaired when a
person is unfairly discriminated against. The determining factor regarding the unfairness of the discrimination is its impact on the person discriminated against.[89]
[21] Relevant considerations in this regard include the position of the victim of the
discrimination in society, the purpose sought to be achieved by the discrimination,
the extent to which the rights or interests of the victim of the discrimination have
been affected, and whether the discrimination has impaired the human dignity of
the victim.[90] [22]

[28] The Appellant is living with HIV. People who are living with HIV constitute
a minority. Society has responded to their plight with intense prejudice.[91] [23] They

have been subjected to systemic disadvantage and discrimination.[92] [24] They have been stigmatised and marginalised. As the present case demonstrates, they have been denied employment because of their HIV positive status without regard to their ability to perform the duties of the position from which they have been excluded. Society's response to them has forced many of them not to reveal their HIV status for fear of prejudice. This in turn has deprived them of the help they would otherwise have received. People who are living with HIV/AIDS are one of the most vulnerable groups in our society. Notwithstanding the availability of compelling medical evidence as to how this disease is transmitted, the prejudices and stereotypes against HIV positive people still persist. In view of the prevailing prejudice against HIV positive people, any discrimination against them can, to my mind, be interpreted as a fresh instance of stigmatisation and I consider this to be an assault on their dignity. The impact of discrimination on HIV positive people is devastating. It is even more so when it occurs in the context of employment. It denies them the right to earn a living. For this reason, they enjoy special protection in our law.[93]

[29] There can be no doubt that SAA discriminated against the Appellant because of his HIV status. Neither the purpose of the discrimination nor the objective medical evidence justifies such discrimination.

[30] SAA refused to employ the Appellant saying that he was unfit for world-wide duty because of his HIV status. But, on its own medical evidence, not all persons living with HIV cannot be vaccinated against yellow fever, or are prone to contracting infectious diseases—it is only those persons whose infection has reached the stage of immunosuppression, and whose CD4+ count has dropped below 350 cells per microlitre of blood.[94] [26] Therefore, the considerations that dictated its practice as advanced in the High Court did not apply to all persons who are living with HIV. Its practice, therefore, judged and treated all persons who are living with HIV on the same basis. It judged all of them to be unfit for employment as cabin attendants on the basis of assumptions that are true only for an identifiable group of people who are living with HIV. On SAA's own evidence, the Appellant could have been at the asymptomatic stage of infection. Yet, because the Appellant happened to have been HIV positive, he was automatically excluded from employment as a cabin attendant.

[31] A further point must be made here. The conduct of SAA towards cabin attendants who are already in its employ is irreconcilable with the stated purpose of its practice.[95] [27] SAA does not test those already employed as cabin attendants for HIV/AIDS. They may continue to work despite the infection, and regardless of the stage of infection. Yet they may pose the same health, safety and operational hazards as prospective cabin attendants. Apart from this, the practice also pays no attention to the window period. If a person happens to undergo a blood test during the window period, the person can secure employment. But if the same person undergoes the test outside of this period, he or she will not be employed.

[32] The fact that some people who are HIV positive may, under certain circumstances, be unsuitable for employment as cabin attendants does not justify the ex-

clusion from employment as cabin attendants of *all* people who are living with HIV. Were this to be the case, people who are HIV positive would never have the opportunity to have their medical condition evaluated in the light of current medical knowledge for a determination to be made as to whether they are suitable for employment as cabin attendants. On the contrary, they would be vulnerable to discrimination on the basis of prejudice and unfounded assumptions—precisely the type of injury our Constitution seeks to prevent. This is manifestly unfair. Mr *Cohen* properly conceded that this was so.

[33] The High Court found that the commercial operation of SAA, and therefore the public perception about it, would be undermined if the employment practices of SAA did not promote the health and safety of the crew and passengers. In addition, the High Court took into account that the ability of SAA to compete in the airline industry would be undermined "if it were obliged to appoint HIV-infected individuals as flight-deck crew members."[96] [28] This was apparently based on the allegation by SAA that other airlines have a similar policy. It is these considerations that led the High Court to conclude that HIV negative status was, at least for the moment, an inherent requirement for the job of cabin attendant and that therefore the Appellant had not been unfairly discriminated against.

[34] Legitimate commercial requirements are, of course, an important consideration in determining whether to employ an individual. However, we must guard against allowing stereotyping and prejudice to creep in under the guise of commercial interests. The greater interests of society require the recognition of the inherent dignity of every human being, and the elimination of all forms of discrimination. Our Constitution protects the weak, the marginalised, the socially outcast, and the victims of prejudice and stereotyping. It is only when these groups are protected that we can be secure that our own rights are protected.[97] [29]

[35] The need to promote the health and safety of passengers and crew is important. So is the fact that if SAA is not perceived to be promoting the health and safety of its passengers and crew this may undermine the public perception of it. Yet the devastating effects of HIV infection and the widespread lack of knowledge about it have produced a deep anxiety and considerable hysteria. Fear and ignorance can never justify the denial to all people who are HIV positive of the fundamental right to be judged on their merits. Our treatment of people who are HIV positive must be based on reasoned and medically sound judgments. They must be protected against prejudice and stereotyping. We must combat erroneous, but nevertheless prevalent, perceptions about HIV. The fact that some people who are HIV positive may, under certain circumstances, be unsuitable for employment as cabin attendants does not justify a blanket exclusion from the position of cabin attendant of all people who are HIV positive.

[36] The constitutional right of the Appellant not to be unfairly discriminated against cannot be determined by ill-informed public perception of persons with HIV. Nor can it be dictated by the policies of other airlines not subject to our Constitution.

[37] Prejudice can never justify unfair discrimination. This country has recently emerged from institutionalised prejudice. Our law reports are replete with cases in which prejudice was taken into consideration in denying the rights that we now take for granted.[98] [30] Our constitutional democracy has ushered in a new era—it is an era characterised by respect for human dignity for all human beings. In this era, prejudice and stereotyping have no place. Indeed, if as a nation we are to achieve the goal of equality that we have fashioned in our Constitution we must never tolerate prejudice, either directly or indirectly. SAA, as a state organ that has a constitutional duty to uphold the Constitution, may not avoid its constitutional duty by bowing to prejudice and stereotyping.

[38] People who are living with HIV must be treated with compassion and understanding. We must show *ubuntu* towards them.[99] [31] They must not be condemned to "economic death" by the denial of equal opportunity in employment. This is particularly true in our country, where the incidence of HIV infection is said to be disturbingly high. The remarks made by Tipnis J in *MX of Bombay Indian Inhabitant v M/s ZY and Another*[100] [32] are apposite in this context:

"In our opinion, the State and public Corporations like Respondent No. 1 cannot take a ruthless and inhuman stand that they will not employ a person unless they are satisfied that the person will serve during the entire span of service from the employment till superannuation. As is evident from the material to which we have made a detailed reference in the earlier part of this judgment, the most important thing in respect of persons infected with HIV is the requirement of community support, economic support and non-discrimination of such person. This is also necessary for prevention and control of this terrible disease. Taking into consideration the widespread and present threat of this disease in the world in general and this country in particular, the State cannot be permitted to condemn the victims of HIV infection, many of whom may be truly unfortunate, to certain economic death. It is not in the general public interest and is impermissible under the Constitution. The interests of the HIV positive persons, the interests of the employer and the interests of the society will have to be balanced in such a case."

[39] As pointed out earlier, on the medical evidence not all people who are living with HIV are unsuitable for employment as cabin attendants.[101] [33] It is only those people whose CD4+ count has dropped below a certain level who may become unsuitable for employment. It follows that the finding of the High Court that HIV negative status is an inherent requirement "at least for the moment" for a cabin attendant is not borne out by the medical evidence on record.

[40] Having regard to all these considerations, the denial of employment to the Appellant because he was living with HIV impaired his dignity and constituted

unfair discrimination. This conclusion makes it unnecessary to consider whether the Appellant was discriminated against on a listed ground of disability, as set out in section 9(3) of the Constitution, as Mr *Trengove* contended or whether people who are living with HIV ought not to be regarded as having a disability, as contended by the *amicus.*

[41] I conclude, therefore, that the refusal by SAA to employ the Appellant as a cabin attendant because he was HIV positive violated his right to equality guaranteed by section 9 of the Constitution. The third enquiry, namely whether this violation was justified, does not arise. We are not dealing here with a law of general application.[102] [34] This conclusion makes it unnecessary to consider the other constitutional attacks based on human dignity and fair labour practices. It now remains to consider the remedy to which the Appellant is entitled.

Remedy

[42] Section 38 of the Constitution provides that where a right contained in the Bill of Rights has been infringed, "the Court may grant appropriate relief." In the context of our Constitution, "appropriate relief" must be construed purposively, and in the light of section 172(1)(b), which empowers the Court, in constitutional matters, to make "any order that is just and equitable."[103] [35] Thus construed, appropriate relief must be fair and just in the circumstances of the particular case. Indeed, it can hardly be said that relief that is unfair or unjust is appropriate.[104] [36] As Ackermann J remarked, in the context of a comparable provision in the Interim Constitution, "[i]t can hardly be argued, in my view, that relief which was unjust to others could, where other available relief meeting the complainant's needs did not suffer from this defect, be classified as appropriate."[105] [37] Appropriateness, therefore, in the context of our Constitution, imports the elements of justice and fairness.

[43] Fairness requires a consideration of the interests of all those who might be affected by the order. In the context of employment, this will require a consideration not only of the interests of the prospective employee but also the interests of the employer. In other cases, the interests of the community may have to be taken into consideration. In the context of unfair discrimination, the interests of the community lie in the recognition of the inherent dignity of every human being and the elimination of all forms of discrimination. This aspect of the interests of the community can be gathered from the preamble to the Constitution in which the people of this country declared:

"We, the people of South Africa, Recognise the injustices of our past;

. . .

We therefore, through our freely elected representatives, adopt this Constitution as the supreme law of the Republic so as to—

Heal the divisions of the past and establish a society based on democratic values, social justice and fundamental human rights . . ."

[44] This proclamation finds expression in the founding provisions of the Constitution, which include "human dignity, the achievement of equality and the advancement of human rights and freedoms."

[45] The determination of appropriate relief, therefore, calls for the balancing of the various interests that might be affected by the remedy. The balancing process must at least be guided by the objective, first, to address the wrong occasioned by the infringement of the constitutional right; second, to deter future violations; third, to make an order that can be complied with; and fourth, of fairness to all those who might be affected by the relief. Invariably, the nature of the right infringed and the nature of the infringement will provide guidance as to the appropriate relief in the particular case. Therefore, in determining appropriate relief, "we must carefully analyse the nature of [the] constitutional infringement, and strike effectively at its source."

. . .

Is Instatement the Appropriate Relief?

[50] An order of instatement, which requires an employer to employ an employee, is a basic element of the appropriate relief in the case of a prospective employee who is denied employment for reasons declared impermissible by the Constitution. It strikes effectively at the source of unfair discrimination. It is an expression of the general rule that where a wrong has been committed, the aggrieved person should, as a general matter, and as far as is possible, be placed in the same position the person would have been but for the wrong suffered. In proscribing unfair discrimination, the Constitution not only seeks to prevent unfair discrimination, but also to eliminate the effects thereof. In the context of employment, the attainment of that objective rests not only upon the elimination of the discriminatory employment practice, but also requires that the person who has suffered a wrong as a result of unlawful discrimination be, as far as possible, restored to the position in which he or she would have been but for the unfair discrimination.

[51] The need to eliminate unfair discrimination does not arise only from Chapter 2 of our Constitution. It also arises out of international obligation.[106] [42] South Africa has ratified a range of anti-discrimination Conventions, including the African Charter on Human and Peoples' Rights.[107] [43] In the preamble to the African Charter, member states undertake, amongst other things, to dismantle all forms of discrimination. Article 2 prohibits discrimination of any kind. In terms of Article 1, member states have an obligation to give effect to the rights and freedoms enshrined in the Charter. In the context of employment, the ILO Convention 111, Discrimination (Employment and Occupation) Convention, 1958 proscribes discrimination that has the effect of nullifying or impairing equality of opportunity or treatment in employment or occupation. In terms of Article 2, member states have an obligation to pursue national policies that are designed to promote equality of opportunity and treatment in the field of employment, with a view to eliminating

any discrimination. Apart from these Conventions, it is noteworthy that item 4 of the SADC Code of Conduct on HIV/AIDS and Employment,[108] [44] formally adopted by the SADC Council of Ministers in September 1997, lays down that HIV status "should not be a factor in job status, promotion or transfer." It also discourages pre-employment testing for HIV and requires that there should be no compulsory workplace testing for HIV.

[52] Where a person has been wrongfully denied employment, the fullest redress obtainable is instatement.[109] Instatement serves an important constitutional objective. It redresses the wrong suffered, and thus eliminates the effect of the unfair discrimination. It sends a message that under our Constitution discrimination will not be tolerated and thus ensures future compliance. In the end, it vindicates the Constitution and enhances our faith in it. It restores the human dignity of the person who has been discriminated against, achieves equality of employment opportunities and removes the barriers that have operated in the past in favour of certain groups, and in the process advances human rights and freedoms for all. All these are founding values in our Constitution.

THE *PHARMACEUTICAL SOCIETY OF SA* AND *NEW CLICKS SA* CASES

Pharmaceutical Society of SA and Others v. Minister of Health and Another; New Clicks SA (Pty) Ltd v. Tshabalala-Msimang NO and Another 2005 1 All SA 326 (SCA)
    New Clicks SA (Pty) Ltd v. Tshabalala-Msimang NO and Another; Pharmaceutical Society of SA and Others v. Minister of Health and Another 2005 4 All SA 80 (C)

Case Summary
The New Clicks Group challenged new pricing regulations, which were implemented by the Minister of Health in terms of legislation. The aim of the regulations was to control the pricing of medicine. The basis of the challenge was that the regulations amounted to administrative action that was unreasonable and unfair to the degree that it violated the right to procedural fairness. The whole issue turned on whether or not the conduct of the Minister of Health in bringing into force the regulations, was in fact reviewable as administrative action.

The matter was first heard in the Cape High Court. Ultimately, at the level of the Constitutional Court, the *New Clicks* decision was to span over all areas of administrative law. However, we are including this case here to the degree that the courts used *ubuntu*. Justice Hlope appeals to *ubuntu* at the end of his judgment. In response, the Supreme Court of Appeal both noted that *ubuntu* has no constitutional status in the final Constitution, and that it is inappropriate to use it to address an issue of statutory interpretation. The following excerpts the Cape High Court decision.

Justice Hlophe

This is an opposed application for leave to appeal against the majority judgment, which was handed down on 27 August 2004. The judgment of the Court was written by Yekiso. I concurred in his judgment. Traverso DJP wrote a separate dissenting judgment. A few days after the judgment was delivered notice of application for leave to appeal was issued. The application for leave to appeal was made in terms of section 20(4)(b) read with section 20(1) of the Supreme Court Act 59 of 1959 and rule 49(1) of the Uniform Rules of Court. Leave to appeal was made to the Supreme Court of Appeal. In terms of the notice thereof various grounds of appeal were set out.

It is not necessary at this stage to refer to the various grounds of appeal save to state that New Clicks South Africa (Pty) Ltd (Applicant), in terms of their notice of appeal, stated the following:

"Having regard to the minority dissenting judgment of Her Ladyship Traverso DJP, there is a reasonable possibility of another Court coming to a different conclusion to that arrived at by His Lordship [Yekiso J]. Her Ladyship, at paragraph [175] of her minority judgment was of the view that the review application should succeed. It is submitted that this, in itself, should be sufficient for leave to appeal against the majority judgment to be granted."

Subsequent to the filing of notice of application for leave to appeal, counsel in the *New Clicks South Africa (Pty) Ltd and Pharmaceutical* matters indicated that they would like to see the judges in order to make arrangements for the date and time of the hearing of the application for leave to appeal. Accordingly, an appointment with counsel was arranged for Thursday 2 September 2004 at 7:30 A.M. in my chambers. There was also some exchange of communication between the parties. We also received Heads of Argument. The legal teams came to meet us in my chambers as arranged. Mr *Gauntlett* SC indicated in my chambers and in the presence of Traverso DJP and Yekiso J that he (Mr *Gauntlett*) had been in contact with President Howie of the Supreme Court of Appeal regarding the date for hearing the matter in the Supreme Court of Appeal. He told us further that President Howie had indicated that if leave were granted he would be able to squeeze in the matter and that it could be heard in mid-November 2004. However, if the issue of leave to appeal was not finalised, the matter would only be heard in February 2005.

The fact that Mr *Gauntlett* had already been in touch with President Howie of the Supreme Court of Appeal regarding the matter pending before the Cape High Court was not well received by the Respondents' legal team. In a letter written by the State Attorney to the Registrar of the Supreme Court of Appeal dated 6 September 2004, it was said *inter alia*:

"The application for leave to appeal has yet to be heard. The Full Bench
that considered the matter will hear an opposed application for leave to appeal on the 20th September 2004. We take strong exception to the attorneys
of New Clicks and PSSA writing to you and to the Judge President when
the application for leave to appeal has yet to be heard. We believe that the
conduct of New Clicks and PSSA is highly irregular. We oppose the request
of New Clicks for a date to be set for the appeal and the directions to be
given at this stage."

Similarly the State Attorney wrote a letter to the Applicants' legal representatives
on 6 September 2004 in terms of which the following was recorded:

"I wish to bring to your notice that my clients are perturbed at the conduct of
your clients. We are not able to comprehend how your clients saw it fit to
write to the Registrar of the Supreme Court of Appeal when the application
for leave to appeal has yet to be heard. As you are no doubt aware, the application for leave to appeal is opposed. It is rather presumptuous of your clients
to assume that the leave to appeal will be granted or that it will be granted to
the Supreme Court of Appeal. We also believe that your clients' conduct is
contemptuous of the Full Bench that has yet to consider the application for
leave to appeal. We will be writing to the Registrar of the Supreme Court of
Appeal to indicate our attitude. We also intend to bring your letter to the attention of the Full Bench that will hear the application for leave to appeal to
register our protest at this conduct."

Of course the Applicants' Attorneys of record replied in terms of a letter dated
7 September 2004. In terms of that letter the attitude of the Applicants' attorneys
was:

"The tone of your telefax under reply is regrettable. However, it appears that
you have misconstrued both the contents of our letter addressed to the Registrar of the Supreme Court of Appeal, as well as the purpose thereof. The suggestion of impropriety in our request to the Registrar of the Supreme Court
of Appeal is misplaced for the following reasons: . . . Given, however, our understanding that the Supreme Court of Appeal roll for the last term of the
year is being decided today [7 September 2004], our concern was to avoid any
prospect of this matter only being heard next year, simply because no request
has been directed to the Supreme Court of Appeal for provision to be made,
should the President of that Court so determine, to accommodate this matter,
even on a contingent basis."

The relevance of the above correspondence is clear. To me it indicates the attitude particularly of the Applicants' legal representatives. I am certainly not an expert in matters of procedure relating to the Supreme Court of Appeal. It is inconceivable, however, in my respectful view, that the President of the Supreme Court of Appeal could be approached on a matter which is still pending before a High Court. The Full Bench of the Cape High Court was and is still seized with the *Pharmaceutical* matter (*supra*). It was improper for the legal representative(s) to be communicating with the President of the Supreme Court of Appeal on a matter in respect of which leave to appeal had not been granted and finalised. It is my view that that was presumptuous and it bordered on contempt for this Court.

On the day on which we met in my chambers legal teams of both sides were present. The Applicants' legal teams were led by Mr *Gauntlett* SC. Mr *Gauntlett's* attitude in my chambers was simply that, because of the minority judgment of Her Ladyship Traverso DJP, it was not necessary at all to go to Court, and that in the light of the minority judgment leave should be granted in chambers to the Supreme Court of Appeal. I made it very clear to Mr *Gauntlett* that his attitude was unacceptable to the Court. There was no reason, in my view, why the application for leave to appeal in the *Pharmaceutical* matter should be dealt with any differently from other similar applications.

Mr *Gauntlett's* submission that the matter should be easily disposed of in chambers was clearly absurd in the light of his contention (see below) that the *Pharmaceutical / Clicks* matter (*supra*) is one of great public importance. Furthermore, this contention is also absurd given the fact that our Constitution is founded on the principles of openness and transparency. The Preamble to the Constitution reads thus:

> ". . . We therefore, through our freely elected representatives, adopt this Constitution as the supreme law of the Republic so as to—
> Heal the divisions of the past and establish a society based on democratic values, social justice and fundamental human rights;
> Lay the foundations for a democratic and open society in which government is based on the will of the people and every citizen is equally protected by law;
> Improve the quality of life of all citizens and free the potential of each person; and
> Build a united and democratic South Africa able to take its rightful place as a sovereign state in the family of nations . . ."

Section 34 of the Constitution provides that:

> "Everyone has the right to have any dispute that can be resolved by the application of law decided in a fair public hearing before a Court or, where appropriate, another independent and impartial tribunal or forum."

Section 38 of the Constitution provides that:

"Anyone listed in this section has the right to approach a competent Court, alleging that a right in the Bill of Rights has been infringed or threatened, and the Court may grant appropriate relief, including a declaration of rights. The persons who may approach a Court are:

(a) anyone acting in their own interest;
(b) anyone acting on behalf of another person who cannot act in their own name;
(c) anyone acting as a member of , or in the interest of, a group or class of persons;
(d) anyone acting in the public interest; and
(e) an association acting in the interest of its members."

Mr *Gauntlett*'s contention is therefore contradictory to the preamble and provisions of the Constitution.

Accordingly, counsel obliged after the Court made it clear to him that his approach was totally unacceptable and that the application for leave to appeal was going to be heard in open Court, in the usual manner, as is the practice in this Division.

Thereafter the legal teams were unable initially to agree on a date whereupon the application was going to be heard. We were then requested by Mr *Gauntlett* to make a ruling. The attitude of all three judges, including Traverso DJP and Yekiso J, was that it was inappropriate for the Court to fix a date for the hearing of an application for leave to appeal if the legal teams could not reach agreement relating to the hearing of the application. After a short discussion between the legal representatives, we were then approached in chambers and the date agreed upon for the hearing of application for leave to appeal was 20 September 2004.

Once counsel were agreed in relation to the date for the hearing of application for leave to appeal, the matter was accordingly set down for hearing on 20 September 2004. An indication was given to counsel in chambers that the matter would be set down for hearing for the whole day if it need be. Indeed, as it turned out to be, the matter was argued until about lunch hour on 20 September 2004. Counsel were given a fair opportunity to argue the matter fully in open Court, which Court was well attended by legal teams, the parties interested in the matter as well as the public, including the journalists. After hearing argument in Court all three judges agreed that it would be appropriate to reserve judgment on the question of whether or not leave should be granted to the Supreme Court of Appeal.

The grounds of appeal were clearly set out in the Notice of Application for leave to appeal. In short, the grounds for appeal were that the majority erred in upholding the validity of the regulations. The Court should have found that the regulations are *ultra vires* and invalid.

Mr *Gauntlett* argued in Court that firstly, the matter was of great/sufficient importance to the practice and the public at large. He submitted that this was one of the important considerations for purposes of granting leave to appeal to the Supreme Court of Appeal. Secondly, he submitted, that there were reasonable prospects of another Court coming to a different conclusion to that arrived at by the majority. The third argument advanced by Mr *Gauntlett* was that leave to appeal was sought to the Supreme Court of Appeal and not to the Constitutional Court. In amplification of this argument Mr *Gauntlett* submitted that the certificate procedure relating to appeals to the Constitutional Court does no longer exist in the light of regulation 19(2) as published in the *Government Gazette* of October 2003, which provides that:

"A litigant who is aggrieved by the decision of Court and wishes to appeal against it directly to the Court on a constitutional matter, shall within 15 days of the order against which the appeal is sought to be brought, and after giving notice to the other party or parties concerned, lodge with the Registrar an application for leave to appeal: Provided that where the President has refused leave to appeal the period prescribed in this Rule shall run from the date of the order refusing leave."

The arguments that were advanced by Mr *Gauntlett* SC as well as Mr *Trengove* SC had been fully canvassed in the majority judgment prepared by my esteemed brother Yekiso J. With respect to counsel there was absolutely nothing new that came out in argument when we heard the application for leave to appeal. All the issues raised were fully canvassed in a long judgment, which was carefully written. Furthermore, the Applicants had no answer to the constitutional point. Section 27 of the Constitution deals with "Health care, food, water and social security." It reads thus:

"27

(1) everyone has a right to have access to—
    (a) health care services, including reproductive health care; . . .

(2) The State must take reasonable legislative and other measures, within its available resources, to achieve the progressive realisation of each of these rights.

(3) No one may be refused emergency medical treatment."

As Yekiso J found in the majority judgment there is no doubt in my view that the *Pharmaceutical* case (*supra*) not only raises issues relating to the transformation of the pharmaceutical industry in general but, above all the case involves serious constitutional issues relating to provision of health care which in terms of section 27 the State is obliged to take reasonable legislative and other measures within its available resources to achieve and realise that goal. There is another constitutional issue namely section 33 of the Constitution. Section 33 provides that:

"33

(1) Everyone has the right to administrative action that is lawful, reasonable and procedurally fair.

(2) Everyone whose rights have been adversely affected by administrative action has the right to be given written reasons . . ."

The Promotion of Administrative Justice Act 3 of 2000 (PAJA) is another constitutional issue as well ie the extent of the operation of PAJA and rule making in particular, whether or not rule making is subject to the provisions of PAJA. There was with respect no cogent answer whatsoever to the argument advanced by Mr *Moerane* SC namely that this is a case of great constitutional importance and that the Applicants should clearly have proceeded to the Constitutional Court particularly in the light of the attitude that the matter was of great public importance which needed to be finalised sooner rather than later. As Mr *Moerane* SC ably pointed out in argument, in this case we have a situation whereby a matter, which will clearly end up in the Constitutional Court, is first referred to the Supreme Court of Appeal. In the words of Mr *Moerane* SC, the Applicants were seeking to approach "Braamfontein via Bloemfontein."

What is the test for purposes of granting leave to appeal? The test was clearly laid down by the Supreme Court of Appeal (then the Appellate Division) in *Zweni v Minister of Law and Order* 1993 (1) SA 523 (A). Harms AJA (as he then was) said at 531B–E:

"The jurisdictional requirements for a civil appeal emanating from a Provincial or Local Division sitting as a Court of first instance are twofold:

(1) the decision appealed against must be a 'judgment or order' within the meaning of those words in the context of section 20(1) of the [Supreme Court] Act; and

(2) the necessary leave to appeal must have been granted, either by the Court of first instance, or, where leave was refused by it, by this Court. Leave is granted if there are reasonable prospects of success. So much is trite. But, if the judgment or order sought to be appealed against does not dispose of all the issues between the parties the balance of convenience must, in addition, favour a piecemeal consideration of the case. In other words, the test is then 'whether the appeal—if leave were given—would lead to a just and reasonably prompt resolution of the real issue between the parties.'"

See also *Swartzberg v Barclays National Bank Ltd* 1975 (3) SA 515 (W) at 518B.

With respect the test for matters of this nature is very clear. It is not the existence or otherwise of a dissenting judgment, no matter how powerful it might be. While it is true that dissenting judgments, especially on questions of law, may be of importance to the development of the law, they should never be elevated into the law. As Corbett CJ (as he then was) warned in a lecture given in 1998, which was subsequently published in 1998 (115) *SALJ* 116 at 120:

> "So take seriously the duty to dissent in appropriate cases. At the same time avoid undue dissension. Remember that you *may* be wrong and that, since you are in the minority, there is a fair chance that you *are* wrong."

This, with respect, is not to say that Traverso DJP was wrong in her dissenting judgment. All I am saying is that the importance of a dissenting judgment should not be exaggerated. The test is, and has always been, as set out in the *Zweni* matter (*supra*) namely whether or not there are reasonable prospects of another Court coming to a different conclusion to that arrived at by the trial Court. Applying this test to the facts of the present case, it is my judgment that there are no reasonable prospects of another Court coming to a different conclusion. More so, if one has regard to provisions of section 39(2) of the Constitution which enjoins the Courts, when interpreting any legislation and when developing the common law or customary law, to promote the spirit, purport and objects of the Bill of Rights, no other Court is likely to arrive at any other conclusion about the validity of the regulations under attack. Furthermore, section 39(1)(*a*) of the Constitution provides:

> "When interpreting the Bill of Rights, a Court, tribunal or forum—
>
> (a)   must promote the values that underlie an open and democratic society based on human dignity, equality and freedom."

One of the values mentioned in section 39(1)(a) is *ubuntu*. *uBuntu* is "a way of life that contributes positively towards sustaining the well-being of a people, community or society." See Bhengu, *uBuntu: The Essence of Democracy* 1996 Novalis Press, Cape Town at 5. Clearly *ubuntu* requires that medicine must be accessible to all South Africans, rich and poor.

In all circumstances of the case I am satisfied that the application for leave to appeal to the Supreme Court of Appeal should be dismissed with costs, including the costs consequent upon employment of two counsel both under Case Numbers 4128/2004 and 4329/2004.

. . .

Supreme Court of Appeal Decision

. . .

[36] It is necessary to have regard to the terms of Hlophe JP's judgment to see whether it contains any clues as to why it had to be delayed. The first seven pages of the judgment deal with the reason why the application for leave was not dealt with in chambers but in open Court. Those reasons are academic and have nothing to do with the question whether or not leave should have been granted. During the course of this discussion Hlophe JP took umbrage to the Applicants' direct approach to the head of this Court to determine the availability of dates before the application had been determined, as if it amounted to some kind of lese-majesty. Apparently he did not appreciate fully that the Applicants were entitled to approach this Court either by way of an appeal or an application for leave to appeal, irrespective of the outcome of their applications before the Court below.

[37] Hlophe JP, when dealing with the merits of the application, himself said that:

"there was absolutely nothing new that came out in argument when we heard the application for leave to appeal. All the issues raised were fully canvassed in a long judgment which was carefully written."

Why then, one may fairly ask, did it take longer to dispose of the application for leave than the application itself? He said that the fact that there was a minority judgment did not mean that another Court might reasonably agree with the minority. (As Antoine de Saint-Exupéry said, "It is harder to judge oneself—and, one may add, the fruits of one's labours—than to judge others.") He proceeded to find (so it would appear) that since the case raises constitutional issues, leave to this Court should not be granted, apparently assuming that a Court of first instance does have the right to choose the appeal forum while all it can decide is whether there were reasonable prospects of success.

[38] Ineluctably, in the light of the nature and scope of the issues, the period of the delay, the lack of explanation, the urgency of the case, the content of Hlophe JP's judgment and the other factors mentioned, the only conclusion can be that the delay was not only regrettable, it was unreasonable—so unreasonable in fact that it could only be interpreted as a refusal of leave.

[39] The judgment of Hlophe JP concluded with a reference to the spirit of *ubuntu* in interpreting statutes. The word appeared in an endnote of the interim Constitution Act 200 of 1993 where it dealt with national unity and reconciliation:

"These can now be addressed on the basis that there is a need for understanding but not for vengeance, a need for reparation but not for retaliation, a need for *ubuntu* but not for victimisation."

It does, however, not appear in the Constitution in express terms. *uBuntu* has many dimensions but its application to statutory interpretation is novel. It ought to apply to the relationship between Courts and the respect required of organs of State and Courts towards citizens and towards each other. One does sense that the Court below was irritated because the Applicants had the temerity to ask for a quick disposition of the applications for leave. There are some who believe that requests for "hurried justice" should not only be met with judicial displeasure and castigation but the severest censure and that any demand for quick rendition of reserved judgments is tantamount to interference with the independence of judicial office and disrespect for the judge concerned. They are seriously mistaken on both counts. First, parties are entitled to enquire about the progress of their cases and, if they do not receive an answer or if the answer is unsatisfactory, they are entitled to complain. The judicial cloak is not an impregnable shield providing immunity against criticism or reproach. Delays are frustrating and disillusioning and create the impression that judges are imperious. Secondly, it is judicial delay rather than complaints about it that is a threat to judicial independence because delays destroy the public confidence in the judiciary. There rests an ethical duty on judges to give judgment or any ruling in a case promptly and without undue delay and litigants are entitled to judgment as soon as reasonably possible. Otherwise the most quoted legal aphorism, namely that "justice delayed is justice denied," will become a mere platitude. Lord Carswell recently said:

> "The law's delays have been the subject of complaint from litigants for many centuries, and it behoves all Courts to make proper efforts to ensure that the quality of justice is not adversely affected by delay in dealing with the cases which are brought before them, whether in bringing them on for hearing or in issuing decisions when they have been heard."

In *Goose v Wilson Sandford and Co* the Court of Appeal censured a judge for his delay in delivering a reserved judgment and said:

> "Compelling parties to await judgment for an indefinitely extended period . . . weakened public confidence in the whole judicial process.
> Left unchecked it would be ultimately subversive of the rule of law."

THE *DIKOKO* CASE

Dikoko v. Mokhatla 2007 (1) BCLR 1 (CC)

Case Summary
FACTS
The Pretoria High Court found that the applicant, Mr. David Dikoko, had defamed the Respondent, Mr. Thupi Zacharia Mokhatla, and ordered Mr. Dikoko to pay

Mr. Mokhatla R110,000 in damages. In the matter before the Constitutional Court the Applicant sought leave to appeal the judgement and order of the High Court.

Mr. Dikoko, the executive mayor, had run up an excessive cell phone bill. The Provincial Auditor-General had informed Mr. Mokhatla, the chief executive officer of the Southern District Municipality incorporating the Southern District Council, of the Applicant's excessive bill. The Applicant and the Respondent eventually agreed to write off a large proportion of the debt. The Auditor-General, however, was not satisfied with this agreement and called the Applicant to appear before the North West Provincial Standing Accounts Committee to provide an explanation for the cell phone bill.

The Applicant explained that he had accumulated the excessive bill because the Respondent had changed the payment system from a monthly payment scheme to a periodic payment scheme. Furthermore, the Applicant stated that the Respondent had done so intentionally so as to cause the Respondent to fall into excessive debt and thereby provide a ground for political opponents to criticize him on the basis of his integrity. The Respondent instituted action against the applicant, claiming that the Applicant's statement to the Accounts Committee was defamatory.

The Applicant entered a special plea raising the defence of privileged statement. The High Court dismissed the Applicant's special plea, reaching the conclusion that the Applicant's statements were in fact defamatory.

The Applicant argued before the Constitutional Court that the civil and criminal immunity provided to councillors for anything submitted to a council, or one of its committees, by the Constitution and relevant pieces of legislation should be extended to municipal councillors performing their function outside of council.

LEGAL ISSUES

The Applicant sought leave to appeal the High Court decision and two orders of relief. Firstly, an interpretation was required of the constitutional provisions that deal with the provision of privileges and immunities to Municipal Councils and their members, together with relevant provisions of the local government legislation, "to provide immunity to persons who are not members of the Provincial Legislature but appear before it to give information." Secondly, the Applicant argued for a reduction of the quantum awarded to the Respondent by the High Court.

DISPENSATION

The Applicant was granted leave to appeal, but the appeal was dismissed with costs.

On the matter of the Applicant's defense of privileged statement, Justice Mokgoro, writing for the majority of the court, found that Applicant's statements before the Standing Committee were not privileged and therefore the Applicant did not enjoy civil immunity. The appeal against the decision of the High Court in this respect therefore had to fail.

On the issue of the quantum of damages, Justice Mokgoro, writing for the minority this time, found that the quantum of damages awarded by the trial court was unreasonable and excessive. She maintained that an award for damages arising out of defamation in the instant case was a constitutional matter. In her view, the trial court had considered only factors that aggravated the seriousness of the defamation and damages. It had not considered the nature of the defamatory statements, the effect of the statements on the Respondent, and the nature and extent of the circulation of the publication. Justices Nkabinde and Sachs concurred with Justice Mokgoro on this issue. Both Justices Sachs and Mokgoro rely on and develop the notion of *ubuntu* as a principle that demands the rethinking of the law of defamation, and particularly the almost sole reliance on damages as a remedy for defamation.

Writing for the majority of the court on the issue of quantum, Deputy Chief Justice Moseneke, set out reasons for disagreeing with the finding of Justice Mokgoro.

Therefore, Deputy Chief Justice Moseneke, writing for the majority, granted the application for leave to appeal and then dismissed the appeal without interfering with the order for damages issued by the High Court, and ordered the applicant to pay the costs of the Respondent.

Justice Mokgoro

. . .

[52] The emerging question is whether this Court has jurisdiction to review the High Court award. First to determine is whether the award of damages is a constitutional issue falling within the jurisdiction of this Court. Should this Court have jurisdiction to review the award, the next question would be whether in our jurisprudence and under the applicable legal principles this Court should do so.

[53] I agree with Moseneke DCJ's finding in paragraph 92 of his judgment that the extent of damages for defamation has implications for the relationship between dignity and freedom of expression. Robust awards will indeed have a "chilling effect" on freedom of expression.

[54] Moseneke DCJ assumes without deciding that the amount of damages in a defamation suit is a constitutional matter. My view is that when a damages award is excessive, as this judgment finds, it has the effect of curbing freedom of speech for fear of repercussions that might flow from exercising that freedom guaranteed and protected in the Constitution. In my view therefore, we are clearly seized with a constitutional matter. What remains to be determined is whether this Court should interfere with the High Court's award.

[55] In that regard, Mr Mokhatla submits this Court should only interfere with the damages award if leave to appeal on the constitutional issue is granted. Having granted leave, there can be no objection on the part of Mr Mokhatla for this Court to redetermine the High Court's assessment.

[56] Even if this Court has jurisdiction to review the quantum, Mr Mokhatla submitted, being in the same position as any appellate Court, it ought not to interfere with the High Court's award merely for the reason that its own assessment would

yield a different amount. What would additionally be required, Mr Mokhatla argues, is for this Court to make a finding that the High Court's award of damages was manifestly unreasonable.

[57] The approach of the Supreme Court of Appeal to the question whether it can replace a trial Court's award of damages has been that the amount of damages to be awarded is at the discretion of the trial Court but that that Court must exercise its discretion reasonably. In *Sandler v Wholesale Supplies Ltd* the Supreme Court of Appeal held that should an appellate Court find that the trial Court had misdirected itself with regard to material facts or in its approach to the assessment, or having considered all the facts and circumstances of the case, the trial Court's assessment of damages is markedly different to that of the appellate Court, it not only has the discretion but is obliged to substitute its own assessment for that of the trial Court. In its determination, the Court considers whether the amount of damages, which the trial Court had awarded, was so palpably inadequate as to be out of proportion to the injury inflicted.

[58] The Supreme Court of Appeal will therefore only interfere with an award of damages if it finds that the award of the trial Court was palpably excessive, clearly disproportionate in the circumstances of the case, grossly extravagant or unreasonable or so high as to be manifestly unreasonable. An appellate Court may therefore interfere if a trial Court is found to have misdirected itself in its assessment of damages.

[59] In *S v Basson* this Court considered the approach that an appellate Court should take to the exercise of a discretion by a trial Court. Noting two different types of discretion, the Court stated: "[A] discretion in the sense that the [C]ourt must have regard to a number of factors before coming to a decision," which I will refer to as a broad discretion, and a "strong" or "true" discretion which is said to exist when the Court has a range of options available to it. Regarding a broad discretion, an appellate Court can interfere if it is of the view that it would have exercised its discretion differently on the merits. With a "strong" or "true" discretion however, an appellate Court can interfere only when shown that the trial Court exercised its discretion on the basis of wrong principles of law or a mistaken view of the facts.

[60] In the approach of the Supreme Court of Appeal, an award of damages is a matter that is best left to a trial Court to determine. The Court has therefore held that it will not interfere with a trial Court's award if it is of the view that on a consideration of all of the relevant facts and circumstances in a particular case it would have come to a different assessment. Rather, the Court has held that it can only substitute its own assessment for that of the trial Court if it is of the view that the trial Court's assessment was manifestly incorrect or if its assessment differs markedly from that of the trial Court. An assessment, which is markedly different to that of a trial Court, indicates that the Court considered that the trial Court had misdirected itself on the law or the facts before it. The trial Court's discretion to award damages is therefore in my view a "true" discretion, in which this Court can interfere if it is

of the view that the High Court, in its assessment, misdirected itself either on the law or on the facts before it.

[61] When the High Court assessed the quantum it took into account and emphasised relevant factors, which demonstrated the serious nature of the defamation. Relying on the dictum in *Skinner v Shapiro (I)* the High Court simply stated without motivation:

"[W]hen this dictum is applied to the facts of the present case it is clear that the plaintiff's position in society; the relationship that existed between the parties; the absence of an apology and the seriousness of the allegations all weigh against the defendant."

After considering that all these factors weighed against Mr Dikoko the Court found that it was reasonable to make an award of damages of R110 000.

Assessment of the Quantum

[62] The law of defamation is based on the *actio injuriarum*, a flexible Roman law remedy, which afforded the right to claim damages from a person whose personality rights, had been impaired by another. The action is designed to afford personal satisfaction for an impairment of a personality right and became a general remedy for any vexatious violation of a person's right to his dignity and reputation. A number of factors arising from the facts and circumstances of the case are taken into account in assessing the amount of damages.

[63] Mr Dikoko has not apologised to Mr Mokhatla for his defamatory statement. The question arises as to what effect an apology should have on the amount of damages to be awarded. In *Mineworkers Investment Co (Pty) Ltd v Modibane* (the *Mineworkers* case) the plaintiff had brought two separate defamation actions against the defendant, which were consolidated and set down together for trial. The order which the plaintiff requested was an order for damages in the event that the defendant did not publish within 10 days of the Court's order an apology and a retraction of the statements which he had made. Willis J proceeded to consider whether a defendant in a defamation action could be ordered to apologise. The Court considered a remedy, which had existed in Roman-Dutch law, known as the *amende honorable*. In describing this remedy he referred to Melius de Villiers in *The Roman and Roman-Dutch Law of Injuries* at 177, which stated the following:

"In the systems of jurisprudence founded on Roman law a legal remedy has been introduced which was entirely unknown to the Romans, known as the *amende honorable*. . . . *This remedy took two forms. In the first place, there is the palinodia, recantatio or retractio,* that is, a declaration by the person who uttered or published the defamatory words or expressions concerning another, to the effect that he withdraws such words or expressions as being untrue; and it is applied when such words or expressions are in fact untrue. In the second place there is the *deprecatio* or apology, which is an acknowledgment by the person who uttered or published concerning another anything which if untrue would be defamatory, or who committed a real injury, that he has done wrong and a prayer that he may be forgiven."

[64] Willis J held further that the remedy had fallen into disuse in our law, mainly because in Roman-Dutch law it was to be enforced by means of civil imprisonment, a remedy of which the Courts disapproved. This did not mean it had been abrogated by disuse; it still formed part of our law and:

"[E]ven if I am wrong in the conclusion that the *amende honorable* is still part of our law, there are other reasons why I believe a remedy analogous thereto should be available. I agree with the submission of Mr *Chaskalson* that if the only other remedy available in a defamation action is damages, then very often an appropriate balance will not be struck between the protection of reputation on the one hand and freedom of expression on the other. It fails in two respects: (i) often, it does not afford an adequate protection to reputation and (ii) it can, at least indirectly, impose restrictions on freedom of expression. Awards of damages can ruin defendants financially and this risk can operate to restrict information being published, which may indeed be in the public interest. The uncertainty as to whether the 'truth plus public benefit' defence will succeed can inhibit freedom of expression. As Hefer JA, as he then was, said in the case of *National Media Ltd v Bogoshi* (*supra* at 1201G–I):

'Much has been written about the "chilling" effect of defamation actions but nothing can be more chilling than the prospect of being mulcted in damages for even the slightest error.'"

Furthermore, the harm done by a defamatory statement is damage to the reputation of a person. A public apology will usually be far less costly than an award of damages. It can set the record straight; restore the damaged reputation giving the necessary satisfaction; avoid serious financial harm to the culprit and encourage, rather than inhibit, freedom of expression.

[65] A somewhat different approach was adopted in *Young v Shaikh*. In that matter statements made during an interview with the defendant on a South African television station on 21 November 2001 and repeated on 26 November 2001, led the plaintiff to claim damages in the amount of R250 000. In his plea the defendant apologised to the plaintiff unconditionally and unreservedly and in addition, tendered to pay his costs up to and including the consideration of his plea. The defendant submitted that the plaintiff should have claimed an apology instead of damages and should have been satisfied with the apology tendered in the plea. As authority for this submission reference was made to the dictum of Willis J in the *Mineworkers* case.

[66] The Court nonetheless held that even if the *amende honorable* were still part of South African law, an apology in the circumstances of that case would not serve the interests of justice. Freedom of expression, it held, does not include the right to attack falsely the integrity of a fellow citizen for selfish reasons that have nothing to do with "public benefit." It further held that if the award which it intended to make might have a chilling effect on possible future and similarly baseless and selfish attacks on the integrity of others it would be an additional reason not to make use of the *amende honorable*. In addition it was found that an apology in a plea given half-heartedly in evidence could not be regarded as adequate. An aggravating factor was that the defendant had not shown any compunction when attacking the plaintiff's integrity and was indifferent to any financial harm, which his baseless accusations could have caused.

[67] The case illustrates that whether or not the *amende honorable* technically still forms part of our law, it is important that once an apology is tendered as compensation or part thereof, it should be sincere and adequate in the context of each case. When considering the purpose of compensation in defamation cases the true value of a sincere and adequate apology, the publication of which should be as prominent as that of the defamatory statement, and or a retraction as a compensatory measure restoring the integrity and human dignity of the plaintiff, cannot be exaggerated. Far more is involved than protecting freedom of speech from inordinate damages claims.

[68] In our constitutional democracy the basic constitutional value of human dignity relates closely to *ubuntu* or *botho*, an idea based on deep respect for the humanity of another. Traditional law and culture have long considered one of the principal objectives of the law to be the restoration of harmonious human and social relationships where they have been ruptured by an infraction of community norms. It should be a goal of our law to emphasise, in cases of compensation for defamation, the re-establishment of harmony in the relationship between the parties, rather than to enlarge the hole in the defendant's pocket, something more likely to increase acrimony, push the parties apart and even cause the defendant financial ruin. The primary purpose of a compensatory measure, after all, is to restore the dignity of a plaintiff who has suffered the damage and not to punish a defendant. A remedy based on the idea of *ubuntu* or *botho* could go much further in restoring human dignity than an imposed monetary award in which the size of the victory is measured by the quantum ordered and the parties are further estranged rather than brought together by the legal process. It could indeed give better appreciation and sensitise a defendant as to the hurtful impact of his or her unlawful actions, similar to the emerging idea of restorative justice in our sentencing laws.

[69] The focus on monetary compensation diverts attention from two considerations that should be basic to defamation law. The first is that the reparation sought is essentially for injury to one's honour, dignity and reputation, and not to one's

pocket. The second is that Courts should attempt, wherever feasible, to re-establish a dignified and respectful relationship between the parties. Because an apology serves to recognise the human dignity of the plaintiff, thus acknowledging, in the true sense of *ubuntu*, his or her inner humanity, the resultant harmony would serve the good of both the plaintiff and the defendant. Whether the *amende honorable* is part of our law or not, our law in this area should be developed in the light of the values of *ubuntu* emphasising restorative rather than retributive justice. The goal should be to knit together shattered relationships in the community and encourage across-the-board respect for the basic norms of human and social inter-dependence. It is an area where Courts should be proactive, encouraging apology and mutual understanding wherever possible.

[70] This case suggests itself as one where perhaps more could have been done to facilitate an apology. The parties worked closely together in the same environment. An apology or retraction by Mr Dikoko could have gone a long way. At no stage did he offer an apology or a retraction of his false and damaging accusations. The evidence that he led before the High Court, testifying to the high regard he had for Mr Mokhatla, was of an abstract nature and fell far short of a direct apology for the specific and baseless charges he had made. This is a case where it might have been appropriate to order an apology if this had been a majority judgment. However, considering that this is a minority judgment it is not appropriate. Having said that, what remains is to consider whether the monetary award made by the High Court can be interfered with.

[71] When assessing damages for defamation, Courts have in the past considered a range of factors arising from the circumstances and facts of the case: the nature and gravity of the defamatory words; falseness of the statement; malice on the part of the defendant; rank or social status of the parties; the absence or nature of an apology; the nature and extent of the publication and the general conduct of the defendant. The Court must therefore have regard to all the circumstances of a case where the assessment is always context specific. The list is non-exhaustive. Although earlier cases of a similar nature give guidance, they must always be applied with the necessary circumspection.

[72] In *Charles Mogale* the SCA found that a Court of first instance had misdirected itself when it did not show what factors had been taken into account in the determination of the award of damages. Similarly, if a trial Court mentions expressly what factors it had taken into account and determined as relevant for assessing the award, it is reasonable to conclude that other factors not referred to at all in the assessment had not been taken into account. In this case Mr Dikoko's defence against what he submitted was an excessive award is that the publication of the statement was limited; the statement was speculative; he did not have the intention to injure Mr Mokhatla and the statement was made in the context of a meeting aimed at overseeing and managing public funds in which councillors should be given the scope to articulate their views and opinions. He argues further that there is no evidence that

the persons at the meeting drew any negative inferences from the statement. None of these defences were shown anywhere in the judgment to have been considered. The factors mentioned and shown to have been considered all weighed against Mr Dikoko, as the Court correctly observed. Those not considered, could, in my view, have mitigated the gravity of the defamation and affected the award and the determination of the quantum accordingly.

[73] When factors that could have a mitigating effect on the seriousness of the defamation are not shown to have been taken into consideration a difficulty arises. The difficulty is that unless shown, this Court will never know. In *Charles Mogale*, the Court stated that:

> "A Court of appeal may also interfere if the Court of first instance materially misdirected itself and in this regard it is important for a Court of second instance to know what factors a trial Court has taken into account in determining the award."

[74] It is therefore important that all relevant factors be taken into account when assessing damages for defamation. Also important is to strike an equitable balance in the determination of the gravity of the damage. It is for this reason too that a trial Court must show that it has considered those relevant factors, which not only aggravate but also mitigate the seriousness of the damages. *Hulley v Cox*, considering quantum in a different context, emphasised the importance of equity in the assessment of damages and held: "The amount . . . should be estimated on an equitable basis on a consideration of all the circumstances."

[75] Equity in determining a damages award for defamation is therefore an important consideration in the context of the purpose of a damages award aptly expressed in *Lynch* as solace to a plaintiff's wounded feelings and not to penalise or deter people from doing what the defendant has done. Even if a compensatory award may have a deterrent effect, its purpose is not to punish. Clearly, punishment and deterrence are functions of the criminal law. Not the law of delict.

[76] In our law a damages award therefore does not serve to punish for the act of defamation. It principally aims to serve as compensation for damage caused by the defamation, vindicating the victim's dignity, reputation and integrity. Alternatively, it serves to console. For the reasons stated above and in particular having disregarded relevant factors, which could have mitigated the damage caused by the defamation, the High Court, in my view, had materially misdirected itself thereby arriving at an unreasonable award. The grounds for this Court to make its own assessment of the damages are therefore sufficient and I proceed to do so.

[77] The High Court had taken into account Mr Mokhatla's position in society; the relationship between Mr Dikoko and Mr Mokhatla; the absence of an apology and the seriousness of the allegations made by Mr Dikoko against Mr Mokhatla.

It said so expressly. Additional relevant factors not mentioned and in my view not given due regard are: the nature of the defamatory statement; the damaging effect that it had on Mr Mokhatla and the nature and extent of circulation of the publication.

[78] The untruthful nature of the statement; denying responsibility for his tardiness and placing all blame on Mr Mokhatla for the predicament which he created for himself are factors which aggravate the damage done not only to Mr Mokhatla's personal reputation, dignity and esteem, but also to his professional integrity. Although Mr Mokhatla has no doubt suffered serious damage to his professional integrity, the damage was in my view not fatal to his career. At the time the proceedings were launched he was municipal manager of the Klerksdorp Municipal Council, a position of high public office, directly relevant to his experience, performance and trustworthiness as CEO of the Council and his integrity as a person and a professional in the management of local government. Although Mr Mokhatla had been defamed largely in local and provincial government circles, having been appointed to this high public office within the same government circles is demonstration that his integrity as a trustworthy public manager in local government is still largely intact despite Mr Dikoko's statement. This is an important mitigating factor, which the High Court should not have disregarded.

[79] Mr Dikoko's statements were made in the Standing Committee and were published only in the local press. The statements therefore had limited circulation. Although Mr Mokhatla contended that this local publication did more damage to his career than would publication at a national level, in that his professional reputation was more at stake in local circles, his professional reputation does not seem to have been fatally dented. As indicated above, his current position as municipal manager after he had left the Council where he served as CEO seems to suggest that he is still held in high esteem in local government circles and in the province. This too, is a factor which, had the High Court taken into account would have influenced its assessment of damages.

[80] In making its award of damages, the High Court, did not exercise its discretion reasonably. It did not take into account factors, which mitigate the damages award. Mr Dikoko contends that an amount of R20 000 to R30 000 would be adequate. The High Court made an award of R110 000. For reasons outlined above I conclude that in the circumstances of this case an award in the amount of R50 000 would have been appropriate. I would therefore have replaced the High Court's order that Mr Dikoko pay damages in the amount R110 000 with an order that he pay damages in the amount of R50 000.

Costs
[81] Given that Mr Dikoko is partially successful I would have proposed there be no order as to costs.

The Order

[82] I would further have proposed that the application for leave to appeal be granted and that the High Court order be set aside and replaced with an order for damages in the amount of R50 000.

Justice Sachs

. . .

[105] In concurring with the judgment of Mokgoro J, I offer reasons for proposing a remedial shift in the law of defamation from almost exclusive preoccupation with monetary awards, towards a more flexible and broadly based approach that involves and encourages apology. Developing the common law in this way would, consistently with our new constitutional ethos, facilitate interpersonal repair and the restoration of social harmony.

[106] The facts of this case illustrate well the limitations of responding to injury to a person's good name simply by making a monetary award. When trying to evade responsibility for his grossly excessive use of a municipal cellphone, Mr Dikoko, the mayor, uttered manifestly silly and self-serving words to the Public Accounts Standing Committee about Mr Mokhatla, the municipal manager. Mr Mokhatla was entitled to see the mayor publicly rebuked, entitled to have any possible doubts about his own integrity cleared up, entitled to a retraction of the slur, and entitled to an apology. But he was not, in my opinion, entitled to R110 000.

[107] Hard-boiled members of the committee, who have heard every exculpatory story under the sun, could scarcely have taken his words seriously. And certainly the readers of the local newspaper, in whose columns his exchange with the committee was repeated, could be expected to have taken his bluster with a large dose of salt. Indeed, made in the context of pitiful evasions to the accounts committee, the utterances were so blatantly incredible and unworthy as to demean their author rather than the person blamed. Above all, they were delivered on the fringes of protected institutional speech, calling for institutional remedies and apology, rather than payment of an incongruously large and punitive sum.

[108] It might well be that the issue of quantum of damages would generally not on its own qualify as being a constitutional one falling within the jurisdiction of this Court. In this case, however, it arises on the periphery of and in connection with issues of a manifestly constitutional character. Here were public figures being called to account by a public institution for behaviour or misbehaviour in an official setting. Even although qualified privilege was not pleaded as a defence to the claim, the context should have had a significant bearing on the appropriateness of any damages to be awarded. The mayor was testifying before a governmental committee. Witnesses before such investigative committees should feel free to speak their mind. As a matter of general principle they should not be made to fear heavy damages suits if they either overstep the mark in the telling, or do not have iron-clad proof to sub-

stantiate their testimony. The chilling effect of punitive awards would not only be felt by officials caught with their metaphorical pants down, but by honest whistle-blowers and by newspapers simply carrying testimonial exposures.

[109] There is a further and deeper problem with damages awards in defamation cases. They measure something so intrinsic to human dignity as a person's reputation and honour as if these were market-place commodities. Unlike businesses, honour is not quoted on the Stock Exchange. The true and lasting solace for the person wrongly injured is the vindication by the Court of his or her reputation in the community. The greatest prize is to walk away with head high, knowing that even the traducer has acknowledged the injustice of the slur.

[110] There is something conceptually incongruous in attempting to establish a proportionate relationship between vindication of a reputation, on the one hand, and determining a sum of money as compensation, on the other. The damaged reputation is either restored to what it was, or it is not. It cannot be more restored by a higher award, and less restored by a lower one. It is the judicial finding in favour of the integrity of the complainant that vindicates his or her reputation, not the amount of money he or she ends up being able to deposit in the bank.

[111] The notion that the value of a person's reputation has to be expressed in rands in fact carries the risk of undermining the very thing the law is seeking to vindicate, namely the intangible, socially-constructed and intensely meaningful good name of the injured person. The specific nature of the injury at issue requires a sensitive judicial response that goes beyond the ordinary alertness that Courts should be expected to display to encourage settlement between litigants. As the law is currently applied, defamation proceedings tend to unfold in a way that exacerbates the ruptured relationship between the parties, driving them further apart rather than bringing them closer together. For the one to win, the other must lose, the scorecard being measured in a surplus of rands for the victor.

[112] What is called for is greater scope and encouragement for enabling the reparative value of retraction and apology to be introduced into the proceedings. In jurisprudential terms, this would necessitate reconceiving the available remedies so as to focus more on the human and less on the patrimonial dimensions of the problem. The principal goal should be repair rather than punishment. To achieve this objective requires making greater allowance in defamation proceedings for acknowledging the constitutional values of *ubuntu-botho*.

[113] *uBuntu-botho* is more than a phrase to be invoked from time to time to add a gracious and affirmative gloss to a legal finding already arrived at. It is intrinsic to and constitutive of our constitutional culture. Historically it was foundational to the spirit of reconciliation and bridge building that enabled our deeply traumatised society to overcome and transcend the divisions of the past. In present-day terms it has an enduring and creative character, representing the element of human solidarity that binds together liberty and equality to create an affirmative and mutually supportive

triad of central constitutional values. It feeds pervasively into and enriches the fundamental rights enshrined in the Constitution. As this Court said in *Port Elizabeth Municipality v Various Occupiers*:

> "The spirit of *ubuntu*, part of the deep cultural heritage of the majority of the
> population, suffuses the whole constitutional order. It combines individual
> rights with a communitarian philosophy. It is a unifying motif of the Bill of
> Rights, which is nothing if not a structured, institutionalised and operational
> declaration in our evolving new society of the need for human
> interdependence, respect and concern."

[114] *uBuntu-botho* is highly consonant with rapidly evolving international notions of restorative justice. Deeply rooted in our society, it links up with worldwide
striving to develop restorative systems of justice based on reparative rather than
purely punitive principles. The key elements of restorative justice have been identified
as encounter, reparation, reintegration and participation. Encounter (dialogue) enables the victims and offenders to talk about the hurt caused and how the parties are
to get on in future. Reparation focuses on repairing the harm that has been done
rather than on doling out punishment. Reintegration into the community depends
upon the achievement of mutual respect for and mutual commitment to one
another. And participation presupposes a less formal encounter between the parties
that allows other people close to them to participate. These concepts harmonise well
with processes well known to traditional forms of dispute resolution in our country,
processes that have long been, and continue to be, underpinned by the philosophy
of *ubuntu-botho*.

[115] Like the principles of restorative justice, the philosophy of *ubuntu-botho* has
usually been invoked in relation to criminal law, and especially with reference to child
justice. Yet there is no reason why it should be restricted to those areas. It has already
influenced our jurisprudence in respect of such widely divergent issues as capital punishment and the manner in which the Courts should deal with persons threatened
with eviction from rudimentary shelters on land unlawfully occupied. Recently it was
applied in creative fashion in the High Court to combine a suspended custodial sentence in a homicide case with an apology from a senior representative of the family of
the accused, as requested and acknowledged by the mother of the deceased.

[116] I can think of few processes that would be more amenable in appropriate
cases to the influence of the affirming values of *ubuntu-botho* than those concerned
with seeking simultaneously to restore a person's public honour while assuaging
inter-personal trauma and healing social wounds. In this connection attention
should be paid to the traditional Roman-Dutch law concept of the *amende honorable*
referred to in Mokgoro J's judgment. Although *ubuntu-botho* and the *amende honorable* are expressed in different languages intrinsic to separate legal cultures, they
share the same underlying philosophy and goal. Both are directed towards promoting

face-to-face encounter between the parties, so as to facilitate resolution in public of their differences and the restoration of harmony in the community. In both legal cultures the centrepiece of the process is to create conditions to facilitate the achievement, if at all possible, of an apology honestly offered, and generously accepted.

[117] Thus, although I believe the actual award made by the High Court in this matter was way over the top, and accordingly associate myself with Mokgoro J's minority finding in this regard, my concern is not restricted to the excessiveness of the amount. It lies primarily with the fact that the law, as presently understood and applied, does far too little to encourage repair and reconciliation between the parties. In this respect the High Court cannot be faulted. The concerns expressed above were not raised in the papers or addressed in argument before it. The Court was simply working with a well-tried remedy in the ordinary way. Unfortunately, the hydraulic pressure on all concerned to go with the traditional legal flow inevitably produces a set of rules that are self-referential and self-perpetuating. The whole forensic mindset, as well as the way evidence is led and arguments are presented, is functionally and exclusively geared towards enlarging or restricting the amount of damages to be awarded, rather than towards securing an apology. In my view, this fixed concentration on quantum requires amendment. Greater scope has to be given for reparatory remedies.

[118] It is noteworthy that in the context of hate speech the Legislature has indicated its support for the new remedy of Apology. Thus the Equality Court is empowered to order that an apology be made in addition to or in lieu of other remedies. I believe that the values embodied in our Constitution encourage something similar being developed in relation to defamation proceedings. In the light of the core constitutional values of *ubuntu–botho*, trial Courts should feel encouraged proactively to explore mechanisms for shifting the emphasis from near-exclusive attention to quantum, towards searching for processes which enhance the possibilities of resolving the dispute between the parties, and achieving a measure of dignified reconciliation. The problem is that if the vision of the law remains as tunnelled as it is today, parties will be discouraged from seeking to repair their relationship through direct and honourable engagement with each other. Apology will continue to be seen primarily as a tactical means of reducing damages rather as a principled modality for clearing the air and restoring a measure of mutual respect.

[119] The present case indicates the traps that preoccupation with money awards lays in front of a defendant. For a defendant to make an apology is to concede the defamation in advance and take the risk of paying heavy damages should the apology not be accepted. Thus if Mr Dikoko had publicly acknowledged that he had wronged Mr Mokhatla, he risked opening himself up to being seriously mulcted. Hence the ambivalence of his evidence. A retraction and apology genuinely offered and generously received, could have sorted the matter out once and for all, and contributed towards improving the way the parties would have been able to get on in future in the close working environment of local government. Yet the manner in which the process was structured appears to have produced a hurt and humiliated loser on the

one side, and a winner (who might find it difficult not to gloat) on the other. Thus the rupture between the protagonists was not healed, it was entrenched.

[120] Giving special emphasis to restoring the relationship between the parties does not, of course, imply that awards of damages should completely fall out of the picture. In our society money, like cattle, can have significant symbolic value. The threat of damages will continue to be needed, as a deterrent as long as the world we live in remains as money-oriented as it is. Many miscreants would be quite happy to make the most fulsome apology (whether sincere or not) on the basis that doing so costs them nothing—"it is just words." Moreover, it is well established that damage to one's reputation may not be fully cured by counter-publication or apology; the harmful statement often lingers on in people's minds. So even if damages do not cure the defamation, they may deter promiscuous slander, and constitute a real solace for irreparable harm done to one's reputation.

DU PLOOY V. MINISTER OF CORRECTIONAL SERVICES

Du Plooy v. Minister of Correctional Services and Others 2004 (3) All SA 613 (T)

Case Summary

FACTS

The Applicant was a prison inmate who was suffering from a terminal illness during his incarceration. Owing to the fact that his life expectancy was only a few months, the applicant applied to be released on medical parole, but his application was refused by the Pretoria Department of Correctional Services.

According to provisions that govern the placing of prisoners on parole, section 69 of the Correctional Services Act, read with "B-Order," the provincial commissioner, is delegated, pursuant to the parole board's recommendation, to determine the placement or release on medical grounds of offenders who are imprisoned for more than ten years for crimes. In this case, however, the decision to refuse the medical parole was taken by the area commissioner.

LEGAL HISTORY

The Transvaal High Court was the court of first instance in this matter.

LEGAL ISSUE

The Applicant sought the review and setting aside of the Department of Correctional Services decision to deny his application to be released on medical parole on grounds that such decision was taken by the wrong body, and was therefore *ultra vires*.

DISPENSATION

The High Court noted that the decision to decline to place the Applicant on medical parole was unlawful, unreasonable, and procedurally unfair because it was made by the wrong functionary. The court found further that such refusal was irrational, conflicted with sections 69 of the Correctional Services Act, as well as sections 10, 12(1)(e), 27(1)(a) and 35(2)(e) of the Constitution. The decision to deny the Applicant medical parole was set therefore aside.

The court noted, however, that as a general rule, an offender cannot expect to escape punishment or seek an adjustment of his term of imprisonment because of ill health. However, in this case, the Applicant's illness was advanced and he was in need of palliative care.

Justice Patel

. . .

[27] In the final analysis, I am of the considered view that the refusal to place the applicant on parole constitutes an infringement of section 10 of the Constitution which provides that everyone has inherent dignity and right to have his or her dignity respected and protected. There is also an infraction of other constitutional provisions, namely:

27.1 Section 12(1)(e). It states:

"Everyone has the right to freedom and security of the person which includes the right:

. . .

(e) not to be treated or punished in a cruel, inhuman or degrading way."

27.2 Section 27(1)(a) provides:

"Everyone has the right to have access to—
(a) health care service . . ."

27.3 Section 35(2)(e) states:

"Everyone who is detained including every sentenced prisoner has the right

. . .

. . .

(e) to conditions of detention that are consistent with human dignity including at least exercise under provision at state expense of adequate accommodation, nutrition, reading material and medical treatment."

[28] The Respondents also violated the Applicant's right to just administrative action by disregarding the provisions of section 33(1) and (2) of the Constitution read with the provisions of the Promotion of Administrative Justice Act 3 of 2000 and also his right to access to information by disregarding the provisions of section

32(1)(a) and (b) of the Constitution read with the pertinent provisions of the Promotion of Access to Information Act 2 of 2000.

[29] The Applicant is critically ill. He is dying. Imprisonment is too onerous for him by reason of his rapidly deteriorating state of health to continue remaining in jail and to be treated at a prison hospital. What he is in need of is humanness, empathy and compassion. These are values inherently embodied in *ubuntu*. When these values are weighed against the Applicant's continued imprisonment, then, in my view, his continued incarceration violates his human dignity and security, and the very punishment itself becomes cruel, inhuman and degrading. Therefore, I am inclined to grant an order in an amended form from that which the applicant seeks in the notice of motion.

[30] The final aspect is the question of costs. Mr *Joubert* contended that the Respondents should bear the costs of this urgent applicant on an attorney and client scale because of the manner in which they dealt with the application and the Respondents' attitude to these proceedings in this urgent Court. The granting of an appropriate cost order lies in the discretion of the Court. In my view, the Respondent's conduct is indeed reprehensible to justify cost on an attorney and client scale because firstly, the Respondents failed to furnish documentation in spite of proper requests made by LHR on the Applicant's behalf. Secondly, adequate notice of these proceedings was given to the Respondents on Tuesday the 9th, and by 2 P.M. on Wednesday the 10th the Respondents failed to deliver their answering affidavit, consequently the matter had to stand down for two days. Thirdly, a bundle of documents was thrust on the Applicant's legal representatives on Thursday morning when the Respondents could have timeously acceded to LHR's request. Fourthly, due to the conduct of the Respondents the matter was delayed and argument only commenced well after 5 P.M.

uBuntu and Entitlement

THE *SHILUBANE* CASE

S v. Shilubane [2005] JOL 15671 T

Case Summary

FACTS

The accused, thirty-five-year-old David Shilubane, entered a plea of guilty and was convicted of stealing seven fowl, to the value of 216 rand, which he subsequently cooked. The accused, a first-time offender, at the time of his sentencing in the Magistrate's Court showed "genuine remorse" and "solemnly undertook never to commit an offence." The presiding magistrate sentenced the accused to nine months imprisonment. However, on review, the High Court questioned the appropriateness of so harsh a sentence and the magistrate conceded that the sentence was, indeed, "disturbingly inappropriate" and, instead, recommended that the High Court set aside the sentence and replace it with a fine of 500 rand or six months imprisonment. Both the state attorney and the deputy director of public prosecutions indicated that the sentence had been inappropriate and that "the learned Magistrate had misdirected himself by imposing a sentence which is shockingly inappropriate." They, jointly, suggested a 600-rand fine or six months imprisonment, three months of which would be suspended for three years, conditions applying.

LEGAL HISTORY

This case is a review by the Transvaal Provincial Division High Court of a judgment handed down in the Magistrate's Court dealing with sentencing of an accused guilty of a "trifling offence."

LEGAL ISSUES

This case deals with "the efficacy of our current penal system and the ability of presiding officers to sentence people . . . appropriately and effectively." The judgment of Justice Bosielo looks to the restorative justice model as an alternative to the retributive penal system in order to determine how best to follow the precedent in *S v. V* 1972 (3) SA 611 (A), which states that "[p]unishment should fit the criminal as well as the crime, be fair to the accused and to society and be blended with a measure of mercy."[1]

DECISION

The judgment of Justice Bosielo (Justice Shongwe concurring), in seeking to implement "the new philosophy of restorative justice," looks to the already existing provisions of the Criminal Procedure Act 51 of 1977, section 300, in order to determine whether compensation offered to the complainant for the 216 rand loss suffered would, in fact, suffice, and render the imposition of any imprisonment redundant. Justice Bosielo, however, regrets that in this matter the requirement that the complainant consent to the compensation (as required by section 300) had not been fulfilled. Continuing, Justice Bosielo highlights the need for judicial officers to continue to innovate alternative, more appropriate sentences in order to circumvent "the problem of over-crowding in prisons."

Justice Bosielo called upon judicial officers to balance the need for an effective criminal justice system, "critical for the maintenance of law and order," with the need for the law to show humaneness in its imposition of sentences.

Justice Bosielo further highlights empirical studies that indicate that the retributive justice model has failed in its efforts to combat crime and that the consequence of the conventional sentence of direct imprisonment often results in the bitter irony of a "counter-productive, if not self-defeating" system of exposing an accused, guilty of a *de minimis* offence who yet retains the potential to be rehabilitated into society, to prison life and its "corrosive and brutalising effect." The result, as Justice Bosielo indicates, is that the prisoner emerges from his or her time served as a newly "hardened criminal."

Justice Bosielo, therefore, makes the recommendation that sentences such as community service be more frequently relied upon where it is patent that the accused poses no real threat to society. Thus, with its focus on rehabilitation into civil society, the model of retributive justice would seem to offer a benefit to society—so advocates Justice Bosielo.

Consequently, Justice Bosielo ordered that the sentence of the magistrate's court be set aside and replaced with a 500-rand fine or "in default of payment, to imprisonment of 6 months, wholly suspended for a period of 3 years," various conditions applying.[2]

Justice Bosielo

[1] This review matter once again puts the spotlight on the vexed debate which is currently raging on fiercely within the various strata of our civil society *viz*, the effi-

cacy of our current penal system and the ability of presiding officers to sentence people convicted of crime appropriately and effectively. This aspect assumes great significance when viewed in the light of the public hysteria generated by the ever-increasing wave of crimes in our society and against the backdrop of another serious social ill *viz*, overcrowding in our correctional centres concomitant with the plethora of other social ills which are spawned by this overcrowding.

[2] The accused herein was convicted, on his plea of guilty, of theft of seven fowl. Notwithstanding the fact that he expressed genuine remorse, that he is a first offender at the age of 35 years and further that he solemnly undertook never to commit an offence, the magistrate sentenced him to direct imprisonment for 9 months. However, in response to my query concerning the appropriateness of the sentence, the learned Magistrate conceded that the sentence of 9 months' direct imprisonment is in the circumstances of this case, disturbingly inappropriate. He recommended that I should set aside the sentence and replace it with a fine of R500 or in default of payment, imprisonment for 6 months.

[3] Having been requested to comment on the sentence imposed *in casu*, the State Advocate, with the concurrence of the Deputy Director of Public Prosecutions, expressed the view that the learned Magistrate misdirected himself by imposing a sentence, which is shockingly inappropriate. In a unanimous opinion, they recommend a fine of R600 or imprisonment for 6 months, half of which is to be suspended for a period of 3 years on suitable conditions.

[4] The guiding light to sentencing still remains the oft-quoted dictum in *S v V* 1972 (3) SA 611 (A) at 614 (also *S v Zinn* 1969 (2) SA 537 (A)) where it is clearly stated:

"Punishment should fit the criminal as well as the crime, be fair to the accused and to society and be blended with a measure of mercy."

The accused herein stole seven fowl from the complainant, which according to his admissions, he cooked. Self-evidently the loss to the complainant amounts to R216 (two hundred and sixteen rand), which is the value of the seven fowl, reflected on the charge sheet. I have little doubt in my mind that, in line with the new philosophy of restorative justice, that the complainant would have been more pleased to receive compensation for his loss. An order of compensation coupled with a suspended sentence would, in my view, have satisfied the basic triad and the primary purposes of punishment. Unfortunately, I am unable to consider this option, as section 300 of the Criminal Procedure Act 51 of 1977 requires the consent of the complainant.

[5] I feel constrained to remark that unless presiding officers become innovative and pro-active in opting for other alternative sentences to direct imprisonment, we will not be able to solve the problem of overcrowding in our prisons. Inasmuch as it is critical for the maintenance of law and order that criminals be punished for their crimes, it is important that presiding officers impose sentences that are humane

and balanced. There is abundant empirical evidence that retributive justice has failed to stem the ever-increasing wave of crime. It is furthermore counter-productive if not self-defeating, in my view, to expose an accused like the one, *in casu*, to the corrosive and brutalising effect of prison life for such a trifling offence. The price which civil society stands to pay in the end by having him emerge out of prison a hardened criminal, far outweighs the advantages to be gained by sending him to jail.

[6] I am of the view that courts must seriously consider alternative sentences like community service as a viable alternative to direct imprisonment, particularly where the accused is not such a serious threat to society that he requires to be taken away from society for its protection. I am particularly fortified in my view by the strong sentiments (with which I respectfully agree) expressed by the former Deputy Minister of Correctional Services, Ms Cheryl Gillwald in the edition of the now defunct *This Day* newspaper of 17 August 2004 under the heading "Crime and Punishment," where she in an illuminating manner stated:

> "Incarceration only becomes a deterrent when society perceives the justice system to be efficient, consistent and effective. Rather than focusing on internment, sentencing should focus on what the most effective rehabilitation route would be for the offender, taking into account the gravity of the offence, assessment of the individual and his/her history, social and employment circumstances."

Speaking for myself such an approach to sentencing will benefit our society immensely by excluding the possibility of warped sentences being imposed routinely on people who do not deserve them.

[7] For the aforegoing reasons, I am in respectful agreement with both the magistrate and the office of the Director of Public Prosecutions that the sentence imposed on the accused is so disturbingly inappropriate that it should be set aside.

In the result, I make the following order:

1. The conviction of the accused is confirmed.
2. The sentence imposed on the accused by the court *a quo* is set aside and substituted with following:

   > "The accused is sentenced to R500 or in default of payment, to imprisonment for 6 months, wholly suspended for a period of 3 years, on condition the accused is not convicted of theft committed during the period of suspension for which he is sentenced to imprisonment without the option of a fine."

Justice Shongwe concurred in the judgment of Justice Bosielo.

THE *BOPHUTHATSWANA* CASE

Bophuthatswana Broadcasting Corporation v. Ramosa and Others [1997] JOL 283 (B)

Case Summary

FACTS

The Applicant in this case was the Bophuthatswana Broadcasting Corporation (BBC), a parastatal organization. The dispute arose from negotiations between the Applicant and the Respondents (employees of the BBC and members of a trade union—Media Workers' Association of South Africa) during which it was agreed that members of the Respondents were to be paid certain retirement packages by an intermediary, SEBO. The Respondents were not paid by SEBO and consequently took to protesting in a group of about six hundred union members outside the entrance to the BBC. The demonstrators sometimes displayed violent behavior towards members of the BBC trying to conduct their daily business and, since many of the protesters were also in the full time employ of the BBC, their protesting activities kept a significant number of BBC workers away from their work place at the BBC.

The Applicant thus sought an urgent interdict to prevent the Respondents disrupting the BBC's working day (the Respondents were demonstrating and holding meetings at the entrance to the BBC). The Applicants also sought to interdict the Respondents from "threatening, intimidating, obstructing or interfering in any manner with the employees of Applicant and the daily business of its Broadcasting Station."

LEGAL HISTORY

This was an urgent application. An interim interdict was granted and the matter was argued on the return date whereupon judgment was reserved.

LEGAL ISSUES

The issue for determination before this court was whether the Applicant had, on the balance of probabilities, proved the three elements of an interdict listed in the judgment as "(a) a clear right on the part of the Applicant; (b) an injury actually committed or reasonably apprehended; (c) the absence of any other satisfactory remedy available to the Applicant."

DECISION

In consideration of the three elements of obtaining a final interdict, the court heard argument advanced by the Respondents that their constitutional right (presumably referring to section 17 of the Constitution; the right to "[a]ssembly, demonstration, picket and petition") is in no way subject to the rights of the Applicant. This argument was rejected by Justice Khumalo, who cited many mixed authorities—from Confucius to St. Matthew's gospel to Justinian, to invoke a judicial concept of reciprocity of action in so far as "to be human is a communal enterprise." This concept, so held Justice Khumalo, is but one element of *ubuntu*, which Justice Khumalo re-iterates is incorporated into the Constitution. The conclusion was that the activities of the Respondents were not "the proper exercise of a right." Justice Khumalo went on to hold that the Applicant had managed to persuade the court, on the balance of probabilities, that the necessary elements of the interdict sought had been proved. The court thus granted the final interdict prohibiting the Respondents from demonstrating at the Applicants' place of business and in any way disrupting or threatening to disrupt, intimidate, or obstruct the employees of the BBC.

Justice Khumalo

This is an application, which is brought on the basis of urgency. An interim order was granted on 7 March 1996 and on the return date the matter was argued and judgment reserved. What follows are the reasons for judgment.

THE FACTS

(a) The Applicant: The Applicant is a parastatal body employing a large number of people. On 5 March 1996 the Acting Chief Executive of the Applicant was in Johannesburg launching a programme on behalf of the Applicant. He received a report from the Managing Director of Buffalo Security Service. On the 6 March 1996 he again received another report from Thansanqa Linda of Buffalo Services. On 7 March 1996 the Acting Chief Executive of Applicant obtained advice from the Provincial Director General to launch these proceedings. The Managing Director of the Applicant states in his affidavit that the Respondents and their followers planned to disrupt the smooth running of the station. This was to commence on the 5 March 1996. He does not give any further details of the plan. Thamsanqa Linda merely confirms that he told the Applicant's Acting Chief Executive officer that Respondents and their followers were demonstrating at the Applicant's main gate and were unruly and influencing their followers to remain at the gate until the Acting Chief Executive came to explain when SEBO would pay their money. From Applicant's replying affidavits it appears that the Respondents received retirement packages, which had been agreed to between Applicant and the Respondents. SEBO was to effect payment. Cathy Throw, an employee of Applicant, states in her affidavit that she received threats from unknown persons accusing her of not taking part in the protest against Applicant. Pogisho Mpotoane, an employee of Applicant, states in his affidavit that unknown male persons asked him over the telephone if he was aware that a resolution was taken at Applicant's gate that there would be a total black-out of all channels on the evening of 6 March 1996. At 14h20 P.M. he was driving out of Applicant's premises and at the main gate first Respondent was aggressive to him and he pulled him by his clothes through the driver's window but Pogisho drove away. In the evening he received threatening calls accusing him of keeping the station open.

(b) The Respondent alleges that certain of Applicant's short-term employees were entitled to certain amounts to be paid by SEBO on 4 March 1996. The said amounts were not paid on 4 March 1996. First Respondent is an office-bearer in the Media Workers Association of South Africa, a trade union to which most of the affected employees belonged. First Respondent then sent out a pamphlet calling a meeting of all affected persons to be held at the gates of Applicant on 5 March 1996. Approximately 600 persons attended the meeting. The meeting resolved to meet daily at the Applicant's gate to receive reports from first Respondent. The Respondents admit that they encouraged 250 persons working for the Applicant to join these meetings. He does not say how these people were encouraged and where this took place. The meeting of 5 March 1996 lasted until 16h30. First Respondent denies having dissuaded Applicant's employees from going to work or having made threats to them. The same group again met at Applicant's gate on 6 and 7 March 1996. First Applicant states that he told the people not to block Applicant's gate and he "specifically called on those present to refrain from any intimidation of any other person whatsoever." One wonders why he had to do so if his followers were peaceful and not blocking the entrance or interfering with persons going in or out of the gate.

THE LAW

It is trite law that before a final interdict is granted the following must be proved:

(a) a clear right on the part of the Applicant;
(b) an injury actually committed or reasonably apprehended;
(c) the absence of any other satisfactory remedy available to the Applicant.

See *Minister of Law and Order, Bophuthatswana and Another v Committee of the Church Summit of Bophuthatswana and Others* 1994 (3) SA 89 (BGD) at 98 and the authorities cited therein. The Applicant is entitled to the peaceful conduct of its business without any hindrance by six hundred other persons occupying the area outside its gates or main entrance. Such hindrance constitutes the "injury committed or reasonably apprehended." Counsel for the Respondents argued that the Respondents had not been shown to do any harm to Applicant. At 99 *op cit* the following is said:

"Moreover, where there is a threatened infringement of an applicant's clear right, he need not wait for the actual infringement to occur, but may and is entitled to approach the Court to restrain the threatened conduct which would establish and found such a breach or contravention of his/her rights."
See *Minister of Justice v SA Associated Newspapers Ltd and Another* 1979 (3) SA 466 (C).

There is in my view no other effective remedy. Counsel for the Respondents suggested that Applicant ought to have resorted to section 384 of Act 56 of 1955. There were 600 persons involved and most of them were not immediately identified by Applicant. That section would certainly not have been a suitable and adequate remedy for Applicant to resort to taking into account the urgency of the matter and the dilatory procedures under the section. See the above case at 99.

CONCLUSION

From the above it is common cause that for three days about 600 persons met outside the gates of the Applicant. There is nothing in the papers that Applicant agreed to these meetings being held at its gate. SEBO owed the Respondents and not the Applicant. The First Respondent was obviously the leader of the group and he called the meeting. The second and third Respondents were present at the meeting and were among the six hundred. Pogisho Mpotoane was interfered with at the gate. 600 people is a big number to crowd up at Applicant's gates. People wanting to gain access could apprehend harm and avoid entering. Employees who came to work were justified in apprehending harm because of the threats. It was obviously inconvenient for the Applicant and its employees to have so many people demonstrating at the gate. The meeting of the 5th March 1996 went well beyond the lunch hour and stopped at 16h30. Respondent admits that many of those present were short-term employees of Applicant. This long meeting with Applicant's officials was clearly obstructive to its normal business. Counsel for the Respondents argued in reply to Mrs Nkabinde that the Respondents were exercising their Constitutional rights and that there was nothing in the Constitution, which states that, the rights of the Respondents to protest and demonstrate are subject to the rights of the Applicants. I cannot agree with this submission. The Constitution of this country has not swept away everything that came before. Confucius who was not a religious person but rather a teacher of social ethics said the following:

"Do not do unto others what you would not want others to do unto you."

See *Encyclopaedia Brittanica: Knowledge in depth* Vol 16 at 656. In this passage Confucius clearly recognises that to be human is a communal enterprise. This statement is repeated somewhat differently in the Gospel according to St Matthew chapter 7 verse 12 as follows:

"Therefore all things whatsoever ye would that men should do to you, do ye even so to them: for this is the law and the prophets."

The concept contained in these passages quoted above forms part of *ubuntu*, which is incorporated in our Constitution. It was Justinian who said:

"Juris praecepta sunt haec: honeste vivere, alterum non laedare, suum cuique tribuere."

A fair translation of the above would be "the precepts (or maxims) of the law are these: to hurt no one, to give everyone his due." See *Institutes of Justinian* 1.1.3. All this forms part of our Constitutional law. As Mr Justice Oliver Wendell Holmes said on the opening page of his *The Common Law*:

> ". . . The law embodies the story of a nation's development through many centuries, and it cannot be dealt with as if it contained only the axioms and corollaries of a book of mathematics."

I cannot agree that crowding at the gate of another's premises is the proper exercise of a right. I am satisfied that Applicants have proved on a balance of probabilities that there was interference with its daily activities, which justified the granting of the interdict. I may mention *en passant* that papers in this application were poorly drawn and affidavits left out much that would have lightened the task of the Court. The order sought was not meticulously prepared. Counsel must take responsibility for the papers they base their arguments on. Mrs Nkabinde blamed everything on the time factor but ignored the fact that after the granting of the interim order nothing was done.

Be that as it may in the result I make the following order:

1. The Respondents are hereby interdicted from demonstrating and holding meetings at the main gate of the Applicant.
2. The Respondents are hereby restrained from threatening, intimidating, obstructing or interfering in any manner with the employees of Applicant and the daily business of its Broadcasting Station.
3. The Applicants are given leave to approach the Court on the same papers supplemented by additional affidavits for the purpose of seeking additional relief in respect of other persons whom the Applicant wishes to cite as Respondents and whose identity had not been established when the present Application was made.
4. Respondents are ordered to pay costs.

THE *BADENHORST* CASE

Badenhorst v. Badenhorst [2005] JOL 13583 (C)

Case Summary

FACTS

The plaintiff here is the husband and the defendant is the wife. The parties were married to each other out of community of property, and had a prenuptial contract.

What was in dispute were the issues of distribution of assets and maintenance, in terms of section 7(3) of the Divorce Act 70 of 1979.

At the beginning of their marriage, the Badenhorsts were helped by the plaintiff's parents with a farm—by way of getting a jump-start in life. The Jubileeskraal farm was owned by JC Badenhorst Trust. At divorce, the defendant argued that because she and the plaintiff had contributed to the improvement of the farm, and because they used the farm to generate income of their own, it was theirs and it had to be redistributed. The defendant argued further that the trust that owned the farm was actually her ex-husband's *alter ego* and had to be redistributed, too. In arguing for the redistribution of the assets, the Respondent relied on the said provision of the Divorce Act.

LEGAL HISTORY
The Cape High Court heard this matter.

LEGAL ISSUES
The first issue was whether a redistribution of the farm was warranted in the circumstances, and the second was whether, applied correctly, the Divorce Act gave the Respondent a right to a redistribution of assets.

DISPENSATION
After a lengthy cross-examination of the Respondent with respect to the farm, as well as the trust, the court found that the Respondent had no claim in these assets and was not entitled to the relief of redistribution. It was noted further that against *ubuntu*, the Respondent displayed attitudes of selfishness, and abused the generosity that was shown to them by the plaintiff's parents.

In dealing with the second issue, the court took into account various factors; among them was that the Respondent was the sole custodian of their children, and that she contributed to the plaintiff's estate. The court therefore found that the Respondent should be supported even though she had no claim in the trust or the farm.

Justice Ngwenya

. . .

[24] The argument that the plaintiff and the defendant are entitled to Jubileeskraal farm is fallacious. It amounts to the abuse of the generosity displayed by the plaintiff's parents to the couple. All indications are that the parents of the plaintiff wanted to give him and his wife, the defendant here, some start in life. While the evidence at my disposal shows that the litigants here were not given hard cash up front, they were given sufficient assets to enable them to have access to cash immediately. For this reason the plaintiff was able to pledge his parents' and later on the JC Badenhorst Trust's asset to the co-operative to access cash. When the defendant referred to "*ons eie kapitaal*," she referred to funds so accessed. She persisted with

her claim for the Jubileeskraal farm throughout. She left me with an irresistible temptation of greed. Her attitude in this regard undermined *ubuntu*, that godly value with which all human beings are ordained. Suffice it to say that Mr *De Villiers* saw some light at the end of the day that her persistence here was untenable.

[25] The Jubilee Trust is a separate legal entity which stands to benefit her own children. If Mr *De Villiers* meant in his submission that I must regard it as a separate entity, and yet take into account that the plaintiff had unlimited access to it, I have grave difficulties with this reasoning. It is contradictory. It implies that I must make an adverse order against the trust via the back door. Simply put he says I must order the plaintiff to transfer an amount of R946 046,50 to the defendant. The defendant will, in turn, thus, have her estate increased to the net value of R1 924 366,50 and that of the plaintiff reduced to R946 046,50. Because the plaintiff has unlimited access to the Jubilee Trust, even if he cannot raise this amount from his own assets, so proceeds this reasoning, he should be able to access trust property to satisfy this order. In my judgment, unless I find the trust to be a sham, I cannot make an order like this. When I find the trust to be such, I hope I will make a clear order to this effect.

THE *TSHABALALA-MSIMANG* CASE

Tshabalala-Msimang and Another v. Makhanya and Others 2008 (3) BCLR 338 (W)

Case Summary

FACTS

This case was brought by the Minister of Health in the National Government, as the First Applicant, and the operator of the Cape Town Medi Clinic center as the Second Applicant. The minister was hospitalized and treated at the Medi Clinic Center. A journalist from *The Sunday Times* obtained her medical records from the Medi Clinic Center and used them to publish an article in *The Sunday Times* titled "Manto's Hospital Booze Binge." This article alleged that the minister used an excess of painkillers and sleeping pills, and that she abused alcohol while in the hospital.

The Applicants sought an order for the return of the documents, and an order interdicting the Respondents from further publishing the contents of the hospital record, or commenting on the minister's treatment at the medical center. The minister argued that publication of her medical records was a violation of her right to dignity and privacy, or defamatory. Further, she argued that by being in possession of her medical records, the Respondents contravened section 17 of the National Health Act 61 of 2003.

The Respondents argued that their article was not based on the original documents, but on reliable sources. In these premises, they denied that they were under an obligation to return such documents. Moreover, they argued that the article written was in the public interest because the Minister of Health was a public figure.

LEGAL HISTORY
This matter was heard in the Witwatersrand High Court.

LEGAL ISSUE
The court was tasked with reconciling the right to freedom of expression and the right to dignity.

DISPENSATION
The court observed that all constitutional rights have equal weight. Reconciling conflicting rights, therefore, may require that one right be limited to the degree that it inhibits the exercise of another right. Such limitation, however, would have to be done in terms of section 36 of the Constitution of the Republic of South Africa.

The court noted further that while there was no hierarchy of rights, the right to human dignity occupied a central place in the Constitution and had to be accorded special protection.

The court then noted that the Respondents had not shown that they were not in possession of the medical records, or that they had not violated provisions of the National Health Act 61 of 2003. It therefore ordered that the Respondents return these documents; because they contained private and confidential information about the minister.

The Applicant sought an order interdicting the Respondent from further publication of the information. To this, the court held that although information may have been obtained through unlawful means, its public interest might nevertheless be a factor that would justify the publication of such information.

Justice Jajbhay

[1] "The time will come when our nation will honour the memory of all the sons, the daughters, the mothers, the fathers, the youth and the children who, by their thoughts and deeds, gave us the right to assert with pride that we are South Africans, that we are Africans and that we are citizens of the world." History has bestowed on our generation in our beloved country the gift of a rare opportunity to manage the birth of our freedom as a nation and to nurture it towards its maturity. This in turn, obliges all of us as citizens of this country to speak, and to act in very special ways. Section 1 of the Constitution informs us that:

> ". . . the Republic of South Africa is one, sovereign, democratic state founded on the following values: (a) human dignity, the achievement of equality and the advancement of human rights and freedoms."

This means that there are in existence dominant values as well as an ethos that binds us as communities to ensure social cohesion. In South Africa we have a value system based on the culture of *ubuntu*.

[2] This in effect is the capacity to express compassion, justice, reciprocity, dignity, harmony and humanity in the interests of building, maintaining and strengthening the community. *uBuntu* speaks to our inter-connectedness, our common humanity and the responsibility to each that flows from our connection. *uBuntu* is a culture, which places some emphasis on the commonality and on the interdependence of the members of the community. It recognises a person's status as a human being, entitled to unconditional respect, dignity, value and acceptance from the members of the community that such a person may be part of. In South Africa *ubuntu* must become a notion with particular resonance in the building of our constitutional democracy.

"The value of human dignity in our constitution is not only concerned with an individual's sense of self-worth, but constitutes an affirmation of the worth of human beings in our society. It includes the intrinsic worth of human beings shared by all people as well as the individual reputation of each person built upon his or her own individual achievements. The value of human dignity in our constitution therefore values both the personal sense of self-worth as well as the public's estimation of the worth or value of an individual. It should also be noted that there is a close link between human dignity and privacy in our constitutional order. The right to privacy, entrenched in section 14 of the Constitution, recognises that human beings have a right to have a sphere of intimacy and autonomy that should be protected from invasion. This right serves to foster human dignity."

. . .

[28] A constant refrain in our Constitution is that our society aims at the restoration of human dignity because of the many years of oppression and disadvantage. While it is not suggested that there is a hierarchy of rights it cannot be gainsaid that dignity occupies a central position. After all, that was the whole aim of the struggle against apartheid—the restoration of human dignity, equality and freedom.

"If human dignity is regarded as foundational in our Constitution a corollary thereto must be that it must be jealously guarded and protected. As this court held in *Dawood and another v Minister of Home Affairs and Others, Shalabi and Another v Minister of Home Affairs and Others, Thomas and Another v Minister of Home Affairs and Others* [2000 (3) SA 936 (CC); 2000 (8) BCLR 837 (CC)]: the value of dignity in our constitutional framework cannot therefore be doubted. The Constitution asserts dignity to contradict our past in which human dignity for the black South Africans was routinely and cruelly denied. It asserts it too to inform the future to invest in our democracy respect for the intrinsic worth of all human beings. Human dignity therefore informs constitutional adjudication and interpretation at a range of levels. It is a value that informs the interpretation of many, possibly all, other rights.

This court has already acknowledged the importance of the constitutional value of dignity in interpreting rights such as the right to equality, the right not to be punished in a cruel, inhuman or degrading way, and the right to life. Human dignity is also a constitutional value that is of central significance in the limitations analysis. Section 10, however makes it plain that dignity is not only a value fundamental to our Constitution, it is a justiciable and enforceable right that must be respected and protected."

. . .

[31] Both section 14 of the Constitution, as well as section 14(1) of the National Health Act envisage that the first applicant has a right to her privacy which would entitle her not to have her private medical information disclosed without her consent to the public. In *Bernstein and Others v Bester and Others NNO*, Ackermann J recognised that privacy is an elusive concept that has been the subject of much debate by scholars. We assert the value of privacy because of our constitutional understanding of what it means to be a human being. An implicit part of this aspect of privacy incorporates the right to choose what personal information of ours is released into the public domain.

"The more intimate that information, the more important it is in fostering privacy, dignity and autonomy that an individual makes the primary decision whether to release the information. That decision should not be made by others."

[32] It is for the above reasons that The National Health Act recognises confidentiality of healthcare records and the privacy attaching to such information. It also recognises the need to protect the information that is contained therein. The National Health Act also regulates the position regarding the keeping, maintenance, access, and disclosure of a user's health records.

[33] In the present matter, the Respondents have not been able to show that they have not contravened the National Health Act and that their continued access of the health records of the first applicant does not result in a continuous contravention of the provisions of the National Health Act. In fact, the contravention of the National Health Act by the Respondents has on these papers been established. *The Sunday Times* does not have any right to the medical records of the first applicant, either to possess or otherwise to have access to them. It also does not have a right to retain any copies of such records or any part thereof. In fact, in terms of the National Health Act these records are to be kept and maintained by the second applicant and access to these records is only permitted in very strict circumstances. It is the first applicant who has the right to authorise access or to deny such access. I see no reason why I should not make an order that would specify that the records pertaining to the treat-

ment and the stay of the first applicant in the Cape Town Medi Clinic of the second applicant, which were in the possession of the Respondents, be returned to the second applicant. It is generally the user under the relevant provisions of the National Health Act that has a right to determine who obtains access to her health records and to information relating to her health status, treatment and stay as a patient in a health establishment. Since the records contain private and confidential information of the first applicant (including information on her health status, treatment and stay in the Cape Medi Clinic) she is entitled to claim that those who are not authorised to have access, return it to either the first applicant or the second applicant.

The relief sought by the first applicant interdicting and restraining the Respondents from further commenting on, and of publishing any comments on the unlawfully obtained records.

. . .

[35] The freedom of the press is celebrated as one of the great pillars of liberty. It is entrenched in our Constitution but it is often misunderstood. Freedom of the press does not mean that the press is free to ruin a reputation or to break a confidence, or to pollute the cause of justice or to do anything that is unlawful. However, freedom of the press does mean that there should be no censorship. No unreasonable restraint should be placed on the press as to what they should publish.

[36] As a general matter, any person is likely to feel violated, harmed and invaded by the publication of unlawfully obtained information. Any reasonable person would probably feel less concerned if their discussions of an upcoming metropolitan council election, or the state of the global economy was unlawfully intercepted and subsequently published, than that person would if their discussion of intensely private matters such as family disputes or medical records were illegally intercepted and published for a larger audience. Similarly, on the public interest side of the equation, the public will certainly be interested and accordingly benefit from discussion of matters which are clearly in the public interest.

. . .

[38] The public has the right to be informed of current news and events concerning the lives of public persons such as politicians and public officials. This right has been given express recognition in section 16(1)(a) and (2) of the Constitution, which protects the freedom of the press and other media and the freedom to receive and impart information and ideas. The public has the right to be informed not only on matters which have a direct effect on life, such as legislative enactments, and financial policy. This right may in appropriate circumstances extend to information about public figures.

[39] The question then is who is a public figure and to what extent may such a public figure rely on his or her right to privacy to prevent publication of matter he or she would rather keep private? Here, Professor McQuoid-Mason offers the following test:

"In short it is submitted that the test whether a person is a public figure should be: has he by his personality, status or conduct exposed himself to such a degree of publicity as to justify intrusion into, or a public discourse on, certain aspects of his private life? However, non-actionable intrusions on his privacy should be limited to those that are in the public interest or for the public benefit, so that unjustified prying into personal affairs, unrelated to the person's public life, may be prevented."

. . .

[45] In her capacity as a Minister the first applicant cannot detract from the fact that she is a public figure. In such a case her life and affairs have become public knowledge and the press in its turn may inform the public of them.

[46] Much of the information that was published was already in the public domain. Here the information although unlawfully obtained, went beyond being simply interesting to the public; there was in fact a pressing need for the public to be informed about the information contained in the medical records of the first applicant. Then, the disclosure made by *The Sunday Times* did not mislead the public about an issue [in] which the public has a genuine concern. And finally, the publication of the unlawfully obtained controversial information was capable of contributing to a debate in our democratic society relating to a politician in the exercise of her functions.

[47] It is important to note that the contents incorporated in the hospital record according to Smuts, can be verified by "reliable sources." Smuts emphasises in her affidavit that the information found in the record was independently known to a few people. These include hospital staff, as well as fellow users.

[48] The Respondents' contention that they have reliable sources to verify the information in the hospital records means that the privacy right that the first applicant enjoys and seeks to assert becomes diluted. At this stage, it is understandable that these witnesses are not prepared to come forward to volunteer this information. Journalists generally rely on these sources. The veracity of this information cannot be weighed at this point in time. However, when the matter reaches these courts cloaked in a different cause of action then this evidence can clearly be tested. In the matter of *NM and Others v Smith and Others* Sachs J sets out:

". . . in *Bogoshi* the SCA developed in a way that was sensitive to contemporary concerns and realities, a well-weighted means of balancing respect for individual personality rights with concern for freedom of the press."

According to the SCA, what mattered was the reasonableness of the publication in the circumstances.

. . .

[50] This is a case where the need for the truth, is in fact overwhelming. Indeed in this matter the personality involved as well as her status establishes her newswor-

thiness. Here, we are dealing with a person who enjoys a very high position in the eyes of the public and it is the very same public that craves attention in respect of the information that is in the hands of *The Sunday Times*. The overwhelming public interest points in the direction of informing the public about the contents incorporated in the medical records in relation to the first applicant, albeit that the medical records might have been unlawfully obtained. In these circumstances I am unable to accede to the requests of the Applicants with regard to paragraphs 3 and 7 of their notice of motion, which in effect would impose a form of censorship in relation to any future publication around the medical record.

[54] It is not clear if any of the Respondents in the present matter took the necessary steps to investigate the illegal status of the medical record that they were armed with. There is an ethical obligation on journalists in matters such as the present to ascertain whether the document that they are armed with, has in fact been legally obtained. Although the publication of the contents incorporated in the confidential records of the first applicant and verified by "reliable sources" were capable of contributing to a debate in our democratic society, I cannot make a specific finding that *The Sunday Times should* have published them. The harm caused to the first applicant, and her family as well as those close to her must have been vast and painful. Newspapers, no less than other players in our society must keep in mind the consequences of their activities. Those involved with the present stories should have thought long and carefully about suitable alternatives before they chose to release this information. I have deliberately set out at the commencement of this judgment the constitutional values that we collectively espouse as a nation governed by the Constitution. The alternatives are to be found there.

THE *KUKARD* CASE

Kukard and Others v. Molapo Technology (Pty) Ltd 2006 (4) BLLR 334 (LC)

Case Summary
FACTS
The Respondents owned a business, and the Applicants were the employees of the Respondents in this business. Due to the business' unprofitable functioning, the Applicants were fired by the Respondents. The Applicants argued that their dismissal was a violation of section 189 of the Labour Relations Act 6 of 1995.

LEGAL HISTORY
The Labour Court heard this matter.

LEGAL ISSUE
Firstly, the court needed to determine whether there was a justifiable reason for dismissing the Applicants. Secondly, the court needed to determine, even if there had

been a justifiable reason to dismiss the Applicants, whether the procedure followed in dismissing the Applicants was fair.

DISPENSATION

On the facts, the court found that the Respondents had a justifiable reason for dismissing the Applicants. However, the evidence before the court showed that the process adopted by the Respondents in their dismissal had traces of unfairness. The Respondents should have allowed the Applicants time for consultation about its decision to dismiss them.

It was the Respondents' failure to allow time for consultation, which rendered the procedure for dismissal unfair. Accordingly, the court ordered the Respondents to pay the Applicants an amount equivalent to three months salary.

Acting Judge Ntseneza

. . .

[36] In the end, deciding the issue of procedural fairness, bearing in mind all the time, that the requirement of the Act is that a meaningful consultation process needs to be followed prior to a dismissal, really depends on whether the evidence points to a bona fide endeavour by all the parties to resolve the question of whether employees can or should be laid off, or whether one of the parties has frustrated the process by refusing to participate. There can be no general rule for whether this has happened, each case obviously depending not only on its own facts, but also on the way in which the evidence of those facts impressed the trier of fact. In a given case, the tight time frames, in the context of that particular case, may be way too unreasonably tight as to have amounted to a formalistic adherence to process, but so devoid of all substance as to render the process hollow for that very reason. In another case, the same tight frames, in the context of the facts of the case, may be found to be reasonable.

[37] Even though I have agonised over the process in this case, and even as I am very sympathetic to Mr *Taylor's* passionate submissions on how the process was heavily loaded against the employees, I am not persuaded that the employer, on the evidence tendered by it, can be held, justifiably, to have followed a process that can be labelled as having been wholly unfair.

[38] I am satisfied that Hart and Peddie's evidence is unblemished in its clarity that the employer, as soon as it contemplated that retrenchment might be necessary, attempted to engage the representative unions with the first consultation on 6 April 2000, six days after the end of March which had signified the discovery of a financial crisis for the employer as a result of which urgent steps became necessary for efforts to be taken to save the company. For six days, the evidence shows, the employer engaged consultants to advise it on what the viable options were to resolve the financial crisis. When, by 6 April 2000, the reality of the grimness of the financial position of the company became known, namely, that even though the company would be

saved, jobs might have to be cut either through voluntary retrenchments or forced removals, the employer decided to hold, and indeed held, intensive consultative meetings on the four days in April over a period of three weeks, with one scheduled meeting of 7 April 2000 not happening because, on the evidence, the union had not held a meeting with its members to consult with them on the issues of the meeting of 6 April 2000.

[39] Evidently, this period was very tight but it is interesting that even Kemp, one of the affected employees, acknowledged that the situation demanded urgency of attention. His issue was that the employer's time frames were too tight. He did not, however, venture to suggest what time frame would have been fairer in the circumstances. That attitude does not, unfortunately, help me. Further, Kemp conceded (contrary to what had been the complaint), that the employer in fact did provide the union with a great deal of information during the consultation process. I therefore have tried with difficulty to find any evidence to justify Mr *Taylor's* suggestion that the employees were not provided with the necessary information.

[40] The evidence also does not support Mr *Taylor's* contention that selection criteria were never discussed with the employees. The detailed memorandum provided (on 20 April 2000) to the union was a consequence of the deliberations on 18 April 2000, culminating in a final list of those to be laid off being drawn on 25 April 2000.

[41] However, there is something in this process that I need to express my views on. I accept that there may be different perspectives held by the employer, on the one hand, and the employees, on the other, about the value attached by each of these constituencies to the significance of the Freedom Day celebrations of 27 April in South Africa's post-Apartheid era. It is an emotive issue that shows the yawning gap that exists still between the beneficiaries of the Apartheid order, mainly whites in general, and their commercial enterprises, on the other hand, and victims of Apartheid, black workers in the main, on the other. For the former, 27 April 2000 was probably just another working day wasted as a public holiday. In this case, for example, it is clear that the employer thought only about the mess his company was in, and processes it felt had to be engaged in that were geared at saving the company from ruin. Not even Freedom Day celebrations were to stop the employer from seeking to force the workers to engage in a process that they felt could wait. For the workers, the celebrations of Freedom Day were evidently clearly so close to their hearts that the mere suggestion that they should have prioritised consultations over celebrations is anathema to them, almost an insensitive suggestion.

[42] Mr *Wesley* argued that the employer was quite alive and sensitive to the importance of these celebrations, but, in his view, the prioritisation of those celebrations over consultations was "inappropriate" and the employer ought not to be blamed for the consequences of the union's choice. For the most part, particularly, with respect to the absence of explanation from Kemp as to why no work could be done by the union in the period from 20 April to 25 April 2000 (the Easter weekend), and

on 26 and 27 April 2000, the latter day being Freedom Day, Mr *Wesley* submitted that the reason given was insignificant. I cannot agree with him that the reason given is an insignificant one in a transformative post-Apartheid South Africa.

[43] There is, in my view, something precipitous about the way in which, over that critical period, this employer conducted itself. The formalistically correct approach—business like if you want—with which the employer dealt with this time in its negotiations process with the workers was insensitive. It failed to appreciate the passion with which workers; black workers in particular, hold the advent of freedom close to their hearts. In so far as I am called to make a value judgment by Mr *Wesley* to the effect that the union failed the Applicants—and not the Respondent—in the process that was not as complete as it could have been, that value judgment must be premised not only on the evidence, but also on what I perceive to be the values of present day South African society. I hold that the values of dignity, freedom and *ubuntu*, values enshrined in our Constitution, place an imperative on employers to be much more sensitive to what is dear and sacrosanct to their employees. In this case, a long Easter weekend culminating in the Freedom Day celebrations of 27 April 2000 was conducive to the employees' desire to celebrate an historic event in the history of the land. I do not consider that it is fair, therefore, to suggest that the choice the workers made is something that they ought to be blamed for.

[44] I do not consider that the employer should have been as inflexible on this as it in fact was. An otherwise fair process, up to the point when the long weekend came about, was somewhat marred by this unfortunate attitude by the employer. It is an attitude, hardnosed it must be said, that unfortunately, in my view, rendered this process not as exhaustive as it could have been, had there been some sensitivity on the part of the employer. It is an insensitivity that does not amount to *mala fides*. It is one, however, that is not a technical deficiency either. It goes to the heart of what should weigh with me heavily as to whether a matter of weeks could have made any difference to the ultimate fate of the employer.

[45] Was it not in the interests of the employer to have opted for a flawless consultation process, one that probably would have taken a few more weeks to complete rather than go ahead on the basis that if the workers chose to celebrate an Easter weekend culminating in Freedom Day celebrations, they had only themselves to blame if they lost their jobs? I think our Courts, in a constitutional democracy like ours, would lose their credibility if they were to hold that a choice like that which was made by the employees in this context, cannot exonerate them from blame if they get dismissed for non-participation in the process to that extent.

[46] I think that if the employer had allowed a period of four to six more weeks of intensive engagements with the workers, holding them to strict timetables, the process would have been flawlessly completed. Because that time was not allowed, the process can be held, and I so hold, to have been unfair to that limited extent. It is a period in relation to which the employer must be prepared to pay compensation to the workers who were dismissed. Because of the decision I have come to, I am

unable to accede to the submission by Mr *Wesley* that I should order the Applicants to pay the Respondent's costs because the Respondent was brought to Court without good reason, expending considerable resources in defending a case it ought never to have had to meet. I disagree. My reasons have been stated.

[47] Before I conclude, I need to remark about the period it has taken for this judgment to come out. In my view, it is not an uncomplicated matter. The situation was compounded by my own ill health, which culminated in a lifestyle altering surgical operation, which I suddenly had to undergo in the July recess period, during which I had meant to complete re-reading the record and revisiting the arguments and my own notes. In so far, therefore, as justice delayed has been justice denied, I apologise. These factors are over and above the fiasco I alluded to at the beginning of this judgment.

[48] The Applicants have been partially successful, although, substantially, the Respondent has successfully resisted their case. In my view, therefore, an appropriate order would be as follows:

48.1 The Applicants' dismissal was for a fair reason;

48.2 The dismissal of the Applicants was not in accordance with a fair procedure;

48.3 The Respondent is ordered to pay the dismissed employees compensation, that is the equivalent of 3 months' remuneration, an amount just and equitable in the circumstances of this case; and

48.4 There will be no order as to costs.

uBuntu and Key Aspects of Living:

Customary Law

THE *BHE, SHIBI,* AND *SA HUMAN RIGHTS COMMISSION* CASES

Bhe and Others v. Magistrate, Khayelitsha and Others; Shibi v. Sithole and Others; SA Human Rights Commission and Another v. President of the RSA and Another 2005 (1) BCLR 1 (CC)

    Bhe and Others v. Magistrate, Khayelitsha and Others; Shibi v. Sithole and Others; SA Human Rights Commission and Another v. President of the RSA and Another 2004 (1) BCLR 27 (C)

Case Summary

FACTS

There were three cases before the court, all raising the same questions of law. These were *Bhe v. Magistrate Khayelitsha, Shibi v. Sithole,* and an application for direct access to the Court by the South African Human Rights Commission (SAHRC) and the Women's Legal Center Trust (WLCT).

The Bhe *Case*

Ms. Bhe and the deceased lived together as husband and wife for twelve years. They had two girl children, who were both minors at the time of their father's death. The deceased died intestate. During their lifetime together as husband and wife, the deceased had acquired a certain immoveable property in Khayelitsha, in which they all lived, and on which Ms. Bhe and her daughters continued to live after the deceased's death. Upon the death of the deceased, his father claimed that he was administrator and sole heir of the deceased's intestate estate in terms of African customary law, because the deceased did not have sons. Further, he wanted to sell the property on which the Appellants resided in Khayelitsha in order to defray the funeral expenses he incurred as a result of the deceased's death.

In interpreting and applying African customary law, the magistrate of Khayelitsha appointed the father of the deceased as administrator and sole heir of the deceased's estate. The magistrate arrived at this outcome through reliance on the Black Administration Act, which gave recognition to the principle of male primogeniture.

The Applicants argued that the principle of primogeniture violates sections 9(1) and 9(3) of the Constitution.

The Shibi Case

The applicant's brother had died intestate and unmarried, with no children and was not survived by any parents or grandparents. As a female, the applicant was excluded from inheriting under the Black Administration Act. Accordingly, the magistrate awarded the deceased's inheritance to his closest male cousin.

The South African Human Rights Commission Case

The South African Human Rights Commission and the Women's Legal Center Trust applied for direct access to the court acting in their own and in the public interest. They sought broader relief than was sought in the *Shibi* and *Bhe* cases— they wanted the whole of section 23 of the Black Administration Act, or sub-sections 1, 2, and 6 of the Black Administration Act to be declared unconstitutional and invalid because of their inconsistency with sections 9, 10, and 28 of the Constitution.

LEGAL ISSUES

There were two issues before the Constitutional Court. The first related to the constitutional validity of section 23 of the Black Administration Act. The second related to the constitutionality of the rule of primogeniture.

DISPENSATION

The High Court found section 23 of the Black Administration Act to be a racist provision and fundamentally unconstitutional and against *ubuntu*, due to its blatant discrimination on the grounds of race and ethnic origin. The Black Administration Act was specifically crafted to give effect to the separation and the exclusion of Africans from people of European descent.

The effect of invalidating section 23 of the BAA was that African customary law was applicable, and the court found this to include the rule of primogeniture.

The Constitutional Court noted that the exclusion of women and extra-marital children from inheriting in terms of the rule of primogeniture amounted to unfair discrimination, and was contrary to the equality clause of the Constitution; and it also violated women's right to dignity. It held further that the Intestate Succession

Act (as altered to make provision for polygamous unions) replaces the impugned section 23, and that the order apply retrospectively as of April 27, 1994, until Parliament has had the opportunity to act.

Although Justice Langa found the rule of primogeniture to be unconstitutional, and conflated the customary practice in question with primogeniture, he emphasized that respect must be given to the many positive aspects of customary law, with their emphasis on family obligations:

> The positive aspects of customary law have long been neglected. The inherent flexibility of the system is but one of its constructive facets. Customary law places much store in consensus seeking and naturally provides for family and clan meetings, which offer excellent opportunities for the prevention and resolution of disputes and disagreements. Nor are these aspects useful only in the area of disputes. They provide a setting, which contributes to the unity of family structures and the fostering of co-operation, a sense of responsibility in and of belonging to its members, as well as the nurturing of healthy communitarian traditions such as *ubuntu*. These valuable aspects of customary law more than justify its protection by the Constitution.[1]

The High Court decision has been included here because Justice Ngwenya argues that primogeniture violates *ubuntu*.

Justice Ngwenya

The crisp point for consideration in this matter is whether a female African person, whose parents were not married, or married according to African law and custom, is entitled to inherit *ab intestatio*, upon the death of her father. The first, second and third Applicants brought this application essentially against the second Respondent, who is the father of the deceased and the grandfather of the first and second Applicants. The first, third and fourth Respondents are interested parties in this matter and no relief is sought against them. They have accordingly filed notices to abide. The fourth applicant has joined in these proceedings as an interested party and in the public interest. Mr *Trengove*, who is assisted by Mr *Paschke* and Ms *Cowen*, represents all the Applicants. Mr *Carolissen* represents the second Respondent, who is opposing this matter.

Facts

With the exception of one issue, which I will deal with in due course, the essential issues in dispute in this matter are common cause. The third Applicant and the deceased lived together as husband and wife for a period of twelve years. The deceased died on 9 October 2002. Two minor children were born out of the relationship. They are the first and second Applicants in these proceedings. The first Applicant was born on 18 May 1994 and is now 9 years old. The second Applicant was born on 3 August 2001. She is two years old now. The first two Applicants, being minors and females, are assisted by their mother, the third Applicant. Needless to say, the first three Applicants are Africans and of Xhosa extraction. The third Applicant does not seek any relief in her own capacity.

The deceased and the third Applicant acquired an immovable property, Erf 39678, Khayelitsha at 35 Jula Street, Makaza in the City of Tygerberg, Western Cape during their lifetime. Over the years that followed, the deceased applied for and obtained a State housing subsidy. He used it to acquire the property and planned to improve and build the house on it, but died before he could do so. The deceased and the three Applicants occupied the property until the deceased died. The first three Applicants continued to live on the property.

Since the death of the deceased, the second Respondent, who lives in Berlin in the Eastern Cape, claims that he is the intestate heir of the deceased by virtue of African customary law and therefore he is entitled to inherit the property of the deceased. Secondly, he says that he is entitled to the guardianship of the two minor children. The issue of custody and guardianship of the first two Applicants however is not one of the issues for consideration in this matter. It would appear that second Respondent has conceded their custody and guardianship to the third Applicant.

The second Respondent has indicated that he intends to sell the property of the deceased to defray the funeral expenses incurred as a result of his death. As a result of this attitude on the part of the second Respondent, the first three Applicants obtained an interdict *pendente lite*, restraining the second Respondent from alienating or encumbering the property in whatever manner.

THE STATUS AND POSITION OF AFRICAN CUSTOMARY LAW IN THE SOUTH AFRICAN LEGAL SYSTEM

By the proclamation of Sir David Baird in 1806, the rights and privileges of the inhabitants of the Cape Colony, as they existed under the government of the Dutch East India Company, were expressly reserved to them. This position referred to the Cape Colony, as it then existed at the time. In so far as the position of African customary law is concerned, Whitfield in *South African Native Law* 2ed 1948 Juta and Co Ltd has this to say:

"In this way Roman-Dutch Law was secured to the European people of South Africa, then mostly of Dutch and French descent, by the first legislative Act of the British Government in South Africa. *The Natives of South Africa surely had an analogous claim to the recognition of their own social law and customs*, particularly as it is now an explicit part of British policy to retain indigenous institutions in Africa and even to avoid tampering with them where it is not strictly necessary to do so in the interest of law and order" (emphasis added).

This appears to be the correct view, because, irrespective of any shortcomings African customary law might have had, it remained a system according to which most Africans lived.

However, this was not to be so. The recognition and application of African customary law in South Africa has been controversial, spasmodic and inconsistent until 1927. In 1927 the then Union of South Africa passed the Black Administration Act 38 of 1927 whereby African customary law was partially recognised throughout the then Union subject to the proviso that it was not repugnant to public policy. In the present day KwaZulu-Natal there was a code of Zulu law, which was considered to be a codification of the Zulu indigenous law. In that province the Black Administration Act, when it refers to African indigenous law, gave further legal recognition to the code of Zulu law whose origin dates back to 1891 by Sir Theophilus Shepstone. In *Mabuza v Mbatha* 2003 (7) BCLR 743 (C) the Court at 751F refers to this repugnancy clause as notorious. This observation I share.

African customary law at best was and is partially recognised and applied intermittently by our Courts. This was despite the provisions of section 11(1) of the Black Administration Act 38 of 1927, which gave the Commissioner's Courts (special Courts established to decide civil dispute between Africans) a discretion to apply African customary law. The High Court required African customary law to be proven by expert evidence as if it was foreign law (see JC Bekker *Seymour's Customary Law in Southern Africa* (5ed) Juta & Co; AJ Kerr *The Customary Law of Immovable Property and Succession* (2ed). Rhodes University; The Application of Native Law in the Supreme Court (1957) *SALJ* 74 at 313; *Mosii v Motseoakhumo* 1954 (3) SA 919 (A); *Ngcobo v Ngcobo* 1929 AD 233). Section 11(1) of the Black Administration Act enjoined the Court to apply African customary law, provided it was not repugnant to public policy or natural justice. Originally this proviso read "not contrary to civilisation." This remained the underlying rationale in the exercise of the Court's discretion. Whatever it meant depended on the presiding judge's value judgment (see also Transvaal Law of 1995 and *Meesedoosa v Links* 1915 TPD 357).

In *Xulu and Another v Minister of Justice and Another* 1956 (2) SA 128 (N) a woman sued for damages by reason of loss of support which she enjoyed from her husband to whom she was married according to African customary law. Holmes J (as he then was) held that such a relationship did not amount to a statutory recognition that a Black woman, married by African customary law, had legal rights to maintenance against her husband according to the laws of South Africa.

Despite the outcry this judgment evoked, it was upheld in *Santam v Fondo* 1960 (2) SA 467 (A) (see 1956 *SALJ* 402, *Annual Survey* 1956 at 200 and 1961 *SALJ* 103). Despite some legislative intervention to this rather regrettable and unfortunate situation, it remained a half-hearted measure (see *Dlikilili v Federated Insurance* 1983 (2) SA 275 (C) at 282; AJ Kerr *Speculum Juris* (1983) 12 at 37). The attitude of our Courts towards African customary law has been a cause for concern. In *Du Plessis v De Klerk* 1996 (3) SA 850 (CC) Mokgoro J said that customary law has lamentably been marginalised and allowed to degenerate into a vitrified set of norms alienated from its roots in the community.

THE CUSTOMARY LAW OF SUCCESSION

The unwritten African customary law is underpinned by male domination. Ownership in African customary law is not individualistic. It is collective. Differently put, every member of the family is the owner of common property through the head of the family. With the exception of the Lobedu clan in Limpopo, the head of the clan must be a male. African customary law of immovable property generally does not have the same consequences as our common law. It is in this area where even legislation has not done much to accommodate the changing needs and demands put to bear on this system of law. Ownership by the family head is akin to trusteeship as regards immovable property under communal ownership. This mode of ownership in this context may be tolerated under such conditions. However, it cannot be on land in urban environment, which is privately owned. Under African customary law there is room for extended family members to participate in whatever decision that has to be taken, as long as the property is communally held. At common law no such space is allowed. Where the immovable property owned by the deceased is under freehold ownership free of communal pressures and sanctions, the head of the family is less accountable to the other family members and his actions are more visibly akin to those of the owner at common law (see Whitfield at 255). The chances of abuse of his position are thus greater. Thus the development of African customary law must take these eventualities into account.

Succession to status is distinct to inheritance, which is in itself treated differently. The word "status" in this context is used in three senses to refer to the head of the family, the head of the house and the head of the clan (see *Seymour's Customary Law in Southern Africa, supra*; AJ Kerr *The Customary Law of Immovable Property and Succession* 2d ed. Rhode's University; Whitfield, *supra*; TW Bennett *Customary Law in Southern Africa First Edition Juta & Co Ltd*; D Coetze *Apparent Conflict in the Indigenous Law of Succession and Inheritance in "Southern Africa in Need of Law Reform"* (AJGM Sanders (ed) Butterworths). It is not necessary for purposes of this case to discuss in great detail the question of inheritance and succession appertaining to a polygamous relationship.

Women do not participate in the intestate succession of the deceased's estate, save the house personal property. Intestate succession in terms of African customary law is based on the principle of primogeniture. The general rule is that only a male who is related to the deceased through a male line, qualifies as intestate heir. In a monogamous family the elder son of the family head is his heir. If the elder son does not survive his father, then his (the elder son's) eldest male descendant is the heir. If there is no surviving male descendant in the line of the deceased's eldest son, then an heir is sought in the line of the second, third and further sons, in accordance with the principle of primogeniture. If the deceased is not survived by any male descendant, his father succeeds him. If his father also does not survive him, an heir is sought in the father's male descendants relating to him through the male line (see Kerr *The Customary Law of Immovable Property and Succession, supra; Southern Africa in Need of Law Reform, supra; Customary Law in Southern Africa, supra;* Whitfield *Native Law in Southern Africa; Mthembu v Latsela* 2000 (3) SA 867 (SCA) paragraph 8).

It is this system of succession and inheritance, which, Mr *Trengove* submits, is unconstitutional, discriminatory and irrational. We are asked to either develop this system commensurate with the constitutional imperative or to declare it to be unconstitutional and therefore invalid. Before dealing with the argument in any detail, it is appropriate at this juncture to refer to the only issue in dispute in this matter.

ISSUE IN DISPUTE

One issue, which arises peripherally and yet remains unresolved on the papers, is whether the first two Applicants are legitimate or not. Counsel for both parties, however, approached the matter as if that dispute has been resolved. In her founding affidavit the third Applicant states that the deceased could not pay lobolo for her and hence they could not get married. On the other hand the second Respondent refutes that allegation and states that the deceased did pay lobolo for the third Applicant and therefore he is entitled to the guardianship and custody of the first Applicant. According to Xhosa custom he can only claim guardianship and custody of his grandchild if the deceased did pay lobolo for her mother even though marriage might not have been consummated (see JC Bekker, *Seymour's Customary Law in Southern Africa* at 251).

In accordance with *Plascon Evans Paints v Van Riebeeck Paints* 1984 (3) SA 623 (A) this issue must be resolved in favour of the second Respondent. This means that the first two Applicants are legitimate. Furthermore, there is one misconception on the part of the third Applicant, which requires correction. She averred that had it not been the inability of the deceased to pay lobolo for her, they would have been married before he died. It has never been a prerequisite under African customary law to pay lobolo before marriage is consummated. There must be agreement, however, as regards lobolo. It may be deferred as long as circumstances do not permit payment. It is not uncommon that lobolo be paid upon the couple's eldest daughter being "lobolaed" (see Bekker *Seymour's Customary Law in Southern Africa* at 112–113). Payment of lobolo alone, however, does not mean that the parties are married. Save what I have said above as regards the legitimacy of the first two Applicants, nothing turns on this point. Whether the first two Applicants are legitimate or not, does not alter the consequences flowing from the status of the legal relationship between their parents at the time of their father's death.

Does the Principle of Primogeniture
Pass Constitutional Muster?

Mr *Trengove* submitted that the lines of differentiation arising out of the principle of primogeniture irrationally differentiates in violation of the right to equality in section 9(1) and against the prohibition of discrimination in section 9(3). Furthermore, he contended that this principle unfairly discriminates on grounds of gender and sex between male and female descendants and other relatives; it differentiates on the grounds of age and birth between the eldest descendant and all other descendants; it differentiates on the grounds of social origin and birth, between legitimate and illegitimate descendants; it differentiates on the grounds of race between African descendants and other descendants.

The starting point in this regard is the Constitution Act of the Republic of South Africa 1996 (Act 108 of 1996), the Constitution. Section 2 of the Constitution reads:

"This Constitution is the Supreme Law of the Republic; law or conduct inconsistent with it is invalid, and the obligations imposed by it must be fulfilled."

In *Mabuza v Mbatha, supra,* the Court said at 752D–F:

"The proper approach is to accept that the Constitution is the Supreme Law of the Republic. Thus, any custom that is inconsistent with the Constitution cannot withstand Constitutional scrutiny. In line with this approach, my view is that it is not necessary at all to say African Customary Law should not be opposed to the principles of public policy or natural justice. To say that, is fundamentally flawed as it reduces African Law (which is practised by the vast majority in this country) to foreign law—in Africa!"

I associate myself with these views. The basic premise in our current constitutional regime is to test any law, be it common law, statute or African customary law against the values enshrined in the Constitution. At issue here is a rule, which is originally derived from unwritten rule of African customary law. The principle of primogeniture; the principle has received legislative recognition in the Black Administration Act and the regulations promulgated thereunder. Section 23(10) of the Act gives the President powers to make regulations not inconsistent with the Act. The Act predates the Constitution. Pursuant thereto, the President made such regulations in 1987. They appeared in the *Government Gazette* 10601 dated 6 July 1987.

The intestate succession regarding an African in South Africa is briefly as follows. Only in exceptional circumstances, to which I shall make reference shortly, does the estate of a deceased African get wound up in terms of the laws of the country like all other race groups. As a general rule, the devolution of the deceased intestate estates of Africans must evolve in accordance with the principle of primogeniture.

The instances where it will devolve otherwise than in accordance with the principle of primogeniture are the following:

(a) When an African was issued with a letter of exemption by the President in terms of section 31 of the Black Administration Act. The letters of exemption mean that a particular African would be exempt from the application of African customary law. I doubt very much that there are any Africans in this day and age who make use of the provisions of section 31. What is curious with this provision is that there are many Africans who are not originally from South Africa, and who are thus not familiar with African customary law as practised by a large majority of African South Africans. Nevertheless, the law, as it stands, dictates that their estates, unless they are exempted in terms of section 31 or under the two instances to which I shall refer, must be administered according to the principle of primogeniture.

(b) When a deceased was a partner in a marriage in community of property or under antenuptial contract.

(c) In instances where the Minister has decided that the estate must be so administered if in his opinion the circumstances are such as to render the application of African customary law inequitable or inappropriate.

I now proceed to deal with the approach of our Courts to the principle of primogeniture, which is under attack in these proceedings. Mr *Carolissen*, on behalf of the second Respondent, submitted that we are bound by the decision in *Mthembu v Letsele and Another* 1997 (2) SA 936 (T), which was confirmed by the Supreme Court of Appeal in *Mthembu v Letsele and Another* 2000 (3) SA 867 (SCA). Mr *Trengove* on the other hand submitted that we are not bound by that judgment. The reason thereof is that while the facts are similar to the facts before us, there is a profound difference. In that case the Court held that the interim Constitution, which was applicable at the time the judgment was handed down, did not take away the right, which accrued before the Constitution came into operation. Mr *Trengove* further submitted that the only reason why the first two Applicants are not entitled to inherit from their father's estate *ab intestatio* in these proceedings is threefold. Firstly, they are Black, secondly, they are females and thirdly, they are illegitimate. As regards the latter, I have already said that, in my judgment, the first two Applicants are legitimate on the second Respondent's own version. However, this does not take the matter any further, because the principle of primogeniture is not altered by their legitimacy. They remain females. In my view, even if they were illegitimate, this would not have been a ground to refuse them the relief in the light of the constitutional era in which we live.

The principle must now be tested against the constitutional values. Section 9 of the Constitution deals with equality and reads:

"(1) Everyone is equal before the law and has the right to equal protection and benefit of the law.

(2) Equality includes the full and equal enjoinment of all rights and freedoms. To promote the achievement of equality, legislative and other measures designed to protect or advance persons, or categories of persons, disadvantaged by unfair discrimination, may be taken.

(3) The state may not unfairly discriminate directly or indirectly against anyone on one or more grounds, including race, gender, sex, pregnancy, marital status, ethnic or social origin, colour, sexual orientation, age, disability, religion, conscience, belief, culture, language and birth.

(4) No person may unfairly discriminate directly or indirectly against anyone on one or more grounds in terms of subsection (3). National legislation must be enacted to prevent or prohibit unfair discrimination.

(5) Discrimination on one or more of the grounds listed in subsection (3) is unfair unless it is established that the discrimination is fair."

The Black Administration Act is not a code of African customary law. It is an Act of Parliament like all other legislation. However, its fundamental premise was racial inequality. In *Moseneke and Others v The Master and Another* 2001 (2) SA 18 (CC) at 29 Sachs J says:

"The Black Administration Act has been described by this Court as:
    'an egregious apartheid law which anachronistically has survived our transition to a non-racial democracy.'
    Subordinate legislation made under it has been referred to as part of a demeaning and racist system, as obnoxious and as not befitting a democratic society based on human dignity, equality and freedom. The Act systematised and enforced a colonial form of relationship between a dominant white minority who were to have rights of citizenship and a subordinate black majority who were to be administered" (see also *DVB Behuising (Pty) Ltd v North West Provincial Government and Another* 2001 (1) SA 500 (CC), 2000 (4) BCLR 347 (CC)).

The State, in terms of section 9(3) of the Constitution, shall not unfairly discriminate on grounds, *inter alia*, of race, gender or sex. The provisions of regulation 2(e) of the regulations promulgated in terms of the Black Administration Act dictate that, on the facts of this case, the first two Applicants cannot inherit because of their gender and race. They are female and Black.

In terms of the Intestate Succession Act 81 of 1987 (the Intestate Succession Act), (which applies to all races in South Africa) if any person dies intestate, either wholly or in part and is survived by a descendant, but not by his spouse, such descendant shall inherit the intestate estate (see section 1(b)). "Descendant" means any descendant of the deceased person irrespective of race, gender or status.

In this case we have the deceased, who died intestate and left two descendants, namely the first and second Applicants. Can they invoke the provisions of the Intestate Succession Act? The answer is no. The reason why the first two Applicants cannot invoke the provisions of the Act is because in terms of section 1(4)(b) intestate includes any part of any estate which does not devolve by virtue of a will or in respect of which section 23 of the Black Administration Act 38 of 1927 does not apply. Differently put, the only reason why the first two Applicants cannot inherit from their father's estate is because, as Mr *Trengove* correctly submitted, they are Black and they are females. This, in my judgment, is *per se* discrimination on grounds of race and gender. It is *prima facie* unfair and therefore offends against the provisions of section 9(1) and (3) of the Constitution. This Court is thus bound to declare such law unconstitutional and invalid. I may add further that, on the facts before us, the second Respondent's attitude leaves too much to be desired. It lacks basic humanity, which is the hallmark of *ubuntu*. We have been urged to develop African customary law.

This constitutional imperative cannot be realised on the face of some provisions contained in the Black Administration Act (if not the Act *in toto*). In the first instance the provisions of section 23 substantially require a revision. In particular the provisions of section 23(10) instruct the President to make regulations consistent with the Black Administration Act. The underlying imperative of the Black Administration Act is that of male preference as against equality of genders and that of African subordination against other races. This is not the occasion, however, where we are called upon to revise the entire Black Administration Act. Suffice it to state that in *Moseneke and Others v The Master and Another, supra,* the Constitutional Court has already expressed its concern with the fact that this Act still remains in our statute book. It is up to Parliament to decide when this Act shall be repealed *in toto*.

For now the following would suffice. We should make it clear in this judgment that a situation whereby a male person will be preferred to a female person for purposes of inheritance can no longer withstand constitutional scrutiny. That constitutes discrimination before the law. To put it plainly, African females, irrespective of age or social status, are entitled to inherit from their parents' intestate estate like any male person. This does not mean that there may not be instances where differentiation on gender line may not be justified for purposes of certain rituals. As long as this does not amount to disinheritance or prejudice to any female descendant. On the facts before us, therefore, the first two Applicants are declared to be the sole heirs to the deceased's estate and they are entitled to inherit equally.

The order I would make here should reflect the constitutional order of the day. Consequently I shall declare those offending provisions of both the Black Administration Act as well as the regulations promulgated thereunder invalid and unconstitutional. Likewise, with the Intestate Succession Act.

In the result I propose the following order:

1. It is declared that section 23(10)(a), (c) and (e) of the Black Administration Act are unconstitutional and invalid and that regulation 2(e) of the Regulations of the Administration and Distribution of the Estates of Deceased Blacks, published under Government Gazette 10601 dated 7 February 1987 is consequently also invalid.

2. It is declared that section 1(4)(b) of the Intestate Succession Act 91 of 1987 is unconstitutional and invalid in so far as it excludes from the application of section 1 any estate or part of any estate in respect of which section 23 of the Black Administration Act 38 of 1927 applies.

3. It is declared that until the aforegoing defects are corrected by competent legislature, the distribution of intestate Black estate is governed by section 1 of the Intestate Succession Act 81 of 1987.

4. It is declared that the first and second Applicants are the only heirs in the estate of the late Vuyu Elius Mgolombane, registered at Khayelitsha Magistrate's Court under reference 7/1/2–484/2002.

5. The second Respondent is ordered to sign all documents and to take all other steps reasonably required of him to transfer the entire residue of the said estate to the first and second Applicants in equal shares. If the second Respondent fails to do so the Deputy Sheriff is authorised and directed to do so in his stead.

6. It is declared that the Applicants are exclusively entitled to reside in the house at 35 Jula Street, Makaza situated at Erf 39678 Khayelitsha in the City of Tygerberg until its distribution and transfer in accordance with this order.

7. It is further ordered that any letters of appointment and administration of the deceased's estate issued to the second Respondent be and are hereby set aside.

8. There is no order as to costs.

Hlophe JP concurred in the judgment of Ngwenya J.

CONSTITUTIONAL COURT JUDGMENT

We only include Justice Ngcobo in this book because he elaborates more fully on *ubuntu* and on the values of indigenous family law. Justice Langa only mentions *ubuntu* in his majority decision.

Justice Ngcobo

[137] This trilogy of cases raises two important questions concerning the application of indigenous law of succession. The first question relates to the constitutionality of

section 23 of the Black Administration Act of 1927 (the Act)[2] [1] read together with the Regulations for the Administration and Distribution of Estates of Deceased Blacks (the regulations)[3] [2] framed under the Act and read further with section 1(4)(b) of the Intestate Succession Act 81 of 1987.[4] [3] These enactments determine the circumstances under which indigenous law of succession is applicable to African people. The second question concerns the constitutional validity of the indigenous law principle of male primogeniture.

[138] In substance, the impugned provisions put in place a succession scheme that applies only to African people and determines when indigenous law of succession applies to them. The scheme was challenged on the grounds that it violates the right to equality and the right to human dignity. The indigenous law of succession, which the scheme makes applicable, involves the principle of male primogeniture. In terms of this principle, the eldest of the male issue succeeds to the deceased family head. This principle was challenged on the grounds that it discriminates against women and other children of the deceased.

[139] I have read the judgment prepared by the Deputy Chief Justice. Regrettably, I am unable to concur in that judgment. He concludes that (a) it is inappropriate to develop the rule of male primogeniture; and (b) the Intestate Succession Act should, in the interim, govern all the estates that were previously governed by section 23 of the Act. I do not agree. In my view, the rule of male primogeniture should be developed in order to bring it in line with the rights in the Bill of Rights. Pending the enactment of the legislation to determine when indigenous law is applicable, both indigenous law of succession and the Intestate Succession Act should apply subject to the Constitution and the requirements of fairness, justice and equity, bearing in mind the interests of minor children and other dependants of the deceased family head.

[140] The factual background relating to these cases has been set out in the main judgment. It need not be repeated here. For the purposes of this judgment, it is sufficient to say that these cases concern the rights of daughters and sisters to a deceased African male to succeed such a deceased male person. In the *Bhe* matter, the right is asserted by the two minor daughters of the deceased. In the *Shibi* matter, that right is asserted by the sister of the deceased. These cases therefore do not concern the right of widows to succeed to their deceased husbands.

THE CONSTITUTIONAL VALIDITY OF SECTION 23 OF THE ACT, REGULATIONS AND SECTION 1(4)(B) OF THE INTESTATE SUCCESSION ACT

[141] Section 23 must be understood in the context of the scheme of the Act. As its name suggests, the Act is aimed at regulating all aspects of life of African people. The Act was one of the pillars of the apartheid legal order, and together with other racially based statutes, it was part of the edifice of the apartheid legal order. The Act has been described as "an egregious apartheid law" that "anachronistically has survived our transition to a non-racial democracy."[5] [4]

[142] Section 23 deals with succession and inheritance to estates of deceased African people. It prescribes circumstances under which the property of deceased African people may devolve according to "Black law and custom."

> "In addition, it makes provision for the State President to make regulations dealing with matters relating to inheritance and succession to estates of deceased African people. It regulates the manner in which estates of deceased African people may be administered and distributed; defines the rights of widows in regard to the use and occupation of certain land; and prescribes tables of succession. The regulations were in effect choice of law rules which determined when indigenous law was applicable to estates of deceased African people. Section 1(4)(b) of Intestate Succession Act excluded estates of African people that fall within the purview of section 23 of the Act from the scope of the Intestate Succession Act."

[143] The unconstitutionality of section 23 of the Act can hardly be disputed.

> "The Act is manifestly racist in its purpose and effect. It discriminates on the grounds of race and colour. Section 23 of the Act, the regulations and section 1(4)(b) of the Intestate Succession Act are interlinked. They stand or fall together. Their combined effect is to put in place a succession scheme that discriminates on the basis of race and colour applying only to African people.
>
> The limitation that this scheme imposes on the right of African people to equality can hardly be said to be reasonable and justifiable in an open and democratic society based on human dignity, equality and freedom. The discrimination it perpetrates is an affront to the dignity of those that it governs."

[144] Section 23 is therefore inconsistent with the right to equality guaranteed in section 9(3) as well as the right to dignity protected by section 10 of the Constitution. The regulations and section 1(4)(b) of the Intestate Succession Act must suffer the same fate.

[145] The High Court only declared invalid section 23(10)(a), (c) and (e) of the Act, Regulation 2(e) and section 1(4)(b) of the Intestate Succession Act. In my view, the whole of section 23 must go. The same goes for the regulations. To this extent, I concur in the judgment of the Deputy Chief Justice.

[146] It will be recalled that in terms of the regulations, in particular, Regulation 2(e), indigenous law of succession is made applicable to intestate estates that do not fall under Regulation 2(b) to (d).[6] [5] And the central feature of indigenous law of succession is the principle of male primogeniture. This is a rule that was applied by the magistrates in the *Bhe* and *Shibi* matters. The constitutionality of this rule was challenged too. It will therefore be convenient to consider the constitutional validity of the rule before considering the remedy that is appropriate in these cases.

THE CONSTITUTIONAL CHALLENGE TO THE PRINCIPLE
OF MALE PRIMOGENITURE

[147] This rule was challenged on the basis that it discriminates unfairly on the grounds of gender, age and birth. In order to evaluate the cogency of the challenge, it is necessary to understand the nature of indigenous law and, in particular, the concept of succession in indigenous law. All of this provides the context in which the constitutional validity of the rule must be determined. But first, what is the place of indigenous law in our constitutional democracy?

PLACE OF INDIGENOUS LAW IN OUR DEMOCRACY

[148] Our Constitution recognises indigenous law as part of our law. Thus section 211(3) enjoins Courts to "apply customary law when that law is applicable, subject to the Constitution and any legislation that specifically deals with customary law." The Constitution accords it the same status that other laws enjoy under it. In addition, Courts are required to develop indigenous law so as to bring it in line with the rights in the Bills of Rights.[7] [6] While in the past indigenous law was seen through the common-law lens, it must now be seen as part of our law and must be considered on its own terms and "not through the prism of common law."[8] [7] Like all laws, indigenous law now derives its force from the Constitution.[9] [8] Its validity must now be determined by reference not to common law but to the Constitution.[10] [9]

[149] But how do we ascertain the applicable rule of indigenous law?

HOW TO ASCERTAIN INDIGENOUS LAW?

[150] There are at least three ways in which indigenous law may be established. In the first place, a Court may take judicial notice of it. This can only happen where it can readily be ascertained with sufficient certainty. Sec-tion 1(1) of the Law of Evidence Amendment Act 45 of 1988 says so.[11] [10] Compare *Carmichele v Minister of Safety and Security* 2001 (4) SA 938 (CC); 2001 (10) BCLR 995 (CC) at paragraphs 37–40. Where it cannot be readily ascertained, expert evidence may be adduced to establish it.[12] [11] Finally, a Court may consult textbooks and case law.[13] [12]

[151] Caution, however, must be exercised in relying on case law and text books.[14] [13] In *Alexkor*[15] [14] we emphasised the need for caution and said:

> "Although a number of text books exist and there is a considerable body of precedent, Courts today have to bear in mind the extent to which indigenous law in the pre-democratic period was influenced by the political, administrative and judicial context in which it was applied. Bennett points out that, although customary law is supposed to develop spontaneously in a given rural community, during the colonial and apartheid era it became alienated from its community origins. The result was that the term 'customary law' emerged with three quite different meanings: the official body of law employed in the Courts and by the administration (which, he points out, diverges most

markedly from actual social practice); the law used by academics for teaching purposes; and the law actually lived by the people."[16] [15]

[152] It is now generally accepted that there are three forms of indigenous law: (a) that practised in the community; (b) that found in statutes, case law or textbooks on indigenous law (official); and (c) academic law that is used for teaching purposes.[17] [16] All of them differ. This makes it difficult to identify the true indigenous law. The evolving nature of indigenous law only compounds the difficulty of identifying indigenous law.

THE EVOLVING NATURE OF INDIGENOUS LAW

[153] Indigenous law is a dynamic system of law which is continually evolving to meet the changing circumstances of the community in which it operates. It is not a fixed body of classified rules. As we pointed out in *Alexkor*: "In applying indigenous law, it is important to bear in mind that, unlike common law, indigenous law is not written. It is a system of law that was known to the community, practised and passed on from generation to generation. It is a system of law that has its own values and norms.

Throughout its history it has evolved and developed to meet the changing needs of the community. And it will continue to evolve within the context of its values and norms consistently with the Constitution."[18] [17]

[154] The evolving nature of indigenous law and the fact that it is unwritten have resulted in the difficulty of ascertaining the true indigenous law as practised in the community. This law is sometimes referred to as living indigenous law. Statutes, textbooks and case law, as a result, may no longer reflect the living law. What is more, abuses of indigenous law are at times construed as a true reflection of indigenous law, and these abuses tend to distort the law and undermine its value. The difficulty is one of identifying the living indigenous law and separating it from its distorted version.

[155] In these cases, no attempt was made to ascertain the living indigenous law of succession. These matters were approached on the footing that indigenous law of succession is that which is described in the textbooks and case law. Whether that is the proper approach to a system of law that is dynamic and evolving is not free from doubt. However, in both the *Bhe* and *Shibi* matters, the magistrates concerned applied the indigenous law of succession as described in *Mthembu v Letsela*[19] [18] and textbooks. It is that law which we must evaluate in these cases. But first, it is necessary to understand the concept of succession in indigenous law.

THE CONCEPT OF SUCCESSION IN INDIGENOUS LAW

[156] The concept of succession in indigenous law must be understood in the context of indigenous law itself. When dealing with indigenous law every attempt should be made to avoid the tendency of construing indigenous law concepts in the

light of common-law concepts or concepts foreign to indigenous law. There are obvious dangers in such an approach. These two systems of law developed in two different situations, under different cultures and in response to different conditions.[20] [19] In *Alexkor* (*supra*) this Court approved the following passage by the Privy Council in *Amodu Tijani v The Secretary, Southern Nigeria*:[21] [20]

> "Their Lordships make the preliminary observation that in interpreting the native title to land, not only in Southern Nigeria, but other parts of the British Empire, much caution is essential. There is a tendency, operating at times unconsciously, to render that title conceptually in terms that are appropriate only to systems that have grown up under English law. But this tendency has to be held in check closely. As a rule, in the various systems of native jurisprudence throughout the Empire, there is no such full division between property and possession as English lawyers are familiar with. A very usual form of native title is that of a usufructuary right, which is a mere qualification of or burden on the radical or final title of the Sovereign where that exists . . . In India, as in Southern Nigeria, there is yet another feature of the fundamental nature of the title to land which must be borne in mind. The title, such as it is, may not be that of the individual, as in this country it nearly always is in some form, but may be that of a community. Such a community may have the possessory title to the common enjoyment of a usufruct, with customs under which its individual members are admitted to enjoyment, and even to a right of transmitting the individual enjoyment as members by assignment *inter vivos* or by succession. To ascertain how far this latter development of right has progressed involves the study of the history of the particular community and its usages in each case. Abstract principles fashioned *a priori* are of but little assistance, and are as often as not misleading."[22] [21]

[157] However, because of our legal background and, in particular, the fact that indigenous law was previously not allowed to develop in the same way as other systems of law, the tendency may at times be unavoidable. But even then, common-law concepts should be used with great caution in indigenous law.

[158] In common law, concepts of "succession" and "inheritance" are sometimes used interchangeably. However, in the context of indigenous law, it is necessary to distinguish these concepts. As Bennett explains:

> "The words 'succession' and 'inheritance' are often used as synonyms, but for analytical purposes they should be distinguished. The latter denotes transmission of rights to property only, and in those societies emphasising material wealth (which will also have a highly evolved notion of property) inheritance predominates. Succession is more general; it implies the transmission of all the rights, duties, powers, and privileges associated with status. So in the case

of customary law one should speak of a process of succession rather than in-heritance."[23] [22]

[159] The significance of distinguishing between "succession" and "inheritance" appears from the following passage by Himonga:

"Succession refers to the process of succeeding to the estate, office or status of the deceased person, while inheritance refers to the process of inheriting the property of the deceased. The person selected as successor does not, in Zambian systems of succession, as in many other African systems, inherit all the property, although he may have the power to administer the estate and a right to the larger portion of it. Otherwise, the right of inheritance belongs to a much wider group entitled to inherit from the deceased according to the operative system of kinship."[24] [23]

[160] Inheritance of property is not always linked to succession to status.[25] [24] The successor does not inherit the family property. He steps into the shoes of the deceased by taking over the control of the family property. That is not to say that the concept of inheritance was unknown. It is not necessary in this case to determine the circumstances in which inheritance to property occurred. Indigenous law of succession is therefore not solely concerned with the transfer of rights in property. The transfer of status and roles traditionally form an essential component of succession.[26] [25]

[161] It is in this context that the terms "succession" and "inheritance" must be understood. But this must be understood against the background of the origin, nature and purpose of the indigenous law of succession.

THE SOCIAL CONTEXT IN WHICH THE LAW DEVELOPED

[162] To understand the concept of succession in indigenous law, it is instructive to look at the social context in which it originated. The rules of indigenous law, in particular, the rule of primogeniture, have their origin in traditional society. This society was based on a subsistence agricultural economy. At the heart of the African traditional structure was the family unit. The family unit was the focus of social concern.[27] [26] Individual interests were submerged in the common weal. The system emphasised duties and responsibilities as opposed to rights. At the head of the family there was a patriarch or a senior male who exercised control over the family property and members of the family.[28] [27] The family organisation was self-sufficient. Within this system, the position of each member of the family was based on an equitable division of labour.

[163] A sense of community prevailed from which developed an elaborate system of reciprocal duties and obligations among the family members. This is manifest in the concept of *ubuntu—umuntu ngumuntu ngabantu*[29] [28]—a dominant value in

African traditional culture. This concept encapsulates communality and the interdependence of the members of a community. As Langa DCJ put it, it is a culture, which "regulates the exercise of rights by the emphasis it lays on sharing and co-responsibility and the mutual enjoyment of rights."[30] [29] It is this system of reciprocal duties and obligations that ensured that every family member had access to basic necessities of life such as food, clothing, shelter and healthcare.

[164] As Ndulo explains:

"Pre-colonial African society in which these rules were developed was based on an agricultural subsistence economy characterised by self-sufficient joint family organisation. In general a woman's position in traditional society was based on an equitable division of labour. Women were primarily responsible for planting; weeding and harvesting while men performed certain heavy tasks such as clearing the bush and farming. Most Africans were born, grew, married and died without ever leaving the region in which their tribe lived. A sense of community prevailed from which developed an elaborate customary law system of reciprocal obligations between family members. For example, in most polygamous marriages each wife represented a separate unit of production. Her husband had a responsibility to give her land and equipment with which to farm and provide her with adequate shelter. She in turn was expected to feed herself and her children and, along with her co-wives, to provide food for her husband. African traditions and customary law served the needs of the tribal communities from which they developed and together the traditional practices and customary rules ensured that all members of the community had access to food, clothing and shelter."[31] [30]

[165] It was in this social context that the rule of succession in indigenous law, in particular, the principle of male primogeniture, developed and operated. The head of the family had the responsibility to provide food, shelter, clothing and basic healthcare for his dependants. And upon his death, someone had to take over this responsibility.

[166] The obligation to care for family members is a vital and fundamental value in African social system. This value is now entrenched in the African (Banjul) Charter on Human and Peoples' Rights. The Preamble to the Charter urges Member States to take "into consideration the virtues of their historical traditions and values of African civilisation which should inspire and characterise their reflection on the concept of human and peoples' rights." Article 27(1) provides that "every individual shall have duties towards his family and society." Article 29(1) provides that an individual shall . . . have the duty: "to preserve the harmonious development of the family and to work for the cohesion and respect of the family; to respect his parents at all times, to maintain them in case of need."

THE NATURE AND PURPOSE OF THE LAW OF SUCCESSION

[167] The main purpose of succession was to keep the family property in the family.[32] [31] This was essential to the preservation of the family unit. Land and livestock were the most important property. They provided the whole family with a source of livelihood and a place to live. They constituted family property and as such belonged to the family. The father was the head of the family and he held the property on behalf of and for the benefit of the family. He was responsible for the maintenance of the family from the property. Upon his death, two objectives had to be achieved: the perpetuation of the family; and getting someone to take over the powers and duties of the deceased family head. This was achieved by providing rules for the transmission of the deceased's rights and obligations to the eldest son.[33] [32]

[168] The indigenous law of succession was concerned with two objectives:

(a) the perpetuation and the preservation of the family; and
(b) getting someone to take over the duties and obligations of the deceased family head. The preservation of the family required the preservation of family property. Family property consisted mainly of land and livestock. These were the primary sources of livelihood. And these were viewed as the property of the family and not that of each individual. The father was viewed as the caretaker and manager of the common property and thus the family head. He was responsible for the maintenance of the family from the family property. To enable the successor to carry out the duties and obligations of the deceased, family property had to be kept in the family.

[169] Indigenous law preserved the family unit and its continuity by transferring responsibilities of the family head to his senior male descendant.[34] [33] This descendant is referred to as *indlalifa* or *successor*.[35] [34] It is this male descendant who is equated with the heir under common law.[36] [35] But there are important differences between the two. *Indlalifa* takes over the powers and responsibilities of the deceased family head. The powers relate to the right to control and administer the family property on behalf of and for the benefit of the family members. The responsibilities relate to the duty to support and maintain all the dependants of the deceased. This process is metaphorically expressed by the phrase "the *indlalifa* steps into the shoes of the deceased family head and takes over control of the family property."

[170] As pointed out earlier, inheritance of property is not always linked to succession to status.[37] [36] In the context of indigenous law of succession it is perhaps more accurate to speak of *indlalifa* as succeeding to the status of the deceased. The status of the deceased includes both his rights and obligations.[38] [37] By providing *indlalifa* with all the powers necessary to continue managing family property, the indigenous law of succession was designed to ensure the welfare of the surviving family. Because *indlalifa* takes over the control of the family assets he is said to "inherit" the

family assets. This description of the process has resulted in the distortion of the role of *indlalifa* and to regard him as the owner of the family assets. Yet he is no more than a person who holds the property on behalf of the family, with powers to administer it on behalf of and for the benefit of the family.[39] [38] He may be said to "inherit" the right to control the family property.

[171] Succession in the context of indigenous law must therefore be understood to refer to the process of succeeding to the status of the deceased. *Indlalifa* steps into the shoes of the deceased.[40] [39] Under indigenous law, the *indlalifa* does not inherit the property. He succeeds to the status and position of the deceased and thus acquires the same rights and obligations that the deceased had. This includes the power to administer the family assets. He holds the family property on behalf of other family members.[41] [40] Once it is accepted that *indlalifa* holds the family property on behalf of and for the benefit of all family members, it cannot be said that he is the owner of the family property or that he inherits it in the sense understood in common law.[42] [41]

[172] The perpetuation and preservation of the family unit and succession to the position and status of the deceased therefore lie at the heart of succession in indigenous law.[43] [42] Like his predecessor, *indlalifa* becomes the nominal owner of the family property, and is required to administer it on behalf of and for the benefit of the family. *Indlalifa* acquires the duty to maintain and support the widow and minor children.[44] [43] In dealing with family property, *indlalifa* has to consult the widow who had the right to restrain him from dissipating family assets.[45] [44] When there are insufficient assets to maintain the family, *indlalifa* had to use his own resources to provide maintenance.[46] [45]

[173] The underlying purpose of indigenous law of succession is therefore to protect the family and ensure that the dependants of the deceased are looked after. This is achieved by entrusting the responsibility of seeing to the welfare of the deceased's dependants to one person in return for the right to control the family property.[47] [46] This system ensures that the dependants of the deceased as well as the members of the family always have a home and resources for their maintenance. This prevents homelessness. Those who cannot support themselves such as minor children have someone to maintain and support them. The right of *indlalifa* to control and administer family property therefore goes with the responsibility to look after the dependants of the deceased. Mbatha, however, observes that "poverty and unemployment, together with the failure to look after the interests of the deceased's dependants have distorted the customary law of succession, undermined its protective value to other family members and forced members to assume the heir's responsibilities for looking after the needy, the sick and the aged."[48] [47]

[174] Succession was based on the principle of male primogeniture. This principle entailed that the eldest male descendant of the deceased succeeded the deceased. Women and other male children were excluded. However, other male children could be considered if the eldest was not available or willing to succeed. *Indlalifa* in-

variably remained in the common home to enable him to carry out his responsibilities. The rationale for the exclusion of women was the fact that:

> "[W]omen were always regarded as persons who would eventually leave their original family on marriage, after the payment of roora/lobola, to join the family of their husbands. It was reasoned that in their new situation—a member of the husband's family—they could not be heads of their original families, as they were more likely to subordinate the interests of the original family to those of their new family. It was therefore reasoned that in their new situation they would not be able to look after the original family."[49] [48]

[175] However, as pointed out earlier, indigenous law is dynamic and it is evolving, adapting itself to the ever-changing circumstance of the communities in which it operates. There are indications that the rule of primogeniture has developed to allow women to be appointed as heads of the families.[50] [49] It may well be that it has also developed to allow a woman to succeed to a deceased family head. However, this aspect need not be investigated in these cases. No evidence was presented in this regard. The indigenous law that is in issue in this case is the official version, in particular, that which was described by the Supreme Court of Appeal (SCA) in the case of *Mthembu*.[51] [50]

THE RULE OF MALE PRIMOGENITURE

[176] Central to the indigenous law of succession, therefore, is the rule of male primogeniture. It was described as follows by the SCA in the judgment of *Mthembu*:[52] [51]

> "The customary law of succession in Southern Africa is based on the principle of male primogeniture. In monogamous families the eldest son of the family head is his heir, failing him the eldest son's eldest male descendant. Where the eldest son has predeceased the family head without leaving male issue, the second son becomes heir; if he is dead leaving no male issue, the third son succeeds and so on through the sons of the family head. Where the family head dies leaving no male issue his father succeeds . . . Women generally do not inherit in customary law. When the head of the family dies his heir takes his position as head of the family and becomes owner of all the deceased's property, movable and immovable; he becomes liable for the debts of the deceased and assumes the deceased's position as guardian of the women and minor sons in the family. He is obliged to support and maintain them, if necessary from his own resources and not to expel them from his home."[53] [52]

[177] Whether this passage reflects the indigenous law of succession actually lived by the people is doubtful.[54] [53] However, that is the law that was applied in

these cases. In the *Bhe* matter, the deceased left no son and therefore in accordance with the rule of male primogeniture his father was declared the successor. Similarly, in the *Shibi* matter, the deceased left no male descendants and his cousin was therefore appointed sole *indlalifa*. It is this rule that came under constitutional challenge. And, as pointed out earlier, it is this version of the rule that we must evaluate.

[178] It is against this background that the constitutional challenge to the rule of male primogeniture must be evaluated. First, I deal with the challenge based on discrimination against younger children.

THE CHALLENGE BASED ON AGE AND BIRTH DISCRIMINATION

[179] The rule of primogeniture was challenged on the basis that it discriminates unfairly against younger children of the deceased. It will be recalled that only the eldest male succeeds. The rule, no doubt, limits the right of the younger children to succeed to the status of the deceased. The question is whether such limitation is reasonable and justifiable under section 36(1) of the Constitution. It is to that question that I now turn.

[180] The primary purpose of the rule is to preserve the family unit and ensure that upon the death of the family head, someone takes over the responsibilities of family head. These responsibilities include looking after the dependants of the deceased and administering the family property on behalf of and for the benefit of the entire family. Successorship also carries with it the obligation to remain in the family home for the purposes of discharging the responsibilities associated with heirship. From the family of the deceased, someone must be found to assume these responsibilities. There may be several conflicting demands. But there is a need for certainty in order to facilitate the transfer of the rights and obligations of the deceased without lengthy deliberations that may be caused by rival claims. The determination of the eldest male as the successor was intended to ensure certainty.

[181] Entrusting these responsibilities to the eldest child is consistent with the role of the eldest child in relation to his siblings. The eldest child has a responsibility to look after his or her siblings. The rule simply recognises this responsibility. Furthermore, one of the cherished values in African culture is respect for elders. Respect is supposed to inculcate good habits such as humility and Courtesy.[55] [54] The old are required to give guidance to the young. This is the basis of mentorship.

[182] Two points need to be stressed here. First, *indlalifa* does not inherit; as that term is understood in common law. What happens is best conveyed by the expression "*indlalifa* steps into the shoes of the family head." Far from getting any property benefit, the *indlalifa* assumes the responsibilities of a family head. He is required to administer the family property for the benefit of the entire family. As pointed out earlier, where there are insufficient assets in the family, *indlalifa* must use his own resources. Second, the selection of the eldest child must also be seen against the flexibility of the rule and the fact that he may be removed from office. If the eldest child considers that he cannot perform the responsibilities, the next eldest takes over the

responsibility. What is more, the *indlalifa* may be held to account to the family, if he does not perform his responsibilities. The family may, if he fails to perform his duties, remove him.

[183] Having regard to all these factors, I am satisfied that the limitation imposed by entrusting the responsibilities of a deceased family head to the eldest child is reasonable and justifiable under section 36(1). It follows therefore that the rule is not inconsistent with section 9(3) of the Constitution by reason of discrimination based on age and birth. It now remains to consider the challenge based on gender discrimination.

GENDER DISCRIMINATION

[184] Under the rule of male primogeniture, only men can succeed to the deceased family head. The eldest son succeeds, failing which, the son's eldest male descendants succeed. If the eldest son has predeceased the father, leaving no descendants, the second son succeeds. If he too predeceased the father, leaving no sons, it goes to the next son. Where there are no male descendants, the father of the deceased succeeds. This is what happened in the *Bhe* matter. If the father predeceased the deceased, it would go to his sons and their dependants in their order of birth. The process therefore excludes women.

[185] That the rule of male primogeniture limits the rights of women to be considered for succession to the position and status of the deceased family head cannot be gainsaid. They are excluded regardless of their availability and suitability to acquit themselves in that position. They are overlooked in circumstances where they may be the only children of the deceased. Nor does it matter that they may have contributed to the acquisition or preservation of the family property.

[186] The question is whether such limitation is reasonable and justifiable under section 36(1) of the Constitution.

JUSTIFICATION

[187] The importance of the right to equality in our constitutional democracy cannot be gainsaid. This Court has in the past emphasised the importance of the right to equality.[56] [55] The right to equality is related to the right to dignity. Discrimination conveys to the person who is discriminated against that the person is not of equal worth. The discrimination against women conveys a message that women are not of equal worth as men. Where women under indigenous law are already a vulnerable group, this offends their dignity.

[188] The rule of male primogeniture might have been justified by the social and economic context in which it developed. It developed in the context of a traditional society, which was based on a subsistence agricultural economy characterised by a self-sufficient family organisation. Within this system, an elaborate network of reciprocal obligations between members of a family existed which ensured that the needs of every member for food, shelter and clothing were provided for. The roles

that were assigned to men and women in traditional African society were based on the type of social structure and economy that prevailed then.

[189] But all of that has changed. As Ndulo explains:

"In the modern economy women fend for themselves and help their husbands accumulate property during the course of their marriage. In essence, they have outgrown the status assigned to them in traditional society. Tribal law has lagged behind these economic and social changes. As more and more women begin working outside the home, earning money and acquiring property, the gap between their legal status under customary law and their economic status in society widens. . . . But as we have seen, the joint family is in a state of decline and Africans are now enmeshed in an exchange economy. Development and industrialisation have caused an irreversible breakdown in the traditional African social order. The society is now highly individualistic, competitive and acquisitive. Customary rules do not operate to the benefit of the women in this type of society. The joint families that remain have lost their self-sufficiency. Modernisation, therefore, has had a negative impact on women. It has caused the breakdown of the tribal community and has destroyed the subsistence economy to such an extent that the protection women enjoyed under customary law is rendered useless. Today widows must support themselves by their own efforts. Application of the traditional concepts of customary law of succession to women in a modern context is unjust and discriminatory—a practice outlawed by the Zambian Constitution. It also ignores the fact that married women help their husbands accumulate property during the course of their marriage and should not, therefore, be denied an absolute right in any portion of it."[57] [56]

[190] The role that women play in modern society and the transformation of the traditional African communities into urban industrialised communities with all their trappings, make it quite clear that whatever role the rule of male primogeniture may have played in traditional society, it can no longer be justified in the present day and age. Indeed, there are instances where in practice women have assumed the role of the head of the family.[58] [57] This may be due to the fact that *indlalifa* is almost always away from the common home, or has decided to establish his home outside the common family home. The rule has therefore lost its vitality to a certain degree.

[191] Jurisprudence from African Courts, which have considered the position of women in the context of succession, further demonstrates that the rule in its present form no longer has any place in modern times.

AFRICAN JURISPRUDENCE
Nigeria

[192] Indigenous law of succession in Nigeria varies from one ethnic group to another.[59] [58] It ranges from the rule of primogeniture to the rule of ultimogeniture

(according to which inheritance is exclusively by the youngest son).[60] [59] The major ethnic groups in Nigeria include Igbo and Yoruba.[61] [60] For the purposes of this comparison, I focus on the Igbo.

[193] Within the Igbo community, succession is based on the principle of male primogeniture. Daughters and wives have no right of succession. The only situation in which a daughter could succeed the deceased is where, for example, she chooses to remain unmarried in her father's house with a view to raising children there. The situation occurs where the deceased leaves a substantial estate and without having a son or other male relative to succeed him. It is said that the purpose of this practice is to save the lineage from extinction. The legal interest vests in her until she gives birth to her own children. If she bears children, only sons, and not daughters, succeed her.

[194] In *Mojekwu v Mojekwu*[62] [61], the Igbo succession rule was challenged on the ground that it discriminated against females. The Court of appeal held that the rule of male primogeniture was unconstitutional and contrary to democratic values. Justice Tobi wrote:

"All human beings—male and female—are born into a free world and are ex-pected to participate freely, without any inhibition on grounds of sex; and that is constitutional. Any form of societal discrimination on ground of sex, apart from being unconstitutional, is antithesis to a society built on the tenets of democracy which we have freely chosen as a people . . . Accordingly, for a custom or customary law to discriminate against a particular sex is to say the least an affront on the Almighty God Himself. Let nobody do such a thing. On my part, I have no difficulty in holding that the 'Oli-ekpe' custom of Nnewi is repugnant to natural justice, equity and good conscience."[63] [62]

Zimbabwe

[195] In Zimbabwe, the Courts initially used the Legal Majority Act[64] [63] to im-prove the position of women. But this trend was later reversed by the Supreme Court. It is instructive to look at those cases that advance the position of women. In *Katekwe v Muchabaiwa*,[65] [64] the Supreme Court of Zimbabwe had occasion to consider the effect of the Legal Majority Act. It held that "Parliament's intention was to create equal status between men and women and, more importantly, to remove the legal disabilities suffered by African women because of the application of customary law."[66] [65] In *Jenah v Nyemba*,[67] [66] the Court held that protection given by the statute is not restricted to single persons but it extended to married African women aged 18 years or over, who primarily were perpetual minors. In coming to this conclusion, the Court relied on subsection 3(3), which provides that the statute "shall apply for the purposes of any law including customary law."[68] [67]

[196] Then in 1987, the Supreme Court confronted head-on the question whether subsection 3(3) of this statute supersedes African law and custom in matters

of succession and allows a woman to succeed as intestate heir. This was in *Chihowa v Mangwende*,[69] [68] a case in which the deceased was survived by two daughters, his wife by whom he had no children, his father and four brothers. The community Court appointed the eldest daughter as the intestate heiress to the deceased's estate. An appeal by the deceased's father to the provincial magistrate failed. Hence the appeal to the Supreme Court.

[197] Confining itself to the question of entitlement to inherit the estate of an African male who dies intestate, a bench of three judges of the Supreme Court held:

> "The Legislature, by enacting the Legal Age of Majority Act, made women who in African law and custom were perpetual minors, majors and therefore equal to men who are majors. By virtue of the provisions of s 3 of the Act women who attain or attained the age of 18 years before the Act came into effect acquired capacity. That capacity entitles them to be appointed intestate heiresses. . . . Now the eldest daughter of a father who dies intestate can take the lot but not for herself only but for herself and her late father's dependants. . . . There is nothing in the wording of subs (3) of s 3 of Act 15 of 1982 which remotely suggests that for the purposes of inheritance a woman can still be regarded as a minor."[70] [69]

[198] However, in a later case, *Murisa NO v Murisa*,[71] [70] the Supreme Court held that the ruling in *Chihowa's* case "did not go so far as to say that a widow could be appointed heir *ab intestatio* to her deceased husband's estate."[72] [71] In reaching its decision, the Supreme Court relied amongst other things, upon the fact that:

> "Customary law does not recognise a widow's right to inherit in a direct fashion from her deceased husband's estate. She may be entitled to support from the estate but not to a share therein. In this context the Legal Age of Majority Act cannot be used to grant her a share in the estate."[73] [72]

[199] *Murisa's* case (*supra*) has been criticised for excluding widows from inheriting from their husbands.[74] [73] It is indeed difficult to reconcile this decision with the *Chihowa* and *Jenah* cases (*supra*). These two cases held that the purpose of the statute was to confer majority status on African women. The effect of the statute was to give them "the same rights of succession as men." And in *Jenah*, the Court held that the protection afforded by the statute is not restricted to single persons but extends to married African women who were perpetual minors. The *Murisa* decision can only be explained on the basis that the absence of blood relation between her and the husband constituted a bar.

[200] In *Magaya v Magaya*,[75] [74] the Supreme Court, in a bench of five judges, overruled its earlier decisions in *Katekwe* and *Chihowa* including *Murisa*, holding that these cases were decided wrongly.[76] [75] The Court considered two questions,

first, whether customary law of succession was exempt from the anti-discrimination provisions of the Constitution; and second, whether the Legal Age of Majority Act conferred substantive rights upon women. In relation to the first question, it found that anti-discrimination provisions of the Constitution do not forbid discrimination based on sex. It further held that "even if they did on account of Zimbabwe's adherence to gender equality enshrined in international human rights instruments," subsections 3(a) and 3(b) of section 23 of the Constitution exempt customary law from the provisions forbidding discrimination.[77] [76]

Tanzania

[201] In Tanzania, three systems of law govern succession, namely, the Indian Succession Act 1865, Islamic law and indigenous law.[78] [77] Each system differs in the rights it accords to women. The Local Customary Law (Declaration)[79] [78] contains rules that regulate intestate succession among patrilineal communities of Tanzania. A distinction is made between self-acquired land and family and clan land. The deceased's children can inherit self-acquired land in diminishing progression as determined by their sexes. Widows are excluded.

[202] Although daughters are entitled to inherit family land, unlike men, they may not dispose of the land. In *Ibernados Ephraim v Holaria d/o Pastory and Gervazi Keizilege*, in the High Court of Civil Appeal 70/89, this rule came under challenge. The High Court found that this rule is discriminatory and inconsistent with article 13(4) of the Constitution of Tanzania, which forbids discrimination against any person.[80] [79]

Ghana

[203] In *Akrofi v Akrofi*,[81] [80] the younger brother of the deceased was appointed *indlalifa* to succeed. The family property consisted of, amongst other things, three farms. The appointment followed a custom in terms of which women were not allowed to succeed to their deceased fathers' estates. A daughter of the deceased challenged the appointment, claiming that she was entitled to succeed her father.

[204] The High Court issued a declarator to the effect that the daughter was "within the range of persons . . . entitled to succeed to her father's estate."[82] [81]

The Court issued the declarator because under the Ghanaian custom in issue the *indlalifa* was determined at a meeting of family members. The ruling of the Court brought the daughter within the range of persons who could be considered for appointment. In rejecting the reasons given by the paramount chief why a woman cannot succeed, the Court said:

> "I consider also the reason given by the paramount chief why a woman cannot succeed to her father's property unsound, because a successor does not acquire an absolute title which will pass to his or her issues. The successor's title at its best is a determinable life interest, that is to say, if he died still possessed of

family property, the same will go to the person appointed by the family. The danger envisaged by the paramount chief will not arise. Further in many states in Ghana, women do succeed to family properties but no one will say by reason of their succession and their possible marriage into other families the properties they inherit or succeed to stand in jeopardy of being lost to their families. Again the paramount chief was pressed as to a settlement of the case of Mamasie Ofei and his sister Felipina Adjei which he conducted, when he and the members of the arbitration had to divide the inheritance of a brother and a sister and to give the sister a share in her late father's estate."[83] [82]

[205] Although the Court did not find that a custom, which excludes women, exists, the Court nevertheless said:

"I am of the view that if there be such a custom and I do not so find, whereby a person is discriminated against solely upon the ground of sex that custom has outlived its usefulness and is at present not in conformity with public policy. Our customs if they are to survive the test of time must change with the times."[84] [83]

[206] *In re Kofi Antubam (Decd): Quaico v Fosu and Another,*[85] [84] the High Court was concerned, amongst other things, with whether the widows and the children of the deceased had any interest in the estate of the deceased, and if they did, the nature and extent of such interest under Akan customary law. The Court found that widows and children have an interest not only in the immovable property but have to be maintained from the whole estate. "Their interests are inextricably mixed up in the indivisible estate and accordingly they are entitled to share in the estate if ultimately the whole estate is converted into money or partitioned."[86] [85]

[207] Concerning the development of customary law, the Court remarked:

"[i]n the last quarter of the last century, customary law in Ghana has progressed and developed in accordance with the tempo of social, commercial and industrial progress. So far as land tenure is concerned, farming rights have been converted into building and residential rights, customs which appear to be repugnant to natural justice, equity and good conscience have been gradually extinguished by judicial decisions. The then legislature played a less effective role in these spontaneous developments engineered by public opinion. The Courts have embraced these developments without adhering strictly to the original customary rigid rules."[87] [86]

And then added:

"Ghana is a developing state with remarkable social and economic transformations which render some of our customary rules antediluvian. If the customary law is to retain its place as the greatest adjunct to statutory law and the common law, it cannot remain stagnant whilst other aspects of the law are in constant motion."[88] [87]

. . .

WHAT CONCLUSION CAN BE DRAWN FROM THE ABOVE ANALYSIS?

[209] Having regard to these developments on the continent, the transformation of African communities from rural communities into urban and industrialised communities, and the role that women now play in our society, the exclusion of women from succeeding to the family head can no longer be justified. These developments must also be seen against the international instruments that protect women against discrimination, namely: the Convention on the Elimination of All Forms of Discrimination Against Women (CEDAW),[89] [88] the African (Banjul) Charter on Human and Peoples' Rights,[90] [89] and the International Covenant on Civil and Political Rights.[91] [90] In particular, CEDAW requires South Africa to ensure, amongst other things, the practical realisation of the principle of equality between men and women and to take all appropriate measures to modify or abolish existing laws, regulations, customs and practices that constitutes discrimination against women.[92] [91] As we observed in *S v Baloyi (Minister of Justice and Another Intervening)*:[93] [92]

> "[t]he Convention on the Elimination of Discrimination Against Women imposes a positive obligation on States to pursue policies of eliminating discrimination against women by, amongst other things, adopting legislative and other measures which prohibit such discrimination. Similarly the African Charter on Human and Peoples' Rights obliges signatory States to ensure the elimination of discrimination against women."[94] [93] (Footnotes omitted.)

[210] This rule might have been justified by the traditional social economic structure in which it developed. It has outlived its usefulness. In the present day and age the limitation on the right of women to succeed to the position and status of the family head, cannot be said to be reasonable and justifiable under section 36(1) of the Constitution. It follows therefore that the rule of male primogeniture is inconsistent with section 9(3) of the Constitution to the extent that it excludes women from succeeding to the family head.

[211] But what should be done with the rule, in particular, should the rule be developed so that it is brought into line with the Constitution? It is to this question that I now turn.

SHOULD THE RULE BE DEVELOPED IN LINE WITH THE CONSTITUTION?

[212] We are dealing here with indigenous law. That law is part of our law. Section 39(2) of the Constitution imposes an obligation on Courts to develop indigenous

law so as to bring it in line with the Constitution, in particular, the rights in the Bill of Rights. In *Carmichele v Minister of Safety and Security and Another*,[95] [94] this Court considered the obligation to develop the common law and held that "where the common law deviates from the spirit, purport and objects of the Bill of Right the Courts have an obligation to develop it by removing that deviation."[96] [95]

[213] The rationale for this obligation was outlined as follows:

> "[t]he Constitution is the supreme law. The Bill of Rights, under the IC, applied to all law. Item 2 of Schedule 6 to the Constitution provides that 'all law' that was in force when the Constitution took effect, 'continues in force subject to . . . consistency with the Constitution'. Section 173 of the Constitution gives to all higher Courts, including this Court, the inherent power to develop the common law, taking into account the interests of justice. In section 7 of the Constitution, the Bill of Rights enshrines the rights of all people in South Africa, and obliges the State to respect, promote and fulfil these rights. Section 8(1) of the Constitution makes the Bill of Rights binding on the Judiciary as well as on the Legislature and Executive. Section 39(2) of the Constitution provides that when developing the common law, every Court must promote the spirit, purport and objects of the Bill of Rights. It follows implicitly that where the common law deviates from the spirit, purport and objects of the Bill of Rights the Courts have an obligation to develop it by removing that deviation."[97] [96]

[214] The Court stressed that:

> "the obligation of Courts to develop the common law, in the context of the section 39(2) objectives, is not purely discretionary. On the contrary, it is implicit in section 39(2) read with section 173 that where the common law as it stands is deficient in promoting the section 39(2) objectives, the Courts are under a general obligation to develop it appropriately. We say a 'general obligation' because we do not mean to suggest that a Court must, in each and every case where the common law is involved, embark on an independent exercise as to whether the common law is in need of development and, if so, how it is to be developed under section 39(2). At the same time there might be circumstances where a Court is obliged to raise the matter on its own and require full argument from the parties."[98] [97]

[215] The *Carmichele* case (*supra*) applies equally to the development of indigenous law. Where a rule of indigenous law deviates from the spirit, purport and objects of the Bill of Rights, Courts have an obligation to develop it so as to remove such deviation. This obligation is especially important in the context of indigenous law. Once a rule of indigenous law is struck down, that is the end of that particular rule. Yet

there may be many people who observe that rule, and who will continue to observe the rule. And what is more, the rule may already have been adapted to the ever-changing circumstances in which it operates. Furthermore, the Constitution guarantees the survival of the indigenous law. These considerations require that, where possible, Courts should develop rather than strike down a rule of indigenous law.

[216] In view of the decision of this Court in *Carmichele,* there are at least two instances in which the need to develop indigenous law may arise. In the first instance it may arise where it is necessary to adapt indigenous law to the changed circumstances. Like the common law, the indigenous law must be adjusted to the ever-changing needs of the community in which it operates.[99] [98] An illustration of this is to be found in the case of *Mabena (supra).*[100] [99]

[217] Two issues arose in the *Mabena* case. The first one was whether failure by the groom's father to participate in marriage negotiations nullified the marriage. The Court held that it did not. It found that in the past there was a need for parents to consent to children's marriages because they provided lobolo but since young men were now in a position to provide for their own lobolo, parental consent is no longer required. The second issue was whether a woman could receive *lobolo.* The Court accepted that there are instances where a woman may act as head of a family and can receive *lobolo.*[101] [100] As a result, the Court had in that case developed indigenous law by incorporating the changing context in which the system operated.

[218] In the second instance, it may be necessary to develop indigenous law in order to bring it in line with the rights in the Bill of Rights. This is the kind of development that is envisaged in *Carmichele (supra).* Where indigenous law is inconsistent with the rights in the Bill of Rights, Courts have an obligation to develop it so as to bring it in line with the rights in the Bill of Rights. Here the Court assesses the rule of indigenous law (the rule of male primogeniture) against the applicable provision in the Bill of Rights. In this instance, the Court is not primarily concerned with the changing social context in which indigenous law of succession operates or the practice of the people. The dearth of authority on what the living indigenous law is should not therefore preclude a Court from bringing a rule of indigenous law in line with the rights in the Bill of Rights. After all:

> "[o]ur Constitution contemplates that there will be a coherent system of law built on the foundations of the Bill of Rights, in which common law and indigenous law should be developed and legislation should be interpreted so as to be consistent with the Bill of Rights and with our obligations under international law. In this sense the Constitution demands a change in the legal norms and the values of our society."[102] [101]

AND INDIGENOUS LAW MUST REFLECT THIS CHANGE

[219] By contrast, the development of indigenous law in order to adapt it to the changed circumstances requires the Court to have regard to what people are

actually doing. It is here where the living indigenous law—law as actually lived by the people—becomes relevant. It is here too where the problem of identifying living indigenous law arises. The Court must have regard to what people are actually doing in order to adapt the indigenous law to the everchanging circumstances. That is not to say that in this process Courts should not have regard to the Constitution. Of course, in the process of developing indigenous law and adapting it to the ever-changing circumstances, Courts are required by section 39(2) of the Constitution to do so in a manner that promotes the spirit, purport and objects of the Bill of Rights.

[220] In these cases we are concerned with the development of the rule of male primogeniture so as to bring it in line with the right to equality. We are not concerned with the law actually lived by the people. The problem of identifying living indigenous law therefore does not arise. At issue here is the rule of male primogeniture, which was applied in the *Bhe* and *Shibi* matters (*supra*). It is that rule which must be tested against the right to equality, and if found deficient, as I have found, it must be developed so as to remove such deficiency.

[221] The rule of male primogeniture may have been consistent with the structure and the functions of the traditional family. The rule prevented the partitioning of the family property and kept it intact for the support of the widow, unmarried daughters and younger sons. However, the circumstances in which the rule applies today are very different. The cattle-based economy has largely been replaced by a cash-based economy. Impoverishment, urbanisation and the migrant labour system have fundamentally affected the traditional family structures. The role and status of women in modern urban, and even rural, areas extend far beyond that imposed on them by their status in traditional society. Many women are *de facto* heads of their families. They support themselves and their children by their own efforts. Many contribute to the acquisition of family assets. The official traditional version of indigenous law does not therefore reflect nor accommodate this changed role and function.

[222] The defect in the rule of male primogeniture is that it excludes women from being considered for succession to the deceased family head. In this regard it deviates from section 9(3) of the Constitution. It needs to be developed so as to bring it in line with our Bill of Rights. This can be achieved by removing the reference to a male so as to allow an eldest daughter to succeed to the deceased estate.

[223] It is now convenient to consider the remedy for the infringement of the right to equality by section 23, the regulations and section 1(4)(b) of the Intestate Succession Act.

REMEDY

[224] Section 23 of the Act, the regulations and section 1(4)(b) of the Intestate Succession Act cannot be allowed to remain on our statute books. To allow them to remain would mean, as the Deputy Chief Justice put it, "that the benefits of the Constitution would continue to be withheld from those who have been deprived of

them for so long."[103] [102] It is true that the regulations in effect are a choice of law mechanism. They regulate the circumstances in which indigenous law applies. Stripped of their racist purpose and effect, some of these provisions are of the kind found in choice of law statutes. However, to cure the constitutional defect in the regulations would require this Court to engage in detailed legislation, a task that belongs to Parliament. Section 23 and the regulations are, in my view, incapable of being cured through the device of "reading-in" or severance.

[225] The determination of the choice of law rule, which regulates the circumstances in which indigenous law is applicable, involves policy decisions. In particular, it involves a decision on the criteria for determining when indigenous law is applicable. There is a range of options in this regard. The choice of law may be based on, among other things, agreement, the lifestyle of individuals, the type of marriage, the nature of the property such as family land, justice and equity, or a combination of all these factors. The Legislature is better equipped to make these policy choices.

[226] In all the circumstances, the appropriate remedy is one of striking down with immediate effect. But once section 23 and the regulations are struck down, there will no longer be any legal mechanism that regulates the circumstances in which indigenous law of succession is applicable. Indigenous law is still widely practised within African communities. However, the transformation of African communities from rural into urban communities and the influence of other cultures may render indigenous law of succession not particularly suitable in certain circumstances. Furthermore, there may be disputes as to whether indigenous law is applicable in a particular situation.

There will be circumstances where its application may result in an injustice. In others it may not. Until such time that the Legislature enacts the relevant legislation, disputes as to whether indigenous law should apply must be managed and regulated.

[227] It now remains to consider the mechanism that can be put in place to regulate the disputes involving the application of indigenous law pending the enactment of relevant legislation by Parliament.

[228] One option is to direct, as the High Courts did and the main judgment proposes, that all intestate estates shall be governed by the Intestate Succession Act in its amended form. This will bring about uniformity in the administration of intestate estates for all races. No doubt, this option recognises that African communities have been transformed from their traditional settings in which the indigenous law developed into modern and urban communities. But that is not true of all communities. And even within this transformative process, a majority of Africans have not forsaken their traditional cultures. These have been adapted to meet the changing circumstances. The law must recognise this.

[229] In my view, there are factors that militate against the application of the Intestate Succession Act only. First, the Intestate Succession Act is premised on a nuclear family system. By contrast, indigenous law is premised on the extended family system. The provisions of this statute are therefore inadequate to cater for the

social setting that indigenous law of succession was designed to cater for.[104] [103] For example, it was not designed to cater for polygynous unions. Second, as pointed out earlier, the primary objective of indigenous law of succession is the preservation and perpetuation of the family unit and succession to the status and position of the family head. This system ensures the preservation of the family unity and that there is always someone to assume the obligation of the family head to maintain and support the minor children and other dependants of the deceased. That is not the object of the Intestate Succession Act. Its application may well lead to the disintegration of the family unit that indigenous law seeks to preserve and perpetuate.

[230] Third, it does not take sufficient account of indigenous law as part of our law. In *Ex parte Chairperson of the Constitutional Assembly: In re Certification of the Constitution of the Republic of South Africa, 1996*, this Court cautioned that a destructive confrontation between the Bill of Rights and legislation, on the one hand, and indigenous law, on the other, need not take place.[105] [104] The application of common law and the Intestate Succession Act only, may well lead to the obliteration of indigenous law. Yet our Constitution recognises its existence, and contemplates that there are situations where it will be applicable. The Constitution expressly guarantees "the survival of an evolving customary law."[106] [105] And, as the Deputy Chief Justice acknowledges, there is a substantial number of people whose lives are governed by indigenous law and who would wish to have their affairs to be governed by indigenous law.[107] [106] People who live by indigenous law and custom are entitled to be governed by indigenous law. The Constitution accords them that right.

[231] There is a further consideration, which, in my view, militates against the interim application of the Intestate Succession Act as the preferred option. The application of this option may lead to an injustice in certain circumstances. Take the case where both parents die simultaneously leaving a number of children, including minor children and other persons who were dependent upon the deceased for maintenance and support. Let us assume that the major asset in the estate is an immovable property, which is a family home. Each child will be entitled to a share in the estate. Let us assume that one or two children insist on getting their share and they cannot be bought out. This will require the family property to be sold and the proceeds to be divided equally amongst the children. Once the house is sold, there will be no shelter for the minor children and other dependants of the deceased. There is no duty on any of the other heirs to provide such shelter. Or take the case of a deceased who is survived by dependants but leaves nothing for the maintenance and support of the dependants. Minor children and other dependants of the deceased may be left destitute with no one to assume responsibility for their maintenance and support.

[232] The inappropriateness of the Intestate Succession Act in certain circumstances is demonstrated by the report of the Law Commission on customary law of succession. In its report it advanced several reasons why the institution of family property should be preserved. The rule of primogeniture is inextricably linked to the institution of a family home and its concomitant family property. These reasons

include: the fact that despite westernisation, the typical African traditional family home still exists; in polygynous unions, distribution of assets in an estate is quite impractical; and many family homes constitute the only means of livelihood and the only homes for family members. If the property concerned should devolve in terms of common law, the family members concerned will be left without a home and livelihood.[108] [107]

[233] In my view, the reasons advanced by the Law Commission demonstrate that the application of the Intestate Succession Act may lead to unjust results in certain situations and that indigenous law still has a role to play. They underscore the need to have both indigenous law and the Intestate Succession Act apply subject to the requirements of fairness, justice and equity. Indeed, the Law Commission recommends that the institution of family property should be preserved. It further recommends that the destination of family property must be made the subject of an enquiry in appropriate circumstances.[109] [108] The enquiry, which is to be conducted by the Magistrates' Court having jurisdiction, must have regard to: (a) the best interest of the family; and (b) the equality of spouses in customary and civil marriages.[110] [109]

[234] Indigenous law imposes an obligation on *indlalifa* to maintain and support the minor children and other dependants of the deceased. This obligation attaches to the *indlalifa* regardless of whether the deceased left sufficient assets for maintenance and support of the family.[111] [110] The obligation is to administer the estate of the deceased on behalf of and for the benefit of the dependants of the deceased. This ensures that there is always someone to look after the dependants of the deceased. Where there are minor children it may therefore be in their best interests, in certain circumstances, that indigenous law be applied. It may serve to prevent the disintegration of the family unit and prevent members of the family from being rendered homeless or sent to an orphanage or an old-age home. Similarly, where the deceased is survived by dependants but leaves no assets to maintain and support his minor children and other dependents, the application of indigenous law may serve to protect the dependants.

[235] Ours is not the only country that has a pluralist legal system in the sense of common, statutory and indigenous law. Other African countries that face the same problem have opted not for replacing indigenous law with common law or statutory laws. Instead, they have accepted that indigenous law is part of their laws and have sought to regulate the circumstances where it is applicable. In my view this approach reflects recognition of the constitutional right of those communities that live by and are governed by indigenous law. It is a recognition of our diversity, which is an important feature of our constitutional democracy. The importance of diversity in our country was emphasised by this Court in *Christian Education South Africa v Minister of Education*,[112] [111] where the Court said:

"[t]here are a number of other provisions designed to protect the rights of members of communities. They underline the constitutional value of acknowledging diversity and pluralism in our society and give a particular texture to the broadly phrased right to freedom of association contained in s 18. Taken together, they affirm the right of people to be who they are without being forced to subordinate themselves to the cultural and religious norms of others, and highlight the importance of individuals and communities being able to enjoy what has been called the 'right to be different.' In each case, space has been found for members of communities to depart from a general norm. These provisions collectively and separately acknowledge the rich tapestry constituted by civil society, indicating in particular that language, culture and religion constitute a strong weave in the overall pattern."[113] [112]

[236] It seems to me therefore that the answer lies somewhere other than in the application of the Intestate Succession Act only. It lies in flexibility and willingness to examine the applicability of indigenous law in the concrete setting of social conditions presented by each particular case. It lies in accommodating different systems of law in order to ensure that the most vulnerable are treated fairly. The choice of law mechanism must be informed by the need to: (a) respect the right of communities to observe cultures and customs which they hold dear; (b) preserve indigenous law subject to the Constitution; and (c) protect vulnerable members of the family. Indigenous law is part of our law. It must therefore be respected and accorded a place in our legal system. It must not be allowed to stagnate as in the past or disappear.

[237] What is equally important is the fact that the traditional social and economic structures have, to a large extent, been replaced by modern social and economic structures. Poverty and greed have undermined the traditional responsibilities of heirs. These days, spouses and children of deceased people are sometimes no longer cared for. As Ndulo observes:

"The joint family is in a state of decline and Africans are now enmeshed in an exchange economy. Development and industrialisation have caused an irreversible breakdown in the traditional African social order. The society is now highly individualistic, competitive and acquisitive."[114] [113]

And Himonga observes:

"The disruption of the traditional self-sufficient joint family organisation poses the problem of the expense and practicability of maintaining extended families. This may in turn affect the extent to which the kinship group is capable of absorbing spouses and their children and providing them with adequate material support after the dissolution of the marriage by the death of one of the spouses or by divorce."[115] [114]

[238] There must be a balancing exercise. The respect for our diversity and the right of communities to live and be governed by indigenous law must be balanced against the need to protect the vulnerable members of the family. The overriding consideration must be to do that which is fair, just and equitable. And more importantly, the interests of the minor children and other dependants of the deceased should be paramount.

[239] In my view, the question whether indigenous law is applicable should in the first place be determined by agreement. After the burial, it is common for the family to meet and decide what should happen to the deceased's estate. If an agreement can be reached there seems to be no reason for any interference. Any dispute relating to the choice of law should be resolved by the Magistrates' Court having jurisdiction. In determining such dispute a Magistrate must have regard to what is fair, just and equitable in the circumstances of the case. And in determining what is fair, just and equitable, the Magistrate must have regard to, amongst other things, the assets and liabilities of the estate, the widow's contribution to the acquisition of assets, the contribution of family members to such assets, and whether there are minor children or other dependants of the deceased who require support and maintenance. Naturally, this list is not intended to be exhaustive of all the factors that are to be taken into consideration; there may be others too. The ultimate consideration must be to do that which is fair, just and equitable in the circumstances of each case.

CONCLUSION

[240] To sum up therefore, pending the enactment of legislation by Parliament to regulate when indigenous law is applicable, the position should be as follows. Where parties agree that succession to the deceased must be governed by indigenous law of succession, that is, the law that must govern the succession. Any dispute as to whether indigenous law is applicable must be resolved by the Magistrates' Court having jurisdiction. The Magistrate must enquire into the most appropriate system of law to be applied. In conducting such an enquiry, the Magistrate must have regard to what is fair, just and equitable and must have particular regard to the interests of the minor children and any other dependant of the deceased.

[241] It is not necessary in this judgment to set out in any detail the order I would have made. Such order is already foreshadowed in the discussion of the remedy. It is sufficient for the purposes of these cases to say the following:

(a) In the *Bhe* matter, Nonkululeko Bhe and Anelisa Bhe are the only children of the deceased. They are both minors. The deceased had no other dependants. In addition, the two minor children and their mother have been occupying the property with the deceased until his death. No useful purpose will be served by referring this matter back to the Magistrate. In all the circumstances, it would be just and equitable that the estates of the deceased devolve according to the Intestate Succession Act.

Both minors are to be declared the sole heirs. Accordingly, I concur in paragraph 11(a) of the order of the main judgment.

(b) In the *Shibi* matter, Ms Charlotte Shibi is the only sister to the deceased. The latter had no parents or brothers or other sisters. Nor did he have any children. This matter has been going for sometime. It must now be brought to finality. In this case too, it is not necessary to refer the matter back to the Magistrate. On the record, it is possible to determine the relief. In all the circumstances of this case, it is just and equitable that the estates of the deceased devolve in accordance with the Intestate Succession Act. I therefore concur in paragraph 11(b) of the order of the main judgment.

(c) In addition, I concur in paragraphs 1; 2; 3; and 5 of the order of the main judgment.

For the majority judgment, see The Dignity Jurisprudence of the South Africa Constitutional Court.

THE *NZIMANDE* CASE

Nzimande v. Nzimande and Another 2005 (1) All SA 608 (T)

Case Summary

FACTS

The Appellant in this case is the brother of the deceased, and the first Respondent (the Respondent) is the deceased's customary law wife. Before his death, the deceased was issued a certificate of occupation of the house in which he resided in Soweto, in terms of regulation 8 of the regulations promulgated under the Black (Urban Areas) Consolidation Act 25 of 1945. This house formed part of the deceased's estate upon his death. The deceased died intestate and there were no children born to the union between him and the Respondent. The deceased's father had pre-deceased him.

According to customary law, as codified by the Black Administration Act 38 of 1927, the brother of the deceased was the heir to the deceased's estate. As such, the Appellant was issued with a certificate of occupation in terms of regulation 8 of the regulations promulgated under the Black (Urban Areas) Consolidation Act 25 of 1945. However, he never took occupation of the property. The Respondent continued to reside on the property. Because the Appellant never took occupation of the property, and because the Respondent continued to reside on the property after the death of her husband, she was granted a certificate of ownership by the Director General in terms of the Conversion of Certain Rights into Leasehold or Ownership Act 81 of 1988.

The Appellant appealed against the granting of this certificate of ownership. He argued that the Director General did not have the authority to grant the certificate of occupation to the Appellant, and that the Conversion of Certain Rights into Leasehold or Ownership Act was intended to convert automatically the occupation rights to a more common law right, such as ownership.

LEGAL HISTORY

The matter first went before an adjudicator. The adjudicator found that granting of the certificate was appropriate in this situation. This Appellant then launched a second appeal to an appeal panel, which came to the same decision. The matter then went to the Witwatersrand High Court.

LEGAL ISSUE

The question with which the court was faced was whether the Director General had discretion to grant the rights of ownership to someone other than the holder of the certificate of occupation.

DISPENSATION

The court dismissed the appeal against the issuing of a certificate of ownership to the Respondent.

After reviewing relevant legislation and case law, the court noted that the Director General had the discretion to consider the question of whether the granting of a certificate of ownership was valid or not. Moreover, the court asserted that the Constitution mandated that in interpreting any legislation, the courts have to promote the spirit, purport, and purpose of the Bill of Rights. This means that the courts are mandated to give effect to the fundamental values of the Constitution—among them equality. Refusing to grant the Respondent who already had the certificate of occupation, the certificate of ownership, would be a violation of the rights of women married in terms of African customary law. This refusal would amount to discrimination against women who were married under customary law and would in turn be a violation of the Constitution.

Justice Jajbhay

HISTORICAL BACKGROUND

. . .

[5] The nature of this appeal requires an examination of the history of land ownership in respect of Black African people in our country. Land ownership was, as a general rule, not available to black persons in urban areas. It was, however, possible for black persons to acquire a right of occupation in these areas. In the period between 1955 and 1968 black persons could obtain a 30-year lease on houses. This 30-year lease scheme was terminated in 1968, when the Regulations governing the Control and Supervision of an Urban Black Residential Area and Relevant Matters (GN R1036 of 14 June 1968) were promulgated.

[6] In terms of the R1036 Regulations, immovable property could lawfully be occupied by persons qualifying for such occupation in terms of permits issued by the local authority.

[7] The R1036 Regulations provided for site permits (regulation 6) where a person was allocated a site and erected a house thereon with his own funds, a residential permit (regulation 7) where a person rented a dwelling from the local authority and a certificate of occupation (regulation 8) where a person bought a house from the local authority.

[8] In 1978, it became possible for black persons to register rights of 99-year leasehold over property in black urban areas. The introduction of the 99-year leasehold signified an important shift in government policy with regard to land ownership for black persons in urban areas: prior to 1978 black persons could only obtain occupational rights to houses with no rights to the land on which the houses had been erected. After the introduction of the 99-year leasehold scheme, black persons could obtain a registered real right to the property as well.

[9] The leasehold scheme did not prove successful for various reasons and in 1986, the Black Communities Development Act 4 of 1984 ("Development Act") was amended to provide for full ownership rights for black persons in urban areas. On 1 January 1989 the Conversion Act was promulgated. In terms of the Conversion Act, the R1036 Regulations were repealed and the provincial administrations were given the task of converting the occupation rights granted by regulations 6 and 8 into leasehold or ownership. This process is still being carried out by the provincial administrations.

[10] With the promulgation of the Conversion Act, and the consequent repeal of the R1036 Regulations, the residential permit (regulation 7) was abolished. The rights conferred by these permits were, however, retained and are protected by statute.

[11] The persons who were living in houses in terms of permits as aforesaid have for years been claiming that the houses have been paid for and that they should be transferred to them free of charge. After protracted negotiations the cabinet decided during November 1992 and October 1993 that the "big house sales campaign" previously established by Circular 17 of 1983, should be extended and that a discount of up to a maximum of R7500 should be given on the sale of all State-financed rented homes. This would ultimately enable the residential properties to be transferred to "the people," whilst at the same time reducing the housing loans owed by the local authorities to the State. The purchase prices of the houses were set to reflect the historic erection costs and would in most cases be covered by the discount. Some of the more recent houses have a purchase price of more than R7000, and in these cases mortgage bonds have to be registered.

[12] In certain areas, township registers have not as yet been opened. In these areas it is not possible to transfer ownership of the houses at this point in time. The right to these houses will be transferred to leasehold, which will automatically at no further costs be converted to ownership as soon as the township registers are opened.

[13] A fundamental concern that was foreseen in the transfer process contemplated above, was to identify the person with whom the local authority should enter into an agreement of sale with the incorporation of the discount benefit. In the case of occupational rights (regulations 6 and 8 of the R1036 Regulations) a statutory procedure was determined. The Conversion Act provided the statutory dispute resolution mechanisms only for regulation 6 and regulation 8 cases. The Gauteng Housing Act, which was promulgated by the Gauteng Province sometime later, together with the regulations thereunder, provided dispute resolution mechanisms for all housing disputes.

NATIONAL HOUSING CODE

[14] In terms of the National Housing Act 107 of 1997 which came into effect on 1 April 1998, the National Minister of Housing had to publish a National Housing Code, which would incorporate a National Housing Policy as well as procedural guidelines in respect of the implementation of such a policy. The National Housing Code was published during March 2000.

[15] In so far as the former black townships are concerned, the National Housing Code sets out the position as follows:

"(b) In certain townships the present situation is as follows: A permit-holder under Regulations 6 and 8 of the Township Regulations (Government Notice R1036 of 1968) has already acquired rights to his/her house. The provinces are required by statute to deal with the conversion of such rights to ownership; or as an intermediate step, where a township register has not yet been opened, to leasehold or subsequent endorsement for ownership. Because a person in this category has in effect already purchased his/her property, there is no need to enter into sales agreement with him/her, and consequently the discount benefit does not apply. However he, or she is entitled to a discount benefit on any unpaid balance of a loan on the selling price, as well as of a loan granted for self-building purposes. The province bears the cost of issuing leasehold or freehold titles to Regulations 6 and 8 permit-holders under the conversion of certain rights to leasehold and freehold (*sic*) Act, 1988 (Act No 81 of 1988).

A tenant under Regulation 7 of the Township Regulations . . . Regulations under the Conversion of Certain Rights to Leasehold and Freehold Act, 1988 (Act No 81 of 1988), prescribe a comprehensive enquiry procedure to be conducted by provinces for purposes of identification in Regulations 6 and 8 cases. Processing Regulation 7 cases is legally the obligation of the municipality. The provinces are also required to handle transactions in the former South African Development Trust areas."

[16] Disputes with regard to the right to acquire regulations 6, 7, and 8 properties are to be dealt with as follows under the National Housing Code:

"9.2.5.1 Enquiry and dispute resolution procedures for application in the areas of former black local authorities.

(a) For Regulation 6 and 8 cases the Conversion of Certain Right to Leasehold and Freehold Act, 1998 (Act No 81 of 1988) requires the Director-General of a province (or a person designated by him or her) to conduct an enquiry into the identity of the affected site and of the claimant(s) thereto. Each of the four previous provinces had its own set of regulations under this Act. These allow for notices and hearings under a quasi-judicial procedure.

(b) For Regulation 7 'council tenant' cases no similar statutory provision is provided for identification and enquiry procedures. It is desirable that municipalities should apply similar disciplines.

(c) Investigations relating to tenancies in formal black municipal areas should like those under the Conversion of Certain Rights to Leasehold and Freehold Acts, 1988 (Act No 81 of 1988) commence by establishing the situation of record as at 31 December 1988 when the repeal of the Township Regulations R1036/68 took effect."

CONVERSION OF CERTAIN RIGHTS INTO LEASEHOLD OR OWNERSHIP ACT 81 OF 1988

[17] Section 1 of the Conversion Act defines words and expressions used. Some of the definitions are self-explanatory. For purposes of this judgement the following definitions require attention:

"'Affected site'—means a site which is or purports to be occupied by virtue of a site permit, a certificate, a trading site permit, or a permit issued by the local authority concerned conferring upon the holder thereof a right which in the opinion of the Director-General concerned are similar to the rights which are held by the holder of a site permit, certificate or trading site permit (section 1(i)). 'Certificate'—means a certificate of occupation issued under Regulation 8(1) of Chapter 2 of the Regulations."

[18] Section 2 of the Conversion Act relates to enquiries and determinations. This section reads as follows:

"(1) The Director-General shall conduct an inquiry in the prescribed manner in respect of affected sites within his province in order to determine who shall be declared to have been granted a right of leasehold or, in the case where the affected sites are situate in a formalised township for which a township register has been opened, ownership with regard to such sites.

(2) . . ."

(3) For the purposes of the declaration under subsection (1) the Director-General may—

(a) give effect to any agreement or transaction in relation to the rights of a holder contemplated in subsection (4)(a) or (b) in respect of the site concerned, between such holder and any other person;

(b) give effect to such agreement or transaction or any settlement or testamentary disposition in respect of such rights, entered into or made before the death of the last such holder;

(c) consider any intestate heir of the last such holder to have been granted a right of leasehold or, in the case where the site is situate in a formalised township for which a township register has been opened, ownership in respect of the site concerned;

(d) give effect to any Court order or sale in execution in relation to the site concerned, notwithstanding that such agreement, transaction, settlement, testamentary disposition or intestate succession could not by virtue only of the provisions of the regulations have been entered into or made or was entered into or was made without the approval of any person whose approval would have been required under the regulations, and notwithstanding that the site permit, certificate or trading site permit concerned had lapsed upon the death of such holder.

(4) At the conclusion of the inquiry and after having considered any relevant claim or objection, the Director-General shall, if he is satisfied that the person concerned is, subject to the provisions of subsection (3), in respect of the site concerned—

(a) the holder of a site permit, certificate or trading site permit; or

(b) the holder of rights which in the opinion of the Director-General are similar to the rights of the holder of a site permit, certificate or trading site permit, determine whom he intends to declare to have been granted a right of leasehold or, in the case where the site is situate in a formalised township for which a township register has been opened, ownership in respect of the site concerned."

[19] Section 3(1) of the Conversion Act reads as follows:

"Any person who considers himself aggrieved by any determination contemplated in section 2 (4) may, within such period and in such manner as may be prescribed, appeal against that determination to the Administrator concerned, who may, after investigation of the appeal and with due regard to the provisions of section 2 (3) and (4), confirm, set aside or vary the determination or make such other determination as in his opinion should have been made."

[20] Section 3 of the Conversion Act deals with appeals against determinations, to be made to a competent Court. An appeal as contemplated above shall be prosecuted as if it were an appeal against a judgment of a Magistrate's Court in a civil matter. All rules applicable to the hearing of such an appeal, ie the High Court Rules, shall be applicable in the instance. The High Court hearing such an appeal may confirm or set aside the determination or make such other determination as in its opinion should have been made by the Administrator.

[21] In terms of section 7 of the Conversion Act the Director-General has the right and power to investigate any local authority's documents and furthermore make enquiries about any entries in the books of record of such local authority. Section 7(2) of the Conversion Act provides a criminal sanction if the Director-General and/or his authorised officials are hindered or obstructed in the performance of their functions in terms of the Conversion Act.

[22] Section 9 of the Conversion Act deals with the authority of the Administrator of a specific province to make regulations regarding notices, the hearing of appeals, the procedure to be followed in the service of any document or notice, and/or in general any matter which the Administrator may consider necessary or expedient to prescribe in order that the purposes of the Conversion Act may be achieved. The Gauteng Province, unlike the other provinces, did not follow the regulation route, but amended the Conversion Act (in so far as it applies in Gauteng) to make the Act suitable for its particular needs.

[23] Section 10 of the Conversion Act deals with the delegation of powers of the Administrator and/or the Director-General. The Conversion Act specifically provides that any delegation made under the Act shall not prevent the exercise of such powers by the Administrator or the Director-General himself, as the case may be.

ASSIGNMENT OF THE CONVERSION ACT TO THE PROVINCES
[24] The administration of the Conversion Act in Gauteng has under Proclamation 41 of 1996, promulgated in *Government Gazette* 17320 of 26 July 1996, been assigned to the Province of Gauteng with effect from 26 July 1996.

[25] In terms of a resolution signed by the Premier of the Gauteng Provincial Government on 28 August 1996, the Member of the Executive Council: Housing and Land Affairs was designated as a competent authority for the administration of the Conversion Act in terms of section 235(c)(ii) of the Interim Constitution.

ESTABLISHMENT OF HOUSING BUREAUS
[26] Housing bureaus were eventually established within the areas of all the local authorities in Gauteng to give effect to the decision to transfer the State-funded properties to their rightful occupiers.

[27] The establishing of housing bureaus were preceded by extensive negotiations by the stakeholders, namely the Provincial Government, the Local Transitional

Council and the community, which was represented by various political groupings, civic organisations and non-governmental organisations.

[28] After the negotiations, an agreement of co-operation was reached between all the stakeholders. It was reduced to writing and issued to all the local authorities as a directive in terms of section 171 of the Local Government Ordinance 17 of 1939.

[29] The stakeholders agreed to the establishment of housing bureaus through a directive in order to finalise a legal process in terms of which the different role-players would contribute to the successful completion of the project. The directive indicates the principles underlying the transfer of residential properties project. The directive in addition sets out in paragraph 8, the procedures to be followed to enable persons to claim ownership of State-funded properties.

The Adjudication of Housing Disputes

[30] The *transfer of residential properties project*, including the *adjudication of housing disputes*, are based on arrangements that were negotiated between the stakeholders.

[31] The procedures to be followed for the resolution of housing disputes were negotiated on the following basis:

31.1 The Conversion Act had prescribed an open, transparent enquiry process for the resolution of disputes with regard to the ownership of regulations 6 and 8 houses.

31.2 That as far as possible the same process should be used for all types of housing involved in the transfer of residential properties project.

31.3 That it was imperative that the process should adhere to the principles of *audi alteram partem*, as well as the rules of natural justice in order to minimise legal challenges to the procedures used.

31.4 The qualifications and other requirements of adjudicators were agreed upon.

[32] Adjudication of housing disputes commenced during 1997. Approximately two years later the adjudication process was enhanced to include the establishment of a dedicated appeal panel. By the end of 2000 and towards the beginning of 2001, the first Gauteng Housing Amendment Act, 2000, as well as the Transfer of Residential Properties Adjudication Regulations, 2000, were promulgated. These instruments served to legislate the adjudication process and procedures.

. . .

The Appellant's Contention

[45] The Appellant's counsel contended that the question to be asked in this matter is "who is the person to be determined to be the holder of the site permit, certificate of occupation or the like?" He continued that "the *de facto* position that presented itself to the appeal panel was accordingly that the Appellant was the holder of the

certificate." Therefore, the argument concluded that having conducted the enquiry the appeal panel ought to have been satisfied that the Appellant was the holder of "a certificate" in respect of the dwelling and that the Respondent was not a person referred to in section 2(4)(a) or section 2(4)(b) of the Conversion Act.

[46] The certificate of occupation which was issued on 7 December 1982 in favour of the Appellant sets out the following:

> "Issued in terms of Regulation 8 of Chapter 2 of the Regulations governing the control and supervision of an urban Bantu residential area and relevant matters. G.N. 1036 dated 14 June 1968.
>
> The right to the use and occupation of the dwelling on the site described below is hereby granted to the holder and his dependants."

In terms of the certificate of occupation, the Appellant and his dependants are recorded as the occupants. No mention is made of the first Respondent.

[47] The Appellant's submission is constructed on the foundation that sections 2(1), 2(3)(a), (b), (c), (d) and 2(4)(a) and (b) of the Conversion Act do not vest a discretion in the hands of the Director-General or his duly authorised delegates in the determination of a matter such as the present one, where the Appellant is already the holder of a certificate of occupation. The argument continues that the Conversion Act was intended to automatically convert the rights held under the R1036 Regulations to more effective common law rights ie rights of leasehold or ownership.

Does the Director-General have discretion to grant the rights to someone other than the holder of a certificate of occupation?

[48] The question that arises is what consequences follow from the conclusion that the Commissioner may have acted on misrepresentation or even perhaps unlawfully, or in terms of a law that will no longer pass constitutional muster? Is the certificate granted by the Commissioner simply to be disregarded as if it had never existed? In other words, should the delegated official now disregard the Respondent's contentions simply because the Appellant was the holder of the certificate? Here, one should commence from the premise that the Appellant is the holder of a certificate. Until the certificate is set aside by a Court in proceedings for judicial review, it exists in fact and it has legal consequences that simply cannot be overlooked.

> "The proper functioning of a modern state would be considerably compromised if all administrative acts could be given effect or ignored depending upon the view the subject takes of the validity of the act in question. No doubt it is for this reason that our law has always recognised that even an unlawful administrative act is capable of producing legally valid consequences for so long as the unlawful act is not set aside" (*Oudekraal Estates (Pty) Ltd v The City of Cape Town and Others*).

[49] The present matter is not a review application. However, there is nothing in the Conversion Act that prohibits the delegated official to consider the substantive validity. Section 2(4) of the Conversion Act authorises the Director-General to "determine whom he intends to declare to have been granted a right." Section 2(3) of the Conversion Act lists some circumstances under which the Director-General may decide to grant the rights to a competing party. There may well be other circumstances to be considered.

. . .

[53] In the matter of *Moremi v Moremi and Another* Schabort J (as he then was) said the following:

"The conversion of rights brought about by the 1988 Act formed part of the legislative process aimed at delivering society from the tenurial fetters of the area of racial segregation and I do not think that the future dispensation contemplated in the 1988 Act envisaged the retention of any possible restrictive notions concerning spouses and occupancy derived from that past—such as those possibly encapsulated in the 1945 Act and the regulations (bearing in mind that it has already been decided but even thereunder spouses married in community of property were in the position of joint 'lessees'—(see *Toho v Diepmeadow City Council and Another* 1993 (3) SA 679 (W)). I would, therefore, think that the statutory lease was not intended to create a right personal to the applicant only, falling outside the joint estate (cf. Hahlo *The South African Law of Husband and Wife* 5th ed. at 167; Barnard, Cronjé and Olivier *The South African Law of Persons and Family Law* 2nd ed. at 241–5). A construction to the contrary could hardly serve the policy of the 1988 Act."

[54] When the Conversion Act was enacted, its object was "to provide for the conversion of certain rights of occupation into leasehold or ownership." This statute served to achieve the objective by providing a mechanism "for the conversion of the previously discretionary permits into more secure rights and the repeal of the regulations promulgated in terms of the Black (Urban Areas) Consolidation Act 25 of 1945, regulating residential, trading and other occupancies" (see Satchwell J in *Phasha v Southern Metropolitan Council of Johannesburg*).

[55] In the exercise of the discretion of the Director-General, Satchwell J in the *Phasha* matter (*supra*) at page 478 paragraphs C–F sets out the following:

"The Director-General is empowered to roam more widely in the conduct of his s 2(1) enquiry. Section 2(3)(a) provides that the Director-General '. . . may give effect to any agreement or transaction in relation to the rights of a holder contemplated in ss (4)(a) or (b) in respect of the site concerned, between such holder or any other person;' and those rights are expressed extremely broadly in that they are rights '. . . which in the opinion of the

Director-General are similar to the rights of the holder of a . . . trading site permit . . . .'

Precise congruence is not required either between the trading site permit of the regulations or the trading site permit of s 1 of the Act or the declaration to be made in terms of s 2 of the Act. The Director-General appears to have a discretion with regard to the agreement or transaction to which he may give consideration, whether or not and to what extent he gives effect to an agreement or transaction, the grounds of similarity between trading site permit rights and non-trading site permit rights, whether the effect of an agreement or transaction results in determination of a right of ownership or the lesser right of leasehold or neither."

[56] In acknowledging the discretion of the Director-General, I believe that Satchwell J affords a generous and purposive interpretation to the Conversion Act. With respect, I promote a similar approach here. The purpose intended is to guarantee a fair and impartial enquiry into the contentions of the contending parties, as to who would ultimately qualify to acquire ownership of the house. The content of the right relied upon by the Appellant must be determined before the Director-General can pronounce on the legality thereof. The content of this right is really the values and practices the right is designed to support.

[57] In the matter of *Motloung v Rokhoeane*, Flemming J (as he then was), determined from the wording of regulation 8(4) made in terms of the Black (Urban Areas) Consolidation Act 25 of 1945 (the R1036 Regulations which were subsequently revoked), that the document (the certificate of occupation) at issue in that case had been issued to the Applicant. This document established a right to occupy and use the premises in question (analogous to *usus* and *habitatio*). The learned Judge further held that this right had the effect of imposing a corresponding burden on the owner of the premises (the town council), and which binds the successors of the owner. In that matter, the holder of the certificate of occupation was held to have the *locus standi* to launch ejectment proceedings against the Respondent, whose "lodging permit" had expired.

The facts in the present matter are clearly distinguishable from the *Motloung* matter (*supra*). Here, the original certificate was granted in favour of the deceased, and more importantly, the first Respondent has enjoyed the uninterrupted use and enjoyment of the dwelling for more than 30 years. In the present matter, the facts further establish that the information supplied by the Appellant in securing the certificate of occupation were incorrect. The certificate indicates that the Appellant, his mother and his dependants will "occupy" the dwelling. This did not occur.

[58] W du Plessis and NJJ Olivier state that:

"'n Houer van 'n perseelpermit, 'n sertifikaat van bewoning en 'n handels-perseelpermit (reg 6 en 8 hfst 2 en reg 2 hfst 3 GK R1036) behou kragtens artikel

11(1) sy GK R1036-regte totdat die regte in huurpag of in huurkontrakte (a(6)(1)) omskep is."

The precondition in the application of this principle is that the underlying certificate of occupation relied upon is not tainted or invalid.

[59] The Commissioner was aware of the fact that the first Respondent resided in the dwelling, in fact she paid the electricity accounts; and at times, she even paid the installments towards the dwelling; at one stage, she was summoned to appear before a surrogate of the Commissioner, and she should "bring all the illegals" along. The Commissioner was of the view that the Appellant should be placed in the stead of the deceased.

[60] The consequence that follows from the conclusion that the commissioner acted on materially incorrect facts, is that the Director-General could consider the contentions of all contending parties in his enquiry. The change in the political and legal landscape inspires such recognition. In dealing with the construction of the Conversion Act, a Court must commence from a strong appreciation that section 39(2) of the Constitution obliges a Court constructing legislation to promote the spirit, purport and objects of the Bill of Rights. This means that individuals affected by legal measures arising out of invalid action should have a fair opportunity to challenge these measures, and to vindicate their rights under the Conversion Act. Once the challenge has been registered (subject to the procedural requirements), the Director-General must initiate an enquiry as to who "shall be declared to have been granted a right."

[61] The Conversion Act enjoins the Director-General to conduct "an inquiry in the prescribed manner in respect of affected sites within his province in order to determine who shall be declared to have been granted a right." It is implicit in the exercise of the Director-General's discretion to investigate whether, or in what circumstances, the action of the commissioner in having granted the regulation 8 certificate to occupy was valid, lawful and justifiable. Once the inquiry has been conducted, then the provisions encapsulated in section 2(4)(b) of the Conversion Act, in the circumstances of the present matter would apply.

[62] Furthermore, a consideration of the facts in the present matter articulate the violation of the rights of women who were married according to African customary law. The first Respondent resided in the dwelling from the time of the death of the deceased (1975) and continued residing there when the certificate was granted. The evidence established that she was not invited to apply for the cession of the certificate of occupation. The significance of not granting the first Respondent an opportunity to contend for the right to occupy the dwelling in 1982, cannot be underestimated. Here, because of the laws applicable at the time, the commissioner did not consider this important factor.

[63] The values indelibly imprinted in our Constitution require that we seriously and consciously consider the lives that women have been compelled to lead by law

and legally-backed social practices. The reality has been and still in large measures continues to be that in our patriarchal culture men find it easier than women to receive income and acquire property. Moreover, social and institutional practice has been to register homes in the names of the male "heads of households," as was done by the commissioner in the present matter. Widows for whom no provision had been made, by will or other settlement were not protected by the common law. The result was that their bereavement was compounded by dependence and potential homelessness—hence the statute (see *Juleiga Daniels v Robin Grieve Campbell NO and Others*).

The Use and Occupation of the Dwelling

[64] In the present matter the certificate of occupation afforded the Appellant the right to the use and occupation of the dwelling. Here, it is common cause that the Appellant neither used nor occupied the dwelling. The first Respondent has enjoyed the uninterrupted use and occupation thereof. The meaning of "occupy" has been considered in various decided cases. In *R v Ghoor and others* De Villiers AJ considered the meaning of the words "occupy" and "occupation" where these appear in section 15(1) of the Group Areas Act. He is reported, in this regard, as having said the following:

> *"They are words capable of a vast variety of meanings depending on the context in which they are used. The present inquiry is, of course, confined to the meaning of the words in relation to land or premises; but even in this relatively narrow sphere the potential diversity of meaning is considerable. . . . One element is common to them all and, it seems to me, common to all meanings of 'occupy' in relation to land or premises, viz a state of control* (my italics).
>
> A person cannot truly be said to occupy a house or room, as distinct from merely being present in it, unless he exercises some form of control over the whole of it. . . .
>
> On the other hand the mere existence of the control element does not necessarily constitute occupation in all possible significations of the word. It is, indeed, the requirement of something more than control in some instances that introduces the variations in meaning, as is illustrated by the above examples. Sometimes control by itself might suffice. Sometimes some use in addition to control is essential and sufficient. Sometimes the additional requirement is habitual physical presence, and sometimes even unbroken physical presence. . . .
>
> *R v Lombard* 1948 (2) SA 31 (T), illustrates that there cannot be occupation without control . . . The importance of the control element is also mentioned by Mason AAJA, in *Madrassa Anjuman Islamia v Johannesburg Municipal Council* 1919 AD 439 at 454 . . .
>
> The real question in such cases being who is using or drawing some benefit from the premises under consideration, a master could vicariously occupy

through his servant, and could in such case even be considered the real occupant to the exclusion of the servant: *Madrassa's* case. . . .

In other cases, however, the object and scope of a statute, and the context in which it uses the word 'occupy,' have led to the conclusion that the Legislature had in mind physical presence (in addition to some form of control, whether of a subordinate or overriding nature)."

[65] Therefore, in this matter, the use and occupation of the dwelling envisaged in the certificate of occupation constituted the habitual physical presence, or physical presence for substantial periods of time, flowing from some form or another of control over the dwelling in question. Bearing in mind the above elements, it follows that the Appellant did neither use nor occupy the dwelling. The fact that he made some improvements does not bring the Appellant within the ambit of these requirements. The Appellant did not indicate a designed or deliberate choice of the dwelling as the *locus* for the activity permitted/granted by the certificate of occupation. Neither was the activity contemplated here exercised. The Appellant resided in another dwelling at the time that the certificate was issued.

[66] In my view, the contention that the Conversion Act was intended to automatically convert the right held under the R1036 Regulations to more effective common law rights—rights of leasehold or ownership—is ill-founded. The subsections referred to in section 2 of the Conversion Act do not contemplate a mechanical adoption on the part of the Director-General in the exercise of his duties. In the examination of the objects and purport of the Conversion Act and the regulations, as well as the Gauteng Housing Act, and the Gauteng Conversion of Certain Rights into Leasehold or Ownership Amendment Act the following can be highlighted:

66.1 The general perspective is that the transfer of residential property calls for more than merely a range of technical solutions to issues of tenure, methods of transfer and allocation procedures.

66.2 In the exercise of his/her duty, the Director-General had to take into consideration the availability, or lack thereof, of new houses in the area, the need for family members' occupation rights to be recognised and protected and the need not to increase homelessness but to decrease it in the defined area.

[67] The provisions of section 2(1) of the Conversion Act enjoins the Director-General "to determine who shall be declared to have been granted . . . ownership with regard to such sites." This means that the Director-General is left with a discretion after having investigated the dispute. The Director-General's discretion must be exercised bona fide, and his judgment should be duly and honestly expressed. In the exercise of this discretion, the Director-General has to:

67.1 identify the "beneficiaries" entitled to obtain transfer of the residential properties;

67.2 resolve disputes that might arise as to the identity of the beneficiaries;

67.3 carry out the administration required in order to cause transfers to take place, including the processing of applications associated with such a transfer;

67.4 establish and carry out procedures and guidelines which will accommodate the particular requirements of the community in the defined area, for example in relation to tenure choices;

67.5 monitor the interim administration of day-to-day transactions occurring in relation to both regulations 6 and 8 permits pending transfer of the immovable property to the beneficiaries;

67.6 undertake the investigations in order to assist in the resolution of disputes; and

67.7 undertake the resolution of disputes.

As stated earlier, the structure and content of both the Conversion Act as well as the Gauteng Housing Act indicate that the inquiry contemplated by the Director-General was not meant to be a mechanical operation. In other words, the Conversion Act does not prescribe an automatic conversion of the certificate. In the present matter, it cannot be stated that the Appellant acquired continuous physical possession of the dwelling. The first Respondent has been the occupant of the dwelling prior to the death of the deceased and she remained in occupation thereafter.

THE DEED OF CESSION

[68] On 6 October 1982, the West Rand Administration Board entered into a "deed of cession" with the Appellant. This document reads as follows:

"Whereas Joshua Petrus Nzimande (hereinafter referred to as the holder) is registered as the holder of a Certificate of Occupation dated 1.1.1976 and issued to him/her by the West Rand Administration Board (hereinafter referred to as the 'Board') in respect of lot number 980 Klipspruit (hereinafter referred to as 'the Lot') in terms of the Regulations governing the control and supervision of a Black Residential Area and whereas by agreement dated 1.1.1977 (hereinafter referred to as 'the Agreement') the Board sold to the Holder the rights of occupation of the improvement situate upon the Lot comprising four-roomed house and whereas the Holder passed away and Petrus Nzimande (hereinafter referred to as the heir) has been appointed heir in the Holder's estate, as certified by the Commissioner of Cooperation and Development in his letter dated 2.10.1981 and referenced 1/4/3/1508/75 and he is lawfully entitled to transfer of the right, title and interest of the Holder in and to the aforesaid certificate of occupation and improvements and I, the undersigned, Petrus Nzimande do hereby accept the cession and transfer of the Holder's right, title and interest in the Certificate of Occupation in respect of Lot number 980 Klipspruit and agree to be substituted as holder thereof with effect from the fixed date, and further agree that I shall be personally liable for all duties and obligations imposed on the Holder of such certificate and under the Regulations governing the control and supervision of an Urban Black Residential Area and for all the Holder's duties and obligations under the said Agreement as from the fixed date."

The deceased passed away on 31 July 1975. The deed of cession stipulated the deceased became the registered holder of a certificate of occupation on 1 January 1976 in respect of the dwelling. The Commissioner did not consider this factual state when the deed of cession was entered into.

The cession agreement was signed by the Appellant and on behalf of the West Rand Administration Board. The deceased died intestate. The Appellant was the recipient of the cession by virtue of the fact that women do not participate in the intestate succession of a deceased's estate according to African customary law. Intestate succession in terms of African customary law is based on the principle of primogeniture. The general rule is that only a male who is related to the deceased through a male line qualifies as intestate heir. In a monogamous family the eldest son of the family head is the heir. If the eldest son does not survive his father then his (the eldest son's) eldest male descendant is the heir. If there is no surviving male descendant in the line of the deceased's eldest son then an heir is sought in the line of the second, third and further sons, in accordance with the principle of primogeniture. If the deceased is not survived by any male descendant his father succeeds him. If his father also does not survive him an heir is sought in the father's male descendants relating to him through the male line (see Kerr *The Customary Law of Immovable Property and Succession* (3 ed) at 99 (Rhodes University); Seymour's *Customary Law in Southern Africa* (4 ed) by JC Bekker and Coetze at 3–4.

[69] In the matter of *BHE and others v Magistrate, Khayelitsha and Others*, Justice Ngwenya asked the question:

"Does the principle of primogeniture pass constitutional muster?"

At page 554, the learned Judge concludes that the principle of primogeniture constitutes discrimination on grounds of race and gender:

"It is *prima facie* unfair and therefore offends against the provisions of section 9(1) and (3) of the Constitution. This Court is thus bound to declare such law unconstitutional and invalid. I may add further that, on the facts before us, the second Respondent's attitude leaves much to be desired. It lacks basic humanity, which is the hallmark of *ubuntu*."

With respect, I associate myself with these views.

[70] The question that needs to be answered in the present matter is whether the deed of cession which was granted in 1982 (in the pre-constitutional era) can be considered in the post-constitutional era? Furthermore, can the deed of cession be filtered through the prism of the Bill of Rights?

[71] In *Du Plessis and others v De Klerk and Another* Mokgoro J stated the following:

> "In that connection, I would like to draw attention briefly to a matter that has been somewhat neglected in the application debate: the implications thereof for South African customary law in particular. Under the pre-Constitutional order, customary law was lamentably marginalised and allowed to degenerate into a vitrified set of norms alienated from its roots in the community. There is hence significant scope for the dynamic application and development of customary law by the Courts in a manner that has 'due regard to the spirit, purport and objects' of chapter 3. . . . Indeed, in a matter involving customary law, a Court is bound to have regard to the values of chapter 3, even where there is no claim of unconstitutionality raised. I am convinced that the observations of Mahomed DP in his concurring opinion in this matter, with respect to the need to actively develop the common law, apply *a fortiori* to customary law."

[72] The impediments in terms of the customary law that existed against the first Respondent operated as an obstacle in her way, and disallowed her to inherit in the estate of her deceased husband. She has at all material times been in occupation of the dwelling. She enjoyed the use thereof. The Appellant enjoys alternative accommodation. The facts of the present matter, coupled with the application of the relevant statutory provisions, as well as the interests of justice and good government justify an order which disregards an act that was done or permitted in terms of an unconscionable agreement even though the Constitution was not operative at the time that the act was so done or permitted. It must be explained that each case must be considered on its own facts. The situation may be different if the Appellant had the use and was in occupation of the dwelling since 1982. It may not be in the interests of justice and good government in the latter circumstances to consider the validity of the certificate of occupation.

The right "acquired" by virtue of the deed of cession by the Appellant falls within the ambit of the following passage in the *Du Plessis v De Klerk* (*supra*) judgment at paragraph [20]:

> "We leave open the possibility that there may be cases where the enforcement of previously acquired rights would, in the light of our present constitutional values, be so grossly unjust and unfair that it could not be countenanced, whether as being contrary to public policy or on some other basis."

THE *CROSSLEY* CASE

Crossley and Others v. National Commissioner, SAPS and Others 2004 (3) All SA 436 (T)

Case Summary

FACTS

After being charged with feeding the deceased to a pride of lions, the Applicants in this matter were charged with murder.

An urgent application was launched by the Applicants to the High Court, in which they sought an interdict to prevent the funeral undertakers from burying the deceased. They also sought an order directing the Sheriff to take charge of the deceased's remains and remove the remains from the family. They argued that the deceased's remains constituted important evidence in their case, and burying him would lead to a loss of this evidence. This loss of evidence would interfere with their right to a fair trial as enshrined in section 35 of the Constitution of South Africa. More specifically, they argued that burying the deceased would compromise their right to challenge forensic evidence of the trial.

Although not joined as a party to the proceedings, the deceased's family, who had an interest in the burial of the deceased, submitted that being prevented from burying the deceased was a violation of their dignity, enshrined in section 10 of the Constitution, as well as their right to religion (section 31(1)(a)) of the Constitution. Even though the deceased's family was not a formal party to the proceedings, the court allowed them to address the court directly.

LEGAL HISTORY

The Transvaal High Court was the court of first instance for this matter.

LEGAL ISSUE

The court was asked to balance the right to a fair trial, the right to dignity and the right to religion.

DISPENSATION

The court concluded that the right to a fair trial, as important as it is under the new Constitution, could not override the right of the deceased and his family to human dignity and the right to practice such an important ritual. Thus the court saw no reason why the deceased's family should be forbidden from burying the deceased.

The court found that the exercise of the right to a fair trial did not require the preservation of every crucial piece of evidence. The right to a fair trial only demands that one has the ability to challenge the evidence presented to the court. The court further emphasized that given the history of South Africa, due respect and recognition must be accorded to African customary laws and practices.

Justice Patel

. . .

[9] The deceased's family members in opposing the application, at this late hour in the day and moment, did not have the benefit of a lawyer to advance submissions on their behalf. The nub of their opposition was that their family's dignity was not respected by the Applicants and their Attorneys in an attempt to halt the burial of the deceased according to their custom. It is an interference with their right to bury the deceased.

Unreservedly, I afforded Mr Mashego to address the Court on behalf of the deceased's family. He did so with solemnity and dignity. To attempt to summarise the relevant portions of his address would do an injustice, so I quote it *verbatim*:

> "Your Lordship we want to make a prayer, we want to pray to this Court to allow this destitute family to bury the deceased tomorrow morning at 06:00 which is customary to us. It is within our custom, your Lordship, that where we stay we dig our graves and it is customary, your Lordship, that if a grave has been dug we do not let it to remain open. It does not have to remain open for any other day after tomorrow 06:00. It is customary, your Lordship.
>
> It is also customary, your Lordship that we have already spoken to our ancestors that a person went missing on the 31st of January—if you count the days—has at last been found. Has at last been found. It is customary again, your Lordship, with us that one elder from the family has to sit on a mattress, not sleep on a bed. This person has been sitting on this mattress from the 31st of January up to date.
>
> It is also customary, your Lordship, that we do not put our lights on, but we have to put a candle on, and we have been putting on this candle. We have come to a stage where we have to put the last candle and that last candle must be put today.
>
> We are in the civilised world, yes we agree, but there is one custom again that we feel we cannot go against. It will be against our ancestors to do that. This custom is the custom that we have already seen the deceased and having seen the deceased, having received the deceased; the deceased is now with us.
>
> It took us by surprise yesterday, at half past 6, that we were told we could not bury him. What makes matter worse is that our dignity as a family is not respected. We are saying so your Lordship because we are speaking of a person who had an identity document, a South African citizen, who was employed. Who was employed or formally employed by one of the Applicants. It is wrong for anybody to say the family was not known. It is incorrect and it is misleading this Court. *Ja*, Mark Scott Crossley, yes. That will be proved in a

Court of law when that trial begins. It is because of those particulars, that we as a family, here, feel our dignity is not respected. That some people are referred to as Respondents here and we are not Respondents. As if the person, the deceased, here came from another country. We feel that our dignity was not respected at all. We will prove in that Court of law, if this matter is raised, that we have telephone numbers of the people in the Scott family that we were able to speak to them though one of our relatives here. That is known, I believe, to the applicant and it should be known by now to even to their attorneys. But we will come to that stage. We will prove that.

I want to add on the question of our custom, when it comes to burying two, three days before what we are doing your Lordship. As I speak now we have already in our own custom slaughtered two cattle that is the message I got about two days ago. We have already slaughtered two cattle. We have already put up tents. We have, what we call, a night vigil. It is customary that we have that night vigil. As I speak now, I believe all the reverends in that particular area are in the tent. They are praying. All they are praying for is they want to see the deceased. The family wants to see the deceased. The children also want to see the deceased.

I want to understand the argument from the legal representative here. We want to pray that we be afforded the opportunity to deal with our customary rights."

. . .

As I listened carefully the debate is based on the time of the deceased's death and the cause of death. It is not based on the identity of the deceased. It is not based on the identity of the deceased because the impression that the Court gave us, was that we first have to identify whether this is the person. And it has been without doubt that this person is the person who we are speaking of. That has not been argued here. But in their argument again they are saying tissue has been removed, if I understand it . . . [by the state doctors, that is the forensic pathologist at the state laboratory, who works for the government.] And presumably that tissue is still there?

On the debate like you had between yourself, Lordship, and counsel, I want to argue strongly that I agree with yourself, you based your argument on the Constitution of this country on the fundamental rights. I want my plea based on that argument here, that you give us judgment to this matter. That we are able to go home, we have had sleepless nights, we did not sleep for the rest of days and nights. We need some peace of mind. We had been traumatised and this is enough. Thank you, your Lordship."

[10] Mr *Kellermann*, for the Applicants, iterated that the Applicants as accused persons will not have the right to challenge and adduce evidence at their criminal trial if Dr Wagner is not afforded an opportunity to conduct forensic examination

on the deceased's remains. This will be tantamount to an infringement of the Applicants' right under section 35(3)(i). Whilst, on the other hand, it appears from Mr Mashego's address that if the deceased's burial is stayed then that will be tantamount to an infringement of their right to dignity (section 10) and their right to practise their religion (section 31(1)(a)).

[11] At first blush, there appears to be a tension between the Applicants' right to a fair trial which embraces their right to adduce and challenge evidence and the deceased's family's rights to have their dignity respected in their wish to bury the deceased according to their religious practices. Where tension emerges between two sets of competing rights, a decision has to be made by striking a fair and just balance. The best way of achieving this is to seek an answer in the enduring constitutional values.

[12] What the Constitution demands is that an accused should be given a fair trial. Fairness is an issue which has to be decided upon the facts of each case, and the trial judge is best placed to take that decision (*Ferreira v Levin NO and Others; Vryenhoek and Others v Powell NO and Others* 1996 (1) SA 984 (CC) at paragraph [153]; *Key v Attorney-General, Cape Provincial Division and Another* 1996 (4) SA 187 (CC) at paragraph [13]). The right to adduce and challenge evidence is an inherent component of a fair trial. The trial judge will surely afford the accused an opportunity not only to comment on evidence tendered by prosecution witnesses but also to cross-examine the State's witnesses. Cross-examination is a formidable weapon for both adducing evidence, that is, to secure favourable testimony from witnesses and challenging evidence, that is, undermining the value of incriminating testimony (see Nico Steytler *Constitutional Criminal Procedure*, Chapter 2, 345 *et seq*).

An accused person's right under section 35(3)(i) is reinforced firstly, by the right to have access to medico-legal reports in order for the accused to exercise his/her right to adduce and challenge evidence in an effective way. Secondly, the accused will have an opportunity to call Dr Wagner or any other pathologist as an expert witness in order to challenge the evidence of the prosecution's forensic expert witness and also to adduce evidence in rebuttal. The accused's right to call a witness is one of the core principles of a fair trial (see *S v Gwala* 1989 (4) SA 937 (N) at 938G).

In my view, it is for the trial Court that will try the accused to ensure that they will be tried fairly by ensuring that they are afforded the right to adduce and challenge evidence. However, if every accused person came to Court on an urgent basis that his/her right to a fair trial is likely to be jeopardised because a crucial piece of evidence needs to be preserved, then in reality the effectiveness of the criminal justice system will be undermined. It will take years before an accused could ever be tried. This will impact negatively on an accused's right to a speedy trial (see section 35(3)(d)) and thereby impede the promotion of the constitutional values of his/her right to a fair trial.

[13] In our constitutional democracy human dignity stands at the forefront in the founding provisions embodied in section 1(a) of the Constitution. Section 7(1) affirms the democratic values of human dignity. Section 10 espouses that:

"Everyone has inherent dignity and the right to have their dignity respected and protected."

And section 15(1) guarantees two rights: the right to hold a religious belief and the right to express such belief in practice (*Christian Education of South Africa v Minister of Education* 2000 (4) SA 757 (CC) at paragraph [19]). Section 31(1)(a) ensures the rights of persons belonging to a religious community to practise their religion with other members of their community.

[14] The deceased's immediate family members, kith and kin and communal family also need their dignity to be respected. A deceased person, until his body has rested, has the right to dignity and that dignity must prevail and should be respected and protected.

Mr Mashego very ably, very profoundly and very touchingly addressed the Court about the religio-customary practices and values of the African people. These practices and values in the context of this country's past were denied recognition and legitimacy, whilst Eurocentric values proclaimed superiority. Both Germanic custom and Christian faith reposed in the common law and determined the *mores* of society. However, Mahomed CJ in *Amod v Multilateral Motor Vehicle Accidents Fund* (*Commission for Gender Equality Intervening*) 1999 (4) SA 1319 (SCA) at paragraph [20] noted:

"This is an untenable basis for the determination of the *boni mores* of society. It is inconsistent with the new ethos of tolerance, pluralism and religious freedom which had consolidated itself in the community even before the adoption of the interim Constitution on 22 December 1993."

And, at paragraph [23] indicated:

"The common law is not to be trapped within the limitations of its past. If it does not do this it would risk losing the virility, relevance and creativity which it needs to retain its legitimacy and effectiveness in the resolution of conflicts between and pursuit of justice among the citizens of a democratic society. For this reason the common law constantly evolves to accommodate changing values and new needs."

[15] The new ethos of equality of religions is encapsulated in section 31(1)(a) of the Constitution. The subsection provides that persons belonging to a cultural or religious community may not be denied the right with other members of that community to enjoy their culture and practise their religion. Section 15(1) and 31(1)(a) confers rights relating to freedom of religion to all. These constitutional provisions guarantee religious freedom not only to individuals but to religious communities as well. South Africa is a secular state. There is no state or preferred religion as such and all religious communities enjoy the same constitutional protection without any

favour, differentiation or discrimination. Secularism does not mean being irreligious, it means respect for all religions even though the State does not identify itself with any religion. Both the Constitution and the State seek to ensure neutrality in a matter that is profoundly personal.

Mr Justice S Saghir Ahmed, who was quoted in *Indian Supreme Court Case on Feigned Conversion SC* 95 vol; at 635, said:

> "Religion is a matter of faith stemming from the depth of the heart and mind. Religion is a belief, which binds the spiritual nature of man to a supernatural being; it is an object of conscientious devotion, faith and pietism. Devotion in its fullest sense is a consecration and devotes an act of worship. Faith in the strict sense constitutes firm reliance on the truth of religious doctrines in every system of religion. Religion, faith or devotion is not easily interchangeable."

The Constitution proclaims that everyone in this country has the freedom of religion including both the right to hold a religious belief and the right to express such a belief in practice (see *Christian Education of South Africa v Minister of Education, supra*). The constitutional provisions lend a collective dimension for an individual to practise his/her belief in a shared religion. The African religio-customary practices and manifestations are essentially shared in community.

[16] African Customary Law, African religious practices and African cultural manifestations need to be recognised positively by the Courts. In this regard, and more particularly in the context of this matter, there is indeed a prophetic resonance in the dissenting judgment of Ngoepe JP in *Bührmann v Nkosi and Another* 2000 (1) SA 1145 (T) at 1161B/C–D:

> "It is well known that there is a strong relationship between people's religion and the way in which, in the manifestation of such a belief, they would want their dead to be buried. For example, one religion requires that the dead be buried within a certain period; practitioners of another conventional religion demand that their dead be buried with their heads facing to the west in anticipation of the great day of re-awakening. All these are manifestations of certain religions and beliefs, apparently aimed at helping the deceased achieve a better hereafter life or world. To acknowledge the Respondent's right to practice and manifest her religion, but bar her from interring her son at a place and in a manner that would give meaning to her right of religion and belief could amount to no more than paying mere lip service to such a right."

[17] In a multi-dimensional society like ours, African customary law, religious practices and cultural manifestations have not featured much or at all in the mainstream of the country's jurisprudence which has largely been dominated by Eurocentric values to the exclusion of almost all other values. Invariably, in the pre-constitutional

era the views and values of a minority prevailed over those of the majority. It lacked legitimacy amongst all those people who were marginalised and kept on the periphery of society. In the High Court of Tanzania, Mwalusanya J in *Republic v Mbushuu and Another* [1994] 2 LRC 335 at 349b–c, said:

"In a *democratic* state like Tanzania, the views of the majority should be respected. This is because for any system to work, it must be credible in the eyes of the people of the country concerned, For this reason the Court's and parliament's attitudes should not be radically different from those of society as a whole."

[18] Thus, it is incumbent upon the Courts to acknowledge the diversity of religious practices, including burial customs of different religious communities in our country. The burial of the deceased in accordance with African religious custom must surely prevail. It accords credence to the very essence of the dignity, not only to the deceased's immediate family, relatives and community but also to the deceased himself.

Before I pronounce this Court's order, there is a further *raison-d'etat* for the order. One of the embodiments and the essence upon which our Constitution and democracy was founded in 1994 was based upon the African idiom of *Ubuntu*. It encapsulates the metaphor "umuntu ngumtu ngabayne abantu" meaning "a person is a person through other people."

In *S v Makwanyane and Another* 1995 (6) BCLR 655 (CC) at paragraph [307], Mokgoro J said that:

". . . an all inclusive value system, or common values in South Africa, can form a basis upon which to develop a South African human rights jurisprudence . . . one shared value, an ideal that runs like a golden thread across the cultural lines, is the value of *ubuntu*—a notional coming to be generally articulated in this Country" (see also: Langa J (as he then was) at paragraph [225]; Madala J at paragraph [237]; Mahomed J (as he then was) at paragraph [263]).

uBuntu embraces humaneness, group solidarity, compassion, respect, human dignity, conformity to basic norms and collective unity, humanity, morality and conciliation.

[19] The late Chief Justice Ismail Mahomed, in welcoming members of the International Court of Justice in Cape Town on 4 February 1998 said:

"Nationally South Africa itself, enriched by *UBUNTU* and reconciliation, and recovering from the pain and the shame of a horribly long nightmare of institutionalised racism which brought it into protracted collision with the central premise of legal civilisation articulated in the United National Declaration of Human Rights awakes to create a new nation bringing dignity and optimism to our species everywhere."

[20] With those profound words of late Chief Justice, I am of the considered opinion that in this democratic era the higher constitutional value of the right to dignity, embedded in every international human rights instrument, embraces not only those who are living but also those who have departed. They too, like the deceased, need to rest undisturbed with dignity. Now, at this penultimate hour the Applicants chose to come to Court by way of urgency for an order to stop the burial of the deceased. If such an order is granted then that will be the gravest disrespect to the deceased and also violate his family's right to dignity as well as interfere with their religious rights and freedom. It will also result in the gravest injustice to his family and community at large.

uBuntu and the Right to Culture

THE *MEC FOR EDUCATION* CASE

MEC for Education: KwaZulu-Natal, Thulani Cele: School Liaison Officer, Anne Martin: Principal of Durban Girls' High School, Fiona Knight: Chairperson of the Governing Body of Durban Girls' High School v. Navaneethum Pillay, Governing Body Foundation, Natal Tamil Vedic Society Trust, Freedom of Expression Institute 2008 (2) BCLR 99 (CC)

Case Summary

FACTS

The Applicant in this case, Ms. Pillay appears on behalf of her daughter, Sunali Pillay, a minor and a pupil at Durban Girls High School (DGHS) at the time the events leading to this matter arose.

In the process of Sunali's application to begin her education at DGHS in 2002, Sunali's mother signed a declaration in compliance with the school's Code of Conduct (the Code), which limited the wearing of certain pieces of jewelry, including the gold nose stud worn by Sunali that gave rise to this litigation. In October of 2004 Sunali returned to school wearing a gold nose stud. She was informed by the third Applicant, the DGHS Principal, Anne Martin, that the nose stud was worn in contravention of the Code.

Sunali was initially given a grace period by the school in order that the new piercing be allowed to heal sufficiently so as to facilitate the easy removal thereof on a daily basis for the duration of the school day. The grace period expired at the end of October 2004. Sunali did not remove the piercing after the deadline. In 2005,

Sunali's mother was asked to submit written motivation as to why her daughter should continue to wear the piercing. The submission by Ms. Pillay indicated that the gold nose stud was worn as part of a South Indian cultural tradition whereby the women in her family had worn similar piercings when they reached an age of physical maturity, in order to indicate that Sunali had reached an age of adult responsibility. The tradition included that at the age of sixteen Ms. Pillay would replace the gold stud with a diamond stud, as part of a religious rite of passage in honor of Sunali. The submission further emphasized that the stud was not for fashion purposes but rather for "long-standing family tradition and for cultural reasons."

In February 2005, the school's Governing Body, the fourth Applicant, took expert opinion on the matter and was advised that it was under no legal obligation to allow Sunali to continue to wear the piercing.

Ms. Pillay was aggrieved by the decision of the fourth Applicant and sought clarity from the Department of Education, only to discover, in May 2005, that the MEC, the first Applicant, supported the decision of the school that the nose ring be removed by May 23, 2005, whereafter failure to comply would result in a disciplinary hearing scheduled for July 18, 2005.

Before the hearing could take place, Ms. Pillay brought the matter before the Equality Court in order to determine whether the refusal to let Sunali wear the piercing constituted unfair discrimination in terms of the Promotion of Equality and Prevention of Unfair Discrimination Act 4 of 2000 (the Equality Act). Ms. Pillay was granted an interim interdict to prevent the school from "interfering, intimidating, harassing, demeaning, humiliating or discriminating against Sunali." The hearing for the granting of a final order was set for September 29, 2005. The final decision of the Equality Court was that a *prima facie* case of discrimination had been made out but that it was not unfair discrimination. Ms. Pillay thus appealed to the Pietermaritzburg High Court (the High Court) against the decision of the Equality Court.

The decision of the High Court (per Judge Kondile, Judge President Tshabalala concurring) was that the action amounted to unfair discrimination and that the Equality Court had erred in so far as it had not properly taken into consideration the "impact of the Constitution and the Equality Act on the Code and that both religion and culture are equally protected under the Equality Act and the Constitution," thereby establishing a case of indirect unfair discrimination. The High Court further emphasized that Sunali was a member of a historically disadvantaged group, an important factor in an impact analysis. The High Court consequently set aside the decision of the Equality Court and declared the ruling of the school a nullity.

LEGAL HISTORY

This is an appeal against the decision of the Pietermaritzburg High Court wherein the earlier decision of the Equality Court was overturned.

LEGAL ISSUES

The issues dealt with by the court *in casu* were complex and varied, ranging from procedural issues of the application for leave to appeal to issues of mootness. The substantive issues canvassed by the court related, in the main, to a determination of whether a combination of what flowed from the Code and the act of the refusal to grant an exemption constituted unfair discrimination for the purposes of the Equality Act, taking into particular consideration the prohibition of unfair discrimination on the grounds of religion and culture.

To this end, a subissue arose, *obiter*, as to whether the determination of a person's religious and cultural beliefs and practices should be a subjective or objective test.

DECISION

The majority decision of Chief Justice Langa first considered that the protection against unfair discrimination on the distinct (but overlapping) grounds of culture and religion in terms of the Equality Act differed from that of the reliance upon the direct constitutional provisions of sections 15 and 30, the self-standing rights of freedom of religion, belief and opinion and cultural practice, respectively, insofar as the Equality Act, unlike sections 15 and 30, requires a further inquiry into whether the establishment of discrimination on such a ground also results in the discrimination being unfair.

In response to the argument by the third and fourth Applicants that there could have been no discrimination as there was no advantaged comparator group, the court held that there was, indeed a comparator. The court went on to determine that the comparator was "those learners whose sincere religious or cultural beliefs or practices are not compromised by the Code, as compared to those whose beliefs or practices are compromised. The ground of discrimination is still religion or culture as the Code has a disparate impact on certain religions and cultures."

In further consideration of the "alleged grounds of discrimination [of] . . . religion and/or culture," the court considered the cultural significance of the piercing. Here a question arose as to the correct test (subjective or objective) to be applied to the determination of a cultural belief or practice (the answer being less clear than the accepted subjective test for a religious belief) the court, *obiter,* determined that it was unnecessary to decide the question as, on the facts, both tests would be passed determining the genuine cultural significance of the piercing for Sunali. It is to this end that the Chief Justice adds two further points relating to cultural convictions. First, Chief Justice Langa links the idea of a cultural right to the idea of the "communality and the inter-dependence of the members of a community" as found in the concept of *"umuntu ngumuntu ngabantu."* Citing the theory of Gyekye, Chief Justice Langa emphasizes the core of *ubuntu* philosophy as being the inextricable link between the source of individuation and the community. This leads Chief Justice Langa to make a second link between the idea of individuation through communal identity and that of human dignity insofar as he states that "dignity and identity are inseparably linked as one's sense of self-worth is defined by one's identity."

The conclusion of the majority was that, on the facts, the nose stud amounted to "a voluntary expression of South Indian Tamil Hindu culture, a culture that is intertwined in the Hindu religion." Having so decided the court then turned to the question of whether the Equality Act and the constitutional right to equality applied also to cultural or religious practices that were voluntary in nature. The court asking the rhetorical question of whether "voluntary practices [are] any less a part of a person's identity or do they affect human dignity any less seriously because they are not mandatory?"

The court further held, upon consideration of argument raised by two of the *amici,* that "freedom of expression" be taken into consideration, both as a standalone right and as a factor going to the determination of fairness of the discrimination. The court held it was unnecessary to decide whether a claim under the Equality Act could include a claim for "freedom of expression." Instead the court reiterated that it had already established a *prima facie* case of breach of Sunali's right to express her freedom of religion and culture (which the court held are both important components of the section 16 Right).

Turning its attention to the main thrust of the argument advanced by the Applicants (pertaining to factors that may place an "undue burden" on the school, in terms of the considerations of the Equality Act, section 14(3)(f), (*g*), and (*h*)), the court determined that while the need for discipline and uniformity was a legitimate aim for a school, the test, as with the similar test of a section 36 analysis, would in part consider, even if, as stated, there is a legitimate purpose, whether indeed that goal was achieved by the limitation and whether there may be any other less restrictive means to achieve the same legitimate goals. The court held that it was not persuaded "that refusing Sunali an exemption achieves the intended purpose. Indeed the evidence shows that Sunali wore the stud for more than two years without any demonstrable effect on school discipline or the standard of education."[1]

In conclusion, the court found that the discriminatory impact on Sunali had been severe and thus constituted unfair discrimination for the purposes of the Equality Act. The court therefore issued a declarator to the effect that Sunali had been unfairly discriminated against. The court further ordered that DGHS put in place certain procedural formalities in order to allow for the uniform application and granting of exemptions in cases such as the one in issue.

Chief Justice Langa

[1] . . . This case raises vital questions about the nature of discrimination under the provisions of the Promotion of Equality and Prevention of Unfair Discrimination Act 4 of 2000 (the Equality Act) as well as the extent of protection afforded to cultural and religious rights in the public school setting and possibly beyond. . . .

THE PARTIES

[2] The first and second Applicants are the Member of the Executive Council for Education in KwaZulu-Natal and the School Liaison Officer for the KwaZulu-Natal Education Department. I will refer to them collectively as "the Department." The third and fourth Applicants are the Headmistress of Durban Girls' High School, Mrs Martin, and Mrs Knight, the Chairperson of the Governing Body of that School. I will refer to the two collectively and the Durban Girls' High School itself interchangeably as either "the School" or "DGHS." Any reference to "the Applicants" is to all four Applicants.

[3] The Respondent is Ms Navaneethum Pillay who appears on behalf of her minor daughter, Sunali Pillay (Sunali). . . .

FACTUAL BACKGROUND

[4] Sunali applied for admission to DGHS for the 2002 school year. Her mother signed a declaration in which she undertook to ensure that Sunali complied with the Code of Conduct of the School (the Code). Sunali was admitted to the School.

[5] During the school holidays in September 2004 Ms Pillay gave Sunali permission to pierce her nose and insert a small gold stud. When she returned to School after the holidays on 4 October 2004, Ms Pillay was informed that her daughter was not allowed to wear the nose stud as it was in contravention of the Code . . .

[6] Mrs Martin told Ms Pillay that Sunali had received a laminated card to indicate that she had been permitted to wear the nose stud only until the end of October 2004. This was in order to allow the piercing to heal so that the nose stud would be capable of being inserted and removed on a daily basis. October came and went and Sunali did not remove the nose stud. When the new academic year of 2005 commenced, Sunali returned to school with the nose stud still in place.

[7] The School then requested Ms Pillay to write a letter motivating why Sunali should be allowed to continue to wear the stud. In a letter dated 1 February 2005, Ms Pillay . . . explained that she and Sunali came from a South Indian family that intends to maintain cultural identity by upholding the traditions of the women before them. The insertion of the nose stud was part of a time-honoured family tradition. It entailed that a young woman's nose was pierced and a stud inserted when she reached physical maturity as an indication that she had become eligible for marriage. The practice today is meant to honour daughters as responsible young adults. When Sunali turned sixteen, her grandmother would replace the gold stud with a diamond stud. She claimed that this was to be done as part of a religious ritual to honour and bless Sunali. Ms Pillay made it clear that the wearing of the nose stud was not for fashion purposes but as part of a long-standing family tradition and for cultural reasons.

. . .

[9] . . . In May 2005 . . . Ms Pillay was informed that the MEC supported the School's approach. The School decided that if Sunali did not remove the nose stud

by 23 May 2005 she would face a disciplinary tribunal. Sunali did not remove the nose stud and a hearing by the disciplinary tribunal was then re-scheduled for 18 July.

[10] The disciplinary hearing in fact never took place as Ms Pillay took the matter to the Equality Court on 14 July and obtained an Interim Order restraining the school from interfering, intimidating, harassing, demeaning, humiliating or discriminating against Sunali. The Equality Court hearing for confirmation of the Interim Order was set down for 29 September 2005.

EQUALITY COURT HEARING

. . .

[12] . . . Asked why an exemption was not granted to Sunali on the basis of the religious reasons given by Ms Pillay, she stated that Ms Pillay had made it clear in her letter that the nose stud was worn as a personal choice and tradition and not for religious reasons.

. . .[14] The Equality Court held that . . . the discrimination was not unfair . . . In reaching its conclusion the Court took into account several factors namely: Ms Pillay had agreed to the Code when she took Sunali to the School; the Code was devised by the School in consultation with the students, parents and educators; and also that Ms Pillay had failed to consult with the School before sending Sunali to it with the nose stud. The Court held that no impairment to Sunali's dignity or of another interest of a comparably serious nature had occurred and concluded that DGHS had acted reasonably and fairly . . . This decision by the Equality Court was taken on appeal by Ms Pillay to the Pietermaritzburg High Court.

THE HIGH COURT

[15] In its judgment, the High Court[2] (Kondile J with Tshabalala JP concurring) held that the conduct of the School was discriminatory against Sunali and was unfair in terms of the Equality Act . . . It held further that the Equality Court had failed to consider properly the impact of the Constitution and the Equality Act on the Code and that both religion and culture are equally protected under the Equality Act and the Constitution . . . and therefore constituted indirect discrimination.

. . .

[17] . . . the High Court noted that Sunali was part of a group that had been historically discriminated against and that the School's contention that its rule prohibiting the wearing of jewellery was a general one applicable to every learner served only to prolong that discrimination . . . The Court held further that the desire to maintain discipline in the School was not an acceptable reason for the prohibition as there was no evidence that wearing the nose stud had a disruptive effect on the smooth running of the School. The High Court found that, in any event, there were less restrictive means to achieve the laudable objectives of the School as it

could simply explain to its learners that Sunali's religion or culture entitles her to wear the nose stud.

[18] The High Court accordingly set aside the decision and order of the Equality Court and replaced it with an order declaring "null and void" the School's "decision, prohibiting the wearing of a nose stud, in school, by Hindu/Indian learners." The School now applies for leave to appeal to this Court against the decision of the Pietermaritzburg High Court.

PROCEEDINGS IN THIS COURT

. . .

[22] Three institutions were admitted as the *amici*. These were: the Governing Body Foundation (GBF); the Natal Tamil Vedic Society Trust (NTVS); and the Freedom of Expression Institute (FXI). . . .

. . .

[28] . . . Ms Pillay . . . also submitted that under the Equality Act it was unnecessary to show a comparator or a dominant group. As long as a rule imposes disadvantage, it can be discriminatory. . . . She argued that there was no evidence that refusing Sunali an exemption, improved discipline at the School. While her primary case was based on equality, she also sought to assert the rights to freedom of expression and freedom of religion as independent claims.

[29] The NTVS and the FXI submitted argument together. They emphasised the importance of culture. While accepting that culture and religion differ, they argued that once a cultural practice is established, it should be treated exactly the same as a religious practice . . . They further argued that freedom of expression could be considered as a separate right but that even if it could not, it was still relevant in interpreting the Equality Act. They contended that Sunali's right to freedom of expression had been unjustifiably limited because Sunali's nose stud posed no risk of substantial disruption to school activities.

[30] The parties were agreed that the case raises a constitutional issue; it was also not disputed that the Applicants have reasonable prospects of success on appeal. There are, however, two issues that must be examined in order to determine whether leave to appeal should be granted. The first is the fact that the Supreme Court of Appeal has been bypassed and the second is the issue of mootness. The central enquiry is whether it is in the interests of justice for leave to appeal to be granted.

[31] It is clear that the issues in this case involve matters that must eventually be decided by this Court. The parties themselves have made this patently clear. These issues have been fully canvassed in two Courts. We have also had the benefit of comprehensive argument, presented by the parties and the three *amici curiae*. In my view, it is not in the interests of justice in this case to require the parties to incur the additional expense of going to the Supreme Court of Appeal before the matter is decided by this Court.

LEAVE TO APPEAL

[32] With regard to mootness, this Court has held that:

> "A case is moot and therefore not justiciable if it no longer presents an existing or live controversy which should exist if the Court is to avoid giving advisory opinions on abstract propositions of law."

> Sunali is no longer at DGHS and the issue is therefore moot. This Court has, however, held that it may be in the interests of justice to hear a matter even if it is moot if "any order which [it] may make will have some practical effect either on the parties or on others."[3] [4] The following factors have been held to be potentially relevant:

>> the nature and extent of the practical effect that any possible order might have;
>> the importance of the issue;
>> the complexity of the issue;
>> the fullness or otherwise of the argument advanced; and
>> resolving disputes between different Courts.

. . .

[34] The guidelines are not mandatory but are exactly what they purport to be—a guide. The following features all demonstrate the non-binding nature of the guidelines: section 8(3) of the South African Schools Act[4] [10] which empowers the Minister to make the guidelines states that they are for the "consideration" of schools; while some of the regulations are couched in mandatory language,[5] [11] the vast majority—including those relating to religious and cultural diversity—use the suggestive word "should"; the section on religious and cultural diversity is solely to "assist" schools in determining their uniform policy;[6] [12] when a governing body adopts a new code, the only requirement is that it "should make [its] decision in terms of these guidelines";[7] [13] and the strongest obligation that exists on governing bodies is that they must "consider" the guidelines.[8] [14]

[35] As already noted, this matter raises vital questions about the extent of protection afforded to cultural and religious rights in the school setting and possibly beyond. The issues are both important and complex, as is evidenced by the varying approaches of the Courts below as well as Courts in foreign jurisdictions. Extensive argument has been presented, not only from the parties but also from three *amici curiae*. There is accordingly no doubt that the order, if the matter is heard, will have a significant practical effect on the School and all other schools in the country, although it will have no direct impact on Sunali. It is therefore in the interests of justice to grant leave to appeal.

WHAT IS AT ISSUE?

[36] The first question is whether the discrimination complained of by Ms Pillay flows from the Code or from the decision of the School to refuse an exemption . . . To my mind, it is the combination of the Code and the refusal to grant an exemption that resulted in the alleged discrimination, not the one or the other in isolation.

[37] There are two problems with the Code, which operate together. The first is that it does not set out a process or standard according to which exemptions should be granted, for the guidance of learners, parents and the Governing Body. The School has itself developed a tradition of granting exemptions in certain circumstances. The second problem is the fact that the jewellery provision in the Code does not permit learners to wear a nose stud and accordingly required Sunali to seek an exemption in the first place.

[38] . . . A properly drafted code, which sets realistic boundaries and provides a procedure to be followed in applying for and the granting of exemptions, is the proper way to foster a spirit of reasonable accommodation in our schools and to avoid acrimonious disputes such as the present one. In sum, the problem is both the decision to refuse Sunali an exemption and the inadequacies of the Code itself.

THE CORRECT APPROACH TO "DISCRIMINATION"
UNDER THE EQUALITY ACT

[39] . . . The Equality Act is clearly the legislation contemplated in section 9(4) and gives further content to the prohibition on unfair discrimination.[9] [15] Section 6 of the Equality Act reiterates the Constitution's prohibition of unfair discrimination by both the State and private parties on the same grounds including, of course, religion and culture.[10] [16] Although this Court has regularly considered unfair discrimination under section 9 of the Constitution, it has not yet considered discrimination as prohibited by the Equality Act. Two preliminary issues about the nature of discrimination under the Act therefore arise.

[40] The first . . . claims brought under the Equality Act must be considered within the four corners of that Act . . . a litigant cannot circumvent legislation enacted to give effect to a constitutional right by attempting to rely directly on the constitutional right.[11] [17] . . . courts must assume that the Equality Act is consistent with the Constitution and claims must be decided within its margins.

[41] The second issue is how the definition of "discrimination" in the Equality Act should be interpreted. Section 1 of the Equality Act defines "discrimination" as:

"any act or omission, including a policy, law, rule, practice, condition or situation which directly or indirectly—

(a) imposes burdens, obligations or disadvantage on; or
(b) withholds benefits, opportunities or advantages from, any person on one or more of the prohibited grounds."

[42] The School, the GBF and, to a lesser extent, the Department argued that in this case, there was no comparator in the form of a group that was treated better than Sunali. They contended that although a comparator is not specifically mentioned in the definition in the Equality Act, it should be implied as a requirement. Absent a comparator therefore, no discrimination could be established. Ms Pillay's response to this line of reasoning spawned a deeper debate about the extent to which the Act must be informed by section 9 of the Constitution and this Court's interpretation of that section.

[43] . . . Section 39(2) of the Constitution . . . does not mean that the Act must be interpreted to restate the precise terms of section 9. The legislature, when enacting national legislation to give effect to the right to equality, may extend protection beyond what is conferred by section 9. As long as the Act does not decrease the protection afforded by section 9 or infringe another right, a difference between the Act and section 9 does not violate the Constitution.

[44] . . . I hold that there is an appropriate comparator available in this case. It is those learners whose sincere religious or cultural beliefs or practices are not compromised by the Code, as compared to those whose beliefs or practices are compromised. The ground of discrimination is still religion or culture as the Code has a disparate impact on certain religions and cultures . . . In my view, the comparator is not learners who were granted an exemption compared with those who were not.[12] [19]

[45] It follows, therefore that the Code, coupled with the decision to refuse Sunali an exemption, will be discriminatory if they imposed a burden on her or withheld a benefit from her.

DISCRIMINATION

[46] . . . This inquiry is similar to an inquiry under sections 15 or 30, but it is not identical because the Court must go on to consider whether the discrimination, if any, was unfair.

[47] . . . religion is ordinarily concerned with personal faith and belief, while culture generally relates to traditions and beliefs developed by a community. However, there will often be a great deal of overlap between the two; religious practices are frequently informed not only by faith but also by custom, while cultural beliefs do not develop in a vacuum and may be based on the community's underlying religious or spiritual beliefs. Therefore, while it is possible for a belief or practice to be purely religious or purely cultural, it is equally possible for it to be both religious and cultural.

[48] . . . The first question is whether Sunali is part of an identifiable religion or culture.

[49] While foreign jurisprudence is useful, the context in which a particular pronouncement was made needs to be carefully examined. Lord Fraser's remarks were crafted in the specific context of the English Race Relations Act and concerned legislation specifically directed at race and ethnicity, not at the concept of culture, broadly understood. They are accordingly, in my view, not a reliable guide in inter-

preting the Equality Act. In addition, discrimination on the basis of race, ethnic or social origin, religion and language is already prohibited by the Constitution and the Equality Act. Our understanding of "culture" must therefore extend beyond the limits of those terms, which seem to have been the focus of Lord Fraser's definition. At the same time, if too wide a meaning is given to culture, "the category becomes so broad as to be rather useless for understanding differences among identity groups." (Footnote omitted.)

[50] . . . Even on the most restrictive understanding of culture, Sunali is part of the South Indian, Tamil and Hindu groups, which are defined by a combination of religion, language, geographical origin, ethnicity and artistic tradition. Whether those groups operate together or separately matters not; combined or separate, they are an identifiable culture of which Sunali is a part.

[51] . . . There were two interrelated areas of contention. The first was whether a claim that a practice has religious or cultural significance should be determined subjectively or objectively.

[52] It is accepted both in South Africa[13] [27] and abroad[14] [28] that, in order to determine if a practice or belief qualifies as religious a court should ask only whether the claimant professes a sincere belief. There is however no such consensus concerning cultural practices and beliefs . . . It is unnecessary in this case to engage too deeply in that debate as both the subjective and objective evidence lead to the same conclusion. It is however necessary to make two points.

[53] Firstly, cultural convictions or practices may be as strongly held and as important to those who hold them as religious beliefs are to those more inclined to find meaning in a higher power than in a community of people. The notion that "we are not islands unto ourselves"[15] [29] is central to the understanding of the individual in African thought.[16] [30] It is often expressed in the phrase *umuntu ngumuntu ngabantu*[17] [31] which emphasises "communality and the inter-dependence of the members of a community"[18] [32] and that every individual is an extension of others. According to Gyekye, "an individual human person cannot develop and achieve the fullness of his/her potential without the concrete act of relating to other individual persons."[19] [33] This thinking emphasises the importance of community to individual identity and hence to human dignity. Dignity and identity are inseparably linked as one's sense of self-worth is defined by one's identity.[20] [34] Cultural identity is one of the most important parts of a person's identity precisely because it flows from belonging to a community and not from personal choice or achievement. And belonging involves more than simple association; it includes participation and expression of the community's practices and traditions.

[54] Secondly, while cultures are associative, they are not monolithic. The practices and beliefs that make up an individual's cultural identity will differ from person to person within a culture . . . While people find their cultural identity in different places, the importance of that identity to their being in the world remains the same. There is a danger of falling into an antiquated mode of understanding

culture as a single unified entity that can be studied and defined from outside. As Martin Chanock warns us:

"The idea of culture derived from anthropology, a discipline which studied the encapsulated exotic, is no longer appropriate. There are no longer (if there ever were) single cultures in any country, polity or legal system, but many. Cultures are complex conversations within any social formation. These conversations have many voices."[21] [35]

Cultures are living and contested formations. The protection of the Constitution extends to all those for whom culture gives meaning, not only to those who happen to speak with the most powerful voice in the present cultural conversation.

. . .

[56] . . . The need for the child's voice to be heard is perhaps even more acute when it concerns children of Sunali's age who should be increasingly taking responsibility for their own actions and beliefs.

[57] . . . It is important to note that the School does not directly challenge the veracity of Ms Pillay's testimony; it simply argues that we should have heard Sunali as well.

[58] In any event, we have the specific admission of Mrs Martin that the nose stud has cultural significance to Sunali although she denies it has independent religious significance . . . she consistently thereafter defied the will of the School in order to adhere to her belief . . . Sunali also endured a large measure of insensitive treatment from her peers, including the prefects of the School, and media exposure, yet continued to stand by her belief. All this points to the conclusion that Sunali held a sincere belief that the nose stud was part of her religion and culture.

. . .

[60] In conclusion, the evidence shows that the nose stud is not a mandatory tenet of Sunali's religion or culture; Ms Pillay has admitted as much. But the evidence does confirm that the nose stud is a voluntary expression of South Indian Tamil Hindu culture, a culture that is intimately intertwined with Hindu religion, and that Sunali regards it as such. . . . This Court has noted that "the temptation to force [grounds of discrimination] into neatly self-contained categories should be resisted."[22] [38] That is particularly so in this case where the evidence suggests that the borders between culture and religion are malleable and that religious belief informs cultural practice and cultural practice attains religious significance.

[61] The final question is whether the Equality Act and the Constitution apply to voluntary religious and cultural practices.

[62] . . . As stated above, religious and cultural practices are protected because they are central to human identity and hence to human dignity which is in turn central to equality.[23] [40] Are voluntary practices any less a part of a person's identity or do they affect human dignity any less seriously because they are not mandatory?

[63] . . . In *Ferreira v Levin NO and Others* and *Vryenhoek and Others v Powell NO and Others*[24] [43] Ackermann J wrote that:

"Human dignity has little value without freedom; for without freedom personal development and fulfilment are not possible. Without freedom, human dignity is little more than an abstraction. Freedom and dignity are inseparably linked. To deny people their freedom is to deny them their dignity."[25]

[64] A necessary element of freedom and of dignity of any individual is an "entitlement to respect for the unique set of ends that the individual pursues."[26] One of those ends is the voluntary religious and cultural practices in which we participate. That we choose voluntarily rather than through a feeling of obligation only enhances the significance of a practice to our autonomy, our identity and our dignity.

[65] Differentiating between mandatory and voluntary practices does not celebrate or affirm diversity it simply permits it. That falls short of our constitutional project which not only affirms diversity, but promotes and celebrates it . . . As this Court held in *Minister of Home Affairs and Another v Fourie and Another; Lesbian and Gay Equality Project and Others v Minister of Home Affairs and Others*:[27] [46]

". . . The development of an active rather than a purely formal sense of enjoying a common citizenship depends on recognising and accepting people with all their differences, as they are . . ."[28] [47]

[66] . . . Indeed, it seems to me that it may even be more vital to protect non-obligatory cultural practices.

[67] It follows that whether a religious or cultural practice is voluntary or mandatory is irrelevant at the threshold stage of determining whether it qualifies for protection. However, the centrality of the practice, which may be affected by its voluntary nature, is a relevant question in determining the fairness of the discrimination.

. . .

UNFAIRNESS

[73] But what is the content of the principle? At its core is the notion that sometimes the community, whether it is the State, an employer or a school, must take positive measures and possibly incur additional hardship or expense in order to allow all people to participate and enjoy all their rights equally.

. . .

THE SEVERITY OF THE INFRINGEMENT

[85] . . . The practice to which Sunali adheres is that once she inserts the nose stud, she must never remove it. Preventing her from wearing it for several hours of each school day would undermine the practice and therefore constitute a significant

infringement of her religious and cultural identity. What is relevant is the symbolic effect of denying her the right to wear it for even a short period; it sends a message that Sunali, her religion and her culture are not welcome.

. . .

[87] While it is tempting to consider the objective importance or centrality of a belief to a particular religion or culture in determining whether the discrimination is fair, that approach raises many difficulties. In my view, courts should not involve themselves in determining the objective centrality of practices, as this would require them to substitute their judgement of the meaning of a practice for that of the person before them and often to take sides in bitter internal disputes. This is true both for religious and cultural practices. If Sunali states that the nose stud is central to her as a South Indian Tamil Hindu, it is not for the Court to tell her that she is wrong because others do not relate to that religion or culture in the same way.

. . .

[89] . . . Ms Pillay stated that the nose stud was not imposed on Sunali; she had wanted her nose pierced since the age of four. The nose stud was not worn for fashion reasons but was inserted as part of a traditional ritual and an expression of her religious and cultural identity. In her first letter to the School, Ms Pillay wrote that the stud "serves not only to indicate that we value our daughters, but in keeping with Indian tradition, that our daughters are the Luxmi (Goddess of Prosperity) and Light of the house." In her testimony Ms Pillay stated that by inserting the stud:

> "we acknowledge our daughters, the women in our family, as a very vital part of family life. We honour them and we honour the divine within them. And that's important. It's important for every child to know that she garners respect."

. . .

[91] As stated above,[29] [83] religious and cultural practices can be equally important to a person's identity. What is relevant is not whether a practice is characterised as religious or cultural but its meaning to the person involved. Pre-determining that importance based on what will often be an imperfect or artificial categorisation reinforces ideas about the respective roles and importance of religion and culture in peoples' lives and fails to accommodate those who do not conform to that stereotype.

. . .

THE CODE LIMITS FREEDOM OF EXPRESSION

[93] . . . The dual purpose of the NTVS and FXI's submission was to stress the relevance of the right to freedom of expression to the case and to show that it had been infringed. They argued that freedom of expression was relevant both as a self-standing right and as a relevant factor in determining unfair discrimination.

[94] . . . It suffices to say that the extent to which discrimination impacts on

other rights will be a relevant consideration in the determination of whether the discrimination is fair and that the ban on the nose stud limited Sunali's right to express her religion and culture which is central to the right to freedom of expression.

. . .

[102] I am therefore not persuaded that refusing Sunali an exemption achieves the intended purpose. Indeed, the evidence shows that Sunali wore the stud for more than two years without any demonstrable effect on school discipline or the standard of education. Granting exemptions will also have the added benefit of inducting the learners into a multi-cultural South Africa where vastly different cultures exist side-by-side.

[103] The only confirmed effect of granting Sunali an exemption is that some of the girls might feel it is unfair. While that is unfortunate, neither the Equality Act nor the Constitution requires identical treatment. They require equal concern and equal respect.[30] [89] They specifically recognise that sometimes it is fair to treat people differently. In *Christian Education*[31] [90] this Court held:

> "It is true that to single out a member of a religious community for disadvantageous treatment would, on the face of it, constitute unfair discrimination against that community. The contrary, however, does not hold. To grant respect to sincerely held religious views of a community and make an exception from a general law to accommodate them, would not be unfair to anyone else who did not hold those views."[32] [91]

[104] This reasoning can and should be explained to all the girls in the School.[33] [92] Teaching the constitutional values of equality and diversity forms an important part of education. This approach not only teaches and promotes the rights and values enshrined in the Constitution; it also treats the learners as sensitive and autonomous people who can understand the impact the ban has on Sunali.

[105] The School and the GBF made two more specific arguments about the effect of the nose stud on the School. First, they argued that the nose stud should be treated differently because it is also a popular fashion item. Second, they contended that even if the nose stud was acceptable, allowing it would necessitate that many undesirable adornments be permitted. I address each in turn.

[106] Asserting that the nose stud should not be allowed because it is also a fashion symbol fails to understand its religious and cultural significance and is disrespectful of those for whom it is an important expression of their religion and culture.[34] [93] In addition, to uphold the School's reasoning would entail greater protection for religions or cultures whose symbols are well known; those are in fact often the ones least in need of protection. It would also have the absurd result that if a turban, yarmulke or headscarf became part of popular fashion they would no longer be constitutionally protected, while they have constitutional protection as long as they remain on the fringes of society. I accept that the popularity of the nose

stud may make it more difficult to determine if a learner is practicing her religion or culture or trying to impress her friends. But once the former is established, as it has been in this case, the mainstream popularity of a religious or cultural practice can never be relevant.

[107] The other argument raised by the School took the form of a "parade of horribles"[35] [94] or slippery slope scenario that the necessary consequence of a judgment in favour of Ms Pillay is that many more learners will come to school with dreadlocks, body piercings, tattoos and loincloths. This argument has no merit. Firstly, this judgment applies only to *bona fide* religious and cultural practices. It says little about other forms of expression. The possibility for abuse should not affect the rights of those who hold sincere beliefs. Secondly, if there are other learners who hitherto were afraid to express their religions or cultures and who will now be encouraged to do so, that is something to be celebrated, not feared. As a general rule, the more learners feel free to express their religions and cultures in school, the closer we will come to the society envisaged in the Constitution. The display of religion and culture in public is not a "parade of horribles" but a pageant of diversity that will enrich our schools and in turn our country. Thirdly, acceptance of one practice does not require the School to permit all practices. If accommodating a particular practice would impose an unreasonable burden on the School, it may refuse to permit it.

. . .

[110] It would be perfectly correct for a school, through its code of conduct to set strict procedural requirements for exemption. It would also be appropriate for the parents and, depending on their age, the learners, to be required to explain in writing beforehand why they require an exemption. That would ensure that these difficult matters are resolved responsibly, fairly and amicably. It seems that the absence of such a procedure in the Code is largely to blame, not only for the manner in which the complaint was raised, but also for the way in which it was resolved. It is a serious obstacle to a search for reasonable accommodation that an appropriate procedure was not in place.

. . .

CONCLUSION

[112] The discrimination has had a serious impact on Sunali and, although the evidence shows that uniforms serve an important purpose, it does not show that the purpose is significantly furthered by refusing Sunali her exemption. Allowing the stud would not have imposed an undue burden on the School. A reasonable accommodation would have been achieved by allowing Sunali to wear the nose stud. I would therefore confirm the High Court's finding of unfair discrimination.

For Justice O'Regan's dissenting judgment, see The Dignity Jurisprudence of the South African Court.

II

Articles on *uBuntu*

This part presents academic contributions to the general body of literature on the notion and value of *ubuntu*.

Towards the Liberation and Revitalization of Customary Law

Albie Sachs

There is an old South African saying: "No free *braaivleis*"; at this scholarly workshop on the future of customary law, I have to make a speech before I can eat, and you have to listen to me before you can do so. In singing for our suppers I will try to make the wait painless by focusing not so much on what I have written, but rather on what I have lived. And I will start with the words from the old song "Wouldn't it be lovely."

Wouldn't it be lovely if we already had a book, between two and three hundred pages long, that contained a comprehensive survey of the interaction between traditional African law and imposed state law? Wouldn't it be lovely if this were a thoroughly researched work with references to existing literature, to commissions, to oral tradition, to the law reports of what used to be called the Native Appeai Court, as well as to the South African Law Reports? Wouldn't it be lovely!

Wouldn't it be lovely if we had a study that examined these questions in a social, economic, cultural and political context, breaking the narrow, self-referential bounds of positivistic legal analysis that looked at the impact on law of the changing character of production and land tenure, and asked pertinent questions about political rights and responsibilities.

Wouldn't it be lovely if a book of that kind was written in elegant prose, beautifully shaped, showing how there had been legal dualism in the Cape, with the Roman Dutch law system coexisting with partial recognition of African Law in the Transkei? On the other hand, the foundation of apartheid was laid for the first time by the British in Natal through the system of indirect rule, and not in the Boer Republics, where there was a unified and integrated legal system, in which the master-servant-relationship provided for separate levels of status within one code, and not for separate codes for separate people.

Wouldn't it be lovely if we had a book of that kind which focused specifically on the story of the changing role and legal status of African women? Wouldn't it be lovely!

The fact is, such a book already exists, and it is lovely! Its title is *African Women: Their Legal Status in South Africa* and it was written by Jack Simons and published in London and Manchester in 1967. How many people have read this book? [A few hands go up.] I see only six out of some fifty people indicated and this at a conference on the very subject that Jack wrote about. It's a wonderfully written and comprehensive book, which anticipates by thirty years the whole debate we are having today and all the dilemmas posed by the new constitutional order. Yet it is virtually unknown in this country. Jack Simons was banned, he was exiled, his book was banned, and it was a criminal offence to distribute it. The knowledge it contained was blotted out, just as other important studies done at that stage are virtually unknown today. We have lost three decades, and we have got to recover them.

Jack Simons was my teacher, in the fullest sense of the word. He was senior lecturer at the University of Cape Town in a subject he inherited under the title "Native Law and Administration" [*natives* were to be administered, and the law was the instrument for doing so]. Turning the course around, he called it "Comparative African Government and the Law," and critically analyzed the different colonial policies in Africa. In those days the map of Africa was painted in colonial colors. Do any of you remember the color for the British colonies? It was red for the real deep colonies, and pink for the protectorates. For the French colonies: green. There was competition over whether there was more green or red on the map. And then, the Belgian Congo as it was called, a kind of mauve, while the Portuguese colonies were painted gold. In his lectures over the years Jack followed the disintegration of the colonial empires and the repainting of the map. Some of us were joyous as each colony gained independence, but he rejected our simple triumphalism, preferring to deal as an engaged and committed South African with the problems of postcolonial states in a scientific and questioning manner. In this way he prepared us for some of the difficulties that postcolonial states were later to encounter.

Perhaps as important as the content of his lectures was his teaching style. His classroom was always packed. It was the only class I knew where students from other faculties came as volunteer listeners, and because the debate was so lively, there was standing room only. This was right through the 1950s, during the height of apartheid. Today no one claims to have supported apartheid. Back then it was different. Apartheid was being projected as the salvation of South Africa, separate development, rights for everybody in his or her spheres. Many of us had a very clear view: Apartheid was rubbish, it was cruel, and it was racist, end of matter. But Jack said our dismissive approach was not good enough. Apartheid had its team of intellectuals, it was getting a certain measure of international support, and it had a strategy. We had to deal with it as a set of ideas, not simply as the political philosophy of a ruling party, and he insisted that we move beyond denunciation and start considering alternative forms of government for South Africa. Could we live as equals in a common society? Was some sort of separation between black and white inevitable? What was meant by the concept of *government*?

I still remember him introducing the strange name of Max Weber to audiences in Cape Town in the 1950s. As soon as Weber's work came out in English translation in the United States, Jack was on to it, and we were discussing various forms of authority in different societies in the world. He always pushed us to use our own experience, problems, pain, conflicts, and debates as a foundation for examining the universal problems of what society was about, what life was for, why we were born, what it meant to live in the world, what it meant to be who we were, to speak our languages, to have our past and our hopes for the future. He took the ugliness of apartheid—its cruelty, viciousness, and oppressiveness—as an instrument to compel us to engage in debate, discussion, evaluation, argument, and more argument. There were supporters of apartheid in the class and he asked them to stand up and defend their positions, not in order to knock them down, but so that their arguments could be counterposed by better arguments or different arguments. The right of people to speak their minds and defend their philosophy was strongly entrenched and that is why everybody loved coming to his class. It was precisely this kind of intellectual buzz we had all expected at university, but seldom encountered. In his own subtle way Jack would, of course, have the last word. He believed that, like everyone else, teachers had to take responsibility for the world they lived and taught in. Yet he would not mark down students because their positions were different from his. He looked for the logic, the clarity, the coherence, the sensitivity of the arguments. When Jack returned to class after being detained without trial during the post-Sharpeville state of emergency, the whole class, to a person, cheered him. What really mattered, as far as he and they were concerned, was the honesty of the debate, not the fixity of the outcome—the dialogue.

I will speak about the three Ds: dialogue, dignity, and difference. We got our new South African Constitution through dialogue, intense hard dialogue, interrupted by breakdowns and rolling mass action. Four years of hard, intense dialogue, and then another two. We solved problems one by one, two by two, three by three. When people call it a miracle, I get irritated. A miracle should come simply through faith; it just happens spontaneously out of its own a-worldly logic, against history, against reason. In reality, we toiled nights and weekends—we met, we thought, we argued, we debated. I used to think that freedom meant a world with no more meetings; in fact, when freedom came along, we had meetings and more meetings and more meetings; there is certainly nothing miraculous about minutes and matters arising. There was hard work, intelligence, listening, sharing, learning to look into the eyes of the other, to see another person there, while that other sees you as a person too. How can we live together in one country? How can we learn to respect each other so that if I get on in life, if I can be what I am and enjoy living as I am, it doesn't mean you can't do the same? These were the fundamental questions. We had to find a framework for achieving all this, and in microcosm I had already seen the process at work in Jack Simons' class. That open debate, that not being afraid of ideas, that confidence that the truth would set us free.

Truth through dialogue; the dialectic of truth. One of the most wonderful set of books I have seen in years has been the multivolume report of the Truth Commission. It's vividly and passionately all over the place. One can argue about this finding or that, but as a narration of a deep, painful, and awful part of our history, it's intellectually and emotionally convincing, and once and for all precludes any future attempts at denial. One thing: if only the British had had something like a Truth Commission after the Anglo-Boer War, how much this country could have been spared? If only there had been the kinds of free-flowing evidence and testimony ringing with truth, if only the many strands had been woven into a common narrative of the war, if only we hadn't ended up with separate peoples, possessing different histories and disparate memories of the Anglo-Boer War, with the gulf remaining as wide as the memories were incompatible.

There was one aspect of the report that left me as a lawyer and a judge particularly worried. My concern was the following: Why does so little of what we call the truth come out in court cases while so much truth came out of this Truth Commission process? Puzzling over the matter, it occurred to me that there are at least four different kinds of truth. We heard this morning about ontology and epistemology. I don't want to be anti-intellectual, but I am not comfortable with these words. I know they are important, and I look forward to reading the excellent paper in which they appeared. But I have invented my own simple rule-of-thumb classifications, which work for me at the moment.

I start with what I call *microscopic truth*. Microscopic truth requires you to isolate an area and exclude all the variables except those that are going to be measured, whether in nature or positive science, or whether in a court case. In a court case you define the issues: did he do it on that day, to that person, with that intent? You limit the number of issues, and then all the measurement, evidence, and testimony, is directed to deciding those particular issues. The testing by means of evidence of tight propositions to establish their degree of irrefutability is fundamental to the development of science, and basic court processes. Yet, those of you who are legal historians will know that legal findings are rarely used as historical findings, that trials are about legal proof, not about historical truth.

Secondly, you have *logical truth*, the truth implicit in a statement that you can extract by inference or the rules of logic. Most of the legal process involves focusing on microscopic truth in a context of logical truth.

The third kind of truth is what I call *experiential* truth. The phrase came to me some years ago when I read M. K. Gandhi's book on his life and struggles in South Africa. Can I ask how many here have read it? Hands up please. Three. A most beautiful book, by a lawyer *nogal*, a vivid part of legal history, social history, philosophical history, a part of world history, and it has been effectively banned in this country. We should be so proud that Gandhi was here, we should claim him, and instead we expurgate him. In any event, his book was called *My Experiments with Truth*. I found his use of the word *experiments* strange. If I recall correctly, he described how in the Old Fort Prison he took a decision not to eat salt and spices with his food, because the African prisoners locked up in another part of the prison didn't get any condiments with their food. [Incidentally, the Old Fort, popularly known as Number Four, is going to be the site of our new Constitutional Court building.] He felt that if he wanted to understand the experience of the humblest, of the most rejected in his society, he mustn't just imagine it; he must live it in his body, in his self. What afterwards got converted into the systematic moral philosophy called Gandhism, in fact didn't start with an idea. It started with an experience and his interpretation of the experience. The idea, the system, the Gandhian philosophy followed. That is the experiential kind of truth, one that is lived and meaningful to millions outside of the classroom, laboratory or court chamber. The experiential is a dimension that is often rigidly excluded as subjective and unscientific from much discourse in South Africa [and especially by organizers of legal conferences!] And yet, I have heard it bubbling impetuously through debates here today. The intense intellectual emotion can't be explained simply in terms of research findings or logic; it can only be understood in terms of experience. It is what it's like to be a member of a section of society that's been told that you are savage, barbaric, and that your culture is nothing. It is the experience of having been compelled physically to live on the outskirts of the city and the margins of the country, and having been poor, without the vote, having your language disregarded and having government taking all decisions for you and subjecting you to countless humiliations. All these inherited and lived experiences accumulate and produce a tremendous urge to say: I am an African, I am who I am, I am proud of my culture, I want continuity with my past, and when I speak, I want to be heard in my own voice. What I want to do is to acknowledge and wipe out the experience of having been wiped out. That is experiential, and it's an important ingredient of our reality, an intensely important ingredient of our reality. It seeps into every aspect of our knowledge, the way we frame problems, and the answers we regard as important. And you can't understand South Africa if you don't understand that. The point is that many communities have different experiences of life, just as within all communities' life experienced in various diverse ways; each has a right to self expression and not about particles and the atom, they cannot and should not exclude emotion, passion, and experience.

That brings me to the fourth kind of truth, what I call *dialogic* truth. That's what the Truth Commission was really about—dialogic truth. As Antjie Krog brought out so beautifully in her book: There isn't a single truth, only the experience of many people put together, layered, interacting, which creates a richer, deeper pattern, one which never is final, since there never is finality to truth. And dialogic truth is, I think, what this conference is essentially about. It is about listening, talking, interacting, hearing. It is not a search for supposedly scientific conclusions, for a unique, experimentally proved, and logical truth, where one position annihilates all others. On the contrary, it's about an open-ended interaction between positions, viewpoints, and experiences; about perspectives, imagination, empathy, observations, and criticisms.

The other two Ds, dignity and difference, are both related to dialogue, and I'll just mention them briefly. I will start with dignity. There used to be an idea that the gateway to civilization could be crossed by all, irrespective of color, provided that they spoke English, ate with a knife and fork, had a Bible, comported themselves with appropriate protocol, and were male—"equal rights for all civilized men." Even today we are expected as Bloke Modisane put it, to be eternal students at the table of good manners, that is, to behave according to rules for the whole world set by the West. Thus we have been hearing much today about Western concepts of human rights. I wish we could drop that phrase. As far as human dignity was concerned, the impact of the West on Africa was nothing short of disastrous. The colonial presence destroyed communities, undermined traditional agriculture, forced people off the land, introduced pass laws and used Parliament—this wonderful instrument—to deny people their fundamental rights. It employed courts of law—these marvelous bodies—to oppress people. Gallows, corporal punishment, and prisons were imported from the West. In our country hundreds of thousands of people were locked up every year simply because they didn't have the right documents. Inequality and division were promoted through the law, not in spite of it (and I am not even referring to the impact of the slave trade). There is no gain, only loss, in tying the origins of our human rights movement to the West.

By their nature, human rights belong to all humanity, not to any single continent. It is true that the term democracy emerged in Greece, which, by the way, was an African country, an Asian country, and a European country, at the same time. Some might even say that there was especially great theorization of the human rights idea in Europe, precisely because of the especially egregious ways in which human rights were violated there—the Holocaust on European soil has yet to be surpassed in ugliness. Undoubtedly, there were freedom fighters in Europe who identified with those struggling against oppression elsewhere in the world, and due credit must also be given to the moral stands taken by committed philanthropists in that continent. But, in fact, the people who fought hardest in South Africa for the acceptance of universal principles, acknowledging the essential dignity for all, and who searched the hardest to find the commonalities uniting black and white, were black South Africans. Not all black South Africans did so, and not all white South Africans opposed them. But overwhelmingly it was on Robben Island, in the trade union movement, in the underground, and in exile where—and not amongst those South Africans who called themselves Europeans—the core values of our new constitutional arrangement were kept alive and were nurtured.

This brings me to a theme that I wish would receive more attention at this conference, namely, the importance of international law as a point of reference for our debates. The principles of international law guided us in the quest for freedom and democracy in South Africa. The organized international community refused to countenance apartheid and firmly denounced the enforced separation of human beings. At the same time, those of us who fought against apartheid [and, in different ways, I include everybody in this room], not only derived support from international law, we contributed to and enriched it. Our Constitution is held up today as a model for the world. Before, it was a case of "even in South Africa." We were the extreme measure of oppression. If something was not done "even in South Africa," it was truly beyond the pale. Nowadays people say: "In South Africa they managed to do it, surely we can do it too." Thus, our Truth Commission is a source of global astonishment. I travel often, and the only thing people want to hear about is the Truth Commission. We've developed something that is deep in the African tradition, of listening, talking, bringing everybody in, of hearing all the different points of view and affirming the dignity of all through equality of discourse. Our Continent then, is not only a universal recipient of values and processes; it is a universal donor as well.

Difference. The idea of not suppressing or exploiting difference, but of welcoming diversity on the basis of equality, is fundamental to our whole new constitutional order. Equality is based upon acknowledging rather than eliminating difference. To say that if I suppress my language, culture, religion, appearance, my beliefs and way of seeing the world, then I can enjoy equality is to deny me the right to be equal as I am. Any uniformity of treatment, which comes at the price of suppressing my true self, involves the denial of the equal concern and respect for myself as I am, with my characteristics that lie at the very heart of equality. Once more, we return to the concept of basic dignity, which means respecting people as they are and as they identify themselves in the world, then I can enjoy my equality, is to deny me the right to be equal as I am. Any uniformity of treatment, which comes at the price of suppressing my true self, involves the denial of the equal concern and respect for myself as I am, with my characteristics that lie at the heart of equality. Once more, we return to the concept of basic dignity, which means respecting people as they are and as they identify themselves in the world. This approach is so simple, and yet because of our racist ways of regarding others, we have made it so difficult.

The question then, is paying due respect to dignity, dialogue, and difference. How do we envisage the future of customary law in South Africa's new constitutional democracy? Here I think it is vital that we focus not on this particular institution or those special rules but on the core values and principles of traditional African law (customary law, indigenous law—the phrase is not crucial, and the people to whom it means the most should be the ones to make the choice). These deep values, which derive from centuries-old African experiences and are of significance for all of us, whatever our origin, have not changed, even though the institutional arrangements made for realizing them in practice have altered substantially. We need to distinguish between these deep enduring and foundational principles, which affirm orderly social cohesion, and the more ephemeral judicial institutions and legal rules, which ensure meaningful day-to-day law enforcement in the concrete circumstances of the time.

Indeed, to apply ancient mechanisms and formulae to rapidly evolving social life can result in the negation rather than promotion of the core values we seek to protect. I believe that Professor Ronald Dworkin has argued along similar lines when looking at how the centuries-old United States Constitution should be interpreted today. He suggests that mechanistic and literal application in contemporary society of the actual words used by the framers of the Constitution in the eighteenth century would frustrate rather than advance the core principles of the constitution-makers. As society evolves so must the rules and mechanisms for defending those values develop. In the case of traditional law, what needs to endure are the deep principles of social respect, coupled with the all-embracing processes involving listening and hearing, allied to profound notions of restitution, of reintegration of defaulters and delinquents into the community, of attempting always to restore equilibrium, and based on the pervasive philosophy that something capable of improvement can be found in every human being.

This profound and all-encompassing social philosophy has on occasion been summed up in the word *ubuntu*, a term that has both the strength and the debility of being open to many different interpretations. At the heart of traditional African legal concern is a sense of human solidarity, of regard for all. No one is cast out or left by the wayside. I am who I am because you are who you are; my personhood is inextricably linked up with yours. We have all to accept responsibility for ourselves, our family, and our community. [Do not ask for whom the horn sounds, it sounds for thee!] Only in this way can we live together in the same social world. Throughout the globe, people exist in atomized and anomic societies, where personal wealth and individual autonomy have become inseparable from personal loneliness. By way of response there has developed a universal ache for the experience of what our Constitution calls *ubuntu*. The concept of not being alone, of being part of the community, should be seen as the central and precious core of traditional African law.

The particular rules used to further social cohesion in the past were directly related to the social, cultural, and family formations of the time. When production was done mainly by household members working together as a family, tending the fields and looking after cattle and the home, then the land and the home were centers of economic life. At the same time, extended families were centers of social and political relationships. The grand families of the traditional leaders became the leading families at the apex of the nation. As in England at the time of Henry VII, constitutional law, or the law of the state, was in essence family law. From the highest to the lowest, rights and responsibilities were determined by land and lineage.

The situation of African life today is enormously different; the household is different, production is different, wealth is different and property is different. Many are widows; others have been abandoned, while yet more see their husbands only every now and then. Both men and women in towns and countryside have ATM accounts, collective pensions, are owners and tenants with individual title, drive motor cars and tractors, receive wages for employment and participate in insurance schemes. They vote, study, play sports, take part in choirs and stokvels,[1] and attend union meetings, and outside the framework of the household. The particular detailed rules that applied to old forms of conserving family wealth and maintaining family cohesion are frequently quite dysfunctional now. If these rules continue to be applied mechanically, particularly in the way that they were formalized and frozen by magistrates, missionaries, and patriarchal male elders in the colonial and apartheid era, they risk undermining rather than affirming the values of *ubuntu* and social solidarity. They will be ignored, or implemented in opportunistic ways to serve new property interests, thereby undermining family solidarity, and creating new family resentments. They will result in unfairness and oppression, especially for African women and even more particularly for African widows, and will simultaneously violate the sense of right that lies at the heart both of traditional law and of the values of the Constitution for which the African people fought so hard. The strength of customary law lay in its original connection with the lives and culture of the people. If customary law is to be revitalized it must accordingly link itself up to the new energies of a people in transition and be sensitive to the real nuances and contradictions of daily life. Its anchor must be the sense of justice and fairness of a community and its star the broad values of the Constitution.

The Constitutional Court has referred to the need to leave the complicated, carried, and ever-developing specifics of how customary law should develop and be interpreted, to future social evolution, legislative deliberation and judicial interpretation. Does that mean that customary law is finished, archaic, and obsolete? On the contrary, the above approach, focusing on core values rather than clusters of formalized rules, implies the liberation and transfiguration of customary law. It re-establishes its organic connection with the community. It ensures its revitalization through imbibing the juices of daily life. It is important that democracy not be regarded as a blunt instrument that clubs customary law on the head. On the contrary, democracy finds protected space for customary law while freeing it at the same time from rigidly established (in colonial and apartheid times, frequently invented) and increasingly out-of-touch formalized codes. To recover its original vitality, customary law must respond to the lives that people lead now, to their sense of justice and fairness, and to multifarious and at times contradictory ways in which an actively and evolving culture impacts on the actual lives of actual people. People are not being forced willy-nilly to *modernize* or *develop*; they are being freed to enjoy all the aspects of the modern world to which they voluntarily choose to have access.

I have seen that approach work—during the eleven turbulent years when I lived and worked in Mozambique. I witnessed the government there trying out a great variety of new modern institutions, none of which functioned, except the community courts. At one level, they were modern courts rooted in contemporary community life, at another they tapped deeply into ancient African tradition. The composition of the courts and the kind of solutions they arrived at were completely new. They were made up of people of standing in the local community, who were called upon to resolve disputes by applying their sense of justice and the principles of the Constitution. Yet the language, process, feel and underlying objectives were ancient. The community streamed to these courts with their problems, looking for practical and fair resolutions of their disputes. They felt embraced and comforted by the informal, African way in which the courts functioned. Although brief records of the proceedings were kept, the oral tradition reigned supreme. The judges always sat in a panel of at least three so as to reduce the scope for corruption and at least one woman would sit in every court. They did not ask: are you Tsonga, Nyanja, or Makonde; are you Catholic or Muslim, were cattle transferred when you got married? They saw in front of them not tribesmen or tribeswomen, or adherents of particular faiths, but husbands and wives in trouble, families broken down, children to be cared for, and property to be divided. I spent hours, weeks and months with these courts, wrote a book and helped make a BBC film about them. Their solutions were eminently fair and practical, and, I might add, always accompanied by African-style homilies on the responsibility of good family members.

I am convinced that something roughly along similar lines would work wonderfully well in South Africa. It could be that in rural areas traditional leaders would be at the helm. Such leaders would link the wisdom for which they have been prepared with the creativity and inventiveness of ordinary people, so as to find practical solutions for practical problems. Men and women of standing in rural areas might not be scholars, they might not even be literate, but in terms of finding balanced, down-to-earth, and culturally sensitive ways of settling disputes, they are without parallel. To my mind it is in their creative and practical hands that the real success of customary law in this country lies. Enabling them to work properly in association with traditional leaders would require an appropriately balanced institutional framework, softening some of the boundaries between formal and informal courts, and giving informal courts appropriate plasticity and scope for their work. Such courts would be guided both by the evolving values of the community and by the enduring principles of the Constitution. Let us, the professors, help with designing the institutional arrangements and legal framework, and not try to codify rules and attempt to determine outcomes. Then, once the courts have functioned and come up with their decisions, and our ranks have been broadened by scholars with their own community-based backgrounds, we can happily explore the new material, attempt to discern patterns and precedents, and write our scholarly works.

Let no one be alarmed. I am not proposing that community courts in the rural areas, headed by traditional leaders and functioning according to the informal procedures of customary law be given powers to send people to jail. Nor should they be permitted to impose corporal punishment. If anybody is threatened by this loss of liberty, there must be due process of law, defense lawyers, charge sheets, a system of appeal, and formal procedures. This is what the Constitution requires. But resolving

family and neighbors' disputes and healing with petty assaults and small thefts requires other techniques and processes. [Please note: I am not speaking now as a
judge who has heard full argument, I am thinking a few spontaneous thoughts
aloud.] We need new local courts. You may call them traditional courts, customary
courts, or community courts, or whatever, but they are courts. They are not just alternative dispute resolution mechanisms; or mediation or arbitration bodies, they
are courts. They form part of the judicial system, they exercise judicial power, enjoy
compulsory authority over those within their jurisdiction and act on behalf of
society as a whole to keep the peace and secure justice for individuals. They need to
be carefully developed and monitored, starting with pilot schemes that may well
vary from rural areas to urban areas and from one province to another. The
experience of the five hundred traditional courts at present recognized by the law
would be of special value. Attention would have to be paid to the fact that the
boundaries between custom and common law have long become soft and permeable.
I know that these terms are used separately in the Constitution. Yet they can be seen
as having been employed in a descriptive and fluid rather than in a normative and
categorical manner. By common law is meant that body of law that has been
regarded as common law; by custom is meant that body of practices, rules, institutions, and values that has been treated as customary law. Both need to be infused
with the values of the Constitution. In the days of segregation, they were kept apart,
both conceptually and institutionally. Today there is no reason not to recognize and
welcome the fact that each has osmotically and irreversibly seeped into and reinforced
the other. Furthermore, both have been profoundly and irrecoverably affected by
legislation; if ever-pure fonts of common law and customary law existed, they do
not exist any more today.

Take the case, for example, of a woman who has been thrown out of the house
with her children by their father, whom both she and the community at large regard
as her husband. The circumstances might be varied. In some cases the judges might
feel that the principles of customary law as they understand them are quite sufficient
to provide an adequate remedy, that is, one which, in the context of the relationship
between two families, will restore social equilibrium and provide adequate protection
for the women and children. In others, the de facto manner in which the conjugal
partnership was established, the lack of interfamilial connections and the absence of
cattle or other wealth transfers, could result in remedies derived purely from the
common law, such as ordering that the woman be allowed to stay on in the house
and the father be obliged to pay maintenance for the children, either in cash or in
kind. In most cases, one could expect elements of traditional and common law to
be fused in the quest for a just and fair solution. What I am suggesting is that law
in practice be allowed to develop in conformity with life practice. This implies that
the law be made to fit the people and not that the people be compelled to ignore active parts of their lives so as to squeeze themselves into the categories of the law. This
requires not rigid and formulaic doctrine, but open participatory procedures and

the application by the local judges of clearly understood and firmly enunciated principles of equity and effectiveness. It also presupposes abandoning the strict legal dualism coupled with choice-of-law approaches that have been adopted in many postcolonial countries. It is not only that as a matter of principle we need to move away from the settler/native dichotomy as highlighted by Professor Mamdani. From a purely pragmatic point of view, it becomes increasingly difficult to separate out the customary and common law dimensions of law as it actually impinges on the lives of rural communities. What appears to be needed is an appropriate fusion rather than artificial separation. Such interaction and engagement between custom and common law and legislation should be brought about gently rather than robustly, and on a case-by-case basis rather than through an aggressively doctrinaire approach. The goal must always be to reconcile and harmonize different legal concepts so as to provide solutions that are regarded as eminently fair and meaningful to litigants and to the community as a whole.

Similarly, I think it is important to avoid an unfortunate but prevalent tendency to put customary law and the constitutional principle of equality on a collision course, that is to say, that for the one to live, the other must die, or to use a less dramatic metaphor, if custom triumphs, equality must fail (or vice versa). I think this is a profoundly mistaken view. Our Bill of Rights is not based on a hierarchy of rights, nor is it an assemblage of categorically defined rights sealed off from each other. Rather, it contemplates the interdependence of mutually supportive rights. Everything depends on the concrete circumstances which trigger the disputes, on their wider significance and impact, and on the intensity with which the underlying values of the open and democratic society as envisaged by the Constitution are promoted or breached in a particular case. Where the exercise of one right inevitably involves trespassing on another, the notion of proportionally becomes central. Thus, it might be difficult to uphold a precept of custom or religion which required different penal treatment for men and for women who committed adultery; the injury to equality would be grave, while the religious rule infringed would be relatively peripheral to the core elements of the faith. On the other hand, if people follow a faith that only allows men to be clerics, it would be hard to justify a court injunction requiring women to be ordained; the state-enforced intrusion on freedom of belief and association would be massive in circumstances where the state as such was not being made directly complicit in sexist practices. Any remedy would have to lie in internal transformation, not external compulsion. The position might be different, however, if the state is directly implicated through being asked to use its machinery to give effect to patriarchal-type discrimination, that is, if the courts are called upon to apply rules of customary or religious law which, looked at from the point of view of constitutional rights, discriminated unfairly between men and women by means of overtly entrenching patriarchal subordination.

It is important in this regard to recognize that what has severely undermined patriarchy in African society is not the law or the Constitution, but the changing character of African life. Thus, the practical question facing the courts today is not so much whether to perpetuate patriarchy as whether to rescue it. It has been undermined by the migrant labor system and by the fact that household farming has ceased to be the centre of production for the great majority of African families. It has been undermined by the reality that there are millions of women who work outside the home and bring in their own income and who have achieved a certain measure of autonomy and independence which they are not easily going to give up. Thus, the constitutionally created Commission for Gender Equality strives precisely to ensure that actual gains made by women in practice are not reversed or taken away by law.

I was at a judicial conference in Bangalore in India recently. It was quite wonderful to be with judges from all over the world. [We used to say: Workers of the world unite! Now we say: Judges of the world unite!] One of the women speakers, a lawyer from Pakistan, dressed in a sari, told us how angry she got when she heard men saying that in defense of culture we had to accept this, that, and the other, and resist the desire of some women to destroy "our culture" with their allegedly Westernized claims for equality. And she said indignantly: "Look around this room, look at all the men, dressed up in their modernized western-type suits, and look at the women." [All the Asian women were wearing saris.] She said: "We defend our culture in our lives, in our languages, in our daily practice. We are the deepest defenders of culture, but the minute we ask for equal rights, then people suddenly start throwing culture at us."

Jack Simons would have patted me on the back for telling that story. He died about two years ago. People who saw this frail, old figure, this *boereseun* become *boere-oupa*, being carried onto the stage to receive belated honors from University of Cape Town, couldn't have imagined the vigour and the fire of the once great teacher. Yet beautiful eulogies were delivered to him at St. George's Cathedral in Cape Town by persons from many different generations he had taught. After the choir had sung "Onward, Christian Soldiers" followed by the "Internationale" [Jack's last pedagogical joke, he had asked for both of them to be sung.] The warmest tributes came from former members of *Umkhonto We Sizwe*. They spoke about uncle Jack, their wise, humane and humorous teacher, who had told them never to just accept ideas, but always to debate and always to argue—they were in the Angolan bush, in danger of ambushes, short of food, threatened by mosquitoes and snakes, by everything, and they were discussing what it meant to be a human being on this earth, what it meant to live in society, what was meant by the concept of government, what was meant by tradition and culture. And let me say, one reason we've got the Constitution that we've got today, was because we had intellectuals like Jack entering into dialogue with the Black Consciousness generation, the streams of passionate young men and women who had crossed the borders as much in search of ideas as of military training, and who welcomed him as a brilliant intellectual freedom fighter in their midst. The then South African government paid Jack the highest accolade that any engaged intellectual can ever receive: they sent bomber planes to try and destroy him.

Jack Simons is one of our heroes. I am happy to use this occasion to pay tribute to him. I think when you read his book, you will see that I have not been exaggerating his virtues. We already have a strong platform from which to work. What is needed now is a dialogue—an exchange of ideas, experiences, and values that will enable us to distill all the precious elements from our rich and varied experiences. We have done so much in South Africa already. I believe that, provided participation is extensive and honest, this is another area where we will prove to ourselves, to Africa and to the world how creative and sensible we can be.

And so, having earned our supper, I invite all of you who are not vegetarians or not worried about cholesterol, to let the *boerewors* roll.

uBuntu and the Law in South Africa

Yvonne Mokgoro

The concept of *ubuntu*, like many concepts, is not easily defined. Defining an African notion in a foreign language and from an abstract, as opposed to a concrete approach, defies the very essence of the African worldview and may also be particularly elusive. Therefore, I will not attempt to define the concept with precision—that task is unattainable. In one's own experience, it is one of those things that you know when you see it. Therefore, like many who have written on the subject, I will put forward some views that relate to the concept itself. However, I can never claim the last word. I intend to put forward some thought-provoking ideas on *ubuntu* and its relation to South African law in general, the South African Constitution, and customary law in particular, as a way to initiate debate for *ubuntu*-ism in a new jurisprudence for South Africa.

THE CONCEPT OF *UBUNTU*

uBuntu, a Zulu word with *botho* as its Sesotho equivalent, has generally been described as a worldview of African societies and a determining factor in the formation of perceptions that influence social conduct.[1] It has also been described as a philosophy of life, which in its most fundamental sense represents personhood, humanity, humaneness, and morality; a metaphor that describes group solidarity where such group solidarity is central to the survival of communities with a scarcity of resources, and the fundamental belief is that *[u]buntu ngumuntu ngabantu, motho ke motho lo batho ba bangwe*, (a human being is a human being because of other human beings).[2] In other words, the individual's existence and well-being are relative to that of the group. This is manifested in anti-individualistic conduct that threatens the survival of the group. If the individual is to survive within the group, there must be a collective effort for group survival. Basically, it is a humanistic orientation towards fellow beings.

Professor Kunene, however, warns against a superficial perception of *ubuntu*.

> For indeed, it is not, enough to refer to the meaning and profound concept of *ubuntu*ism merely as a social ideology. *uBuntu* is the very quality that guarantees not only a separation between men, women and the beast, but the very fluctuating gradations that determine the relative quality of that essence. It is for that reason that we prefer to call it the potential of being human.[3]

The potential, he states, can fluctuate from the lowest to the highest level during one's lifetime. At the highest level, there is constant harmony between the physicality and spirituality of life. The harmony is achieved through close and sympathetic social relations within the group. Thus, the notion, a human being is a human being because of other human beings, implies that during one's lifetime, one is constantly challenged by others, practically, to achieve self-fulfillment through a set of collective social ideals. Because the African worldview is not easily and neatly categorized and defined, any attempt to define *ubuntu* is merely a simplification of a more expansive, flexible, and philosophically accommodative idea.

The meaning of *ubuntu*, however, becomes much clearer when we examine its practical effect on everyday life. For example, a society based on *ubuntu* places strong emphasis on family obligations. Family members are obliged to help one another. The concept of family is a broad nuclear family, which includes the extended family. People are willing to pool community resources to help an individual in need. This is captured in some of the African aphorisms such as, *[m]otho ke motho lo batho ba bangwe* (people live through the help of others) and, *a botho ba gago e nne botho seshabeng* (let your welfare be the welfare of the nation).

Group solidarity, conformity, compassion, respect, human dignity, humanistic orientation and collective unity have, among others, been defined as key social values of *ubuntu*. Because of the expansive nature of the concept, its social value will always depend on the approach and the purpose upon which it is relied. Thus, its value has also been viewed as its basis for a morality of cooperation, compassion, communalism, concern for the interests of the collective respect, and respect for the dignity of personhood, with emphasis on the virtues of that dignity in social relationships and practices. For purposes of an ordered society, *ubuntu* is a prized value, an ideal that age-old traditional African societies could achieve. The age-old traditional societies had their own customary institutions that functioned on well-adjusted principles and practices.

Despite the effect some of the various social forces have had on African societies, the suitability of those original principles and practices is often questioned, and in my view correctly so. Through modernity, the traditional cohesion of African societies has been largely eroded. It can be argued that the social field for an *ubuntu* legal system is not particularly fertile. It can also be argued that the values of *ubuntu*, if consciously harnessed, can enhance the creation of the envisaged value system of the new and contemporary South African jurisprudence. Indeed, as Ali Mazrui observes, "Africa can never go back completely to its pre-colonial starting point but there may be a case for re-establishing contacts with familiar landmarks of modernisation under indigenous impetus."[4]

UBUNTU AND SOUTH AFRICAN LAW

Although South Africa is a multicultural society, indigenous law has not been featured in the mainstream of South African jurisprudence. Although an opportunity existed under the reforms of the Special Courts for Blacks Abolition Act 34 of 1986 and the Law of Evidence Amendment Act 4 of 1988, which among other things, empowered mainstream courts to take judicial cognizance of indigenous law, not much has become of that either. Without a doubt, some aspects or values of *ubuntu* are universally inherent to South Africa's cultures. It would be anomalous if dignity, humaneness, conformity, and respect were foreign to any of South Africa's cultural systems. On the other hand, the various methods, approaches, emphasis, and attitude are concepts unique to African culture.

I believe we should incorporate *ubuntu* into mainstream jurisprudence by harnessing it carefully, consciously, creatively, strategically, and with ingenuity so that age-old African social innovations and historical cultural experiences are aligned with present-day legal notions and techniques if the intention is to create a legitimate system of law for all South Africans.

Including *ubuntu* will enhance the legitimacy of a jurisprudence, which is required to manage the challenges that constitutionalism with entrenched human rights poses for us. Hence, there is much room for law reform. As part of a new law management strategy, we need to carefully prioritize current problems and develop new research methods to find a pragmatic and integrated solution.

UBUNTU AND THE CONSTITUTION

The Interim Constitution (1993) sets the tone for socio-political transformation in South Africa. It created "a historic bridge between the past of a deeply divided society, characterized by strife, conflict, untold suffering and injustice, and a future founded on the recognition of peaceful co-existence . . . for all South Africans."[5]

To realize the peaceful coexistence recognized by the Interim Constitution, despite the injustices of the past, there is a need for understanding, not vengeance, and a need for reparation, not retaliation. Specifically, that constitution recognized the need for *ubuntu* and not victimization.

In its preamble the Interim Constitution declared:

"Whereas there is a need to create a new order in which all South Africans
will be entitled to a common South African Citizenship . . . where there is
equality between men and women and people of all races so that all citizens
shall be able to enjoy and exercise their fundamental rights and freedoms."

The Interim Constitution further declared, "it is necessary for such purposes
that provision should be made for the promotion of national unity and the restruc-
turing and continued governance of South Africa . . . ." Therefore, the Interim Constitution established a new socio-political order with national unity and a common
citizenship, and where all and not only a few should enjoy and exercise their fundamental rights and freedoms.

Finally, despite the potential for disorder that the permissive guarantee of rights
and freedoms may have after decades of oppression and repression, these guiding
values aim to set the tone for peaceful coexistence. The Preamble specifically
required the need for *ubuntu*, but not victimization. The values of *ubuntu* are an integral part of the value system established by the Interim Constitution. With respect
to individual human rights and freedoms, the Interim Constitution did not establish
a system where these rights and freedoms are exercised and claimed arbitrarily,
despite the claims and existence of concomitant rights of others.

The limitations clause, a rights-balancing mechanism, provided specific criteria to
be considered when conflicting rights and interests are claimed.[6] As such, the limitations
clause could also be a mechanism for peaceful coexistence between individual claimants.

The constitutional principles in the Interim Constitution, which resulted from a
solemn pact among the negotiators at Kempton Park, insisted that the new Constitution take its cue from the Interim Constitution. Like the latter, the new Constitution
is the supreme law of the land and contains a Bill of Rights described in section 7(l)
as the "cornerstone of democracy in South Africa."[7] The new Constitution established
democratic values, such as human dignity, equality, promotion of human rights and
freedoms, multiparty democracy to ensure accountability, and responsiveness and
openness of law. The values in the new Constitution arguably coincide with some
key values of *ubuntu*-ism, for example, human dignity, respect, inclusivity, compassion, concern for others, honesty, and conformity. The *ubuntu* values of collective
unity and group solidarity are translated into the value of national unity demanded
by the new South African society.

The collective unity, group solidarity, and conformity tendencies of *ubuntu* can
promote a new patriotism and personal stewardship crucial to the development of
a democratic society. A number of other similar survival issues in the law, which are
brought about by the challenges of constitutionalism, are easily identifiable. It is
around these issues that law reform can harness the ideas of *ubuntu*-ism to achieve
appropriate responses to the demands of constitutionalism.

uBuntu-ism can be employed to create responsive legal institutions for the advancement of constitutionalism and a culture of human rights in South Africa by:

Promoting the values of the new Constitution by translating them into more familiar *ubuntu* values and tendencies;
Harnessing some unique *ubuntu* value, tendency, approach, or strategy;
Promoting or aligning these aspects of *ubuntu* with core constitutional demands.

UBUNTU AND AFRICAN INDIGENOUS LAW

For the first time in South Africa's history, indigenous law and its application has acquired constitutional status. Section 211, which takes its cue from the Interim Constitution, recognizes the institution of traditional leaders and the systems of indigenous law that they observed. It specifically enjoined courts to apply this law, where it is applicable, but subject to the Constitution and applicable legislation.[8]

The Constitution brings to an end the marginal development of customary law or indigenous principles. It addresses the need to bring outdated and distorted customary law institutions in line with the values of the Constitution. Indigenous law is replete with such institutions, which deserve to be discarded or realigned and developed. *uBuntu*-ism, which is central to age-old African customs and traditions, abounds with values and ideas that have the potential for shaping not only current indigenous law institutions, but South African jurisprudence as a whole. Examples that come to mind are:

The original conception of law was perceived not as a tool for personal defense against an adversary, but as an opportunity given to all to survive under the protection of the order of the communal entity;
Communalism which emphasizes group solidarity and interest groups generally, with all the rules that sustain it, as opposed to individual interests, with its individualistic tendencies, with its likely utility in building a sense of national unity among South Africans;
The conciliatory character of the adjudication process which aims to restore peace and harmony between members rather than the adversarial approach to litigation, which emphasizes retribution and seems repressive. The importance of group solidarity requires restoration of peace between litigants, rather than an all-out victor and an all-out loser;
The idea that law, experienced by an individual within the group, is bound to individual duty as opposed to individual rights, demands, or entitlement. Closely related is the notion of individual sacrifice for group interests and group solidarity so central to *ubuntu*-ism and possibly useful for the development of a jurisprudence of socio-economic rights.

The shared values of *ubuntu*-ism and the Constitution, and the significant and effective approaches, methods, techniques, and strategies of the former can play a crucial role in shaping and formulating a new indigenous law and jurisprudence to meet the demands and challenges of constitutionalism for indigenous law. How exactly these values can be used to form jurisprudential responses to the current challenges brought by competing demands in a complex and rapidly changing South Africa requires close examination of current shortcomings of existing institutions, their mechanisms, and their strategies.

Section 39(2) of the new Constitution provides that in the interpretation of the Bill of Rights or any legislation, courts have a specific injunction to develop indigenous law, taking into account the spirit, purpose and object of the Bill of Rights. Since the values of the Constitution, and at least the key values of *ubuntu*-ism seem to converge, indigenous law may need to be aligned with these converging values. It is, however, not only the system of indigenous law which needs this realignment. South African law as a whole is constantly placed under the scrutiny of the Constitution. Therefore, the values of *ubuntu* can provide the necessary indigenous impetus.

CONCLUSION

When Chief Justice Mahomed addressed the World Jurist Association Seminar in Cape Town in February of this year [1998], he summed up the significance of African values:

> "The ageless emotional and cultural maturity of Africa is less dramatic but not less significant or potentially powerful in influencing, in shaping and in formulating the constitutional ethos which must inform and define judicial responses to jurisprudential challenges arising from competing demands in a complex and rapidly changing society. That maturity expresses itself through a collectivist [emotion] of communal caring and humanism, and of reciprocity and caring."[9]

These African values, which manifest themselves in *ubuntu*, are inconsonance with the values of the Constitution in general and those of the Bill of Rights in particular. The Human Rights violations and indignities of the past have not well served the legitimacy and respect for South African law.

The advent of constitutionalism has seen unconstitutional laws and actions invalidated and set aside. Institutions of democracy, which had been created by the Interim Constitution to advance a culture of democracy and human rights, have also swung into much action. However, less than four years of constitutionalism has not and cannot have achieved the necessary popular for South Africa; nor did it and could it have restored fully the dignity of our legal system. In the true spirit of *ubuntu*, no one, especially not lawyers, can afford to sit back and watch our newfound constitutionalism slide into disrepute. Quite obviously, the complete restoration of the reputation of South African law and jurisprudence requires considerable modification of existing rules. We will thus have to be ingenious in finding or creating law reform programs, methods, approaches, and strategies that will enhance adaptation to such unprecedented change.

The values of *ubuntu*, I would like to believe, if consciously harnessed, can be central to a process of harmonizing indigenous law with the Constitution and can be integral to a new South African jurisprudence.

A Call for a Nuanced Constitutional Jurisprudence: South Africa, *uBuntu*, Dignity, and Reconciliation

Drucilla Cornell

What I hope to do in this article is to try to reconfigure the relationship between dignity and *ubuntu*, and then show how we might rethink this relationship in some crucial court cases in South Africa. Dignity famously comes from Immanuel Kant's distinction between who and how we are as sensible beings in the world, subjected to the determination by the causal laws of nature in our lives as sensual creatures.[1] Yet in our lives as creatures capable of making ourselves, subject to the law of the categorical imperative, we can also make ourselves legislators of the moral law and moral right. We are free and because we are free we are of infinite worth. The categorical imperative in Kant is a demand put on us that could be succinctly summarized: who I am only has a claim to dignity because I comply my life with who I should be, and the categorical imperative is a practical imperative that commands the "should be." Since it is only in the realm of morality that we find our freedom, there is no contradiction in Kant between subjecting ourselves to that command and our freedom.

DIGNITY AS AN IDEAL

Many thinkers, particularly feminists, have questioned Kant in terms of his dualism: the dualism between the noumenal and the phenomenal self. Yet on a much broader understanding of Kantian insight, it turns on the notion that dignity itself, since it is part of practical reason and not theoretical reason, is inevitably related to the ideal of humanity, an ideal that is inseparable from freedom. But our freedom need not be defined so rigidly as in Kant as only the subject of moral reason placed under the categorical imperative. Our dignity and the demand for its respect can stem from actual resistance, but also from the broken dreams that mark our commitment to moral ideals. Painted with a very broad brush, dignity inheres in the evaluations we all have to make of our lives, the ethical decisions we consciously confront, and even the ones we ignore. Dignity lies in our struggle to remain true to our moral vision, and even in our wavering from it. In the case of South Africa, those who broke under torture did not lose their dignity, precisely because they cannot lose their dignity, since it is a postulate of practical reason that never can be fatally undermined by our actual existential collapse before horrifying brutality. As Zora Neale Hurston's character, Nanny, in *Their Eyes Were Watching God* describes dignity:

> Ah was born back due in slavery, so it wasn't for me to fulfill my dreams of whut a woman oughta be and to do. Dat's one of de hold-backs of slavery. But nothing can't stop you from wishin'. You can't beat nobody down so low till you can rob 'em of they will. Ah didn't want to be used for a work-ox and a brood sow and Ah didn't want mah daughter used dat way neither.[2]

Again, if we give Kantian dignity its broadest meaning, it is not associated with our actual freedom but with the postulation of ourselves as beings who not only can but must confront moral and ethical decisions, and in making those decisions, we give value to our world. In the context of South Africa, the remembrance of the postulation of dignity as an ideal that we can never lose is particularly important, for dignity simply is at the level of the ideal. Dignity and its respect is also a demand placed on us as we shape our practical, ethical, and political reality. It is human beings in their practical activity who give value to the world. In Kant, freedom is inscrutable; if it could be reduced to a set of positive characteristics, it would no longer be freedom, but would come to be known as a cognizable object falling under the laws of nature. Beyond the inscrutability of our freedom, dignity and the respect it demands does not require the elaboration of common identities and shared characteristics, with the corresponding boundaries of who is in and who is out. Indeed such an elaboration goes against the grain of dignity since all value scales that attempt to codify the meaning of richer identities have long been associated with the hierarchical brutality of colonization. It is important to note here that dignity is an ideal, not a value, because unlike a value it cannot be weighed; there is no such thing as thick and thin dignity.

It is precisely because dignity remains at the level of an ideality associated with the ideal of humanity that it is difficult to use as a sole justification for, what in South Africa are known as, second- or third-generation rights. But I want to make a stronger point here, which is that dignity should not be used as the ideal or translated into a legal principle to justify such rights. The reason for this is that we undermine both the ideal and critical aspect of dignity when we attempt to say and elaborate the conditions under which it can be lost. This, for example, is the problem with Martha Nussbaum's attempt when she seeks to elaborate what a fully human life is, with its attendant understanding that if we are denied certain conditions, we lose our dignity, because then we are no longer "dignified."[3] Feminist conflations between dignity and what is dignified are particularly problematic, for then there is the danger of denying dignity to other women because of the oppressive conditions under which they live. We seek to say that those conditions should be changed in the name of their dignity and not because they have lost their dignity due to those conditions. This distinction may seem subtle, but I believe it is crucial for both transnational feminism, and for the jurisprudence of South Africa. However, dignity is enough for a wide range of cases; for example, it certainly can be used to reject state-imposed execution as constitutionally legitimate. We can move from Kant to the rejection of the death penalty because, as in suicide, the subject of rights is annihilated, and without at least an idealized subject of rights, there can be no rights in the first place.

Elsewhere I have defended a revision of the Kantian notion of dignity, so as to reconcile Kant with the right to die.[4] But for now, I want to emphasize that for Kant, the notion of law and the founding principle of legality can only be a hypothetical experiment in the imagination, in which self-legislating human beings contracted to their own restraint on the basis of mutual accordance of each other's dignity as free persons, limited only by the internal restrictions of dignity as an ideal. As a result, Kant could not himself easily justify anything close to second- or third-generation rights. Throughout a philosophical lifetime, John Rawls sought to demonstrate that perhaps we could take the Kantian hypothetical social contract so as to reach much more sweeping egalitarian conclusions. Whether or not he was successful is open to debate. But my point here is simply that even in Kant, just like in his predecessors and contemporaries, modern Anglo-European political philosophy presumes at least on the level of the individual, a social contract as the only legitimate constitutive power of a constituted government. The definition of a legitimate legal authority turns on this idealized social contract with its highly specific understanding of how a Bill of Rights and other constitutional mandates can be legitimated only from within this imagined basis of a contract with an imagined, already individuated, individual. This understanding of law through social contract is, in my opinion, simply inadequate to the second- and third-generation rights guaranteed in the South African Constitution.

Kant can get us to the notion of democracy as friendship, but only in the following sense: I am your friend because I am a friend to myself, as a being, who can make himself or herself a person who struggles to make what I am who I should be.

UBUNTU

In her most theoretically innovative moments, Justice Yvonne Mokgoro has suggested that *ubuntu* provides us with a very different notion of the founding of the principle of law. The Law of law or the founding principles of legality are not reducible to the internal limiting principles of the social contract, based on maximizing the negative freedom of all. Instead, the Law of law is rearticulated to recognize that democracy as friendship can only be found in solidarity by reinforcing the community that sustains it:

> *uBuntu*(-ism), which is central to age-old African custom and tradition however, abounds with values and ideas which have the potential of shaping not only current indigenous law institutions, but South African jurisprudence as a whole. Examples that come to mind are: The original conception of law perceived not as a tool for personal defense, but as an opportunity given to all to survive under the protection of the order of the communal entity; communalism which emphasises group solidarity and interests generally, and all rules which sustain it, as opposed to individual interests, with its likely utility in building a sense of national unity among South Africans; the conciliatory character of the adjudication process which aims to restore peace and harmony between members rather than the adversarial approach which emphasises retribution and seems repressive. The lawsuit is viewed as a quarrel between community members and not as a conflict; the importance of public ritual and ceremony in the communication of information within the group; the idea that law, experienced by an individual within the group, is bound to individual duty as opposed to individual rights or entitlement. Closely related is the notion of sacrifice for group interests and group solidarity so central to *ubuntu*(-ism); the importance of sacrifice for every advantage or benefit, which has significant implications for reciprocity and caring within the communal entity.[5]

uBuntu, understood as an ideal irreducible to one based in an imagined social contract, could potentially promote a different set of ideals for interpreting the Bill of Rights in South Africa. Such an interpretation would not have to swim upstream against the grain of negative liberty implied in the Western social contract tradition.

We could rephrase the Kantian language of friendship through *ubuntu* as follows. In Kant, I am a friend to myself because of the dignity of my humanity. Under *ubuntu*, I am a friend to myself because others in my community have already been friends to me, making me someone who could survive at all, and therefore be in the community. It is only because I have always been together with others and they with me that I am gathered together as a person and sustained in that self-gathering. We have a responsibility to that community which is irreducible to one-on-one correspondence between rights and duty, because I am not at all a person without this community. Obligation and duty in this sense goes beyond that allowable under social contract theory.

This more sweeping sense of obligation can help us understand how the beneficiaries of racism can be held responsible for correcting it, even by asserting and defending what at first glance might seem as an unequal, and because unequal, unfair position vis-à-vis other members of the community.

The closest we come to this ideal of *ubuntu* in the European tradition is in Hegel, where the objective community, or *Sittlichkeit*, always precedes and constitutes the subject of rights. Hegel of course did not deny subjective rights, as we understand them—as first-generation rights defended through dignity—and neither does Yvonne Mokgoro. But I'd like to suggest here that to understand Mokgoro at her most provocative is to grasp her argument that African ideals of solidarity and mutual sustenance could potentially provide a new and important way to think about the law of law, or the grounding principle of legality itself. G. J. van Niekerk makes a similar argument in her defense of the idea that the basic principles of indigenous law remain implicated in a different notion of the ground of law, one that is foreign to social contract theory.[6] She describes those principles as the harmony of the collectivity, the principle of the superhuman or spiritual forces superior to the human, and what she calls the identity postulate. The identity postulate is an odd way for her to name her principle, since her point is that transformation and indeed contradictory ways of thinking can be taken into these principles in a "both-and" ethical attitude that can seek harmony without rationalization.

In some of the most sophisticated postcolonial theory today, this "both-and" attitude is defended as being against the historicism that, following Hegel, seeks to tell us that we must reject as an anachronism pieces of our lives, including, for example, the belief in spiritual and agential beings in the world of humans, because they can be thoroughly replaced with the rationality of mature enlightenment which becomes secular at the level of ontology. Dipesh Chakrabarty, for example, argues that this "both-and" attitude is what allows us to keep alive contemporaneous "future nows" in Heidegger's sense, which can be present at hand and yet, seemingly contradictory.[7]

uBuntu and social contract theory are in tension with one another, but if postcolonial theory has anything to teach us, it is that that tension can be productive, even as we attempt reconfigurations of possibly divergent notions of the Law of law and the axiomatic principles they generate. It is important to note here that when Mokgoro translates *ubuntu* into an ideal of the South African Constitution, she does so by way of what I have called a conversion principle.[8] By a conversion principle, I mean an act of recollective imagination that not only recalls the past as it remembers the future, but also projects forward as an ideal the very principles that read into the past, that is, in this case, *ubuntu*. A conversion principle generally both converts the way we understand the past, and converts or translates any current practice of interpretation as we attempt to realize it in the reconstruction of law and legal principle. Given Mokgoro's profound concern with discrimination against women, she is, on my reading of her, converting the world-view and ideal of *ubuntu* into law by both recollecting it and then also re-imagining it in accordance with a constitution that is explicitly teleological and thus performative in that it attempts to actualize the democratic values of human dignity, equality, and freedom.

Certainly there are questionable aspects of *ubuntu*, particularly for feminists, such as for example the notion of subsidiarity. Subsidiarity, as the philosopher Augustine

Shutte has defined it, carries a benevolent paternalism that has often treated women in customary law as if they were minors under the care of their husbands.[9] It is evident that her feminist aspirations would lead Mokgoro to question subsidiarity, at least as it has been applied to women. But she does so by reminding us that social custom, including the day-to-day, on-the-ground status of women, is dynamic, even if at times certain aspects of customary law have become rigidified. Thus there are sources within the practice of social custom itself that can be imagined and reimagined so as to reconfigure the norms of customary law. As I understand her, Mokgoro is proceeding from two directions. The first is to convert *ubuntu* into a constitutional principle and thereby to synchronize it with dignity. The second is to reimagine *ubuntu* from within the practices of customary law, as they are engaged in by women themselves.

Of course, there is a more limited way to read Mokgoro, but one that I think is unfair to her more sweeping arguments that African values, such as *ubuntu*, are important in any jurisprudence that will seek to justify second- and third-generation rights. The more limited way to read Mokgoro is to argue that she is simply defending the notion that, as a matter of equality, we should respect the role and importance of African values in a society that has completely repudiated the very notion that black Africans had anything of ethical worth to add to the legal or moral culture to which they were subjected. Justice Albie Sachs has clearly joined Mokgoro in this more limited understanding of *ubuntu*, firmly stating that *ubuntu* is a constitutionally acknowledged principle. As he also eloquently states:

> Above all, however, it means giving long overdue recognition to African law and legal thinking as a source of legal ideas, values, and practice. We cannot, unfortunately, extend the equality principle backwards in time to remove the humilities and indignities suffered by past generations, but we can restore dignity to ideas and values that have long been suppressed or marginalised.[10]

Sachs has been criticized for establishing no normative basis for his system of human rights in his own two works on human rights. Famously, he is echoing the Marxist-inspired sentiment that a vote without bread is a hollow right indeed. Indeed, Dennis Davis has accused him of entirely rejecting "a transformative legal enterprise that facilitates the scope of societal transformation and enhances the democratic character of politics and informs participation in all forms of social life."[11] He accuses Sachs of having as his goal the centralized reconstruction of socio-economic life through law. For all of the fancy talk, this criticism boils down to Davis' belief that Sachs never got over Marxist notions of legal development that Chakrabarty would call historicist, in the sense in which law plays a major role in undoing the capitalist relations of production and slowly leads the masses into their emancipation from lingering superstition. Simply put, Davis is suggesting that in his 1991 and 1992 books on human rights, Albie Sachs is a socialist and will always remain one. I hope that that is the case, since I believe the future of South Africa is better thought of as a democratic socialist society, rather than a social democracy along the lines of modern European states such as Norway, Sweden, and Finland. Despite the more serious criticism of his work on law in Mozambique, articulated, for example, by Mahmood Mamdani in his book *Citizen and Subject*, I think a fair assessment of Sachs is that he is both slowly moving away from what Mamdani calls an oversimplified model of the modernization of law in African countries[12] and moving towards a more complex jurisprudence that is actually quite close to the principles of constitutional interpretation defined by Lourens du Plessis.[13] But for now, I want to suggest provocatively that the spirit of *ubuntu* does reside in Sachs's jurisprudence, despite the fact that he himself does not use *ubuntu* as the basis for his rejection of capital punishment.[14] Instead he proceeds through an explicitly literalist interpretation of the right to life in the constitution. In other words, the right to life for Sachs forecloses state-enforced execution. There are problems with this literalist reading of the right to life as Ronald Dworkin has pointed out—life has both a natural and an expressive moment and that it is this expressive moment, and not simply natural existence, that makes us think of human life as intrinsically valuable.[15] Sachs is aware of Dworkin's writing, and returns to it in his decision on the allocation of kidney machines under conditions of scarce resources.[16] I do not want to belabor this point too much, because I believe Sachs's jurisprudence does not tend overall toward literalist or contextualist interpretations of the constitution, and that ultimately he would agree with the language in Mokgoro's concurrence. Mokgoro directly asserts that the death penalty is a form of vengeance incompatible with *ubuntu*.[17] But she also writes:

> with the entrenchment of a bill of fundamental rights and freedoms in a supreme constitution, however, the interpretive task frequently involves making constitutional choices by balancing competing rights and freedoms. This can often only be done by reference to a system of values extraneous to the constitutional text itself where these principles constitute the historical context in which the text was adopted and which helped to explain the meaning of the text. The constitution makes it particularly imperative for courts to develop the entrenched fundamental rights in terms of a cohesive set of values, ideal to an open and democratic society.[18]

I do not have the space in this article to defend it here, but my interpretation of Sachs's jurisprudence is that it relies heavily on the synchronization of three ideals: dignity, equality, and *ubuntu*. The spirit of *ubuntu* indeed pervades Sachs's attempt to *harmonize* (a word he frequently uses) the particularly difficult right of cultural belonging and religious belief, as in his argument in the *Prince* case,[19] in which a young Rastafari practitioner sought to enter the formal legal profession in South Africa despite his professed use of cannabis for religious purposes. Sachs makes it clear, in his language, "where there are [religious] practices that might fall within a general legal prohibition, but that do not involve any violation of the Bill of Rights, the Constitution obliges the State to walk the extra mile."[20] Sachs's point is that this extra mile should be taken precisely because of his insight (which echoes Chakrabarty's) that religious belief and practice and rational assessment and justification simply do not proceed at the same register, and that human beings cannot and should not be called to rationalize those beliefs or clean them up through reason, unless they fall afoul of the need to affirm the basic principles of the Bill of Rights. Particularly in this case, I am suggesting that Sachs's opinion reflects the spirit of *ubuntu* in two ways that go beyond the simple recognition that dignity should have a subjective component that demands that we respect people's representations of themselves. The first way in which Sachs's opinion reflects *ubuntu* takes us back to what Van Niekerk has described as the identity postulate associated with *ubuntu* thinking. What I am suggesting here is that Sachs, in this opinion, recognizes the "both-and" as an ontic orientation in the world that is sometimes difficult for Westerners to comprehend. That is, I believe in the constitution and in ancestor worship and I do not believe that these two registers can be gathered together in a coherent whole. Secondly, I'm suggesting that Sachs is seeking the harmonization of legal ideals so as to respect reconciliation and social harmony and democracy as friendship that puts a strong demand on us. My question to Sachs would be why he did not rely on *ubuntu* in his decision in the allocation of kidney machines under conditions of scarce resources, particularly since he is insisting that the very nature of the right involved has to turn on the recognition of our actual interdependence as human beings, and on the notion of human interdependence as "defining the circumstances in which the rights may most fairly and effectively be enjoyed."[21] Sachs instead relies on Martha Minow and Ronald Dworkin.[22] Although Dworkin's insight into the dominion of life is certainly relevant to making these kinds of decisions, Dworkin's insistence on integrity and coherence makes him reluctant ever to acknowledge tragedy as inevitable in a world in which we live under conditions of massive inequality. *uBuntu* cannot only note the interdependence, it can also help us understand the tragedy of how we are all diminished in our humanity at the time of that relatively young man's inevitable death. *uBuntu* is associated with *seriti*, which names the life force by which a community of persons are connected to each other. In a constant mutual interchange of personhood and community, becomes indistinguishable from *ubuntu* in that the unity of the life force depends on the individual's unity with the community. As one philosopher of *ubuntu* explains:

> it is as if each person were a magnet creating together a complex field. Within that field any change in the degree of magnetization, any movement of one, affects the magnetization of all.[23]

In my interviews in South Africa, this concept of *seriti*, as a force field that shapes who we can be and diminishes us if we cannot live up to the demand it imposes upon us for care and responsibility, was emphasized again and again. We have actually physically lost something; we are in a sense drained of our humanity if we allow one of us to be denied access to a kidney machine simply because he or she can no longer afford it. Justice Mokgoro, in her concurring opinion in *Makwanyane*,[24] seems to rely on something like this notion of *seriti*, in that the toll of vengeance is not only felt by the one murdered, but extends to those who murder him or her, and beyond that to all those who live in a society shaped by that kind of vengeance. It is difficult, if not impossible, for many legal thinkers trained in the Anglo-American tradition to live with the proposition that a legal decision can be fair and yet tragic. But I believe that this is consistent with *ubuntu* thinking in the "both-and" sense that I described earlier, and that the South African Constitution in particular needs to keep alive this "both-and" sense in that many of the socio-economic rights guaranteed by the constitution are simply beyond their actualization in the current economic reality of South Africa. Keeping the ideal alive often involves marking that tragedy.

CONCLUSION

Ultimately a jurisprudence rich enough for the South African constitution will have to reach beyond the ethical individualism of Ronald Dworkin, and even the radical egalitarian Kantianism of John Rawls. Social contract theory, even in its best form, can only take us so far. But it is not simply a matter of dignity that we respect indigenous traditions in South Africa. My more provocative suggestion is that *ubuntu* thinking—and I'm sure there will be many other such ideals to be recollected and reimagined in African legal and ethical philosophy—is crucial to the fundamental purpose of the South African Constitution, which is to develop an interpretation of the Bill of Rights that goes way beyond the limited notion of such a bill as only a defense against state intrusion and based on negative freedoms. The promotion of a democratic community of friendship that always remains to come, even as we seek to bring it into being today, brings a nuanced jurisprudence that entails a complex reconciliation of the inevitable tensions that makes it stronger, between customary law and the Western ideals of liberalism, all of which should inform the constitution.

Doing Things with Values:

The Case of *uBuntu*

Irma J. Kroeze

In an earlier article,[1] I argued that the approach of the Constitutional Court to values in constitutional interpretation is flawed. I argued that the way the court approaches values is indicative of a textualist approach and that values are employed to enhance the objectivist paradigm underlying constitutional interpretation. In that paper, I also mention the brief flirtation with *ubuntu* as a constitutional value. This article is an attempt to explore this idea further.

The idea or philosophy of *ubuntu* was introduced into South African constitutional law by the postamble to the Interim Constitution.[2] The relevant portion of that provision reads as follows:

> The adoption of this Constitution lays the secure foundation for the people of South Africa to transcend the divisions and strife of the past, which generated gross violations of human rights, the transgression of humanitarian principles in violent conflicts and a legacy of hatred, fear, guilt and revenge.
>
> These can now be addressed on the basis that there is a need for understanding but not for vengeance, a need for reparation but not for retaliation, a need for *ubuntu* but not for victimisation.

Although the idea of *ubuntu* as a constitutional value was discussed in the *Makwanyane* case,[3] it was not developed further in subsequent cases and was not included in the final Constitution.[4] However, academic writers[5] and popular culture[6] would seem to indicate that the idea is far from dead and buried. Hence the continued interest in *ubuntu* within the legal and philosophical context.

The purpose of this article is threefold. First, it examines the way in which *ubuntu* is used and understood in case law and in legal-academic writing. Second, the question is raised as to why this idea was never developed further in constitutional jurisprudence. Third, this is part of the broader inquiry into the Constitutional Court's approach to values in constitutional interpretation generally.

UBUNTU AS A LEGAL CONCEPT

There is little doubt that *ubuntu* is a concept of some religious and cultural significance in the African philosophy and culture.[7] But it is in the transformation of that concept into a legal one that the interesting questions arise. In the legal context, the *ubuntu* concept is used to give content to rights (as a constitutional value) and to limit rights (as part of the values of an open and democratic society). But in the process of functioning within the rights discourse, the concept is also changed. It is that change that provides an interesting perspective.

uBuntu in Case Law

As was stated earlier, *ubuntu* was first used as a constitutional value in the *Makwanyane* case. Seven of the judgments refer to *ubuntu* in some form or another. It is instructive to refer to these judgments in some detail.

President Arthur Chaskalson refers to *ubuntu* as a concept that is primarily relevant to the field of political reconciliation but states that it is, nevertheless, not without relevance to the case at hand.[8] He states that "[t]o be consistent with the value of *ubuntu*, ours should be a society that 'wishes to prevent crime (not) to kill criminals simply to get even with them.'"[9] The quote in this instance is from the judgment of Justice Brennan in the American case of *Furman v. Georgia*."[10] Chaskalson does not indicate how American jurisprudence is relevant to *ubuntu*, nor does he indicate exactly how *ubuntu* is relevant to the case at hand.

This is an interesting dilemma. On the one hand, Chaskalson's judgment leaves the impression that the values of *ubuntu* are basically the same as those in American jurisprudence. In which case it raises the question of exactly why it is then necessary to refer to *ubuntu* at all. On the other hand, it might be that there are differences, which begs the question as to why the American case is quoted at all.

Justice Pius Langa also refers to the postamble, but indicates that the Constitution does not define the concept of *ubuntu*. He then explains his own understanding of what the concept means:

> The concept [of *ubuntu*] is of some relevance to the values we need to uphold.
> It is a culture that places some emphasis on communality and on the
> interdependence of the members of a community. It recognises a person's status
> as a human being, entitled to unconditional respect, dignity, value and accept-
> ance from the members of the community such person happens to be part of. It

also entails the converse, however. The person has a corresponding duty to give the same respect, dignity, value and acceptance to each member of that community. More importantly, it regulates the exercise of rights by the emphasis it lays on sharing and co-responsibility and the mutual enjoyment of rights by all.[11]

Langa then proceeds to point out that *ubuntu* emphasizes the value of life and human dignity and that "heinous crimes" are the exact opposite of *ubuntu*. In the same way, cruel, inhuman, and degrading treatment is "bereft of *ubuntu*."[12] Langa acknowledges that the concept is mostly used without explanation of its content, but points out that it is always regarded as something to be desired, a "commendable attribute."[13] An interesting aspect of his judgment is a reference to a Tanzanian case as apparent confirmation of the meaning of *ubuntu*.[14]

The judgment by Langa is indicative of much of the debate around *ubuntu*. While there is consensus that it entails some form of communality, the specifics are not dealt with. And while all agree that it is indeed a "commendable attribute" there is no indication what content that would give to a concept like human dignity, for example. There is no indication that the emphasis on communality in any way changes the typically liberalist concept of dignity.

Justice Madala also deals with *ubuntu* as a concept that "permeates the Constitution generally" and is of the opinion that the concept includes "the ideas of humaneness, social justice and fairness."[15] For Madala the idea of *ubuntu* is specifically linked to punishment. He is of the opinion that the reformative theory of punishment "accords fully with the concept of *ubuntu*."[16] In his opinion the long tradition of taking extenuating circumstances into consideration when passing sentence is an example of how *ubuntu* has always been part of South African law.[17]

Justice Mahomed refers to the concept of *ubuntu* in startlingly unusual language. His views read as follows:

> The need for *ubuntu* (as referred to in the post-amble) expresses the ethos of an instinctive capacity for and enjoyment of love towards our fellow men and women; the joy and the fulfillment involved in recognizing their innate humanity; the reciprocity this generates in interaction within the collective community; the richness of the creative emotions which it engenders and the moral energies which it releases both in the givers and the society which they serve and are served by.[18]

However, apart from stating that it is against this background that the Constitution must be interpreted, he does not indicate if and how the concept is relevant to the death penalty. It is, consequently, difficult to understand how this advances the idea of a uniquely African set of constitutional values.

By far the most extensive elaboration regarding *ubuntu* can be found in the judgment of Justice Mokgoro. Mokgoro argues, as point of departure, that the ideal of *ubuntu* is a "shared value and ideal that runs like a golden thread across cultural lines" in South African society.[19] Although the legal system has not always recognized this, it is nevertheless consistent with the "inherited traditional value systems of South Africans in general."[20] *uBuntu* can be explained in the following way:

> Generally, *ubuntu* translates as 'humaneness.' In its most fundamental sense it translates as personhood and 'morality'. Metaphorically, it expresses itself in *umuntu ngumuntu ngabantu*,[21] describing the significance of group solidarity on survival issues so central to the survival of communities. While it envelops the key values of group solidarity, compassion, respect, human dignity, conformity to basic norms and collective unity, in its fundamental sense it denotes humanity and morality. Its spirit emphasises respect for human dignity, marking a shift from confrontation to conciliation. In South Africa *ubuntu* has become a notion with particular resonance in the building of a democracy. It is part of our rainbow heritage, though it might have operated and still operates differently in diverse community settings. In the Western cultural heritage, respect and the value for life, manifested in the all-embracing concepts of 'humanity' and 'menswaardigheid,' are also highly prized. It is values like these that section 35 requires to be promoted. They give meaning and texture to the principles of a society based on freedom and equality.[22]

In Mokgoro's view, this is entirely consistent with values articulated in the American and Hungarian constitutions as well as the values contained in international human rights documents.[23] Mokgoro has also written on *ubuntu* in the academic context. She points out that *ubuntu* is firstly a "philosophy of life" based on personhood, humanity, humaneness, morality, and group solidarity.[24] Some of these aspects are, in Mokgoro's view, universal to all cultures in South Africa, but the unique aspect of *ubuntu* lies in its approaches, attitudes, and methods.[25] These must be included in South African law.[26]

And although *ubuntu* is not mentioned in the Constitution, the values included "coincide with some key values of *ubuntu*-ism.[27] Of all the judges, Mokgoro is the most insistent that *ubuntu* is not a value system reserved for one section of the population alone. She is at pains to indicate that, although the emphasis is on communality, the values are basically universal. That is why she can blithely refer to "morality" as the fundamental meaning of *ubuntu*. From a critical perspective one might well ask: which morality? But in her judgment there is an almost unreflective assumption that all South Africans share a common morality and a common understanding of what dignity entails.

The *Makwanyane* case remains virtually the only case in which *ubuntu* is discussed in any kind of detail. Subsequent cases for the most part either simply quote the postamble without any discussion or refer to the discussion in *Makwanyane*.[28] And this should not come as a surprise—emphasizing the universal nature of the values of *ubuntu*, paradoxically, also makes them irrelevant.

Academic Discussion of *uBuntu*

Various academic writers have welcomed the inclusion of a reference to *ubuntu* in constitutional jurisprudence. A number of these will be discussed here, although this is far from an exhaustive overview.

Van Niekerk argues that the spirit of *ubuntu* is an integral part of indigenous law[29] in that it is precisely this concept of *ubuntu* that distinguishes indigenous law from primitive law, religious law or "mere" customary law.[30] She regards *ubuntu* as "a fundamental value; an inherent belief system which underscores . . . indigenous legal orders in Africa."[31] As such it is closely linked with "African humanism." But Van Niekerk warns that *ubuntu* can only be understood within the context of a specific worldview: "[T]he welfare of the individual is inextricably linked to the welfare of the collectivity and that, in turn, is inextricably linked to an harmonious relationship with the ancestors and with nature."[32]

This results in a high regard for human dignity that is not based on efficiency or functionality, as well as a high regard for the family.[33] It also undermines the strong liberalist distinction between private and public. This, in Van Niekerk's view, results in a very definite differentiation between "western legal orders" and "indigenous African legal orders":

> Because of the weak position of 'we', as opposed to the strong position of 'I' in western cultures, western legal orders are characterised by analysis, discrimination, differentiation, individualism, intellectualism, objectivism, inductive reasoning, scientific thought, generalisation, conceptualism, legalism, organisation, self-assertion, and impersonality. By contrast, indigenous Japanese and indigenous African legal orders, because of a well developed we-consciousness, are characterised as synthetic, totalising, integrative, non-discriminative, non-systematic, dogmatic, intuitive, non-discursive, subjective, communalistic and spiritually individualistic.[34]

On a general level, the strong distinction between "western" and "other" legal orders is probably overstated. For one thing it is extremely difficult to determine which are Western legal systems and which are not. But, apart from that, given the wide variety of legal systems that form part of the Western tradition, it is unlikely that they can be regarded as homogenous systems that all share these characteristics in the same way. That would negate the cultural and hermeneutic differences as well as critical voices that shape these legal systems.

One of the strangest views on *ubuntu* links this concept to psychosocial behavior.[35] De Kock and Labuschagne contend that *ubuntu* is not unique to Africa but can be traced to "the admittedly embryonic altruistic inclination of humankind."[36] Even more startling is the idea that *ubuntu* "shows vestiges of a prenatal womb memory," which makes it a universal phenomenon. This has an up- and a downside:

> "Thus in the socio-juridical value structures in traditional African societies there is an unmistaken pre-rational [sic] and emotionally vivid dimension which, paradoxically, subverts individuality, personal autonomy and mundane humaneness in the very essence and moral fibre of a *Rechtsstaat* and a human-rights culture."[37]

Despite this apparent drawback, the authors regard *ubuntu* as a way to establish a human rights culture.[38]

The idea of *ubuntu* as "African humanism" is also found in the views of Mqeke.[39] When it comes to the application of law, *ubuntu* is embodied in the principle of reconciliation and in the concept of group rights. According to Mqeke, the African Court system fostered the principle of reconciliation because it operated in "the framework of a strong symbiotic association between law, religion, kinship and culture."[40] The idea of group rights indicates both a way of life and a problem-solving technique.

As a result of these two principles, Mqeke states that, in customary law, "all interested adult males" have the right to take part in legal proceedings,[41] and "every adult male" has the right to freedom of thought.[42] Similarly, the right to a good name could be enforced by the head of a family or "the legal guardian of a female"[43] whatever that might mean. The right to life could only be violated in the case of witchcraft or for "serious political offences."[44]

What is astonishing about Mqeke's account is the explicit and uncritical assumption of the patriarchal nature of customary law. To be able to say that all males have rights in customary law and that therefore "customary law (is) not incompatible with human rights"[45] takes a special kind of logic. At the very least one would assume that this is discrimination based on gender and therefore presumptively unconstitutional.

UBUNTU AND THE POLITICS OF FORM

When the idea of *ubuntu* was introduced into South African constitutional law, it was immediately hailed as a way of incorporating "undistorted values historically disregarded in South African judicial law-making" into the mainstream jurisprudence.[46] In a general sense it was hoped that a "value-laden" approach to constitutional interpretation generally would result in a move away from literalism to a more contextual approach.[47] Unfortunately this has not been the case.[48] More specifically, *ubuntu* as constitutional value was touted as the beginning of a truly South African approach to constitutional interpretation. But, as was stated earlier, the idea of *ubuntu* as a constitutional or legal concept was not developed further after the *Makwanyane* case. Many explanations may be offered as to why this should be the case. In my view, however, the apparent demise of *ubuntu* is the result of what Pierre Schlag calls "the politics of form," and the form in question is normative legal thought.[49]

The Politics of Form

Schlag argues that traditional legal discourse determines the boundaries within which acceptable legal discourse can take place.[50] It does this by deprivileging and subordinating the form of the discourse. The form is treated as inconsequential and, as such, neutral.[51] The traditional thinker can, therefore, immediately move to the substantial legal questions without concern over the form. But this is a fantasy. The form of legal discourse is a profoundly political act—"a manifestation of social power congealed in linguistic form."[52]

This implies that the form of legal discursive practices is of extreme importance. Indeed, the form of traditional legal thought systematically transforms new ideas into just another theory, just another technique.[53] Because the cognitive practices are left undisturbed, the new ideas are coopted, distorted, and neutralized by those practices.[54] As a result "[t]he realm of conceivable social relations, the permissible channels of change, the character of the community have already been established by the politics of form."[55]

But what kind of legal thinking is at stake here? Schlag calls this normative legal thinking—the intellectual enterprise of norm-selection and norm-production[56] that is exercised with the pretence that the form is irrelevant.[57] And because the form is invisible, it is also impossible for normative legal thinking to recognize its own formalism.[58] The point is that normative legal thinking is "largely a performative enterprise"—where the form (the language) is used to induce specific kinds of social action.[59] And the kind of social action it induces is almost always conservative:

> Normative legal thought is thus an extremely conservative enterprise—
> conservative in the sense that it tends to reproduce whatever regime is already
> in place.[60]

The Case of *uBuntu*

The real question is, of course, what the connection is between the politics of form and South African interpretation regarding *ubuntu*. My contention is that the formalism in constitutional adjudication is the reason why *ubuntu* has not been used in further judgments. The way in which the concept has been used and defined in the *Makwanyane* case made it impossible to use the concept in subsequent cases. This is the result of three basic rhetoric moves employed by the Constitutional Court—moves that are very familiar to traditional legal thinking. This is not to suggest that the Court employed these moves consciously and deliberately in order to achieve a particular outcome. The point is that these are traditional moves: part of the form and therefore invisible to the performer.

The first move has already been alluded to and need only be restated briefly. Most of the judgments and writers seem to be at pains to show that the values of *ubuntu* are no different from those found in any other civilized society or legal system. Whether this is true or not is not actually the point. The point is that, once you regard *ubuntu* as just a local example of a universal phenomenon, it is no longer a separate concept that needs to be articulated and applied. The only difference then lies in its emphasis on community and there is no indication that this has had any effect on concepts such as dignity, freedom, and justice.[61]

For the sake of argument one can assume that *ubuntu* was intended to play the role of the "other" in South African jurisprudence—a concept that would challenge the accepted theories and methods. But once the "otherness" is denied for the sake of broad acceptance, it cannot play that role. The result is that the "other" is erased and becomes irrelevant. That is the real result of the consensus politics of the Constitutional Court and the formalist insistence on universal truths and definitions.

The second rhetorical move revolves around the way in which *ubuntu* is defined in judgments and in academic writing. If one studies the definitions supplied above, it is immediately clear that defining *ubuntu* is no simple undertaking. To summarize, *ubuntu* is said to include the following values: communality, respect, dignity, value, acceptance, sharing, co-responsibility, humaneness, social justice, fairness, personhood, morality, group solidarity, compassion, joy, love, fulfillment, conciliation, and so on. The problem with this kind of bloated concept is that it tries to do too much. The concept simply collapses under the weight of the expectations!

But that is not the primary problem. The real problem is that the terms included in the definitions are by and large empty. That is not to suggest that a term like "humaneness" has no meaning, but merely that it has no self-evident meaning. Words do not have meaning in themselves and the people who employ them give them meaning within a context. And this is the real failure of the definitions used by the Constitutional Court in particular—they are over-loaded with empty concepts. But it is impossible to divorce the concept of *ubuntu* from the context within which it has meaning:

> We forget that *ubuntu* must be understood within the context of a mainly feudal socio-economic system in which the chief, the chiefdom, the clan and the extended family, were crucial providers of wealth and values . . . Given the fact that the 'global village' is nothing like a 16th century 'African village' consisting of a network of extended families, what is the effect and wisdom of recommending *ubuntu* to blacks in 1999?[62]

The result of this is that the concept becomes endlessly manipulable. As the language games become increasingly complex, they also manage to hide the rhetorical moves that allow judges to use concepts in an abstract way and thus deny their own responsibility.[63]

The third rhetoric move is by far the most important. In most cases it quickly becomes clear that *ubuntu* is presented in such a way that it is clearly an alternative to liberalism: if liberalism is individualistic, *ubuntu* must be communitarian; if liberalism emphasizes individual rights, *ubuntu* must stress group rights; competition versus compassion; confrontation versus conciliation; and so on. But this keeps the debate stuck in the liberalist dichotomies and hierarchies. It limits the choices to either liberalism or communitarianism.[64] It is forced into the politics of form prescribed by liberal formalism. And that denies the idea of *ubuntu* for any transformative potential.

It is one of the most consistent traditional ideas that one should make a simplistic choice between liberalism and communitarianism. This is not by chance—it is the way traditional legal thinking operates. It starts by setting up endless sets of apparently conflicting values or ideas (public or private; subjective or objective; individual or community) and then representing the only option as a choice between these dichotomies. But what if these are not the only choices? And who says that they must be necessarily conflicting? They only seem that way because that is the politics of form.

The conclusion seems clear—*ubuntu* was rendered ineffective as a constitutional value because it did not fit within the discourse of traditional legal thinking. By trying to force it into the mould required, the Court has effectively destroyed its uniqueness and, as a result, its usefulness.

VALUES IN CONSTITUTIONAL INTERPRETATION

What has been said about *ubuntu* is not meant to suggest that there is something wrong with the concept as such—quite the opposite. What it is intended to illustrate is that there is something wrong with the Constitutional Court's approach to constitutional values. It does not do any good to invoke values like "little divinities" without at least thinking about what values are and what their role is in constitutional adjudication. This does not mean that a complete and all-embracing theory of values should be constructed before anything can be done, but simply that all the value talk needs actually to be about values.

Schlag has suggested that, before values can be used in law, one needs to address the ontological status of values first.[65] It is, for example, necessary to determine whether the values in question are ontologically deep[66] or ontologically superficial.[67] This will determine the response to the invocation of values. But it does not advance the issue at all if the ontological depth of particular values is blithely presupposed.

Second, one needs to question the performative roles of values.[68] Values, such as *ubuntu,* for example, can perform the role of "concept, image, ideal, motivation, totem, icon, affect, coercive device (and so on)"[69] and it would be a mistake to confuse one with the other. Values play many roles, not the least of which is the following:

> Values and value-talk can operate as a form of collective denial, a way of not taking into account the social or historical situation . . . Values and value-talk can be a way of arresting troubling and disturbing inquiries.[70]

It seems clear that the judgments dealing with *ubuntu* all assume the ontological depth of the value, although subsequent disagreement on the death penalty might suggest otherwise. But it is in its performative role that the interesting aspect comes to the fore. It seems clear that the value of *ubuntu* was used to stop debate by appealing to an unquestioned origin or ground—an attempt to assume a broad consensus on values that was in no way apparent.

In this regard the problem regarding *ubuntu* serves as an example of a much larger problem regarding constitutional interpretation, namely the approach to constitutional interpretation in general. The current approach is, in my mind, not so much one of "judicious avoidance"[71] as it is a case of "complacent pragmatism."[72] Complacent pragmatism employs three techniques: "immunising value choices by obscuring these choices and the power relations they support; making coercion invisible by assuming a majority perspective on choices; and making an appeal to common-sense notions of (values)."[73]

It does not take much to see that this is exactly what the court has been doing. First, the abstract reasoning about values obscures the social and cultural choices that underlie these values. By treating them as a-contextual concepts, the impression is created that this is not about power at all. It also serves to mask those inequalities that are part-and-parcel of the value being invoked.[74] Second, the judgments and writings on *ubuntu* seem to suggest a consensus that is, at the very least, never established. But by assuming a majority or consensus understanding of the values, all dissenting voices are ignored and this serves to entrench existing practices:

> Complacent techniques display a tendency to essentialist or conceptualist thinking, where real value choices and real power relations are obscured by abstract and supposedly scientific reasoning about abstract rights.[75]

CONCLUSION

> The historical achievement of science and technology has rendered possible the translation of values into technical tasks—the materialization of values.[76]

One of the key insights of neo-Marxism has been that contemporary society is capable of neutralizing any critical or alternative voice by flattening it out. Illustrated with reference to art as the "great refusal," writers like Marcuse indicate that works of alienation are incorporated into the society as part and parcel of that society. The result is that "they become commercials—they sell, comfort, or excite."[77] In this way the anarchist tendencies of certain movements (such as the Punk movement) is transformed into just another fad, a fashion statement. Revolutionary movements "become cogs in a culture-machine which remakes their content."[78]

The same dynamic is at work in contemporary legal thinking and constitutional jurisprudence. Once new and innovative ideas, such as *ubuntu*, are forced into the politics of form of liberal legalism, it is flattened out so that a numbing sameness seems to take over. Very soon the new ideas become just another "flavor of the month" method of achieving the dreams of liberalism.

In the process the philosophical naivety of constitutional jurisprudence is revealed. Values are accepted as immutable, debate-stopping certainties without any apparent awareness of their ontological status as cultural artifacts. Nor is there a hermeneutic sensitivity regarding constitutional interpretation—it is as if the "linguistic turn" in legal philosophy had not taken place. And this is not without consequences:

> Once emancipated from their generative history, values tend to become the ethical equivalent of currency endlessly recyclable, ready for appropriation by any force, ready to underwrite any end. The identities of values become uncertain, their roles indiscriminate.[79]

Exploring *uBuntu*:
Tentative Reflections

Drucilla Cornell and Karin van Marle

In March 2004, the *uBuntu* Project, a project developed out of the Stellenbosch Institute for Advanced Studies, held a one-day conference to discuss the role of *ubuntu* in the new South Africa, and particularly the feasibility of translating *ubuntu* into law. Our article has a modest goal: We seek mainly to articulate the central questions raised in that conference and to deepen the possible significance of those questions for a nuanced constitutional jurisprudence in South Africa.

In this essay we proceed as follows: First, we address the issue of the nature of African philosophy and how an understanding of this relates to debates about *ubuntu*. Central to this discussion is an examination of Derrida's writing on the archive as this relates to the recollection and re-imagination of African gnosis. Second, we attempt to expand from this discussion of gnosis and explore whether *ubuntu* can be used as a justiciable principle. Third, to show how *ubuntu* might be deployed, both as a founding legal ideal and as a working legal principle, we examine Justice Mokgoro's opinion in the *Khosa* case.[1]

uBuntu is a controversial value or ideal in South Africa. Philosophers such as Shutte have forcefully argued that *ubuntu* should be adopted as a new ethic for South Africa.[2] On the other hand, critics of *ubuntu* have argued against those who would make *ubuntu* an essential ethical ideal or moral value in the new South Africa. Broadly construed, those criticisms range from the claim that *ubuntu* was once a meaningful value, but now gives nothing to young South Africans, to the claim that *ubuntu* is inherently patriarchal and conservative. Still others argue that *ubuntu* is such a bloated concept that it means everything to everyone, and as a bloated concept it should not be translated into a constitutional principle. Although *ubuntu* was included in the epilogue of the interim Constitution, there have not been many attempts to incorporate *ubuntu* into postapartheid jurisprudence. Where Courts have referred to *ubuntu*, they treated it as a unidimensional concept and not as a philosophical doctrine.[3]

The debate over whether or not *ubuntu* can be translated into a justiciable principle turns not only on the definition one gives to *ubuntu*, but also on how and why *ubuntu* can be considered an African or South African value. One panel at the conference focused exclusively on the question of whether *ubuntu* is a South African value, and even more broadly an African value or ideal, and what this would mean for the future of the Constitution. The three panelists agreed that *ubuntu*, or something very close to it, appears in most African languages. It is beyond the scope of this article to try to address the complex ethno-philosophical questions of whether or not *ubuntu* actually represents a key ethical principle or ideal in African philosophy in general. However, we realize, at the very least, that the question of what is and what can constitute an African philosophy lies at the very heart of this discussion. A related question is what role African philosophy, including African political and ethical philosophy, should play in the development of a constitutional jurisprudence for a new South Africa. To help us respond to these questions, we turn to the work of two philosophers: Valentin Yves Mudimbe and Jacques Derrida.

AFRICAN GNOSIS: WHAT IS AFRICAN PHILOSOPHY?

Mudimbe has suggested the word *gnosis* to configure African ethno-philosophy.[4] And why is African philosophy necessarily ethno-philosophy? Mudimbe powerfully argues that the question of what African philosophy is must be pursued through a genealogy of its social and historical origins, including a genealogy of the anthropological methods used to articulate African gnosis and the epistemological context in which it has been made possible.

These intellectual explorations must inevitably deal with the troubling social and historical reality that the very question of what constitutes African philosophy cannot be separated from the brutal imposition of colonialism on the continent of Africa. Mudimbe attempts to analyze the complexity of epistemological legitimation. Who, in the last few centuries at least, has been given the right and credentials to write, describe, and produce opinions of what is African philosophy? In addressing this question about right and credentials, we must also grapple with the issue of how African gnosis, to use Mudimbe's word, has inevitably and inextricably been bound up with the social and scientific constructs of a Western episteme. As Mudimbe reminds us, one aspect of colonialism is that it seeks to organize and transform the non-European world through European constructs. But this does not mean that gnosis is reducible to European constructs. Mudimbe's definition of gnosis, at least, gives us a word that yields a form of knowledge that cannot be reduced to doxa, or opinion, or episteme understood as a scientific or social scientific construct associated with the so-called modern West. Gnosis, as Mudimbe defines it:

means seeking to know, inquiry, methods of knowing, investigation, and even acquaintance with someone. Often the word is used in a more specialised sense, that of higher and esoteric knowledge, and thus it refers to a structured, common, and conventional knowledge, but one strictly under the control of specific procedures for its use as well as transmission.[5]

There is clearly much more work to be done in terms of the historical genealogy and, indeed, the anthropological investigation into what African philosophy is or can be, and perhaps most importantly what it ethically should be, in the struggle of African nations to define themselves in the purportedly postcolonial world. But for our purposes, at least, we want to accept the postulate that there is a form of knowledge—gnosis that allows us to engage in an ontological, or what Mudimbe calls anthropou-Iogos—hermeneutic that could facilitate investigation into African or South African indigenous systems.

But, how does one pick up the project that Mudimbe has started for us? The answer is two-fold. First, there is a sense that we are investigating the way the meaning of values and ideals comes out of an engagement with the past and with interpretation about the meaning of that past as it relates to the configuration of such values and ideals. Second, the South African Constitution has been conceived through different metaphors, one of which is the archive.[6] This metaphor seems to be the best way to grapple with the promise of the Constitution. And so, we begin with a more general consideration of the archive.

FEVERISH WORDS AND THE ROLE OF ARCHIVE

The problem of the *archive* and what counts as archival material, haunts all historical and anthropological research and is for obvious reasons important in our exploration of and reflections on *ubuntu*. Derrida argues that what an archive is resists conceptualization, more appropriately being rendered or configured as an impression. The archive *impresses* the past on us, and yet the way in which it does so inescapably involves the one who is recording or describing the impression in its transmission as authoritative. What the archive encodes is how the past makes an impression on human beings. It encodes how we are to remember in terms of both an internal memory that constitutes a *we*, and also at the same time in terms of a purportedly legitimating memory for those who are outside the *we* that is therefore constituted. In his work on the archive, Derrida describes his own use of the word *impression* instead of concept as follows:

> We have no concept, only an impression, a series of impressions associated with a word. To the rigor of the concept, I am opposing here the vagueness or the open imprecision, the relative indetermination of such a notion. 'Archive' is only a notion, an impression associated with a word and for which, together with Freud, we do not have a concept. We only have an impression, an insis-

tent impression through the unstable feeling of a shifting figure, of a schema, or of an in-finite or indefinite process.[7]

However, the disjointedness of the archive takes on a particular meaning in terms of Africa. As Mudimbe shows us in his excellent genealogy of African ethno-philosophy, the recording of this philosophy originates with anthropological testimony about it. There is a central problem with this testimonial as to how African rituals, practices, and social encounters are described, namely that the impression made by the natives on the anthropologists are given expression and articulation in terms of Western epistemological schemas. Thus, Africa comes to be invented by anthropologists and shaped by the changing trends within that discipline.[8]

Mudimbe demonstrates that even the political movements, such as negritude, which have affirmed the uniqueness of African philosophy, only do so through an archive that comes to them from Western anthropologists engaging in a study of a form of knowledge that was primarily oral—passed down in ritual, aphorisms, and parables—and therefore not presented as the form of knowledge some today would recognize as the discipline of philosophy. But does this mean that African philosophy does not exist? Does this mean, further, that there is no sense in trying to trace the geography of reason? Not at all. Indeed, we would argue that the opposite is the case, since what have been considered the governing ideas of philosophical reason have now been localized and consigned to the West. Mudimbe offers us a genealogy of how African philosophy came to be, and continues to be invented and reimagined in part through the reworking of its genealogy. His work is exactly that: a genealogy of how African philosophy came to be as ethno-philosophy.

Derrida adds to Mudimbe's explorations a philosophical understanding of how what is true to Africa may be unique in form and therefore have its own unique genealogy, and yet can still present us with the more general dilemma of the archival, which is not simply a problem for Africanists, but for all who engage with the significance, both politically and ethically, with the geography of reason and of the meaning of memory. We can, however, make use of Derrida's obsession (or, to use his word, *fever*). We see how a past and with it an identity impresses itself upon us so that we inherit that impression as it constitutes us as a *we*. We also see that the archive is inherently troubled in that it always involves *us* in interpreting the trait of being, and indeed authorizing it as that which is a mark of an identity. The archive in that sense both encircles and marks us, and it is through that encirclement that we endlessly find ourselves in a spiral of reinterpretation that opens out into a future as we continuously reaffirm what are and what are not the authoritative traits of an identity.

Derrida reminds us of the force of remembering any trait of being that we call identity and the consignation that orders the archive:

This archontic function is not solely toponomological. It does not only require that the archive be deposited somewhere, on a stable substrate, and at the disposition of a legitimate hermeneutic authority. The archontic power, which also gathers the functions of unification, of identification, of classification, must be paired with what we will call the power of consignation. By consignation, we do not only mean, in the ordinary sense of the word, the act of assigning residence or of entrusting so as to put into reserve (to consign, to deposit), in a place and on a substrate, but here the act of consigning through gathering together signs. It is not only the traditional *consignatio*, that it, the written proof, but what all *consignatio* begins by presupposing. Consignation aims to coordinate a single *corpus*, in a system or a synchrony in which all the elements articulate the unity of an ideal configuration. In an archive, there should not be any absolute dissociation, any heterogeneity or secret, which could separate (*secernere*), or partition, in an absolute manner. The archontic principle of the archive is also a principle of consignation, that is, of gathering together.[9]

The archive, then, in a sense shelters and keeps safe the impression of the past, and this act of self-repetition is inevitably a promise to the future, since what is preserved is meant to be preserved, not only for those living, but also for those to come. What is preserved is a confirmation of its significance (using that work deliberately to keynote both meaning and importance):

> The injunction, even when it summons memory or the safeguard of the archive, turns incontestably toward the future to come. It orders to promise, but it orders repetition, and first of all self-repetition, self-confirmation in a yes, yes. If repetition is thus inscribed at the heart of the future to come, one must also import there, in the same stroke, the death drive, the violence of forgetting, superrepression (suppression and repression), the anarchive, in short, the possibility of putting to death the very thing, whatever its name, which carries the law in its tradition: the archon of the archive, the table, what carries the table and who carries the table, the subjectile, the substrate, and the subject of the law.[10]

What is known as African is inseparable from an ethical and political contest over what African can or should be. That this knowledge is inevitably political and ethical explains the obsession, or what Derrida calls the fever, over how words like *ubuntu* come to be given meaning and significance as part of a tradition that marks both the importance of what is, either or both, African or South African. It is, of course, also a debate over who has the right to name what is African or South African and from where that right comes.

Sheltering, for Derrida, is always a matter of both preserving and of protecting a legacy. This protection, since it can never be complete, carries within it what Derrida calls the *secret*. But, gnosis, as Mudimbe has defined it, is a kind of secret knowledge in a special sense in that it has been accessible at least in certain times and places only by certain people (priests and priestesses, for example) with permission to access realms of being and forms of knowledge to which others cannot ascend. There is yet another sense in which gnosis is secret, in that it resists translation into the very anthropological language that gave it its being. As Mudimbe explains:

> Gnosis is by definition a kind of secret knowledge. The changes of motives, the succession of theses about foundation, and the differences of scale in interpretations that I have tried to bring to light about African gnosis witness to the vigour of a knowledge which is sometimes African by virtue of its authors and promoters, but which extends to a Western epistemological territory.[11]

Is there anything there that matters as African? And who is the *we* that will decide that question? Those who think that the answer has to be *no*, that there is nothing there that can be identified as African, may have been misled by the wisdom of deconstruction, and therefore may have missed the heart of deconstruction, and even of genealogy. Why? Because they inscribe themselves in a process of denial that is inseparable from the horrifying realty of the colonialism that identified Africa with all that was dark, unthinkable, and only knowable as what should not be for itself and thus must be overcome in the name of civilization. Our point is to show that the idea of an African philosophy cannot be summarily dismissed, which is why we point to some of the most sophisticated thinking on the notion of identity and its connection to the process of archivalization. For us, the debate over the meaning of *ubuntu* and, more significantly, its identification as both African and South African, is feverish because it is integral to the struggle over what Africa or South Africa can or should come to be in the future. We more than understand the risk of essentializing Africa. But we believe that the only cure for this risk is through the kind of re-evaluation through anthropology and genealogy that Mudimbe calls for. Otherwise we simply fall back into formulations that carry within them the worst aspect of the colonial project: the full-scale trivializing of the traditional mode of life and the spiritual framework of the African *Weltanschauungen*, and denial of the gnosis through which we struggle to articulate and interpret its meaning.

THE CONSTITUTION AS ARCHIVE

Commentators have employed various metaphors to describe the South African Constitution. The image of the Constitution as bridge, as used in the post-amble of the interim Constitution and also further developed, for example, by the late Mureinik[12] and the late Justice Mahomed,[13] has frequently been recalled to stand in service of constitutional claims to reconciliation, healing, and unity. Du Plessis chooses three other images in his reflection on the Constitution in the context of reconciliation, memory, and justice, namely the Constitution as promise, monument, and memorial.

For Du Plessis, a constitution serves the dual function of narration as well as authorship of a nation's history. He relates what he calls "the potency with which [a constitution] can mould a politics of memory" to "the authority with which it can shape the politics of the day."[14] However, he concedes that the Constitution is but one of many participants in telling a nation's history and accordingly also one of many determinants of a nation's future. He explains that the possibility of the Constitution's promise is dependent on how the Constitution deals with memory, thereby drawing a connection between past and future, and, one could say, reasserting the point that future events should also influence constitutional memory.

Du Plessis, like others,[15] focuses on the tensions within the Constitution as a form of redemption. Following the work of Snyman, he describes the Constitution as simultaneously monumental and memorial.[16] Although monuments and memorials share a concern with memory, they differ significantly in the way they remember. Monuments celebrate and memorials commemorate. For example, after a war has been won, a monument will be created, celebrating the heroes and achievements of war. Memorials are created to commemorate the dead. In discussing the Constitution as monument, Du Plessis refers to the Constitution as "hardly a modest text."[17] Both interim and final constitutions make reference and lay claim to the achievement of a "peaceful transition" to a "non-racial democracy" to the recognition of the "injustices of our past" and the honoring of "those who suffered for justice and freedom in our land" to the need for healing the "divisions of the past" and for building a "united and democratic South Africa."[18] Du Plessis also refers to the entrenchment of the values of democracy, human dignity, equality, and freedom as "monumental flair."[19] To conclude his discussion of the Constitution as monument, he refers to some of the Constitutional Court's decisions, most notably *S v. Makwanyane*,[20] in which capital punishment was declared unconstitutional. He describes the various decisions as "imbued with value statements" that not only focused on constitutionalism nationally, but also internationally. Du Plessis continues to argue that, although no one should be cynical about the monumental achievements of the South African Constitution, one should also embrace the "restrained constitution." For Du Plessis, the restrained constitution is the constitution as memorial, namely the idea that a written constitutional text cannot alone provide justice, but rather reminds us to strive for justice.[21]

Du Plessis's metaphorical description of the Constitution can be useful in the tentative refiguring of the Constitution through yet another image, the Constitution as archive.[22] With reference to the meaning of archive as the place where things commence, the place from which order is given and the place that contains memory, an easy link between archive and Constitution can be made. As the archive traces only particular aspects of the past, the Constitution similarly traces only particular aspects of the South African past and nation. Also, the principles and ideals embodied in the Constitution are already interpretations of the past and the nation's idealized aspirations for the new South Africa. Like the archive cannot fully contain memory, the Constitution cannot encapsulate all that must be remembered of the old South Africa. The Constitution as monument risks the death drive of the Constitution, the drive to destroy all traces without any remainder of what is other to the past of the country it engraves. The Constitution, figured as archive, works against the death drive of the Constitution as monument.

To return to Derrida's work on the archive, Derrida himself reminds us that the word *archive* has at its root in a nomological principle:

> But rather the word 'archive'—and with the archive of so familiar a word. This name apparently co-ordinates two principles in one: the principle according to nature or history, there where things commence—physical, historical, or ontological principles—but also the principle according to the law, there where men and gods command, there where authority, social order are exercised, in this place from which order is given—nomological principle.[23]

As we have seen earlier, Derrida's careful work on the meaning of the archive always shows us that the reality to which the archive testifies is always beyond itself in that it points to a future implicit in the ambiguity of the word itself; implicit in the sense that the command of a nomos, an ethical command, is always beyond the simple *there* that is always purportedly being discovered. Thus, a constitution understood as an archive that always carries within it this ambiguity turns us to a future of struggle in which we confront the inescapability of our responsibility for the meaning we give to the archive as a nomological principle.[24]

One aspect of understanding the Constitution as an archive is that the struggle over the values and ideals of the South African Constitution should be made explicit as crucial to the continuous transfiguration of the social and political reality of the new South Africa. For what is being constituted in the new South Africa, if not a new nomos that continuously shapes and reconfigures both the meaning of what is new and South African? This *new* carries within it a commandment to the moral memory of apartheid, which it partially, at least, defines itself against. An interesting feature of the South African Constitution is that it points to this new nomos that must be brought into being. Thus, it does not turn, as many other constitutions do, on a past that legitimates its basis. It is explicitly future-oriented and thus purposive in a sense that it seeks to bring the new nomos into being. Mokgoro's demand for the ontological transparency of the ideals and values through which this new nomos will come into being shows her profound commitment and fidelity to the purposive self-understanding of the South African Constitution. In her concurring opinion in the Constitutional Court's decision to reject the death penalty, Mokgoro explicitly called for making the values that inform constitutional decision explicit in the decisions themselves. To quote Mokgoro:

> In order to guard against what Didcott 1, in his concurring judgment, terms the trap of undue subjectivity, the interpretation clause prescribes that Courts

seek guidance in international norms and foreign judicial precedent, reflective of the values which underlie an open and democratic society based on freedom and equality. By articulating rather than suppressing values that underlie our decisions, we are not being subjective. On the contrary, we set out in a transparent and objective way the foundations of our interpretive choice and make them available for criticism. Section 35 seems to acknowledge the paucity of home-grown judicial precedent upholding human rights, which is not surprising considering the repressive nature of the past legal order. It requires Courts to proceed to public international law and foreign case law for guidance in constitutional interpretation, thereby promoting the ideal and the internationally accepted values in the cultivation of a Human Rights jurisprudence for South Africa. However, I am of the view that our own (ideal) indigenous value systems are a premise from which we need to proceed and are not wholly unrelated to our goal of a society based on freedom and equality.[25]

As Derrida reminds us, the archive is a troubled word, precisely because of the ambiguity inherent in the two meanings of beginning. But this trouble can be good for a constitution understood as an archive of what must be other to the past of apartheid, and that in this other is always a future-oriented affirmation of the very ideals that mark the past as a wrong to be overcome. Mokgoro's call that constitutional decisions make the values and ideals of the Constitution explicit can, at least, turn us back to an understanding of constitutionalism as in service of democratic struggle in which what is constituted is, at least in part, the space for the contest over ideas and values that seek to keep the just promise of the South African Constitution alive. Ideals and values should not be conflated, and the significance of the difference between these terms was debated in the seminar. Values are defined as what are actually liked, prized, esteemed, or approved of by actual groups or individuals. In utilitarianism, for example, values are the basic measure of the worthiness of any moral proposition. Ideals, alternatively, mark a place of irreducibility to what is actually valued or prized. It is this irreducibility that can always demand transformation of current tastes and desires in the name of the horizon that the ideal holds out. Obviously the Constitution understood as archive, which demands that the ethical moment always be recognized, in its commandments would include struggle over both values and ideals. Mokgoro's call for ontological transparency, then, is crucial if the Constitution seeks to redeem the past of apartheid, and yet to do so in such a way as to remember that justice itself is always an ideal to be struggled for, never one that can be realized once and for all even in the best of constitutions.

UBUNTU BEHIND THE LAW

One crucial aspect of African philosophy which is articulated by anthropologists, theologians and philosophers, who disagree on every other aspect of African philosophy, is its focus on metadynamics and the relationship, or active play of forces, as the nature of being. *uBuntu* in a profound sense, and whatever else it may be, implies an interactive ethic, or an ontic orientation in which who and how we can be as human beings is always being shaped in our interaction with each other. This ethic is not then a simple form of communalism or communitarianism, if one means by those terms the privileging of the community over the individual. For what is at stake here is the process of becoming a person or, more strongly put, how one is given the chance to become a person at all. The community is not something outside, some static entity that stands against individuals. The community is only as it is continuously brought into being by those who make it up, a phrase we use deliberately. The community, then, is always being formed through an ethic of being with others, and this ethic is in turn evaluated by how it empowers people. In a dynamic process the individual and community are always in the process of coming into being. Individuals become individuated through their engagement with others and their ability to live in line with their capability is at the heart of how ethical interactions are judged.

However, since we are gathered together in the first place by our engagements with others, a strong notion of responsibility inheres in *ubuntu*. Since our togetherness is actually part of our creative force that comes into being as we form ourselves with each other, our freedom is almost indistinguishable from our responsibility to the way in which we create a life in common with each other. If we ever try to bring *ubuntu* into speech, we might attempt to define it as this integral connection between freedom as empowerment, which is always enhanced and indeed only made possible through engagement with other people. Each one of us is responsible for making up our togetherness, which in turn yields a process in which each person can come into their own.

This interactive, ontic orientation reveals how freedom can be understood as indivisible. As Mandela himself wrote: "Freedom is indivisible. The chains on any one of my people are the chains on all of them. The chains on all of my people are the chains on me."[26] Without justice and without all of us transforming ourselves so as to be together in freedom, our individuality will be thwarted since we will all be bound, if differently so, in a field of unfreedom. Again to quote Mandela:

> A man who takes away another man's freedom is a prisoner of hatred. He is locked behind the bars of prejudice and narrow-mindedness. I am not truly free if I am taking away someone else's freedom, just as surely as I am not free when my freedom is taken from me. The oppressed and the oppressor alike are robbed of their humanity.[27]

Mandela refers to the word *humanity* as an ideal in that *ubuntu*, as it is associated with justice and freedom, is something to live up to. On the other hand, the dynamic, interactive ethic that *ubuntu* expresses has as much to do with reshaping our humanness through the modality of being together as it does with defining what are, for example, the essential attributes of our humanity that make us moral beings. This understanding that our humanness is shaped in our interactions with one another and within a force field created and sustained by those interactions, explains one of the most interesting aspects of *ubuntu*, which is the notion that one's humanness can be diminished by the violent actions of others, including the violent actions of the state. We can at least make sense of why *ubuntu* was so crucial in the decision rejecting the constitutionality of the death penalty in South Africa. In a society in which the death penalty is allowed, state murder is institutionalized and this form of vengeance becomes part of the field in which we have to operate. Vengeance feeds on itself, whether it is perpetuated by the state or the individual. Freedom as understood by *ubuntu* thinking, then, is not freedom from; it is freedom to be together in a way that enhances everyone's capability to transform themselves in their society.[28] Since *ubuntu* is an ontic orientation within an interactive ethic, it is indeed a sliding signifier whose meaning in terms of a definition of good and bad is always being re-evaluated in the context of actual interactions, as these enhance the individual's and community's powers. In this sense, the ultimate irony may be that it is precisely the bloatedness of *ubuntu*, to use the word of one of its critics, is actually its strength.[29] We do not pretend to be giving the ultimate definition of *ubuntu*, because indeed that would go against the spirit of *ubuntu*, but instead we simply choose to emphasize certain key aspects as these were articulated in the seminars and the interviews conducted by one of the authors. Let us return now to the role *ubuntu* might play in the constitutional jurisprudence of the new South Africa. To do so we raise two further questions.

UBUNTU AND THE SOUTH AFRICAN CONSTITUTION

The first question, which was addressed over and over again in the seminar, is: Who is the *we* of the nation state of South Africa? The afternoon panel raised this question with particular attention to the inadequate representation of black South African ideals, such as *ubuntu* in the final version of the Constitution. To remind the reader, *ubuntu* appeared in the 1993 postamble to the Constitution, but was not carried over into the 1996 Constitution. The panelists are not alone in this concern. Moosa argues that:

> The omission of *ubuntu* must therefore mean that the Constitution was de-Africanised in the re-drafting process. With that the religio-cultural values of African people are also devalued. Thus the desire to formulate a core legal system, which encapsulates the multiple value systems in South Africa, was not necessarily accomplished in the final Constitution.[30]

The second question, which is undoubtedly related to the first, is: Can *ubuntu* be operationalized as a legal principle or justiciable right in the South African legal system? Before returning to these questions, we simply want to suggest that debates over *ubuntu* on both sides assume the possibility of an ontological hermeneutic that can interpret the gnosis of indigenous systems of law in South Africa, and articulate them so as to begin the debate as to their relative importance within the South African legal system.

Our suggestion here is that the ethnographic or anthropological aspect of work, such as the *uBuntu* Project, not only includes the interviews conducted by and with young black South Africans as to the meaning and significance of *ubuntu*.[31] Of course, it does include these materials. But there is a broader claim that we also seek to emphasize. Mudimbe, rightfully to our minds, points to a form of anthropological knowledge as inherent in the understanding of what African philosophy and legal theory can be. The attempt to articulate and interpret the meaning of *ubuntu* and the struggle over its political and ethical importance in the new South Africa demand an interdisciplinary inquiry into the conditions that have shaped the meaning of the debate. Anthropology and philosophy in this sense become intertwined at the very foundation at how this debate can take place in the first place.

Obviously, the question of whether African traditions have been adequately addressed in the South African Constitution turns on the possibility of interpreting the meaning of *ubuntu*. As we will see, it also informs whether or not *ubuntu* can be operationalized in constitutional law. There is a deep sense in which we cannot even get to the possibility of addressing the two questions on the role of *ubuntu* and constitutional jurisprudence, unless we have some understanding of how we can articulate and interpret the ethics of an African or South African *Weltanschauung*. Our claim here is that the interdisciplinary approach of the *uBuntu* Project is necessary for the rethinking of what kind of philosophy African philosophy might be, and that this kind of rethinking of philosophy may be important, not only for African philosophy, but for what philosophy, including political and legal philosophy, should become in the twenty-first century.

In our discussions in the seminar, the question of the relationship between *ubuntu* and law turned to some degree on the understanding of what a legal principle is. Indeed, Cornell's debate with Justice Sachs on the question of whether or not *ubuntu* could be operationalized turned on the question of how one defines a legal principle, as well as what principles should be included in constitutional jurisprudence. Sachs has been criticized in his work on human rights for not providing, in his attempt to reconcile competing rights situations, underlying principles of political or ethical morality to support the hierarchy that would allow us to resolve such conflicts as more than a matter of strategy.[32]

Richard Dworkin has famously argued, for example, that we can only reconcile competing rights, and indeed competing principles and ideals, such as liberty and equality that inform most modern legal systems, if we have underlying ethical principles that allow us to configure the way in which those principles, rights and ideals can be understood in relation to one another. In the case of Dworkin, for example, the constitutional ideals of liberty and equality can only be reconciled if they turn on a deeper level of commitment to both of the two principles making up what he has termed ethical individualism. Those two principles, quoting Dworkin, are as follows:

> The first principle is the principle of equal importance: It is important, from an objective point of view, that human lives be successful rather than wasted, and that this is equally important, from that objective point of view, for each human life. The second is the principle of special responsibility: Though we must all recognise the equal objective importance of the success of a human life, one person has a special and final responsibility for that success—the person whose life it is.[33]

Our point here is not to endorse ethical individualism. Indeed, we do not think that ethical individualism provides us with principles adequate to the task of building the new South Africa. But it is important to show that the actual rights in a constitution inevitably implicate deeper principles and that in a case of competing rights we will need to make explicit an appeal to those deeper principles in trying to identify a hierarchy between them. Sachs, like many other judges of the Constitutional Court, defends dignity as the ultimate principle of the Constitution. Although we agree with Sachs's critics that Sachs is not always clear on the relationship between rights and the Constitution and its underlying principles, it was evident in the seminar that Sachs is defending dignitarianism as the fundamental principle of the South African Constitution. Dignity has been defended by the Constitutional Court as not only an underlying principle, but also as a right, and thus dignity also functions on many different levels in the constitutional jurisprudence of South Africa. The court in Dawood said:

> Human dignity . . . informs constitutional adjudication and interpretation at a range of levels. It is a value that informs the interpretation of many, possibly, all, other rights . . . Section 10, however, makes it plain that dignity is not only a value fundamental to our Constitution; it is a justiciable and enforceable right that must be respected and protected. In many cases, however, where the value of human dignity is offended, the primary constitutional breach occasioned may be of a more specific right such as the right to bodily integrity, the right to equality or the right not to be subjected to slavery, servitude or forced labour.[34]

Sachs is certainly willing to have the spirit of *ubuntu* pervade constitutional law and indeed, to the degree it is cited in actual legal cases, recognizes that it is a constitutionally cited principle. At least in the seminar he seemed to argue that it would damage *ubuntu* to turn it into a judicial principle or right, although, as we will see shortly, Sachs seems to be rethinking his position on *ubuntu* and constitutional law.

Drucilla Cornell responded in a twofold way. First, she agreed with Sachs that dignity is a crucial principle in the South African Constitution. Broadly construed, dignity is a metaphysical fact of humanity that cannot be lost and yet can be violated. To recognize dignity as a metaphysical fact does not mean that there cannot be wrongs against dignity, because the ultimate wrong to dignity is to refuse to other human beings the status of being human. Clearly, in the context of apartheid, South African blacks were denied the status of being human. Dignity is a crucial principle and, more specifically, an ever important reminder that skin color or any other supposedly biological attribute can never be a reason to deny anyone their inclusion in the idea of humanity.[35] But social realities should also not be allowed to undermine the truth of that metaphysical fact. In other words, we never want to make the argument that, because of the social conditions in which someone lives, they could lose their dignity as if it is simply the positive attribute of being a human being that is there or not. Thus, we cannot use dignity in and of itself to call for the promotion of sweeping egalitarian transformation as if there were positive conditions that must be there as part and parcel of requirements of dignity.

This understanding of dignity can help us explain why Immanuel Kant himself never argued for the second and third generational rights that are included in the South African Constitution. In Kant, the metaphysical fact of dignity turns on the ideal aspect of our humanity, which inheres in humanity, placing itself under the moral law and thus achieving freedom of self-legislation by so doing. Only through such self-legislation do we rise above the determinants of our natural life, and thus a community of self-legislators would, at least on the level of the hypothetical imagination, be able to constitute a moral community as an ideal in which freedom would be a self-limiting principle. By self-limiting principle, we mean my freedom would be limited by your freedom and that we would agree to this limitation because of the moral nature of freedom itself. The social contract ideal in Kant yields an integral relationship between duty and right.[36] My rights are also my duties to you, but my duties to you, since they are limited by the very rights they entail, will never go beyond this one-to-one correspondence between rights and duties. Kant gives us a moral notion of the law of a modern legal system as formed in and through this experiment in the hypothetical imagination of a moral social contract based on maximizing the negative freedom of all. *uBuntu*, as it has been defined by Mokgoro, gives us a very different notion of the founding principle of law and with it a very different notion of rights and responsibility.

UBUNTU AS A FOUNDING PRINCIPLE OF LAW

To quote Justice Mokgoro:

> *Ubuntu*(-ism), which is central to age-old African custom and tradition, however, abounds with values and ideas which have the potential of shaping not

only current indigenous law institutions, but South African jurisprudence as a whole. Examples that come to mind are: The original conception of law perceived not as a tool for personal defence, but as an opportunity given to all to survive under the protection of the order of the communal entity; communalism which emphasises group solidarity and interests generally, and all rules which sustain it, as opposed to individual interests, with its likely utility in building a sense of national unity among South Africans; the conciliatory character of the adjudication process which aims to restore peace and harmony between members rather than the adversarial approach which emphasises retribution and seems repressive. The lawsuit is viewed as a quarrel between community members and not as a conflict; the importance of group solidarity requires restoration of peace between them; the importance of public ritual and ceremony in the communication of information within the group; the idea that law, experienced by an individual within the group, is bound to individual duty as opposed to individual rights or entitlement. Closely related is the notion of sacrifice for group interests and group solidarity so central to *ubuntu*(-ism); the importance of sacrifice for every advantage or benefit, which has significant implications for reciprocity and caring within the communal entity.[37]

Clearly, Mokgoro's rendering of the understanding of *ubuntu* as it relates to traditional law gives us a very different conceptualization of the law than even the one embodied in the Kantian ideal of the social contract. One question that was raised in the seminar was, should *ubuntu*, as defined by Mokgoro, function at the highest level of the legal imaginary, as the material of the experiment in the imagination of what the *we* of South Africa should be constituted to be. Further, by keeping the emphasis on freedom in *ubuntu*, this other understanding of the founding principle of law could even be inclusive of dignity and explain why dignity is so important in the Constitution of South Africa, without forcing dignity to do more work that it can do, at least when it is grasped as a metaphysical fact, a postulate of reason and not an attribute of persons. We will not try to answer the sweeping nature of that first question. Yet, it is clear that *ubuntu*, as it is defined by Mokgoro, as a founding principle of law, would not have the same kind of one-to-one correspondence of right and duty that it does under social contract theory. Obligation, and even a legally imposed duty, can go beyond that allowable under social contract theory, since the enhancement of a just community is crucial to the freedom of all in that community and for the quality of life more generally. Responsibility could thus entail the acceptance of measures that would be deemed unfair under traditional Western conceptions of the social contract that usually start with fairness, even if they disagree about the content of fairness. Thus, for example, beneficiaries of racism in South Africa could be held to a duty to correct it that might be formally unfair, such that they could be expected, for example, to pay higher electricity bills than blacks. Thus, they would not be treated equally, at least under a so-called neutral theory of equality and fairness. Mokgoro clearly does not want to limit the use of *ubuntu* to a vague spirit that pervades the Constitution. She had forthrightly and correctly argued, to our mind, that the founding principles of the Constitution and the ideals they uphold must be made explicit in actual legal decisions. It is important to remember here our earlier discussion of responsibility and freedom in which the creative power of the individual is both deepened and enhanced by being in a community that takes support for people seriously. This sort of enhancement may not be reduced to any self-interested benefit on the individual level in any immediate sense. The idea is that in a just community the shared force will realize our shared humanity, which is, of course, a benefit beyond price.

But it is not only its ability to defend a notion of obligation that goes beyond social contract that might make *ubuntu* important. It is also in its emphasis on the just quality of the community and the enhancement of that just quality that distinguishes *ubuntu* from other notions of community that reduce it to an imagined social contract between already individuated persons. In her opinion, in the *Khosa* case, Mokgoro did not justify her decision through the use of *ubuntu*, yet her conclusions in the case reflect an *ubuntu*-inspired jurisprudence. The fate of the people in this case recalled the following words of Weil, quoted by Christodoulidis in another context: "You do not interest me. No man can say these words to another without committing a cruelty and offending against justice."[38] The facts of the *Khosa* case were a clear example of where the state through the law, through parliamentary legislation, confirmed that claim. The message was that, if you are not a citizen of this country, "you do not interest me," or at least interest me "enough," to care for your well-being.[39]

In this decision, the court had to confront a challenge to a certain provision of the Social Assistance Act 59 of 1992. The Applicants in both matters were Mozambique citizens who were permanent residents in South Africa. In the case of the first applicant, the mother, applied for child support grants for her children under the age of seven and another grant, a care dependency grant, for a child aged 12 who suffered from diabetes. The second Applicant applied for an old-age grant. The Applicants in both matters were denied the grants because they were not citizens of South Africa. In a decision to uphold the validity of an order of the High Court, Mokgoro ruled that the High Court's order should indeed be upheld and the court itself had the responsibility to read the words *permanent resident* into the challenged sections of the Social Security Act. The Applicants argued that sections 26, 27, and 28 of the Constitution use the word *everyone* in the first two cases and the words *every child* in the third case, and that delimiting access to social service grants violated the Constitution on its face in which it is written that everyone is eligible.

Mokgoro obviously could have limited the reach of her decision to the group before her, who were both Mozambicans. There is a tragic past that the South Africa of apartheid rule had with Mozambique. Many of the freedom fighters of the African National Congress, including members of a guerilla army formed by Mandela, fled to Mozambique and based their operations there. The result was an ongoing set of military interventions into Mozambique that violated the integrity of the country and to this day continues to make life in Mozambique difficult. One classic example is that a relatively large amount of Mozambican land is still heavily mined. The mines were installed by the South African government under apartheid and now those lands are of little industrial or agricultural use. Due to this tragic past, Mokgoro could have made a special exception for Mozambican refugees, but she chose not to rest her decision on that past or the special responsibility that might grow out of it. Instead, she took the message of the Constitution to heart because the relevant sections gave the rights to *everyone*, and that it was this word that demanded interpretation.

There might be something else at play in her decision that is more important than the pure legal discussion—something beyond law and legal language, something beyond the rights that Weil captured as follows:

> At the bottom of the heart of every human being, from earliest infancy until the tomb, there is something that goes on indomitably expecting, in the teeth of all experience of crimes committed, suffered, and witnessed, that good and not evil will be done to him. It is this, above all, that is sacred in every human being . . . This profound and childlike and unchanging expectation of good in the heart is not what is involved when we agitate for our rights. The motive which prompts a little boy to watch jealously to see if his brother has a slightly larger piece of cake arises from a much more superficial level of the soul. The word justice means two very different things according to whether it refers to the one or the other level. It is only the former one that matters.[40]

A certain politics and ethics might be at play, a concern with protecting and enhancing lives, striving for a society where no one, but at the very least the state, is not allowed to say "you do not interest me." The inspiration for this politics and ethics could be the notion of *ubuntu* at least hinted at in the following excerpt from Mokgoro's judgment:

> Sharing responsibility for the problems and consequences of poverty equally as a community represents the extent to which wealthier members of the community view the minimal well-being of the poor as connected with their personal well-being and the well-being of the community as a whole.[41]

Mokgoro argues strongly that the grants in all cases should be ordered and that it was not enough to accept the compromise that was offered by the Respondents, that they would allow these particular Mozambicans access to the grants. Mokgoro accepted the Applicants' argument that the refusal of these grants denied them the right to life and dignity under the Constitution. There is a deep sense in which, for Mokgoro, the humanity of the residents could not be denied because they were not citizens and in that sense her argument, in our mind, rightfully appeals to dignity. To quote Mokgoro again:

> This Court has adopted a purposive approach to the interpretation of rights. Given that the Constitution expressly provides that the Bill of Rights enshrines the rights of "all people in our country," and in the absence of any indication that the section 27(1) right is to be restricted to citizens as in other provisions in the Bill of Rights, the word "everyone" in this section cannot be construed as referring only to "citizens."[42]

Mokgoro explicitly rejects the American solution in this problem, which is to treat citizens differently than noncitizens. Indeed, the Respondents made the argument that many developed countries, and not just the United States, made distinctions between citizens and noncitizens in the granting of social welfare grants. Mokgoro distinguished her own decision from the U.S. Supreme Court by arguing that the reasonableness by which differentiations and exclusion in legislations are judged in South Africa is a much higher standard of judicial review than the one used by the U.S. Supreme Court, which is based on rationality. In the United States, this rationality standard is used in all cases except those involving suspect classification or in the case of gender, which operates under an intermediate standard of review. But what makes Mokgoro's decision particularly important for us is that she not only emphasizes the wrong to the individuals; she also insists that the purposive nature of the South African Constitution is rooted in the promotion of a just community, which again is irreducible to a social contractual understanding of the relationship between rights and duties.

Here we sound again Mokgoro's note that our responsibility to our community is not simply because it protects our entitlements. Instead, we are responsible for the quality of that community and the promotion of a just community becomes a goal for everyone in South Africa, even if it demands assuming what seems to be an unfair imposition of requirements not simply to make up past wrongs, but to achieve a justice that ultimately enhances everyone's power, if power is understood through the ethical force field of *ubuntu*. Again, we are returned to the idea that freedom is indivisible.

We think that the best understanding of her argument, if it proceeds through *ubuntu*, is that permanent residents, through their actual engagements with South Africa, have become a part of the ethical interactions that make up the country and that they, as a result, should be considered part of the promise for justice offered by the Constitution.[43] The purposiveness of the Constitution of South Africa, which explicitly seeks "to free the potential of each person" is simultaneously working to free the potential of the community toward justice. In this sense, the purposiveness is about the kind of community the Constitution promotes as integral to the freeing of that potential. A just community for Mokgoro is a strong community, and a strong community strengthened by the capability and potential of individuals, certainly. But by promoting the indivisibility of freedom, the community established keeps itself from being diminished by the denial of humanity to anyone who is thrown in its lot with it. Thus, what is lost in terms of the burden placed on citizens to sustain those who are not citizens is well made up for Mokgoro by the promotion of a just community, which is the only kind of community under *ubuntu* that can strengthen all of us together. Here we have a classic example of some citizens having to assume a responsibility, which might seem under a more liberal notion of fairness to be unjust, because they are taking on additional burdens on behalf of others in the community, without receiving any apparent reciprocal benefit. Yet, the situation is viewed as one where assuming such extra burdens is in the end in their moral interest because who they are as free individuals is inseparable from the freedom guaranteed *to everyone*. Indeed, one can even read Mokgoro's insistence that the Constitutional Court should itself read in the words *permanent residents* into the challenged sections of the social legislation as an *ubuntu*-inspired understanding of the role of the Constitutional Court.

The Constitutional Court is also responsible in its service as part of South Africa to promote justice for everyone. Thus, the court should not just relinquish its responsibility to make sure that the change takes place now so that the destitute individuals should get their grants (although, of course, Mokgoro is very concerned that they do get their grants), but instead the change should be enforced by the court in its responsibility to bring into being a just and equitable community. If the court was simply to turn back the legislation to the legislature, not only would the individuals involved be harmed, but the court would be diminished in its responsibility to be just in the name of the community itself. As we have written, Mokgoro did not use the word *ubuntu* here, but when she writes that extra burdens must be assumed by citizens and that others who do not have those burdens still have equal right to access to social benefits, she is not only promoting a fair community but, as she writes, a caring community. And this close connection between a just and caring community is part and parcel of her understanding of what the nomos of the new South Africa demands of its citizens:

> At the time the immigrant applies for admission to take up permanent residence, the state has a choice. If it chooses to allow immigrants to make their homes here, it is because it sees some advantage to the state in doing so. Through careful immigration policies it can ensure that those admitted for the purpose of becoming permanent residents are persons who will profit, and not be a burden to, the state. If a mistake is made in this regard, and the permanent resident becomes a burden, that may be a cost we have to pay for the constitutional commitment to developing a caring society, and granting access to socio-economic rights to all who make their homes here. Immigration can be controlled in ways other than allowing immigrants to make their

permanent homes here, and then abandoning them to destitution if they
fall upon hard times. The category of permanent residents who are before
us are children and the aged, all of whom are destitute and in need of social
assistance. They are unlikely to earn a living for themselves. While the self-
sufficiency argument may hold in the case of immigrants who are viable in the
job market and who are still in the process of applying for permanent resident
status, the argument is seemingly not valid in the case of children and the aged
who are already settled permanent residents and part of South African society.[44]

Crucial to the debate on whether or not *ubuntu* can be operationalized in the
Constitution are two questions about constitutionalism itself. As John and Jean Comaroff have written:

> The Constitution of the Republic of South Africa, adopted in 1996, has been
> accorded hallowed status in the formation of the postcolonial polity. Translated
> into all official languages under the legend *'One law for One nation'*—the italics
> are in the original—the text is shelved, in many homes, alongside family bibles
> and books of prayer. Yet, almost from the start, there have been doubts about
> its ability to constitute either *One Nation or One Law*; these italics are ours.
> Even its comprehensibility has been questioned: a mass circulation black news-
> paper in Johannesburg, for example, has referred to it as a Tower of Babel,
> pointing out that its vernacular versions are utterly opaque—and, hence, bab-
> ble to those whom it was meant to enfranchise.[45]

Through their careful ethnographic work, the Comaroffs have pointed to how
contradictions between the *one* people of the Constitution and the many peoples of
South Africa's indigenous legal systems cannot be reconciled by any of the current
ideals of liberal multiculturalism, including the liberal ideals read into the South
African Constitution itself. The Comaroffs point to how on-the-ground struggles
are constantly disrupting any easy liberal solution to what they rightly, in our mind,
designate as claims to polysovereignty: actual claims to self-government in current
law being made by different peoples in South Africa. Our first point is that we agree
with the Comaroffs, that the Constitution has not and should not be fitted into a
liberal mode that belies the complexity of actual struggle, yet simultaneously this
should not imply a rejection of constitutionalism altogether. The Comaroffs clearly
not only embrace constitutionalism, but they have defended it as a substantive
rather than proceduralist form of democratic jurisprudence. The jurisprudence is
democratic in that the Court is actually participating in the configuration of values
and ideals. These values and ideals both become embodied in law and also symbol-
ically rein force visions of what kind of polity the new South Africa hopes to
become. Indeed, from the beginning of his work on the tribal legal systems, John
Comaroff has emphasized the importance of aesthetically informed political practices

of tribal intuitions, including those related to law-making practices, such as community conciliation and the like. Obviously, we need to look more into how the operation of tribal law in South Africa has appealed to a very different notion of law, including the *law of law* than the one we associate with modern legal systems justified by one version or another of the social contract. What we want to emphasize here is that the Comaroffs continually point us to the importance of remembering that the constant effort to make sense of the Constitution should itself be seen as a political struggle.

In a recent decision, *Port Elizabeth Municipality v. Various Occupiers*,[46] the Constitutional Court had to decide whether the municipality acted lawfully when it evicted residents from privately owned land within the municipality. The municipality responded to a petition signed by 1,600 people in the neighborhood seeking an eviction order from the South Eastern Cape Local Division of the High Court. The High Court granted the order, after which the occupiers took the matter on appeal to the Supreme Court of Appeal. The Supreme Court upheld the appeal and set aside the eviction order. The municipality then applied to the Constitutional Court for leave to appeal against the decision of the Supreme Court. In a decision by Justice Sachs, the court did not grant leave to appeal. Sachs placed the question of eviction within an historical context, referring to the "pre-democratic era" where the law would have responded to illegal squatting in a drastic manner, which led to not only the dignity of black people being assaulted, but also to the creation of large well-affluent white urban areas that coexisted alongside black areas where blacks lived in poverty and insecure social conditions.[47] In a new democratic era under a supreme Constitution with an entrenched Bill of Rights, squatting was decriminalized and evictions were made subject to a number of requirements. A significant feature of the new era is that homeless people must be treated with dignity and respect. However, he added that it is not only the dignity of the poor that is affected when evicted and forcibly removed; the whole society is demeaned by such actions. Sachs argued that Courts had a new role to play in balancing illegal eviction and unlawful occupation, that they are called upon to go beyond their "normal functions, and to engage in active judicial management."[48] He highlighted the Constitution's requirement that everyone must be treated with "care and concern" within a society based on human dignity, equality, and freedom. He argued that cases must be decided not on generalities, but in the light of their own particular circumstances.[49] With explicit reference to *ubuntu*, he said the following:

> The spirit of *ubuntu*, part of the deep cultural heritage of the majority of the population, suffuses the whole constitutional order. It combines individual rights with a communitarian philosophy. It is a unifying motif of the Bill of Rights, which is nothing if not a structured, institutionalised and operational declaration in our evolving new society of the need for human interdependence, respect and concern.[50]

In this opinion, Sachs seems to have come closer to Mokgoro than he appeared to be in the seminar, in that we can read him to allow *ubuntu* to be an important ethical directive in the sense of the law of law underlying the entirety of the Constitution.

CONCLUSION

Some contemporary advocates of agonism, a word embraced by Arendt, who argued that we must allow for radical plurality as the very basis of democratic politics, have resisted the ideal of constitutionalism itself as against this agonism. The critique that has become well known is that the law and the Constitution can only carry a poison that induces a kind of sclerosis of the agonal energies of politics.[51] What was raised in the seminar was not this critique of the life-dissipating effects of constitutionalism, but instead recognition that is precisely the depth of the challenge to South African sovereignty: Polysovereignty could at least potentially spur new and innovative interpretations of the Constitution.

There is no reason in principle that *ubuntu*, as it is understood, as a founding principle of the law of law, cannot be operationalized. What would it mean if both dignity and *ubuntu* were configured together as operational principles as well as founding principles? We want to at least raise the suggestion here that *ubuntu* could not be translated as dignity has into an individual right because it goes beyond the notion of individual entitlement. The legal system of South Africa does not give standing only to individuals who have been harmed, but also to those individuals and communities who want to promote the public good. Therefore, even the idea of standing, so different than the one in the United States, can best be interpreted through *ubuntu*. We understand that in this essay we are only beginning to think of how *ubuntu* is being operationalized, but we also want to suggest that *ubuntu*, understood as a principle that could be operationalized, might well serve to promote ethically sound interpretations of difficult (at least for traditionally liberal jurisprudences) clauses of the Constitution, such as the limitations clause. After all, the limitations clause imposes a limit on when individuals can pursue their rights. How can we understand that limit? It is difficult to understand that limit, indeed, in the traditional liberal framework, even one inspired by Immanuel Kant, which reduces all rights and duties to a one-to-one correspondence in the social contract. Thus, it at least deserves much more exploration as to how *ubuntu* could be operationalized in the Constitution.

More importantly, it would provide a nuanced jurisprudence that would not only include African or South African values and ideals as important to the new South Africa, as a matter of fairness to those whose ideals have been marginalized, but also because those principles, ideals and values may well provide with solutions to dilemmas in South Africa that are not solvable by liberalism. It could be argued that certain aspects of customary law and features of the African Charter on Human and Peoples' Rights (African Charter) are concrete manifestations of ubuntu. Pieterse notes the influence of *ubuntu* in the humanist and collective emphasis in the customary law areas of restorative justice, the extended family, the notion of belonging and property.[52] He also relates the inclusion of social, economic and cultural rights alongside civil and political rights; the inclusion of the right to development; the protection of peoples' rights and the concept of duties in the African Charter to *ubuntu*. These rights, as well as the armonization of rights and responsibilities, illustrate the interdependence of individuals and communities and underscore the notion that individual rights cannot be meaningfully exercised in isolation of broader community rights.[53]

Perhaps the most empowering aspect of *ubuntu* is that, by taking its interactive ethic seriously, we should not shy away from the actual attempt to operationalize this powerful ideal because of fears of failure to do so adequately. Indeed, the very spirit of *ubuntu* might suggest to us that, while such failures are to be expected, the true enactment of this sort of ethic is itself constructed through the ongoing participation of the community in such struggles, including failures of operationalization and efforts to resolve them, to create a new South Africa.

Some Thoughts on the *uBuntu* Jurisprudence of the Constitutional Court

Narnia Bohler-Müller

In this contribution I revisit the *ubuntu* jurisprudence of the South African Constitutional Court. After analyzing the various extant critiques of the *ubuntu* reasoning of the court, I offer below a careful reading of three recent cases: *Khosa v. Minister of Social Development* 2004 6 SA 505 (CC) (hereinafter *Khosa*), *Port Elizabeth Municipality v. Various Occupiers* 2004 12 BCLR 1268 (CC) (hereinafter *PE Municipality*) and *Dikoko v. Mokhatla* CCT62/05 (hereinafter *Dikoko*) in order to decipher to some extent the court's vision of a constitutional community of "belonging together" post-*Makwanyane*.[1] More specifically, I explore the singular judgments of Justices Sachs and Mokgoro in order to illustrate how it is possible to assess their attempts to think the law and post-apartheid community differently as a reflection of something truly new.

THE PROBLEM OF *UBUNTU*

The ideal of a new constitutional community can be glimpsed already in *Makwanyane*, where the Justices of the Constitutional Court used the African principles of *ubuntu*, community, and unity to argue that the death penalty should be abolished. In a thorough critique of this judgment and its "frightening" lack of jurisprudence rigor, Van der Walt argues that:

> a rigorous jurisprudence must remain dissatisfied with the feel-good flavour
> of a jurisprudence that has done little more than add a local, indigenous and
> communitarian touch to the Christian, Kantian or Millsian respect for the

individual that informs Western jurisprudence. A rigorous jurisprudence would ask more probing questions regarding *ubuntu*.[2]

Van der Walt thus rejects Justice Sachs's somewhat "rosy portrayal" of African jurisprudence[3] and conducts his own research into aspects of African culture that endorse the *lex talionis* and executions, and hereby refutes to a certain extent Sachs's own more romantic version of African culture and practice. He concludes that using *ubuntu* without question as a constitutional value in *Makwanyane* may have served the immediate purpose of abolishing the death penalty, but it can be argued in future that this decision was based on a spurious interpretation of *ubuntu*.[4]

For Van der Walt, the use of *ubuntu* in South African constitutional jurisprudence in the future would require a good deal of honest critical thinking "to distil from the feudal, hierarchical, and thus vertical trappings of this concept, a different understanding of constitutionality."[5] We must, indeed, be cautious when embracing a concept that may very well lead to the swallowing up of singularities into an integrated and harmonious whole,[6] something akin to cultural nationalism or the ideology of nation-building. Van der Walt thus wishes to draw our attention to the problem of discourses of unity that reduce or nullify the possibilities of plurality.[7] Van der Walt's thinking on plurality is based on J. L. Nancy's concept of multiple exposures of singularities and a radical horizontality where no one and nothing occupies an elevated position in society. Where "there will no longer be an above from which to hang the ropes of hangmen."[8]

Lenta also cautions that the Constitutional Court's resort to *ubuntu* (in *Makwanyane*) can be seen as providing cover for the operations of power in the case:

> although the Court's resort to *ubuntu* seems to contain ethically laudable sentiments—the valorisation of excluded identity, tradition and forms of community—on a Foucauldian reading, its political effect is to substitute long prison sentences in the place of execution, which Foucault perceives as a new form of domination.[9]

Lenta's concerns here resonate somewhat with those expressed by Van der Walt. The truth of the matter is that if *ubuntu* remains a "bloated" concept[10] that can mean "all things to all men,"[11] it can also be (mis)used in the exercise of power. In essence, "*ubuntu*-speak" can be easily manipulated, used to enforce social and legal conformity and to silence dissenting voices and, it can, Lenta suggests, become a new form of domination. As Van der Walt correctly points out, *ubuntu* in a certain sense does not sound any different from the centuries-old, tight hierarchical order endorsed by the order of the *Corpus Christi* in medieval Europe.[12] What, then, sets *ubuntu* apart from other Western values? What separates *ubuntu* from authoritarian discourses that demand respect and obedience from the "collective"?

I have written about *ubuntu* elsewhere and do not want to repeat any of those arguments here.[13] My aim is rather to add to the growing volume of work on this African philosophy and the value it may possibly hold for social, political, and legal transformation in post-apartheid South Africa (I have, once again, to thank my ex-student Zolelwa Tuswa for challenging me to think more carefully about transformation). Keeping in mind the warnings issued above and the dangers inherent in asserting *ubuntu* as a conservative value that may restrict the expression of political and other differences, I submit that the strategy of using *ubuntu* to enrich human rights and constitutional discourse should be seen having both political and ethical dimensions. I therefore remain convinced that the reconceptualization of *ubuntu* may take us beyond strategy to a future-oriented utopianism pointing to an "elsewhere" beyond our current conceptions of the legal and political as purely instrumental struggles for individual and group power.[14] In this sense the notion of *ubuntu* is both conservative and subversive in nature, and it is the potential of the latter—its subversiveness and resistance to the *status quo* of liberal individualism—that I would like to explore in more detail.

In John Murungi's words:

Each path of jurisprudence represents an attempt by human beings to tell a story about being human. Unless one discounts the humanity of others, one must admit that one has something in common with all other human beings . . . what African jurisprudence calls for is an ongoing dialogue among Africans on being human, a dialogue that of necessity leads to dialogue with other human beings. This dialogue is not an end in itself. It is a dialogue with an existential implication . . . .[15]

My own understanding of ethical community through *ubuntu* or the ongoing dialogue of what a "shared humanity" means is not reducible to western communitarianism or theories of social consensus or cohesion. MO Eze (different Eze mentioned below) similarly submits that the "common good" in African value systems is not conceived through consensus, but through what he terms "realist perspectivism."[16] According to Eze, consensus neither accommodates nor promotes autonomy and alterity, but suppresses these core values of human identity.[17] Realist perspectivism, on the other hand, takes into account the perspectives and viewpoints of others:

The realist perspectivism that I advocate illustrates in a more coherent way, more than consensus, how common good is arrived at in the African traditional system. This kind of perspectivism shuns unanimity but seeks for the understanding of the other before arriving at judgement. It is humanistic insofar as the focus is the human person and . . . [seeks] ways to reconcile and accommodate different perspectives in such a way that does not oppress or possess.[18]

uBuntu reconceived, redefined, and relocated as a philosophy of the individual-in-relationship sees the revitalized individual as a gift to the world where her freedom becomes an "act of responsibility to the community."[19] This disposition, outlook or attitude does not rely on uniformity or sameness within community, but plays out as a question of *who I can become* as an individual in an ethical community: In exposing ourselves to others, encountering the difference and diversity of lives, we inform and enrich our own lives. Essential to these encounters is the space between "You" and "I" as "[t]o be a person is not to be the same as the other but to be in harmony with all that is. There is a distance and relation where the 'I' and the 'We' are engaged in a perpetual encounter with the other."[20] Accordingly, my humanity becomes real when I encounter the sovereign humanity of the other, and the I-It relationship is transformed into an I-Thou relationship. Being together is thus not dependent on assimilating otherness, but rather signifies a new kind of community beautifully described by Costas Douzinas:

> The other as a singular, unique finite being puts me in touch with infinite otherness. In this ontology, community is not the common belonging of communitarianism, a common essence given by history, tradition, the spirit of the nation. Cosmos is being together with one another, ourselves as others, being selves through otherness.[21]

Although Douzinas is not writing about *ubuntu* in this context, his work on reclaiming the ancient Greek spirit of the *cosmos* may assist in informing the way in which *ubuntu* is understood as both immanence and transcendence. In explaining the metaphysics of *ubuntu* philosophy, M. Ramosa points out that this African philosophy rests upon an understanding of cosmic harmony or wholeness.[22] African and European thinking on community may then very well offer similar insights, but these insights arise out of "dissimilar experiences" and thus cannot be collapsed into one another.[23]

> Having made an effort to address the problem of *ubuntu* without resolving any of the necessary tensions, I now turn to the ways in which the Constitutional Court has used this "problematic" concept in order to rethink the notion of a new South African community.

THE PROMISE OF *UBUNTU*

Since her judgment in *Makwanyane,* Justice Mokgoro has indicated a firm commitment to using *ubuntu* as a constitutional value or ideal.[24] Having noted this, it is therefore surprising that she does not explicitly refer to *ubuntu* in the *Khosa* case. Nowhere in her judgment does she give voice to her need to operationalize *ubuntu*, although it does seem that her understanding of *ubuntu* implicitly informs her arguments to extend the payment of social grants to noncitizens residing in South Africa.

In *Khosa* the Constitutional Court was faced with a challenge to the Social Assistance Act (59 of 1992). The Applicants were Mozambican citizens who were permanent residents in South Africa. The first Applicant, a mother of two children, applied for a child support grant and a care dependency grant for a child suffering from diabetes. The second Applicant applied for an old-age grant. Both Applicants had been denied their grants, as they were not citizens of South Africa. In this case, Mokgoro upheld a decision of the High Court that it was the court's responsibility to read the words *permanent resident* into the challenged provisions of the Social Assistance Act. The Applicants argued that sections 26, 27, and 28 of the final Constitution use the word *everyone* in the first two sections and *every child* in the third, and that it would be unconstitutional to limit access to social grants to citizens alone.

Cornell and Van Marle critically analyze this case and the assumptions underlying Mokgoro's attempts to rethink citizenship. They argue convincingly that Mokgoro's reasoning reveals a certain politico-ethical stance.[25] There appears in her judgment a deep sense that the humanity and dignity of these Applicants should not be denied as the purposive nature of the South African Constitution is rooted in the promotion of a just community. Although, as mentioned, Mokgoro does not use the word *ubuntu* in this case, her insistence that everyone is responsible for ensuring the well-being of persons within their community appears to reflect such thinking. She is therefore not only promoting a fair community, but a *caring* one. In her view, there is a connection between a just and caring community:

> Through careful immigration policies it can ensure that those admitted for the purpose of becoming permanent residents are persons who will profit, and not be a burden to, the state. If a mistake is made in this regard, and the permanent residents become a burden, that may be a cost we have to pay for the constitutional commitment to developing a caring society, and granting access to socio-economic rights to all who have homes here. Immigration can be controlled in ways other than allowing immigrants to make their permanent homes here, and then abandoning them to destitution if they fall upon hard times.[26]

Echoing Mokgoro's concerns with the development of a just and caring community, Justice Albie Sachs makes explicit reference to *ubuntu* in *PE Municipality* in justifying his refusal to uphold an eviction order that would result in the homelessness of a large number of squatters. He highlights in his judgment the (constitutional) requirement that everyone must be treated with "care and concern" within a society based on the values of human dignity, equality and freedom. He also reminds us that the Constitution places a demand upon the judiciary to decide cases, not on generalities, but in the light of their own particular circumstances:

The spirit of *ubuntu*, part of the deep cultural heritage of the majority of the population, suffuses the whole constitutional order. It combines individual rights with a communitarian philosophy. It is a unifying motif of the Bill of Rights, which is nothing if not a structured, institutionalised and operational declaration in our evolving new society of the need for human interdependence, respect and concern.[27]

Sachs thus places the question of eviction within its historical context by referring to predemocratic laws that enabled drastic responses to illegal squatting, assaulting the dignity of black people and allowed the creation of affluent white areas.[28] Sachs then contrasts this position to the "new era" where homeless people must be treated with dignity and respect, as it is not only the poor whose dignity is affected when evicted and forcibly removed, but also the whole of society is demeaned by such actions.

In an insightful critique of this judgment, Bekker notes that Sachs's laudable sentiments (once again) do not directly address what he means when he uses terms such as *ubuntu* and "human interdependence."[29] There is, Bekker submits, a "gap" between what is understood by human interdependence in Western and African law,[30] and the use of the term needs to be explored more fully in order to determine what human interdependence actually means (politically and legally) to the Constitutional Court.

Be that as it may, Mokgoro and Sachs argue, albeit in different ways and from different perspectives, that *ubuntu* can, and should, become central to a new constitutional jurisprudence and to the revival of sustainable African values as part of the broader process of the African renaissance. They also articulate in these judgments their vision of a just and caring postapartheid community. Although there does exist to some extent a lack of jurisprudential rigor in their judgments in *Khosa* and *PE Municipality*, my submission remains that their efforts could be seen in a positive light as at least an attempt to move beyond a liberal conception of human rights discourse.

As reflected upon above, adherence to the value of *ubuntu,* whether implicitly or explicitly, demands that we deal with individuals in the context of their historical and current disadvantage and that equality issues must address *the actual conditions of human life,* for example life as a noncitizen or a squatter, but nevertheless life with and through others.

Ideally, all members of any community should have the right to feel welcomed, to participate fully in a process of becoming within a just and caring environment that supports life with others in a process of unfolding and enfolding, in the words of Ramose.[31] Both Mokgoro and Sachs appear to share this vision, and in their own unique ways maintain that the Constitution should facilitate a sense of responsibility towards others since our togetherness is a creative force that comes into being as we form ourselves with each other. This vision is further explored by both judges in the recent case of *Dikoko v. Mokhatla* (decided on August 3, 2006).

In this case the Applicant, Dikoko, appealed against the judgment and order of the High Court in which it was found that he had defamed Mokhatla. The High Court ordered the Applicant to pay the respondent damages in the amount of R110 000. I do not address the question of privilege as a defense to claims of defamation here, but merely want to draw attention to some comments made by Justices Mokgoro and Sachs on the quantum of damages.

In this case Justice Moseneke held, for the majority, that an excessive award of damages would have the effect of deterring free speech and expression and assumes, without deciding, that the issue of quantum in a defamation suit is a constitutional matter. He concludes, however, that there are no special circumstances in this particular case that justifies interference with the High Court award for damages.[32]

However, Mokgoro, in a minority judgment with Justices Nkabinde and Sachs concurring, considered the issue of whether the quantum of damages awarded by the High Court was excessive. She concludes that the High Court did not exercise its discretion reasonably in taking into account mitigating factors and determined that an award of 50,000 rand would have been more reasonable.[33]

In examining whether the Roman-Dutch remedy *amende honorable* (in terms of which a public apology was rendered by the defendant) is still a part of South African private law, Mokgoro links this remedy to *ubuntu*:

> The primary purpose of a compensatory measure, after all, is to restore the dignity of a plaintiff who has suffered the damage and not to punish a defendant. A remedy based on the idea of *ubuntu* or *botho* could go much further in restoring human dignity than an imposed monetary award in which the size of the victory is measured by the quantum ordered and the parties are further estranged rather than brought together by the legal process.[34]

In essence, Mokgoro maintains that in emphasizing restorative rather than retributive justice in the spirit of *ubuntu*, we should keep in mind the goal of knitting together shattered relationships in the community and that the courts should be proactive in encouraging "respect for the basic norms of human and social interdependence."[35]

In a separate judgment, Sachs goes as far as to propose that the law of defamation should be developed so as to move away from an almost exclusive preoccupation with monetary awards, which are unsuitable to restoring the damage done to a person's reputation and which often serve to drive parties further apart rather than to reconcile them. He then suggests that the law of defamation should be developed to encompass an approach that encourages apology, which, he argues, is better suited to reconciling the parties:

> There is a further and deeper problem with damages awards in defamation cases. They measure something so intrinsic to human dignity as a person's

reputation and honour as if these were market place commodities. Unlike business, honour is not quoted on the Stock Exchange.[36]

In his view, the goal of the remedy should be reparation rather than punishment. He holds that this approach would accord more with the constitutional value of *ubuntu*, which is consonant with the notion of restorative justice; the key elements of which he identifies as encounter, reparation, reintegration and participation:

> The key elements of restorative justice have been identified as encounter, reparation, reintegration and participation. Encounter (dialogue) enables the victims and offenders to talk about the hurt caused and how the parties are to get on in future. Reparation focuses on repairing the harm that has been done rather than on doling out punishment. Reintegration into the community depends upon the achievement of mutual respect for and mutual commitment to one another. And participation presupposes a less formal encounter between the parties that allows other people close to them to participate. These concepts harmonise well with processes well-known to traditional forms of dispute resolution in our country, processes that have long been, and continue to be, underpinned by the philosophy of *ubuntu – botho*.[37]

In his argument, Sachs articulates (as in *PE Municipality*) the need for human interdependence, respect, and concern in an evolving society[38] but then also goes further to emphasize the need for *restorative justice* by "seeking simultaneously to restore a person's public honour while assuaging inter-personal trauma and healing social wounds."[39]

In addressing the application of the *amende honorable,* Sachs notes that although *ubuntu* and *amende honorable* are expressed in different languages, they share an underlying philosophy, namely the promotion of a face-to-face encounter between the parties in order to facilitate the public resolution of their conflict and to restore a sense of harmony. Both legal cultures thus aim to facilitate the achievement of "an apology honestly offered, and generously accepted."[40]

Although Justice Moseneke perhaps correctly points out that both Mokgoro and Sachs raise issues "which never confronted the trial Court and therefore do not properly arise before us,"[41] I am of the view that the discussions dealing with the role of *ubuntu* as a constitutional value add substantially to this growing jurisprudence and were not in vain. Mokgoro and Sachs have directed us in this judgment to their understanding of what a new South African community should look like and they have given us some idea of how to do this differently. Bekker agrees that the judgment is commendable, not because it is necessarily correct but "by reason of the fact that it represents the first real and genuine attempt to give real meaning and substance to the concept of *ubuntu* in a specific context."[42] Bekker is particularly enamored with the emphasis placed by the justices on reconciliation and restorative justice as these concepts "unlike other elements of *ubuntu,* can therefore be successfully linked to values intrinsic to both the original indigenous law as well as Western law."[43] *uBuntu* is thus rendered more understandable and acceptable to the Western mind.

It may very well be true that *ubuntu* in its "current all-embracing form will not be able to provide the Courts with an effective, workable constitutional value,"[44] but I submit that "pinning" the meaning of *ubuntu* down in order to render it more useful and less "worthless," diminishes the *potential* of this African philosophy as "ideal," future-oriented, revolutionary—a rebellion against the *status quo* of western liberalism. E. C. Eze—a different Eze from the one mentioned above[45]—is particularly critical of hegemonic or "civilizing" impulses to "tame" whatever is not easily rationalized in Western terms. In his view, idea(l)s should not be separated from the way they are practiced:

> to speak of ideals or ideas as universally neutral schemes or models which we historically perfectly or imperfectly implement, obscures the fact that these ideals and ideas are already part and parcel of—ie, always already infused with historical practices and intentions out of which ideals are, in the first place, constituted as such—judged worthy of pursuit. Ideals do not have meaning in a historical vacuum.[46]

I submit that it is possible to read the judgments in *Khosa, PE Municipality,* and *Dikoko* as "revolutionary" in the sense that Justices Mokgoro and Sachs write against strict legal convention in reimagining a new form of community for South Africans. In their interpretation of the Bill of Rights they make an effort to go beyond conceptions of rights and individual freedoms as instruments to be selectively enjoyed by the middle classes "who could afford higher education, fill management positions and engage in research."[47] By invoking the value and ideal of *ubuntu* Justices Mokgoro and Sachs at the very least acknowledge in the *Khosa* and *PE Municipality* cases the potential of human rights to be meaningful in the struggle against oppression and disempowerment. Perhaps the aim is not to "replace one master's voice with another"[48] but to introduce voices that represent the experiences of the deprived and oppressed. In his way human rights can be transformed from a discourse of state power into the language of struggle.[49]

While I do depict these judgments in a positive light, I also agree that there is a need for unfailing vigilance. We must remain vigilant against the invocation of an image of community as homogenous, a denial of both singularity and plurality. Euphoric discourses of unity and solidarity are undeniably dangerous and totalitarian as homogeneity tends to silence dissenting voices.

The emphasis should rather be on beginning anew—an ethics (and politics), not only of difference, but also *of and for the future.*

CONCLUSION

I have referred above to Mokgoro and Sachs's judgments in three constitutional cases as examples of a jurisprudence that reflects something beyond the confines of traditional Western law. Keeping in mind warnings against being over optimistic about law's ability to restore and reconcile, these explorations may ignite new hope for a different future, not leaving us endlessly isolated from one another. And in emphasizing the need to adopt a vision of hope for the future, Cornell and Van Marle insist that we should not give up for fear of failure:

> Perhaps the most empowering aspect of *ubuntu* is that, by taking its interactive ethic seriously, we should not shy away from the actual attempt to operationalise this powerful ideal because of fears of failure to do so adequately. Indeed, the very spirit of *ubuntu* might suggest to us that, while such failures are to be expected, the true enactment of this sort of ethic is itself constructed through the ongoing participation of the community in such struggles, including failures of operationalisation and efforts to resolve them, to create a new South Africa.[50]

A lot can go wrong when we defend ideals such as *ubuntu*. It is a risky business and the traps are numerous, but if we dare to risk failure, if we dare to ask what good we are without others, if we dare to imagine a revitalized philosophy of *ubuntu*, if we dare to do it differently, we may have stories worth telling future generations of South Africans. Stories of hope.

> What good am I then to others and me.
> If I've had every chance and yet still fail to see.
> If my hands are tied must I not wonder within.
> Who tied them and why and where must I have been?
> What good am I if I say foolish things.
> And I laugh in the face of what sorrow brings.
> And I just turn my back while you silently die.
> What good am I?
>
> Bob Dylan "What Good am I?"
> 1989 Special Rider Music *Oh Mercy*

The Reemergence of *uBuntu*:
A Critical Analysis

Thino Bekker

The constitutional concept of *ubuntu* was introduced for the first time in the South African legal landscape in the highly discussed and watershed case of *S v. Makwanyane*.[1] After *Makwanyane*, *ubuntu* was the new buzzword amongst legal practitioners and academics, which has also led to a substantial academic discourse on this highly controversial topic.[2]

After the initial interest that was invoked by the decision in *Makwanyane*, the concept of *ubuntu* as a constitutional value seemed to have withered away to an historical artifact of a newly born democracy. The courts, especially the Constitutional Court, seemed in some way reluctant to develop the principle of *ubuntu* further after *Makwanyane*.

Three recent civil Constitutional Court cases, however, have given rise to the reemergence of the concept of *ubuntu*, and hopefully a renewed academic stimulation of this highly dynamic subject. These cases are *Port Elizabeth Municipality v. Various Occupiers*,[3] *Bhe v. Magistrate, Khayelitsha; Shibi v. Sithole; South African Human Rights Commission v. President of the Republic of South Africa*,[4] and *Dikoko v. Mokhatla*.[5]

In this article the potential of *ubuntu* as a constitutional value in the development of both the public and private law spheres will be investigated with specific reference and critical discussion of the *Makwanyane* case as well as the aforementioned three civil Constitutional Court cases. An argument will be made out that *ubuntu* can play an important role in the development of both the public law as well as the private law spheres, but only if the concept is properly redefined to fit into the current legal system and the community it purports to serve.

THE TRUE NATURE OF *UBUNTU*

The first very important thing to note when investigating the true nature of *ubuntu*, lies in the fact that this concept is not easily definable. Bohler-Müller for example states that: "Like life and love, *ubuntu* is a difficult word or concept to define,"[6] and Archbishop Emeritus Desmond Tutu is of the opinion that "*ubuntu* is very difficult to render into Western language."[7]

Perhaps the best definition of the multilayered character of *ubuntu* can be found in the following observations of Justice Mokgoro:

> Generally *ubuntu* translates as "humaneness." In its most fundamental sense it translates as personhood and "morality." Metaphorically, it expresses itself in *umuntu ngumuntu ngabantu*,[8] describing the significance of group solidarity on survival issues so central to the survival of communities. While it envelops the key values of group solidarity, compassion, respect, human dignity, conformity to basic norms and collective unity, in its fundamental sense it denotes humanity and orality. Its spirit emphasises respect for human dignity, marking a shift from confrontation to conciliation. In South Africa *ubuntu* has become a notion with particular resonance in the building of a democracy.[9]

In essence, it is a humanist approach to fellow beings.[10]

It is furthermore perhaps significant to note that (while specific reference was made to *ubuntu* in the 1993 Interim Constitution[11]) there is no mention of this concept in the final 1996 Constitution.[12] Mokgoro is of the view that some of the founding values specifically spelt out in the 1996 Constitution, such as human dignity, equality, promotion of human rights and freedoms, multiparty democracy to ensure accountability, responsiveness, openness, and the rule of law arguably coincide with some key values of *ubuntu*-ism.[13]

The logical question that arises from this is: Does *ubuntu* as a constitutional value serve any real purpose anymore? Irma Kroeze is of the opinion that once you regard *ubuntu* as just a local example of a universal phenomenon, it is no longer a separate concept that needs to be articulated and applied.[14] She further argues that the concept is bloated and "simply collapses under the weight of the expectations," that the terms included in the definition of *ubuntu* has no self-evident meaning and that the concept therefore becomes endlessly manipulable.[15]

The arguments of Kroeze have considerable merits. The main problem is that the concept of *ubuntu* may, in the words of English, "simply mean all things to all men."[16] It is submitted that this problem can only be resolved if the concept of *ubuntu* is considerably redefined and that only certain relevant key components of it are emphasized by our courts in such a definition. This aspect will be discussed in more detail later in this article.

UBUNTU AS CONSTITUTIONAL VALUE
IN THE PUBLIC LAW SPHERE

Makwanyane illustrates the serious deficiencies of *ubuntu* as a constitutional value in its current form. Van der Walt, for example, argues convincingly that the Constitutional Court judges in *Makwanyane* in effect failed to link *ubuntu* as a constitutional value effectively to their reasoning of why the death penalty should be abolished.[17] One also has to agree with his argument that the separate judgments in this case did not offer us any real insight regarding the "specific and singular meaning of *ubuntu* for the question of the constitutionality of capital punishment."[18]

It is submitted that *Makwanyane* was in effect a politically motivated (consciously or unconsciously) decision that many will argue was essential at the time to protect the legitimacy of the newly found South-African constitutional order. The Constitutional Court, however, had to justify its decision on nonpolitical grounds and therefore attempted (unsuccessfully) to "use" the concept of *ubuntu* as constitutional value in its reasoning process. As this case has already been the subject of considerable academic discourse, it will not be discussed in any further detail in this article.

UBUNTU AS CONSTITUTIONAL VALUE
IN THE PRIVATE LAW SPHERE

uBuntu as constitutional value in the private law sphere came to the fore for the first time in the Constitutional Court case of *Port Elizabeth Municipality v. Various Occupiers*.[19]

The applicant in this matter was the Port Elizabeth Municipality which (responding to a petition signed by 1,600 people in the neighborhood) sought an eviction order against 68 people (including 23 children) who occupied twenty-nine shacks erected on privately owned land within the Municipality. At the time of institution of the legal proceedings, the occupiers had been living on the property for periods ranging from two to eight years on dwellings erected without the consent of the Municipality. The respondents indicated that they were willing to leave the property if given reasonable notice and provided with suitable alternative land on which they could reside. The Municipality stated that it was aware of its obligation to provide housing and that it had embarked on a comprehensive housing development program. The Municipality, however, submitted that if alternative land was made available to the occupiers they would effectively be queue-jumping, that this would disrupt the housing program and be forcing the Municipality to grant them preferential treatment.

The High Court held that the occupiers were unlawfully occupying the property and that it was in the public interest to terminate their occupation. The matter was taken to the Supreme Court of Appeal who upheld the appeal and set aside the eviction order, one of the reasons being the apparent unavailability of suitable alternative land. The Municipality then applied to the Constitutional Court for leave to appeal against the order of the Supreme Court of Appeal and asked the court to make a ruling on whether a municipality, when seeking the eviction of unlawful occupiers, was constitutionally bound to provide alternative accommodation or land.

Justice Sachs delivering the judgment of the court (all other ten judges concurring) held that, due to the lengthy period during which the occupiers have lived on the land, the fact that there is no need to evict the occupiers in order to put the land to some other productive use, the absence of any real attempts by the Municipality to consider the problems of the occupiers and the fact that the occupiers represented a relatively small group of people who appeared to be genuinely homeless, it was not just and equitable to order the eviction of the occupiers and dismissed the application for leave to appeal with costs.[20]

In the court's judgment Justice Sachs stated that the spirit of *ubuntu*, which formed part of the deep cultural heritage of the majority of the South African population, suffuses the whole constitutional order and that it combines individual rights with a communitarian philosophy. He went on to state that:

> It is a unifying motif of the Bill of Rights, which is nothing if not a structured, institutionalised and operational declaration in our evolving new society of *the need for human interdependence, respect and concern.*[21] (emphasis added)

It is significant that this is the only reference made to *ubuntu* in all of the court's judgment. This may give rise to the assumption that *ubuntu* is only used by some of the Constitutional Court judges as a catchphrase in an attempt to strengthen a certain judgment, without developing the concept as a constitutional value.

It is submitted that it is quite clear from the aforementioned quotation from Justice Sachs that no new contribution was made to the understanding of the concept of *ubuntu* or the potential role that it may play in future adjudication. It is submitted that the Constitutional Court had the ideal opportunity in this case to do just that. Where Justice Sachs, for example, considered whether it was "just and equitable" to grant an eviction order against the occupiers, he referred to the values of humanity and respect without any reference to *ubuntu* and the possible contribution it could make in the circumstances.[22]

What is of further interest is the reference made by Justice Sachs to the need in our evolving new society for "human interdependence." There is, however, no explanation by the court of what this aspect entailed with regard to the facts of the case. It is submitted, with the greatest of respect, that statements like these (without any elaboration) do not take into account the inherent differences that exist between western law and original indigenous law.

The reason for this statement is the fact that there still exists a vast difference between human interdependence in a Western society and human interdependence in an original indigenous society. It is submitted that in a Western society it still relates to a large extent to the notion of exercising one's rights with due regard to the rights of others as well as mutual respect for each other, as long as one's own personal space is not invaded. The individual in Western societies is the cornerstone of the society and not the group as such.

In original South African indigenous societies, the position is completely the opposite. In these societies the emphasis is placed on the group and not the individual. It is the group that has rights not the individual and human interdependence here relates to the fact that the individual cannot survive without the group. Everything that individuals do in these societies are for the ultimate well-being of the group and not the individuals within the group.

This opinion is held with due regard to some of the modern post-apartheid viewpoints in terms whereof the original Western conceptualization of rights are questioned[23] (maybe rightly so), and that the differences as set out above are perhaps not as rigid as stated. It is however submitted that there is still at present a definite gap between the concepts of human interdependence in a Western society and human interdependence in an original indigenous society that may be bridged in time, but effectively renders the concept (at present anyway) ineffective as a constitutional value (on its own or part as the concept of *ubuntu*).

If this distinction is borne in mind it follows logically that the concept of *ubuntu*, where it relates to human interdependence is destined to fail as constitutional value in the interpretation of a constitution that is largely based on a western society with a western value system. This only reiterates the point that the concept of *ubuntu* in its entirety and specifically where it relates to certain indigenous aspects will not be able to provide the courts with a workable constitutional value.

THE *BHE, SHIBI,* AND *SOUTH AFRICAN HUMAN RIGHTS COMMISSION* CASES

In the Cape High Court case of *Bhe v. Magistrate Khayelitsha*[24] and the Pretoria High Court case of *Charlotte Shibi v. Mantabeni Freddy Sithole*[25] the Applicants successfully challenged both the constitutionality of sections 23(10)(a), (c), and (e) of the Black Administration Act[26] as well as the customary principle of primogeniture.

The Applicants in both these proceedings then applied to the Constitutional Court in the case of *Bhe v. Magistrate, Khayelitsha; Shibi v. Sithole; South African Human Rights Commission v. President of the Republic of South Africa*[27] for confirmation of the orders of the respective divisions of the High Court.

The Constitutional Court declared section 23 (as well as the regulations promulgated thereunder) to be inconsistent with the Constitution and therefore invalid. It also declared the rule of male primogeniture as applied in customary law "to be inconsistent with the Constitution and invalid to the extent that it excluded or hindered women and extra-marital children from inheriting property."[28]

Langa DCJ, for the majority, only once (fleetingly) refers to the concept of *ubuntu* where he states that customary law provides a setting for the "nurturing of healthy communitarian traditions such as *ubuntu*."[29] Bohler-Muller, however, points correctly to the fact that, although Langa DCJ highlighted the constitutional values of dignity and equality, he did not make any express mention of *ubuntu* as a constitutional value or the effects it would have on the decision reached. She is of the opinion that there is perhaps a tendency on the part of judges to avoid delving too deeply into values that are political and ethical in nature and that *ubuntu* seems to be one of those values that does not fit comfortably into the objective system of legal rules and the controllable reality of the law.[30]

Justice Ncgobo also only referred very briefly to the concept of *ubuntu* in a customary law setting,[31] but made no contribution towards the developing thereof as a constitutional value. He apparently made use of the values of *ubuntu* as justification for his opinion that the customary rule of primogeniture should be constitutionally developed in terms of section 39(2) of the Constitution.

If one looks critically at the judgment of the Constitutional Court in the *Bhe* case the conclusion can be made that, although reference was made to *ubuntu*, no new insight into the concept as constitutional value was provided.

DIKOKO V. MOKHATLA

It is submitted that the Constitutional Court made a real breakthrough in the judgment of *Dikoko v. Mokhatla*[32] with regard to the interpretation of *ubuntu* as a constitutional value.

This case came to the Constitutional Court as an application for leave to appeal against a judgment of the Pretoria High Court in terms whereof Mokathla was awarded satisfaction in the amount of 110,000 rand[33] against Dikoko for certain defamatory statements made by him. The Constitutional Court was asked, firstly, to decide whether the Court had the necessary jurisdiction to hear the appeal, secondly, if Dikoko enjoyed immunity for the defamatory statements made by reason thereof that it was subject to the privilege enjoyed by municipal councilors and, thirdly, whether the *quantum* awarded by the Pretoria High Court was excessive under the circumstances.

Deputy Chief Justice Moseneke, delivering the majority judgment of the court, granted the application for leave to appeal, but dismissed the appeal with costs. Moseneke agreed with the decision by Justice Mokgoro who held that the appeal dealt with a constitutional matter[34] but that Dikoko was not entitled to the privilege claimed, one of the reasons being that the defamatory statements did not relate to the legitimate business of the National Council of Provinces.[35] He also held that the damages awarded were of such a (fair) nature that there was no reasonable prospect that the court could alter the amount.[36]

Justice Mokgoro delivered a minority judgment to the effect that the damages awarded by the Pretoria High Court was unreasonable in the circumstances, as it did not take sufficient cognizance of all the relevant mitigating circumstances.[37] Justice Mokgoro therefore held that she would have replaced the damages awarded by the Pretoria High Court in the amount of 110,000 rand with an amount of 50,000 rand.[38]

What is however of particular interest, is the specific reference made by Mokgoro in relation to the role that *ubuntu* can play as a constitutional value in the relevant circumstances. In an analysis of whether the ancient Roman-Dutch remedy of *amende honorable* (in terms whereof a public apology was rendered by a defamator) still form part of our law, she linked this remedy indirectly to the concept of *ubuntu*. Mokgoro held that:

> In our constitutional democracy the basic constitutional value of human dig-
> nity relates closely to *ubuntu* or *botho*, an idea based on deep respect for the
> humanity of another. Traditional law and culture have long considered one of
> the principal objectives of the law to be the restoration of harmonious human
> and social relationships where they have been ruptured by an infraction of
> community norms. It should be a goal of our law to emphasise, in cases of
> compensation for defamation, the re-establishment of harmony in the
> relationship between the parties, rather than to enlarge the hole in the defen-
> dant's pocket, something more likely to increase acrimony, push the parties
> apart and even cause the defendant financial ruin. The primary purpose of a
> compensatory measure, after all, is to restore the dignity of a plaintiff who has
> suffered the damage and not to punish a defendant. A remedy based on the
> idea of *ubuntu* or *botho* could go much further in restoring human dignity
> than an imposed monetary award in which the size of the victory is measured
> by the quantum ordered and the parties are further estranged rather than
> brought together by the legal process. It could indeed give better appreciation
> and sensitise a defendant as to the hurtful impact his or her unlawful actions,
> similar to the emerging idea of restorative justice in our sentencing laws.[39]

Mokgoro went on to state that two basic considerations should be borne in mind in defamation cases. The first consideration is that the reparation sought by a plaintiff is essentially for injury to his honor, dignity, and reputation and not to his pocket. The second is that the courts should attempt to reestablish a dignified and respectful relationship between the parties. She links this to *ubuntu* in the following way:

> Because an apology serves to recognize the human dignity of the plaintiff,
> thus acknowledging, in the true sense of *ubuntu*, his or her inner humanity,
> the resultant harmony would serve the good of both the plaintiff and the de-
> fendant. Whether the *amende honorable* is part of our law or not, our law in
> this area should be developed in the light of the values of *ubuntu* emphasising
> restorative rather than retributive justice. The goal should be to knit together

shattered relationships in the community and encourage across-the-board respect for the basic norms of human and social inter-dependence. It is an area
where Courts should be pro-active encouraging apology and mutual
understanding wherever possible.[40]

Justice Sachs, in a separate dissenting judgment, elaborated on this approach of
Mokgoro. He is of the opinion that greater allowance should be made in defamation
proceedings for acknowledging the constitutional values of *ubuntu*. He explained
the contribution of *ubuntu* as a constitutional value as follows:

> *Ubuntu-botho* is more than a phrase to be invoked from time to time to add a
> gracious and affirmative gloss to a legal finding already arrived at. It is intrinsic to
> and constitutive of our constitutional culture. Historically it was foundational to
> the spirit of reconciliation and bridge-building that enabled our deeply trauma-
> tized society to overcome and transcend the divisions of the past. In present day
> terms it has an enduring and creative character, representing the element of hu-
> man solidarity that binds together liberty and equality to create an affirmative
> and mutually supportive triad of central constitutional values. It feeds pervasively
> into and enriches the fundamental rights enshrined in the Constitution.[41]

Focusing on the facts beforehand, Justice Sachs then drew a parallel between
ubuntu and the rapidly evolving international notions of restorative justice which
strives for a justice system based on reparative rather than purely punitive principles.[42]
He stated that the key elements of restorative justice have been identified as encounter
(enabling victims and offenders to talk about the hurt caused and how the parties are
to get along in the future), reparation (focusing on repairing the harm caused rather
than punishing), reintegration into the community (depending upon the achievement
of mutual respect and commitment to one another) and participation (allowing
people close to the parties to participate). Sachs went on to state that these concepts
harmonize well with processes related to the traditional forms of dispute resolution
in our law, "processes that have long been, and continue to be, underpinned by the
philosophy of *ubuntu-botho*."[43]

Justice Sachs further pointed out that although the concept of *ubuntu* (like the
principles of restorative justice) has usually been invoked in relation to criminal law,
there is no reason why it should be restricted to this area. As one of the examples of
how *ubuntu* has already influenced our jurisprudence, Justice Sachs referred to the
case of *S v. Joyce Maluleke*[44] where Justice Bertelsmann discussed the advantages of
drawing upon traditional African legal processes so as to achieve reconciliation and
closure, similar to the developing notions of restorative justice in various international
jurisdictions. Justice Bertelsmann in this case also cited Justice Bosielo as calling for
innovative and proactive presiding officers to seek alternatives to imprisonment that
are based on restorative justice principles.[45]

Judge Sachs went on to state that although *ubuntu* and the *amende honorable* are expressed in different languages intrinsic to separate legal cultures, they share the same underlying goal and philosophy. Both are namely, according to him, directed towards the promotion of the face-to-face encounter between the parties in order to facilitate the public resolution of their differences and to restore harmony in the community. Both legal cultures therefore aim to create conditions to facilitate the achievement of "an apology honestly offered, and generously accepted."[46]

Justice Sachs further emphasized the point that his main concern was not the fact that the amount awarded by the Pretoria High Court was way over the top, but that our law, as presently understood and applied, does far too little to encourage repair and reconciliation between parties involved in legal proceedings. He is also of the opinion that the fixed concentration by the courts on quantum requires an amendment and that greater scope has to be given for reparatory remedies.

Justice Sachs concluded his judgment with the following passage:

> What is needed, then, is more flexibility and innovation concerning the relation between apology and money awards. A good beginning for achieving greater remedial suppleness might well be to seek out the points of overlap between *ubuntu-botho* and the *amende honorable*, the first providing a new spirit, the second a time-honoured legal format. Whatever renovatory modalities are employed, and however significant to the outcome the facts will have to be in each particular case, the fuller the range of remedial options available the more likely will justice be done between the parties. And the greater the prospect of realising the more humane society envisaged by the Constitution.[47]

The statement of both Justices Mokgoro and Sachs must be highly commended, not because it is necessarily correct, but by reason of the fact that it represents the first real and genuine attempt to give real meaning and substance to the concept of *ubuntu* in a specific context.

It is then also submitted that Justices Mokgoro and Sachs inadvertently emphasized those elements of *ubuntu* that may render the concept practically effective as a constitutional value in South African law, namely reconciliation and restorative justice. As reiterated by both Justices Mokgoro and Sachs, the elements of reconciliation and restorative justice play a major role in original indigenous law. According to this element of indigenous law, it is not so much the individual that is harmed where his or her rights are infringed upon, but the group as a whole. It is therefore necessary to restore the harmony within the group.

As Justice Sachs correctly pointed out, the concept of reconciliation and restorative justice is also rapidly evolving in the Western world, South Africa included. This holds true for both the public law sphere (where the concept is primarily used to provide for alternatives to effective prison sentences) and the private law sphere (where the concept may be used as an alternative to huge damage awards).

The concept of reconciliation and restorative justice, unlike some of the other elements of *ubuntu*, can therefore be successfully linked to values intrinsic to both the original indigenous law as well as Western law. As such it can play an important role as a constitutional value in the future adjudication of both public law and private law disputes. In this regard the sentiments of Cornell where she envisages a "nuanced jurisprudence that entails a complex reconciliation of the inevitable tensions between customary law and the Western ideals of liberalism,"[48] may be a reachable goal.

With specific reference to the law of defamation, the statements of Justices Mokgoro and Sachs however, may at present still be rather idealistic and unrealistic. For an apology to be a realistic solution (either on its own or as a supplement to another remedy) in defamation cases, there will need to be a substantial mind shift in current legal thinking and the perceptions of the majority of the South African community.

In the first instance it may promote the defamation of individuals rather than to prevent it from happening. A person can defame anyone without fear in the knowledge that he will probably only be required to apologize "sincerely" and all will be forgotten.

Secondly, how are the courts going to ascertain whether an apology was "honestly offered"? It may be argued that a defamator who stares a large damages award in the face, may suddenly be quite prepared to falsely offer an "honest" apology without meaning it!

What these judgments did achieve, however, is the ideal starting point from which the courts can begin to bring about a mind shift in current legal thinking and the perceptions of the community from the current notions where everything is calculated in rand and cent towards an approach where the emphasis is rather placed on the reconciliation and the restoration of harmony in the community.

It is submitted that, in defamation cases, the ideal should be to arrive at a point where damages for satisfaction are completely abolished and the courts will look at the actual damages sustained by the plaintiff. If the plaintiff's reputation was damaged to such an extent that he can actually prove that he sustained calculatable damages, he should be awarded a monetary sum equivalent to such damages. However, if there was no real damage to the reputation of the plaintiff (as was apparently the case with *Dikoko v. Mokathla*) the only objective should be an attempt to reconcile the parties and in this regard an apology in the form as prescribed by the *amende honorable* may just bring about this result in future (even though it may be unrealistic at present).

CONCLUSION

It is submitted that the concept of *ubuntu* in its present all-embracing form will not be able to provide the courts with an effective, workable constitutional value. To achieve this, the concept will have to be redefined to link the value systems of both the original indigenous law and Western law with each other. This is also the main reason why the courts have struggled after *Makwanyane* to develop and define *ubuntu* as a constitutional value. All references to the concept by the courts were therefore void of any real substance.

The minority judgments of Justices Mokgoro and Sachs in *Dikoko v. Mokathla*, however, may have broken this deadlock. It also provided us with a possible practical and workable definition of *ubuntu*, namely reconciliation and restorative justice between parties involved in litigation proceedings.

The question may of course be asked of why the term *ubuntu* should be used to describe this constitutional value when one can just as well refer to the well-known values of *reconciliation* and *restorative justice*? It is submitted that the term *ubuntu* should be retained as it provides our courts with a constitutional value with a local flavor intrinsically linked to our troubled past and the consequent and ongoing bridge-building process of our nation. With this in mind our courts can then also develop the concept in a specific way relating to a uniquely African value system and not just blindly follow international trends in this regard.

Hopefully the courts will embrace this key element of *ubuntu* in future court proceedings and develop it in the relevant context of the particular case instead of reverting back to the all-embracing and seemingly worthless definition of *ubuntu* that was used in previous cases.[49]

African Customary Law in South Africa:
The Many Faces of *Bhe v. Magistrate Khayelitsha*

Chuma Himonga

Bhe v. Magistrate Khayelitsha[1] (hereafter referred to as *Bhe*) is as much of a landmark decision as it is multifaceted. Apart from being the first Constitutional Court case to decide on the constitutionality of the principle of male primogeniture in customary succession law, which in its official version has been the subject of litigation in other prominent cases across Africa,[2] the case contains pronouncements on several issues pertaining to customary law within the framework of the Constitution and human rights in regional and international treaties that South Africa has ratified. Among the prominent ones are: the rights of women living under customary law; the relationship between customary law and the previously dominant legal system, the common law;[3] the old African continental issue of how to reform customary law in a pluralistic legal system,[4] which in South Africa's constitutionally entrenched cultural and legal pluralism takes on an additional dimension;[5] the official and living dimensions of the concept of customary law and their implications for the application and development of this system of law; and the roles of the courts and the legislature in the alignment of customary law with the Constitution. These facets represent what I have entitled the many faces of *Bhe,* although the pronouncements made in relation to each one of them are different in weight.

Furthermore, at least in the sphere of customary succession law, *Bhe* will probably be numbered among the most cited constitutional cases in this country and internationally. For sure, *Bhe* will be among the most written about constitutional decisions, gathering from the many issues it touched on. And this writing will most likely be on what it achieved or did not achieve.

The foregoing description of the faces of *Bhe*, however, also shows that it is almost impossible to do justice to this decision as a whole in a single article, and this paper is no exception. A selective approach to its discussion is, therefore, inevitable.

The aim of this article is to comment on selected aspects of *Bhe*, taking into account both the majority and minority judgments. These are: the protection of the rights of African women and gender equality in succession; the development of customary law as envisioned by the Constitution; the approach adopted to reform the customary law of succession; conflict of laws and the need for innovation in dealing with customary law in South Africa that *Bhe* has revealed. The selection of these issues is arbitrary and determined by the interests of the author and the limits of space. But it is also probably true that the issues chosen represent some of the major concerns in current customary law debates. The paper will attempt to evaluate the majority and minority judgments and show how they have affected the various subjects under discussion. Some of the issues, such as the dimensions of living and official customary law and the roles of the courts and the legislature in reconciling customary law with the Constitution, are not dealt with under specific headings as they permeate the discussion of the other issues.

The discussion of the selected issues will be preceded by a brief outline of the majority decision, while that of the minority will be incorporated into the discussion where appropriate. The legal framework in which the case arose and the general position occupied by customary law in the Republican Constitution are not dealt with, as these are clearly laid out by the judgments.[6] Nevertheless, various aspects of these two subjects will be introduced in the discussion of the selected issues when necessary.

THE DECISION

Bhe was heard together with two other cases. These were *Shibi v. Sithole and Minister for Justice and Constitutional Development* and *South African Human Rights Commission and Women's Legal Centre Trust v. The President of the Republic of South Africa and Minister for Justice and Constitutional Development*. Both *Shibi* and *Bhe* concerned the constitutionality of the customary law of succession embodied in the Black Administration Act[7] (hereafter referred to as BAA), including the principle of primogeniture. The only difference between them is that the female excluded from succession to the deceased's estate in *Shibi* was the deceased's sister as compared to the deceased's daughters in *Bhe*. On the other hand, the Applicants in *South African Human Rights Commission* applied for direct access to the Constitutional Court to have the whole of the Black Administration Act declared unconstitutional, on the ground that its provisions infringed the rights to equality and human dignity, and the court granted direct access to the Applicants.

It is necessary to point out at the outset that *Bhe* only concerns succession to the intestate estates of black South Africans, which were previously regulated by customary law in terms both of their distribution and administration.

According to the internal conflict of law rules governing intestate succession, before they were invalidated by *Bhe,* the following estates fell to be distributed and administered under customary law: (a) movable property of a black "allotted by him to or accruing under customary law to any woman with whom he lived in a customary union or to any house,"[8] (b) "[a]ll land in a tribal settlement held in individual tenure upon quitrent conditions by a Black,"[9] and (c) estates of blacks that devolved under regulation 2 (e) of the BAA. This regulation stated that any deceased estate of a black which did not fall to be distributed in terms of regulations 2 (a), (c), and (d) would be distributed according to Black law and custom.[10] The estates which were covered by regulations 2 (a), (c), and (d) were those of blacks whose estates were distributed as though they had been Europeans, and their estates were then distributed in accordance with the Intestate Succession Act[11] (hereafter referred to as ISA). The following categories of deceased estates of blacks qualified to be distributed under the ISA in terms of regulation 2 (a), (c), and (d):

(a) If the deceased was at the time of his death the holder of a letter of exemption issued under the provisions of section 31 of the BAA, exempting him from the operation of customary law;

(c) If the deceased, at the time of his death was—
   (i) a partner in a civil marriage in community of property or under antenuptial contract; or
   (ii) a widower, widow or divorcee, as the case may be, of a civil marriage in community of property or under antenuptial contract and was not survived by a partner to a customary union entered into subsequent to the dissolution of such marriage; and

(d) if the deceased was survived by any partner—
   (i)   with whom he had contracted a marriage which was out of community of property; or
   (ii) with whom he had entered into a customary union; or
   (iii) who was at the time of his death living with him as his putative spouse,[12] and where the Minister considered it, in the circumstances of the case, to be inequitable or inappropriate to apply customary law.

Section 1(4)(b) of the ISA then excluded all the estates to which customary law applied in terms of section 23 of the BAA from its application.

Generally the indicators as to whether customary law or the ISA applied were, according to these regulations, the nature of the marriage and the type of matrimonial property adopted by the spouses. In a civil marriage in community of property,[13] the ISA was deemed to apply whereas in a customary marriage or in a civil marriage out of community of property[14] customary law was deemed to apply.

An important rule of customary law under these regulations was the principle of male primogeniture, which excluded women from succession and inheritance and also preferred older over junior males as heirs.[15]

The court set aside the High Court orders in the two cases before the High Court (i.e. *Bhe* and *Shibi)* and made orders that encompassed the third application as well. Among other things, it held the following:[16]

(a) Section 23 of the BAA and the relevant regulations[17] were discriminatory, contrary to section 9(3) of the Constitution, and not "reasonable and justifiable in a democratic society based on dignity, equality and freedom."[18] It accordingly invalidated them.

(b) The exclusion of women and extra-marital children from inheriting in terms of the principle of primogeniture amounted to unfair discrimination against these classes of people contrary to section 9(3) of the Constitution, and the principle of primogeniture also violated the right of women to dignity, contrary to section 10 of the Constitution.[19]

(c) Section 1(4)(b) of the ISA was unconstitutional, because it excluded from the application of section 1 of that Act any estate or part of the estate to which section 23 of the BAA applied.

(d) The ISA would apply to the estates that were previously governed by the impugned provisions of the BAA and the regulations and the principle of primogeniture.

(e) In fairness and justice, the order invalidating the impugned provisions will apply retrospectively to 27 April 1994. This would ensure that in respect of the estates of the people who died after the interim Constitution became operative, all affected women, men, and children would benefit from the decision. The only exceptions are those estates in which the transfer of ownership to a *bona fide* heir[20] was completed before the date of the Court's order, and the deceased estate was not subject to litigation challenging the constitutional validity of the customary law of inheritance.

(f) The Master of the High Court would no longer be precluded from dealing with estates of blacks that were previously regulated by the impugned provisions and, except for estates that were being wound up in terms of section 23 of the BAA at the time of the order, all estates would be wound up in terms of the Administration of Estates Act[21] in the future.[22]

SELECTED ASPECTS OF *BHE*

Women's Rights and Gender Equality

This is the largest part of the face of *Bhe*, in terms of its importance and in being the aspect of the case that set the proceedings into motion.

As already stated, the principle of male primogeniture precluded women from inheriting either as daughters or as widows from the deceased head of the family. The untold suffering that rules of inheritance under customary law have brought upon women in changing social and economic conditions has been the subject of much writing and research on the African continent.[23] In South Africa, this problem came to the fore with the infamous decision of the High Court[24] and the Supreme Court of Appeal in *Mthembu v. Letsela*[25] discussed below.[26]

Bhe sought to protect the inheritance and equality of women in relation to succession in four distinct ways. These are the invalidation of the principle of primogeniture, the refusal to suspend the invalidation of the principle of primogeniture, the distribution of estates by agreement and the rejection of the case-by-case approach.

INVALIDATION OF THE PRINCIPLE OF PRIMOGENITURE
The court invalidated the relevant provisions of the BAA and its regulations and the official customary law principle of male primogeniture.

Official customary law denotes the customary law that is recorded in textbooks, court precedents and codified in legislation, while living (unofficial) customary law means the customary practices or norms observed by people living under customary law in their day-to-day lives. These forms of customary law are often different from each other.[27]

The constitutionality of the principle of male primogeniture had been challenged in the High Court in 1998 in *Mthembu v. Letsela*[28] on the basis, *inter alia*, that it discriminated on the grounds of sex and gender. The application was brought on behalf of the deceased's female child and was being contested by the deceased's father who claimed to be the heir to the deceased. The High Court held that although the principle was *prima facie* discriminatory; it did not amount to unfair discrimination contrary to the Constitution because the law placed a concomitant duty upon the heir to support the deceased's widow and children. On appeal to the Supreme Court of Appeal, the Court refused to decide the constitutional challenge and to develop the rule of primogeniture on the grounds, *inter alia*, that the interim Constitution did not operate retroactively and that the legislature was best suited to develop customary law respectively. With regard to the first ground, the court reasoned that the rights of the heir in the estate had vested on the death of the deceased, which was on 13 August 1993 and before the interim Constitution took effect.[29]

The dismissal of the application by the High Court and the Supreme Court of Appeal meant that for the next six years or so until the decision in *Bhe*, women were denied their inheritance rights under customary law. In fact, it seems that cases similar to *Mthembu* that were already before the courts were dismissed and dealt with under customary law.[30]

In invalidating the principle of primogeniture and the statutory provisions that supported it, the court overruled *Mthembu*.[31] In order to fill the *lacuna* left by the rule, the court extended the ISA to all estates that were previously governed by customary law as a temporary measure until the legislature enacted legislation dealing with the customary law of succession. It also declared section 1(4)(b) of the ISA to be unconstitutional, as already stated.

Section 1 of the ISA spells out the beneficiaries to a deceased estate.[32] Surviving spouses and the children of the deceased are the primary beneficiaries. The members of the extended family (i.e. the deceased's relatives other than his or her surviving spouse and children) only inherit if there are no primary heirs surviving.

However, the ISA provided for monogamous marriages only, but customary marriages are potentially polygynous in nature. In order to protect women in polygynous marriages as well, the court modified section 1(1)(c)(i) and (4)(f) of the ISA with the following results:

(a) the determination of a child's share must have regard to the existence of more than one surviving spouse;

(b) provision must be made for each surviving spouse to inherit the minimum;[33] and

(c) all the surviving spouses are to share the estate equally where the estate is not enough to provide the prescribed minimum to each of the surviving spouses.[34]

Thus until the legislature enacts the legislation to replace this remedy, as the case may be, all women in South Africa will, in theory, enjoy inheritance rights under the ISA regardless of whether they are married under customary law or civil law or whether they live in the rural hinterland or in town. From the experience of other African countries concerning delays in the enactment of legislation reforming customary law, it could be a number of years before we see the anticipated legislation on succession. The women living under customary law are, therefore, guaranteed their newly acquired rights for some time to come.

However, it is necessary at this stage to consider the impact on the position of women under *Bhe* of the fact that customary law is a system of law that operates at official and non-official levels. It is submitted that the extent to which women will benefit from the decision may depend on whether they are governed by official or living customary law.

It is clear from both the majority and minority decisions in *Bhe* that the rule of primogeniture that was replaced by the ISA or developed by the majority and minority[35] respectively is the official rather than the living customary law version of the rule. This means that the court has not dealt with the situation of women under living customary law or tested the constitutionality of this form of law with regard to women's rights and gender equality. The court's dealings with living customary law basically stopped at the point where the existence of the dichotomy between official customary law and living customary law was acknowledged.[36]

Although it is acknowledged that the flexibility of living customary law makes it more likely for it to adapt to the new constitutional values and human rights than official customary law[37] and, therefore, more likely to protect women's rights, it cannot be assumed that all living customary law is consistent with the constitutional principles and values and that it does not require constitutional scrutiny. Thus the court's failure to engage with living customary law may, with due respect, signify its failure to advance the rights of the majority of women living under this system of law in the area of succession, and to meaningfully transform their lives in line with the Constitution.

By dealing with official customary law only, the court seems to have done what it in fact objected to—a piecemeal reform of customary law, albeit in another context.[38] More importantly, in the words of *Stewart*, the court merely tinkered "with [the] officially or judicially constructed versions of customary law [in order] to make this version of customary law more women friendly [by aligning] it with international human rights instruments [and] with the Constitution [which] is women friendly."[39] Unfortunately, this approach does not "address the reality of women's experiences on the ground with local customs and practices, which may be either negative or positive experiences."[40]

At another place, *Stewart* underscores the political and rather meaningless nature of changes to customary law that focus on official customary law:

> The focus of law reform tends to be on the ossified written versions of the so called rules of custom and on the superior Courts' versions of custom which can be adjusted, adapted, amended, criticised and generally played with, thereby keeping the 'big players' happy. That is precisely the game that is played if the re-examination of customary law is superficial and not located in the way that it operates at the level of people's and, in this case, women's daily access to resources and the exercise of rights over those resources.[41]

This argument is in no way meant to suggest that the Constitutional Court in *Bhe* was pandering to politicians or some other interest groups in reaching its decision. It merely suggests that the decision, partly because of its stature as the decision of the Constitutional Court, may be used by appropriate authorities as an excuse for not addressing the position of women under customary succession law further, or soon enough, to the disadvantage of the majority of women whose interest or rights are not encompassed by the majority decision. What we have in mind is a situation where the legislature, for example, does nothing to bring about the law anticipated by the court, because it feels that *Bhe* has solved all the problems of women, or worse still, it simply lifts the decision into the anticipated legislation for reasons of convenience.

The possibility of the first scenario happening could probably have been avoided if the court had, along with its remedy, put the legislature to terms to enact the legislation in question within a fixed period of time as it has done in other cases in the past.[42] The second scenario was, obviously, beyond the court's control. But should either of these scenarios happen,[43] *Bhe* will end up being something that the court did not anticipate—a tragic decision for most women living under customary law for reasons already stated above.

The sum of this argument is that, because the court's decision dealt only with official customary law, its relevance is limited to people living under that form of customary law as opposed to those living under living customary law. Consequently, if *Bhe* ever gets to be understood or perceived as though it solved the problems of all women in inheritance under customary law consistently with the Constitution, it will detract from the need for a comprehensive reform of the customary law in a manner that is relevant to all women living under customary law. It therefore lies with everyone concerned with the position of all women, but especially those living under the form of customary law that was not addressed by the court, to ensure that the limits of *Bhe* in this regard are understood, and that the decision will not have unforeseen or unintended consequences for certain categories of women.

REFUSAL TO SUSPEND THE INVALIDATION OF THE PRINCIPLE OF PRIMOGENITURE

The court refused to suspend the declaration of invalidity of the impugned provisions of the BAA and the principle of male primogeniture to a future date until Parliament rectified the problem. The court reasoned that this would condemn those (women and extramarital children) who had suffered unfair discrimination in the past to the mercy of the legislature, and already the legislature had proved unhelpful in providing solutions to the problem.[44] For nearly ten years since the new constitutional dispensation, it had done nothing to legislate on the customary law of succession to alleviate the plight of vulnerable members of the family under the law.[45] The court thus took a different course from that which was taken by the Supreme Court of Appeal in *Mthembu v. Letsela* that simply deferred the issue of reforming the principle of primogeniture to the legislature.

However, since the court in *Bhe* declined to develop customary law, and in view of the importance of the problem and the need to find a permanent solution quickly, one wonders whether deferring to the legislature (in the way that it did) without putting it to terms as to when it should produce the necessary legislation was the best solution. The question of the development of customary law itself is dealt with below.

DISTRIBUTION OF THE ESTATE BY AGREEMENT

The flexibility introduced into the distribution of estates by *Bhe* by allowing family agreements is laudable, indeed, not only for the purposes of creating space for the spontaneous development of living customary law for its own sake,[46] but also for promoting the development of a system of law that is more relevant to the lives of most people, especially women, as stated above.

Both the majority and minority judgments held that the parties could agree on how the estate could be distributed, albeit, in different contexts. The majority held that although the ISA replaced the customary law that previously regulated intestate estates of blacks, the application of that Act did not "preclude an estate devolving in accordance with an agreement reached among all interested parties but in a way that is consistent with its provisions."[47] The minority on the other hand held that both the ISA and customary law would apply to the estates in question, but the choice of law process would be directed by the agreement of the parties in the first instance, and by the decision of a magistrate with jurisdiction in the event of a dispute between the parties about the applicable law.

As already stated, living customary law is often different from official customary law. In its judgment the minority alluded to the fact that living customary law may already have adjusted to the rights of women under the Constitution.[48] If this were to be true, then family agreements would serve a double purpose—the creation of a space for the spontaneous growth of living customary law and contributing towards the development of customary law that is consistent with the Constitution. Such a system of law also runs less of a risk of being ignored by the communities because they do not identify themselves with it and becoming mere paper law that has no relevance to their experiences in real life, again to the disadvantage of those the new law seeks to protect, the women and children.[49]

However, the majority decision was alert to the problem that family agreement could be abused to the disadvantage of some family members and made provision to counteract this problem.

The problem lies in the danger that the court's idea of family agreements may instead create an avenue for the continued application of customary law, which was invalidated, to the detriment of women, especially widows, who in both matrilineal and patrilineal kinship systems do not take part in the decision-making process concerning the distribution of the estates of their deceased husbands.[50] And if they take part in this process nevertheless, their views are not determinative. In other words, the intersections between the semi-autonomous social field[51] of the family operating under living customary law and the official (state) institutions do not always safeguard the interests or rights of women as expected or anticipated by state-sponsored law reforms. This is borne out by a comparative study in Zambia, which revealed that family decisions about the administration of estates sometimes undermine the interests of widows in their deceased husbands' estates.[52]

Furthermore, the pressure of the family on women and on widows, in particular, to negotiate the distribution of estates and to apply customary law instead of the ISA is likely to be heightened by the fact that the majority decision did not accommodate the interests of the extended family in the inheritance of the estate. The extended family members who previously inherited estates under customary law or who were, at least, supported from deceased estates by heirs, may see the flexibility created by the court in the administration of the estate by agreement as a way of regaining inheritance rights they have lost to surviving spouses and children of the deceased under the court's order. This practice has been observed in Zambia, admittedly, even though the Intestate Succession Act,[53] which reformed the customary law of succession, provides for the extended family to inherit a portion of the deceased's estate.[54]

For these reasons, the majority decision's alertness to the need to protect vulnerable family members when agreements are used as the vehicle of distribution is noteworthy. It stated that:

> Having regard to the vulnerable position in which some of the surviving family members may find themselves, care must be taken that such agreements are genuine and not the result of exploitation of the weaker members of the family by the strong. In this regard, a special duty rests on the Master of the High Court, the magistrates and other officials responsible for the administration of estates to ensure that no one is prejudiced in the discussions leading to the purported agreements.[55]

Thus, in order to protect weak family members, especially women and children, from the unintended consequences of family negotiations with regard to the distribution of the estate by agreement, it will be necessary to monitor the effect of the involvement of the family closely through, for example, socio-legal research.[56]

In contrast, the minority's decision to use the parties' agreement to determine the law to be used to distribute the estate does not make any reference to the need for caution aimed at protecting vulnerable family members. It is therefore problematic from this point of view.

REJECTION OF THE CASE-BY-CASE APPROACH

It had been urged upon the majority to develop the offending principle of primogeniture as a way of reconciling this rule of customary law with the Constitution. However, the Court viewed this as involving the development of customary law on a case-by-case approach and rejected it. Among the reasons for this was that the case-by-case approach would not "guarantee the constitutional protection of the rights of women and children in the devolution of intestate estates."[57] What was required, according to the majority, was a "more direct action to safeguard the important rights that have been identified."[58]

The action taken by the court under this heading to protect women can be criticized on the ground that it precluded the majority from developing customary law, especially living customary law, which, as shown above, was necessary to protect a greater number of women than is now protected by the decision. As shown in the next section, objection to the case-by-case approach to the development of customary law was one of the reasons why the majority declined to develop customary law.

From the foregoing, in theory, *Bhe* has definitely improved the situation of some women living under customary law in the area of succession. However, whether or not women will enjoy the rights acquired from the remedy of the court in practice will depend, firstly, on whether they live under official customary law or living customary law, as already stated and, secondly, on how well the law can be implemented. The latter is beyond the scope of this article.[59]

Development of Customary Law

The clearest provision for the development of customary law is section 39(2) of the Constitution.[60] It states that, "When interpreting any legislation, and when developing the common law or customary law, every Court, tribunal or forum must promote the spirit, purport and objects of the Bill of Rights."

The discussion of the judgment on the development of customary law under this heading is restricted to the question whether the court could have developed living customary law. This will entail analyzing the reasons why the court did not develop this system of law and a consideration of the possibilities that were open to it to do so. In the preceding section it was shown that women's rights would have been more extensively protected if the court had dealt with living customary law as well. This is, of course, not the only significance to be attached to the development of living customary law by the courts as a way of resolving conflict between customary law and the Constitution. Not developing customary law may also mean that the court has to invalidate the rule that conflicts with the Constitution and replace it with the common law, as happened in *Bhe* (i.e. the majority judgment) and other cases before it.[61]

This, in turn, creates the problem that in a legal system in which the continued existence of legal pluralism is assured by provisions in the Constitution, including provisions in the Bill of Rights, customary law is slowly but surely being wiped out and replaced by the common law. This problem has been discussed elsewhere,[62] and will not form the subject of this article. Suffice it to say that it is beyond question that customary law forms a part of the South African legal system, that it occupies an equal position with the common law in the legal system and that, as much as possible, it must be preserved. In regard to the latter, the minority rightly referred to the Constitutional Court's decision in *Ex parte Chairperson of the Constitutional Assembly: In re Certification of the Constitution of the Republic of South Africa, 1996*[63] and said:

> This Court cautioned that a destructive confrontation between the Bill of Rights and legislation, on the one hand, and indigenous law, on the other, need not take place. The application of common law and the Intestate Succession Act only, may well lead to the obliteration of indigenous law. Yet our Constitution recognises its existence, and contemplates that there are situations where it will be applicable. The Constitution expressly guarantees 'the survival of an evolving customary law.'[64] And . . . as the [majority] acknowledges, there is a substantial number of people whose lives are governed by indigenous law

and who would wish to have their affairs to be governed by indigenous law. People who live by indigenous law and custom are entitled to be governed by indigenous law. The Constitution accords them that right.[65]

Against this background, it would be expected that a court should develop, rather than expunge or invalidate, customary law, let alone replace it with the common law unless it is impossible to develop it.

What then were the reasons for the court not developing customary law in Bhe?

The court tendered three reasons for rejecting the argument urging it to develop customary law.[66] The first reason was the difficulty of determining the true content of the current customary law (i.e. living customary law). The second was that adopting this approach would have entailed the development of customary law on a case-by-case basis, which was not only very slow but created other problems, such as uncertainty in the law and the lack of uniformity in the application of the law by the courts.[67] Thirdly, it considered the legislature to be best suited to deal with the defects in the customary law of succession. We are interested in the first two.

ASCERTAINING CUSTOMARY LAW

The proof and ascertainment of living customary law is an acknowledged problem.[68] However, considering that the Constitution recognized this system of law, with full knowledge on the part of its drafters of this fact, suggests that the difficulty of ascertaining customary law should never be a legitimate reason for a court not discharging its duty under the Constitution to develop it. And, as the majority itself acknowledged,[69] there are cases[70] in which the courts have done this, using the existing methods to ascertain customary law. The minority judgment also referred to these methods.[71] They are the methods contained in the Law of Evidence Amendment Act,[72] and the use of textbooks and precedent (with the necessary caution about not using textbooks or precedents of the pre-democratic dispensation that distort customary law).[73] It would therefore appear that the court could have ascertained living customary law using these methods, and developed it, if necessary. Some of these methods might have required the court to call witnesses and hear evidence that had not been introduced by the parties on its own account. It is submitted that if there were to be any procedural or technical reasons barring this course of action, they would have to be disregarded in terms either of section 36 of the Constitution or other relevant law. This would be on account of the need for the Constitutional Court to protect the human rights of people at the least cost to themselves possible.

In any case, it seems that if the court was so inclined it would, at least, have developed the official customary law before it, as did the minority. The minority pointed out, rightly, that it was not necessary to ascertain living customary law in order to develop the form of customary law (i.e. official customary law) that was before the court.[74]

CASE-BY-CASE METHOD

One of the main concerns of the majority of the court was that the case-by-case method induced uncertainty and the lack of uniformity in the law. But the court does not interrogate the significance of the values of certainty and uniformity in the application of the law within the context of the new dispensation. While these are important values of the common law, it is doubtful that their continued value and impact on the status of other legal systems can be assumed in a society that has a constitutionally entrenched legal pluralism. In so far as they may not be shared by all the legal systems recognized in the country (customary law is by its very nature flexible, which predisposes it to uncertainty), there may be a need to subject the values in question to constitutional scrutiny, in the same way as the interpretation of public policy was subjected to constitutional scrutiny in *Ryland v. Edros*.[75] This would ensure that the values of one system of law (for example, the common law) are not used to frustrate the legitimate existence of other systems of law in the new legal system. In *Ryland v. Edros,* one of the earliest cases to make sense of the meaning of legal pluralism in the new constitutional dispensation, the High Court rejected the prevailing interpretation of the concept of public policy that preferred the values of one sector of the South African society (whites) over another. Consequently the court for the first time recognized the Muslim contract of marriage as producing legal consequences that could be enforced by the courts.[76]

Furthermore, with regard to certainty, the majority seems to have overlooked its own earlier pronouncement about the nature of customary law in *Alexkor Ltd and Another v. Richtersveld Community and Others*,[77] where it stated that "indigenous law is not a fixed body of formally classified and easily ascertainable rules [and that] by its very nature it evolves as the people who live by its norms change their patterns of life."[78] In fact, to insist on certainty in customary law is to further the rigidity and, therefore, ossification of customary law, as well as the perpetuation of official customary law, all of which seem to undermine the right to culture entrenched in the Bill of Rights.[79]

Finally, it seems that a case-by-case approach would have commended itself to a court that was concerned about taking upon itself the role of finding a permanent solution to conflicts between customary law and the Constitution and thereby usurping the role of the legislature. This approach would have enabled the court to do justice to the case before it while leaving the search for a permanent solution to the legislature.[80] Two other actions were, however, necessary to meet the court's concerns if it had taken the case-by-case approach.

Firstly, in order to deal with the court's concerns about the need to halt violations of fundamental rights while we await the legislature's action, it should have invalidated the official customary law (as it, indeed, did); developed the living customary law, if necessary, after ascertaining it as suggested above and applied it to the case before it. Secondly, it should have put Parliament to terms by requiring it to complete the process of legislation within a fixed period, as already stated. In the meantime, all cases similar to *Bhe* would be dealt with under the doctrine of precedent, applying the principles of customary law developed by *Bhe*, or principles as developed in subsequent cases on a case-by-case basis.

Alternatively, it seems that the court could still have achieved the desired "direct action" to safeguard the important rights that had been identified by applying the ISA in *Bhe* or similar cases as an exception, while leaving the case-by-case approach as the main method of developing customary law. This is not an unprecedented approach. It is applied to the common law when it is necessary to bring about a faster development to the law in a given area than would otherwise be the case if the matter were left to precedent.[81]

It is submitted on the basis of the foregoing arguments that it is difficult to understand why the majority did not develop official and living customary law in this case. Developing both forms of customary law would not only have protected the rights of women more effectively but also the new status of customary law in the legal system (in that it would not have to be struck down unnecessarily whenever it conflicts with the Constitution).

Approach to the Reform of Customary Law

The reform of customary law in postcolonial Africa has been a pre-occupation of African governments, albeit at different paces and degrees of political will.[82] *Bhe* joined the law reform arena by introducing a temporary change to the customary law of succession until Parliament enacts legislation to regulate this area of the law.

The court was aware of the argument that applying the ISA would obliterate customary law contrary to the status accorded it in the Constitution. Drawing support from the proposals of the South African Law Commission on the Customary Law of Succession,[83] the court alluded to the Commission's assumption that the ISA had the capacity to accommodate "much of the customary law of succession,"[84] and apparently saw this as one way of meeting the obliteration argument above. It accordingly replaced the substantive customary law in issue by the ISA, and the customary law on administration of estates by the Administration of Estates Act.[85] It then sought to adjust the ISA, in order to accommodate customary law.

It is noteworthy, however, that in the end the court only accommodated polygynous marriages,[86] an institution that is apparently already waning,[87] and customary law to be brought in through family agreements. With regard to the latter, it left it open to interested parties to agree on how the estate should be distributed. In so doing, it hoped to foster the "spontaneous development of customary law," obviously, under the frame of reference of constitutional values.[88] But, as already stated, this spontaneous development would only be allowed if the agreements were consistent with the provisions of the ISA.[89]

Thus the majority effectively accommodated a very small amount of customary law, leaving out apparently important aspects of customary law, such as family property and the needs of the deceased's extended family for support.[90] In this respect, the court followed the path taken for the reform of the customary law of marriage by the Recognition of Customary Marriages Act,[91] which also accommodated but a small portion of customary law and replaced the rest with the common law governing a civil marriage.[92]

Gauging from these two initiatives concerning the most important areas of customary law (i.e. marriage and succession), it seems that South Africa is poised to adopt the method of law reform whereby customary law is replaced by the common law, if the latter is compatible with the Constitution. In this case, one thing seems to be certain: State intervention will not have the last word; the people living under customary law will continue to feed and grow their own system of law. Hopefully, this growth will take place within, and be informed by, the new terms of reference set by the Constitution and its values.

The majority approach to law reform may be contrasted with the minority decision. It held that the official principle of male primogeniture be developed (and developed it) and that both customary law and the ISA should be applied "subject to the Constitution and the requirements of fairness, justice and equity, bearing in mind the interests of minor children and other dependants of the deceased family head."[93]

Both this and the case-by-case approach advocated by the minority seem to be more accommodative of customary law than the approaches taken by the majority.[94] But both the minority approach and that of the majority concerning the notion of family agreements seem to represent a flexible and open-ended approach that may contain the initial gems of innovative law reform in our plural legal system. This is emphasized below.

The application of both customary law and the ISA proposed by the minority, obviously, raises the question of conflict of laws, to which we now turn.

Conflict of Laws

As already pointed out, *Bhe* invalidated the conflict of laws dealing with succession contained in section 23 of the BAA and its regulations. By applying the ISA to estates previously governed by customary law, the court removed all conflicts between customary law and common law in this area. This development has overtaken the South African Law Commission's proposals on the application of customary law of 1999.[95] Until those proposals become law,[96] or the anticipated legislation on intestate succession comes into existence, the majority decision of the court will continue to apply.

On the other hand, the minority's decision that both customary law and the ISA would apply to the distribution of estates maintains the need for choice of law rules to determine the applicable system.

The choice of law rules proposed by the minority is that, first and foremost, the agreement of the parties will determine the applicable law. In the event of a dispute preventing such an agreement, the Magistrate Court having jurisdiction will determine the dispute, having "regard to what is fair, just and equitable in the circumstances of the case." And in determining what is fair, just and equitable, the Magistrate should have regard to, amongst other things, the assets and liabilities of the estate, the widow's contribution to the acquisition of assets, the contribution of family members to such assets, and whether there are minor children or other dependants of the deceased who require support and maintenance.

The agreement of the parties as to whether to apply common law (i.e. the ISA in this case) or customary law to a case before the court is not new in South Africa. The current choice of law rules for determining the application of customary in areas other than succession have been developed by the courts over the years and they use agreement as one of the guidelines.[97] Similarly, the parties' agreement ranks first in a hierarchy of statutory rules for determining conflicts between systems of customary law.[98] Agreement also ranks first for resolving both conflicts between customary law and common law and between systems of customary law, in the proposed Application of Customary Law Bill,[99] which is aimed at reforming the current choice of law rules. What is new in the minority's approach, however, is the inclusion of the constitutional values of fairness, justice and equity to be considered when the Magistrate Court has to decide the applicable law. It is submitted that the agreement of the parties should equally be informed by these underlying values.

It may furthermore be observed that in the South African context, the approach, which incorporates the agreement of the parties to choose their own law, seems to be compatible with the Constitution concerning the right of individuals to participate in a cultural life of their own choice.[100]

The Need for Innovation and Creativity

Bhe has revealed the difficulties of reconciling customary law with the Constitution within the context of South Africa's constitutionally protected cultural and legal pluralism. This seems to suggest the need for innovative and creative approaches on the part of the court s and the legislature when seeking to align customary law with the Constitution. Two examples from the preceding discussions will suffice.

There seems to be a conflict between the need to accommodate customary law in the reformed laws with the imperative to protect women's constitutional and other human rights. While the inclusion of family agreements or the agreement of the parties as to what law to apply contributes to the greater accommodation of customary law in the legal system in line with the Constitution, it works against the protection of women's rights and gender equality unless extra measures are taken to guard against this. The same goes for the case-by-case approach, which, though friendly to the accommodation of customary law in the reformed law, does not seem to be compatible with the protection of women's rights because of its slow nature.

These somewhat inherent tensions seem to call for deep reflection, innovation and creativity on the part of the courts and the legislature. Unfortunately, it has been observed that the courts are rather uncritical and superficial in their engagement with customary law and its development.[101] This may not be far from the truth as far as the legislature is concerned, if one looks at the way the Recognition of Customary Marriages Act simply imported the common law to regulate a big portion of matters previously regulated by customary law.[102] It is hoped that the suggestions made in this paper will contribute towards innovative approaches to aligning customary law to the Constitution.

CONCLUSION

This article provides a broad-based commentary on the majority and minority decisions in *Bhe*. Apart from highlighting the prominent features of this ground-breaking case in some respects, this article has shown its multifaceted nature. In my view, the majority and minority decisions have touched on nearly all important aspects of customary law. This is bound to affect the development, in one way or another, of the various aspects of the law concerned through judicial or legislative interventions in the future.

I also hope that the complexity of the issues pertaining to customary law that are evident in the entire judgment of *Bhe*, including those aspects of it that were not dealt with in this article, will challenge the court s and the legislature, which are charged with the development of jurisprudence and law befitting a constitutionally protected legal pluralism, into seeking innovative and creative solutions for resolving conflicts between customary law and the Constitution when these occur.

Notes

INTRODUCTION

1. John Murungi, "African Jurisprudence: hermeneutic reflections," in *A Companion to African Philosophy*, ed. Kwasi Wiredu (Oxford: Blackwell Publishing, 2006), 525–6.

2. See Hobbes, *The Leviathan.*

3. H. L. A. Hart, *Essays in Jurisprudence and Philosophy* (Oxford: Claredon Press, 2001), 80–82, 111–116, 135, 161, 163–164, 185.

4. Kant, "On the Relationship of Theory to Practice in Political Right" in *Kant, Political Writings*, ed. H. S. Reiss, (Cambridge: Cambridge University Press, 2001).

5. Ifeanyi Menkiti, "On the normative conception of a person," in *A Companion to African Philosophy*, ed. Kwasi Wiredu (Oxford: Blackwell Publishing, 2006), 326.

6. Kwasi Wiredu, "Mortality and Religion in Akan Thought," in *Philosophy and Cultures*, eds. Henry O. Oruka and D. A. Masolo (Nairobi: Bookwise Publishers, 1983), 6–13; and in *Cultural Universals and Particulars* (Bloomington: Indiana University Press, 1996), quoted in D. A. Masolo, "Western and African Communitarianism," in *A Companion to African Philosophy*, ed. Kwasi Wiredu (Oxford: Blackwell Publishing, 2006), 496.

7. *MEC for Education: KwaZulu-Natal and Others v. Pillay and Others* 2006 10 BCLR 1237 N at para 53.

8. D. A. Masolo (*supra* n. 6), 483 and 493.

9. John Murungi (*supra* n. 1), 522–3.

10. *Bhe and Others v. Magistrate, Khayelitsha and Others* [2003] JOL 11805 (c) at 17.

11. To quote Rawls on the "Veil of Ignorance":

> As a device of representation its abstractness invites misunderstanding. In particular, the description of the parties may seem to presuppose a particular metaphysical conception of the person; for example, that the essential nature of persons is independent of and prior to their contingent attributes, including their final ends and attachments, and indeed their conception of the good and character as a whole (*Political Liberalism* [New York: Columbia University Press, 1996], 27).

Also, see discussion in Drucilla Cornell, *Moral Images of Freedom* (New York: Rowman & Littlefield Publishers, 2007), 11–37.

12. Mabogo More, *"South Africa under and after Apartheid," in* A companion to African Philosophy, ed. Kwasi Wiredu (Oxford: Blackwell Publishing, 2006), 149 and 156–157.

13. John Murungi (*supra* n. 1), 525.

14. *S v. Makwanyane and Another* 1995 (6) BCLR 665 (CC) at para 306; Justice Mokgoro stated that:

> The broad legal profession, academia and those sectors of organised civil society particularly concerned with public interest law, have an equally important responsibility and role to play by combining efforts and resources to place the required evidence in argument before the Courts. It is not as if these resources are lacking; what has been absent has been the will, and the acknowledgement of the importance of the material concerned.

15. Notwithstanding the other provisions of the new Constitution and despite the repeal of the previous Constitution, all the provisions relating to amnesty contained in the previous Constitution under the heading "National Unity and Reconciliation" are deemed to be part of the new Constitution for the purposes of the Promotion of National Unity and Reconciliation Act, 1995 (Act 34 of 1995), as amended, including for the purposes of its validity.

16. *Makwanyane* (*supra* n. 14) at para 308.

17. George Carew, "Economic globalism, deliberative democracy" in *A Companion to African Philosophy,* ed. Kwasi Wiredu (Oxford, Blackwell Publishing, 2006), 460 and 463.

18. John Murungi (*supra* n. 1), 525.

19. *Makwanyane* (*supra* n. 14) at para 307.

20. On file with author.

21. *Makwanyane* (*supra* n. 14) at para 316.

22. *Id.* at para 222.

23. *Id.* at para 226.

24. *Id.* at para 227.

25. *Id.* at para 241.

26. *Id.* at para 260.

27. *Id.* at para 131.

28. *Id.* at paras 358–85.

29. Johan van der Walt, *Law and Sacrifice: Towards a Post Apartheid Theory of Law,* (London and Johannesburg: Birbeck Law Press, 2005), 113.

30. *Tom Bennet, "'Official' vs 'Living' Customary Law: Dilemmas of Description and Recognition," in* Land, Power and Custom: Controversies Generated by South Africa's Communal Land Rights Act, eds. A. Claasens and B. Cousins (Cape Town: UCT Press, 2008).

31. *S v. V.* 1972 (3) SA 611 (A) at 614 and *S v. Zinn* 1969 (2) SA 537 (A) at 542.

32. *S v. Shilubane* [2005] JOL 15671 (T).

33. *Id.* at paras 5–6.

34. *Port Elizabeth Municipality v. Various Occupiers* 2005 (1) SA 217 (CC).

35. Prevention of Illegal Eviction (PIE) from and Unlawful Occupation of Land Act 19 of 1998.

36. Thino Bekker, "The Re-emergence of *ubuntu*: A Critical Analysis" *South African Public Law* 21, no. 2 (2006): 337.

37. *PE Municipality* (*supra* n. 34) at para 23.

38. *Id.* at para 29.

39. *Id.* at para 32.

40. *Id.* at para 37.

41. *City of Johannesburg v. Rand Properties (Pty) Ltd* 2007 (SCA) 25 at para 78.

42. *Id.* at paras 63–4.

43. *City of Johannesburg* (*supra* n. 41) at para 15.

44. *PE Municipality* (*supra* n. 43) at para 37.

45. *Dikoko v. Mokhatla* 2006 (6) SA 235 (CC) at para 63.

46. *Id.* at para 68.

47. *Id.* at para 69.

48. *Id.* at paras 116–7.

49. *Id.* at paras 121.

50. *Barkhuizen v. Napier* 2007 (5) SA 323 (CC).

51. *Id.* at para 51.

52. *Id.* at para 72.

53. *Id.* at para 73.

54. *Id.* at para 135.

55. Many thanks to Professor Dale Huchison for his incisive commentary on the significance of the *Barkhuizen* case. For an interesting discussion of the *Barkhuizen* case, see Jaco Barnard Naudé, "Oh What a Tangled Web We Weave . . . Hegemony, Freedom of Contract, Good Faith in Transformation—Towards a Politics of Friendship in the Politics of Contract," *Constitutional Court Review* 1 (2009): 1.

56. John Murungi (*supra* n. 1), 525.

UBUNTU, RESTORATIVE JUSTICE, AND THE CONSTITUTIONAL COURT

1. Bertelsmann J citing Bately and Maepa at paragraph 30 of this judgment.

2. Although this case does not make explicit mention of the word *ubuntu*, in light of what has been said in the introduction to this book about the role of the restorative justice model in relation to *ubuntu*, the authors consider the following judgment, relied upon subsequently by Justice Sachs in the *Dikoko v. Mokhatla* 2007(1) BCLR 1 (CC) judgment, to be of great import.

Deputy Chief Justice Moseneke

3. The powers and duties of the Inspector-General of Intelligence are prescribed by section 7(7) of the Committee of Members of Parliament on and Inspectors-general of Intelligence Act 40 of 1994 (Intelligence Services Oversight Act). Important powers and duties include, *inter alia*, monitoring compliance by any intelligence service with the

Constitution, applicable laws, and relevant policies on intelligence and counter-intelligence; reviewing the intelligence and counter-intelligence activities of any intelligence service and performing functions designated to him or her by the President or any Minister responsible for a service. The Agency is an intelligence service as defined in section 1 of this Act.

4. The applicant did not proceed with this application. Its remaining relevance is that the papers in that application were incorporated by reference to the papers before the High Court in the second suspension application.

5. Section 101 of the Constitution provides:

"(1) A decision by the President must be in writing if—
   (a) it is taken in terms of legislation; or
   (b) it has legal consequences.
(2) A written decision by the President must be countersigned by another Cabinet member if that decision concerns a function assigned to that other Cabinet member."

6. Section 37 of the PSA provides for the remuneration of officers and employees. Section 37(2) states the following:

"Subject to such conditions as may be prescribed—

. . .

(d) any special service benefit may be granted to a head of department or class of heads of department before or at the expiry of a term contemplated in section 12(1)(a) or (b), or any extended term contemplated in section 12(1)(c), or at the time of retirement or discharge from the public service."

7. Act 3 of 2000.

8. The interpretation of the Constitution and legislation enacted to give effect to the Constitution give rise to constitutional issues. See, for example, *Alexkor Ltd and Another v The Richtersveld Community and Others* 2004 (5) SA 460 (CC); 2003 (12) BCLR 1301 (CC) at para 23; *National Education Health and Allied Workers Union v University of Cape Town and Others* 2003 (3) SA 1 (CC); 2003 (2) BCLR 154 (CC) at paras 14–15; *Department of Land Affairs and Others v Goedgelegen Tropical Fruits (Pty) Ltd* CCT 69/06, 6 June 2007, as yet unreported, at para 31.

9. Section 198(a) of the Constitution.

10. Section 199 of the Constitution provides:

"(1) The security services of the Republic consist of a single defence force, a single police service and any intelligence services established in terms of the Constitution.

. . .

(4) The security services must be structured and regulated by national legislation."

11. Section 198(c) of the Constitution provides: "National security must be pursued in compliance with the law, including international law."

12. The Intelligence Services Act 38 of 1994 preceded ISA. ISA had the effect of repealing certain provisions of, *inter alia*, the PSA; the Labour Relations Act 66 of 1995; the Basic Conditions of Employment Act 75 of 1997; the Employment Equity Act 55 of 1998 and the Medical Schemes Act 131 of 1998.

13. Section 8 of ISA provides:

> "(1) The Minister may, subject to this Act—
>
>> (a) appoint any person as a member of the Intelligence Services or the Academy;
>>
>> (b) promote, discharge, demote or transfer any member:
>
> Provided that such appointment, promotion, discharge, demotion or transfer in respect of a Deputy Director-General or equivalent post may only be effected in consultation with the President.
>
> (2) A prescribed document signed by the Minister and certifying that any person has been appointed as a member is prima facie proof that such person has been so appointed."

14. The text of section 3B(1)(a) is contained in para 39 above. Section 3B(2) refers to the President, as indicated in section 3B(1)(a), as the relevant executing authority.

15. Act 66 of 1995.

16. Section 2(b) of the Labour Relations Act states that this Act is not applicable to members of the Agency.

17. Act 75 of 1997. Section 3(1) of this Act states:

> "This Act applies to all employees and employers except—
>
>> (a) members of the National Defence Force, the National Intelligence Agency and the South African Secret Service . . . ."

18. The text of section 12(4) of the PSA is contained in para 54 above.

19. *Transnet Ltd v Rubenstein* 2006 (1) SA 591 (SCA); [2005] 3 All SA 425 (SCA) at para 18; *Alfred McAlpine & Son (Pty) Ltd v Transvaal Provincial Administration* 1974 (3) SA 506 (A) at 531E-532A; *Pan American World Airways Incorporated v SA Fire Accident Insurance Co Ltd* 1965 (3) SA 150 (A) at 175C.

20. See para 31 above. It should be noted further that the PSA does not claim to cover the entire field. On its own terms, its application, however complementary, is subject to other legislative provisions that establish the Agency.

21. See *Pharmaceutical Manufacturers* above n 39 at para 85 and *Prinsloo v Van der Linde and Another* 1997 (3) SA 1012 (CC); 1997 (6) BCLR 759 (CC) at para 25.

22. In essence, the applicant in this matter is seeking specific performance of a service contract. Christie in *The Law of Contract* 4 ed (Butterworths, Durban 2001) at 606 defines specific performance as, inter alia, an order to perform a specific act or to pay money in pursuance of a contractual obligation. Analogously, section 193 of the Labour Relations Act contemplates re-instatement, re-employment or compensation for dismissals that are found to be unfair. See also *Schierhout v Minister of Justice* 1926 AD 99 and *Rogers v Durban Corporation* 1950 (1) SA 65 (D).

23. Christie *id* at 614. See also *Schierhout id* at 107 and *Rogers* at 65.

Justice Sachs

24. Section 179(1)(a) of the Constitution provides:

"There is a single national prosecuting authority in the Republic, structured in terms of an Act of Parliament, and consisting of a National Director of Public Prosecutions, who is the head of the prosecuting authority, and is appointed by the President, as head of the national executive."

25. Section 207(1) of the Constitution provides:

"The President as head of the national executive must appoint a woman or a man as the National Commissioner of the police service, to control and manage the police service."

26. Section 209(2) of the Constitution provides:

"The President as head of the national executive must appoint a woman or a man as head of each intelligence service established in terms of subsection (1), and must either assume political responsibility for the control and direction of any of those services, or designate a member of the Cabinet to assume that responsibility."

27. The relevant part of section 198 of the Constitution provides:

"The following principles govern national security in the Republic:

. . .

(c) National security must be pursued in compliance with the law, including international law.

. . ."

28. I expressly refrain from dealing with the factors that would justify terminating the appointments of the National Director of Public Prosecutions and the National Commissioner of the Police where different constitutional and statutory considerations apply.

29. Section 23(1) provides: "Everyone has the right to fair labour practices."

30. See, for example, Rawls *Justice as Fairness: A restatement* (Harvard University Press, Cambridge 2001) at 116:

"[A] requirement of a stable constitutional regime is that its basic institutions should encourage the cooperative virtues of political life: the virtues of reasonableness and a sense of fairness, and of a spirit of compromise and a readiness to meet others halfway. These virtues underwrite the willingness if not the desire to cooperate with others on terms that all can publicly accept as fair on a footing of equality and mutual respect."

UBUNTU UNDER THE INTERIM CONSTITUTION: LIFE, DEATH, AND *UBUNTU*

1. See *The Dignity Jurisprudence of South Africa* casebook for Justice O'Regan's judgment.

Justice Mokgoro

2. Act No 12 of 1979.

3. See Jesse Choper quoted in *Rights and Constitutionalism; The New South African Legal Order;* Van Wyk D. *et al,* Juta, 1994 p. 9. The suggestion is that the judiciary is not wholly removed from the political process, where it plays a supervisory role, restraining the majority will through judicial review.

4. Mbigi, L., with J. Maree, *uBuntu—The Spirit of African Transformation Management,* Knowledge Resources, 1995, pp.1–16.

5. See analysis in the English translation of Decision No 23/1990 (X31) AB of the Hungarian Constitutional Court.

Justice Chaskalson

6. The Preamble to the Constitution records that the new order will be a "constitutional state in which . . . all citizens shall be able to enjoy and exercise their fundamental rights and freedoms." The commitment to recognition of human rights is reaffirmed in the concluding provision on National Unity and Reconciliation.

Justice Langa

7. See the remarks of Lord Bridge in *Bugdaycay v Secretary of State* 1987(1) All ER 940 at 952b.

8. See para 82 of Chaskalson P's judgment.

9. *S v Tuhadeleni and Others* 1969(1) SA 153 (A) at 172D–173F; Baxter, *Administrative Law*, page 30 (1984).

10. Brandeis J in his dissenting opinion in *Olmstead v. United States*, 277 US 438, 485 (1928) put it succinctly: "Our Government is the potent, the omni-present teacher. For good or for ill, it teaches the whole of our people by its example."

11. In his Oliver Wendell Holmes lecture at the Harvard Law School, reprinted under the heading "Federalism and State Criminal Procedure," 70 Harv. L. Rev. 1, 26 (1956). The passage was referred to with approval in *Coppedge v. United States*, 369 US 438, 449 (1962).

12. [1991] LRC (Const) 553 at 566b–d, per Nyalali CJ, Makame and Ramadhani JJA.

13. See paragraphs 130 and 131 of Chaskalson P's judgment. The concept has been referred to also by Madala J, Mahomed J, and Mokgoro J in their separate concurring judgments in this matter.

14. Per Brennan J in *Furman v Georgia, supra*, at 305.

Justice Sachs

15. *Cf.* 1969 SALJ 455 and 1970 SALJ 60; *S v Van Niekerk* 1970 (3) SA 655.

16. *The International Law of Human Rights*, Oxford 1983, reprinted 1992, at p. 93 referring to *James, Young and Webster v U.K. Judgment of the European Court of Human Rights* on 13/08/81.

17. See the postamble, also referred to as the epilogue or afterword, where reference is made to the "need for *ubuntu*."

18. Junod, *Henri A—The Life of a South African Tribe* 2nd Edition published Macmillan 1927 at p. 436.

19. 1889 CLJ 87, extracts from *Maclean's Handbook.*

20. John Henderson Soga, *The Ama-Xosa: Life and Customs,* published Lovedale Press, South Africa; London, KeganPaul, at p. 46.

21. Hammond-Tooke D: *The "other side" of frontier history: a model of Cape Nguni political process, in African Societies* in *Southern Africa* ed. Leonard Thompson, London 1969, at p. 255.

22. Soga *supra* at p. 46.

23. *Bantu Law and Western Civilisation in South Africa—A Study in the Clash of Cultures* (1934 Yale University MA Thesis).

24. 1889 CLJ 89, 1890 CLJ 23 at 34.

25. J M Orpen, *History of the Basutus of South Africa,* Cape Argus 1857, Reprinted UCT 1955.

26. Molema *SM: Montshiwa (1815–1896) Barolong Chief and Patriot* (published C. Struik 1966).

27. Donald R. Morris, *The Washing of the Spears—A History of the Rise of the Zulu Nation under Shaka and Its Fall in the Zulu War of 1879* 174–5 (Jonathan Cape 1965; Random House, 1995).

AMNESTY, RECONCILIATION, AND *UBUNTU*

1. Act 200 of 1993, which is referred to in this judgment as "the Constitution."

2. Described in the epilogue to the Constitution as "a date after 8 October 1990 and before 6 December 1993." "Cut-off date" is defined in section 1 of the Act to mean, "the latest date allowed as the cut-off date in terms of the Constitution as set out under the heading 'National Unity and Reconciliation.'"

3. Section 3(1)(a).

4. Section 3(1)(b).

5. Section 3(1)(c).

6. Section 3(1)(d).

7. Section 3(3).

8. Sections 3(3)(a), 12, and 14.

9. Sections 3(3)(c), 23, and 25. The recommendations of the committee are themselves considered by the President who then makes recommendations to Parliament. This is considered by a joint committee of Parliament and the decisions of the joint committee, after approval by Parliament, are implemented by regulations made by the President.

10. Section 3(3)(b).

11. Section 17(3). It is common cause that the Committee on Amnesty, in fact appointed by the President, includes three judges of the Supreme Court.

12. Section 19.

13. Section 20(1).

14. Sub-section 6 which is referred to in sub-sections 8 and 9 simply provides that the Committee must by proclamation in the Gazette make known the full names of any person to whom amnesty has been granted, together with sufficient information to identify the act, omission or offence in respect of which such amnesty has been granted.

15. Section 71(1) of the Constitution. *Executive Council, Western Cape Legislature, and Others v President of the Republic of South Africa and Others* 1995 (4) SA 877 (CC); 1995 (10) BCLR 1289 (CC) at para 41; *Premier, KwaZulu-Natal, and Others v President of the Republic of South Africa and Others* 1996 (1) SA 769 (CC); 1996 (12) BCLR 1561 (CC) at para 12; *The Azanian Peoples Organisation and Others v The Truth and Reconciliation Commission and Others*, (CPD) Case No 4895/96, 9 May 1996, not yet reported, at 20–1 ("the *AZAPO* case").

16. Section 71(2) of the Constitution.

17. Sections 33(1)(a)(ii) and 35(1) of the Constitution.

18. The meaning of that concept is discussed in *S v Makwanyane and Another* 1995 (3) SA 391 (CC); 1995 (6) BCLR 665 (CC) at paras 224–27, 241–51, 263, and 307–13.

19. See the fourth paragraph of the epilogue to the Constitution.

20. Immanuel Kant paraphrased in Isaiah Berlin's essay on "Two concepts of Liberty" in *Four Essays on Liberty* at 170 (Oxford University Press 1969). See also Ackermann J in *Ferreira v Levin NO and Others; Vryenhoek and Others v Powell NO and Others* 1996 (1) SA 984 (CC); 1996 (1) BCLR 1 (CC) at para 53.

21. *The Oxford English Dictionary*, 2nd Ed, Vol I at 406.

22. *Webster's New Twentieth Century Dictionary*, 2nd Ed at 59.

23. *Wharton's Law Lexicon*, 14th Ed at 59.

24. *Supra* n 35.

25. De Vattel, *The Law of Nations or the Principles of Natural Law Applied to the Conduct and to the Affairs of Nations and of Sovereigns,* trans. by Fenwick (Carnegie Institute of Washington, 1916) at 351, paras 20–2, quoted by Friedman JP and Farlam J in the *AZAPO* case, *supra* n. 15 at 24.

26. At paragraphs 44 and 45 *supra*.

UBUNTU, SOCIOECONOMIC RIGHTS, AND PERSONHOOD

Justice Sachs

1. Section 7(1) and (2) of the Bill of Rights state that:

(1) This Bill of Rights is the cornerstone of democracy in South Africa. It enshrines the rights of all people in our country and affirms the democratic values of human dignity, equality and freedom.

(2) The state must respect, protect, promote and fulfil the rights in the Bill of Rights.

Similarly, section 39 states that when interpreting the Bill of Rights a court must promote the values of an open and democratic society based on human dignity, equality and freedom.

2. The full text of section 25 reads as follows:

"Property

(1) No one may be deprived of property except in terms of law of general application, and no law may permit arbitrary deprivation of property.

(2) Property may be expropriated only in terms of law of general application—

(a) for a public purpose or in the public interest; and

(b) subject to compensation, the amount of which and the time and manner of payment of which have either been agreed to by those affected or decided or approved by a court.

(3) The amount of the compensation and the time and manner of payment must be just and equitable, reflecting an equitable balance between the public interest and the interests of those affected, having regard to all relevant circumstances, including

(a) the current use of the property;

(b) the history of the acquisition and use of the property;

(c) the market value of the property;

(d) the extent of direct state investment and subsidy in the acquisition and beneficial capital improvement of the property and

(e) the purpose of the expropriation.

(4) For the purposes of this section

(a) the public interest includes the nation's commitment to land reform, and to reforms to bring about equitable access to all South Africa's natural resources; and

(b) property is not limited to land,

(5) The state must take reasonable legislative and other measures within its available resources, to foster conditions that enable citizens to gain access to land on an equitable basis.

(6) A person or community whose tenure of land is legally insecure as a result of past racially discriminatory laws or practices is entitled to the extent provided by an Act of Parliament, either to tenure which is legally secure or to comparable redress.

(7) A person or community dispossessed of property after 19 June 1913 as a result of past racially discriminatory laws or practices is entitled, to the extent provided by an Act of Parliament, either to restitution of that property or to equitable redress.

(8) No provision of this section may impede the state from taking legislative and other measures to achieve land, water and related reform, in order to redress the results of past racial discrimination, provided that any departure from the provisions of this section is in accordance with the provisions of section 36(1).

(9) Parliament must enact the legislation referred to in subsection (6)."

3. *First National Bank of SA Limited t/a Westbank v Commissioner for the South African Revenue Services and Another; First National Bank of SA Limited t/a Westbank v Minister of Finance* 2002 (4) SA 768 (CC); 2002 (7) BCLR 702 (CC).

4. *Id.* at paras 50–52. Footnotes omitted.

5. United Nations Housing Rights Programme, Report No 1, *Housing Rights Legislation: Review of International and National Legal Instruments* (2002) at 1. The UN-Habitat report concludes its Introduction by stating:

"Housing rights rest upon the firm foundations of international human rights law, as well as the subsequent interpretative development of the standards, principles and norms embodied in that law. Indeed, the concept of housing rights has expanded beyond traditional, and often rudimentary, perceptions of those rights. The diversity in texts regarding housing rights may pose numerous ramifications for the international and national legal regimes. Yet, one clear priority remains: the imperative of consolidating promotional activities through an expanded focus on the global protection of housing rights."

6. Section 25(4)(a).

7. Section 25(5).

8. Section 25(6).

9. Section 25(7).

10. *Government of the Republic of South Africa and Others v. Grootboom and Others* 2001 (1) SA 46 (CC); 2000 (11) BCLR 1169 (CC) at para 74.

11. As Van der Walt correctly points out it does not change the institution of private property. Nor does it create what has been referred to as a "servitude of trespass" (see *Betta Eindomme (Pty) Ltd v. Ekple-Epoh* 2000 (4) SA 468 (WLD) at para 8.2). See Van der Walt *Exclusivity of Ownership, Security of Tenure and Eviction Orders: A Critical Evaluation of Recent Case Law* (2002) 18 *SA Journal on Human Rights* 372 at 397 *f*.

12. As Yacoob J pointed out in *Grootboom*:

"Land invasion is inimical to the systematic provision of adequate housing on a planned basis. It may well be that the decision of the State structure, faced with the difficulty of repeated land invasions, not to provide housing in response to those invasions, would be reasonable. Reasonableness must be determined on the facts of each case." (supra n 20 at para 92)

The term land invasion, however, must be used with caution. It can be stretched to cover widely dissimilar cases, like the present where a relatively small number of people have erected shacks and lived on undeveloped land for relatively long periods of time, or the situation in *Grootboom* where although a thousand desperate people occupied a hillside due to be developed for low-cost housing, no intent to jump the queue was shown and a remedy was not refused, or the circumstances revealed in *Port Elizabeth Municipality v Peoples Dialogue on Land and Shelter* (above n 7) at 1085, where the trial court held that eviction subject to conditions should be ordered because there had been a deliberate and premeditated act culminating in the unlawful invasion and occupation of a large tract of land.

13. Horn AJ in *Port Elizabeth Municipality* (above n 7) at 1081. The judge was quoted with approval by Olivier JA in *Ndlovu and Bekker* (above n 6). See also Van Der Walt (above n 21) at 378.

14. Echoing the provisions of sections 25(1) and 26(3) of the Constitution, its preamble declares:

"WHEREAS no one may be deprived of property except in terms of law of general application, and no law may permit arbitrary deprivation of property;

AND WHEREAS no one may be evicted from their home, or have their home demolished without an order of court made after considering all relevant circumstances;

AND WHEREAS it is desirable that the law should regulate the eviction of unlawful occupiers from land in a fair manner, while recognising the right of land owners to apply to a court for an eviction order in appropriate circumstances;

AND WHEREAS special consideration should be given to the rights of the elderly, children, disabled persons and particularly households headed by women, and that it should be recognised that the needs of those groups should be considered;"

The definition section (section 1) states that "building or structure" includes any hut, shack, tent, or similar structure or any other form of temporary or permanent dwelling or shelter. An "unlawful occupier" means a person who occupies land without the express or tacit consent of the owner or person in charge. Magistrate's courts are included in the definition of courts to whom powers under PIE are entrusted (sections 1 and 9). It is made a criminal offence to evict an unlawful occupier except on the authority of an order of a competent court (section 8(1)). Section 3 prohibits receipt of payment for organising unlawful occupation of land. Section 5 makes special provision for emergency evictions. Extensive provision is made in section 7 for the appointment of mediators. The Minister designated by the State President is given power to make regulations where they are required or where it is necessary or desirable to achieve the objectives of the Act (section 12).

15. Section 4 reads:

"Eviction of unlawful occupiers—

(1) Notwithstanding anything to the contrary contained in any law or the common law, the provisions of this section apply to proceedings by an owner or person in charge of land for the eviction of an unlawful occupier.

(2) At least 14 days before the hearing of the proceedings contemplated in subsection (1), the court must serve written and effective notice of the proceedings on the unlawful occupier and the municipality having jurisdiction.

(3) Subject to the provisions of subsection (2), the procedure for the serving of notices and filing of papers is as prescribed by the rules of the court in question.

(4) Subject to the provisions of subsection (2), if a court is satisfied that service cannot conveniently or expeditiously be effected in the manner provided in the rules of the court, service must be effected in the manner directed by the court: Provided that the court must consider the rights of the unlawful occupier to receive adequate notice and to defend the case.

(5) The notice of proceedings contemplated in subsection (2) must—

(a) state that proceedings are being instituted in terms of subsection (1) for an order for the eviction of the unlawful occupier;

    (b) indicate on what date and at what time the court will hear the proceedings;

    (c) set out the grounds for the proposed eviction; and

    (d) state that the unlawful occupier is entitled to appear before the court and defend the case and, where necessary, has the right to apply for legal aid.

(6) If an unlawful occupier has occupied the land in question for less than six months at the time when the proceedings are initiated, a court may grant an order for eviction if it is of the opinion that it is just and equitable to do so, after considering all the relevant circumstances, including the rights and needs of the elderly, children, disabled persons and households headed by women.

(7) If an unlawful occupier has occupied the land in question for more than six months at the time when the proceedings are initiated, a court may grant an order for eviction if it is of the opinion that it is just and equitable to do so, after considering all the relevant circumstances, including, except where the land is sold in a sale of execution pursuant to a mortgage, whether land has been made available or can reasonably be made available by a municipality or other organ of state or another land owner for the relocation of the unlawful occupier, and including the rights and needs of the elderly, children, disabled persons and households headed by women.

(8) If the court is satisfied that all the requirements of this section have been complied with and that no valid defence has been raised by the unlawful occupier, it must grant an order for the eviction of the unlawful occupier, and determine—

    (a) a just and equitable date on which the unlawful occupier must vacate the land under the circumstances; and

    (b) the date on which an eviction order may be carried out if the unlawful occupier has not vacated the land on the date contemplated in paragraph (a).

(9) In determining a just and equitable date contemplated in subsection (8), the court must have regard to all relevant factors, including the period the unlawful occupier and his or her family have resided on the land in question.

(10) The court which orders the eviction of any person in terms of this section may make an order for the demolition and removal of the buildings or structures that were occupied by such person on the land in question.

(11) A court may, at the request of the sheriff, authorise any person to assist the sheriff to carry out an order for eviction, demolition or removal subject to conditions determined by the court: Provided that the sheriff must at all times be present during such eviction, demolition or removal."

16. It is not necessary for the purposes of this judgment to decide whether the manner in which the SCA in this matter discusses the disjunctive "or" between section 4(1) (a) and (b) is fully accurate. See para 9 in that judgment.

17. Horn AJ in *Port Elizabeth Municipality* (above n 7) at 1084.

18. While the provisions of PIE give temporary continuity to transit camps established under section 11(4) of PISA. PIE makes no substitute infrastructural provision for transitional support for evicted persons. This gap in the law creates problems for municipalities seeking to ensure that evictions are carried out in a just and equitable manner. Though in the age of forced removals transit camps had a dolorous history, the role of places for temporary settlement could be quite different today. They could serve to cushion removals and place the persons concerned in a position to re-establish themselves pending access to secure housing. See, Pienaar and Muller "The impact of the Prevention of Illegal Eviction from and Unlawful Occupation of Land Act 19 of 1998 on homelessness and unlawful occupation within the present statutory framework," (1999) 10 *Stellenbosch Law Review* 370 at 393.

19. *Grootboom* at para 44. The issue in *Grootboom* was whether or not the housing programme was reasonable. In the present matter the focus is whether an eviction order would be just and equitable. Yet though the text and context in each case is different, what they have in common is the need to focus on the question of human dignity and to ensure that the programmes at issue are sufficiently flexible to respond to those in desperate need and to cater appropriately for immediate and short-term requirements (at para 52). In the words of Yacoob J: "The Constitution will be worth infinitely less than its paper if the reasonableness of State action is determined without regard to the fundamental constitutional value of human dignity . . . . In short, I emphasise that human beings are required to be treated as human beings" (at para 83).

20. The reported cases indicate that homeless people tend to erect their shelters on relatively deserted land, rather than on open spaces like golf courses, public commons or private gardens. They seek to tuck themselves away in places from which they are unlikely to be evicted, rather than to choose spots, which would inevitably and immediately provoke confrontation.

21. For the purposes of this case it is not necessary to go into the question, which divided the SCA in *Ndlovu and Bekker* (n 6), namely, whether the operation of PIE is restricted to poor, homeless persons who out of necessity arising from past laws have occupied the land of others without consent.

22. Section 6(6) read with sections 4(8), (9), and (12).

23. *Port Elizabeth Municipality* (above n 7).

24. Olivier J in *Ndlovu and Bekker* (n 6) at para 56.

25. A perusal of the orders made in the many cases brought under PIE in the different divisions of the High Court indicates a great variety of responses. Innovative orders have been made both in the High Court as a court of first instance, and the SCA as a court of appeal.

Thus, Browde AJ in *Transnet t/a Spoornet v. Informal Settlers of Good Hope and Others* 2001 (4) All SA 516 (WLD) concludes his judgment as follows at 524:

> "It is clear to me that what is required is further investigation into the matter since an order for eviction would merely exacerbate an already tragic situation. I therefore make the following order namely:
>
> 1. The application is postponed *sine die*.
> 2. The applicant is ordered to conduct a survey to enable it (and the court when the matter is reinstated) to assess the needs and the rights of the

persons presently illegally occupying the Rail Reserve and the prospect, if any, of relocating the communities to a safer and healthier site.

3. Respondents ie the two respondent communities, represented by the Legal Resources Centre and the third respondent are ordered to take all reasonable steps to assist the applicant in carrying out the survey referred to in paragraph 1 hereof.

4. The costs of the application thus far incurred are reserved for decision by the court which hears the application if and when it is reinstated."

26. As Mokgoro J has explained:

"Generally, *ubuntu* translates as 'humaneness.' In its most fundamental sense it translates as personhood and 'morality.' Metaphorically, it expresses itself in *umuntu ngumuntu ngabantu*, describing the significance of group solidarity on survival issues so central to the survival of communities. While it envelops the key values of group solidarity, compassion, respect, human dignity, conformity to basic norms and collective unity, in its fundamental sense it denotes humanity and morality. Its spirit emphasises a respect for human dignity, marking a shift from confrontation to conciliation. In South Africa *ubuntu* has become a notion with particular resonance in the building of a democracy. It is part of our *rainbow* heritage, though it might have operated and still operates differently in diverse community settings. In the Western cultural heritage, respect and the value for life, manifested in the all-embracing concepts of 'humanity' and 'menswaardigheid', are also highly prized. It is values like these that [s 39(1)(a)] requires to be promoted. They give meaning and texture to the principles of a society based on freedom and equality." [Footnotes omitted.]

See *S v Makwanyane and Another* 1995 (3) SA 391 (CC); 1995 (6) BCLR (CC) at para 308.

27. The eloquent opening words by the Vice President of the German Federal Constitutional Court and the presiding judge in its second senate, Judge Mahrenholz, and his colleague, Judge Sommer in the second abortion case heard by that Court in 1993, illustrate certain inherent limitations of the law; some legal dilemmas cannot be resolved, they can only be managed more or less well.

"Legal regulation of the termination of pregnancy strikes to the innermost core of human life and touches fundamental questions of human existence. It is characteristic of the human condition that sexuality and the desire to bear children do not coincide. Women have to bear the consequence of this divergence. At all times and in all cultures, including those with different moral and religious value systems, they have sought and found ways out of the crisis of unwanted pregnancies. They have not let themselves be deterred by the heaviest and most cruel punishments, or even by the risk to their own lives, from terminating the unborn life when they did not want a child. In accordance with their changed station in society, women today resolve this fundamental conflict primarily in terms of whether, in their own estimation, they are able to fulfil the responsibilities of motherhood.

Any regulation of the termination of pregnancy raises questions about the sphere of inviolable autonomy of the individual on the one hand, and the right of the state to regulate on the other; here *the legislature finds itself at the limit of its capacity to regulate in any way an aspect of human life. It can introduce a better or worse regulation, but it cannot 'solve' the problem; in this sphere the state can no longer be confident that it can lay down the 'correct' legislation.*" [My emphasis]

See *Die Entscheidung des Bundesverfassungsgerichts zum Schwangerschaftsabbruch vom 28 Mai 1993* reported in full in a special issue of *Juristenzeitung* (JZ.) of 7 June 1993 at 43. Translated and quoted by Van Zyl Smit in "Reconciling the irreconcilable? Recent developments in the German law on abortion" *Medical Law Review* (1994) 3 at 302. Here the problem is not one of competing values but of competing interests with deep historical roots.

28. Mediation, as a process, is notoriously difficult to define. See the general discussion in Laurence Boulle and Miryana Nesic, *Mediation Principles, Process, Practice* (Butterworths, Durban 1997) at 3–7. Nupen offers the following crisp definition: "Mediation is a process in which parties in conflict voluntarily enlist the services of an acceptable third party to assist them in reaching agreement on issues that divide them." Nupen "Mediation" in *Dispute Resolution,* ed. Paul Pretorius (Juta, Cape Town 1993) at 39.

29. See the Labour Relations Act 66 of 1995 and the discussion in Boulle and Rycroft, (supra n. 38), chapter 8.

30. For a helpful synoptic account of such developments see Van Zyl, *Divorce mediation and the best interests of the child* (HSRC, Pretoria 1997) at 142–153.

31. The parties were asked to answer the following questions:

"(i) Is it competent for a court seized at first instance of an application under the Prevention of Illegal Eviction and Unlawful Occupation Act 19 of 1998, where the parties to the matter have not availed themselves of the procedures laid down in section 7 of the Act:

(a) to order that mediation or a similar form of alternative dispute resolution be followed; and

(b) to decide the case only if the alternative dispute resolution process does not resolve the dispute between the parties within a specified time.

(ii) If so, is it competent for a court to make such an order on appeal where such an order has not been made by the court of first instance?

(iii) If so, would it be competent and appropriate in the circumstances of this case for this Court to make such an order?"

32. Section 7 reads as follows:

"Mediation

(1) If the municipality in whose area of jurisdiction the land in question is situated is not the owner of the land the municipality may, on the conditions that it may determine, appoint one or more persons with expert-

ise in dispute resolution to facilitate meetings of interested parties and to attempt to mediate and settle any dispute in terms of this Act: Provided that the parties may at any time, by agreement, appoint another person to facilitate meetings or mediate a dispute, on the conditions that the municipality may determine.

(2) If the municipality in whose area of jurisdiction the land in question is situated is the owner of the land in question, the member of the Executive Council designated by the Premier of the province concerned, or his or her nominee, may, on the conditions that he or she may determine, appoint one or more persons with expertise in dispute resolution to facilitate meetings of interested parties and to attempt to mediate and settle any dispute in terms of this Act: Provided that the parties may at any time, by agreement, appoint another person to facilitate meetings or mediate a dispute, on the conditions that the said member of the Executive Council may determine.

(3) Any party may request the municipality to appoint one or more persons in terms of subsections (1) and (2), for the purposes of those subsections.

(4) A person appointed in terms of subsection (1) or (2) who is not in full-time service of the State may be paid the remuneration and allowances that may be determined by the body or official who appointed that person for services performed by him or her.

(5) All discussions, disclosures and submissions which take place or are made during the mediation process shall be privileged, unless the parties agree to the contrary."

33. Even in pre-constitutional times some judges recognised the need to take account of the drastic effects of eviction. As Goldstone J pointed out in *S v Govender* 1986 (3) SA 969 (T) at 971, the power to make an ejectment order under section 46(2)(b) of the Group Areas Act 36 of 1966 was a wide one and one which might, and in most cases would, seriously affect the lives of the person or persons concerned. Such an order should not therefore be made without the fullest enquiry. Many considerations might be relevant to the exercise of the court's discretion, for example the nature of the area concerned; the attitude of the neighbours; the policy and views of the Department of Community Development or any other interested Department of State; the attitude of the landlord; the prospects of the permit being issued for continued lawful occupation of the premises; the personal hardship which such an order may cause and the availability of alternative accommodation.

34. See *Plascon Evans Paints Ltd v Van Riebeeck Paints (Pty) Ltd* 1984 (3) SA 623 (A).

35. Section 6(1)(a) provides that:

"Eviction at instance of organ of state.—

(1) An organ of state may institute proceedings for the eviction of an unlawful occupier from land which falls within its area of jurisdiction, except where the unlawful occupier is a mortgagor and the land in question is sold in a sale of execution pursuant to a mortgage, and the court may

grant such an order if it is just and equitable to do so, after considering all the relevant circumstances, and if —

    (a) the consent of that organ of state is required for the erection of a building or structure on that land or for the occupation of the land, and the unlawful occupier is occupying a building or structure on that land without such consent having been obtained."

Given the conclusion that we will reach, it is not necessary to decide whether the requirements stipulated in section 6(1)(a) and (b) are disjunctive or conjunctive. See the discussion in the SCA judgment at para 9.

36. 1st, 2nd, 5th, 7th, 8th, 9th, 10th, and 11th Respondents.

37. 3rd, 6th, and 12th Respondents.

38. 4th Respondent.

39. See (above n 20) at para 58.

Justice Mokgoro

40. Section 1 of the Constitution states in the relevant part:

"The Republic of South Africa is one sovereign democratic state founded on the following values:

    (a) Human dignity, the achievement of equality and the advancement of human rights and freedoms."

41. 2001 (1) SA 46 (CC); 2000 (11) BCLR 1169 (CC).

42. *S v Makwanyane and Another* 1995 (3) SA 391 (CC); 1995 (6) BCLR 665 (CC) at para 327.

43. Above n. 10 at para 35.

44. Ex Parte Chairperson of the Constitutional Assembly: In re Certification of the Constitution of the Republic of South Africa, 1996 (4) SA 744 (CC); 1996 (10) BCLR 1253 (CC) at paras 76–8; *Soobramoney v Minister of Health, KwaZulu-Natal* 1998 (1) SA 765 (CC); 1997 (12) BCLR 1696 (CC); *Grootboom* (above n 46); *Minister of Health and Others v Treatment Action Campaign and Others* (2), 2002 (5) SA 721; 2002 (10) BCLR 1033 (CC).

45. *Id. Soobramoney* at para 22; *Grootboom* at para 74; Treatment Action Campaign at paras 23 and 39.

46. Section 26 provides:

"26. Housing

    (1) Everyone has the right to have access to adequate housing.

    (2) The state must take reasonable legislative and other measures, within its available resources, to achieve the progressive realisation of this right.

    (3) No one may be evicted from their home, or have their home demolished, without an order of the court made after considering all the relevant circumstances. No legislation may permitarbitrary evictions."

47. Section 25(5) of the Constitution provides:

> "The state must take reasonable legislative and other measures, within its available resources, to foster conditions which enable *citizens* to gain access to land on an equitable basis." (Emphasis added.)

48. Some rights in the Bill of Rights such as political rights in section 19; citizenship rights in section 20; the right to a passport and to enter, remain and reside in the Republic in sections 21(3) and 21(4); freedom of trade, occupation and profession in section 22; and certain labour rights in section 23 are qualified as being available to smaller groups of people than "everyone."

49. Above n 47 at para 9; *S v Mhlungu and Others* 1995 (3) SA 867 (CC); 1995 (7) BCLR 793 (CC) at para 8.

50. Section 7(1) of the Bill of Rights provides: "[The] Bill of Rights is a cornerstone of democracy in South Africa. It enshrines the rights of *all people in our country* and affirms the democratic values of human dignity, equality and freedom." (Emphasis added.)

51. *Commissioner for Inland Revenue v NST Ferrochrome (Pty) Ltd* 1999 (2) SA 228 (T) at 232.

52. Above n 46 at para 41.

53. *Id.* at para 44.

54. The Respondents referred to the position in the United States, Canada and the United Kingdom.

55. See section 5(9).

56. See para 65 below.

57. See, for example, *Mathews v Diaz* 426 US 67, 78 (1976). See also para 66 [*sic*] below.

58. Section 25(1).

59. Section 28(c) of the Immigration Act.

60. Section 9(2) and 9(3)(d) of the Immigration Act.

61. *Larbi-Odam and Others v Member of the Executive Council for Education (North-West Province) and Another* 1998 (1) SA 745 (CC); 1997 (12) BCLR 1655 (CC) at para 24.

62. *S v Tsotsobe and Others* 1983 (1) SA 856 (A) at 866E; *S v Zwane and Others* 1989 (3) SA 253 (W) at 256I.

63. 189 F.3d 598 (7th Cir 1999).

64. *Id.* at 609.

65. *City Council of Pretoria v Walker* 1998 (2) SA 363 (CC); 1998 (3) BCLR 257 (CC) at para 27.

66. *Bel Porto School Governing Body and Others v Premier, Western Cape and Another* 2002 (3) SA 265 (CC); 2002 (9) BCLR 891 (CC) at para 46.

67. Section 9(3) provides:

> "The state may not unfairly discriminate directly or indirectly against anyone on one or more grounds, including race, gender, sex, pregnancy, marital status, ethnic or social origin, colour, sexual orientation, age, disability, religion, conscience, belief, culture, language and birth."

68. Section 9(5) states:

"Discrimination on one or more of the grounds listed in subsection (3) is unfair unless it is established that the discrimination is fair."

See also *Harksen v Lane NO and Others* 1998 (1) SA 300 (CC); 1997 (11) BCLR 1489 (CC) at para 53.

69. 1997 (4) SA 1 (CC); 1997 (6) BCLR 708 (CC) at paras 41–3.

70. 2001 (1) SA 1 (CC); 2000 (11) BCLR 1211 (CC) at para 27.

71. Above n 74 at para 52.

72. Above n 66.

73. *Id.*

74. *Id.* at para 20.

75. Above n 75.

76. *Harksen* (above n 73) 373 at para 51.

77. *National Coalition* (above n 73) at para 41.

78. 1996 (4) SA 197 (CC); 1996 (6) BCLR 752 (CC) at para 42.

79. Gerald M. Rosberg, *The Protection of Aliens from Discriminatory Treatment by the National Government* (1977) *Supreme Court Review* 275 at 311.

80. Connie Chang, "Immigrants Under the New Welfare Law: A Call for Uniformity, A Call for Justice" (1977) 45 *University of California Los Angeles Law Review* 205 at 223.

81. To use the terminology from *Plessy v. Ferguson* 163 US 537, 551 (1896) and *Brown v Board of Education* 347 US 483, 494 (1954), the exclusion of foreigners from state welfare programmes not only operates to stamp them with a "badge of inferiority", but marginalises them by sending a messageof second-class status in the communities in which they reside.

82. Section 28(1)(c) reads:

(1) Every child has the right—
    . . .
    (c) to basic nutrition, shelter, basic health care services and social services."

83. See Van der Walt *The Constitutional Property Clause* (Juta, 1997) 92–5; Rautenbach *General Provisions of the South African Bill of Rights* (Butterworths, 1995) 84–5 and 106–07; De Waal et al *The Bill of Rights Handbook* 4 ed. (Juta, 2001) 451; Liebenberg "Socio-economic Rights" in *Constitutional Law of South Africa,* ed. Chaskalson *et al.* (Juta, 1999) 41–7 to 41–8; Pierre De Vos, "Pious Wishes or Directly Enforceable Human Rights? Social and Economic Rights in South Africa's 1996 Constitution" (1997) 13 *SAJHR* 67 at 79–80; Marius Pieterse "Towards a Useful Role for Section 36 of the Constitution in Social Rights Cases? *Residents of Bon Vista Mansions v Southern Metropolitan Local Council*" (2003) 120 *SALJ* 41.

84. Section 172(1)(a) of the Constitution provides:

"(1) When deciding a constitutional matter within its power, a court—
    (a) must declare that any law or conduct that is inconsistent with the Constitution is invalid to the extent of its inconsistency."

85. Section 172(1)(b) reads:

"(1) When deciding a constitutional matter within its power, a court—
(b) may make any order that is just and equitable, including—
(i) an order limiting the retrospective effect of the declaration of invalidity; and
(ii) an order suspending the declaration of invalidity for any period and on any conditions, to allow the competent authority to correct the defect."

86. *National Coalition* above n 13 at para 87.

87. *Id.*

Justice Ngcobo

88. *President of the Republic of South Africa and Another v Hugo* 1997 (4) SA 1 (CC); 1997 (6) BCLR 708 (CC) at para 41.

89. *Harksen v Lane*, (above n 19), at para 50.

90. *Id.*, para 51.

91. Charles Ngwena, *HIV In the Workplace: Protecting Rights to Equality and Privacy* (1999) 15 *SA Journal of Human Rights* 513 at 514.

92. See section 34 of the Promotion of Equality and Prevention of Unfair Discrimination Act, 2000, 4 of 2000.

93. Section 6(1) of the Employment Equity Act, which section came into effect on 9 August 1999, specifically mentions HIV status as a prohibited ground of unfair discrimination; section 7(2) prohibits the testing of an employee for HIV status unless the Labour Court, acting under section 50(4), determines that such testing is justifiable. Section 34(1) of the Promotion of Equality and Prevention of Unfair Discrimination Act, 2000, 4 of 2000, which section came into effect on 1 September 2000, requires the Minister of Justice and Constitutional Development to give special consideration to the inclusion of, amongst other things, HIV/AIDS as a prohibited ground of discrimination; the schedule to that Act lists, as part of an illustrative list of unfair practices in the insurance services, "unfairly disadvantaging a person or persons, including unfairly and unreasonably refusing to grant services, to persons solely on the basis of HIV/AIDS status." The National Department of Education has, in terms of section 3(4) of the National Education Policy Act, 27 of 1996, issued a national policy on HIV/AIDS which, amongst other things, prohibits unfair discrimination against learners, students and educators with HIV/AIDS. The National Department of Health has, in terms of the National Policy for Health Act, 116 of 1990, issued a national policy on testing for HIV. The Medical Schemes Act, 131 of 1998 obliges all medical schemes to provide at least a minimum cover for HIV positive persons. Finally, a draft code of good practice on key aspects of HIV/AIDS and employment issued under the Employment Equity Act has been published for public comment. This draft code has, as one of its goals, the elimination of unfair discrimination in the workplace based on HIV status.

94. See above para 11(c).

95. I accept, of course, that the obligations of an employer towards existing employees may be greater than its obligations towards prospective employees.

96. Above n 7, at para 28.

97. *S v Makwanyane and Another* 1995 (3) SA 391 (CC); 1995 (6) BCLR 665 (CC) at para 88.

98. For example, in *Moller v Keimoes School Committee* 1911 AD 635, a case involving a challenge to segregation in public schools following an objection by a group of white parents to their children having to attend the same school as black children, de Villiers CJ, at 643–4, declined to ignore colour "prepossessions, or . . . prejudices" in construing a statute. Relying on such prejudice, he found that a white parent would not have been "a consenting party to an Act by which European parents could be compelled to send their children to a school which children of mixed origin can also be compelled to attend." In *Minister of Posts and Telegraphs v Rasool* 1934 AD 167, a case involving a challenge to segregation of counters at a post office following an objection by a group of whites to being served at the same counter as Indians, Stratford ACJ, at 175, held that "a division of the community on differences of race or language for the purpose of postal service seems, *prima facie*, to be sensible and make for the convenience and comfort of the public as a whole, since appropriate officials conversant with the customs, requirements and language of each section will conceivably serve the respective sections." In *Williams & Adendorff v Johannesburg Municipality* 1915 TPD 106, a case involving a challenge to segregation in the use of tramcars, while the majority found that segregation was unlawful because it was unauthorised by the empowering statute, Bristowe J held, at 122, that regard might "be properly paid to the feelings and the sensitiveness, even to the prejudices and foibles of the general body of reasonable citizens" in determining whether segregation was lawful. Bristowe J held further that, having regard to "the existing state of public feeling the segregation of natives, even though not coming within bye-law 12, may be essential to an efficient tramway system." Curlewis J, also dissenting, held, at 128, that "apart from dress and behaviour it is possible that it may be established that the use, for instance, by natives of the ordinary tramcars would be so distasteful and revolting to the rest of the community that the council as a common carrier would be justified in refusing to carry them as passengers in the same cars as Europeans." *The State v Xhego and Others* 83 Prentice Hall H76 concerned the admissibility of confessions. Some ten African accused challenged confessions made by them on the grounds that they had been induced by threats or force on the part of the police. Rejecting the evidence of the accused, van der Riet AJP observed, at 197, that "[h]ad the evidence been given by Europeans, it might well have prevailed against the single evidence of warrant officer de Beer" because there were many other policemen who were allegedly involved in the assault but who gave no evidence to contradict the accused. The evidence of the accused was rejected, however, because "the native, in giving evidence, is so prone to exaggeration that it is often impossible to distinguish the truth from fiction." The Court also noted that there were other factors that "militated strongly against the acceptance of the allegations of the accused, again resulting largely from the inherent foolishness of the Bantu character." In *Incorporated Law Society v Wookey* 1912 AD 623, a case involving an application by a woman to be admitted as an attorney, even though the statute in question did not expressly exclude women from practising as attorneys, relying upon the history of the profession, namely that it is a profession which has always been practised by men, the Court found that the word "person" should be construed to refer to men only, to the exclusion of women.

99. *uBuntu* is the recognition of human worth and respect for the dignity of every person. See also the comments of Langa J, Mahomed J, and Mokgoro J in *S v Makwanyane*, above n 29, at paras 224, 263, and 308 respectively.

100. AIR 1997 (Bombay) 406 at 431.

101. Above para 15.

102. See *August and Another v. Electoral Commission and Others* 1999 (3) SA 1 (CC); 1999 (4) BCLR 363 (CC) at para 23.

103. *National Coalition for Gay and Lesbian Equality and Others v Minister of Home Affairs and Others* 2000 (2) SA 1 (CC); 2000 (1) BCLR 39 (CC) at para 65. In terms of section 7(4) of the interim Constitution, where the rights contained in Chapter 3 were infringed, persons referred to in paragraph (b) of section 7(4) were entitled to apply to Court "for appropriate relief."

104. In Re Kodellas *et al* and Saskatchewan Human Rights Commission *et al*; Attorney-General of Saskatchewan, Intervenor (1989) 60 DLR (4th) 143, 187, Vancise JA said: "A just remedy must of necessity be appropriate, but an appropriate remedy may not be fair or equitable in the circumstances." This statement must be understood in the context of section 24(1) of the Canadian Charter, which provides that anyone whose rights, guaranteed in the Charter, have been infringed may apply to court "to obtain such remedy as the court considers appropriate and just in the circumstances." The Canadian Constitution, therefore, makes a distinction between "appropriateness" and "justness." Our Constitution does not.

105. *Fose v Minister of Safety and Security* 1997 (3) SA 786 (CC); 1997 (7) BCLR 851 (CC) at para 38.

106. In terms of section 231(2) of the Constitution, an international agreement is binding on the Republic of South Africa once it has been ratified.

107. South Africa has ratified the following Conventions dealing with discrimination: The African Charter on Human and Peoples' Rights, 1981; the Convention on the Elimination of All Forms of Discrimination Against Women, 1979; the International Covenant on Civil and Political Rights, 1966; the International Convention on the Elimination of All Forms of Racial Discrimination, 1966; and ILO Convention 111, Discrimination (Employment and Occupation) Convention, 1958. South Africa has signed, but not ratified, the Convention on the Political Rights of Women, 1953 and the International Covenant on Economic, Social and Cultural Rights, 1966.

108. In terms of the Code of Conduct on HIV/AIDS and Employment in the Southern African Development Community (SADC), 1997.

109. In the context of an employee who is unfairly dismissed, Nicholas AJA expressed the rule as follows:

"Where an employee is unfairly dismissed he suffers a wrong. Fairness and justice require that such wrong should be redressed. The [Labour Relations Act, 28 of 1956] provides that the redress may consist of reinstatement, compensation or otherwise. The fullest redress obtainable is provided by the restoration of the status quo ante. It follows that it is incumbent on the Court when deciding what remedy is appropriate to consider whether, in the light of all the proved circumstances, there is reason to refuse reinstatement."

UBUNTU AND ENTITLEMENT

1. *S v V* 1972 (3) SA 611 (A) at 614 as quoted by Bosielo J *in casu*.

2. Although this case does not make explicit mention of the word *ubuntu*, in light of what has been said in the introduction to this book about the role of the restorative justice model in relation to *ubuntu*, the authors consider the following judgment, relied upon in *S v. Joyce Maluleke* (http://www.restorativejustice.org) and subsequently by Justice Sachs in the *Dikoko v. Mokhatla* 2007 (1) BCLR 1 (CC) judgment, to be of great import.

UBUNTU AND KEY ASPECTS OF LIVING: CUSTOMARY LAW

1. At para 45 of the *Bhe* case.

Justice Ngcobo

2. Act 38 of 1927.

3. Government Gazette 10601 GN R200, 6 February 1987 as amended by Government Gazette 24120, GN R1501, 3 December 2002.

4. Section 1(4)(b) of the Intestate Succession Act provides that:
"'[I]ntestate estate' includes any part of an estate . . . in respect of which section 23 of the Black Administration Act, 1927 (Act No. 38 of 1927), does not apply."

5. *Western Cape Provincial Government and Others: In re DVB Behuising (Pty) Ltd v North West Provincial Government and Another* 2001 (1) SA 500 (CC); 2000 (4) BCLR 347 (CC) at para 1.

6. See para 36 of the main judgment.

7. Section 39(2) of the Constitution provides that ". . . when developing the common law or customary law, every court, tribunal or forum must promote the spirit, purport and objects of the Bill of Rights." See also *Ex Parte Chairperson of the Constitutional Assembly: In re Certification of the Constitution of the Republic of South Africa*, 1996 (4) SA 744 (CC); 1996 (10) BCLR 1253 (CC) at para 197. Compare *Carmichele v Minister of Safety and Security* 2001 (4) SA 938 (CC); 2001 (10) BCLR 995 (CC) at paras 37–40.

8. Compare *Carmichele v Minister of Safety and Security* 2001 (4) SA 938 (CC); 2001 (10) BCLR 995 (CC) at paras 37–40.

9. *Id* at para 51. Compare *Pharmaceutical Manufacturers Association of South Africa and Another: In re Ex Parte President of the Republic of South Africa and Others* 2000 (2) SA 674 (CC); 2000 (3) BCLR 241 (CC) at para 44.

10. Section 2 of the Constitution states that, "[t]his Constitution is the supreme law of the Republic; law or conduct inconsistent with it is invalid, and the obligations imposed by it must be fulfilled." See also *Mabuza v Mbatha* 2003 (4) SA 218 (T); 2003 (7) BCLR 743 (T) at para 32.

11. Section 1(1) provides that "[a]ny court may take judicial notice of the law of a foreign state and of indigenous law in so far as such law can be ascertained readily and with sufficient certainty: Provided that indigenous law shall not be opposed to the principles of public policy and natural justice: Provided further that it shall not be lawful for any court to declare that the custom of lobola or bogadi or other similar custom is repugnant to such principles." In view of the constitutionalisation of indigenous law, there are substantial doubts as to whether the first proviso still applies. See also *Mabuza id.*

12. Above n 7 at para 52; *Masenya v Seleka Tribal Authority & Another* 1981 (1) SA 522 (T); *Hlophe v Mahlalela and Another* 1998 (1) SA 449 (T) at 457E–F; and *Mabuza* (above n 9).

13. Above n 7 at para 54; and *Mabuza id* at 448D–F.

14. *Alexkor Ltd and Another v Richtersveld Community and Others id.*

15. *Id.*

16. *Id* at para 52 n 51.

17. Above n 7 at para 52; Bekker and De Kock, "Male primogeniture in African customary law—are some now more equal than others?" (1998) 23 *Journal for Juridical Science* 99 at 112–113. See also *Mabena v Letsoalo* 1998 (2) SA 1068 (T) at 1074–1075B.

18. Above n 7 at para 53.

19. 2000 (3) SA 867 (SCA); [2000] 3 All SA 319 (A) at para 8.

20. *Alexkor* (above n 7) at para 56.

21. [1921] 2 AC 399.

22. *Id* at 402–404.

23. Bennett, *A Sourcebook of African Customary law for Southern Africa* (Juta, Cape Town 1991) at 383.

24. Himonga, "The Law of Succession and Inheritance in Zambia and the Proposed Reform," (1989) *International Journal of Law and the Family* 3 160 at 161.

25. Bekker and De Kock, "Adaptation of the Customary Law of Succession to Changing Needs" (1992) 25 *Comparative and International Law Journal of Southern Africa* 366 at 368; and Maithufi, The constitutionality of the rule of primogeniture in customary law of intestate succession (1998) *Tydskrif vir Hedendaagse Romeins-Hollandse Reg* 142 at 147.

26. Ndulo, "Widows under Zambian Customary Law and the Response of the Court" (1995) *Comparative and International Law Journal of Southern Africa* 90 at 92.

27. *Magaya v Magaya* 1999 (1) ZLR 100 (S) at 108E–G.

28. Bennet, *Human Rights and African Customary Law under the South African Constitution* (Juta, Cape Town 1995) at 5; and *id.*

29. As Mokgoro J put it in *S v Makwanyane and Another* 1995 (3) SA 391 (CC); 1995 (6) BCLR 665 (CC) at para 308: "*ubuntu* . . . metaphorically, it expresses itself in *umuntu ngumuntu ngabantu*, describing the significance of group solidarity on survival issues so central to the survival of communities. While it envelops the key values of group solidarity, compassion, respect, human dignity, conformity to basic norms and collective unity, in its fundamental sense it denotes humanity and morality. Its spirit emphasises respect for human dignity, marking a shift from confrontation to conciliation." (Footnotes omitted.) Further, Mohamed J held in *Makwanyane* at para 263 that "[t]he need for *ubuntu* expresses the ethos of an instinctive capacity for and enjoyment of love towards our fellow men and women; the joy and the fulfilment involved in recognizing their innate humanity; the reciprocity this generates in interaction within the collective community; the richness of the creative emotions which it engenders and the moral energies which it releases both in the givers and the society which they serve and are served by." See also *Makwanyane* at para 237.

30. *Id* at para 224.

31. Above n 25 at 99.

32. South African Law Commission Project 90 *Report on Customary Law of Succession,* 2004 at 15; Bekker and De Kock, (above n 22) at 366; and Bennett (above n 25) at 382.

33. Bennett, (above n 22) at 383.

34. Ndulo, (above n 25) at 100.

35. Maithufi, (above n 24) at 147.

36. In this judgment the term *indlalifa* will be used as it is more appropriate in the context of succession in indigenous law.

37. Bekker and De Kock, (above n 24) at 368; and Maithufi, (above n 24) at 147.

38. South African Law Commission Project 90, (above n 31) at 17; and *Magaya,* (above n 26) at 109E–G.

39. *Chihowa v Mangwende* 1987 (1) ZLR 228 (SC) at 231H–232D; and *Magaya* (above n 26) at 110B–E.

40. *Mgoza and Another v Mgoza* 1967 (2) SA 36 (A) at 440E–G.

41. Above n 38.

42. Above n 26 at 109E–H.

43. Bekker and De Kock (above n 24) at 366 and 368.

44. Rautenbach, "Law of succession and inheritance" in *Introduction to Legal Pluralism in South Africa Part 1 Customary Law,* ed. Bekker 109 at 110.

45. Bekker, *Seymour's Customary Law in Southern Africa* 5th ed. (Juta, Cape Town 1989) at 298.

46. Above n 39 at 440E–F.

47. Mbatha, "Reforming the Customary Law of Succession" (2002) 18 *South Africa Journal on Human Rights* 259 at 260.

48. *Id* at 261.

49. Above n 26 at 109B–E.

50. *Mabena* (above n 16) at 1073J.

51. Above n. 18.

52. *Id.*

53. *Id* at para 8.

54. *Mabena* (above n 16) at 1074E–F, where the court found that female family heads were on the increase. See also paras 73–74 and 83 below.

55. Nhlapo, "The African family and women's rights: Friends or foes?" (1991) *Acta Juridica* 135 at 141–142.

56. *S v Makwanyane and Another* 1995 (3) SA 391 (CC); 1995 (6) BCLR 665 (CC) at paras 155–156; *Shabalala and Others v Attorney-General, Transvaal, and Another* 1996 (1) SA 725 (CC); 1995 (12) BCLR 1593 (CC) at para 26; *Brink v Kitshoff NO* 1996 (4) SA 197 (CC); 1996 (6) BCLR 752 (CC) at paras 33–40; *Fraser v Children's Court, Pretoria North, and Others* 1997 (2) SA 261 (CC); 1997 (2) BCLR 153 (CC) at para 20; *National Coalition for Gay and Lesbian Equality and Another v Minister of Justice and Others* 1999 (1) SA 6 (CC); 1998 (12) BCLR 1517 (CC) at paras 15–25; *National Coalition for Gay and Lesbian Equality and Others v Minister of Home Affairs and Others* 2000 (2) SA 1 (CC); 2000 (1) BCLR 39 (CC) at para 58; *Hoffmann v South African Airways* 2001 (1) SA 1 (CC); 2000 (11) BCLR 1211 (CC) at para 27; and *Satchwell v President of the Republic of South Africa and Another* 2002 (6) SA 1 (CC); 2002 (9) BCLR 986 (CC) at paras 17–18.

57. Above n 25 at 99–100.

58. Above n 49 at 1074F–G.

59. Elias, *Nigerian Land Law and Custom* (Routledge and Kegan Paul Ltd, London 1951) at 216–235; Ezeilo, *Laws and practices relating to women's inheritance rights in Nigeria: An overview* at 11, www.wacolnig.org/LawAndPracticesRetakingToWomens InheritNig.doc (accessed on 1 June 2004).

60. Elias, *id* at 216.

61. Ezeilo (above n 58) at 11.

62. [1997] 7 NWLR 283.

63. *Id* at 305A–D.

64. Act 15 of 1982.

65. 1984 (2) ZLR 112 (S).

66. *Id* at 117G–H.

67. 1986 (1) ZLR 138 (SC).

68. *Id* at 143A.

69. Above n. 38.

70. *Id* at 231E–F and at 232H–233A–B.

71. 1992 (1) ZLR 167 (S). This case was decided by a bench of three judges.

72. *Id* at 170A–B.

73. *Id* at 170A–B.

74. Stewart, "Untying the Gordian knot! *Murisa v Murisa* S-41–92: A Little More Than a Case Note," (1992) 4 no 3 *Legal Forum* at 8.

75. Above n 26.

76. *Id* at 111B.

77. *Id* at 105G–106B.

78. *Land and property rights of widows: A case study of inheritance customary law in Tanzania*, at 6, www.widowsrights.org (accessed on 12 October 2004).

79. No 4 Order, 1963.

80. Article 13(4) of the Constitution of the United Republic of Tanzania, 1977 provides that "no person shall be discriminated against by any person or any authority acting under any law or in the discharge of the functions or business of any state office."

81. 1965 G.L.R 13.

82. *Id* at 17.

83. *Id* at 16.

84. *Id.*

85. 1965 G.L.R 138.

86. *Id* at 148.

87. *Id* at 144.

88. *Id.*

89. Articles 1, 2, and 5(a). South Africa signed the Convention on 29 January 1993 and ratified it on 14 January 1996.

90. Article 18(3). South Africa signed the Charter in 1995 and ratified it in 1996.

91. Articles 2(1) and 26. South Africa ratified the Covenant on 10 March 1999.

92. Articles 2 and 5 of the CEDAW.

93. 2000 (2) SA 425 (CC); 2000 (1) BCLR 86 (CC).

94. *Id* at para 13.

95. Above n 6.

96. *Id* at para 33.

97. *Id.*

98. *Id* at para 39.

99. See the development of the common law relating to delictual liability for an omission in cases such as *Minister van Polisie v Ewels* 1975 (3) SA 590 (A); *Administrateur, Natal v Trust Bank van Afrika Bpk* 1979 (3) SA 824 (A); and *Schultz v Butt* 1986 (3) SA 667 (A). See generally Corbett, "Aspects of the Role of Policy in the Evolution of our Common Law," (1987) 104 *South African Law Journal* 52.

100. Above n 49.

101. *Id* at 1074F–G.

102. *Daniels v Campbell NO and Others* 2004 (7) BCLR 735 (CC) at para 56.

103. See para 108 of the main judgment.

104. Above n 46 at 285.

105. *Ex Parte Chairperson of the Constitutional Assembly* above n 6 at para 202.

106. *Id.* at para 197.

107. See para 107 of the main judgment.

108. South African Law Commission Project 90, above n 31 at 83.

109. *Id.*

110. *Id* at 86.

111. Above n 39.

112. 2000 (4) SA 757 (CC); 2000 (10) BCLR 1051 (CC).

113. *Id* at para 24.

114. Above n 25 at 100.

115. Above n 23 at 165.

UBUNTU AND THE RIGHT TO CULTURE

1. For the minority judgment of Justice O'Regan, see *The Dignity Jurisprudence of South Africa.*

Justice Langa

2. *Pillay v MEC for Education, KwaZulu-Natal, and Others* 2006 (6) SA 363 (EqC); 2006 (10) BCLR 1237 (N).

3. *Independent Electoral Commission v Langeberg Municipality* 2001 (3) SA 925 (CC); 2001 (9) BCLR 883 (CC) at para 11. See also *AAA Investments Pty (Ltd) v Micro Finance Regulatory Council and Another* 2007 (1) SA 343 (CC); 2006 (11) BCLR 1255 (CC) at para 27.

4. Act 84 of 1996.

5. For example: "The uniform *must* allow learners to participate in school activities with comfort, safety and decorum" (regulation 11); "*No* child may be refused admission to a school because of an inability to obtain or wear the school uniform" (regulation 14). (Emphasis added.)

6. Regulation 29.

7. Regulation 23.

8. Preamble to guidelines.

9. See the long title of the Equality Act which reads:

"To give effect to section 9 read with item 23(1) of Schedule 6 to the Constitution of the Republic of South Africa, 1996, so as to prevent and prohibit unfair discrimination and harassment; to promote equality and eliminate unfair discrimination; to prevent and prohibit hate speech; and to provide for matters connected therewith."

10. Section 6 reads: "Neither the State nor any person may unfairly discriminate against any person." The "prohibited grounds" on which discrimination is barred, are defined in section 1 which repeats the list in section 9(3) of the Constitution.

11. *Minister of Health and Another NO v New Clicks South Africa (Pty) Ltd (Treatment Action Campaign and Another as* Amicus Curiae*)* 2006 (2) SA 311 (CC); 2006 (1) BCLR 1 (CC) at paras 96 (Chaskalson CJ) and 434–437 (Ngcobo J); *South African National Defence Union v Minister of Defence and Others* CCT 65/06, 30 May 2007, as yet unreported at para 51. See also *NAPTOSA and Others v Minister of Education, Western Cape, and Others* 2001 (2) SA 112 (C) at 123I–J; 2001 (4) BCLR 388 (C) at 396I–J.

12. This is the conclusion reached by O'Regan J at para 164 below.

13. *Prince v President, Cape Law Society, and Others* 2002 (2) SA 794 (CC); 2002 (3) BCLR 231 (CC) (*Prince II*) at para 42. The majority in *Prince II* did not express any disagreement with this part of Ngcobo J's judgment.

14. See, for example, *Syndicat Northcrest v Amselem* [2004] 2 SCR 551 (SCC) at para 43; *Ross v New Brunswick School District No 15* [1996] 1 SCR 825 at paras 70–71; BVerfGE 33, 23 at 29; *Thomas v Review Board of the Indiana Employment Security Division* 450 US 707 (1981) at 715–716; *United States v Ballard* 322 US 78 (1944) at 86–87; and *In re Chikweche* 1995 (4) SA 284 (ZSC) at 289J.

15. *Port Elizabeth Municipality v Various Occupiers* 2005 (1) SA 217 (CC); 2004 (12) BCLR 1268 (CC) at para 37.

16. A recognition of the importance of the community to the individual is by no means unique to African thought. See, for example, Kymlicka, *Multicultural Citizenship: A Liberal Theory of Minority Rights* (Claredon Press, Oxford 1995) at 89–90 quoting and discussing Margalit and Raz "National Self Determination" (1990) *Journal of Philosophy* 439 at 447–449; Donders *Towards a Right to Cultural Identity?* (Intersentia, Antwerpen 2002) especially at 30–31 and Almqvist *Human Rights, Culture and the Rule of Law* (Hart Publishing, Oxford and Portland 2005) especially at 4042.

17. This translates literally as "a person is a person through other people."

18. *Bhe and Others v Magistrate, Khayelitsha, and Others (Commission for Gender Equality as* Amicus Curiae*); Shibi v Sithole and Others; South African Human Rights Commission and Another v President of the Republic of South Africa and Another* 2005 (1) SA 580 (CC); 2005 (1) BCLR 1 (CC) at para 163 (Ngcobo J).

19. Gyekye, *Person and Community: Ghanaian Philosophical Studies* (1992) reprinted as *Person and Community in African Thought* in *Philosophy from Africa: A Text with Readings* 321 (Oxford University Press, Cape Town 1998).

20. See, for example, *Affordable Medicines Trust and Others v Minister of Health and Others* 2006 (3) SA 247 (CC); 2005 (6) BCLR 529 (CC) at para 59 and *National Coalition*

for Gay and Lesbian Equality and Another v Minister of Justice and Others 1999 (1) SA 6 (CC); 1998 (12) BCLR 1517 (CC) at para 26.

21. Chanock, *Human Rights and Cultural Branding: Who Speaks and How in Cultural Transformation and Human Rights in Africa* 41 (Zed Books, London 2002). See also Benhabib *The Claims of Culture: Equality and Diversity in the Global Era* 3–9 (Princeton University Press, 2002).

22. *Harksen v Lane NO and Others* 1998 (1) SA 300 (CC) at para 50; 1997 (11) BCLR 1489 (CC) at para 49.

23. See above n 34

24. 1996 (1) SA 984 (CC); 1996 (1) BCLR 1 (CC).

25. *Id* at para 49. While the majority in *Ferreira v Levin* distanced themselves from Ackermann J's broad construction of freedom as a self-standing right, there is nothing to suggest they questioned his link between freedom and dignity.

26. See Woolman "Dignity" in Woolman et al (eds) *Constitutional Law of South Africa* 2 ed (Juta, Cape Town 2006) at 36–11.

27. 2006 (1) SA 524 (CC); 2006 (3) BCLR 355 (CC).

28. *Id* at para 60.

29. At para 53.

30. *Fourie* above n 46 at paras 60, 95 and 112; *Pretoria City Council v Walker* 1998 (2) SA 363 (CC); 1998 (3) BCLR 257 (CC) at paras 81 (Langa DP) and 130 (Sachs J); *President of the Republic of South Africa and Another v Hugo* 1997 (4) SA 1 (CC); 1997 (6) BCLR 708 (CC) at para 41; *Prinsloo v Van der Linde and Another* 1997 (3) SA 1012 (CC); 1997 (6) BCLR 759 (CC) at para 32.

31. Above n 36.

32. *Id* at para 42.

33. This matter was pertinently dealt with in *Multani* above n 72 at para 76.

34. *Id* at paras 71 and 74.

35. This term was employed by O'Connor J in *Oregon v Smith* to describe the majority's list of extreme examples of possible religious exemptions, which they employed to justify their decision that neutral rules would not violate the First Amendment. See *Oregon v Smith* above n 87 at 902.

TOWARDS THE LIBERATION AND REVITALIZATION OF CUSTOMARY LAW

Albie Sachs

This article is the transcript of a predinner address delivered by Justice of the Constitutional Court Albie Sachs at the Southern African Society of Legal Historians Conference on "Law in Africa: New Perspectives on Origins, Foundations and Transition." The conference was held at Roodevallei Country Lodge, Pretoria, 13–15 January 1999. The article has been lightly edited for publication in this book.

1. Stokvels are clubs or syndicates serving as rotating savings clubs. Members contribute money on a periodic basis, and this money is given to a different member of the club each months.

UBUNTU AND THE LAW IN SOUTH AFRICA

Yvonne Mokgoro

This is a revised version of a paper presented by Yvonne Mokgoro, Justice of the Constitutional Court of the Republic of South Africa, at the colloquium, "Constitution and Law," organized by the Law Faculty, Potchefsroom University for Higher Christian Education (PU for HCE), South Africa, October 31, 1997.

1. Gena Johann Broodryk, "*uBuntu* in South Africa" (unpublished Ph.D. diss., University of South Africa, Pretoria, 1997), ch. 1.

2. Lovemore Mbigi and Jenny Maree, *uBuntu: The Spirit of African Transformation Management* 1–7 (Johannesburg: Sigma Press, 1995).

3. Professor Kunene, "The Essence of Being Human—An African Perspective" (inaugural lecture, University of Natal, Durban 10, August 16, 1996).

4. Mbigi and Maree (*supra* n. 2), 5.

5. South African Constitution, chapter 16 (National Unity and Reconciliation is the postscript of the Constitution).

6. *Id*, section 33.

7. 1996 South African Constitution, chapter 2, section 7, d.i.

8. *Id*. chapter 12, section 211, cl. 3.

9. "Chief Justice Hails New Const and African Values" in *De Rebus: The South African Attorneys' Journal* 78 (February 1997).

A CALL FOR A NUANCED CONSTITUTIONAL JURISPRUDENCE: SOUTH AFRICA, *UBUNTU*, DIGNITY, AND RECONCILIATION

Drucilla Cornell

This essay is based on two texts: Drucilla Cornell, "A Call for a Nuanced Constitutional Jurisprudence: *uBuntu*, Dignity, and Reconciliation in Suid-Afrikaanse Publiekereg" *South African Public Law* 19 (2004): 661, and Drucilla Cornell and Karin Van Marle, "Exploring *Ubuntu*—Tentative Reflections in African" *Human Rights Law Journal* (2005): 195–220. The author and the editors would like to thank Karin Van Marle for allowing them to reproduce portions of the latter text. Drucilla Cornell is Professor of Political Science, Women's Studies, and Comparative Literature at Rutgers University.

1. See Immanuel Kant, *Groundwork on the Metaphysics of Morals* (Cambridge: Cambridge University Press, 1998).

2. Zora Neale Hurston, *Their Eyes Were Watching God* 15 (New York: Harper & Row Publishers, 1990).

3. Martha Nussbaum, *Women and Human Development: The Capabilities Approach* (Cambridge: Cambridge University Press, 2000).

4. Drucilla Cornell, "Who bears the right to die" in *Sovereignty and Death*, ed. Thurschwell (forthcoming).

5. Yvonne Mokgoro, "*uBuntu* and the law in South Africa" (paper delivered at the first Colloquium "Constitution and Law," Potchefstroom, October 31, 1997, and published in the previous chapter of this book).

6. G. J. van Niekerk, "A Common Law for Southern Africa: Roman Law or Indigenous African Law?" in *Roman Law at the Crossroads,* eds. J. E. Spruit, W. J. Kamba, and M. O. Hinz (Kenwyn: Juta & Co. Ltd., 2000), 83.

7. For more information see Dipesh Chakrabarty, *Provincializing Europe* (Princeton: Princeton University Press, 2000).

8. Cornell, *Transformations: Recollective Imagination and Sexual Difference* (New York: Routledge, 1993), 37–40.

9. Augustine Shutte, *uBuntu: An Ethic for a New South Africa* (Pietermaritzburg: Cluster Publications, 2001), 107, 148, 182.

10. Albie Sachs, *Protecting Human Rights in a New South Africa* (Oxford: Oxford University Press, 1991) and *Advancing Human Rights in South Africa* (Oxford: Oxford University Press, 1992).

11. Dennis Davis, "Deconstructing and Reconstructing the Argument for a Bill of Rights within the Context of South African Nationalism" in *The Post-Apartheid Constitutions,* eds. Penelope Andrews and Stephen Ellmann (Athens: Ohio University Press, 2001), 205.

12. See Mahmood Mamdani, *Citizen and Subject* (Princeton: Princeton University Press, 1996), 131–132.

13. See Lourens du Plessis and Hugh Corder, *Understanding South Africa's Transitional Bill of Rights* (Kenwyn: Juta & Company, 1994).

14. *S v. Makwanyane* (n. 9) at paras 350–357.

15. See Ronald Dworkin, *Life's Dominion* (New York: Vintage Books, 1994).

16. *Soobramoney v. Minister of Health, Kwa-Zulu-Natal,* concurring opinion of Justice Sachs at para 55.

17. *S v. Makwanyane* (n. 9), concurring opinion of Justice Mokgoro at para 313.

18. *Id.* at para 302.

19. *Prince v. President,* Cape Law Society 2002 2 SA 794 (CC).

20. *Id.,* dissenting opinion of Justice Sachs at para 149.

21. *Soobramoney (supra* n. 16) at para 54.

22. *Id.* at paras 54 and 55.

23. Setiloane, *The Image of God among the Sotho-Tswana* 52 (Rotterdam: A. A. Balkema, 1976), 52; cited in *Battle Reconciliation: The* uBuntu *Theology of Desmond Tutu* (Cleveland: The Pilgrim Press, 1997), 50.

24. *S v. Makwanyane* (n. 9).

DOING THINGS WITH VALUES: THE CASE OF *UBUNTU*

Irma J. Kroeze

This article is based on a paper delivered at the Twentieth World Congress of the International Association for Philosophy of Law and Social Philosophy held at the Vrije Universiteit, Amsterdam from June 19–23, 2001. It was first published in *Stellenbosch Law Review* 2 (2002) at 252. It is reproduced here with the permission of Juta Law and the editors of the Stellenbosch Law Review.

1. "Doing Things with Values: The Role of Constitutional Interpretation" in *Stellenbosch Law Review* (2001): 265–276.

2. The last (unnumbered) section of the Constitution of the Republic of South 1993, entitled National Unity and Reconciliation.

3. *S v. Makwanyane* 1995 3 SA 391 (CC).

4. Constitution of the Republic of South Africa, 1996; hereinafter the Constitution.

5. See Mokgoro, "*uBuntu* and the Law in South Africa," *Potchefstroom Elektroniese Regstydskrif* 1 (1998) (http://www.puk.ac.za/lawper/). Mokgoro states that, although the concept of *ubuntu* was not included in the final Constitution, the values included "coincide with some key values of *ubuntu*(-ism)."

6. A very general search of the Internet resulted in 3,330 hits on the search term *ubuntu*. These include web pages relating to everything from education to business, religion, and law.

7. See, for example, Michael Battle *Reconciliation: The uBuntu Theology of Desmond Tutu* (Cleveland, Ohio: Pilgrim Press, 1997).

8. From a CLS perspective the very strong distinction between law and politics is very interesting, but this can, unfortunately, not be investigated here.

9. *Makwanyane* (*supra* n. 3) at para 131.

10. *Furman v. Georgia* 408 US 238 (1972), 305.

11. *Makwanyane* (*supra* n. 3) at para 224.

12. *Id.* at para 225.

13. *Id.* at para 227.

14. This was the case of *DPP v. Pete* [1991] LRC (Const) 553; see *Makwanyane* (*supra* n. 3) at para 224.

15. *Makwanyane* (*supra* n. 3) at para 237.

16. *Id.* at para 241–243.

17. *Id.* at para 244.

18. *Id.* at para 263.

19. *Id.* at para 307.

20. *Id. at* para 310–311. It is interesting to note that Mokgoro is not claiming that *ubuntu* is a concept unique to African people—in her view, it is a concept that is shared by all South Africans. This is a truly fascinating claim that she never substantiates.

21. This idiom is translated in various ways. One translation is: A person is a person through other people.

22. *Makwanyane* (*supra* n. 3) at para 308.

23. *Id.* at para 309.

24. Mokgoro 1998 PER 2.

25. The learned judge does not indicate what these unique approaches, attitudes, and methods are or what their influence would be.

26. Mokgoro 1998 PER 4.

27. Mokgoro 1998 PER 7.

28. See, for example, *S v. Williams* 1994 4 SA 126 (C) at 135; *Azanian Peoples' Organisation (AZAPO) v. Truth and Reconciliation Commission* 1996 4 SA 562 (C) 566 and 677; *Dulabh v. Department of Land Affairs* 1997 4 SA 1108 (LCC) 1126; *Williamson v. Schoon* 1997 3 SA 1053 (T) 1070; *Ryland v. Edros* 1997 2 SA 690 (C) 708; *Christian Education SA v. Minister of Education* 2000 4 SA 757 (CC) at para 50; Inkatha Freedom Party Truth and Reconciliation Commission 2000 3 SA 119 (C) 123.

29. Various authors use different terms to refer to indigenous law, such as African customary law. This term will be used here, as it is the one Van Niekerk uses.

30. Van Niekerk, "A Common Law for Southern Africa: Roman Law or Indigenous African Law?" CILSA (1998): 158–173, 167.

31. *Id.* 158, 167.

32. *Id.* 158, 168.

33. *Id.* 158, 169.

34. *Id.* 158, 171; see also sources quoted here.

35. De Kock and Labuschagne, "*uBuntu* as a conceptual directive in realising a culture of effective Human Rights" THRHR (1999): 114–120, 119.

36. *Id.* 114, 119.

37. *Id.* 114, 119.

38. *Id.* 114, 120.

39. Mqeke, "Customary law and human rights" *South African Law Journal* (1996): 364–369, 364 .

40. *Id.* 364, 365.

41. *Id.* 364, 366.

42. *Id.* 364, 368.

43. *Id.* 364, 368.

44. *Id.* 364, 369.

45. *Id.* 364, 369.

46. *Makwanyane* (*supra* n. 3) at para 306.

47. See, for example, du Plessis and de Ville, "Bill of Rights interpretation in the South African context" *Stellenbosch Law Review* 63 (1993): 389; see also sources quoted there.

48. See Kroeze, *Stellenbosch Law Review* (2001): 265–276.

49. See Pierre Schlag, "Normativity and the Politics of Form" *U. Penn. L. Rev.* (1991): 801–932; Schlag, "Normative and Nowhere to Go in Laying Down the Law—Mysticism, Fetishism, and the American Legal Mind" (1996): 17–41; Schlag, " '*Le hors de texte c'est moi*': The Politics of Form and the Domestication of Deconstruction" *Cardozo L. Rev.* (1990): 1631–1674.

50. The discussion that follows is not meant to be a detailed discussion of Schlag's viewpoint, but will merely serve as a summary of his arguments. The assumption is that readers are familiar with Schlag's work.

51. Schlag, "*Le hors de texte c'est moi*," 1632–1633.

52. *Id.*, 1633.

53. *Id.*, 1637.

54. *Id.*, 1647.

55. *Id.*, 1671.

56. This should be very Jakmiliar to those who study constitutional jurisprudence. The court is constantly engaged in this process—articulating or "finding" a value or values and then choosing one over the other. In this judgment of Chaskalson in *Makwanyane* (*supra* n. 3) at para 104: "The limitation of constitutional rights for a purpose that is reasonable and necessary in a democratic society, involves the weighing up of competing values . . ."

57. Schlag, "Normative and Nowhere," 27–28.

58. *Id.,* 30.

59. *Id.,* 32.

60. Schlag, "Normativity," 873.

61. Once again I am not suggesting that it cannot have an effect on these concepts, but merely that this has not been demonstrated.

62. Maluleke, "The Misuse of *'ubuntu'" Challenge* (1999): 12–13.

63. For an elaboration on this, see Schlag, "Normative and Nowhere," 17–41.

64. This is a common problem. Any criticism of liberalism is regarded as an argument in favor of communitarianism, as if these are the only two choices. See, for example, Van Blerk, *Jurisprudence: An Introduction* (1998), 153, 214–215. Van Blerk misunderstands the CLS criticism of liberalism as a defense of communitarianism.

65. Schlag, "Values," in *Laying Down the Law: Mysticism, Fetishism, and the American Legal Mind,* 42–59, 57 (New York University Press, 1996).

66. Ontologically deep values constitute the dominant forms of being for a person or group in that they are "sedimented cultural formations that constitute the very way in which our social and intellectual lives are fashioned." See Schlag, "Values," 51.

67. Ontologically superficial values are subordinate or derivative in that they are "epiphenominal, normatively pleasing illusion(s) akin to magical thinking." See Schlag, "Values," 51.

68. *Id.,* 53–55.

69. *Id.,* 54.

70. *Id.,* 54–55.

71. "Judicious avoidance" is the term Currie uses to describe the (in his view welcome) approach of the Constitutional Court to interpretation—one that avoids the construction of theoretical systems. See Currie, "Judicious Avoidance" *SAJHR* (1999): 138–165.

72. See Van der Walt, "Tradition on Trial: A Critical Analysis of the Civil-law Tradition in South African Property Law" *SAJHR* (1995): 169–206. See also Singer, "Property and Coercion in Federal Indian Law: The Conflict Between Critical and Complacent Pragmatism" in *S. Cal. L. Rev.* (1990): 1821; "The Pragmatist and the Feminist" *S. Cal. L. Rev.* (1990): 1710.

73. Van der Walt (1995), 193.

74. The best example in this regard is patriarchal assumptions and underpinnings in the case of *ubuntu.*

75. Van der Walt, "Tradition on Trial," 196.

76. Herbert Marcuse, *One Dimensional Man: Studies in the Ideology of Advanced Industrial Society* (1964), 231–232.

77. *Id.,* 64.

78. *Id.,* 65. See also Marcuse, *The End of Utopia in Five Lectures: Psychoanalysis, Politics, and Utopia* (1970), 62–82.

79. Schlag, "Values," 58.

EXPLORING *UBUNTU*: TENTATIVE REFLECTIONS

Drucilla Cornell and Karin van Marle

This article was first published in *African Human Rights Law Journal* (2005): 195–220.

1. *Khosa v. Minister of Social Development* 2004 6 SA 505 (CC) (Khosa).

2. See, for example, Agustine Shutte *Philosophy for Africa* (Cape Town: UCT Press 1995), especially ch. 10 and 11.

3. M. Pieterse "'Traditional' African Jurisprudence" in C. Roederer and D. Moelendorf *Jurisprudence* (Juta & Company, 2004), 442.

4. V. Y. Mudimbe, *The Invention of Africa: Gnosis, Philosophy, and the Order of Knowledge* (Bloomington: Indiana University Press, 1988) 186.

5. *Id.*, ix.

6. See K. van Marie, "Constitution as Archive," unpublished paper delivered at a workshop on "Law, time and reconciliation," Glasgow, May 2004; copy on file with the authors.

7. Jacques Derrida, *Archive Fever: A Freudian Impression* (Chicago: University Of Chicago Press, 1996) 29.

8. Foucault has captured this dilemma that inheres in the ethno-philosophy of Africa and its inevitable domination by a Western framework as follows: "Ethnology has its roots, in fact, in a possibility that properly belongs to the history of the European culture, even more to its fundamental relation with the whole of history . . . There is a certain position of the Western ratio that was constituted in its history and provides a foundation for the relation it can have with all other societies . . . Obviously, this does not mean that the colonising situation is indispensable to ethnology: neither hypnosis, nor the patient's alienation within the fantasmatic character of the doctor, is constitutive of psychoanalysis; but just as the latter can be deployed only in the calm violence of a particular relationship and the transference it produces, so ethnology can assume its proper dimensions only within the historical sovereignty—always restrained, but always present—of European thought and the relation that can bring it face to face with all other culture as well as with itself" (Michel Foucault, *The Order of Things* (1973) 377 as cited in Mudimbe (*supra* n. 4) 16).

9. Derrida, 3.

10. *Id.*, 79.

11. Mudimbe, 186.

12. E. Mureinik, "A Bridge to Where? Introducing the Interim Bill of Rights," *South African Journal on Human Rights* 10 (1994): 31. For a critique on the bridge metaphor, see for example, A. Van der Walt, "Dancing with Codes—Protecting Developing and Deconstructing Property Rights in a Constitutional State," *South African Law Journal* 118 (2001): 258.

13. *AZAPO and Others v. President of the Republic of South Africa and Others* 1996 8 BCLR 1015 (CC) (AZAPO).

14. L. M. du Plessis, "The South African Constitution as Memory and Promise" in *Transcending a Century of Injustice,* ed. C. Villa-Vicencio (2000), 63.

15. See, for example, H. Botha, "Democracy and Rights: Constitutional Interpretation in a Post-realist World," *Journal of Contemporary Roman-Dutch Law* 63 (2000): 561; K. Klare "Legal Culture and Transformative Constitutionalism," *South African Journal on Human Rights* 14 (1998): 146.

16. Snyman, "Interpretation and the Politics of Memory," *Acta Juridica* 312 (1998).

17. Du Plessis, 64.

18. *Id.*

19. *Id.*

20. *S v. Makwanyane* 1995 3 SA 391 (CC).

21. Du Plessis, 65.

22. Van Marie.

23. Derrida, 1.

24. See Cornell, *The Philosophy of the Limit* (1992), 62–90.

25. *Makwanyone* (*supra* n. 20) at para 304.

26. N. R. Mandela, *Long Walk to Freedom* (1995), 624.

27. *Id.*

28. In a forthcoming article, Cornell will be engaging in a discussion of the integral connection between *ubuntu* and the capabilities approach developed by Amartya Sen. For preliminary thinking by Cornell on the capabilities approach, see D. Cornell *Defending Ideals: War, Democracy, and Political Struggle* (New York: Routledge, 2004), ch. 4.

29. I. J. Kroeze, "Doing Things with Values II: The Case of uBuntu," *Stellenbosch Law Review* 13 (2002): 260.

30. E. Moosa, "Tensions in Legal and Religious Values in the 1996 South African Constitution" in *Beyond Rights Talk and Culture Talk: Comparative Essays on the Politics of Rights and Culture,* ed. M. Mamdani (New York: St. Martin's Press, 2000), 131.

31. For example, as well as the ethnographic and jurisprudential aspects of the project, there is an activist dimension. A group of young women who were initially conducting interviews in local townships on the meaning of *ubuntu* organized themselves into a committee to found an *ubuntu* women's centre in Khayamandi.

32. D. M. Davis, "Deconstructing and Reconstructing the Argument for a Bill of Rights within the Context of South African Nationalism" in *The Post-apartheid Constitutions: Perspectives on South Africa's Basic Law,* eds. P. Andrews and S. Ellmann (Athens: Ohio University Press, 2001), 194.

33. R. Dworkin, *Sovereign Virtue: The Theory and Practice of Equality* (Place: Publisher, 2000), 5.

34. *Dowood and Another v. Minister of Home Affairs and Others* 2000 3 SA 936 (CC). See also *Ex Porte Chairperson of the Constitutional Assembly: In re Certification of the Constitution of the Republic of South Africa* 1996 4 SA 744 (CC) (Certification) at paras 76–8; *Soobramoney v. Minister of Health, KwaZulu-Natal* 1998 1 SA 765 (CC) (Soobramoney); *Government of the Republic of South Africa v. Grootboom* 2001 1 SA 46 (CC) (Grootboom); *Minister of Health and Others v. Treatment Action Campaign and Others* (2) 2002 5 SA 721 (CC) (TAC).

35. For a general discussion of dignity, see the introduction and ch. 4 of D. Cornell *Between Women and Generations: Legacies of Dignity* (New York: Palgrave, 2005).

36. For an excellent discussion of Immanuel Kant's defense and elaboration of the ideal of the social contract, see Immanuel Kant, "On the Common Saying: That May Be Correct in Theory, But It Is of No Use in Practice" in *Practical Philosophy,* ed. M. Gregor (Cambridge: Cambridge University Press, 1999), 273.

37. Y. Mokgoro, "*uBuntu* and the Law in South Africa," *Potchefstroom Electronic Law Journal* 1 (1998).

38. E. Christodoulidis, "Reconciliation as potentiality," (unpublished paper read at a conference on "Time, reconciliation and the law," Glasgow, May 2004, copy on file

with authors); the quote is from Simone Weil's essay, "On Human Personality" in *Selected Essays,* ed. R. Rees (Oxford: Oxford University Press, 1962), 9–34.

39. *Id.*

40. S. Weil, "Human personality," 10; Burns, "Justice and Impersonality: Simone Weil on Rights and Obligations," *Laval Théologique et Philosophique* 49 (1993): 480.

41. *Khosa* (*supra* n. 1) at para 74.

42. Mokgoro in *Khoso* (*supra* n. 1) at para 47.

43. The judgment explicitly declines to address the position of other excluded groups, such as temporary residents, asylum seekers and illegal immigrants, hinting instead that such groups can legitimately be excluded from social assistance benefits. See *Khosa* (*supra* n. 1) at para 59.

44. *Khosa* (*supra* n. 1) at para 65.

45. J. and J. Comaroff, "Reflections on Liberalism, Policulturalism and ID-ology: Citizenship and Difference in South Africa," New Social Forms Seminar Series, University of Stellenbosch Department of Sociology and Social Anthropology (15 August 2003).

46. *Port Elizabeth Municipality v. Various Occupiers* 2004 12 BCLR 1268 (CC).

47. *Id.* at paras 8–10.

48. *Id.* at para 36.

49. *Id.* at para 31.

50. *Id.* at para 37.

51. See S. Wolin, *Tocqueville Between Two Worlds: The Making of a Political and Theoretical Life* (Princeton: Princeton University Press, 2003).

52. Pieterse (*supra* n. 3) 449.

53. *Id.*, 456–457.

SOME THOUGHTS ON THE *UBUNTU* JURISPRUDENCE OF THE CONSTITUTIONAL COURT

Narnia Bohler-Müller

This article was originally published in *Obiter* 28, 3 (2007): 590–599.

1. See *S v. Makwanyane* 1995 3 SA 391 (CC), hereinafter *Makwanyane*.

2. Van der Walt, *Law and Sacrifice: Towards a Post-Apartheid Theory of Law* (Johannesburg: Wits University Press, 2005), 111. See also Van der Walt, "Vertical Sovereignty and Horizontal Plurality: Normative and Existential Reflections on the Capital Punishment Jurisprudence Articulated in *S v. Makwanyane*," *SAPL* 20, no. 2 (2005): 253.

3. Van der Walt, *Law and Sacrifice,* 113.

4. *Id.*, 114.

5. *Id.*, 114.

6. *Id.*, 114.

7. *Id.*, 115.

8. *Id.*, 120.

9. Lenta, "Just Gaming: The Case for Postmodernism in South African Legal Theory" *SAJHR* 17 (2001): 191. See also Lenta, *Just Gaming,* 173.

10. Kroeze, "Doing Things with Values II: The Case of *uBuntu*," *Stellenbosch Law Review* 13 (2002): 260.

11. English, "*uBuntu*: The Quest for an Indigenous Jurisprudence," *SAJHR* 12 (1996): 641, 646.

12. Van der Walt, *Law and Sacrifice,* 115.

13. See Bohler-Muller, "The Story of an African Value," *SAPL* 20, no. 2 (2005): 266.

14. Cornell, *Beyond Accommodation: Ethical Feminism, Deconstructions, and the Law* (New York: Rowman & Littlefield Publishers, 1999).

15. Murungi, "The Question of African Jurisprudence: Some Hermeneutical Reflections" in *A Companion to African Philosophy,* ed. K. Wiredu (Oxford: Blackwell Publishing, 2004), 519, 525.

16. Eze, "*uBuntu*: A Communitarian Response to Liberal Individualism?" (unpublished master's thesis at University of South Africa, Pretoria, 2005), 98.

17. *Id.,* 99.

18. *Id.,* 107. Eze uses the philosophy of science to explain realist perspectivism, similar to the work of Harding on standpoint epistemology. See Harding, *The Science Question in Feminism* (Ithaca: Cornell University Press, 1986).

19. Eze, 140.

20. Eze, 123.

21. Douzinas, *Human Rights and Empire: The Political Philosophy of Cosmopolitanism* (New York: Routledge-Cavendish, 2007), 294.

22. Ramosa, *African Philosophy Through* uBuntu, rev. ed. (2002), 50.

23. *Id.,* vii–viii.

24. See Mokgoro, "*uBuntu* and the Law in South Africa," *Buffalo Human Rights Law Review* 20 (1998).

25. Cornell and Van Marle, "Exploring *uBuntu*: Tentative Reflections," *African Human Rights Law Journal* 5, no. 2 (2005): 195. The politics and ethics seem to be telling us that no one—including the state—is allowed to say "you do not interest me" (214).

26. *Khosa* at para 65.

27. *PE Municipality* at pars 37.

28. *Id.* at paras 8–10.

29. Thino Bekker, "The Re-emergence of *uBuntu*: A Critical Analysis," *SAPL* 21 (2006): 333.

30. *Id.,* 339.

31. See Ramose 2002 where he writes about *ubuntu* as an African philosophy of both belonging (being "enfolded" in the community) and becoming (the "unfolding" of the self within community).

32. *Dikoko v. Mokhatla supra* at para 102.

33. *Id.* at para 80.

34. *Id.* In a footnote, Mokgoro refers to the Promotion of Equality and Prevention of Unfair Discrimination Act 4 of 2000. This Act makes provision in section 21(2)(j) for an equality Court to make an order that an unconditional apology be made if it determines under section 21(1) that unfair discrimination, hate speech or harassment has taken place.)

35. *Dikoko v. Mokhatla supra* at para 69.

36. *Id.* at para 109.

37. *Id.* at para 114.

38. *Id.* at para 113; and Justice Sachs refers here to two cases, *Makwanyane* and *PE Municipality.*

39. *Dikoko v. Mokhatla supra* at para 116; and both Mokgoro and Sachs point out similarities between the Roman Dutch concept of *amende honorable* and *ubuntu-botho.*

40. *Id.* at para 60.

41. *Id.* at para 86.

42. Bekker, 21 *SAPL* 342 (2006).

43. *Id.* 342.

44. *Id.* 344.

45. "The Colour of Reason: The Idea of 'Race' in Kant's Anthropology" in *Postcolonial African Philosophy: A Critical Reader,* ed. Eze (Cambridge, Mass.: Blackwell Publisher, 1997), ch. 4.

46. Eze 12–13 as quoted in Appiagyei-Atua, "A Rights-centred Critique of African Philosophy in the Context of Development" *AHRLJ* 5 (2005): 335.

47. Appiagyei-Atua *AHRLJ* 5 (2005): 343.

48. *Id.,* 357.

49. For a general critique of the (mis)use of human rights in the exercise of power, see Douzinas, where he states that, paradoxically, "the ideal, transcendent position of natural law, natural and human rights has been reversed, turning them into tools of public power and individual desire" (8).

50. Cornell and Van der Marle, "Exploring *uBuntu*" (*supra* n. 25), 220.

THE REEMERGENCE OF *UBUNTU*: A CRITICAL ANALYSIS

Thino Bekker

This article was first published in *SAPR/PL* 21 (2006): 333.

1. *S v. Makwanyane* 1995 3 SA 391 (CC).

2. See, for example, Cornell, "A Call for a Nuanced Constitutional Jurisprudence: *uBuntu*, Dignity, and Reconciliation," *SAPR/PL* (2004): 666; De Kock and Labuschagne, "*uBuntu* as a Conceptual Directive in Realizing a Culture of Effective Human Rights," *THRHR* 62 (1999): 114; Bohler-Müller, "What the Equality Courts Can Learn from Gilligan's Ethic of Care: A Novel Approach," *SAJHR* (2000): 623; Barrie, "*ubuntu ungamntu ngabanye abantu:* The Recognition of Minority Rights in the South African Constitution," *TSAR* (2000): 271; Mchunu, "The need for Traditional African Jurisprudence in the South African Legal System," The Magistrate 31 (1996): 55; Kroeze, "Doing Things with Values: The Role of Constitutional Values in Constitutional Interpretation," *Stell. L. Rev.* 12 (2001): 265; Van Niekerk, "A Common Law for Southern Africa: Roman Law or Indigenous African Law," *CILSA* (1998): 158; Mqeke, "Customary Law and Human Rights," *SALJ* (1996): 364; Hoctor, "Dignity, Criminal Law and the Bill of Rights," *SALJ* (2004): 304.

3. 2005 1 SA 217 (CC).

4. 2005 1 BCLR (CC).

5. As yet unreported.

6. "The Story of an African Value," *SAPR/PL* (2005): 266.

7. Tutu, *No Future Without Forgiveness* (South Africa: Image, 1999), 34.

8. In translation: means "a human being is a human being because of other human beings." Mokgoro explains this as follows: "In other words, the individual's existence and wellbeing, is relative to that of the group. This is manifested in anti-individualistic conduct which threatens the survival of the group." See Mokgoro, "*uBuntu* and the Law in South Africa," *Potchefstroom Elektroniese Regstydskrif* 1 (1998) (http://www.puk.ac.za/lawper/).

9. *Makwanyane* (*supra* n. 1) at para 308.

10. Mokgoro (*supra* n. 8), 2.

11. Act 200 of 1993.

12. The only mention of *ubuntu* in the 1996 Constitution is made in ch 6, but only for purposes of the Promotion of National Unity and Reconciliation Act 34 of 1995.

13. Mokgoro (*supra* n. 8), 7.

14. Kroeze (*supra* n. 2), 260.

15. *Id.,* 261.

16. English, "*uBuntu*: The Quest for an Indigenous Jurisprudence" *SAJHR* (1996): 646.

17. Van der Walt, "Vertical sovereignty and horizontal plurality: Normative and existential reflections on the capital punishment jurisprudence articulated in *S v. Makwanyane*," *SAPR/PL* 253 (2005): 256–260.

18. *Id.,* 257.

19. See n. 2.

20. At para 59.

21. At para 37.

22. At para 56.

23. See, for example, Le Roux, "Bridges, Clearings and Labyrinths: The Architectural Framing of Postapartheid Constitutionalism," *SAPR/PL* (2004): 629; Van der Walt, "The Public Aspect of Private Property *SAPR/PL* (2004): 676; Botha, Equality, Dignity, and the Politics of Interpretation," *SAPR/PL* (2004): 724.

24. 2004 2 SA 544 (C).

25. Case no 7292/01 (as yet unreported).

26. 38 of 1927.

27. See n. 3.

28. At para 136.

29. At para 45.

30. Bohler-Müller (*supra* n. 5), 278–279.

31. Where he states at para 163 that "This concept encapsulates communality and the interdependence of the members of a community."

32. See n. 4.

33. Rand is the basic unit of money in South Africa.

34. At para 29.

35. At para 49.

36. At para 102.

37. At para 73–80.

38. At para 80.

39. At para 68.

40. At para 69.

41. At para 113.

42. This can be described as what Bohler-Müller (*supra* n. 2) refers to as "compassionate justice" at 635.

43. At para 114.

44. As yet unreported. In this homicide case a suspended custodial sentence was combined with an apology from a senior representative of the family of the accused, as requested and acknowledged by the mother of the deceased.

45. In *S v. Shilubane* [2005] JOL 15671 (T).

46. At para 60.

47. At para 121.

48. Cornell (*supra* n. 2), 675.

49. That the Constitutional Court may do just that in future reflects from the majority judgment delivered by Moseneke DCJ: "Sachs J finds that monetary compensation alone is often not appropriate relief for defamation and that courts need to explore the wide and creative possibilities afforded by restorative justice as contemplated by the indigenous values of *ubuntu* or *botho. Persuasive as this line of reasoning may be,* it raises issues which never confronted the trial court and therefore do not properly arise before us" at para 86 (my emphasis).

AFRICAN CUSTOMARY LAW IN SOUTH AFRICA: THE MANY FACES OF *BHE V. MAGISTRATE KHAYELITSHA*

Chuma Himonga

Chuma Himonga LLB (Zambia), LLM, Ph.D. (London) is Professor of Law at the University of Cape Town, South Africa.

1. 2005 (1) BCLR 1 (CC).

2. See, for example, *Mthembu v. Letsela* [2000] 3 All SA 219 (SCA), 2000 (3) SA 867 SCA (South Africa); *Magaya v. Magaya* 1999 (1) ZLR 100 SC (Zimbabwe); and other cases cited by the minority judgment (at paras 191–207), especially *Mojekwu v. Mojekwu* [1997] 7 NWLR 283 (Nigeria); *Chihowa v. Mangwende* 1987 (1) ZLR 228 (SC) at 231H–232D (Zimbabwe); *Murisa NO v. Murisa* 1992 (1) ZLR 167 (SC) (Zimbabwe); and *Bernardo Ephrahim v. Holaria d/o Pastory and Gervazi Kaizilege* High Court of Tanzania at Mwanza (PC) Civil Appeal 70/89 (Tanzania).

3. In this paper, common law is used broadly to refer to the laws historically of western origin, including Roman-Dutch law, case law, and statutory law.

4. The future of law in Africa. Record of proceedings of the London conference, 28.12.1959–8.1.1960 (A. N. Allott ed) (1960); A. N. Allott "What is to be done with African customary law? The experience of problems and reforms in anglophone Africa from 1950" in *Journal of African Law* 28 (1984): 56–71.

5. For critical discussions of this subject in South Africa, see L. Mbatha, "Reforming the Customary Law of Succession," *SAJHR* 18 (2002): 259; M. Pieterse, "It's a Black Thing: Upholding Culture and Customary Law in a Society," *SAJHR* 17 (2001): 364; M. Pieterse, "Killing It Softly: Customary Law in the New Constitutional Order," De Jure 33 (2000): 35; C. Himonga. "The Advancement of African Women's Rights in the First Decade of Democracy in South Africa: The Reform of the Customary Law of Marriage

and Succession," *ACTA Juridica* (forthcoming) (2005); and C. Himonga and R. Manjoo, "What's in a Name? The Identity and Reform of Customary Law in South Africa's Constitutional Dispensation" in *Governance in African Tradition,* ed. M. O. Hinz (2005).

6. See especially paras 35–100.

7. 38 of 1927.

8. S 23(1) of the BAA.

9. S 23(2) of the BAA. Section 2 of the Upgrading of Land Tenure Rights Act 112 of 1991 (read with schedule 1) provides for the upgrading of quitrent to ownership. This part of the BAA had therefore already been overtaken by events at the time of *Bhe*.

10. See also section 1(4)(b) of the ISA.

11. Act 81 of 1987.

12. In South African law, a putative marriage is a void civil marriage, but to which the law allocates some legal consequences, such as the legitimate status of children born of such marriage; see, for example, *Moola v. Auselbrook* No 1983 (1) SA 687 (N) and *Ngubane v. Ngubane* 1983 (2) SA 770 (T).

13. See Matrimonial Property Act 88 of 1984.

14. In such cases the marriage out of community of property was assumed to be an indication that the spouses wished customary law to apply. For statutory provisions on marriage out of community of property, see Matrimonial Property Act.

15. That is, section 23(10)(a), (c), and (e) and regulation 2(e) of Regulations for the Administration and Distribution of the Estates of Deceased Blacks GN R200 of February 1987. The nature of this principle is discussed in *Bhe* (see paras 88–97).

16. See *Bhe* paras 131–133.

17. See notes 8, 9, and 15 above.

18. See section 36 of the Constitution, which provides for the circumstances in which the rights in the Constitution may be limited.

19. See paras 91–94.

20. That is, the heir, who was unaware that the constitutional validity of section 23 of the BAA was being challenged.

21. 66 of 1965.

22. See also *Moseneke v. The Master* 2001 (2) SA 18 (CC) in which the Court invalidated s 23(7)(a) and Regulation 3(1) (GN R200 of February 1987) of the BAA that differentiated between the administration of deceased estates of blacks and other people as being unfairly discriminatory and thus contrary to the Constitution.

23. For example, the research and publications of Women and the Law in Southern Africa Research Trust (WLSA) covering six southern African countries: Botswana, Lesotho, Swaziland, Mozambique, Zambia and Zimbabwe. Monographs on the findings of this research were published by WLSA in each country in 1994.

24. The case was heard by two High Courts reported in *Mthembu v. Letsela and Another* 1997 (2) SA 936 (T) and 1998 (2) SA 675 (T), respectively, before it went on appeal.

25. The decision of the Supreme Court of Appeal is reported as *Mthembu v. Letsela and Another* 2000 (3) SA 867 (SCA); [2000] 3 All SA 219 (A).

26. For a discussion of the problems of the rule of primogeniture in modern conditions and within the constitutional framework of South Africa see *Bhe* paras 88–97.

27. See M. Chanock, *Law, Custom and Social Order in Malawi and Zambia* (Porthsmouth, NH: Heinemann, 1985).

28. 1998 (2) SA 675 (T).

29. *Mthembu (supra* n. 25) at paras 33 and 35.

30. See *Bhe* at para 24.

31. *Id.* at para 100.

32. For a full statement of the section, see *Bhe* at paras 39 and 40.

33. See *Bhe* para 125.

34. *Id.*

35. The minority sought to develop rather than invalidate the rule (see para 222).

36. P. J. Stewart, "Rights, Rights, Rights: Women's Rights? Reconceptualising, Reconsidering Rights," in *Ret Og Skonsmhed I En Overgangstid* ed. A. W. Bentzon (1998), 161.

37. The minority judgment of the Constitutional Court in *Bhe* recognizes this when it states, citing its own decision in *Alexkor Ltd and Another v. Richtersveld Community and Others* (2003 (12) BCLR 1301 (CC) and 2004 (5) SA 460 (CC)) that "[i]n applying indigenous law, it is important to bear in mind that, unlike common law, indigenous law is not written . . . . It is a system of law that has its own values and norms. Throughout its history it has evolved and developed to meet the changing needs of the community. It will continue to evolve within the context of its values and norms consistently with the Constitution" (at para 153).

38. See para 113.

39. See Stewart *(supra* n. 36).

40. *Id.*

41. See Stewart *(supra* n. 36), 164.

42. For example, *Moseneke (supra* n. 22); *Fraser v. Naude and Others* 1999 (1) SA 1 (CC); 1998 (11) BCLR 1357 (CC).

43. In this regard, it may be worth observing that the South African Law Commission has already proceeded on the basis partly of *Bhe* to reform the law on administration of estates, thereby treating *Bhe* as though it were a permanent decision. See South African Law Commission Discussion Paper 110 Project 134 on the Administration of Estates (October 2005), 10, para 4.2.1.

44. See para 114.

45. The first Bill to reform the customary law of succession was introduced to Parliament in 1998, but was later withdrawn. No legislative action has been taken to reform the substantive customary law of succession other than the ongoing investigation by the South African Law Commission, see South African Law Commission Discussion Paper 93 Project 90 on the Customary Law of Succession (2000).

46. See para 130.

47. *Id.*

48. See para 215. See also *Mbatha (supra* n. 5) at 271.

49. See Himonga *(supra* n. 5); South African Law Commission Discussion Paper 93 Project 90 on the Customary Law of Succession (2000) at 13, para 3.1.5.

50. See also C. Himonga, "Protecting the Minor Child's Inheritance Rights (Zambia)," *The International Survey of Family Law* 457 (2001): 471.

51. For a discussion of this concept see C. Himonga and C. Bosch, "The Application of African Customary Law under the Constitution of South Africa: Problems Solved or Just Beginning?" *South African Law Journal* 117, 306 (2000): 322.

52. See C. Himonga, "Protection of Widows and Administration of Customary Estates in Zambian Courts" in *Gros-plan sur les femmes en Afrique. Afrikanische Frauen im Blick,* eds. G. Ludwar-Ene and M. Reh (Bayreuth, Germany: Bayreuth University 1993), 159.

53. Chapter 59 of the Laws of Zambia.

54. See, for example, C. Himonga, "Zambia: Protecting the Minor Child's Inheritance Rights" *The International Survey of Family Law* 457 (2001): 471–472.

55. See para 130.

56. See Himonga (*supra* n. 5).

57. See para 113.

58. *Id.*

59. For a discussion of this subject, see Himonga (*supra* n. 5).

60. The development of customary law based on section 8(3) of the Constitution is a source of controversy; see, for example, T. W. Bennett, *Customary Law in South Africa* 91 (Juta & Company, 2004); C. Rautenbach, "Some Comments on the Status of Customary Law in Relation to the Bill of Rights," *Stellenbosh Law Review* 14 (2003): 107; Himonga and Bosch (*supra* n. 51).

61. See, for example, *Zondi v. President of RSA and Others* 2000 (2) SA 49 (N); 1999 (11) BCLR 1313 (N). For further discussion of the development of customary law see Himonga and Bosch (*supra* n. 51), 314–318 and references therein; Bennett (*supra* n. 60), 91–94 and references therein.

62. See, for example, Pieterse, "It's a Black Thing" (*supra* n. 5); Pieterse, "Killing It Softly" (*supra* n. 5); *Himonga* and *Manjoo* (*supra* n. 5); Bennett (*supra* n. 60) 91; Rautenbach (*supra* n. 60); A. J. Kerr, "Customary Law, Fundamental Rights and the Constitution," *South African Law Journal* 111 (1994): 720.

63. 1996 (4) SA 744 (CC); 1996 (10) BCLR 1253 (CC) at para 197.

64. *Id.* at para 197.

65. *Id.* at para 230.

66. See paras 111 and 112.

67. *Id.*

68. See, for example, Himonga and Bosch (*supra* n. 51); G. van Niekerk, "Indigenous Law and Narrative: Rethinking Methodology," *CILSA* 32 (1999): 208.

69. See para 111.

70. For example, *Mabena v. Letsoalo* 1998 (2) SA 1068 (T); *Hhlophe v. Mahlalela* 1998 (1) SA 449 (T).

71. See paras 150 and 151.

72. 45 of 1988. According to this Act, the methods are: taking judicial notice of customary law in so far as such law can be ascertained readily and with sufficient certainty [and] is not opposed to the principles of public policy and natural justice, and the hearing of evidence from witnesses, sections 1(1) and (2).

73. See para 151.

74. See paras 218 and 220.

75. 1997 (2) SA 690 (C).

76. See also *Amod v. Commission for Gender Equality and Multilateral Motor Vehicle Accidents Fund* 1999 (4) SA 1319 (SCA).

77. *Alexkor* (*supra* n. 37) at para 53.

78. See para 52.

79. Culture denotes flexibility. It has also been argued elsewhere that the right to culture contemplates the recognition of living customary law by the Constitution as opposed to official customary law, see Himonga and Bosch (*supra* n. 51), 318–331.

80. See also C. van Nierkerk, "State Initiatives to Incorporate Non-state Laws into the Official Legal Order: A Denial of Legal Pluralism?" *CILSA* (2001): 349, commenting on *Moseneke* (*supra* n. 22) at 359 (where she implicitly supports the case by case approach while Parliament developed the impugned statutory provision concerned in that case).

81. See Himonga and Manjoo (*supra* n. 5).

82. For example, reforms in Tanzania that culminated in the Law of Marriage Act 5 of 1971; reforms in Ghana that culminated in the Ghana Intestate Succession Law 1985 (PNDCL 111); reforms in Zambia that culminated in the Intestate Succession Act of 1989 (n 53) and the Wills and Administration of Testate Estates Act (chapter 60 of the Laws of Zambia); the reform in Zimbabwe that resulted in the Administration of Estates Amendment Act of 1997, Act 6 of 1997; and the South African Recognition of Customary Marriages Act 120 of 1998.

83. South African Law Commission Discussion Paper 93 Project 90 on the Customary Law of Succession at para 4.6.1 (2000).

84. See para 120. The Commission's proposed Intestate Succession Bill seeks to establish a uniform system of intestate succession that will be regulated by a modified Intestate Succession Act to accommodate customary law.

85. 66 of 1965 (at paras 131–134 regarding administration of estates).

86. See para 125.

87. According to the findings of the South African Law Commission's Special Project Committee on Customary Law that investigated and proposed the reform of the customary law of marriage in 1998 under South African Law Commission Project 90 (1998), *Harmonisation of the Common Law and the Indigenous Law Report on Customary Marriages* (84), and L. Mbatha, "Summary of findings on how black South Africans marry" (unpublished paper), the practice of polygyny is dying out. The latter study was done in three of South Africa's provinces (Gauteng, North West, and Northern Province) and it included an urban/rural variable. It is undated, but it appears that it was conducted shortly before the enactment of the Act in 1998.

88. See para 130.

89. *Id.*

90. See the minority judgment, paras 165, 166, and 170–175.

91. See *supra* n. 82.

92. For a discussion see Himonga (*supra* n. 5).

93. See para 139.

94. See Himonga and Manjoo (*supra* n. 5).

95. See South African Law Commission Project 90, Harmonisation of the Common Law and the Indigenous Law Report on Conflicts of Law (September 1999) and the annexed Application of Customary Law Bill (110–111).

96. See section 5(1) of the Bill provides for devolution of assets. It states that:

(1) Customary law shall be applied to the devolution of a deceased estate if all relevant factors including the deceased's ways of life an, for purposes of deciding interests in land, the place where that land is situated, indicate that the deceased had his or her closest connection to that law unless it appears—

(a) that the deceased had executed a will, in which case the terms of the will must be applied;

(b) taking account of the factors referred to in this paragraph, that it would be more appropriate to apply the common law; or

(c) that the application of customary law would result in unjust or unfair consequences.

(2) Notwithstanding paragraph (1)(a) customary law may be applied to the interpretation of the terms of a will executed by a person normally subject to customary law.

97. See Bennett (*supra* n. 60), 53.

98. See section 1(3) of the Law of Evidence Amendment Act 54 of 1988.

99. See clauses 4 and 6 of the Bill respectively. For example, clause 4 of the Bill states: "When deciding whether customary law is applicable, a court may give effect to an express or implied agreement between the parties that customary law should apply, unless the court is satisfied that it is inappropriate to do so"; see South African Law Commission Project 90, Harmonisation of the Common Law and the Indigenous Law Report on Conflicts of Law (*supra* n. 95).

100. See sections 30 and 31 of the Constitution. See also Himonga and Bosch (*supra* n. 51) 314. As customary law is undeniably a part of the African cultural tradition, the right to culture may be interpreted as including a right for a person to choose between customary and common law or any other recognized system of law. See Bennett (*supra* n. 60), 78–80.

101. See, for example, E. Bonthuys, "The South African Bill of Rights and the Development of Family Law," *SALJ* 119 no. 748 (2002): 757–761, 778–779; C. Himonga, *Implementing the Rights of the Child in African Legal Systems: The Mthembu Journey to Justice*" 9 International Journal of Children's Rights 89–122 (2001).

102. For an identification of some of the alternative and more innovative approaches that could have been explored by the legislature, see Pieterse, "Killing It Softly" (*supra* n. 5), 42–47.

Glossary

African, Latin, and other words and phrases used in Part I of this book.

A botho ba gago e nne botho seshabeng (Tswana/Sotho): let your welfare be the welfare of the nation

a quo: from where, as such

amende honourable: an apology publicly and openly honestly offered

amicus curiae: in the United States, a third party allowed to submit a legal opinion to the court

amicus: friend, friendly

audi alteram partem: hear the other side

audi principe: the right to be heard before the event

boereoupa (Afrikaans): Afrikaans grandfather or a grandfather who is a farmer

boereseun (Afrikaans): Afrikaans boy or the son of a farmer

boerewors (Afrikaans): a traditional Afrikaans grilling sausage composed of beef larded with pork fat

bona fide: in good faith

botho (Tswana) = ubuntu: civility, humaneness ,personhood, morality, a person is a person through or because of (other) people

botshelô bo tswêlwê ke botshelô thlôgô ke thlôgô: a life yields to a life, a head to a head

braaivleis (Afrikaans): barbecue

contra bones mores: against good morals; offensive to the public conscience and sense of justice

culpa: fault, guilt

dano (Luos): ubuntu

de facto: in fact / the way things really are

de jure: by law

de minimis: trifling

de minimis non curat lex: the law does not concern itself with trifles.

déclaration des droits de l'homme et du citoyen (French): Declaration of the Rights of Man and the Citizen

deprecatio: a plea for pardon

dolus eventualis: intent in the form of foreseeing the possibility of a consequence resulting from one's primary act but nevertheless acting and reconciling oneself with the possibility that this consequence might result

dominium: ownership

en passant (French): in passing

être singulier pluriel (French): the singular plural existence

functus officio: having performed his or her function

God seën SuidAfrika (Afrikaans): God bless South Africa

Grundnorm (German): foundation, fundamental norm

habitatio: the right to live or dwell in

homo loquens: speaker, human speech

homo scriptans: writer

hunhu (Shona): ubuntu

in casu: in the event, in this case

in toto: in total

Indlalifa: successor

inter alia: among other things

inter personas: among people

inter vivos: among the living

ius ad bellum: law towards war, laws that regulate the reasons for going to war

ius in bello: law in war, laws that regulate war

ius talionis: the law of retaliation

juris praecepta sunt haec: honeste vivere, alterum non laedare, suum cique tribuere: The precepts of the law are these: to live honestly, to harm no one, to give everybody their due.

juris praecepta: precepts of the law

kgosi ke kgosi ka batho: the sovereignty of the king derives from and belongs to its subject

l'horisontalité des morts (French): the horizontality of mortals

letgotlo le lefa ka setopo: a mouse pays with its carcass (meaning, a murderer pays with his life)

lex talionis: the law of retaliation (an eye for an eye)

mens rea: guilty mind, mindset of a criminal

menswaardigheid (Afrikaans): human worth, human dignity

molao: character of law

molato ga obole (Sotho/Tswana): a debt or feud is never extinguished until the equilibrium has been restored; you can never run away from your debt or transgression because when you come back those who you owe or transgressed against will take you to task

moordbende (Afrikaans): murder gang

motho ke motho lo batho ba bangwe (Tswana): people live through the helping of others

ndiri nokuti eiri ndinorara nokuti tinor arowa (Shona): I am because we are; I exist because the community exists.

Nkosi sikelel' iAfrika: God bless Africa

nogal (Afrikaans): quite, rather

nomine officio: in an official or representative capacity

nomos: names

noodtoestand as regverdedigingsgrond in die strafreg (Afrikaans): necessity is a ground of justification in criminal law

obiter and obiter dictum: Any statement in the judgment of a court of law on a point of law that is not, or is not part of, the principle of the judgment

palinodia, recantatio, retractio: declaration by the person who uttered defamatory words or expressions concerning another, to the effect that he withdraws such words or expressions as being untrue

panta rei: everything flows

partage (French): division, to share

pendante lite: pending litigation

prima facie: at first sight

raison d'être (French): reason for coming into existence

Recht (German): it has two distinct meanings: 1. *right* in the subjective sense that I have a *right* arising from a contract or the constitution; 2. *law* in the objective sense of a governing legal norm; for example, the common law of contract or the statutory law of trade marks

relation sans relation (French): a relation without relation

separare: to sever or separate

seriti (Tswana): dignity, life force by which a community of persons are connected to each other

setopo ka setopa: a corpse for a corpse

sic: thus

Sittlichkeit (German): morality, ethics

status quo: current condition or situation, the situation in which

sui generis: in a class of its own

supra: above

taolo: commandment, regulation

ubuntobotho: tolerance for those with whom one disagrees and respect

ubuntu ngumuntu ngabantu, modio ke modia ba batho ba bangwe: a human being is a human being because of other people.

ultra vires: beyond powers, without authority

Umkhonto we sizwe: Spear of the Nation

umuntu ngumuntu ngabantu (Zulu): communality and the interdependence of the members of a community; every individual is an extension of others.

umuntu = ubuntu: a human being, communality

unsere Logik (German): our logic

unsere rationale Logik (German): our rational logic

usus: practice, right of use

vis-à-vis (French): face to face, opposite

Weltanschauung (German): world view, world outlook, philosophy of life

Index

just ideas

Roger Berkowitz, *The Gift of Science: Leibniz and the Modern Legal Tradition*

Jean-Luc Nancy, translated by Pascale-Anne Brault and Michael Naas, *The Truth of Democracy*

Drucilla Cornell and Kenneth Michael Panfilio, *Symbolic Forms for a New Humanity: Cultural and Racial Reconfigurations of Critical Theory*

Karl Shoemaker, *Sanctuary and Crime in the Middle Ages, 400–1500*

Michael J. Monahan, *The Creolizing Subject: Race, Reason, and the Politics of Purity.*

Drucilla Cornell and Nyoko Muvangua (eds.), *uBuntu and the Law: African Ideals and Postapartheid Jurisprudence.*